Starting a Business

ALL-IN-ONE

2nd Edition WITHDRAWN

by Kathleen R. Allen, PhD; Peter Economy; Paul and Sarah Edwards; Lita Epstein; Alexander Hiam; Greg Holden; Peter Jaret; Jeanette Maw McMurtry, MBA; Joyce Mazero; Jim Muehlhausen, JD; Bob Nelson, PhD; Steven D. Peterson; Jim Schell; Barbara Findlay Schenck; Michael H. Seid; John A. Tracy, CPA; Tage C. Tracy, CPA; and Eric Tyson, MBA

for dummies®

A Wiley Brand

Starting a Business All-in-One For Dummies®, 2nd Edition

Published by: **John Wiley & Sons, Inc.**, 111 River Street, Hoboken, NJ 07030-5774, www.wiley.com

Copyright © 2019 by John Wiley & Sons, Inc., Hoboken, New Jersey

Published simultaneously in Canada

For general information on our other products and services, please contact our Customer Care Department within the U.S. at 877-762-2974, outside the U.S. at 317-572-3993, or fax 317-572-4002. For technical support, please visit https://hub.wiley.com/community/support/dummies.

Wiley publishes in a variety of print and electronic formats and by print-on-demand. Some material included with standard print versions of this book may not be included in e-books or in print-on-demand. If this book refers to media such as a CD or DVD that is not included in the version you purchased, you may download this material at http://booksupport.wiley.com. For more information about Wiley products, visit www.wiley.com.

Library of Congress Control Number: 2019939297

ISBN 978-1-119-56521-5 (pbk); ISBN 978-1-119-56524-6 (ebk); ISBN 978-1-119-56520-8 (ebk)

Manufactured in the United States of America

C10013325_082219

Contents at a Glance

Table of Contents

Introduction

Welcome to *Starting a Business All-in-One For Dummies,* Second Edition!

It's a good bet that you share the popular dream of starting your own business and being your own boss. Increasingly, this dream is becoming more relevant to the challenges of the economy that has emerged. It's not just a pie-in-the-sky dream anymore; starting a business is a reality that has created opportunity and satisfaction for many people who decided to take the plunge — just as it can for you.

This book presents and explains a wide variety of information, all aimed at enlightening you on what you need to know and ensuring your success. Whether you need know-how and advice on turning your idea into reality, creating a business plan and business model, finding funding, picking a legal structure, setting up your books, marketing and promoting, or staying in business for the long haul, you'll find the help you need here. Most of this book is applicable to you whether your business is a local business, a start-up corporation, a franchise, or based out of your home.

The aim of this book is to provide you with the very best ideas, concepts, and tools for starting and successfully operating your business. Using the info here, you should be able to create exactly the kind of business you've always dreamed of and find exactly the level of success you've always wanted.

About This Book

This book is a generous conglomeration of material from a number of *For Dummies* business books, carefully selected with an eye toward getting the new business owner/entrepreneur up and running. Your current level of business experience (or lack thereof) doesn't matter. Don't worry about not having years of management experience under your belt or about not knowing the difference between a *balance sheet* and an *income statement.*

For a fraction of the amount you'd pay to get an MBA, this book provides you with an easily understandable road map to today's most innovative and effective business techniques and strategies. The information you find here is firmly grounded in the real world. This book isn't an abstract collection of theoretical mumbo-jumbo that sounds good but doesn't work when you put it to the test. Instead, you'll find only the best information, the best strategies, and the best techniques — the same ones that top business schools teach today.

This book is also meant to be at least a little fun — running a business doesn't have to be a bore! In fact, maintaining a sense of humor can be vital when facing the challenges that all new business owners face from time to time.

Within this book, you may note that some web addresses (URLs) break across two lines of text. If you're reading this book in print and want to visit one of these web pages, simply key in the web address exactly as it's noted in the text, pretending as though the line break doesn't exist. If you're reading this as an e-book, you've got it easy — just tap the web address to be taken directly to the web page.

Foolish Assumptions

This book makes a few assumptions about you. For example, you have at least a passing interest in starting your own business. (Duh.) Maybe you've already started a business and are looking for tips to refine the techniques you're already developing. Or perhaps it's something you think you may want to try and are looking to read up on it before you make your move. In any case, you've come to the right place.

It's also safe to assume that you can — or believe you can — produce and deliver products or services that people will be willing to pay you for. These products and services can be most anything. You're limited only by your imagination (and, of course, your bank account, about which you'll soon be reading quite a bit).

Finally, this book assumes that you're eager to scoop up and implement new tips and tricks and that you're willing to acquire some new perspectives on the topic.

Icons Used in This Book

Icons are handy little graphic images that are meant to point out particularly important information about starting your own business. Throughout this book, you find the following icons, conveniently located along the left margins:

REMEMBER

Remember the important points of information that follow this icon, and your business will be all the better for it.

TECHNICAL STUFF

This one points out slightly advanced material that you can safely skip if you're in a hurry. But by all means, read these if you want to stretch yourself a bit.

TIP

This icon directs you to tips and shortcuts you can follow to save time and do things the right way the first time.

WARNING

Danger! Ignore the advice next to this icon at your own risk!

Where to Go from Here

If you're new to starting a business, you may want to start at the beginning of this book and work your way through to the end. A wealth of information and practical advice awaits you. Simply turn the page and you're on your way! But you can start anywhere. If you already own and operate a business and are short of time (and who isn't?), feel free to use the table of contents and the index to zero in on particular topics of interest to you right now.

Regardless of how you find your way around this book, the sincere hope of this endeavor is that you'll enjoy the journey.

For answers and helpful tips online, go to www.dummies.com and search for "*Starting a Business All-in-One For Dummies* Cheat Sheet" in the Search box.

1

Moving from Idea to Reality

Contents at a Glance

IN THIS CHAPTER

» Analyzing the feasibility of your business idea

» Figuring out your industry

» Doing research on your industry

» Determining where you fit in

» Targeting a new product for the market

Chapter **1**

Your Business in Context

This chapter starts at the very beginning, looking at how to step back and see a potential start-up business in the context within which it operates. If you've already started your business and are committed to it, or if you know exactly what kind of business you want to run and nothing will change your mind, or if your idea is to start rather small, with a modest idea that doesn't require finding much funding to get you going, you can skip this chapter. Good luck to you.

But it could be to your advantage to stick around anyway, because the fact is, not every business is a good idea at the time and place where it is born. You could save yourself some heartache by examining the external factors that will affect your business whether you like it or not. If you choose the right business at the right time and the right place, your chances of success are much higher.

Every successful business operates inside an environment that affects everything it does. The environment includes the industry in which the business operates, the market the business serves, the state of the economy, and the various people and businesses the business interacts with. Your business doesn't exist in a vacuum. Now, more than ever before, understanding your industry is a critical component of your business venture's success.

If you position your company well inside a growing, healthy industry, you have a better chance of building a successful venture. By contrast, if your business niche is a weak position in a hostile, mature industry, your fledgling business may be doomed. Conducting a feasibility analysis can be a good way to get a clear picture of the landscape. The first section of this chapter provides an overview of this process.

An Overview of Feasibility Analysis

A *feasibility analysis* consists of a series of tests that you conduct as you discover more and more about your opportunity. After each test, you ask yourself whether you still want to go forward. Is there anything here that prevents you from going forward with this business? Feasibility is a process of discovery, and during that process you will probably modify your original concept several times until you get it right. That's the real value of feasibility — the way that it helps you refine your concept so that you have the highest potential for success when you launch your business.

Today, you can often go for financing on the strength of a feasibility study alone. Certainly in the case of Internet businesses, speed is of the essence. Many an online business has gotten first-round financing on its proof of concept alone and *then* done a business plan before going for bigger dollars in the form of venture capital. But even if your business is a traditional one, feasibility can help you avoid big early mistakes.

Executive summary

REMEMBER

The *executive summary* is probably the most important piece of a feasibility analysis because, in two pages, it presents the most important and persuasive points from every test you did during your analysis. An effective executive summary captures the reader's attention immediately with the excitement of the concept. It doesn't let the reader get away; it draws the reader deeper and deeper into the concept as it proves your claim that the concept is feasible and will be a market success.

The most important information to emphasize in the executive summary is your proof that customers want what you have to offer. This proof comes from the primary research you do with the customers to find out what they think of your concept and how much demand there is. The other key piece to emphasize is your description of your founding team. Even the greatest ideas can't happen without a great team, and investors put a lot of stock in a founding team's expertise and experience.

TIP

For an online business, you may want to prepare what's called a *proof of concept*. This is essentially a one-page statement of why your concept will work, emphasizing what you have done to prove that customers will come to your site. That may be in the form of showing hits to your beta site or a list of customers signed up and ready to go when the site is finished. Similarly, if you're developing a new product, your proof of concept is your market-quality prototype.

Business concept

REMEMBER

In this first part of the body of your feasibility analysis, you are developing your business concept. Essentially you are answering these questions:

>> What is the business?

>> Who is the customer?

>> What is the value proposition?

>> How will the benefit be delivered?

It's important to be able to state your business concept in a few clear, concise, and direct sentences that include all four of the components of the concept. This is what is often called your *elevator pitch* — a conversation that begins when the elevator door closes and ends when the door opens at your floor. That means you have only a few seconds to capture your listener's attention, so you better be able to get it all out quickly and confidently. If you're preparing a feasibility analysis that will be shown to investors, you should state your business concept right up front in the concept section. Then you can elaborate on each point as a follow-up. Here's an example:

> Rural Power Tools is in the power equipment business, providing contractors and developers solutions to power needs in remote areas through rental equipment outlets.

As you find out more about your business concept, you'll also want to consider the various spin-off products and services you may be able to offer.

WARNING

One-product businesses often have a more difficult time becoming successful than multi-product/service companies. You don't want to put all your eggs into one basket if you can help it, and you want to give your customer choices.

Industry analysis

Testing whether or not the industry in which you will be operating will support your concept is an important part of any feasibility analysis. Here you look at the status of your industry, identify trends and patterns of change, and look at who the players in terms of competitors may be. Also, don't forget that one way to *find* a great opportunity is to study an industry first. More details on how to do an industry analysis are covered in the section "Researching an Industry," later in this chapter.

Market/customer analysis

Here you will be testing your customer. Ideally, inside your industry, you find a market segment appropriate to your business. Then you identify a niche that is not being served so that you have an entry strategy with the lowest barriers possible and the highest probability of success. In this part of the analysis, you also look at what your potential customer wants and what the demand for your product/service is. You will also consider a variety of different distribution channels to deliver the benefit to the customer. To find out more, see the section "Defining Your Market Niche," later in this chapter.

Genesis or founding team analysis

Investors look very carefully at the founding team because even the best concept won't happen without a team that can execute it. In this part of the analysis, you want to consider the qualifications, expertise, and experience of your founding team, even if that consists of only yourself. Be aware that today's business environment is so complex and fast-paced that no one person has all the skills, time, and resources to do everything him- or herself.

Product/service development analysis

Whether you're planning to offer a product or a service or both (and that's usually the case), it's going to take some planning. Consider which tasks must be accomplished to prepare the product or service for market, whether that is developing a product from raw materials and going through the patent process or developing a plan for implementing a service concept. Identify these preparatory tasks and figure out a realistic timeline for completion of them. Put that timeline in your analysis.

Financial analysis

In this part of the feasibility analysis, you figure out how much money you need to start the business and carry it to a positive cash flow. You also distinguish among the types of money, which will be important in defining your financial strategy. You can find out more about finding funding in Chapter 2 of Book 2.

Feasibility decision

After you have gone through all the various tests that comprise the feasibility analysis, you are ready to make a decision about going forward. Of course, throughout the process of doing the tests, you may have decided to stop — because of something you found out from analysis of the industry, market, product/service, and so forth. But if you're still on the mission, now's the time to define the conditions under which you go forward.

Timeline to launch

You always need to end a feasibility analysis with an action plan so that you're sure that at least something will happen. Establishing a list of all tasks to be completed and a time frame for completing them will increase the probability that your business will be launched in a timely fashion. The research you have done along the way will help you make wise decisions about the length of time it takes to complete everything and open the doors to your business.

Understanding Your Industry

New industries emerge on a regular basis. In fact, with e-commerce holding so much of the attention of young businesspeople today, you may well ask, "Is e-commerce an industry?" That's a great question. If you define an industry as a group of related businesses, then all e-commerce businesses have one thing in common: the Internet. But retail businesses, manufacturers, wholesalers, and service companies are all on the Internet, so every member of the value chain is found in one location.

All retail businesses have retail in common, and all manufacturers have manufacturing in common. Are retail and manufacturing industries as well? Within retail, you find clothing retailers and book retailers among many others. Is clothing an industry? Is publishing an industry? The answer to all these questions is yes.

Actually, there are layers of industries, starting with the broadest terms and working down to the more specific terms. Take an e-commerce business that almost everyone knows: Amazon.com. If you consider e-commerce to be an industry, a grouping of like businesses, then Amazon is definitely part of that industry. Within e-commerce, Amazon is also a retail business that happens to be using the Internet as its marketing/distribution channel. Within retail, it operates in the publishing, music, toys, and video industries, among others. What this means to you is that when you study Amazon's industry, you're really looking at multiple distinct industries, and it's important to understand what's going on in each.

TIP

You need to study the industry you have chosen for your feasibility study. Start at the broadest level of industry definition and work your way down to the segment that includes the product or service that you are providing.

Using a framework of industry structure

One way to begin to look at the industry you're interested in is to use a common framework. One useful framework is based on the work of W.H. Starbuck and Michael E. Porter, two experts on organizational strategy. This framework steps you through analyzing your potential industry by assessing the outside forces that work upon it and then assessing the countermeasures that you'll need to implement against those outside forces. According to Starbuck and Porter, new businesses must be constantly on the lookout for forces that affect them in every area.

The business environment, especially the entrepreneurial environment, often looks like a battlefield. But for every threat there's a countermeasure. The first step is to look at what these outside forces really are.

Carrying capacity, uncertainty, and complexity

This first environmental factor explains why so many industries today are changing, moving more rapidly, and making it more difficult for businesses to succeed. *Carrying capacity* refers to the extent to which an industry can accept more businesses. Industries can become oversaturated with too many businesses. When that happens, the capacity of businesses to produce their products and services exceeds the demand for them. Then it becomes increasingly difficult for new businesses to enter the industry and survive.

Uncertainty refers to the predictability or unpredictability of the industry — stability or instability. Typically volatile and fast-changing, modern technology industries produce more uncertainty. But these same industries often produce more opportunities for new businesses to take advantage of.

Complexity is about the number and diversity of inputs and outputs in the industry. Complex industries cause businesses to have to deal with more suppliers, customers, and competitors than other industries. Biotechnology and telecommunications are examples of industries with high degrees of complexity in the form of competition and government regulation.

Recognizing threat to new entrants

Some industries have barriers to entry that are quite high. These barriers come in many forms. Here are the main ones:

- **Economies of scale:** These are product volumes that enable established businesses to produce goods more inexpensively than a new business can. A new business can't compete with the low costs of the entrenched firms. To combat economies of scale, new firms often form alliances that give them more clout.

- **Brand loyalty:** If you're a new business, you face competitors that have achieved brand loyalty, which makes it much more difficult to entice customers to your products and services. That's why it's so important to find a market niche that you can control — a need in the market that is not being served. That will give you time to establish some brand loyalty of your own. Later in this chapter you find out more about niches, and Chapter 4 in Book 5 covers branding in detail.

- **High capital requirements:** In some industries, you encounter high costs for the advertising, R&D (research and development), and plants and equipment you need to compete with established firms. Again, new companies often overcome this barrier by outsourcing expensive functions to other firms.

- **Buyer switching costs:** Buyers don't generally like to switch from one supplier to another unless there's a good reason to do so. That's why once a person invests the time to learn and use the Windows environment, for example, he or she is reluctant to start all over with a different platform. Entrepreneurs must match a need *that is not being met with the current product on the market* to get the customer to switch.

- **Access to distribution channels:** Every industry has established methods for getting products to customers. New companies must have access to those distribution channels if they are going to succeed. The one exception is where the new business finds a new method of delivering a product or service that the customer accepts — for example, the Internet.

- **Proprietary factors:** Established companies may own technology or a location that gives them a competitive advantage over new companies. However, new ventures have often entered industries with their own proprietary factors that enable them to enjoy a relatively competition-free environment for a brief time.

>> **Government regulations:** In some industries, a long and expensive governmental process, such as FDA approval for foods and drugs, can be prohibitive for a new business. That's why many new ventures form strategic alliances with larger companies to help support the costs along the way.

>> **Industry hostility:** In some industries, rival companies make it difficult for a new business to enter. Because they typically are mature companies with many resources, they can afford to do what it takes to push the new entrant out. Again, finding that niche in the market where you're giving the customer what your competitors are not helps your company survive, even in a hostile industry.

Identifying threat from substitute products/services

Remember that your competition comes not only from companies that deal in the same products and services that you do, but also from companies that have substitute products. These products accomplish the same function but use a different method. For example, restaurants compete with other restaurants for consumer dollars, but they also compete with other forms of entertainment that include food. You could go out to dinner at a restaurant, take in a movie, and stop off at a pub for a nightcap. But there are movie theaters now where you can do all three of these things.

Spotting threat from buyers' bargaining power

Buyers have the power to force down prices in the industry when they are able to buy in volume. Established companies, if they are worth their salt, have this kind of buying power. New entrants can't purchase at volume rates; therefore, they have to charge customers more. Consequently, it's more difficult for them to compete.

Distinguishing threat from suppliers' bargaining power

In some industries, suppliers have the power to raise prices or change the quality of products that they supply to manufacturers or distributors. This is particularly true where there are few suppliers relative to the size of the industry and they are the primary source of materials in the industry. Don't forget that labor is also a source of supply, and in some industries such as software, highly skilled labor is in short supply; therefore the price goes up.

Being aware of rivalry among existing firms

Highly competitive industries force prices down and profits as well. That's when you see price wars, the kind you find in the airline industry. One company lowers its prices and others quickly follow. This kind of strategy hurts everyone in the industry and makes it nearly impossible for a new entrant to compete on price. Instead, savvy new businesses find an unserved niche in the market where they don't have to compete on price.

Deciding on an entry strategy

The structure of your industry will largely determine how you enter it. Failing to consider the structure of your industry can mean that you spend a lot of time and money only to find that you have chosen the wrong entry strategy. By then, you may have lost your window of opportunity. For the most part, new ventures have three broad options as entry strategies: differentiation, niche strategy, and cost superiority.

» **Differentiation:** With a *differentiation* strategy, you attempt to distinguish your company from others in the industry through product/process innovation, a unique marketing or distribution strategy, or through branding. If you are able to gain customer loyalty through your differentiation strategy, you will succeed in making your product or service less sensitive to price because customers will perceive the inherent value of dealing with your company.

» **Niche strategy:** The *niche* strategy is perhaps the most popular strategy for new ventures. It involves identifying and creating a place in the market where no one else is — serving a need that no one else is serving. This niche gives you space and time to compete without going head to head with the established players in the industry. It lets you own a piece of the market where you can establish the standards and create your brand.

» **Cost superiority:** Being the low-cost leader is typically difficult for a new venture because it relies heavily on volume sales and low-cost production. A new venture can take advantage of providing the lowest-cost products and services when it's part of an emerging industry where everyone shares the same disadvantage.

Researching an Industry

Getting to understand your industry inside and out is critical to developing any business strategies you may have. Yes, it's a lot of work, but it will pay off many times over.

TIP

Today, it's much easier than it used to be to research an industry because of all the sources available on the Internet. Of course, not everything posted on a website is necessarily true or from a creditable source. Anyone can easily put up a website and tout that he or she is an expert in whatever, and if you don't do any checking, you may end up relying on an unreliable source. So, how do you check on your sources? Here are some things you can do:

>> Ask yourself whether the site or author is a recognized expert in the field.

>> Ask people who are familiar with the industry you're researching whether they've ever heard of that site or that person.

>> Compare what that site or person has said with what others are saying. If you find a number of sources that seem to agree, you're probably okay. Of course, don't assume that just because many people are saying something, it's necessarily true — that's how rumors get started.

REMEMBER

By the way, when you present information to potential lenders or funders that you've gathered from someone else's research in your feasibility study (covered earlier in this chapter) or business plan (see Chapter 1 in Book 2), you need to give credit to that person with a full citation of the title, author, source, date, and page. Things become a bit trickier with websites because sometimes all they give is the URL. Great sites like Inc. (www.inc.com/) and Bloomberg Businessweek (www.bloomberg.com/businessweek) always attribute articles to their authors and the hard copy source. Be wary of sites that don't do this. Always be aware that not all sites archive information, so what you find one week may be gone the next. That's why it's important to have a citation that includes more than just the URL. Consult a website like www.easybib.com for help on citing resources.

TIP

When it's time to analyze your industry, you'll find a wealth of information out there. One good place to start is with the Standard Industrial Classification Code List at www.sec.gov/info/edgar/siccodes.htm. This site lets you search for your industry and industry segment and then gives you the 4-digit SIC code that represents that portion of the industry. This code can prove useful for finding information at many sites you may choose.

Checking out the status of your industry

REMEMBER

As you begin to do your research, you will probably find yourself overwhelmed with data and unsure which is important and which is not. Here's a list of questions to guide you in defining the critical information about your industry:

>> **Is the industry growing?** Growth can be measured in many ways: number of employees, revenues, units produced, and number of new companies entering the industry.

>> **Who are the major competitors?** You want to understand which companies dominate the industry, what their strategies are, and how your business is differentiated from them.

>> **Where are the opportunities in the industry?** In some industries, new products and services provide more opportunity, whereas in others, an innovative marketing and distribution strategy will win the game.

>> **What are the trends and patterns of change in your industry?** You want to look backward and forward to study what has happened over time in your industry to see if it foreshadows what will happen in the future. You also want to see what the industry prognosticators are saying about the future of the industry. But the best way to find out about the future of your industry is to get close to the new technology that is in the works yet may not hit the marketplace for five years.

>> **What is the status of new technology and R&D spending?** Does your industry adopt new technology quickly? Is your industry technology-based or driven by new technology? If you look at how much the major firms are spending on research and development of new technologies, you'll get a pretty good idea of how important technology is to your industry. You'll also find out how rapid the product development cycle is, which tells you how fast you'll have to be to compete.

>> **Are there young and successful companies in the industry?** If you see no new companies being formed in your industry, it's a pretty good bet that it's a mature industry with dominant players. That doesn't automatically preclude your entry into the industry, but it does make it much more expensive and difficult.

>> **Are there any threats to the industry?** Is there anything on the horizon that you or others can see that makes any part of your industry obsolete? Certainly, if you were in the mechanical office equipment industry in the early 1980s, you should have seen the writing on the wall with the introduction and mass acceptance of the personal computer.

>> **What are the typical gross profit margins in the industry?** The *gross profit margin* (or *gross margin*) tells you how much room you have to make mistakes. Gross margin is the gross profit (revenues minus cost of goods sold) as a percentage of sales. If your industry has margins of 2 percent, like the grocery industry has (sometimes even less), you have little room for error, because 98 percent of what you receive in revenues goes to pay your direct costs of production. You only have 2 percent left to pay overhead. On the other hand, in some industries gross margins run at 70 percent or more, so you end up with a lot more capital to expend on overhead and profit.

Competitive intelligence: Checking out the competition

One of the most difficult tasks you'll face is finding information about your competitors. Not the obvious things that you can easily find by going to a competitor's physical site or website (although of course you should do those things), but the really important stuff that can affect what you do with your business concept. Things like how much competitors spend on customer service, what their profit margins are, how many customers they have, what their growth strategies are, and so forth.

If you're in competition with private companies (which is true most of the time), your task is that much more difficult because private companies don't have to disclose the kinds of information that public companies do.

Here's some of the information you may want to collect on your competitors:

» The management style of the company

» Current market strategies — also what they've done in the past because history tends to repeat itself

» The unique features and benefits of the products and services they offer

» Their pricing strategy

» Their customer mix

» Their promotional mix

With a concerted effort and a plan in hand, you can find out a lot about the companies you'll be competing against. This section provides a step-by-step strategy for attacking the challenge of competitive intelligence.

Pound the pavement

If your competition has bricks-and-mortar sites, visit them and observe what goes on. What kinds of customers frequent their sites? What do they buy, and how much do they buy? What is the appearance of the site? How would you evaluate the location? Gather as much information as you can through observation and talking to customers and employees.

Buy your competitors' products

Buying your competitors' products helps you find out more about how your competition treats its customers and how good its products and services are.

If you think that it sounds strange to buy your competitors' products, just remember, as soon as yours are in the marketplace, your competitors will buy them.

Rev up the search engines

Go to the Internet and hit the search engines. Just type in the names of the companies you're interested in and see what comes up. True, this is not the most effective way to search, but it's a start, and you never know what you'll pull up that you otherwise may not have found.

TIP

Try to go beyond Google. In addition to Google (www.google.com), you might try Bing (www.bing.com), Yahoo! (www.yahoo.com), DuckDuckGo (www.duckduckgo.com), and Ask (www.ask.com). And be sure to check out your competition's social media activity on sites like Facebook (www.facebook.com), Pinterest (www.pinterest.com), Instagram (www.instagram.com), and Twitter (www.twitter.com). Finally, see whether anyone is saying anything about your competitors on the customer review site Yelp (www.yelp.com).

Check information on public companies

TIP

In most industries, public companies are the most established companies and often the dominant players, so it's a good idea to check them out. They can also serve as benchmarks for best practices in the industry. There are a host of online resources related to public companies. Here are two to get you started:

>> **D&B Hoovers** (www.hoovers.com): This source provides detailed profiles of public companies. Visit the site to find out about current pricing.

>> **U.S. Securities and Exchange Commission** (www.sec.gov): This site contains the SEC's EDGAR (Electronic Data Gathering, Analysis, and Retrieval) database about companies. It's not terribly user friendly but has great information. Try Free Edgar, www.freeedgar.com, which is a good place to research public companies and those that have filed to go public.

Use online media

Here are some great online sources that you may want to check out:

>> **Inc.** (www.inc.com): This database of the fastest-growing private companies in the U.S. contains information you won't find elsewhere on revenue, profit-and-loss percentages, numbers of employees, and so forth for the past eight years.

» **Fuld + Company** (www.fuld.com): This site gives you advice on how to seek competitive intelligence and has many links to information on specific industries.

» **ProfNet** (www.profnet.com): This site provides a direct link to experts at universities, colleges, corporations, and national laboratories. You may be able to find an expert in your industry and contact that person. Check the site for current pricing.

» **ProQuest eLibrary** (www.elibrary.com): This is a great site if you're looking for articles, reference works, and news wires. You can request a free trial; check the site for current pricing. If you're near a local university, you may be able to access it from the university's library computers.

Look for data at government websites

You can find an extensive network of government sites with mostly free information on economic news, export information, legislative trends, and so forth. You may want to go directly to often-used sites like the following:

» **U.S. Department of Commerce** (www.commerce.gov): Here you'll find everything you ever wanted to know about the U.S. economy.

» **U.S. Census Bureau** (www.census.gov): This is the home of the stats based on the census taken every ten years. The amount of information available here is very impressive.

» **Bureau of Labor Statistics** (www.bls.gov): This is another site full of information on the economy, in particular, the labor market.

Go off-line for more research

The Internet is not the only place you can find important information. Here are two off-line options you ought to consider:

» **Industry trade associations:** Virtually every industry has its own trade association with a corresponding journal or magazine. Trade associations usually track what's going on in their industries, so they are a wealth of information. If you are serious about starting a business in your particular industry, you may want to join a trade association, so you'll have access to inside information.

» **Network, network, network:** Take every opportunity to talk with people in the industry. They are on the front lines on a daily basis and they will give you information that is probably more current than what you'll find in the media or on the web.

Defining Your Market Niche

Markets are groups of customers inside an industry. Take a look at Figure 1-1 and you can see that in conducting your feasibility analysis (covered earlier in this chapter), you work your way down from the broad industry to the narrower market niche.

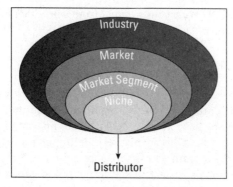

FIGURE 1-1: Finding your niche.

© John Wiley & Sons, Inc.

Narrowing your market

Within each broad market are segments. For example, the broad market of people who buy books contains segments of customers for

» Travel books (or any other broad category of books)

» Kids' books

» Books appealing to seniors

» Audiobooks

Within a market segment, you can find niches — specific needs that perhaps aren't being served — such as

» Travel books geared toward people with disabilities

» Kids' books that target minorities

» Books that teach seniors how to deal with technology

» Audiobooks that provide current journal articles to professionals

Market niches provide a place for new businesses to enter a market and gain a foothold before bigger companies take notice and begin to compete. Having a niche all to yourself gives you a quiet period during which you alone serve a need of the customer that otherwise is not being met. As a result, you get to set the standards for the niche. In short, you're the market leader.

REMEMBER

As you zero in on your market, take care that the niche you ultimately choose is big enough to allow your business to make money. The niche you select must have enough customers willing to buy your product from you, enabling you to pay your expenses and turn a profit.

Defining your target market is about identifying the primary customer for your products or services — the customer most likely to purchase from you. You want to identify a target market because creating customer awareness of a new product or service is time-consuming and costly, requiring lots of marketing dollars — dollars that few start-ups have at their disposal. So, instead of using a shotgun approach and trying to bag a broad market, aiming at the specific customers who are likely to purchase from you is far more effective. More important still, going to the customer who's easiest to sell to helps you gain a foothold quickly and start to build brand recognition, which makes selling to other potential customers easier.

Your first definition of a target customer will probably be fairly loose — an estimate. For example, suppose you target customers are "professional women." That's a fairly broad estimate. But as you conduct market research, you come to know your primary customer well. In this example, the picture may emerge of "a woman in law, medicine, or business, between 35 and 55 years of age, married, with children."

The basic questions to answer about your potential customers are:

» What are their demographics: Age, education, ethnicity, income level?

» What are their buying habits? What do they buy? When? How?

» How do customers hear about your products and services? Do your customers buy based on TV ads, magazines, social media, web advertising, word-of-mouth, referrals?

» How can your new business meet customers' needs? What customer need is your product now meeting?

Where do you find the answers to these important questions? Your market research — actually talking with potential customers — provides answers.

REMEMBER

Not all customers are individuals; many are other businesses. In fact, the greatest dollar volume of transactions conducted on the Internet today is business-to-business. If a distributor, wholesaler, retail store, or manufacturer is paying you, your customer is a business, not an individual consumer. Businesses as customers can be described in pretty much the same way that you describe a person. Businesses come in a variety of sizes and revenue levels. Like consumers, they also have buying cycles, tastes, and preferences.

Don't forget that if your customer is another business, that business may not be the actual end user of your product or service. So then you also have an end user to deal with. The *end user* is the ultimate consumer, the person who uses the product or service. For example, here is a typical channel for distributing a product:

Manufacturer > Distributor > Retailer > Consumer

If that distribution channel is filled with your products — refrigerators, for example — who is your customer? It's the distributor who purchases the fridge from you to distribute to retailers. The retailer, in turn, is the distributor's customer. The consumer, who actually uses the fridge, is the retailer's customer and your end user. (The easiest way to identify the customer is to find out who pays you — follow the money.)

REMEMBER

Just because the end users aren't technically your customers doesn't mean that you can ignore them. You need to know as much about the end user as you do about the customer, because you must convince the distributor that a market for the product exists and that the end user will buy enough product so that the distributor and retailer can make a profit. Thus, you must conduct the same kind of research on the end user that you do on the distributor.

Developing a niche strategy

One primary reason to define and analyze a target market is to find a way into the market so that you have a chance to compete. If you enter a market without a strategy, you're setting yourself up for failure. You are the new kid on the block. If customers can't distinguish you from your competitors, they're not likely to buy from you. People generally prefer to deal with someone they know.

Niche strategy is probably the premier strategy for entrepreneurs because it yields the greatest amount of control. Creating a niche that no one else is serving is the key. That way, you become the leader and can set the standards for those who follow. Niche strategy is important because, as the sole occupant of the niche, you can establish your business in a relatively safe environment (the quiet period) before you develop any direct competitors. Fending off competitors takes a lot of marketing dollars, and when you're a start-up company, you have numerous better uses for your limited resources.

How do you find a niche that no one else has found? By talking to customers. The target market from which your business opportunity comes also holds the keys to your entry strategy. Your potential customers tell you what's missing in your competitors' products and services. They also tell you what they need. Fulfilling that unmet need is your entry strategy.

Zeroing In on a Brand-New Product

Many entrepreneurs would like to deal in products, but they're not quite sure how to get started. Of course, you could import products from other countries or buy your products from domestic manufacturers. But if you like the idea of manufacturing and distributing a brand-new technology or other type of product, then you have three choices: invent something, team up with an inventor, or license an invention.

Become an inventor

If you're the kind of person who likes to tinker and play around with new ideas that might become inventions, then your role might be to invent a new product. Most entrepreneurs and start-up businesspeople, however, are not inventors — not because they don't have the ability to invent, but because their focus is elsewhere.

The mindsets of businesspeople and inventors tend to be quite different, and it's unusual to find both in the same person. Not only are the mindsets different, but the skills required by each are very different. In general, pure inventor types aren't interested in the commercial side of things. They invent for the love of invention. Unless an entrepreneur comes along and points out an opportunity, many inventors never see their inventions reach the marketplace.

REMEMBER

Many types of inventors — engineers, scientists, and so forth — would rather spend their time in the laboratory than consider business issues like markets and customers. You have to ask yourself what role feels right to you and do that. You can always find the other talents in someone else.

Team up with an inventor

Entrepreneurs often team up with inventors to commercialize a new product. Often the opportunity to pair up with an inventor comes out of the industry in which you're working. You hear about someone who's working on something; you investigate and discover an interesting invention.

Don't hesitate to approach an inventor, but remember a couple important things:

>> Inventors are paranoid about their inventions. They are sure that someone is out to steal their ideas.

>> Inventors typically aren't business oriented and don't want to become business people. Their love is inventing, so don't expect them to be partners in a business sense.

TIP

Be sure your attorney structures a beneficial arrangement with your inventor that doesn't hamstring your efforts to commercialize the invention. You are each bringing something very important to the mix, so be sure you can work together well. For much more on the details of inventing, check out *Inventing For Dummies* by Pamela Riddle Bird and Forrest M. Bird (Wiley).

License an invention

Companies, universities, the government, and independent inventors are all looking for entrepreneurs to commercialize their inventions. You gain access to these inventions through a vehicle known as licensing. *Licensing* grants you the right to use the invention in an agreed-upon way for an agreed-upon time period. In return, you agree to pay a royalty to the inventor, usually based on sales of the product that results from the invention.

TIP

The government owns many core technologies developed for the military and the aerospace program, among others. You can license these core technologies and create a new application for use in a different industry. Alternatively, visit the technology licensing office of most major research universities and you'll find more opportunities. For example, the Stanford University Office of Technology Licensing (`http://otl.stanford.edu`) evaluates, markets, and licenses technology owned by Stanford University. Universities are a gold mine of new technology you can tap into.

Chapter **2**

Refining and Defining Your Business Idea

Almost all successful businesses begin with a good idea. The idea may be based on a brand new product or service. Or, it may introduce an existing product or service into a new niche. Great business ideas are born when someone figures out a better way to make something or to provide customers what they need or want. Successful business ideas don't have to be world-shaking. But no matter how modest or extensive they are, they have to appeal to customers in order to succeed.

Writing a business plan is one of the most important steps in shaping an idea and putting it to its first test (see Chapter 1 in Book 2 for details). The process of writing a business plan can help you identify both the strengths and weaknesses of your idea. Doing so can enable you to tweak your idea to make it as strong as possible. Count on the following pages to fuel your idea-generating process with tips and tools for taking stock of your personal resources, asking others for advice, brainstorming ideas alone or in a group, putting your possibilities through a make-it-or-break-it reality check, and, finally, weighing the likelihood that investors, customers, and colleagues will want to buy into your business proposition.

Recognizing the Power of a Good Idea

Facebook started with a good idea. So did Whole Foods. Toyota had a pretty good idea when it developed a hybrid engine. Apple did too, when the company decided to build a touch screen device big enough to read, draw, and write on. Today, Tesla is an engine of innovative ideas. So is Google. Even simple ideas — like creating a website where people with accommodations to rent connect with people who want to rent them — can grow into billion-dollar businesses.

Good ideas aren't limited to major companies. The young couple who decides to open a doggy day care in a town where a lot of people commute to work may have a great idea, too. Or, there's the home brewer who realizes that a small-town ale can make it big. Even the local caterer who decides to take her business on the road in the form of a fleet of food trucks may be able to turn that idea into profit.

REMEMBER

When coming up with a good business idea, keep these five key characteristics in mind:

>> A good business idea meets a real need or desire.

>> It offers something new (or at least a little different).

>> It's grounded in reality, not wishful thinking.

>> It can generate money.

>> It's something you want to do.

Read on to begin the process of developing and fine-tuning your business idea to make sure it can stand up to the harsh realities of the marketplace.

Knowing the difference between passion and profitability

Plenty of profitable businesses owe their success to a personal passion. A baker who starts a successful bakery, a musician who opens a recording studio, a teacher who starts a nonprofit tutoring service all have passion in common. That's great. Excitement and confidence are crucial to making a business a success.

So is a good dose of reality.

WARNING

Being excited about what you want to do is no guarantee of success. Businesses that begin with passionate optimism sometimes go belly-up. Personal passion can carry you away, blinding you to the hard realities that any business faces in making it in today's highly competitive world. The bottom line of all for-profit businesses is ultimately — you guessed it — profit. If you're hoping to turn a personal passion into a successful business, you need to ask yourself a simple question: Can it make a profit?

The question may be simple. Answering it isn't always so easy.

TIP

If you're sitting down to write a business plan because you already have a knock-'em-dead idea, now's the good time to give it a test run. Use the following questions:

>> Does the idea meet a real need or desire?

>> What's new or different about the idea?

>> Who are your customers likely to be?

>> What do you offer your customers that no one else does?

>> How much are they willing to pay?

>> Who are your competitors?

>> What's the best thing about the idea?

>> What's the biggest weakness?

>> What will be the biggest challenge you face in turning your idea into a reality?

>> How long will it take to get a business up and running?

>> Is this idea scalable, meaning can you provide more to meet demand, and if so, how?

>> Is this something you really want to do?

Turning a side gig into a business

Lots of people have their day jobs — you know, the work that pays the rent — and then they have the thing they really like to do, whether it's making pottery, volunteering at the animal shelter, or collecting dolls. And most of them would love nothing more than turning their side interests into a profit-making business.

Good for them, but it takes more than passion to start a successful business. Most successful entrepreneurs will tell you that they were surprised to discover what goes into making a business work. Often, the surprise is how little they knew about the nuts and bolts of operating a business. Consider the example of a woman who developed her baking skills at home and then started a highly successful northern California bakery. She knew the craft of baking. She knew the equipment she needed to go from home baking to commercial baking. What she wasn't prepared for was managing a staff. In the first year, personnel problems plagued her bakery and almost scuttled her business.

TIP

If you're thinking of turning something you love to do into a business, take time to ask yourself some basic but important questions. You can use the following questions to begin the process of exploring what you need to turn passion into profitability:

>> What is your product or service? (Be as specific as possible.)

>> How will you make money? (Be as specific and creative as possible.)

>> How will you reach your customers or clients?

>> Where will you conduct your business?

>> Will you need employees? How many? What jobs will they do?

>> What kinds of equipment will you need to get started?

>> How much money will you need to get up and running?

>> What are your monthly operating expenses likely to be?

>> How much money will you need to earn each month to be successful?

>> What are your biggest strengths to start this business?

>> What are your greatest weaknesses?

>> What can you do to turn those weaknesses into strengths (or at least work around them)?

>> Who are your competitors? What are their strengths and weaknesses?

>> What are the potential risks a business like this faces? How can you minimize the risks?

Planning ahead: Great ideas take time

Most ideas require time to take off. A musician who decides to go professional needs to find gigs (and probably music students). An accountant who decides to leave her company and start her own business needs to set up an office and line up clients. An inventor with the next big thing needs to arrange for manufacturing, distribution, and marketing. They all take time. And while the clock ticks, cash goes out — but no or few revenues come in.

REMEMBER

The more realistic you are about how much time your idea will take and how much you'll need to spend before revenue kicks in, the better prepared you'll be. Looking ahead, especially with a new venture, requires a fair amount of guesswork, but be as realistic as possible. Detail what you're working to achieve and all the major steps you'll need to take, often referred to as *mileposts* you'll need to pass, in order to succeed. Then establish a timeline for when you'll be able to reach each one. The result? A diagram of the runway for your business or business idea.

Checking out the competition

TIP

The saying goes that there's nothing new under the sun. It also applies to most new businesses. Unless it's a totally new and disruptive innovation, chances are a similar business to the one you're planning to launch already exists. One easy way to test your new idea is to check out how other people doing roughly the same thing are faring. In some cases, all you have to do is ask. Unless people perceive you as a competitive threat, they're usually willing to share details about their businesses. If not, you can uncover information in other ways, such as the following:

>> **Check websites of similar businesses for information about products and services, including pricing.** If appropriate, peruse online customer reviews of your competitors, which can provide invaluable tips on how you can do better.

>> **Search the web for business articles about the kind of business you're planning.** Be sure to check publication dates, because business reports can go quickly out of date. If you don't find what you need online, head to your local library to browse the periodical shelves.

>> **Investigate how similar businesses present and market their goods or services.** If you're starting a local business, check out your competitors' presence in local media and online. If you're going after a national or international market, analyze how other businesses in your arena use major media, their own websites, social media, business partnerships, and collaborations to present their offerings.

>> **Check out local business organizations.** Most cities and even small towns have Chambers of Commerce and economic development organizations with websites you can study. If you don't find what you need there, make a visit to the bricks-and-mortar office to talk to a representative about your business sector, its major players, its current conditions, and its untapped opportunities.

>> **Talk to prospective customers.** If you're starting a local business, ask friends and family what they consider important as prospective customers and what wants or needs aren't being addressed. If you're planning a retail business, visit similar stores and observe how customers move through the aisles and what they do and don't buy.

Brainstorming New Business Ideas

Not all new businesses start with an idea. Some begin with a group of talented people in search of an idea. Others begin when an individual decides to join the self-employed ranks and begin to think, "But what will I do?"

Plenty of would-be entrepreneurs have caught themselves thinking, "Why didn't I think of that?" or "How in the world did they come up with that idea?" Great ideas may look lucky or random, but when you look a little closer, you're likely to find that considerable time and effort went into making them happen. Those visionaries everyone admires were able to foresee market needs and respond with precisely matched product and service solutions.

REMEMBER

Brainstorming isn't just for when you're starting out. Even after you're off and running, you must constantly stay on the lookout for ways to revitalize existing offerings or add new products or services to stay ahead of the competition. That's especially true these days, with the accelerating pace of technological change.

The following sections can help you generate brand-new ideas to build a business around and possibly be the next visionary. They provide you with tried-and-true methods for revving your creative engine — whether alone or in a group — and snaring great ideas for your next business venture.

Reimagining your business environment

A survey of 500 of the fastest-growing companies in the United States showed that nearly half grew directly out of the founders' previous work environments. In other words, the founders created these companies after looking around at what they were doing and thinking, "There *has* to be a better way to do this." Solutions to challenges also often come from within. After all, who knows your business and your customers' wants and needs better than you and your employees? With that knowledge, ask: What would you do, what products and services would you offer, and how would you produce and present your products if you were starting from scratch to address the problems and fulfill the desires that your business addresses?

WARNING

As you dream up new business ideas, be aware of potential roadblocks. For example, many companies require employees to sign *noncompete agreements*. These agreements usually prohibit former employees from engaging in competitive businesses for a set period of time. If you've signed one, make sure your new venture doesn't violate its terms.

Also, watch out for tunnel vision. Although people inside the company are an invaluable source of new ideas, there are many examples of companies that recognized the challenges they faced but were unable to come up with effective strategies to meet them. The reason: People inside a company who are used to the way things work often have trouble thinking outside the box. Even sole proprietors and small business people run into the same problem. They're so close to the company and its way of doing business that they can't see the forest for the trees.

TIP

One way around the problem of tunnel vision is to invest in the talents of an outside consultant — someone who sees your business and its challenges with fresh, unbiased eyes. Another approach, if you have employees in a variety of positions, is to ask someone from an unrelated part of the business to look at the problem and suggest solutions.

REMEMBER

When considering new business possibilities, keep in mind that 99 percent of all businesses (both old and new) fall into one of three broad categories:

>> **Products for sale:** Consider the range of products that your industry offers.

- Can you think of innovative ways to make them better?

- Can you imagine a product that completely replaces them?

- What new product would knock you out of business if the competition offered it first?

>> **Services for hire:** Consider the services that your industry offers.

- Do you notice problems with consistency?

- What isn't being done that should be?

- What do customers complain about?

- What new services would threaten your business if the competition offered them first?

>> **Distribution and delivery:** Ask yourself similar questions about your distribution and delivery systems.

- What are the most serious bottlenecks?

- Can you think of clever ways to improve distribution?

- Can you envision a radically new delivery system? (Think Amazon and its proposed drone delivery program.)

Inspiring team creativity (with or without donuts or bagels)

The best creative thinking isn't necessarily done alone. Put a few heads together, and you may whip up a mental hurricane. The outcome depends on the nature of the group of individuals you assemble (the more dynamic, inspired, freewheeling, and innovative, the better) and the communication skills that the session leader brings into the room.

WARNING

The quickest way to kill an idea is to say anything akin to any of the following:

>> It won't work.

>> We're not ready for that.

>> It isn't practical.

>> It's already been done.

>> That's just plain stupid.

The group you assemble needs to remain open to all ideas presented in order to develop a healthy idea-generating environment.

Applying the LCS system to nurture new ideas

To nurture brand-new ideas and allow them to grow, use the three-part *LCS system:*

>> *L* is for *likes,* as in, *"What I like about your idea . . . ."* Begin with some positive comments to encourage people to let loose with every creative idea that comes to mind. Not every idea will work. But even zany ideas can spark more practical and effective ones.

>> *C* is for *concerns,* as in, *"What concerns me about your idea . . . ."* Sharing concerns begins dialogue that opens up and expands the creative process. As you point out a concern, someone else in the group is likely to offer a creative solution.

>> *S* is for *suggestions,* as in, *"I have a few suggestions . . . ."* Offering suggestions moves the brainstorming session along and may lead to the generation of a brand-new set of ideas.

Assembling a brainstorming session

With the LCS system fresh in your minds, your group can take on a brainstorming session following these steps:

1. Start with a small group of people you trust and admire.

You can turn to friends, relatives, professional acquaintances — anyone you think may contribute a new and useful perspective.

2. Invite a couple of ringers.

Consider inviting a few people beyond your small group who can stretch the group's thinking, challenge assumptions, and take the group in new and unexpected directions, even if these individuals may make you feel a bit uncomfortable.

3. Choose the right time and place.

The same old places can lead to the same old thinking, so be inventive. To inspire creativity, change the scene. Larger companies often hold brainstorming sessions at off-site retreats. If you're a small company or sole proprietor, you can still meet in a place that inspires creativity, such as a park or local coffeehouse (as long as it's not too crowded or noisy). Whatever location you choose, be sure to have everything you need for brainstorming — from an old-fashioned scratchpad to an iPad or digital voice recorder — handy.

4. Establish ground rules.

Explain what you want the group to achieve. Introduce the LCS system (see the previous section) so that participants have a tool that allows them to make positive contributions to the session. Emphasize the fact that at this stage in planning, there are no bad ideas. The group should be encouraged to be as freewheeling as possible.

5. Act as the group's conductor.

Keep the process moving without turning into a dictator. Use these tactics:

- Encourage alternatives: *How else can we do that?*
- Stimulate visionary thinking: *What if we had no constraints?*
- Invite new perspectives: *How would a child see this?*
- Ask for specifics: *What exactly do you mean?*
- Clarify the next steps: *How should we proceed on that?*

6. **Record the results.**

Designate a person to take notes throughout the session or record the session to review later. Remember, the best ideas are often side comments, so capture the offbeat comments as well as the mainstream discussion. Every idea, even ones that seem zany, can lead to something useful. Assign someone the task of taking digital pictures of white boards. Sometimes a great idea passes by so quickly that people only later say, "Hey, what was that idea we had?"

7. **Review your notes and thoughts while they're still fresh.**

Set aside time after the brainstorming session to distill the discussion down to three or four ideas that you want to continue working on.

Identifying Business Opportunities

Maybe the idea behind some highly successful businesses began with a flash of inspiration that came out of nowhere. But not many. Most were developed by painstakingly surveying the territory and looking for a new or better product or service, a new way to deliver value to customers, or a new business model. Some great business ideas grow out of a confluence of new technological innovations (think iPad). Some are inspired by regulatory changes (think the solar power industry). Some are born out of passion (think of the artist who opens a gallery). These sections provide tips to assist you in recognizing opportunities that just may lead to an unbeatable business idea.

Tuning in to what customers have to say

The Internet — and specifically online review sites — can be an excellent source of inspiration for new business opportunities. Customers, it turns out, have very strong opinions about what they've bought or what they want, and they're not afraid to voice them. Just look at the reviews on Amazon, Yelp, HomeAway, and other consumer sites. Those reviews, good and bad, can tell you exactly what customers like, what they don't like, and what they'd like to see in products and services. Their input is a gold mine of information.

Say that you're interested in designing and producing a computer program that will make it easier for people to compose their own songs. Several such programs already exist. Go onto the sites that sell them, such as Musician's Friend, and you'll find plenty of chatter from satisfied and unsatisfied customers. Their likes and dislikes can help you decide what your product needs to offer in order to compete with products already in the marketplace.

The people who write online reviews of products and services are often outliers. Either they loved what they bought or they hated it, which is why they're motivated to take the time to write a review. The bulk of customers falls somewhere in between. Online reviews can give you a good sense of the two ends of the spectrum. Most of your potential customers are likely to lie somewhere in between.

Pursuing changes that open up new opportunities

Many fledgling businesses succeed by jumping on new opportunities that arise through technological, social, policy, or other changes. Change can be scary, but it can also open new doors. Spotting that door — and being the first to open it — requires skill and a little daring. For example, when Apple launched the iPad, a whole new industry of apps and accessories sprang into existence, created by designers and developers perceptive and daring enough to plunge into a new technology and a new marketplace.

As Internet bandwidth increased and the potential for streaming video appeared on the horizon, companies like Amazon, Netflix, and Hulu seized the opportunity, establishing themselves as leaders and leaving some competitors — remember Blockbuster Video? — in the dust. Today, with baby boomers retiring, a host of companies are looking for ways to strike gold by opening high-end retirement communities, providing healthcare consulting services, or offering products and services that promise to keep people youthful even as they age.

Any time the government breaks up a monopoly, new arenas for competition arise. Regulatory changes and new tax incentives also open the door to opportunity, if you're smart and agile enough to take advantage. As part of your brainstorming (covered earlier in this chapter), ask your team to consider ongoing or likely changes that could open up new opportunities.

There are many ways to spell business success. True, many companies succeed by creating a brand-new product or service. But opportunities also materialize for selling existing products or services to new customers or by creating a new business model that makes an existing product or service more appealing to established or new customers.

These days, many companies prosper by finding clever ways to make people's personal or working lives easier or more efficient. Think no-iron shirts. Think parking garages that offer car washes. Think dictation software that does away with the need to type. Think apps for making restaurant reservations. Evaluate your promising business idea to see whether you can take advantage of new opportunities to improve the efficiency or effectiveness of your customers' lives.

Narrowing your choices

After some combination of brainstorming, market analysis, and a few random flashes of brilliance, you may accumulate a drawerful of promising business ideas. Following are two guidelines to help you separate the real opportunities from the fluff:

>> **Focus on the ideas that you're really excited about.** Your passion is what will keep you motivated on the road to success.

>> **Pursue ideas that you can follow through on.** If you feel you don't have the means or the drive to take an idea from the drawing board to the real world, scrap it.

TIP

To help you choose among your ideas, use the following questions for each possibility you're considering. Tally your answers and consider any idea with a score of 24 or higher worthy of serious consideration. The one exception to the scoring: If your promising idea scores high on every question except for number 3 (Is this the kind of business you really want to pursue?), it may be a great idea for someone else — but not for you.

1. **Describe your promising idea in two sentences.**

2. **Being as honest as you can, rate the idea on a scale of 1 to 10 with 1 being "the only thing we could come up with in a pinch" and 10 being "the best thing since sliced bread."**

3. **Think seriously about what you would have to do to turn your idea into reality.**

   Is this the kind of idea — and the kind of business — you really want to pursue? Rate your interest on a scale of 1 to 10 with 1 for "so-so" and 10 for "very high."

4. **Imagine sitting down and persuading an investor to put down hard-earned cash to help turn your idea into a real business.**

   How easy would it be to convince a skeptical outsider that your idea has the potential to make money? Choose your answer from 1, meaning "very difficult," to 10, meaning "a breeze."

5. **Being as objective as you can, ask yourself what odds your idea has of becoming a real business venture.**

   Rate your chances from 1, meaning "it's a long shot," to 10, meaning "it's a guaranteed overnight success."

REMEMBER

Use the preceding questions as a first test for any business idea. If the idea scores high, it still has to pass other hurdles, but at least you know that it's an idea worth pursuing.

After you answer the preceding questions, separating the promising ideas from all the others, it's a good idea to answer some basic questions that reveal pretty quickly whether or not an idea has what it takes to become a real, live business.

TIP

Use the following questions to fill in details and to flesh out some of the issues around your preliminary business propositions. If you give your answers some careful thought, they'll reveal to you the likelihood of an idea breaking through as your winning business concept.

>> Describe your business opportunity in two sentences.

>> List the three most important features of the product or service you propose.

>> What basic customer needs does your product or service fill?

>> Briefly describe who is likely to buy your product or service.

>> List two or three existing products or services that already meet a similar need.

>> Why would customers choose your product or service over others?

>> How will you reach your customers?

>> How do you plan to make money?

REMEMBER

If you find yourself struggling to come up with answers to the preceding questions, your idea may be too sketchy to evaluate. That doesn't mean you have to abandon the idea, but you should take the time to understand the opportunity more fully before taking it to the next stage in the business development process. For example, if you can't easily describe the customer need you're filling or how you plan to make money, you still have homework to do.

Putting a Promising Idea to the Test

Asking questions like "Is this really such a good idea?" and "Who am I kidding, anyway?" doesn't mean you lack confidence. What asking these types of questions does mean is that you've come to the time to step back and make sure that the road you're on is leading you where you want to go. In short, you need a reality check.

In many ways, writing a business plan is a series of reality checks (see Chapter 1 in Book 2 for details). By making you carefully think through every aspect of your business — from the product or service you offer to the competitors you face and the customers you serve — the business-planning process brings you face to face with the realities of doing business. Read on for tips on bouncing your ideas around with people who may be able to help refine them, as well as useful ways to appraise your personal strengths and weaknesses when it comes to carrying out your ideas.

Doing your first reality check

After you settle on the idea that can power your business plan, take time out to conduct an honest evaluation. If that sounds easy, think again. Most would-be entrepreneurs are excited by their ideas. Excitement and a can-do spirit help drive success. But a dose of skepticism and honesty are also essential.

Ask these basic questions:

>> Is the idea that will power your business plan clearly stated? (If not, spend a little time refining it. Writing your idea down, and revising what you've written, is one way to get clarity.)

>> Is it doable? (If you have any doubts, rethink the scale of your undertaking, or make a list of what you'll need to make it doable.)

>> What excites you most about the idea?

>> What worries you about the idea?

>> What are the biggest hurdles to implementing your business idea? (A realistic list should probably include at least three items.)

>> How is your idea different from other great ideas out there in the marketplace?

>> Can you tweak the idea to make it even more powerful?

Anticipating disruptive innovations: Opportunities and cautions

Today's blockbuster idea may be next year's bankruptcy if new and unforeseen innovations or business models suddenly disrupt its business arena. Want an example? Remember the Flip video camera? Relatively inexpensive and a snap to use, it gobbled market share from established camcorder companies and soared in valuation. Then suddenly an altogether unanticipated competitor, the smartphone, disrupted the Flip camera. Smartphone cameras came installed, at no additional price, with video capability. As obituaries for Flip put it, the once-popular camera ended up "eating iPhone's dust."

REMEMBER

Disruptive innovations can be a source of both trouble (if you're not prepared) and opportunity (if you know how to seize the moment). The rise of the Internet, for example, spelled the demise of money-making classified ad sections in newspapers; however, it gave birth to Craigslist, eBay, and a host of other online services.

To begin to think about how the idea that will power your business plan could be affected by innovations coming through the pipeline:

>> **Make a list of all the technologies involved in the industry you're in or hope to enter.** Among them, identify the technologies that are undergoing — or are likely to undergo — innovative changes. How could those changes affect your business, either as a threat or an opportunity?

>> **Give some thought to your industry or business arena.** Has it undergone sweeping changes in the past? What drove those changes? Are there signs that it could be transformed again? In what ways? How would these scenarios of change affect the idea behind your business?

>> **Make a list of the assumptions that your business idea is founded on.** Question each of these assumptions. What if the founding assumptions behind your idea aren't as solid as you think? What could change? Take the car insurance business, for example. A big underlying assumption is that people like the convenience of owning their own car. But what if they don't? What if more and more people decide that getting a Zipcar or car2go is easier than hassling with car ownership? What happens when self-driving cars are a reality and you can hail one via app?

Don't expect to come up with definitive answers here. The idea is to recognize that disruptive changes can come along in almost any industry and marketplace. The more you question your assumptions and assess the implications of technological changes coming along, the better prepared you'll be.

Getting a second opinion

To help determine whether or not you're on solid ground, discuss your business idea and preliminary plans with someone outside your company. What you're really seeking is a *mentor* with most or all of the following characteristics:

>> Someone who has experience in the business area you're considering, or at least experience in a similar business

>> Someone with the courage to tell you the truth, whether it's "That's a great idea. Go for it!" or "If I were you, I'd take a little more time to think this over"

>> Someone you respect and admire and from whom you can take candid criticism without feeling defensive

Consider turning to colleagues you've worked with in the past, teachers or professors, friends from college, or other associates.

WARNING

Friends and family members sometimes can offer the advice and perspective you need, but emotional ties can get in the way of absolute honesty and objectivity. If you go this route, set some ground rules in advance. Be specific with your requests. Then, ask for suggestions, comments, and constructive criticism and be prepared to hear both the good and the bad without taking what you hear personally.

TIP

In addition to a mentor, consider designating someone to act as the devil's advocate to guarantee that you address the flip side of every issue that you're considering. This person's task is to be critical of each idea on the table — not in a destructive way, but in a skeptical, show-me-the-money, I'll-believe-it-when-I-see-it, how-is-this-new-or-better kind of way. In larger companies, you can accomplish this goal by creating two teams — one to defend the idea and the second to critique it. Ask the opposing team members to think of themselves as a competing firm looking to find weaknesses in the new venture.

Conducting a self-appraisal

Whether your idea will be the genesis for launching or growing a one-person business, a small business, or a business that aspires to be the next Google or Facebook, you still have one very important question to answer: Do you have what it takes to turn this opportunity into a success story?

The CEOs who became multimillionaires before they turned 25 and the entrepreneurs cruising around in sports cars issuing orders on their cellphones while the value of their stock values soar share some common traits: talent *and* hard work. To succeed, you must exhibit both, and to be a high-flyer or, for that matter, to be self-employed, you need discipline, confidence, and the capacity to live with the uncertainty that's part and parcel of being out on your own.

TIP

As a first step toward appraising your strengths and weaknesses, respond to the following 20 statements as candidly as you possibly can, rating yourself either poor, fair, good, or excellent for each one. There's no such thing as a perfect score. The point of the exercise is to identify your strongest and weakest areas so that you can capitalize and compensate accordingly.

- Setting goals and pushing yourself to achieve them on time

- Making decisions and completing tasks

- Organizing a complex schedule and getting things done efficiently

- Staying focused on the specific task at hand

- Juggling several tasks at one time

- Judging a person's character

- Getting along with other people and bringing out the best in them

- Listening to several sides of an issue and then making a decision

- Leading a team, even when there is disagreement among the members

- Understanding what motivates other people

- Resolving disputes among people

- Saying what you mean and meaning what you say

- Keeping your cool even when everyone else is losing his or hers

- Telling someone no

- Tending to the details of a project

- Looking at the big picture

- Acting decisively under pressure

- Adapting to changing circumstances

- Taking risks

- Taking responsibility, even when things go wrong

As you review your responses, watch for the following:

- Areas that receive "poor" ratings represent your weakest areas. Be alert for the need to compensate for these personal shortcomings.

- Areas that receive "excellent" ratings represent your greatest strengths and the personal resources you can call upon when you start your business venture.

REMEMBER

Not all personal strengths and weaknesses will contribute equally as you turn your idea into a business success. For example, if you're planning to be a sole proprietor who works mostly alone, the ability to manage a staff doesn't matter much, but self-motivation is absolutely essential. Or, if your success will depend on face-to-face presentations and individualized service, interpersonal skills will be indispensable.

TIP

As you respond to the preceding statements, place a star next to the six traits that you think are most important for turning your idea into a business success. For the moment, ignore how you rate yourself in each of those areas. Focus clearly on what it will take to propel your idea into a reality. Next, see how your personal strengths and weaknesses apply to the needs of your proposed business idea. Take the top six traits and align them with your personal abilities.

REMEMBER

Just because you're personally weak in an important area doesn't mean you don't have what it takes to turn your idea into a business. But it does unveil areas in which you'll either want to develop certain traits or enlist others to add necessary strengths. For example, if you aren't good with details, but details are important to the success of your business idea, this exercise alerts you to the fact that you may need to hire a personal assistant or cajole a colleague into tying up all the loose ends.

Chapter **3**

Creating a Business Model

S o what is a business model, anyway? Is it the way you make money? Yes, in part. Is it competitive advantage? Yes, in part. Is it your business plan? Not really. Simply put, a *business model* is your profit formula. It's the method you use to acquire customers, service them, and make money doing so. You can break down a business model into three primary areas: Offering, monetization, and sustainability. What is your offering? How will you monetize the offering? How will you sustain it?

Many businesspeople mistakenly believe that a business plan and a business model are one and the same. They're not. Your business model is the core concept upon which you build your business plan. Therefore, your business model should be a significant portion of your business plan. Too many business plans gloss over the business model in favor of lengthy financial projections and operational details that go along with business plans. Without a solid business model, though, these projections and details are likely premature. (Chapter 1 of Book 2 is devoted to business plans.) In today's turbulent environment, having a strong business model is more important than ever. This chapter outlines an accessible way to refine the essence of your business.

THE EVOLUTION OF BUSINESS MODELS

The notion of a business model may be relatively new, but the study of business in general has been going on for centuries. The notion of a business plan has been around since the late 1800s. Since then, business planning has grown from a mere notion to a science. Colleges offer courses in business planning. Software and templates have been created, and the general business public is well skilled in the practice.

Next came the concept of entrepreneurship. If you look at the rise of entrepreneurship, you see that it's grown from a vague concept in the 1960s to a major discipline in which you can now get a business degree. If you talk to recent college graduates about careers, a significant and growing percentage of them want to work for an entrepreneurial company or want to start a company of their own one day. Never before has entrepreneurship been celebrated the way it is today — both in the real world and in the academic world, where special programs and degrees are offered in entrepreneurship.

The study of business models can be called *advanced entrepreneurship*. The business model picks up where entrepreneurship leaves off and may well become the next wave of interest within the business community.

REMEMBER

Ideally, you should consider your business model before even starting to plan how your business will accomplish what it aims to accomplish. That's why business models are discussed in Book 1, which focuses on the foundations of your business idea, and business plans are discussed in Book 2, where you start up your business.

Identifying Who Needs a Business Model

Whether you're an army general or a donut shop owner, every organization has and needs a business model. Schools have business models. Not-for-profit organizations have business models. Families have business models. Even governments have business models.

There used to be an old saying in business: "It takes 15 years to become an overnight success." The gist of this saying was that a business owner needed to toil in anonymity for 15 years before becoming tremendously successful. Today, business moves much faster, and tremendous profitability can be achieved almost overnight. Commerce is worldwide and moves significantly faster now, creating better opportunities for better businesses. There's simply no need to slog it out for 15 years.

As businesses became very successful quickly, people started to ask, "How can this happen?" The only logical answer was superior business models. With financial stakes resembling lottery winnings, business models gained more and more attention.

Why is a business model suddenly necessary? People have operated successful businesses for centuries without a business model — or have they?

Sun Tzu (author of *The Art of War*) is widely believed to have provided Napoleon with a quantum shift in thinking, which led to the development of the model through which Napoleon's early successes were won. It's argued that when he moved away from the fundamentals of his business model and started to rely heavily on plans that didn't take into account the sustainability of his actions, he was defeated. The one thing Sun Tzu espoused loudly and often was to consider all aspects and influences of the job at hand. This concept elevated management to a high art. Sun Tzu believed it was critical not only to lay a great plan but also to be flexible and make excellent decisions when things became fluid.

REMEMBER

Business models aren't a fad. A strong business model is at the heart of a strong business and is the key to its profitability. Business models take all the complexity of a multibillion-dollar business and boil it down to an easy-to-communicate profitable essence. For your organization to operate at maximum effectiveness, an up-to-date and innovative business model is a necessity.

Common Aspects of All Business Models

REMEMBER

Whether your business model is cutting edge or based on 100-year-old principles, all business models answer the following questions:

>> **What problem are you trying to solve?** People don't need a new widget; they need a new widget to solve a problem. No one asked for an ATM. Customers wanted additional banking hours. The ATM solved this problem. Start with the job the customer is trying to accomplish, but without a good solution. These unserved or underserved markets provide the best opportunity for a great business model.

>> **Who needs this problem solved?** The answer to this question is the customer you'll be serving. In the case of the ATM, the market is very large — everyone with a bank account. In the case of pet cloning, the market is much smaller — people with $50,000 who loved their deceased pet enough to re-create it.

>> **What market segment is the model pursuing?** A *market segment* is a group of prospective buyers who have common needs and will respond similarly to your marketing. Nike makes shoes for many market segments, among them running, basketball, training, and soccer. Traditional marketing focuses on demographic segments while modern marketing focuses on buyer behaviors. (Flip to Book 5 for more on marketing and promotion.)

>> **How will you solve this problem better, cheaper, faster, or differently than other offerings?** Duluth Trading Company offers "ballroom jeans" that offer extra room in the right places so you can crouch without the ouch. Clever, unique offerings like these are superior to a better mousetrap.

>> **What is the value proposition?** What problem do you solve for the customer in relation to what you charge to fix it? Ballroom jeans have a clever niche and solve a problem for a defined segment, but if the price is $250 per pair, the value proposition is weak. Your product solves a problem for the customer. Hopefully, the customer values the solution and will pay you much more than it costs you to make the product. The larger this spread, the greater your value proposition.

>> **Where does your offer place you on the value chain?** Many creative business models — like Skype, ProFlowers, and eBay — have redefined the value chain by eliminating or shifting the partners that contribute to the final offering.

>> **What is your revenue model?** Factors such as how you'll charge for the product, how much you'll charge, and which portions of your offerings will be the biggest money makers all determine your revenue model. For instance, most airlines have radically changed their revenue models to charge separately for items that used to be bundled into the ticket price, effectively making them free. Items like checked bags, extra legroom, in-flight food, and even carry-on bags now generate billions of dollars in revenue for airlines.

>> **What is your competitive strategy?** You don't want to just jump into the shark tank. You need a plan to differentiate yourself from competition — via marketing, sales, and operations — that allows you to effectively outshine the competition.

>> **How will you maintain your competitive edge?** After you distance yourself from competitors, how will you hold off their attempts to copy your winning strategies? The best business models create barriers to maintain their hard-earned competitive advantage.

>> **What partners or other complementary products should be used?** Henry Ford was famous for creating companies to make everything included in his cars. Toyota relies on a partner network to engineer and manufacture most of the components for its cars. Savvy relationships with partners can enhance your business model.

>> **What network effects can be harnessed?** If you owned the only fax machine, it wouldn't be worth much because you couldn't send or receive a fax. Network effects enhance the value of everyone's purchase when the network of users grows. Nightclubs and Facebook rely on their large network of users to increase the value of their offer.

REMEMBER

The best business models aren't merely an idea. A great business model solves problems for customers creatively and generates more profit than was previously thought possible.

Business Models in Their Simplest Form

You have an overwhelming number of factors and concerns to consider when creating a business model. It can be daunting. Here's a simple three-part method to break down a model:

>> **What is the offering?** Are you selling roses on the side of the road or the fractional use of private jets? Why do customers need your offering? How is it different from customers' other options to solve their problem? Are you selling your product to the best market and in the best niche? Book 1, Chapter 4 talks more about the basics of creating a powerful offering.

>> **How will you monetize the offering?** Twitter has a powerful offering providing hundreds of millions of users valuable communication tools. However, Twitter has struggled to turn this offering into money. You must have more than just a product people want. You must be able to charge a price that generates significant margin and be able to sell it. Sharper Image was a company whose products were priced at a level that afforded high margins; however, not enough customers bought them. You must be able to execute your sales strategy in order to complete the monetization of the offering.

>> **How will you create sustainability?** Blockbuster Video had an exceptionally profitable business model for nearly two decades, but the company was unable to sustain it once it missed the digital video streaming boat. Factors such as maintaining/growing competitive advantage, the ability to innovate, and avoiding pitfalls affect the sustainability of the business model.

Examples of Business Models

There are business models hundreds of years old and models only a handful of years old, such as Internet freemium models. Some of the most profitable companies didn't invent new business models; they borrowed a business model from another industry. The Gillette razor and blades model has been highly profitable for Hewlett-Packard's inkjet printer business and Verizon's cellphone business. The cheap chic business model works for Trader Joe's in the grocery business and IKEA in the home furnishing business. Sometimes, one little tweak to an existing business model can yield powerful results in a new industry.

Table 3-1 shows a partial list of common business models. These examples should get your creative juices flowing as you begin to create your business model. Review the list for small ideas you can work into your model rather than copying a model lock, stock, and barrel.

TABLE 3-1   ## Types of Business Models

Type of Model	Description	Example Companies and Products
Razor and blades	Consumer purchases a low-margin item like a razor handle or inkjet printer. Sale of necessary consumables such as replacement blades or ink are sold at a very high markup.	Gillette, Hewlett-Packard printers, Keurig coffeemakers
Inverted razor and blades	Initial purchase has a high margin, but consumables are sold at a low margin to entice initial purchase or contrast to razor and blade competitor.	Kodak inkjet printers, Apple iPhone & iTunes combination. Apple makes very low margins on iTunes but high margins on hardware.
Cheap chic	Marketing of stylish but inexpensive merchandise. Typically allows for high margins because merchandise sells at low price points but has an expensive feel.	Target, Trader Joe's, IKEA
Bricks and clicks	Extension of in-store shopping to include online ordering with in-store pickup or items found exclusively online.	Best Buy, local mystery bookstore with online shop
Multilevel marketing	Leverage friends, family, and other personal networks to recommend products and act as a sales force. Works best for products needing recommendation to facilitate purchase.	Avon, Mary Kay, Amway
Franchise	Sell the right to use the business model in exchange for a percentage of revenues.	McDonald's, Holiday Inn, NFL

Type of Model	Description	Example Companies and Products
Anticipated upsell	High percentage of buyers ultimately purchase more than they expected. For instance, most new home buyers end up spending 1.2 times the base price of the home after extras.	Homebuilders, car dealerships, steel fabricators
Loss leader	This model offers velocity items for a very low margin in anticipation of additional sales at a higher margin.	Gas stations, $1 menus
Subscription model	One of the more popular models because of recurring revenue. Typically involves creating a significant asset and renting a piece of it.	Health clubs, software as a service
Collective	Similar to a franchise. Involves many businesses coming together for purchasing, marketing, or operational purposes but with looser ties than a franchise. Typically, collectives aggregate buying power and don't pay ongoing royalties like a franchise.	Ace Hardware, Carquest
Productization of services	Standardizing a predetermined bundle of services typically bought together and selling for a fixed price similar to a product. Many times it includes an element of flat-fee pricing as well.	A consultant charges $5,000 for a business plan analysis rather than charging $200 per hour, prepaid legal plans
Servitization of products	Making a product part of a larger service offering.	Rolls-Royce sells aircraft engines, not as distinct components but as complete solutions based on aviation miles. All operations and maintenance functions are included in this "Power by the Hour" plan.
Long tail	Based on Chris Anderson's famed 2004 *Wired* magazine article. Selecting a tiny niche and serving it in ways mass marketers can't. Hopefully, the tiny niche grows into a much larger one.	Fat Tire beer, YouTube bands, left-handed online store, micro-breweries
Direct sales	Bypass the traditional sales channels to target end users. Methods include door-to-door sales and company-owned stores.	Kirby Vacuums, Girl Scout cookies, outlet mall stores
Cut out the middle man	Removal of intermediaries in a supply chain, such as by skipping the warehouse distributor in the traditional three-step distribution chain.	AutoZone, Dell Computer, farmer's markets

(continued)

Creating a Business Model

TABLE 3-1 *(continued)*

Type of Model	Description	Example Companies and Products
Freemium business model	Product is offered for free. Typically 8% of users upgrade to become paying customers of virtual goods or to get expanded access.	Fortnite video game, shareware software, McAfee security
Online auctions	Create a community of buyers and sellers by using an auction-type selling process versus a set sales price.	eBay, Ariba
Hotel California model	Create a must-have product that traps customers into buying unrelated high-profit items.	Concessions at amusement parks, sporting events, movie theaters
Network effect	Create a product in which the value to each user becomes higher as more people use it.	Social networks
Crowdsourcing	Leveraging users to co-create products and sell to other users.	CafePress, Frito Lay new flavors, Kickstarter
Users as experts	Gives users access to technology and tools typically reserved for company employees. Users then create their own designs or versions of the product.	Cook-your-own-steak restaurants, LEGO
Premium	Offer high-end products that appeal to brand-conscious consumers.	Tiffany, Rolls-Royce
Nickel and dime	Price the most cost-sensitive item as low as possible and then charge for every little extra.	Airlines
Flat fee	The opposite of nickel and dime. Most or all incidental purchases are bundled into one fee.	Sandals Resorts, Southwest Airlines

Finding Success with a Business Model

In its simplest form, a business model is your profit formula. It's the method you use to acquire customers, service them, and make money doing so.

Every business has a business model, in fact, even if nobody ever bothers to write it down. That's because the business model is the basic structure of the business — what service it provides or what product it creates or sells to make money.

Generally, business models focus on the creation of profitable revenue and the delivery required to keep the revenue flowing. Most operational, finance, and human resource issues are peripheral to the creation of profitable revenue, and so they're separate from the business model. Here are some examples of business models in action:

>> Domino's focuses on inexpensive pizza, delivered fast. Jimmy John's has used a similar model in the sandwich business.

>> Toyota began the push of manufacturers leveraging lean manufacturing in order to produce better quality cars at a lower cost. After Toyota proved the model successful, many other companies followed Toyota's lead.

>> Walmart strives to consistently lower purchasing and operating costs and then pass the savings on to consumers. As this business model wooed customers away from established retailers, many retailers and non-retailers have imitated Walmart's model.

>> Zappos.com did what most thought impossible. It created an online business (selling shoes) where physically handling the product was important and virtualized it online. Zappos has set a new standard of online customer service by allowing customers to have several pairs of shoes delivered to their door, try them on in the convenience of their home, and send any or all of them back at no charge.

>> Dollar Shave Club has ignited a monthly club business model craze for everything from the monthly delivery of socks and t-shirts to baby clothes and feminine hygiene products. Even Walmart has jumped onto the monthly club bandwagon.

>> Zipcar competes with other car rental companies by renting cars by the hour in busy metropolitan areas for quick trips. Cars can be returned to any Zipcar drop-off location.

>> Crowdspring.com uses a unique business model for graphic design by leveraging crowdsourcing. Rather than pick vendors based upon the quality of their previous work, the customer posts how much she will pay for the project and vendors actually complete the design. Low resolution samples are shown to the buyer, and then a winner is chosen.

Your secret sauce for making money

At its most basic level, your business model is the formula that allows you to make money. You can think of it as the combination of everything you do — your secret sauce — to provide your customers with value and make a profit doing so. The more differentiated and proprietary your combination is, the more profitable you'll be.

Set yourself apart through differentiation

Differentiated business models offer customers products, services, or other value that stands out from the competition. Consider the following examples:

>> **Bigbelly** doesn't just make trash containers; Bigbelly's trash containers harness solar power to compact trash five times more than a typical container. This capability allows cities like Chicago, Philadelphia, and Boston to collect trash far less often and save fuel, manpower, and vehicle wear and tear.

>> **Camp Bow Wow** offers more than kenneling or dog-sitting. Dogs play together much like children at recess. Customers pay a premium for their dogs to have a good time rather than be cooped up all day.

>> **The Huffington Post** is an Internet-only news outlet.

>> **Walk-In Lab** doesn't accept insurance. Instead, the company provides low-cost medical testing to the uninsured.

Make your model difficult to copy

A proprietary business model is a differentiated model that's difficult or impossible for a competitor to emulate. Typically, proprietary models create methods to

>> **Deliver products and services better, cheaper, or faster through a business process known only to that company.** Examples include the following:

- Toyota's lean manufacturing process.

- Walmart's heavy investing in technology during the 1980s to create a logistical system that brought goods to market significantly more cheaply than its competitors.

>> **Create a closed ecosystem where ongoing use of your product is highly desirable or required.** A powerful ecosystem attracts new customers and discourages old customers from leaving. Here are some examples of successful closed ecosystems:

- The iTunes ecosystem (iPhone, iCloud, and iTunes) that created a proprietary business model for Apple.

- Amazon's Kindle, which created a large library of books on the proprietary format, making it difficult for customers to purchase any other product.

>> **Find a way to serve customers others thought were unprofitable.** Consider the following:

- Vistaprint attacked the micro business printing market thought unprofitable by most competitors. The combination of an Internet sales process and large-scale combining of orders allowed Vistaprint to grow rapidly in a contracting market.

- SafeAuto offers minimum coverage to drivers the big insurers deem too risky and too financially unstable to cover.

>> **Do business in a way competitors thought was unprofitable or impractical.** Your business model can be well protected if your competitors think you're nuts for trying. Here are some business models that had competitors shaking their heads:

- FedEx started as a Yale business school project for founder Fred Smith. Everyone, including Smith's professor (who gave the project a C), thought delivering packages overnight was an awful idea. Not dissuaded, Smith pursued the concept and spent years building the infrastructure to deliver packages efficiently and quickly. By the time it was clear that overnight package delivery was a good business model, Smith had a ten-year head start.

- Nearly every computer maker attempted a tablet computer and failed. It was well known that tablet computers were a niche product for hospitals and a select few customers. Apple ignored the gloom and doom and launched the iPad anyway. The product was a huge success and left competitors scrambling to create their own tablet computers.

>> **Create a product or service that's patented, trademarked, or difficult to duplicate.** Consider these examples:

- The Xerox 914 copier used a proprietary process to duplicate documents. It's quite possible that Xerox wouldn't have grown to become a Fortune 500 company if it had simply sold the 914 machine outright. Renting the machines was a much better business model. It cost Xerox around $2,000 to build one machine. Instead of selling it, Xerox rented the machines for

$95 per month plus 5 cents per copy for each one over the first 2,000 per month. Large customers like General Motors were copying up to 100,000 documents per month (that's a $4,995 rental per month).

- Nochar (www.nochar.com) makes an unpatented polymer that turns nasty liquid spills of anything from diesel fuel to nuclear waste into a solid. The proprietary product isn't patented because the company doesn't want to reveal the formula, even to the patent office. Nochar has built a successful business based on a product its competitors simply can't figure out how to copy.

REMEMBER

Becoming the absolute best in your field creates a product or service that's difficult to duplicate. If you're having brain surgery or a cavity filled, you want the most talented person performing the function. The same holds true for any skilled trade. People always want the best, and they're willing to pay a premium for it.

Same industry, different business models

McDonald's, Wendy's, and Burger King are all in the fast-food hamburger business. However, the three burger joints have very different business models. Because of their different business models, the methodologies, psychologies, ideologies, and profit formulas of these businesses differ greatly.

Each of these burger businesses uses a different "secret sauce" — not on its burgers, but on its business model. For instance, McDonald's owns more corner lots than any other company in the world. Clearly, its business model entails acquiring valuable real estate in addition to selling hamburgers.

DURAFLAME BURNS THE COMPETITION

Most proprietary business models are simply a series of excellent business practices well executed. In the late 1960s, California Cedar Company needed a way to discard shavings from its pencil factory. Through research and development, the company discovered a process to turn these unwanted scraps into the Duraflame log, a product that now generates $250 million in annual revenue. However, California Cedar Company didn't stop at the invention of this product. The true genius of the business model wasn't how to make the first artificial log; it was using waste to make it. In the 1970s, sawmills had to *pay* to haul off their sawdust. California Cedar went to virtually every sawmill on the Pacific coast and significantly undercut its sawdust waste hauling contract in exchange for a long-term commitment. California Cedar created a business model in which it was paid to accept its primary raw material.

Wendy's focuses on freshness and more upscale customers than McDonald's mass customer approach, and Wendy's charges accordingly. Wendy's business model focuses on maximizing margin per customer. Like McDonald's, Wendy's is currently focused on a single brand. In the past, Wendy's grew its business by adding new brands, such as Tim Horton's, Baja Fresh, and Arby's. Eventually, Wendy's sold or spun off these businesses.

In recent years, Burger King has struggled with its business model and place in the market. Many years ago, competitors took away Burger King's primary differentiator of making its burgers exactly the way customers want them ("Hold the pickle, hold the lettuce"). Now Burger King is struggling to find a business model that works. Burger King closed hundreds of stores and at times has fallen to third place behind McDonald's and Wendy's in sales despite having thousands more stores than Wendy's. It seems that Burger King's issues are with its own business model and not the hamburger business in general. While Burger King has struggled, several other hamburger chains have thrived; examples include Red Robin, Rally's, Checkers, In-N-Out, and Five Guys.

How your business model sets you apart from the competition

Your business model is at the core of your business's capability to make profit. Many of the factors that differentiate your business flow directly from your business model. For instance, Walmart and Target sell similar products to similar customers. However, their business models differ significantly.

At the core of Walmart's business model is its "always low prices" promise. To deliver on this promise, Walmart must maintain low costs in all aspects of its business:

>> Low-cost employees

>> Low-cost health insurance

>> Low-cost real estate

>> Low-cost purchasing by creating custom products or beating up vendors for the best deal

>> Logistical efficiencies that lower costs

Walmart's business model aims to be the low-cost provider. The company's desire to provide goods at the lowest cost cascades into many aspects of its operations. Because the chain is focused on the lowest cost, its stores may not be as modern or attractive as those of Target, and its products may not be as trendy as what you can find at Target. Walmart also has a reputation for paying lower wages than Target. The company's business model decisions keep costs at the absolute minimum but have caused significant human resource issues, including potential unionization, lawsuits, and negative publicity. Walmart's business model dictates that keeping costs low always comes first.

Target, on the other hand, has chosen a business model that can be summed up as *cheap chic.* Target spends its organizational energy trying to find hip but inexpensive products for its customers. Of course, Target must remain cost competitive, but the niche it has carved out doesn't require that it charge the lowest possible cost on all items. The money that Walmart makes with sheer volume of transactions, Target makes in higher margin per item. Just think for a second how much the $10 potato peeler with the designer handle in a choice of trendy colors actually costs Target.

REMEMBER

Just like Target and Walmart, your business model differentiates you from the competition. The stronger your business model, the stronger your capability to make outstanding profits.

Considering your competitive advantage

Competitive advantage allows a firm to perform at a higher level than others in the same industry or market — or with anyone competing for the customer's limited budget. Competitive advantage can serve as a powerful catalyst for your business. Competitive advantage allows you to outsell, outprofit, and outperform others in the same industry or market. When you're analyzing the strength of a business, if you look only at competitive advantage, your analysis will be incomplete.

People often mistakenly use the term *competitive advantage* as a synonym for the term *business model.* The reality is that competitive advantage is a portion of your business model, but not all of it. A business model is more encompassing than your competitive advantage. For instance, you can have excellent competitive advantage but still have a weak business model. If Starbucks decided to maximize coffee poundage sales by lowering the price of a cup of coffee to $0.50, its competitive advantage may rise slightly. However, the lower price would result in a significantly different, and worse, business model for Starbucks.

Obtaining your competitive advantage

According to Michael Porter, the Harvard professor responsible for the concept, competitive advantage is obtained through cost leadership, differentiation, and/ or focus.

Cost leadership

Cost leadership means your firm has the capability to deliver similar goods or services as your competitors for a lower cost. This doesn't mean a lower sales price, but a lower cost of goods sold. If one firm has the capability to deliver a widget at a cost of $8 and it costs another firm $10 to deliver a similar widget, the first one has a cost advantage. If your cost advantage is the best in your industry, you have cost leadership. You can gain cost leadership in countless ways; here are just a few:

>> **Access to natural resources:** Middle Eastern oil or Chinese cheap labor are examples.

>> **Scale:** Walmart can buy Pampers cheaper than anyone else.

>> **Vertical integration:** Intel designs, fabricates, and markets chips.

>> **Technological leverage:** Many analysts attribute Walmart's rise in the 1980s to technological superiority in logistics.

>> **Proprietary processes:** Rolls-Royce uses a secret metallurgy process to make super-durable jet engine blades.

Differentiation

Differentiation means that the customer feels your product has superior and different attributes than the competition's. Customers pay much more for a cup of Starbucks coffee than for a cup of joe at the diner because they view Starbucks coffee as a differentiated product. Many times, you can charge extra for the differentiated attributes of your offering, creating additional margin. Businesses can create differentiation by using any of the following tactics:

>> **Superior branding** (Coach, Tiffany's, Rolex)

>> **Unique supplier relationships** (Eddie Bauer Edition Ford Explorer)

>> **First mover advantage** (iPad, Walkman, Crest toothpaste)

>> **Location** (remember the retail mantra "location, location, location"?)

>> **Scale** (not many companies can build an airplane or a skyscraper)

>> **Intellectual property** (Hemi engines, Intel Inside)

Focus

You can also gain competitive advantage through your focus. A business can't serve too many masters. You can translate intense focus on a market, niche, or attribute into a significant advantage. Examples include the following:

>> Taiwan Semiconductor's exclusive focus on fabrication

>> Amgen's focus on biopharmaceuticals (rather than all types of drugs)

>> Starbucks's focus on coffee rather than becoming just another restaurant

>> Rally's focus on drive-through hamburgers

>> A doctor's focus on heart surgery

Enhancing your competitive advantage

To fully leverage a strong competitive advantage, you must shore up the other aspects of your business model as well. The following sections detail several other factors that a strong business model must take into account. As a savvy business-person, you must go further than competitive advantage analysis and explore all aspects of the business model. By doing so, you can unleash the maximum potential of the business.

Innovation

You need to take into account your company's capability to innovate in order to fully evaluate its business model. Without innovation, your competitive advantage will weaken or disappear. Do you think Apple will continue to dominate the tablet market for ten more years? Without future innovation, competitors will catch Apple and eat into its market share. Not that long ago, BlackBerry had a dominant share of the cellphone market. A few years later, BlackBerry was teetering on bankruptcy.

Customer segments

What customer segment will the product attack? Competitive advantage is somewhat generic in regard to who the customer will be. It assumes that you'll find the right one. However, chasing the wrong customers or market segment can destroy an otherwise solid business model.

Targeting your competitive advantage to the right customer or market segment makes a big difference, as the following examples demonstrate:

>> Motorola had a product well suited for the military market in the Iridium satellite phone, but the company blew billions trying to market it to nonmilitary consumers who were unwilling to buy a $3,000 phone.

>> After NASA was exposed for purchasing $129 pencils for space missions, Paul Fisher took it upon himself to invent a pen that would write in space. He succeeded, calling his invention the Space Pen. For many years, Fisher sold his pen to NASA for $4 (it cost him $1.98 to manufacture). However, the market for the space pen as a collectible item turned out to be much larger for Fisher. The pen sells many more units today for $20 than it did to NASA for $4.

>> Ivan Getting conceived of the GPS system in the 1950s. It took nearly 50 years and $12 billion to create a system for tracking military personnel, missiles, ships, tanks, and the like. The consumer electronics industry sold more than one billion GPS-enabled devices in just 15 years.

Pricing

What will you charge for the product? How high or low will the margin be? The answers to these questions are critical factors of the business model, but they aren't addressed directly in competitive advantage. For example, Amazon has competitive advantage in its capability to distribute product conveniently and efficiently. However, what would happen if Amazon focused on the convenience of the online experience but charged 15 percent more than bricks-and-mortar competitors? No one knows the answer, but these factors would affect Amazon's competitive advantage.

Capability to sell

Without a proven and repeatable sales process, most business models fail. Unfortunately, the world doesn't care if you have a better mousetrap. All products and services must be *sold*. It's easy to forget this inconvenient truth as you look at the long line outside the Apple store with customers clamoring to buy. However, don't forget all those iPhone and iPad commercials on television, the publicity, paid product placements on shows, and countless other efforts to drive demand. All these things help to create that long line of eager buyers.

In order to finalize the marketing process, someone must purchase your product. A solid sales and marketing system must be used to realize the full potential of your offering. See Book 5 for more about marketing.

Potential pitfalls

Competitive advantage doesn't take potential pitfalls into account. Taser pioneered the stun gun business, holds many patents, owns the best brand in the business, and gets sued for $1 million nearly every week. Taser has a good business model despite this pitfall. However, if you look only at Taser's competitive advantage without regard to pitfalls, Taser's business looks much more attractive than it actually is.

Continuity

A significant issue for mid-sized and small businesses is the capability to operate without the day-to-day input of the owner. If the business falls apart without the owner in the building, the business model is weak and the owner will never be able to sell the business.

Say Tom has a business that nets him $900,000 per year. The business has significant competitive advantage as witnessed by its profitability. However, the instant Tom stops showing up, the business nets $0. Many doctors, lawyers, accountants, architects, and other professionals face the same issue. The competitive advantage of these businesses is strong, but the business model still needs some work.

Chapter **4**

Finding Your Target Market

The most important step toward creating a great business is creating a product or service that customers want and will buy. This is called a *powerful offering.* The first step in creating a powerful offering is selecting the right market. Picking the proper combination of industry attractiveness, niche attractiveness, and customer attractiveness creates the best market for your product.

REMEMBER

By combining industry attractiveness, niche attractiveness, and customer attractiveness, you can understand the overall market potential. This chapter refers to this combination as the *market attractiveness* from this point forward. Market attractiveness is one of the most important aspects of your business. It's difficult to imagine a strong business that sells to lousy customers in a bad industry and small niche market.

Gauging the Target Market

You should find a profitable and sufficiently large market segment. However, in order to have a successful and durable business, you need to find a large market that's unserved or underserved. Finding this underserved market is paramount.

Anyone can find huge markets to attack. Hey, let's sell coffee! The market is large and growing, right? However, several large and successful companies already own pieces of this market. In general, it's unwise to attack an established competitor in the exact same market segment. Traditionally, the first mover or incumbent wins.

REMEMBER

If you want to go after the coffee market, you need to find a viable market segment that's unserved or underserved by Starbucks and similar companies. You can break down any target market into four pieces to make things easier:

>> **How attractive is the industry itself?** For instance, software companies tend to be more profitable than construction companies. Professor Scott A. Shane conducted research for his book *The Illusions of Entrepreneurship: The Costly Myths That Entrepreneurs, Investors, and Policy Makers Live By* (Yale University Press). That research offers significant data that some industries are more viable and profitable than others. Of course, other areas of the business model have great effect on the overall profitability.

>> **How attractive is the niche within the industry?** Typically, packaged software developers are more profitable than custom software developers. You want to pick a niche that offers the best potential profitability.

>> **How attractive is the customer segment?** The high-end customer targeted by Starbucks is more profitable than the customer targeted by McDonald's. An attractive customer doesn't have to be a wealthy customer. An attractive customer is the one who can make your business model work best. For instance, many profitable business models are being created for the unbanked (people without checking accounts). See Chapter 3 in Book 1 for an introduction to business models.

>> **Is the niche big enough to provide a good opportunity for you to enter it and sell enough product or services, at a price point that will allow you to create a viable business?** Prosthetic limbs for pet dogs may seem like a great idea, but can you sell enough of them at a high enough price to be able to make any money doing it?

Determining Industry Attractiveness

An *industry* is the broadest category or definition of the business you'll be in. Examples of industry include the following:

>> Automotive aftermarket manufacturing

>> Business consulting

>> General contracting

>> Home remodeling

>> Lawn and garden distribution

>> Legal services

>> Medical

>> Pet care

>> Residential landscaping

>> Software development

Within a broad industry are often-defined industry segments that further refine the offering. Here are some examples:

>> The vehicle manufacturing industry has segments for heavy-duty trucks, electric automobiles, recreational vehicles, and more.

>> The restaurant industry has segments for fast food, fine dining, casual dining, and so on.

>> Clothing manufacturers have segments for athletic wear, men's suits, lingerie, women's business attire, and bridal gowns, among others.

>> The medical doctor industry has segmentation for general practitioners, surgeons, podiatrists, holistic practitioners, ophthalmologists, and hundreds more.

>> The HVAC (heating, ventilation, and air conditioning) industry has segments for light-duty, boilers, and heavy-duty systems.

You're much more likely to be successful in a "good" industry than a "bad" one. In a good industry, most companies are successful; examples include software development, mineral extraction, and insurance. In a bad industry, margins are historically low and/or competition is overly intense; examples include airlines and construction. However, you can find numerous examples of companies that entered unattractive industries and were successful because their business model was strong in other areas. Examples include Waste Management (garbage), Apple (computer hardware), Nike (shoes), and Vistaprint (commercial printing).

REMEMBER

You have a much greater chance of success if you pick an attractive industry. Consider these factors:

>> Is this industry, as a whole, growing or shrinking?

>> Will this industry be strong in ten years?

Finding Your Target Market

>> How many incumbents are in this industry, and how strong are they?

>> Do you see an opportunity for this industry to overlap into a different existing market (convergence)?

>> Could the industry provide powerful synergies with an existing part of your business?

Book 1, Chapter 1 talks more about researching your chosen industry.

After you identify an attractive industry, you identify the best subset of that market, or niche, and then identify the best customers to serve within that niche. Working in an attractive industry is helpful, but it isn't a prerequisite. Many great business models have been created in bad industries by carving out attractive customer segments, niches, or both.

For example, Vistaprint created an excellent business model serving customers no one wanted (microbusinesses) in an industry no one wanted to be in (printing). Vistaprint succeeded by leveraging a highly differentiated sales, distribution, and cost model.

There's an old saying: "Everyone thinks they know how to run a restaurant because they know how to eat." Every industry and business can be learned. However, if you're unfamiliar with an industry, count on some hard work to get up to speed.

TIP

As you choose your industry, keep in mind that the business landscape is always changing. Gas stations used to fix cars; now they sell donuts and sandwiches. If you look into the future, it can help you determine whether your chosen industry has peripheral growth opportunities or potential threats.

WHAT'S THE DIFFERENCE BETWEEN A MARKET AND AN INDUSTRY?

Many businesspeople use the term *market* as a catch-all for the combination of *industry, segment, niche,* and *customer* (in other words, who will pay you for your product). Although simply referring to *the market* is easier, it's better to break things down into more discreet pieces so you can gain additional insight into your model. These concepts, however, do bleed into one another. If your industry niche is electric cars, your customer segment is probably dictated by the fact that you make electric cars. The two complement and bleed into each other.

Market is best used when *industry, segment, niche,* or *customer segment* simply doesn't fully cover all the bases. *Industry* should refer to the industry and the industry segment.

Finding the best industry

Picking an attractive industry for your business model may seem simple. The key lies in research (see Book 1, Chapter 1 for more ideas on how to conduct your research). One thing you should do is gather as much independent information as possible regarding current and future trends. By doing so, you're able to make the best choice of industry for your model. Here are some places to find industry data and trends:

>> Paid services such as Gartner (www.gartner.com) and Forrester Research (www.forrester.com)

>> General business publications and news outlets like Bloomberg Businessweek (www.businessweek.com), Inc. (www.inc.com), Barron's (www.barrons.com), and CNN Business (http://money.cnn.com)

>> Books

>> Industry trade publications

WARNING

Watch out for bias when using trade publications as a resource. Such publications put the most positive spin on the industry. For instance, travel industry trade publications were likely still positive on the industry in 2000 even though Internet sites like Priceline.com and Expedia.com were beginning to destroy portions of the business.

>> Industry associations

>> Personal experience

>> The IRS or state government (look for the number of businesses in an industry starting or filing bankruptcy)

REMEMBER

Without proprietary information, you're picking your industry with the same data as your competition. Business is inherently risky. No amount of research is a substitute for time in the marketplace. At some point, you will have done your homework and taken your best guess, and you will need to take the leap.

Working in unserved or underserved markets

Unserved or underserved markets offer significantly better opportunities than most. Underserved markets have growth potential and less competition. Position yourself in an underserved market and your business model will be much stronger. Markets are underserved because

>> **The market is growing and too few vendors serve the market.** Most new businesses chase this classic market. Markets like Android application

development, social media platforms, 3D printing, and passenger space travel are examples.

» **The market is stagnant or shrinking and vendors flee.** An overcorrection by competition can create opportunities.

» **The market is considered unattractive.** Some possible reasons:

- **Perceived profitability:** Rent-A-Center profits in a market others consider too dicey.

- **Perceived size:** Walmart found a market serving towns under 20,000 in population while competitors focused on large cities.

- **Being unsexy:** Markets like portable toilets, paper manufacturing, and salt mining have far less sex appeal than iPhone application development and can offer opportunities because of this lack of appeal.

REMEMBER

Some markets are underserved for a reason. Carefully examine the market opportunity, take off the rose-colored glasses, and be brutally honest with yourself — and then pick based on all the criteria.

Looking for Niche Attractiveness

After you pick an attractive industry for your business model (see the preceding section), it's time to find an attractive niche. Your niche market is a subset of the overall market you participate in.

Know the power of a good niche

Picking the right niche may be more important than picking the right industry. For example, Vistaprint was founded in 1995 when the traditional printing business was getting crushed. Thousands of printers went out of business during the 1990s and early 2000s. During that time, Vistaprint grew into a billion-dollar business. How could Vistaprint grow when other printers were dramatically shrinking? Vistaprint targeted micro and small businesses considered too small for traditional printers. Combined with ingenious leverage of technology, Vistaprint turned unprofitable small customers into one of the most profitable printing operations in the world.

Unlimited niches exist

Good news! You can find unlimited niches within any market. At the core of many successful companies' strategies was the creation or refinement of a new niche. Here are some examples:

>> **Panera Bread:** Healthier, higher-quality sandwiches aimed at the fast-food industry.

>> **Häagen-Dazs:** High-end ice cream at triple the price versus other ice creams in the frozen dessert industry.

>> **Starbucks:** Not just a cup of joe — an experience. You could argue that Starbucks is in the restaurant industry, and it is. However, Starbucks also competes against convenience stores for coffee sales. The niche in either case is the customer who wants the full Starbucks coffee experience.

>> **McDonald's:** Fast, consistent food. This niche in the restaurant business is mature and crowded today, but when McDonald's started, it was a new and untapped market. By catering to customers who wanted consistency in fast food, McDonald's dominated this niche.

>> **Coach:** Everyday luxury. Coach bags are more stylish than a department store brand but priced much more reasonably than high-fashion brands. This half high-fashion, half department-store niche has worked well for Coach and other everyday luxury brands.

>> **iPad:** An email and Internet toy. Apple found a great niche between a laptop, Gameboy, and smartphone.

How many different niches can the hamburger business support? A lot more than anyone expected. The hamburger was invented around 1890, and the first hamburger restaurants began appearing in the 1920s. Since then, dozens of spins on making a hamburger have appeared. Here's a partial list of hamburger chains and their niches.

Chain	Niche
McDonald's	The kids' burger chain
Wendy's	The adults' burger chain
Red Robin	Gourmet burgers
White Castle	Craveable sliders
Rally's	Drive-through only
Steak 'n Shake	Sit-down burgers with a diner feel
Five Guys	Simple, fresher burgers and fries

Markets have a habit of splitting

As markets mature, they tend to split into more and more niches. Niches that used to comprise a small portion of the market can become huge. Fifty years ago, abrasive cleaners such as Comet dominated the household cleaner market. In 1977, the Clorox Company introduced the niche cleaner Soft Scrub. The product had a limited market for those looking for an occasional alternative to hard abrasives. Over time, cream cleaners became the largest segment of the household cleaner market. Now you can find niche cream products such as Cerama Bryte stovetop cleaner for specialty uses.

If you think of the overall market as a bell curve in which the largest market exists in the fat portion of the bell curve, the best niches exist on the fringes of the market. Think of the left fringe as low-cost options and the right edge as high-cost options. Figure 4-1 shows bell curves for the household cleaner market.

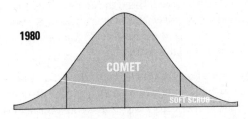

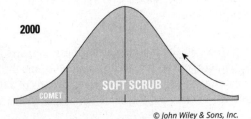

FIGURE 4-1:
Bell curves for the household cleaner market.

© John Wiley & Sons, Inc.

At one time, dry cleaners like Comet held the bulk of the market. Soft Scrub entered the market as a liquid specialty cleaner on the right fringe of the market. Soft Scrub garnered customers who didn't want the harsh abrasive in a dry cleaner. Over time, the appeal of liquid cleaners versus dry cleaners grew, and Soft Scrub replaced Comet as the main portion of the market (the fat part of the bell curve). Comet was relegated to the least attractive portion of the market (the left fringe), appealing to cost-sensitive customers willing to use old-fashioned cleaners.

Both edges of the bell curve offer a variety of niches. Walmart found a niche on the left fringe by providing buyers in small towns a low-cost department store. Today, Walmart represents the fat part of the bell curve, and dollar stores have carved out a niche on the left fringe.

TIP

Generally, your business model should *not* attempt to enter a market in the fat portion of the bell curve. These established markets have strong, established players that are typically tough to beat at their own game. Instead, find a fringe to attack (shown in Figure 4-2). Most likely, the established players won't want to leave their large markets to mess with your little niche . . . yet.

FIGURE 4-2:
Entering the market on the fringes.

ENTER THE MARKET HERE

© *John Wiley & Sons, Inc.*

NICHE MARKETS AREN'T ALWAYS LOGICAL

Creating a niche may be easier than you think. Take the iPad for example. The iPad should *not* have worked for lots of reasons:

- Tablet computers had been tried by dozens of companies, including Apple, without success.

- Smartphones do more than an iPad does.

- An iPad isn't quite a laptop and doesn't allow easy typing.

- Smartphones are portable; an iPad is much less portable.

- Isn't an iPad just a giant iPod?

One hundred million iPads later, all these reasons don't matter. Apple's secret with the iPad was niching the product differently than all the previously failed tablet computers. Previous tablets tried to be computers in tablet form. The iPad is *not* a personal computer — it's a giant iPod. The iPad does many things well, but being a PC isn't one of them. Apple was smart enough to see the unmet demand for unserved customers looking for fast-boot Internet, easy email access, a screen big enough to read, enough portability to be acceptable, and a cool factor to create a brand-new niche.

In Al Ries and Jack Trout's classic marketing book, *The 22 Immutable Laws of Marketing* (HarperBusiness), they say that your goal as a marketer is to create a Kleenex or Jell-O type brand. Kleenex is a tissue. Jell-O is gelatin. Xerox is a photocopier. These brands created new niches and dominated the niche to such an extent that the market renamed the category after the brand. This is the gold standard of niche creation.

Find unserved or underserved markets

The best way to create a good niche is to find an unserved or underserved market. All blockbuster products do this. No one bought a cellphone for what it was; people bought it for what it *did* — made them feel safer and more productive while driving, for example. The underserved market for cellphones wasn't one for better phones; it was for the capability to communicate in situations where it was previously impossible.

What does *underserved* mean? If the market was obviously underserved, an existing player in the market would fill the void. Some guesswork is involved in predicting what underserved means. You have to use your business judgment and then guess. Only the market knows what's needed, and the only way to find out is to take it to the market.

Sometimes it's easy to identify an underserved market. A fast-growing suburb needs gas stations, restaurants, and services in prime retail locations. Exponential growth in the use of smartphones creates users faster than the applications needed to serve them.

If you choose a niche in an easy-to-identify growth area, keep in mind that competitors can easily find this niche, too. Count on lots of competition.

Instead of going for the obvious niche, be willing to take some chances and pick a less obvious niche. If everyone is chasing mobile phone growth by writing iPhone and Android apps, take a chance on Microsoft apps. For smaller companies, having a less competitive niche can be far more advantageous than being a very small fish in the big pond.

How can you find these elusive unserved or underserved markets?

>> **Personal experience:** Many great products and companies have been created by an entrepreneur's discontent with the status quo. Fred Smith wondered why letters couldn't be delivered overnight when he conceived FedEx. While traveling in Italy, Starbucks's Howard Schultz wondered why European-style cafes wouldn't work in America.

>> **Friends and relatives:** If you aren't the cutting-edge type, look to friends who are. What products and services are they buying and why? What problems do they wish they could solve?

>> **Research trends:** You don't need to catch a trend to find a great niche; however, catching a trend can make your niche much better because the growth is built-in.

>> **Hired experts:** Professional business plan writers, business model consultants, futurists, or other gurus can help you find a niche.

>> **Luck:** Angie's List was founded in 1995 when the Internet didn't exist for very many people. Angie's List was simply a monthly booklet sent to members with reviews of home contractors. Its popularity was concentrated in historic neighborhoods where repairs were frequent and expensive. Angie's List was a nice little business that never envisioned the tidal wave that would carry it to become the leader in its niche. When the Internet turned the Angie's List business model upside down, it also made it better. Instead of a localized printer of recommendation booklets, Angie's List built a comprehensive website.

Checking Out Customer Attractiveness

You can create an attractive market niche (see the preceding section), but have it destroyed by bad customers. *Attractive customers* have a strong need for your offering, value the solution to their problem more than your product costs (that's a *strong value proposition*), have disposable income to spend on your offering, pay their bills on time, and exist in sufficient numbers to make your venture profitable.

Most business models have customers that are neither exceptionally attractive nor exceptionally unattractive. Most business models don't need to focus on customer attractiveness for long because the old mantra "all customers are good customers" is true most the time. However, you do have to study customer attractiveness.

The most prominent example of gaining the most attractive customer is the retail mantra "location, location, location." What does an outstanding retail location get you? Outstanding customers, that's what. A high-end retail mall has the same industry attractiveness and niche attractiveness regardless of where it's located. Whether the mall is located in the hottest new suburb or the middle of farmland, the industry and niche attractiveness remain the same. However, the high-income customers available in the hot new suburb are typically viewed as more attractive than those in rural locations.

REMEMBER

More affluent customers don't make a market segment more attractive. Typically, more affluent customers can afford to pay a higher price for goods and services. High margin typically follows these higher prices, but may well be set off by higher overheads and lower volumes owing to a higher degree of exclusivity. Simply chasing affluent customers isn't always the best strategy. Remember the old adage, "Sell to the masses, live with the classes. Sell to the classes, live with the masses."

For example, Rent-A-Center is in the same industry as Best Buy. The two companies have some niche overlap, but they serve significantly different customers. Best Buy serves customers who can afford to purchase a television in full. These customers have either cash or pre-arranged financing like a credit card. Rent-A-Center caters to customers with lesser credit availability. Rent-A-Center extends credit to buyers deemed undesirable by traditional retailers like Best Buy. Rent-A-Center accepts monthly or weekly payments from customers until the item is paid in full. Due to the differences in the customer segments they serve, Rent-A-Center's business model is significantly different from Best Buy's:

» Best Buy serves a larger number of buyers who are more financially stable and makes money with a traditional retail business model — buying and selling merchandise.

» Rent-A-Center is closer to a specialty finance company that happens to sell appliances. Because Rent-A-Center doesn't collect payment in full upfront, the company has many profit areas that Best Buy doesn't have. Finance fees, high interest rates on loans, repossession fees, and more account for the bulk of Rent-A-Center's profit.

Many businesses would consider the customers of Rent-A-Center less than desirable. However, Rent-A-Center has created a profitable business model selling to these supposedly less-than-desirable customers. Because the Rent-A-Center model accounts for sporadic and occasional nonpayment, it's a workable business model.

REMEMBER

As a businessperson, you must eliminate or account for bad customers in your business model. If you meet ten business owners in the construction industry, you'll probably meet someone whose business was destroyed by a slow-paying or nonpaying customer. The wrong customers can destroy a workable business model.

Interestingly, you can have a customer niche within your customer niche. Your products are marketed to target a certain segment or niche. However, customers within any niche, no matter how tight, are widely varied. Coach bags fill a niche between the everyday bags you can find at JCPenney's and the high-end bags you can find in Paris. Within this niche you can find Louis Vuitton customers slumming it a bit and middle-class folks looking for a bit of everyday luxury.

The question you need to answer is which of the sub-segments the marketing is directed to. In the case of Coach bags, the marketing is clearly directed at the middle-class buyer looking for everyday luxury.

Here's another example: Starbucks attracts the most affluent and desired customers in the coffee industry. However, within Starbucks niche are buyers who stretch themselves financially to buy a $5 latte and buyers who spend hundreds of dollars every month at Starbucks. The niche Starbucks markets to is customers who want Starbucks as a lifestyle choice rather than just a cup of coffee.

Finding Your Place on the Industry Value Chain

You want to find the best place on the industry value chain. Every firm involved in getting a product from initial creation to purchase and consumption by the end consumer adds value in the form of activities, incurs costs, and has a resulting margin. Some positions in this value chain offer a greater opportunity than others.

Different industries value the places on this value chain differently. For instance, clothing retailers enjoy a more profitable position on their value chain than the clothing manufacturers. In automobiles, retailers tend to make less than the manufacturers. In some industries, no desirable places on the value chain are available, making the overall market less attractive for your business.

Consider a cup of coffee. Several operators add value to your daily cup of joe. However, the market rewards some activities much more richly than others. If your business model is to be the most successful, you want to assume a position on the value chain that offers the best potential profits. Table 4-1 shows the value chain for coffee.

TABLE 4-1   Value Chain for Coffee

Firm	Value Added	Key Activities
Coffee bean grower	Operations	Farming
Shipper	Logistics	Transportation and logistics
Coffee roaster	Operations	Converting beans into drinkable coffee
Marketers (Folgers, Starbucks)	Sales	Branding, sales, customer service
Retailer	Sales	Merchandising

Coffee prices go up and down, but the principles involved don't change. Suppose that whole green Columbian coffee beans sell for $1.97 a pound. Assume the farmer has costs equal to about half that. The farmer's margin is 98.5 cents per pound of coffee. The roaster buys the coffee from the farmer for $1.97 a pound and transports it, roasts it, and grinds it. The cost of logistics and transportation is around 2 cents per pound. The roaster then sells it to a coffee service, consumer products company, or retail outlet. Unbranded wholesale coffee sells for around $5 per pound. If the coffee roaster's cost of operations is about half the $3.03 per pound value added, then the coffee roaster makes a margin of around $1.51. If the coffee is branded (Starbucks, Folgers, Seattle's Best), add a dollar or two to the value added. Note that almost all the value added by branding drops to profit/margin. Finally, a company like Starbucks, Folgers, Kroger, or a coffee service delivers the coffee to the consumer. Folgers coffee sells for $9.99 a pound (Starbucks, $13.95 per pound). Therefore, the retail seller of Folgers has added about $4 of value (mostly margin). This comprises the entire value chain for a one-pound bag of coffee.

Table 4-2 shows the value added by each function and the approximate margin. Note that the marketing and sales related functions are much more handsomely rewarded than the functions that make the product.

TABLE 4-2   **Value Added for Coffee**

Firm	Cost Added per Pound	Margin Earned per Pound	Total Value Added
Coffee bean grower	$0.985	$0.985	$1.97
Shipper	$0.015	$0.005	$.02
Coffee roaster	$1.52	$1.51	$3.03
Marketers (Folgers, Starbucks)	$0	$2	$2
Retailer	$2	$2	$4

WARNING

Some places on the coffee value chain are much more profitable than others. To maximize the effectiveness of your business model, find the most profitable portion of the value chain. Usually, the closer you are to the end user or consumer, the greater the opportunity for margin. Don't misconstrue this statement. The best business models may not be retail models. But as manufacturing has shifted to low-wage countries, the value add for manufacturing and related activities has gone down dramatically. As the capability to add value for manufacturing has decreased, the capability to add value through sales, distribution, and branding has increased. This shift has provided opportunities for savvy entrepreneurs.

Savvy entrepreneurs have also created new positions on the value chain to carve value away from existing players. For example, in the field of law, several new players have emerged to carve out a portion of the value chain traditionally owned by lawyers. Law firms in India specialize in large-scale complex research only. Some firms audit bills from law firms in an attempt to save their clients money. Both of these industries used to be part of the law firm value chain.

Ironically, there seems to be very little correlation between the amount of work or the difficulty of work and the amount of value added in the value chain. As you can see from the coffee example, the hardest work is done by the farmer. The farmer takes the risk of bad weather, has the highest number of employees, and puts in the most hours proportionately. However, the farmer makes the least amount of money on the value chain.

REMEMBER

Certain portions of the value chain tend to add more value than others. Note that value added is the difference between sales price and cost. An item may have a large percentage of the total sales price to the end consumer, but add little value on the chain.

Chapter 5

Considering a Franchise

Three constants have fueled the growth of franchising over its long history: the desire to expand, the limitations on human and financial capital, and the need to overcome distance. Although you may think of franchising mostly in the context of your neighborhood fast food outlets, franchising has transformed how people purchase products and services today. More than 120 distinct industries use franchising today, and because of that it is nearly impossible to drive down any major street in the world and not pass by some business that is part of a franchise network. This chapter begins your exploration of franchising, not by looking at any particular franchise but by giving you some of the basics so you can better understand what franchising is all about.

Understanding What a Franchise Is

Franchising is, in a word, a *license*. It is a system for independently owned businesses to share a common brand, distribute products and services, and expand. It's a contractual relationship between a brand owner (the franchisor) and an independent local business owner (the franchisee).

For example, BrightStar Care doesn't "franchise" medical and non-medical home care assistance, FASTSIGNS does not franchise printing, Wetzel's Pretzels does not franchise pretzel shops, and Dat Dog does not franchise hotdogs, sausages, and beer. What each "franchises" is a system that delivers quality branded products and services to consumers. And they do so through a network of independently owned and operated businesses that deliver a consistent customer experience.

Playing by brand standards to create consistency

A franchise occurs when a *franchisor* licenses its trade name and intellectual property — the *brand* and its operating methods (its system of doing business) — to a person or group who agrees to operate their business to the franchise system's brand standards. The franchisor defines the brand promise it wants delivered to consumers, provides the franchisee with initial and continuing support, and then ensures compliance by the franchisee on how it delivers on that brand promise. The magic of franchising is that consistent brand standards can be achieved at each location without the franchisor being involved in the day-to-day management of the franchisee's business.

In exchange, the franchisee pays an initial *franchise fee* to join the system and a continuing fee known as a *royalty* to remain a part of the franchise system.

People have grown accustomed to the consistency that comes from shopping at branded locations. From the comfort of knowing exactly what you will find when you check into a Courtyard by Marriott, to the quality of the chicken at a Popeyes Louisiana Kitchen, or a haircut at Sport Clips, people know what they will get when they purchase under a franchisor's brand. The number of companies and industries bringing goods and services to consumers through franchising is growing, limited only by the imagination of the people who understand its potential application.

Setting your sights on success

Franchising creates opportunities for business ownership to create personal wealth and generates local jobs. It also consistently delivers products and services on a global basis to the brand standards established by the franchisor.

As you explore becoming a franchisee, be wary of statistics that talk about the "success rate" in franchising. As late as 2000, the International Franchise Association (IFA) published statistics that claimed that franchisees had a success rate of 95 percent — versus a *failure* rate of 85 percent for nonfranchised start-ups in their first five years in business. Those statistics turned out to be inaccurate and misleading.

WARNING

The IFA has frequently reminded franchisors to not use those out-of-date and misleading statistics, but unfortunately, some franchisors, franchise brokers, and franchise-packaging firms (one-stop shops that offer "cookie-cutter" franchise advice) continue to use them to attract potential franchisees. What should be important is how well a franchise system is doing, and it is irrelevant in choosing any franchise opportunity whether or not franchising in general is doing well. You should be very wary of working with anyone who still uses invalid claims of franchise industry success statistics. In fact, it's strongly recommended that you don't work with them at all.

Franchising can be a very effective method of getting into business, but that depends on how carefully the franchise system is structured and supported. Even in highly successful franchise systems, locations *can* fail for a host of reasons. It is up to prospective franchisees to conduct a proper examination of every franchise opportunity that interests them.

Recognizing the Importance of Brands in Franchising

The *brand* is a franchise system's most valuable asset, because consumers decide what and whether to buy based on what they know, or think they know, about the brand. Unless consumers have a personal relationship with the local owner of a franchise, they probably don't give any thought to who owns the local business. In their minds, they are shopping at a branch of a chain. This fact is evident in the signs most franchisors require franchisees to post in their locations notifying the public that the location is owned and operated by a local business owner. In the consumer's mind, a company's brand equals its reputation.

Franchisors focus much of their support effort, time, energy, and money ensuring consistency at each of their locations. This promise of consistency is a major advantage for new franchisees because it is meant to assure them a ready flow of customers. A good brand can communicate a positive message to the customer. Equally so, a bad brand experience can paint a negative message for the entire brand. With a great brand, consumers can visualize and almost feel the experience they will receive even before they enter the local business.

A positive brand recognition is what every franchisee hopes for. With a well-known successful brand, new franchisees don't have to build brand awareness for their business because the franchisor and the other franchisees have already taken care of that. Having a reputation for a positive brand experience is one of the major advantages found in well-established franchise systems.

REMEMBER

But brands are not born fully grown. Smaller franchise systems or those with limited brand recognition in markets can't deliver consumer acceptance until the local franchisee creates a reputation for a positive brand experience in their market. This is an issue for new franchisees because they may be required to build brand recognition by spending more on advertising and promotion than where the franchise system's brand is well known. When prospective franchisees review the franchisor's offering, the amount of advertising specified by a franchisor is only the minimum amount they expect will be required — but most certainly is not the maximum amount a new franchisee may need to invest. (Flip to Chapter 4 in Book 5 for more about branding.)

Identifying the Three Types of Franchising

The three basic types of franchising are as follows, which the following sections examine in greater detail:

» Traditional or product-distribution franchising

» Business-format franchising

» Social franchising

Traditional franchising

The industries in which you most often find traditional franchising include soft drinks, automobiles and trucks, mobile homes, automobile accessories, and gasoline. The franchisee is typically selling products manufactured by the franchisor. Some examples include Coca-Cola, Ford Motor Company, and John Deere.

Although traditional franchises look a lot like *supplier-dealer relationships,* the difference is in the degree of the relationship. In a traditional franchise, the franchisee may handle the franchisor's products on an exclusive or semi-exclusive basis, while the supplier-dealer may handle several products, even competing ones. For example, Tempur-Pedic mattresses may be offered by a national dealer network that also offers other bedding brands in its retail stores.

The traditional franchisee is closely associated with the franchisor's brand and generally receives more services from its franchisor than a dealer would from its supplier. Frequently the franchisee provides some pre-sale preparation before a product is sold (such as you find with Coca-Cola, where the franchisee manufacturers and bottles the soda) or some additional post-sale servicing (such as you find at a Ford dealer with your periodic maintenance programs).

In a traditional product-distribution franchise, the franchisor licenses its trademark and logo to its franchisees, but it typically does not provide franchisees with an entire system for running their businesses. Measured in total sales, traditional franchising is larger than business-format franchising, covered in the next section.

Business-format franchising

The *business-format* franchisee gets a complete system for delivering a franchisor's product or service. The major difference between a traditional franchise and a business-format franchise is that business-format franchisees operate their business based on a business system largely prescribed by the franchisor. The role of the franchisor is to define the business system and establish the brand standards, whereas the role of the franchisee is to independently manage its business on a day-to-day basis to achieve those brand standards.

McDonald's doesn't franchise hamburgers, and Domino's doesn't franchise pizza. What they provide to their franchisees is a system of delivering their branded products and services. Although traditional franchising is larger than business-format franchising, because the size of the individual transactions is larger, more than 80 percent of all franchise locations in the United States are the business-format type.

It is the franchisee's execution to a franchisor's brand standards that produces consistency — the foundation for a business franchisee's success. Interim HealthCare, Sport Clips, PostNet, PuroClean, Twin Peaks, and Firehouse Subs are all examples of business-format franchises. The business-format franchisor provides a detailed system, and franchisees are trained and supported in their independent management of their business.

The confidential operating and procedures manuals (the how-to guides of every great franchise) provide the franchisees with the information they will need to establish, operate, and manage their businesses. The goal in a franchise system is for customers to get the same brand experience each and every time they shop in one of the franchise's locations, and the manual is one of the tools to achieve that important goal.

Although the franchisor provides a comprehensive business system, it is the franchisee's responsibility to manage all the day-to-day affairs of the business. After all, the franchisee is an independent business owner simply operating under a license.

REMEMBER

Although franchisors may specify uniforms and other brand standards related to how a franchisee's staff looks (think tattoos, beards, piercing, cleanliness), franchisors don't generally provide any other human resource requirements. Who a franchisee hires, how much they are paid, what benefits they receive, which hours they work, and how they are promoted and disciplined are all the sole responsibility of the franchisee. Because human resources are the sole and exclusive responsibility of the franchisee and not the franchisor, franchisors and franchisee are generally not considered joint-employers and are not liable for each other's actions or inactions.

Social franchising

Social franchising is the newest form of franchising. *Social franchising* is the application of business-format franchising's techniques and methods to the delivery of products and services to address the needs of people who live at the base of the economic pyramid (BOP). The term *BOP* refers to the estimated three billion people in the world who live on less than $2.50 per day. Social franchise systems generally focus on the lack of access to basic needs such as safe drinking water, adequate food supply, authentic drugs, quality healthcare, education, sanitation, and energy. These products and services have historically been delivered primarily by governments, churches, and nongovernmental organizations (NGOs) with mixed results.

NGOs provide a beneficial and important service in bringing critical products and services to the poor. But traditional methods used to provide this type of support are less sustainable than those found in social franchisors. Traditional methods typically lack the level of brand standards found in franchising, and NGOs usually don't typically focus their resources on training and supporting local operators as do social franchisors.

The social franchise model is emerging as a powerful tool for the international development community because of its potential to scale (expand). All the elements found in commercial franchising — including agreements, manuals, training, headquarters and field support, consistent supply chains, brand standards, and enforcement — are also found in a social franchise system.

A significant problem facing both social franchisors and NGOs is the frequent inability of consumers to afford the products and services, and the necessary reliance by the system on donations and other financial contributions. Because most NGOs use a top-down structure (the opening of locations), this often leads to an insufficient focus on ensuring that local product and service providers can sustain the standards found in commercial enterprises like social franchising.

Evolution in social franchise systems is generally driven by the same reasons found in commercial franchising — changes in consumers and competition. In an NGO, changes are frequently caused at the direction of donors and the unique products and services they want the NGO's system to deliver. This, above all else, is one of the reasons that NGOs are not able to achieve the sustainability found in franchising.

TIP

Just two examples of social franchises are Living Goods (https://livinggoods.org/) and VisionSpring (https://visionspring.org/). For more details on social franchising, check out www.socialsectorfranchising.org/.

Being Aware of the Roles and Goals of Franchisors and Franchisees

The franchisor and franchisee are in distinctly different businesses — they merely share a brand. In a franchise, the franchisor licenses to the franchisee an operating system, and the franchisee provides the products and services to consumers.

As a licensor, the business of a franchisor is to develop, license, support, and expand an indirect system of distribution of its branded products and services. As required under the law, it is the franchisor's responsibility to establish brand standards and enforce how the franchisee meets those brand standards sufficient to protect consumers. In contrast, the business of franchisees is to independently manage and operate their business to the brand standards established by the franchisor.

In this interdependent relationship, the franchisor generally has no contractual right to manage or supervise the day-to-day business affairs of its franchisees, and its rights to enforce its standards are limited to those agreed to in the contract between the parties. The franchise relationship effectively runs on trust, as the ability of a franchisor to enforce its brand standards is ultimately limited to its right to default and terminate noncompliant franchisees — a relatively high bar under the law.

The world through franchisor lenses

Who a franchisor is may vary. It can be a large or small company with a long history of successful operations or it can be a start-up with little or no experience. Some examples include the following:

» Roark Capital is a private equity firm with over $6.5 billion in equity capital. Some of its portfolio companies include 1-800-Radiator, Anytime Fitness, Arby's, Auntie Anne's, Batteries Plus Bulbs, Bosley's, CARSTAR, Carvel, Cinnabon, CKE Restaurants, Corner Bakery Café, Econo Lube N' Tune & Brakes, Great Expressions Dental Centers, Il Fornaio, Jimmy John's, Maaco, Massage Envy, McAlister's Deli, Meineke, Merlin, Miller's Ale House, Moe's Southwest Grill, Naf Naf, Orangetheory Fitness, Pet Supermarket, Pet Valu Pet Store, Primrose Schools, Pro Oil Change, Schlotzsky's, Take 5 Oil Change, and Waxing the City.

» Foumami, Dat Dog, Beverly Hills Rejuvenation Center, and America's Escape Game are small and relatively new to offering franchises.

» Firehouse Subs, Sport Clips, FASTSIGNS, BrightStar Care, and 7-Eleven are larger, well-established franchisors.

All great franchisors provide their franchisees with a uniform operating system and train and support them to independently manage and operate their business. When looking at franchising, consider that new businesses don't usually fail because their products or services are of low quality — they fail because of unknowns and lack of resources. Established franchisors have made and survived their mistakes, and that is one of the benefits of working with established companies — you can generally avoid a lot of the minefield of blunders that start-up businesses usually face.

Franchisors don't set standards, nor do they provide assistance, out of the kindness of their hearts. It is important to them that their franchisees deliver a consistent, sustainable, and replicable quality of products and services to consumers. They need the system to grow, prosper, make profits, and achieve a solid return on investment at every level, and to achieve that they design their systems so that franchisees can easily execute to their brand standards. If they do that well, franchisees can make money, stay in business, expand, and pay fees. The franchisor's brand value grows as more people shop at its branded units — and because of everyone's success, additional investors will want to become franchisees.

The franchisee's end of the bargain

When you invest in a franchise, you are not buying a franchise. You can't because all the franchisor is providing to you is a license allowing you to use its brand name and methods to operate your business, and you only get those rights for a specified period of time.

As a franchisee, you own the physical assets of your business: the land, building, equipment, and so forth. You are not buying the franchisor's brand or systems, and in some franchise systems, the franchisor may even retain the right to purchase your assets when the franchise relationship ends.

It may not sound like much of a deal, but here's what you get when you join a well-established franchise system:

>> Brand standards and enforcement by the franchisor

>> A proven and successful way of doing business

>> A recognized brand name

>> Training and ongoing field and headquarters support

>> Research and development into new products and services

>> Professionally designed local, regional, and national advertising and marketing programs

>> Often, a chance to invest in additional franchises

>> A shortcut around the common mistakes of start-up businesses

>> Often, a buying cooperative or negotiated lower costs from suppliers for many of the things you need to run and operate the business (ingredients, advertising, insurance, supplies, and so on)

>> Your fellow franchisees as a network of peer advisors

>> Sometimes a protected market or territory in which to operate your business

Franchisors don't always provide their franchisees with a defined area around their location in which no other company-owned or franchisee-owned business are allowed to operate. Many do, but even then the market area provided may not be an *exclusive territory* and may only be a *protected territory.* An exclusive or protected territory may be defined by the following:

>> The radius or area around the franchisee's location

>> The number of households or businesses in an area

>> The number of people who live in an area

>> Zip codes

>> Counties

>> Metes and bounds using highways, streets, or other geographic measures

TECHNICAL STUFF

Metes and bounds is an old English term still used in real estate today. A *mete* defines the measurement or distance, and the *bound* describes the physical feature like a road or a river. You will see it frequently used to describe territories in franchising.

>> Any other method that defines the area in which no other same-branded location may be established or in which the franchisee has some protection

From the franchisor's perspective, if the territory is too large, the total market will not contain enough locations to achieve brand recognition. From the franchisee's perspective, if it is too small or if other locations are too close, there may not be enough customers to support the business.

The goal for franchisors when granting any type of territorial protection is to ensure that they have the right to develop sufficient locations in an area to achieve brand penetration — the number of locations in an area sufficient to service the market and to ensure that consumers see the brand frequently.

Even when a franchisee is granted territorial rights, it may not be permanent and may only be provided for a limited period of time. Some franchisors may also require franchisees to reach certain levels of performance to maintain those rights. And in some systems, a protected territory may overlap with another. If you are a prospective franchisee, make sure you read the contract, and consult with a lawyer to make certain you understand the territorial rights the franchise agreement provides.

Reviewing Franchise Relationships

The number of franchisors, the variety of industries represented in franchising, and the range of investments available create opportunities for the smallest single-unit mom-and-pop operator to a large multimillion-dollar investor group or established businesses that are looking to add a franchise investment to its portfolio.

Flying solo: Single-unit franchises

A *single-unit* or *direct-unit franchise* is just what it says it is: As a franchisee, you obtain the right to own and operate one franchised business from a franchisor.

Over the years, most franchise systems have grown one franchise at a time. It is the classic method and, until the past few decades, was the most common type of relationship in franchising. As people looked for a way to get to their dream of independence through business ownership, franchising became their chosen vehicle. In a single-unit franchise, the franchisee (often along with family members) generally manages and supervises the business on a day-to-day basis. It is how their family makes a living.

There are more single-unit franchisees looking for opportunities than there are multi-unit investors (covered later in this chapter). Also, because the locations are managed directly by the franchisee and generally are a significant part of the franchisee's family income, single-unit operators tend to be better focused on operating their locations to brand standards and contributing to the neighborhoods in which their businesses are located. That's because they usually live in the community, their children go to the same schools, they attend the same houses of worship, and their customers are their neighbors.

Growing a family one franchise at a time

As single-unit franchisees prosper (see the preceding section), eventually they will want to acquire another franchise from the same franchisor. After all, they have an understanding of the business, have a relationship with the franchisor, can project the return that an additional unit can generate, and know the types of locations that work best. Initial training likely won't be needed, and some of the key employees they already have may be perfect managers in their second and third locations.

As they add additional locations, their little chain now can leverage off of the prior locations by sharing staff, inventory, storage, and back-of-house resources like bookkeeping and payroll processing. Investing in additional franchises is a terrific way to grow, because with experience their risk is generally lower than when they made their initial franchise decision, and even though they have more franchises, the relationship between the franchisor and franchisee is substantially the same.

However, growing one location at a time is different from agreeing to operate multiple locations from the beginning, because you don't usually obtain a reduction in initial or continuing fees and you'll continue to share the market with other franchisees. But with more units and more money invested, you will tend to be noticed more often by the franchisor and its staff because they are hoping you will continue to grow and grow and grow.

It's important to understand that franchisors will periodically update their franchise agreements, and franchisees who acquire additional franchises are likely to find variations between their original contract with the franchisor and the new franchise agreement for later units. Your franchisor may also include *cross defaults* in the agreements, meaning that if you can be terminated at one location, the franchisor reserves the right to terminate all your franchises at the same time — even if every other location is operating perfectly.

REMEMBER

As with all franchise agreements, you should have a qualified franchise attorney work with you. They may be able to also help you negotiate some changes to your agreements, including personal guarantees, cross defaults, and changes in fees that other franchisees may be required to pay.

Multi-unit developers

Instead of growing one location at a time, many franchisees instead choose to become multi-unit franchisees right from the start. By entering into a *multi-unit development agreement*, a developer obtains the right and the obligation to open a specific number of locations during a defined period of time and usually within a specified contiguous geographic area.

For example, say you want to open ten hair salons in your town. You can go to the franchisor and buy one franchise at a time (see the preceding section), but you have certain risks:

>> You may have to share the market with other franchisees from the system. And by the time you're ready to grow, the best locations for your brand may have been taken by other franchisees, or worse, the franchisor may have achieved critical mass in your market and is no longer offering additional opportunities where you want to grow.

>> Even if the franchisor is offering a better "deal" to multi-unit developers, it may not be offering that same deal to single-unit franchisees, and you likely won't have the necessary leverage you need to negotiate the changes you want.

To avoid these risks, you can enter into a multi-unit development agreement and agree to open and operate your multiple locations, say over the next several years, and the franchisor will grant you an exclusive market to develop your little chain.

TIP

If possible, you want your multi-unit development agreement to include *market exclusivity,* ensuring that you are the only franchisee operating in your area. Frequently, though, there may already be locations up and running in the area you want, and you'll need to decide whether market exclusivity is important to you prior to making your investment decision.

A multi-unit developer will typically pay the franchisor a fee for the right to enter into a multi-unit development agreement. As you sign a franchise agreement for each new location, generally a portion of the multi-unit development fee is credited by the franchisor against your initial franchise fee.

Expect that your development obligations will be specific. For example, instead of simply agreeing to ten units over five years, your agreement will usually have precise dates that you must meet, such as requiring that you have your locations open and operating on January 1, July 1, and so on during the term. These opening dates are important to the franchisor, so if you think the time provided for development is too restrictive or ambitious, this is something you and your attorney should discuss with the franchisor before you sign the development agreement.

WARNING

Don't expect the franchisor to allow you to slip on your opening dates later on — missing those dates might trigger certain terminations and cross default rights by the franchisor, including the loss of your development rights and the fee you have paid.

Frequently, the initial franchise fee for locations developed after the initial franchise in a development agreement will be reduced from the franchisor's standard initial fee. However, how the franchisor applies your development fee to the initial franchise fees you will owe varies from company to company.

In most franchise systems, as the franchisee signs a new single-unit franchise agreement and pays the initial fee, a pro-rata portion of the development fee paid will be applied to the initial franchise fee due. In other situations, you will receive no credit and you may pay the full initial franchise fee for each location.

You can expect that the development agreement may modify some portions of your franchise agreements. In addition to changing the initial franchise fees you may be charged, the franchisor may offer a reduced royalty after a certain number of locations have been developed, and changes in training, site selection, and development are common. You can also expect your franchisor to require you to have a general manager overseeing your units, and it may require you to have someone on staff to conduct the training of your staff.

Advantages for the multi-unit developer include the following:

>> You gain the ability to shift personnel from one location to another depending on where the staff is needed.

>> You may be able to establish a commissary or kitchen and combine the preparation of products for all the locations or save on freight and other costs by buying in greater quantities at a lower cost and storing inventory in a centralized warehouse, allowing for smaller retail locations and lower real estate costs.

>> General managers overseeing multiple locations may reduce management costs at each location. Franchisees may only need an assistant manager, and with consolidated back-of-house support staff, including a trainer, internal costs on a unit basis can be reduced.

Why are two agreements needed? Because the multi-unit development agreement and the franchise agreement serve different purposes. The multi-unit development agreement lays out the rights and obligations being granted to open the locations, and the franchise agreement governs how each location, as part of the franchise system, will operate.

REMEMBER

Make certain that the market you select can handle the number of locations you've committed to open, that you have the financial backing to live up to your development obligations, if the first location gets off to a slower start than anticipated, and most certainly, that you are ready and able to operate each location per the terms of the individual franchise agreement.

Master franchising

When you become a *master franchisee*, you become a franchisor in an area and are authorized to offer subfranchises through your master franchise license. As with any franchisor, your master franchisor will prepare and provide to prospective franchisees its own franchise disclosure document (FDD) and agreements that will contain information about you and your services.

In most master franchise relationships, the first thing you will likely be required to do is open and operate a few locations of your own. Once that has been accomplished, you will then be allowed to offer franchise rights to other franchisees (called *subfranchises*) to open and operate franchises in your market.

You will sign a master franchise agreement with the franchisor and usually pay a *master franchise fee.* Because your subfranchisees pay you their initial franchise fees and continuing royalty, typically you share a portion with your franchisor. The percentage split will vary widely depending on the franchise system. There is no standard master franchise relationship:

>> The subfranchisee may execute a franchise agreement directly with the franchisor or with the master franchisee.

>> The franchisor may or may not have the right to approve the new subfranchisee.

>> The subfranchisee may receive training and continuing support from the franchisor, the master franchisee, or both.

>> The subfranchisee may pay fees directly to the master franchisee, to the franchisor, or a combination of both.

Of all the types of franchising relationships, the master franchise or subfranchise relationship is the most complex.

WARNING

With the exception of foreign franchisors entering into the United States, don't expect a lot of U.S.-based franchisors to offer a master franchise relationship today. Although it is still used to some extent by U.S. franchisors internationally — and the trend is shifting away from master franchising to multi-unit development relationships, as technology and other advancements have made it possible to better directly support franchisees internationally — its popularity is waning.

The hired gun: Area representatives

Both an area representative and a master franchisee acquire a territory in which to solicit and support franchisees, and both share in the initial and continuing fees collected from franchisees with the franchisor. The difference is that the area representative is not a franchisor, does not deliver his or her own FDD, and doesn't execute any agreements with the franchisees. In essence, an area rep is a commissioned sales and field support person for the franchisor.

As in a master franchise relationship, the area representative pays the franchisor a market development fee for the opportunity to develop and provide services to a specific minimum number of units, during a specified time period in a defined area. Once recruited, the franchisees sign their single-unit and multi-unit development agreements with their franchisor.

For many of the same reasons discussed in the preceding section, the use of area representatives is on the decline. An area rep can recruit franchisees quickly. But because they share in the franchisor's fees, rather than earn their income as an employee, there is a strong argument that they tend to depress the exit or enterprise value of the franchisor despite their potential advantage in recruitment. When the franchise system is sold, the buyer of the system will value the continuing revenue stream available, and sharing of royalties with an area representative will reduce the value of the system to the buyer.

Area reps also are focused more on expansion and less on supporting the franchisees. Should that occur, the franchised businesses in their area — if not in the entire franchise system — suffer, and there is the potential for a higher level of closures and litigation.

There are ways to address some of the downsides of an area representative relationship by structuring the rep's role and modifying their fee arrangement to be based on the performance of the locations in their area. Still given the downside risks and the availability of alternative growth strategies, it's expected that the use of area representatives will continue to decline.

Nuances of the Franchisor/Franchisee Relationship

The franchise relationship is contractual, and franchisees and franchisors are not partners. Franchisors don't have a fiduciary responsibility to their franchisees. That means that the franchisor can do things to benefit itself and other franchisees, even if these things aren't beneficial to all franchisees.

REMEMBER

In great systems, franchisors and franchisees frequently discuss issues both one-on-one and communally through *franchisee advisory councils* (FACs). But it is essential to understand that it is the sole right of the franchisor to make the brand decisions.

FACs give franchisees a voice in the system's direction and provide the franchisor with advice in evolving and improving its systems. Often, one of the FAC's functions is to review ideas for new products and services, whether the ideas come from the franchisor or from a franchisee. FACs are also frequently involved in advertising review and menu or product testing, and help the franchisor to make changes to improve the system.

You may often hear franchisees referred to as entrepreneurs, and franchisees may view themselves as entrepreneurs. But franchisees are not *true* entrepreneurs because if they were they would naturally want to make all the decisions about how the franchise system should operate and would want to break free from the constraints that franchise systems impose on them. Successful franchisees are "formula entrepreneurs" willing and able to invest in a system and follow the system's direction. To achieve consistency a franchisor has to make decisions about how the business operates globally. Franchisees may think that they have the next great idea, and often they do, but the franchisor must look at those great (and sometimes not-so-great) ideas and make system-wide decisions.

For franchisees who *are* true entrepreneurs, the restrictions of a franchise system can be overwhelming and may even make the franchisor appear like a dictator. This can lead to disputes and disruptions in the franchise relationship.

If you invest in a franchise, you might not become rich. Not all franchises systems are successful, not all franchisees are profitable, and many franchisors and franchisees fail.

Owning any business is hard and comes with risk. For franchisees, even though you are supposed to get a proven systems and training when you hook up with a solid franchisor, no one guarantees your success. Often, the variable in this equation is you. Business ownership is not a passive investment and it requires long hours and dedication. Even with the best franchise system and the most popular brand name, the franchisee is often the key ingredient to making the business successful.

For emerging franchisors, how they design and develop their franchise system is essential to their ability to grow and support their franchise system successfully. Unfortunately, there is no legal baseline on who can become a franchisor, and how you structure your franchise system is up to you — and no one else.

Are you discouraged? Scared? Confused? Don't worry. The rest of this book is designed to help you in many ways. Franchising, when done right and entered into with eyes open, can be a profitable, highly enjoyable way to spend your future.

Considering the Pros and Cons of Franchising

You may occasionally see franchisors or franchise brokers using generalized statistics about the success of franchising. These statistics were based on studies by the U.S. Department of Commerce or the U.S. Small Business Administration conducted in the 1980s and 1990s that misled potential franchisees by making them think franchising was a surefire, safe investment, regardless of the franchisor. The International Franchise Association has asked its members and the press to no longer quote those statistics.

Most franchisors will publish statistics about their own franchise systems, and that information can be instructive and very beneficial because a well-designed franchise program *can* be an exceptional investment. But cookie-cutter franchise systems that are poorly managed are not good investments and need to be avoided. If any franchisor or broker quotes from these out-of-date and misleading industry success statistics, our best recommendation is for you not to do business with them and move on. Most franchisors are legitimate businesses looking for qualified franchisees. These franchisors don't mislead prospective franchisees by quoting discredited industry statistics.

Instead consider some of the advantages and disadvantages of your making a franchise investment.

The advantages

Your chance of success in franchising can only be as strong as the franchise system you select and how well you manage your business. Well-structured and managed franchise systems that support their franchisees generally offer the benefits discussed in this section.

Overall competitive benefits

The public has become accustomed to a certain level of quality and consistency when shopping at any branded locations. What's meant by *branded location* is a business that the public thinks of as a *chain* because each location has the same name, decor, products, services, menu items, and so on. In a branded location you expect that the customer experience will be the same regardless of the location.

REMEMBER

Whether a company's product is superior or mediocre, if its locations are successful, the secret for its success will likely be in its consistency. Great branded systems offer consumers consistent, sustainable replication of their brand promise, regardless of where you shop.

No matter where they are, even if they're overseas, consumers believe that they understand the level of quality they will receive when they shop at a branded location. This perception about branded chains gives new franchisees an established customer base on the day they open their doors — often even before they begin their retail advertising. Branding enables franchisees to compete with well-established, independent operators and even against other franchised and nonfranchised chains.

The advantage of brand recognition can also extend to the ability of a franchisor to establish system accounts that benefit the franchise system. Companies and even government agencies frequently look for franchise systems that have a network of locations because they trust that each franchisee will operate at the same level of consistency and commitment. The franchisor will often establish system relationships, including the price that the business will pay for the products and services. In this way, the customer can have its needs serviced wherever the franchise system has a location.

Pre-opening benefits

Although the cost of entrance into a franchise system includes a franchise fee, often cited as a disadvantage, the franchisee that joins and pays the initial franchise fee can expect to benefit from the franchisor having tested operating systems that will be consistently applied in each location. The franchisees will receive initial and often advanced training for management and staff, operations manuals, marketing and advertising programs, site-selection tools, store design, construction programs, reduced cost of equipment, and other support necessary for them to successfully launch their business. Additionally, franchisees can ask their franchisor and a network of other franchisees in the system questions when issues come up.

TIP

Over time, most franchisees discover how valuable the advice other franchisees give can be. After all, they have likely faced the same issue you're having trouble with — and best of all, they had the same issue in the same exact business and franchise system you have joined.

Ongoing benefits

Once a franchisee is open, support from the franchisor's home office and *field consultants* (franchisor support personnel assigned to assist and consult with a franchisee) can be powerful. Because the franchisee is part of a system where everyone is buying the same inventory and other goods, the system can enjoy the purchasing power that comes from joining with others. This can often result in lowered operating costs. Franchisees benefit from professionally designed point of sale computer systems that help them track their sales and often their costs. Having professionally designed marketing materials, advertising, grand-opening programs, and other marketing materials that independents could never afford is a major advantage.

Also, with multiple franchisees in a market, the ability to advertise is enhanced because the cost is shared across the locations in the system. Franchise systems have the ability to test and modernize their products and services to keep ahead of the competition that smaller independent businesses simply couldn't afford. In addition, when a franchisor can establish critical mass in a market by developing multiple locations, franchise systems can dominate local markets.

The disadvantages

Before investing in any franchise you need to understand some of the disadvantages that come in a franchise relationship.

Loss of independence

For some people, one of the most serious disadvantages of becoming a franchisee is their loss of independence. If you need to make all your own decisions about the products and services your business will be selling, franchising is likely the wrong choice for you. Franchise systems are structured in such a way that the franchisor sets the rules and the franchisees will independently manage their business to meet the franchisor's brand standards included in the franchise system's manual.

Overdependence on the system

Loss of independence, if taken to extremes, leads to another disadvantage: overdependence on the franchise system. Franchising succeeds when financial and emotional risks motivate franchisees to take the franchise system and execute it better. Great franchisees do not change the system — they simply deliver better on the franchisor's brand promise.

However, when franchisees need to totally rely on the system for their success, and cannot independently manage their business on a day-to-day basis, their overdependence can cause problems. Franchisees need to balance system restrictions with their personal ability to manage their own businesses. For example, when franchisees depend on national advertising exclusively and do not invest in local marketing, they are shortchanging their business by relying too heavily on what the franchisor is bringing to the party. If every time an issue comes up, they cannot independently make decisions and instead call the franchisor or another franchisee for advice, all parties are going to suffer.

Other franchisees who are "bad apples"

The principal reason for the success of franchising is the public's perception of quality and consistency throughout the chain. When the public receives great service at one location, the assumption is that the system has great service at every location. This consumer expectation is also one of the potential major frailties of any chain, including franchising. Franchisees are judged not only by *their* performance but also by the performance of other franchisees.

WARNING

Poorly performing fellow franchisees or company-owned locations can damage a franchisee's business even where it does not share the same market. If the hotel room is dirty in one location or, even worse, if the press reports that the hotel has rodents, the public assumes that the problem exists throughout the system.

Consider how you feel about a brand when one or more locations across the country have a problem reported on Yelp or other social media sites. Because of the Internet and social media, no brand today is truly local, and what happens across the country or even across the ocean is going to impact how the public views your local operation.

Elevated income expectations

Although good franchisors and franchise sales staff try to prevent it, some potential franchisees have unrealistic expectations about the income they are going to earn. If franchisees' earnings expectations are unrealistic, they will regret their investment in dollars, time, and effort and may become a negative influence on the system. Having realistic expectations is important to any investment decision. It is essential, therefore, that you carefully prepare for yourself financial projections for your business to determine whether or not the franchise you are evaluating can meet your financial needs.

Because of the rules that govern franchising, franchisors are often restricted from commenting on the financial projections prepared by prospective franchisees. Doing so may put them outside the boundaries established by the FTC's Franchise Rule governing financial performance representations. Franchisees with their advisors should base projections on realistic expectations and information gained through the franchisor's disclosure document, the Internet, and other franchisees and other sources.

Franchising inelasticity

Franchise systems are bound together through the legal agreements between the franchisor and each franchisee and developer. Often, these agreements contain restrictions that potentially impact the franchisor's ability to make strategic decisions.

For example, if an independent nonfranchised business finds a perfect location for a new store, it is free to open at that location. In a franchise system, the franchisor must first look to the legal agreements between itself and the franchisees in the market to see if that new location will encroach on any franchisees contractual rights. If the franchisor has granted the franchisees protected territories, and the potential location is in one of those territories, the franchise system may lose that market opportunity — and will often lose that location to a competitor who does not have the same restrictions. A similar situation can arise if the new product or service the franchisor wants to introduce into the system requires the franchisee to make a capital investment and the franchisee does not have the contractual obligation to do so.

The franchise agreement

Every franchise agreement contains rights and obligations that both the franchisee and franchisor have agreed to meet. For franchisees the agreement can contain provisions they need to understand before they sign on the dotted line.

These rights and obligations can be a double-edged sword. Sometimes they can make franchising successful, but sometimes they can also be disadvantages to some franchisees. The restrictions may be on the product and services they are allowed to offer, limitations on size and exclusivity of their territory, the possibility of termination for failure to follow the system, the added investment often required for reimaging, remodeling, or new equipment as a condition of renewal, the cost of transfer and renewal, and restrictions on independent marketing. Also, the added costs for royalties, advertising, additional training, and other services potentially reduce a franchisee's earnings.

WARNING

Many franchisors today are reducing the size of the territory they grant to franchisees. Some grant exclusivity for only a short period of time, and others are eliminating protected territories altogether. In the long run, having a fully developed market is a benefit to the franchise system, although it may have an impact on a particular unit in sales.

2

Planning for Your Business

Contents at a Glance

Chapter **1**

Writing a Business Plan

The fact that you've opened this book means the idea of writing a business plan has made it onto your to-do list. That's a big step in the right direction. Now come the questions. What exactly is a business plan? What should it include? How should it be organized? And do you really need one?

This chapter answers all those questions and more. It offers plenty of reasons why business planning is essential — when you start your business and at every growth stage along the way. It helps you think about the audience for your plan, what its key components should be, and how to go about putting it together. It also updates you on changes and challenges facing business planners in today's rapidly transforming business arena.

Selling Yourself on the Importance of Business Planning

Nearly all business experts agree on one thing: the importance of drafting a business plan. Yet plenty of business leaders plunge into the competitive arena without a formal plan. Why? There are plenty of excuses posing as reasons. There are entrepreneurs so carried away by their enthusiasm that they figure their passion and optimism are enough to build a successful company. Others say they were just too busy to develop a formal business plan. But operating without a plan can prove even more time-consuming in the long run. These sections clarify in plain English the importance of having a business plan.

Tallying up the benefits of a business plan

Some of the benefits you can gain from business planning include

>> An opportunity to test your business idea to see whether it holds real promise of success (see Chapter 2 in Book 1)

>> Clarity about your business mission, vision, and the values that can help you steer your business through times of growth or difficulty

>> A description of your *business model,* or how you plan to make money and stay in business (see Chapter 3 in Book 1), along with a road map and timetable for achieving your goals and objectives

>> A portrait of your potential customers and their buying behaviors (see Chapter 4 in Book 1)

>> A rundown of your major competitors and your strategies for facing them

>> A clear-eyed analysis of your industry, including opportunities and threats, along with an honest assessment of your company's strengths and weaknesses

>> Benchmarks you can use to track your performance and make midcourse corrections

>> An explanation of your marketing strategies (head to Book 5 for more on marketing and publicity)

>> An analysis of your revenues, costs, and projected profits, along with cash flow projections that help you anticipate your funding needs until the time when revenues flow in to cover expenses (see Book 3 for more about finances)

>> An assessment of risks and the forces of change that can threaten your success or present opportunities to capitalize upon

>> A résumé you can use to introduce your business to employees, suppliers, vendors, lenders, and others

Knowing what can go wrong without a plan

WARNING

The many benefits of having a business plan should be enough to convince you. But in case you're still wavering, consider what can go wrong if you don't take time to plan. You risk

>> Running out of cash because you haven't projected start-up or expansion costs and the amount of funding you'll need before sufficient revenue rolls in

>> Missing sales projections because you don't really know who your customers are, what they want, or how they shop and buy

>> Becoming overwhelmed or sidetracked by too many options because you never took the time to focus on a mission and vision for your company

>> Going bankrupt because you don't have a rational *business model* or a plan for how to make money

REMEMBER

Time spent putting together a solid business plan is time well spent. Don't be overwhelmed by the task you're launching. The basic components of a business plan are fairly simple and the benefits are many.

The Anatomy of a Business Plan

Business plans are as varied as the companies that compile them. Some run dozens of pages. Others barely fill a few sheets. The following sections introduce the basic components that you can adapt to create a plan to meet your needs.

Business plan contents from beginning to end

Although business plans come in all sizes and formats, they typically share a similar framework. The following components, presented in the order they generally appear, are the elements you'll choose from as you build your plan:

>> **Table of contents:** This guide to key sections in your business plan is especially useful if your plan exceeds ten pages.

>> **Executive summary:** This summary of key points in your business plan is important if your plan runs more than ten pages, and you want to convey the major points up-front. You want to keep it clear, captivating, and brief — in fact, aim to keep it to no more than two pages.

>> **Business overview:** This section describes your company and the nature of your business. It may include your company's mission and vision statements as well as descriptions of your values, your products or services, ways your company is unique, and what business opportunities you plan to seize.

>> **Business environment:** This section includes an analysis of your industry and the forces at work in your market; a description of your direct and potential competitors; and a close look at your customers, including who they are, what they want, and how they buy products or services. It describes forces beyond your control that affect your business success.

>> **Business description:** In this section, include information about your management team, organizational structure, new or proprietary technology, products and services, business operations, and marketing potential.

>> **Business strategy:** This section is your road map to success. It brings together information about your business environment, business model, goals and objectives, and resources, and then lays out your strategy for start-up, growth, or turnaround.

>> **Marketing plan:** This section is where you describe your brand, value proposition, and how you plan to reach prospects, make sales, and develop a loyal clientele. (See Book 5 for more about marketing.)

>> **Financial review:** This section includes a detailed review of the state of your current finances and what you expect your financial picture to look like in the future. It typically contains financial statements, including an income statement, your balance sheet, and a cash-flow statement. (Book 3 has more about finances.)

>> **Action plan:** Here you detail the steps involved in implementing your business plan, including the sequence of actions and how they align with your goals and objectives.

>> **Appendices:** This section includes detailed information that supports your business plan. It may include analyses, reports, surveys, legal documents, product specifications, and spreadsheets that deliver information that supports your business plan but which is of interest to only a small number of your readers.

Business plan FAQs

If you're like most people who are launching the business-planning process, the following questions are on your mind:

>> **Do you really need to include all these sections?** Nope. Your business plan should include only what's important to you and your company. If your plan is short — or written mostly for your own purposes — you can skip the executive summary and table of contents, for example. Or if it's a one-person business, you may not need to describe its organization (unless you need a little help in getting organized!).

TIP

For most businesses, however, all the other sections are important. By putting your mission, vision, values, product offering, goals, and competitive advantages into words, you clarify and strengthen ideas about what you really plan to do with your business. That exercise can be extremely valuable for any company, no matter how big or small.

>> **Do you really need to write it all down?** The one-word answer is yes. Creating a written plan forces you to think through issues that you may otherwise ignore. For example, when you write your business plan, you commit to how you're going to make money; you define your customers and your strategy for reaching them; you analyze your competition and how your offerings compare to theirs; you list opportunities to seize and threats to protect against; and you establish a set of goals and objectives — along with your action plan for achieving success. And when you're done, you have it all in writing for quick, easy, and frequent reference.

>> **How long should your plan be?** As long as it needs to be — and not a single word longer. A business plan as thick as a good novel doesn't impress anyone. In fact, a plan that size is likely to scare people off. What really impresses investors, clients, employees, and anyone else who may read your plan is clear, straightforward, and to-the-point thinking. Don't go overboard in the cutting room or leave anything important out of your plan purely for the sake of keeping it brief, but do condense every section down to its most important points. Even comprehensive plans usually fit on 20 to 30 pages, plus appendices. Most 100-page business plans are about 75 pages too long.

Setting Out Your Planning Objectives

To get your business where you want it to go, you need a map to follow, which is what your business plan is all about. To navigate a new course for your company, you need to start with an assessment of where your business is right now. After you assess your current situation, you need to define where you want to arrive and what financial, operational, marketing, and organizational strategies you'll follow to achieve success. The following sections lead the way.

Planning for a new business

Every new business — whether a tech start-up or new business in a long-standing arena — begins with a new idea and high hopes. A business plan helps you evaluate your new idea, potential market, and competition, addressing these critical questions:

>> Does this new venture have a good chance of getting off the ground?

>> How much money will the business need to get up and running?

>> Who are your customers, and what's the best way to reach them?

>> Who are your competitors, and what's the best way to outrun them?

>> Why will people choose this product or service over other options?

Planning for a solo business

Millions of people work for themselves in businesses called *sole proprietorships.* They range from accountants and attorneys to app developers, artists, and musicians. Many never consider drafting a business plan, which is too bad. A business plan helps zero in on key questions:

>> Are you prepared for running a company of one?

>> How can you turn what you love doing into a profitable business?

>> What resources do you need to get your business off the ground?

>> What should you charge for your product or service?

>> What affiliations could you explore to strengthen the business?

Chapter 2 in Book 1 includes a section on turning a side gig into a business.

Planning to address changing conditions

No business today is immune to change. New technologies, disruptive innovations, and global, economic, and political turbulence prompt many established businesses to plan how to retool themselves. The critical questions a business plan must address are as follows:

>> What are the drivers of change that present your business with internal or external threats or opportunities?

>> How can you reshape your business, its technology, its products or services, and its customer interactions to better compete in its transformed environment?

>> What steps do you need to take to achieve your goals for change?

Planning for growth

Successful companies can't rest on their laurels. To remain successful, they have to maintain their competitive edge. And to grow, they need to seize new opportunities, whether by introducing products, expanding into new locations or market segments, improving efficiencies and profitability, or embracing new innovations. For companies charting a strategy to grow, a business plan must address several key questions:

>> How are you planning to deepen customer loyalty?

>> Where do the best opportunities for growth lie?

>> If you're aiming to reach new market areas or new consumer segments, who are your competitors in these new markets?

>> Can you take advantage of technological innovations?

>> How can you revise operations and processes to scale into a larger business or to improve profitability?

>> How can you best compete to grab new market share?

Identifying Your Business Plan Audiences and Key Messages

Your business plan is the blueprint for how you plan to reach your business goals. To help focus your efforts, consider which groups of people will have the greatest impact on your success. Those groups will be the primary audiences for your business plan. For example, if you need capital investment, investors will be your primary audience. If you need to build strategic alliances, you want your plan to address potential business partners. You and your team are another key audience for the plan, of course, because it will serve as your guide.

After you know *whom* you want to reach with your business plan, you can focus on what those readers need to know and what messages you want them to receive. These sections help you define your audience and your messages before you begin to assemble your plan.

Your audience

All the people who have an interest in or who can help you succeed in your business venture — from investors and lenders to employees, customers, and suppliers — represent *audiences* for your business plan. Depending on the situation you face and what you want your company to achieve through its plan, certain audiences will be more important than others:

>> If your company seeks investment capital, your all-important target audience is likely to be filled with potential investors.

>> If your plan includes the introduction of stock options (possibly in lieu of higher salaries), your current and prospective employees and stakeholders are a primary target audience.

>> If you're launching a business that needs clients to get up and running — the sooner the better — major customers may comprise one of your plan's primary audiences.

>> If you're self-employed in a one-person business, your plan may be to focus on you and you alone as you chart your course and anticipate problems before they arise.

TIP

The following is a checklist of the most common audiences for a business plan:

>> **Yourself and those individuals in your close circle:** To focus and gain support for your efforts, establish your goals, chart your course, anticipate problems, reduce distractions, build on strengths, and stay on track to success.

>> **Your board of directors or advisors:** To share growth plans and how you can achieve them.

>> **Investors and lenders:** To provide proof of good long-term financial prospects, positive and growing revenue and profit projections, and strong strategies and financial management. For investors, also to convince that your business is postured for strong and rapid growth.

>> **Senior management team:** To present growth plans and how each manager's area contributes to success.

>> **Current employees:** To present a business overview with emphasis on growth plans and how team members can participate and benefit from business changes, growth, and profitability.

>> **New hires:** To present a business overview with emphasis on brand and business culture, growth plans, and how team members can participate and benefit from business changes, growth, and profitability.

>> **Independent contractors:** To present a business overview with emphasis on brand and business culture, quality, growth plans, and how remote team members collaborate and contribute.

>> **Vendors and suppliers:** To present a business overview that describes what your company is and does, its distinctions and value proposition, and how its capabilities, operations, and finances posture it as a strong business partner in business alliances.

>> **Customers or clients:** To present a business overview that describes what your company is and does, its distinctions and value proposition, and how its capabilities, operations, and finances posture it for long-term strength.

>> **Donors (for nonprofits):** To present the organization's goals, operations, the importance of its work, the extent of its volunteer and client network, and how it uses funds and ensures financial accountability.

>> **Distributors:** To present a business overview with emphasis on brand strength, product lines, competitive advantage, market area, growth plans, and financial strength.

>> **Regulators:** To present a business overview with emphasis on operational, financial, and legal issues.

>> **Advocacy groups:** To share key strategies for addressing the interests or requirements of each group and how your business has the operational and financial strength to succeed.

Your message

After you target the audiences for your plan, the next step is to focus on the key messages you want each group to receive. For example:

>> A person who owns shares in a company wants to know growth plans.

>> A banker considering a loan request wants to see proof of strong revenue and profit prospects.

>> Employee groups want to see how they'll benefit from the company's growth and profits.

>> Regulators focus on operational and financial issues.

TIP

Take time to clarify the primary messages you need to convey to your key audiences. Refer to the preceding section for samples of messages that various audiences are likely to consider important. Then, identify the three most important audiences you intend to address with your business plan and the key points you want to convey to each.

Establishing Your Plan's Time Frame

Your *time frame* represents how far into the future you want your business plan to reach. You want your business to grow successfully for years and years into the future, but each business plan covers a unique planning period. Some are designed to get a company to a defined sales level, a funding objective, or the achievement of some other business goal. All good plans should span a time frame that has a realistic start and finish, with a number of measurable checkpoints in between. The sections that follow help you determine how far into the future your plan should extend and the milestones that you can use to chart your progress.

Setting your schedule

How far out your planning horizon should span depends on the kind of business you're in and the pace at which your industry is moving. Some ventures have only six months to prove themselves. At the other end of the spectrum, organizations with substantial endowments, such as nonprofits, are in for the long haul with business plans that look at five- or ten-year horizons. Typical business plans, however, tend to use one-year, three-year, or five-year benchmarks.

REMEMBER

Business planning is an ongoing process. At least annually — and sometimes more often — most companies review, revise, and even completely overhaul their plans. As you establish your time frame, don't cast it in cement. Instead, think of your schedule as something you commit to follow unless and until circumstances change and you make a conscious decision to revise it.

Defining milestones

Establishing goals and establishing measurable objectives is a critical part of business planning. But knowing your goals and objectives isn't enough. You also need to establish and hold yourself accountable to a schedule that includes specific milestones to reach along the way to success.

TIP

Answer the following questions. Then use your responses to establish your business plan time frame, along with key milestones that take into account your business trends and cycles and the competitive and financial realities of your business.

>> Identify three milestones that represent essential steps you need to take to get your business up and running or to reach your business turnaround or growth goals. Estimate a time frame for each.

>> Is the success of your business tied to a major business trend or change? If so, what is the time frame?

>> Is your business seasonal in nature? When do you need to have your product or service available to take advantage of the peak season?

>> How soon do you need to make your product or service available to stay ahead of your competition?

>> When do you absolutely need to start making a profit?

Preparing for the Real World

You're about ready to dive into the business-planning process. By now you're pretty certain about the purpose and benefit of your plan, and you have a fairly clear idea of who you want to read your opus when it's ready, and what you want them to do as a result. You may even have a preliminary idea of your planning timeline. (If any of that sounds like Greek, look back at the preceding sections in this chapter.)

Take a minute to become aware of some of the resources you can turn to for additional tips and tools.

Locating informative resources

You're certain to have plenty of questions as your business planning gets underway. Here's a list of places you can check out:

TIP

>> **The Internet:** You can find tons of information on markets, customers, competition — you name it. Just make sure the material is current and from reliable sources. Reputable industry, government, or university reports are among the best resources for tracking market shifts and trends.

Also, spend time studying customer comments on review and rating sites. Look to see what customers like and don't like about products and services already on the market. Study your own customer reviews, if you have them, and also study what people say about competing offerings. Every complaint you see represents a potential business opportunity.

>> **The library:** The periodical section of most libraries has business journals and other useful publications, and the reference shelves contain books on demographics, industry trends, and other factual resources.

- >> **Business schools:** Colleges, universities, and organizations (including the Small Business Association [SBA]) offer courses that can develop your planning, financial, and management skills. Also, many business school professors are willing to discuss specific planning issues.

- >> **Industry trade journals:** Yes, the subscriptions can be pricey, but they're often worth the investment and sometimes available at libraries.

- >> **Newspapers:** No matter your business, *The New York Times, The Wall Street Journal,* and local papers keep you on top of issues and trends.

- >> **Trade shows and industry symposiums:** These gatherings are usually great places to get news about products, services, customers, and competitors — all under one roof.

- >> **U.S. Small Business Administration (SBA):** This rich resource is for just about everything you want to know about starting and running a small business. Look at www.sba.gov.

- >> **Search and research companies:** Using these resources comes with a price, but sometimes a LEXIS/NEXIS search or a market-research study is the only way to access must-have data.

- >> **Professional groups:** Almost every profession has a guild or group, from the American Medical Writers Association to the Society of Wetland Scientists. Find the group that serves your business arena and check out the website and membership requirements.

- >> **Business networking groups:** These groups are comprised of members with experience, insights, and even business referrals to share.

- >> **Local business organizations:** Your local Chamber of Commerce and economic development organization are good vehicles for networking, staying abreast of local and state issues, and obtaining business and regional information.

Seeking expert advice

When you can't find answers to specific questions, ask for advice. For example, if you're thinking of starting a business, ask someone who runs a similar business to fill you in on what you need to know. If you want to break away from the corporate grind and go into business for yourself, schedule a lunch with someone who made a similar move to discover what it takes. You're sure to get an earful of useful input to incorporate in your planning.

TIP

As you interview industry contacts — or people with experience in similar businesses — follow these steps:

>> **Prepare your questions in advance.** With advance planning, you won't waste time or forget to discuss something really important.

>> **Explain exactly why you're asking for help.** You can't expect people to be open with you if you aren't honest with them.

>> **Be prepared to listen.** Even if you hear something you don't want to know, listen anyway. Anybody who warns you about potential obstacles is doing you a big favor.

>> **Keep the conversation open-ended.** Always ask whether you should be thinking about other issues or addressing other topics.

>> **Build your network of contacts.** Ask for introductions to others who may be helpful or for suggestions for sources of useful information.

Chapter **2**

Finding the Funding

Two common attitudes about start-up funds make the search for funds much more difficult. They are

>> The more money I get, the better. I can use as much as I can get.

>> My business plan numbers are just estimates — the investor will tell me what I need.

If you're thinking like this, stop right now. First of all, why seek more investment money than you absolutely need? Every bit of capital invested in your business costs you some equity (ownership) in your company. Besides, having too much money may lead you to make poor decisions because you don't think as carefully as you should about how you spend that money.

Secondly, although it's true that your business plan financials are estimates, they had better be *good* estimates based on your research. Your investor may discount your estimate of rapid sales growth, but he or she wants to know that you've carefully considered all your numbers and that they make sense.

In this chapter, you see how to raise capital for your business the smart way — and you start with a plan.

Starting with a Plan

Before you talk to anyone — even your grandmother — about money, have a plan in place, a set of strategies for targeting the right amount of money from the right sources. Here are some guidelines for putting together a plan that works:

>> Seek what you actually need, not what you think you can raise.

>> Look at how your company grows and define the points when you'll most likely need capital.

>> Consider the sources of money available to you at each stage.

>> Make sure that the activities of your business let you tap into the correct source of money at the right time. For example, if you know that you are planning an initial public offering (IPO) in three years, start putting in place the systems, controls, and professional management that you'll need before the IPO takes place.

>> Monitor your capital needs as you go so that you don't have to return to the trough too many times. Every time you go back for another round of capital, you give up more stock in your company, and the percentage you own declines.

You can come out a winner if you prepare for your future capital needs. Just follow the lead of one technology company that produces custom productivity and e-commerce applications. This company keeps itself in a good position to raise capital by

>> Creating value in the form of long-term customers and great products

>> Running a profitable business

>> Keeping cash flow positive

If you do these three things, you will probably not have difficulty raising growth capital whenever you need it. If you have a start-up venture, strive to achieve these goals from day one.

When you're financing a traditional business

Traditional businesses (non-Internet businesses) typically follow fairly predictable financing cycles. Take a look at Figure 2-1 to see the stages of financing for a typical business.

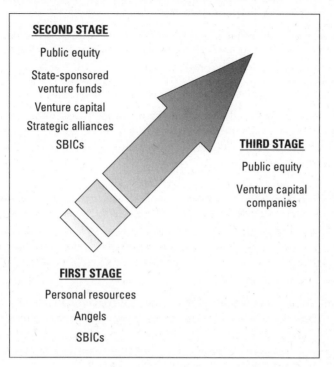

SECOND STAGE

Public equity

State-sponsored
venture funds

Venture capital

Strategic alliances

SBICs

THIRD STAGE

Public equity

Venture capital
companies

FIRST STAGE

Personal resources

Angels

SBICs

FIGURE 2-1:
Three stages
for financing the
typical business.

© John Wiley & Sons, Inc.

First-stage funding is about getting seed capital to finish preparing the product and the business for launch. It's also the stage where you seek funding to begin operations and reach a positive cash flow. In the second stage, you're usually looking for growth capital. Your business has proven its concept and now you want to grow. Alternatively, your customers have demanded that your company grow to meet their needs (that's a nice thing when it happens). To successfully use second-round financing, you need to be out looking for capital in advance of needing it.

Third-stage funding generally results in an acquisition or a buyout of the company. It's the harvest stage for the entrepreneur who wants to take his or her wealth out of the business and possibly exit, or for investors who want to exit. In general, if you take on *venture capital* (a professionally managed pool of money), you are probably looking at a buyout or IPO within three to five years. That's because a buyout or IPO provides the cash your investor needs to get out of the investment.

When you're financing for e-commerce

It's pretty easy to look at the funding stages of a traditional business, but the Internet has brought about some business models that don't fit those stages well, if at all. Internet-based businesses (whose primary location is the Internet) require a strategy that is part formula and part artistic achievement. Such a strategy is ill defined at best. And sometimes it's difficult to judge which concept is going to get funding before it launches, and which will have to bootstrap for a while to prove its concept.

REMEMBER

Grabbing early brand recognition from competitors online takes a lot of money, a professional management team, and the capability to grow in a hurry. If that's your business, here are some suggestions for maneuvering through the capital maze:

>> **Don't take the easy money.** You want the smart money. It's okay to fund a traditional business with money from friends, family, and lovers. Doing so isn't a good idea, however, when you're seeking early stage capital for an Internet concept. Who is funding your business is as important as how much they're giving you. Be sure that you associate with people who attract the right kind of money to your venture.

>> **Get an introduction to the money source through one of your advisors.** Be sure you exercise due diligence (fancy words for doing your homework — investigating the money source) on the investor to find one that has worked with your type of business before and has compatible firms in its portfolio that provide synergies with yours.

>> **Don't get married on the first date.** Large quantities of money are available for great Internet concepts. If you have such a concept, you may have more *term sheets* (agreements listing what an investor is willing to do) than you know what to do with. It's tempting to grab the first term sheet under the assumption that the first is always the best. The agreement may be for the most money, maybe not, but the investor may not be the most compatible with your business. Compatibility is even more important than money, because the money source has a lot to say about what happens to your business. So, consider all your options before selecting one. Remember that the most important person to get to know in any potential investment firm is the partner you will be dealing with. If you don't have a good feeling about that person, you may want to look elsewhere.

>> **Take the deal that moves you on to the next stage.** The biggest deal doesn't always win. What you're looking for is enough money to get you comfortably to the next round of financing and an investment firm that adds value to what you're doing in the form of introductions, contacts, advice, and so forth.

>> **Get your website up as quickly as possible.** Don't wait for the perfect site. Get up and running and start receiving feedback from potential customers. You need to keep the momentum going and collect data on the people who visit your site. This is important information to have when you talk to your investor.

>> **Buy the best management you can get with your capital.** Investors are practically unanimous: The management team is more important than the business concept itself. When you obtain money, invest in the best management you can get. If you have to bootstrap with your own funds, seek a strategic alliance with a company whose great management you can leverage.

Tapping Friends and Family

The majority of entrepreneurs — well over 70 percent — start their businesses with personal savings, credit cards, and other personal assets like the proceeds from second mortgages and sale of stock portfolios. Why is that? With all the venture capital and private investor money out there for the taking, why do you have to use your own resources? The answer is simple: Your new company is just too big a risk — it's unproven, and you don't know for certain if the market will accept it. The only people who'll invest in your business at this point are you and people who know and believe in you.

TIP

But what if you don't have a network of friends and family willing to give you money, or from whom you prefer not to take money? What do you do then? One thing you do is *bootstrap* — beg, borrow, and barter for anything that you can from products to services to an office site. One way to bootstrap is to avoid hiring employees as long as possible (employees are typically the single biggest expense of any business). Here are some other tips:

>> Look for an office suite where you can share facilities and equipment with other tenants.

>> Share office space with an established company that is compatible with yours. You may even be able to barter or trade services.

>> To reduce cash needs, consider leasing rather than buying equipment.

>> Barter with established companies for services.

>> Get your customers to pay quickly. Sometimes a new company can get customers to pay a deposit upfront, providing capital for the raw materials you need to make the product.

>> Ask your suppliers for favorable payment terms, and then pay on time. Those relationships become important to your business as it grows. You may find it necessary to request smaller amounts of credit from several suppliers until you establish your business.

REMEMBER

If you do decide to take money from friends and family, do it in a businesslike manner. That is, have an attorney draw up a contract that protects both sides. Investing in a business venture is a risk and should only be undertaken by people who can bear to lose their investment, should that occur. Family money is the most expensive money you'll ever use because you pay for it for the rest of your life!

Finding an Angel

The second most common source of capital for starting and growing a business is an angel, also known as a private investor. Angels are members of the informal risk capital market — the largest pool of capital in the United States. So, how do you find one of these gift-givers from heaven? Unfortunately, that's the hard part because angels tend to keep a lower profile than any other type of investor. Entrepreneurs typically find angels through referrals from someone else. That's why networking with people in your industry is so important when you begin thinking about starting a business. You need to build up a personal network to tap when it's time to look for private investment capital.

How to spot an angel

There was a time when angels were into the investment for the long haul. Times have changed; angel investors have, too. Today, angel investors look a lot like professional venture capitalists. Angels typically ask you for the same credentials that a venture capitalist wants:

>> A business plan

>> Milestones

>> A significant equity stake in the business

>> A seat on the board of directors

The similarity between an angel and a venture capitalist came about because of the long bull market in the late 1990s when venture capital funding reached astronomical levels. Flush with cash, the venture capitalist stopped looking at deals that were less than $3 million to $5 million, leaving the playing field wide open for angels to step in, with the promise of a quicker turnaround.

Angels used to be characterized as middle-aged, former entrepreneurs who generally operated solo and invested near their homes. They usually funded deals for less than a million dollars and stayed in the investment for several years. Today, angels come in all ages, even turning up among the twenty-something Internet crowd who hit it big with their first ventures. Angels also band together to increase the size of their investment pools and take on larger deals. Networks like The Tech Coast Angels, based in California, consider themselves to be seed venture capitalists. They have become as sophisticated in their investment methods as any professional venture capitalist — exercising more due diligence and sometimes looking for a quicker return on their investment, often to the detriment of the business. In other words, they need to be cashed out of their investment before the growing business is in a position to do so. Entrepreneurs typically work with longer growth and performance horizons than venture capitalists and many of the new breed of angels. So their goals are often in conflict.

How to deal with angels

In many ways, you deal with angels the same as you deal with professional venture capitalists. You start with a good referral from someone who knows the angel well. Then:

>> **Make sure your goals and your angel's goals are the same.** Otherwise, you may risk the goals you've set for the business. Try to avoid an angel who wants to get in and out in three years or less. You can't build an enduring business in that time frame. Besides, you need to find a way to buy out the investor at that point, and that may mean selling the business or offering an IPO, which may not have been your original plan.

>> **Exercise your own due diligence (investigation, background check) on the angel.** Don't be afraid to ask for references from other companies the angel has invested in. Talk to those entrepreneurs to find out what their experience was.

>> **Look for an angel who provides more than money.** You want contacts in the industry, potential board members, and strategic assistance for your business. These things are as important as money.

>> **Get the angel's commitment to help you meet certain business milestones that you both agree on.**

GETTING READY TO DEAL

One of the more important rules about negotiation is, "He who has the most information wins." Negotiating the best funding deal really is about 1) understanding the needs of the other party, 2) knowing what you want, and 3) knowing your alternatives if you can't come to an agreement. Here's a checklist of information you should have at your fingertips when you negotiate for funding:

1. How much money do you need for start-up and years one through five?
2. How will you use the funds?
3. What sources of money will you seek and why?
4. If you seek debt funding, what will you use as collateral?
5. Are you willing to personally guarantee the debt?
6. What funds have been invested to date and by whom? Are these funds debtor equity?
7. If you have received outside investment capital, what did the investor receive in return for the investment?
8. Which outside investors have you approached or will you approach? What were the results?
9. Under what legal form is the company organized and how does this help the principals and investors?
10. What tax benefits does the legal structure provide for the company, the principals, and the investors?
11. What is the financial vehicle being offered to the investors?
12. What is the payback period for the investor and the projected return on investment (ROI)?
13. What is the proposed exit strategy for the investors? The principals?
14. Have your financial projections been reviewed by an accountant?
15. What leases and loan agreements do you currently have?

Daring to Use Venture Capital

Venture capital is a professionally managed pool of funds that usually operates in the form of a limited partnership. The managing general partner pulls together a pool of investors — individual and institutional (pension funds and insurance companies, for example) — whose money he or she invests on behalf of the partnership. Typically, venture capitalists invest at the second round of funding and are looking for fast growth and a quick turnaround of their investment. Consequently, their goals often conflict with the entrepreneur's goals for the company.

In the late 1990s, it appeared that all the rules about what a good investment is changed as venture capitalists began focusing on Internet companies and investing in ideas rather than intellectual property. They rushed to invest in companies like Amazon.com, Buy.com, and e-Toys, companies that weren't projecting profits for several years. But as stock valuations of these companies plummeted to near zero levels in late 1999 and early 2000, venture capitalists began rethinking their strategies. They didn't stop investing in Internet companies; they just started doing a better job of evaluating the opportunities.

What is still true about venture capital is that it funds less than 1 percent of all new ventures, mostly in technology areas — biotechnology, information systems, the Internet, and computer technology. To see how you may be able to use venture capital to your advantage, you first need to understand the cost of raising capital and the process by which it happens.

Calculating the real cost of money

Raising money for your business, whether private or venture capital, is a time-consuming and costly process. That's why many entrepreneurs in more traditional businesses (non-high-tech or non-Internet) opt for slower growth, using internal cash flows as long as they can. But if you've decided to speed up your start-up or growth rate with outside capital, you need to have reasonable expectations about how that can happen. Here's what you need to know:

>> Raising money always takes longer than you planned, at least twice as long. Count on it.

>> Plan to spend several months seeking funds, several more months for the potential investor to agree to fund your venture, and perhaps six more months before the money is actually in your hands.

>> Use financial advisors experienced in raising money.

>> Understand that raising money takes you away from your business a lot, probably when you most need to be there. So be sure to have a good management team in place.

Start looking for money before you need it!

After you find what you think is the ideal investor — you're compatible, you have the same goals for the future of the company, and you genuinely like each other — the investor may back out of the deal. That's right, after you've spent months trying to find this investor and even more time exercising due diligence (yours and the investor's), the investor may change his or her mind. Perhaps the investor stumbled across something unfavorable; more likely, he or she couldn't pull together the capital needed to fund your deal.

Always have a backup if you sense that the deal may be going sideways.

Investors often want to buy out your early investors, including your friends and family, typically out of the belief that first-round funders have nothing more to contribute to the venture. Investors also don't want to deal with a bunch of small investors. A buyout like this can turn into an awkward situation if you haven't explained to your early funders that it's a possibility. And if you don't agree to the buyout of the first round, understand that your investor may walk away from the deal.

It takes money to make money. Truer words were never spoken. The costs of finding your investor, including preparing and printing the business plan, travel, and time, all are paid upfront by you. If you're seeking a lot of money — several million — you probably need to have your financials prepared or reviewed by a CPA, and you need to prepare a prospectus, an offering document spelling out the risks and rewards of investing in your business opportunity. Again, these are costs you bear upfront.

After you receive the capital, the cost of maintaining it, ranging from paying interest on loans to keeping investors apprised of what's going on with your business, can usually be paid out of the proceeds. You'll also have back-end costs if you are raising capital by selling securities (shares of stock in your corporation). These costs include investment-banking fees, legal fees, marketing costs, brokerage fees, and any fees charged by state and federal authorities. The total cost of raising equity capital can reach 25 percent of the total amount of money you're seeking. You see it definitely takes money to make money.

Tracking the venture capital process

The process that venture capitalists go through to analyze your deal, decide to make the deal, put together a term sheet, and exercise their due diligence can be quite complex and vary from firm to firm. In general, the process follows a predictable pattern, however. But first, consider what venture capitalists are looking for.

A venture capitalist invests in your company for a specified period of time (typically five years or less) with the expectation that at the end of that time, he or she gets the investment back plus a substantial return, in the neighborhood of 50 percent or more. The amount of return is a function of the risk associated with your venture. In the early stages, the risk is high, so the venture capitalist wants a higher return. Later, when your business has proven itself and you're looking for second-round financing, the risk is less, so you have more clout in your negotiations.

The venture capitalist also probably wants a seat on your board of directors — a say in business strategy and policy.

Approving your plan

The first thing venture capitalists do is scrutinize your business plan, particularly to see whether you have a strong management team consisting of people experienced in your industry and committed to the launch of this venture. Then they look at your product and market to ensure the opportunity you've defined is substantial and worth their effort and the risk they're taking. If you have a unique product that is protected through patents, you have an important barrier to competitors that is attractive to the venture capitalists, who also look at the market to ensure a significant potential for growth — that's where they make their money, from the growth in value of your business.

If the venture capitalists like what they see, they'll probably call for a meeting at which you may be asked to present your plan. They want to confirm that your team is everything you say it is. The venture capitalists may or may not discuss initial terms for an agreement at the meeting. It is likely they'll wait until they've exercised due diligence.

Doing due diligence

If you've made it past the meeting stage, and the venture capitalists feel positive about your concept, it's time for them to exercise due diligence, meaning they thoroughly check out your team and your business concept (or business, as the case may be). Once they're satisfied that you check out, they'll draw up legal documents detailing the terms of the investment. But don't hold your breath waiting. Some venture capitalists wait until they know they have a good investment opportunity before putting together the partnership that actually funds your venture. Others just take a long time to release the money. In any case, you can certainly ask what the next steps are and how long they'll take.

TIP

One more surprise lies in store: It's unlikely that the money will be released to you in one lump sum. Study your term sheet carefully: It probably states that the money will be released in stages triggered by you achieving certain predefined goals.

Crafting the deal

Always approach a venture capitalist from a position of strength. If you sound and look desperate for money, you won't get a good deal. Venture capitalists see many business concepts, but most of them aren't winners. Your power at the negotiating table comes from proving that your concept is one of the winners.

REMEMBER

Every deal is comprised of four parts:

1. The amount of capital to be invested

2. The timing and use of the money

3. The return on investment to the investors

4. The level of risk

The amount of capital the venture capitalist provides reflects need. However, it also depends on the risks involved, how the money will be used, and how quickly the venture capitalist can earn a return on the investment (timing). The amount of equity in your company that the venture capitalist demands depends on the risk and the amount of the investment.

Selling Stock to the Public: An IPO

The aura and myths surrounding the IPO (selling stock in your company on a public stock exchange) have grown with the huge IPOs undertaken by up-start dot-com companies that don't have an ounce of profit to their names. The glamor of watching your stock appear on the exchange you've chosen and the attention you get from the media make you forget for a moment all the hard work that led to this point and all the hard work that you can expect to follow as your company strives every quarter to satisfy stockholders and investment analysts that you're doing the right things.

It's no wonder so many naïve entrepreneurs announce their intention to go public within three years (if not sooner) of starting their businesses. If they knew more about what it's really like to launch a public company, these starry-eyed adventurers would think twice. You need to be doing your homework — reading, talking to people who have done it — before making the decision to do an IPO. Once you decide to go ahead, you set in motion a series of events that have a life of their own. Yes, you can stop the IPO up to the night before your company is scheduled to be listed on the stock exchange, but doing so will cost you a lot of money and time, not to mention bad publicity.

An IPO is really just a more complex version of a private offering. You file your intent to sell a portion of your company to the public with the Securities and Exchange Commission (SEC) and list your stock on one of the exchanges. When you complete the IPO, the proceeds go to the company in what is termed a *primary offering.* If, later on, you sell your shares (after restrictions have ceased), those proceeds are termed a *secondary distribution.*

Considering the pros and cons of going public

The real reason that many entrepreneurs choose to take their companies public is that an IPO provides an enormous source of interest-free capital for growth and expansion. After you've done one offering, you can do additional offerings if you maintain a positive track record. Other general advantages that companies derive from becoming publicly held are

>> More clout with industry types and the financial community

>> Easier ways for you to form partnerships and negotiate favorable deals with suppliers, customers, and others

>> The capability to offer stock to your employees

>> Easier ways for you to harvest the wealth you have created by selling some of your shares or borrowing against them

WARNING

But becoming a public company also has several disadvantages that you should carefully consider. Some of them include

>> The cost exceeds $300,000, and that doesn't include the commission to the underwriter (the investment bank that sells the securities).

>> The process is extremely time-consuming, taking most of your week for more than six months.

>> Everything you and your company do becomes public information.

>> You are now responsible first and foremost to your shareholders, not to your customers or employees.

>> You may no longer have the controlling share of stock in your company.

>> Your stock may lose value because of factors in the economy even if you're running the company well.

>> You face intense pressure to perform in the short term so that revenues and earnings rise, driving up stock prices and dividends to stockholders.

>> The SEC reporting requirements are a huge and time-consuming burden.

Deciding to go for it

If you've weighed all the advantages and disadvantages and still want to go forward with an IPO, you need to have a good understanding of what happens during the months that precede the offering. In general, the process unfolds in a fairly predictable fashion.

Choosing the underwriter

You need to choose an underwriter that serves as your guide on this journey and, you hope, sells your securities to enough institutional investors to make the IPO a success. Like meeting a venture capitalist, you need to secure an introduction to a good investment banker through a mutual acquaintance and investigate the reputation and track record of any investment banker you're considering. Many disreputable firms out there are looking for a quick buck. You also want to find an investment banker who'll stay with you after the IPO and look out for the long-term success of the stock.

Once chosen, the investment banker drafts a letter of intent stating the terms and conditions of the agreement. The letter includes a price range for the stock, although this is just an estimate because the going-out price won't be decided until the night before the offering. At that point, if you're unhappy with the price, you can cancel the offering. You will, however, be responsible for some costs incurred.

Satisfying the SEC

You file a registration statement with the SEC. Known as a *red herring*, this prospectus presents all the potential risks of investing in the IPO and is given to anyone interested in investing. Following the filing of the registration statement, you place an advertisement, known as a *tombstone*, in the financial press announcing the offering. Your prospectus is valid for nine months after the tombstone is published.

You need to decide on which stock exchange your company will be listed. Here are the two best known in the U.S.:

>> National Association of Securities Dealers Automated Quotation (Nasdaq)

>> New York Stock Exchange (NYSE)

The NYSE is the most difficult to qualify for listing. The NYSE is an auction market where securities are traded on the floor of the exchange so that investors trade directly with one another. By contrast, the Nasdaq is a floorless exchange that trades on the National Market System through a system of broker-dealers from respected securities firms.

TIP

You may also want to look at regional exchanges like the Chicago Stock Exchange. They are generally less expensive alternatives.

Taking your show on the road

Many consider the *road show* to be the high point of the entire IPO process. It is exactly what it sounds like, a whirlwind tour of all the major institutional investors over about two weeks. The entrepreneur and the IPO team present the business and the offering to these potential investors, whom they hope to sign on. The goal is to have the offering oversubscribed so that it can be sold in a day.

One of the more important skills you need to have or develop if you intend to go the IPO route (or seek money from any source) is how to talk to money people. These people have seen so many presentations from so many people begging for their resources that they are jaded. You have to work hard to capture their attention, and that's not an easy thing to do.

TIP

Here are some suggestions based on the lessons taught by Jerry Weissman, whose company, Suasive (formerly Power Presentations), has been behind some of the most famous IPOs in history — Cisco, Yahoo!, and Compaq, to name a few:

>> **Tell a great story.** Investors want to hear why this is the best investment opportunity they've ever seen. In short, they want to know what's in it for them, their return on investment. Entrepreneurs, by contrast, are more focused on what's in it for the customer.

>> **The entrepreneur must tell the story.** Not only must the entrepreneur/CEO tell the story, but he or she needs to write it as well. No one has the passion for the business that the founder does, and that passion means a higher valuation for the business. So, tell your own story, and tell it with energy and passion.

>> **Don't exaggerate your story.** Keep in mind that investors have heard it all, so you need to tell them what makes your company stand out from the crowd. And don't hide potential problems or negatives your business may have. Recognize them and then tell investors what you intend to do about them.

Finding the Funding

>> **Get their attention.** You can grab attention in many ways, but one of the best is to show your audience that you have a solution to a problem they're experiencing. For example, Scott Cook of Intuit (Quicken, QuickBooks) started his story with a question: "How many of you balance your own checkbooks?" Every investor raised his or her hand. "How many of you like doing it?" Not one hand was raised. He explained that millions of people around the world dislike that task, but he had a product that would solve the problem. That approach definitely caught the investors' attention.

Dealing with failure

Once in a while, even when you've done all the right things, the IPO can fail, like the Texas company that developed a computer that would stand up to the toughest environments — places like machine shops and hot restaurant kitchens. When the founder decided to raise money through a first registered stock offering on the Internet, it was a long and costly undertaking (more than $65,000) to secure the necessary approvals from the SEC. But finally the company began selling shares through its website, its sights set on raising between $1.5 million and $9.9 million. The offering period was 90 days, and at the end of that time the company had raised only about $300,000. Attempts to do a traditional offering failed as well, and the company filed for Chapter 7 bankruptcy. The total bill for the IPO was about $250,000, for which the company received nothing.

REMEMBER

Just because you start an IPO doesn't guarantee that you'll finish it. Many entrepreneurs cancel their IPOs the night before they come out because they are unable to raise sufficient capital during the road show.

Finding Other Ways to Finance Growth

Equity is not the only way to finance the growth of your business. Debt vehicles — IOUs with interest — are another way to acquire the capital you need to grow. When you choose this route, you typically hand over title to a business or personal asset as collateral for a loan bearing a market rate of interest. You normally pay principal and interest on the note until it's paid off. Some arrangements, however, combine debt and equity. For example, a *debenture* is a debt vehicle that can be converted to common stock at some predetermined time in the future. In the meantime, the holder of the debenture receives interest on his or her loan to the company.

Here are some of the more common sources of debt financing for growth:

>> **Commercial banks:** Banks are better sources for growth capital than for start-up capital, because by the time you come to them, your company has, in all likelihood, developed a good track record. Banks make loans based on the Five C's: character of the entrepreneur, capacity to repay the loan, capital needed, collateral the entrepreneur can provide to secure the loan, and condition of the entrepreneur's overall financial health and situation. For entrepreneurs with new ventures, character and capacity become the overriding factors.

>> **Commercial finance companies:** Also known as *asset-based lenders,* these companies are typically more expensive to use than commercial banks by as much as 5 percent above the prime interest rate. But they are also more likely to lend to a start-up entrepreneur than a commercial bank is. And when you weigh the difference between starting the business and not starting because of money, a commercial lender may not be that expensive.

>> **Small Business Administration:** For more than 60 years the SBA (www.sba. gov) has provided many forms of financial assistance to small businesses. This assistance includes grants, counseling, and loan guarantees. SBA loan programs are designed to help small businesses obtain funding when they can't obtain suitable financing through traditional means. The SBA doesn't directly make loans to small businesses. Instead, it provides a guarantee to banks and other authorized lenders for loans provided to qualifying businesses.

This guarantee protects the lender by promising to repay a portion of the loan in the event the borrower defaults. Therefore, an SBA loan application is not submitted directly to the agency but rather through an authorized lender. Note that not all lenders offer SBA loans, and authorized lenders may not offer all the several types of SBA loans. Because the SBA is a government agency, its programs frequently change based upon current fiscal policy. The following are three of the more typical SBA loan programs currently being offered:

- **SBA 7(a) loans:** This is the SBA's traditional loan program. Currently, 7(a) loans have a maximum of $5 million and no minimum. The SBA guarantees 75–85 percent of the loan, depending on the loan amount.

- **SBA Express:** SBA Express aims to reduce all the paperwork associated with a traditional SBA loan. If you qualify at a bank, you can borrow up to $350,000 without going through the standard SBA application process. In fact, this program promises to give you a decision within 36 hours. Because the SBA guarantees these loans only to 50 percent of their face value, not all the SBA-qualified lenders have signed on to the program.

- **Microloan program:** This program provides up to $50,000 to help small business with funding for various needs, such as working capital, inventory, and equipment acquisition. The SBA provides funds to specially designated intermediary lenders — nonprofit, community-based organizations with experience in lending and providing other technical and management assistance. These intermediaries administer the microloan program for eligible borrowers. Each intermediary lender establishes its own credit requirements. Often these lenders require some sort of collateral as well as the personal guarantee of the business owner.

Guarding Your Interests

Trade secrets generally include sensitive company information that can't be covered by patents, trademarks, and copyrights. Business plans are often considered trade secrets. The only method of protecting trade secrets is through contracts and nondisclosure agreements (NDA) that specifically detail the trade secret to be protected. No other legal form of protection exists. If you have any concerns about sharing your business plan with anyone outside your circle of trust, including employees or investors, consider creating a contract or a NDA.

Contracts

A contract simply is an offer or a promise to do something or refrain from doing something in exchange for consideration, which is the promise to supply or give up something in return. So you are asking your employees to not reveal your company's trade secrets in exchange for having a job there (and not getting sued if they do reveal them).

In addition to using contracts with employees and others who have access to your trade secrets, make sure that no one has all the components of your trade secret. For example, suppose you develop a new barbecue sauce that you intend to brand and market to specialty shops. If you're producing in large volumes, you obviously can't do all the work yourself, so you hire others to help. To avoid letting them know how to reproduce your unique barbecue sauce, you can do three things:

>> Execute a contract with them binding them to not disclose what they know about your recipe.

>> Provide them with premixed herbs and spices so they don't know exactly what's in the recipe.

>> Give each person a different portion of the sauce to prepare.

Nondisclosure agreements

Many entrepreneurs and small business start-ups try protecting their ideas through a *nondisclosure agreement (NDA)*. An NDA is a document that announces the confidentiality of the material being shared with someone and specifies that the person or persons cannot disclose anything identified by the NDA to other parties or personally use the information. Providing an NDA to anyone you are speaking to in confidence about your business plan, or any other trade secret, is a good idea. Without it, you have no evidence that you provided your proprietary information in confidence; therefore, it can be considered a public disclosure — that is, no longer confidential.

You definitely want to work with an attorney when you construct your NDA, because it must fit your situation. Generic NDAs do not exist. If you want an NDA to be valid for evidence purposes, it must include the following:

>> *Consideration,* or what is being given in exchange for signing the document and refraining from revealing the confidentiality

>> A description of what is being covered (be sure this is not too vague or broad)

>> A procedure describing how the other party will use or not use the confidential information

Whom should you have sign an NDA? Anyone who will become privy to your trade secret:

>> **Immediate family:** Spouses, children, and parents do not usually require NDAs, but it wouldn't be a bad idea to have them sign one anyway.

>> **Extended family and friends who will not be doing business with you:** To meet the consideration requirement for the NDA, you typically offer $1 in compensation.

>> **Business associates or companies with which you might do business:** Consideration, in this case, is the opportunity to do business with you. For example, if you show your business plan to a potential investor or creditor, the consideration is the stake in the business or the return on investment.

>> **Buyers:** Buyers typically don't sign NDAs because doing so may preclude them from developing something similar, or they may already be working on a similar concept. For example, a toy manufacturer may not sign NDAs from inventors if it has a large R&D department that continually works on new ideas for toys. Chances are it's working on something that will be similar enough to potentially infringe on an inventor's product.

REMEMBER

The truth is, an NDA is only as good (and reliable) as the person who signs it. Fighting a violation of an NDA in the courts is difficult and expensive, so when you're ready to talk about your business plan with outsiders, sometimes the best thing you can do is be careful whom you talk to.

Chapter **3**

Setting Your Franchise's Wheels in Motion

Franchising is most successful when each and every location in the chain operates in a way that ensures customers a consistent level of quality and service, regardless of which location they're visiting.

But being consistent isn't an easy thing to do (in the business realm, that is). The location's design has to feel right to the customers, and the business needs to be placed where it's convenient for customers to shop. The quality of the products and services you deliver to the customers can't vary much at all from their last experience — they're coming for the experience of shopping with you, which requires your management and staff to be up to the task of delivering on your brand's promise to them. Giving customers that level of reliability is what franchisees do (or should, anyway) every day.

To reach that level of delivery, you have to know where you should place your business; find the vendors that have the products you need; and understand how to recruit, train, motivate, and manage your staff. Great franchisors teach you how to do all these things. In short, great franchisors share their formula for success.

Surveying Your Options for Locale

Depending on your franchise, you will be confronted with a host of different types of locations in which to establish your business. Good franchisors look closely at successful operations in their system and provide franchisees with profiles of what they consider ideal locations. Some franchisees rent office space in high-rise office buildings, others work from home, but most select from an ever-growing list of options, covered in this section.

Considering common site options

Here are some of the types of locations you typically will be looking at for your franchise.

Malls

Malls — as you surely know — are large, enclosed shopping facilities anchored by two or more major retail stores and servicing a large geographic area. A mall is typically easily accessible by automobile via major arteries or interstate highways and is surrounded by a very large parking lot.

WARNING

Selecting a well-developed mall requires a franchisee to balance the benefits and the drawbacks. The principal drawback of a mall is the cost, which includes not only the rent but also a host of additional expenses, such as common-area maintenance — your share of caring for the public space. Malls also charge merchants association fees, used for advertising for all the tenants in the mall. You also usually have to operate during the hours that the mall is open.

On the plus side, malls are natural draws and attract large numbers of potential customers from as far as 25 or more miles away, depending on traffic patterns and competing malls. You can expect that some malls will include a percentage of your sales as rent (that's on top of your *base rent*). In addition to your franchisor having a say on what your location looks like, the better malls may restrict your ability to reimage.

Neighborhood shopping centers

A supermarket typically anchors a neighborhood shopping center with a variety of convenience-oriented small retail and service stores. These centers usually provide reasonable rents and draw from a trade area of from one to three miles, depending on population access and concentration.

Most neighborhood shopping centers have few signage restrictions — though upscale centers or those in upscale towns can be as tough as regional malls when it comes to signage and décor — and are the type of location that retail and service franchise systems target for their franchisees.

Community centers

Community centers are also convenient for local populations. They usually have two or more anchors, a supermarket, a drugstore, and other general merchandise retailers. They serve local populations up to six or seven miles away, depending on ease of travel and accessibility. They have appeal similar to the neighborhood centers but are much larger — and hence, may have more signage limitations for their on-street pole signs.

These are the types of centers that most often have available *out-parcels* (spaces for smaller, free-standing buildings out on the parking lot). The quick-service restaurant business uses out-parcels, as do other businesses that need to be closer to the street to be seen by passing motorists.

Lifestyle centers

Usually found near affluent residential communities, these open-air centers feature upscale national specialty chain stores, dining and entertainment, and fountains and other ambient design elements that make browsing the internal, uncovered walkways enjoyable — whenever the weather permits.

In these setups, traditional anchor stores typically aren't dominant the way they are at malls. Multiplex cinemas, small department stores, large bookstores, and large-format specialty retailers are usually the biggest individual draws. These centers combine some lower-priced, impulse-purchase vendors trading off of the high traffic counts along with higher-priced, destination-type merchants. Often, these centers have parking at each of the retail stores and sometimes larger parking lots as well. They draw from up to 13 miles, depending on traffic patterns and convenience.

WARNING

Be careful in choosing a site in a lifestyle center. They are excellent venues for compatible concepts, but they can be expensive mistakes if your concept is not a good fit with the *lifestyles* of the majority of the center's visitors. Most of the time, your franchisor will know whether these centers are a good bet for you.

Power centers

Power centers are open air and usually located near a regional or super-regional center. They include at least three big-box stores (or *category killers*), such as Walmart, Target, Home Depot, or Costco. Power centers draw customers from a five-mile radius. A trend in many markets is to convert underproducing regional centers to power centers, because people like the convenience of the regional centers but prefer the option of parking in front of the store of their choice.

Other centers

Constantly evolving variations of developments exist where retailing, entertainment, employment, tourism, bargain hunting, and other activities come together. For example:

>> *Theme/festival* centers are heavy on entertainment and restaurant businesses for leisure and tourist activities.

>> *Outlet* centers have great bargains and sometimes draw busloads of people from very far away.

>> *Mixed-use* centers combine many activities in the same area: retail, restaurants, employment, transportation, sports, recreation, office, hotel, cultural, and other activities in various integrated combinations.

>> *Specialty* centers can focus on restaurants, car care, off-price, and other specific types of businesses on a planned development parcel.

As with the more typical centers just listed, you want to be part of or nearby these centers to take advantage of the customer flows they create.

Shopping areas

A concentration of stores serving a local community is considered a *shopping area*. Downtown, also known as a central business district (CBD), is a shopping area that benefits from the traffic from office workers, visitors to downtown, and people who live in the downtown area. Because of the traffic and their prime locations, these sites can be expensive in some cities and often suffer from lack of customer parking. Because most of the traffic in downtown areas is usually created by office workers, the hours during the weekdays are busiest, with most customers coming in before work, during lunch, and after work. This inconsistent traffic pattern makes staffing a bit problematic. Except for a few cities that have re-created their downtowns as entertainment destination areas or festival marketplaces for residents from the suburbs — as Baltimore did — these areas are often quiet in the evenings and on weekends and holidays.

Off-street sites

Many franchisors are able to expand their systems by opening locations in off-street venues or captive-audience venues. These types of sites usually aren't easily accessible to customers just driving or walking down the street. They represent significant opportunities for many franchisees today and a growing trend in franchising. These locations include gas stations, convenience stores, hospitals, airports, train and bus stations, colleges, large department stores, offices, factories, and movable kiosks at seasonal and recreation locations, sporting arenas, parks, and malls.

The strength of captive-audience (also called *mass-gathering*) locations is that the merchant benefits from customers drawn to the location by something other than the product they're offering. You might not go to a baseball game to eat, but you'll be hungry by the sixth inning. The biggest drawback to a mass-gathering site is that customer flow is tied to the ebb and flow of people in the host environment. When the ballplayers go out on the road or when the season ends, you're out of luck. Colleges are governed by the academic calendar, so get ready to twiddle your thumbs a bit during summer vacation, unless many students attend summer school. Still, the traffic can be so high during the busy periods that these locations are highly sought after.

REMEMBER

If an airport location opens up, more road warriors go through a main terminal, concourse, or food court than through a regional terminal. Not every mass gathering opportunity is the same — do your homework.

Also, many mass gatherings may not be available to you because those locations are controlled by concession companies or other large businesses that sign long-term contracts with those venues. Check with your franchisor to see whether alternative venues are available to you in the area you've selected. Also, see whether your franchise agreement excludes you from looking at mass-gathering locations altogether — many do.

At-home sites

Although home locations aren't sites in the traditional sense, more and more franchisees are choosing this option, where the franchisor allows them to work out of their homes. Many franchise systems, especially smaller service franchises that never have customers coming to their offices — for example, carpet cleaning, janitorial, maintenance, and repair services — not only allow their franchisees to work from their homes but actually encourage it.

Working from home reduces a franchisee's cost of doing business and is convenient. For many franchisees, it's perfect. They can get up early, do their paperwork, and plan their day — all before taking a shower. In the evening, after dinner, they can relax in their offices, watch some TV, and prepare for the next day. And because they don't have any other office, they may be able to deduct the costs associated with their home office on their tax returns. (Check with your accountant and tax preparer to determine what is deductible.)

Dual branding: Sharing your space

When two or more businesses share the same premises, it's called *dual branding:* Two or more franchises with different concepts set up shop next to one another or within the same location, offering customers a one-stop shopping experience. Think of a food court.

Yum! Brands, the parent company of KFC, Pizza Hut, Taco Bell, and WingStreet, often places two or three of its brands in one location. So do gasoline companies that often combine their gasoline stations with a convenience store offering sandwiches, doughnuts, and other food, along with a quick oil change or car wash businesses (often with multiple brands all at once).

A dual-branded location may be able to use labor and real estate more efficiently because, if done well, it expands a location's *daypart.* (In the restaurant industry, breakfast, lunch, and dinner are called dayparts.) For example, doughnut chains, as you might expect, are usually busiest during the breakfast daypart and slow down during the lunch and dinner dayparts. Some, like Dunkin' (formerly Dunkin' Donuts), have begun to expand their offerings to expand their traditional dayparts to include lunch. Other concepts are slow during the breakfast daypart but busier during the lunch or dinner daypart. By dual-branding a location, the operator hopes to capture traffic generated by the other product offering and use the location more fully.

REMEMBER

If you choose one of these dual-branded sites, you still pay an initial franchise fee and royalties and remain accountable to the same standards. Make sure your franchisor offers equipment, signage, and design specifications to fit these new locations. Compare the costs — and sales/profit potential — with those of single-branded locations. These sites are usually tucked inside another location and take up less square footage. The smaller space may mean less staff and possibly lower overhead. Some operate seasonally. But just because they're smaller doesn't mean they're cheaper. Some — such as limited-access highway travel centers — are on prime properties. The bidding can be fierce and the occupancy costs high.

Finding Your Franchise's Habitat

Finding a good retail or restaurant location in today's market is not always easy. Many of the best spots have already been taken, and competition for the available real estate is brisk. Given rapidly changing consumer traveling patterns, opening your franchise in the right location matters because if your operations and your location are great, you have the best of both worlds.

REMEMBER

Although a good location is important, a good or even great location won't make up for a bad operator. Given the choice between the old adage "location, location, location" and "operations, operations, operations," lean toward the latter.

Defining your location is a vital part of your business plan. Anyone financing your venture — even your moneybags uncle — will want to know where the cash is going, what the site will look like, why it will attract customers, how much customer traffic will pass the site, whether there's adequate parking, and who your neighbors and competitors will be.

You may luck into a site just by driving through town looking for FOR SALE or FOR LEASE signs. A better approach is to use a local commercial real estate broker familiar with the unique aspects of your market. You will find that many, or most, of the better sites never have FOR SALE or FOR LEASE signs on the property. The local brokers become aware of them or dig them out for you based on their business networks and experience.

TIP

Be sure your broker learns about your franchise system and site requirements or restrictions imposed by your franchisor. Another resource is the exhibitions where shopping center developers lay out their construction plans. Contact the International Council of Shopping Centers at `www.icsc.org`.

Finding out what constitutes a good site

First, you need to understand from your franchisor the criteria that are important for your type of business. You may think the best place to open your doors is where the crowds are right now, such as in a shopping mall or adjacent to a busy highway. You may be right — for now. But with all the acquisitions, mergers, and market pullouts happening with major retailers and grocers, that major draw your business is dependent on may go away and take your customers with it. At one point being close to a Sears store was a terrific choice because of its customer draw — that has changed considerably.

No one can offer a stock definition of a "good" site, because different businesses require different kinds of locations. Some generalities do hold up, however. If you're investing in a retail franchise, focus your search on a location that gets in your customers' faces. If it's in the path of people commuting to work, near an entertainment arena, or in an office complex, customers can see your business, recognize your brand, and more easily come in to buy your products and services.

For some businesses, though, getting the best corner in town, with high visibility and terrific customer access in a strong, anchored shopping center, for example, is not only unnecessary but also the path to rapid disaster. Carpet cleaners, janitorial services, building-repair services, direct-mail companies, lawn-care services, pest-control businesses, moving companies, tool-delivery services, and home-inspection services, among other service providers, don't usually need high-visibility retail space (and can't afford it, either). Their needs run more to good-looking trucks, delivery access, access to postal facilities, highway access, warehouse facilities, and good telephone service than to locations where their customers shop. After all, most of these service providers go to their customers — the customers don't come to them.

TIP

If you don't need to be at the corner of State and Main, you'll likely have more options, lower rent, and a more accommodating landlord.

WARNING

Also consider your potential neighbors and nearby competitors. If you're operating a child care center, you don't want to be next door to a liquor store. Being near a strong anchor store like a Target or a grocery store could help drive customers to your location, as long as the anchor store doesn't monopolize available parking spaces or offer the same products or services as your store. If direct competitors are in the same retail center or shopping plaza, consider choosing a different location — unless your potential site out-positions them by being more visible or more convenient for the customers you're competing for. But clustering with similar businesses may on occasion be advantageous, especially when the area is known for restaurants or the regulations for the sale of alcohol make those areas essential.

Some developers or landlords may not want or allow two business of the same type (for example, two pizza parlors) in the same complex, either for reasons of tenant mix or exclusivity rights granted in a lease. So, even if you don't mind moving in a few doors down from a competitor, the landlord may not be willing or able to rent to you. Understand these restrictions up front so you don't invest a lot of time and money on a site you can't get into.

Using the franchisor as your compass

Most franchisors can offer a big advantage: experience. The staff at a mature franchisor can help you identify the kinds of locations that usually work — and those that don't. For example, staff members know whether a franchise can be effectively home-based initially or even long term, whether an office is attractive or whether a retail franchise fares better tucked inside a suburban mall or flaunted center stage on a main thoroughfare. So, your first step in selecting a location is to discuss viable options with your franchisor. The company may allow a variety of locations, or it may stick to only one type.

A good franchisor points you in the right direction and can share with you the demographics that profile your potential customers:

>> Who are the system's target customers and where do they live?

>> How many customers do you need, say, of a particular age and income that can drive to your business in a certain amount of time?

>> How far are customers willing to travel to buy your goods or services?

>> How and when do customers typically interact with the chain — are you opening a coffee shop aimed at commuters, a fitness center catering to professionals on their lunch hour, a child care center that needs to be near residential areas, or a destination concept like a spa?

>> How much are your target customers willing to pay for what you sell?

REMEMBER

A good franchisor wants you to find a location that meets the needs of your target customers. Many franchisors use mapping software for locating areas best suited for your type of business. But you still need to double-check any information the franchisor supplies against your own research. Think of this as a check-and-balance. You check on the accuracy of the data, and your information provides a balance to what the franchisor offers. Frequently your knowledge of your market will be a better gauge than even the best mapping software — don't rely exclusively on one source of information.

Many franchisors bombard new franchisees with *site criteria* — a list that spells out specifications for a particular franchise — inside and out, so that the site meets the franchise system's standards. You may be required to have x number of square feet, x number of parking spaces, x number of seats, x number of grills, venting requirements, and so on. Retail and restaurant franchisors, especially, expect their franchisees to comply with their design standards — without variation. On the other hand, an office-based franchise may not care whether you have wood floors or carpeting, mahogany desks or oak. A consistent look at each of the locations may not be important to franchisors, as long as the locations meet their overall quality standards.

Will your franchisor ultimately help you find this crown jewel of a site? Typically, a franchisor will educate you about its site criteria, provide you with site criteria forms, and ask you to find the location and do the required research — before you present the site package to the franchisor for review. Then the franchisor will evaluate your information and possibly visit the location before approving or disapproving your choice.

Check your franchise agreement to see whether and how the franchisor must approve a franchisee-selected site and the time limit for the franchisor to render a decision. Standard contracts allow a franchisor to accept or reject your request to open at a particular location. This decision, like everything else in franchising, reflects the need for consistency.

In almost every franchise agreement, the franchisor is only approving or rejecting a site, not guaranteeing it. This is true even if the franchisor found the location for you — you didn't have to accept it, did you? The franchisor's approval indicates only that the site is acceptable to the franchisor but ultimately, the selection of the site is your responsibility.

TIP

The more hands-on support the franchisor provides in site selection, the better your chances of finding a successful site. Look at your franchise agreement to find out what your franchisor will do for you. Ask the other franchisees in the system how good the franchisor's site-selection assistance actually was.

Typically, the franchisor will approve a general area for your location and expect you to search within those boundaries for a location, unless the franchisor already has a site in mind. After you find a site, the franchisor's role is to accept or reject it. Other franchisors — especially start-up franchisors — may physically accompany you on your site hunting. The staff may jump in the car with you, plot demographics, and talk to landlords. Some franchisors may already have located the site, built the building, outfitted it with equipment and fixtures, and made it available for you to buy or lease.

Crunching data to evaluate a site on your own

Investigating a site for your franchise is like following the scientific method. Suppose you hypothesize that a given site may be a good location. You need facts to support your hypothesis before you can reach any conclusions. The factors that influence site success fall into four primary categories:

>> Demographics and employment

>> Activity generators

>> Physical and traffic

>> Competition

Most demographics studies today can present information based on census tracts, block groups, zip codes, a radius measured in miles from a center point, drive-time polygons, and many other configurations. For retail and restaurant franchises, the drive times are usually best (except for walk-up locations) because most people will drive to your business — either coming from someplace or going to someplace else. Given a specified amount of time (3 minutes, 20 minutes, and so on), some computer programs that franchisors use can draw an irregular polygon based on vehicle speeds on the various roads and highways and then provide demographic and employment information for the contained area. These polygons usually vary dramatically from the comparable circles of 1, 5, 10, or 20 miles. The size of an area you should measure is most important. If your customers are quick-lunch types who typically drive no more than a couple of minutes each way to get lunch, measuring the employment population 10 minutes out won't help you. The franchisor can usually give you assistance in determining the size of your *trading area* (the area where you draw the majority of your customers).

WARNING

As you look for a site, keep your eyes peeled for red flags. A location that keeps turning over or that has been on the market for a long time should raise eyebrows. You may want to consider a different location if pedestrians would have to cross a busy street or drivers would need to make a U-turn to get around a median to get to the site. If anything — seriously, *anything* — smells fishy, investigate before you sign a lease. Do *not* let your desire to find a site and open your store trap you into selecting a substandard location.

Protected Areas, Exclusive Areas, and Encroachment Policies

You must understand what, if any, protections your franchise agreement provides for your site and the surrounding area. You need to understand the concepts of *territorial exclusivity* and *encroachment* before — not after — you sign your franchise agreement.

Suppose you open a franchise on the corner of Fifth and Main. Some years later, another franchisee from the same system opens a franchise on Fourth and Main. The new franchise is so close that you can see your customers going in and out of the new location. That's called *encroachment.* Whether encroachment is allowed depends on your franchise agreement.

Carefully examine the language of your franchise agreement. Are you getting a protected territory, an exclusive territory, or do you have no territorial rights? If your franchise agreement grants you only a site address franchise (meaning your protected territory is no bigger than the four walls of your store), the franchisor could conceivably establish or allow other franchisee- or company-owned locations nearby that will compete with you. Obviously, encroachment can potentially have an adverse impact on your business.

Your franchise agreement may grant you an exclusive or protected area. Say your franchisor has granted you an *exclusive* territory stretching one mile around your location or for a specific trade area outlined on a map. The franchisor then is prohibited from allowing another franchisee- or company-owned location to open closer than a mile from your store.

Encroaching from another franchisee- or company-owned location opening in your *protected* territory may be allowed. Your franchisor may also sell products in other locations — such as a supermarket or a convenience store — in your protected territory.

With an exclusive territory, encroachment can occur through Internet sales (if customers can buy through e-commerce the same products you sell) or catalog sales (from catalogs mailed into your market). It can also happen if your franchisor's affiliate allows others to offer similar products and services in your neighborhood under a different business name. It depends on what the franchise agreement says about your territorial protection.

Some franchise agreements state that a franchisor or its affiliate may sell items through other channels of distribution (like catalog or online sales) or establish other units under different names and trademarks in direct competition with a franchisee. Because e-commerce sales don't require the establishment of a location, they may not legally be encroachment unless specified. Never assume you have rights not provided in the agreement.

One of the reasons you chose to be part of a branded system is that you don't want to be the only one of your brand in the market. Left all alone, you'll be vulnerable to competitors who will have no problem with opening next door to you, especially if you're part of a weak brand with little penetration and you're unable to advertise sufficiently. Good franchisors try to achieve a balance to create brand recognition in the marketplace and, therefore, create more demand for the products and services of the franchised brand so that everyone in the chain can benefit.

REMEMBER

You need to know — before you sign the franchise agreement — whether the franchisor will be able to open locations in your market area. Heed this caution: Contracts normally tell you what the franchisor is granting, such as the right to operate a site, but sometimes don't plainly tell you what it's not granting, such as no right to exclusivity outside of the site, no right to conduct business on the Internet, and no right to prohibit the franchisor or another franchisee from operating from a site close to your site. What you're getting is just as important as what you're not getting.

REMEMBER

Never rely on a franchise salesperson's statements about what the system generally does or doesn't do regarding its locations. Even if they make sense when saying that the franchisor would never open a location so close to you that it would adversely affect your business, get the language in writing in the franchise agreement (as with everything else that's important to you).

Although it may not be a contractual obligation, some franchisors have an encroachment policy, and you should see whether your franchise system does. With an *encroachment policy,* a franchisor allows a franchisee to protest a new store's development, and then based on research — which generally the franchisee pays for — the franchisor may reconsider whether or not to open that new location close to yours. Keep in mind that a policy is not the same as a contractual obligation, and the franchisor can change or even eliminate a policy, which it can't do for obligations contained in a written agreement.

If it seems that the encroachment will cause a prolonged and material adverse impact, a franchisor may decide not to allow the development of the new location. If it appears that the encroachment will cause a minor or temporary impact, the franchisor may allow the unit to be developed but may also assist the affected franchisee to make up for the lost sales. Other franchisors simply cite the terms of the affected franchisee's agreement and allow the unit to open — regardless of the extent of the impact.

REMEMBER

Find out the franchisor's policies and practices on protected territories and encroachment impact before signing the franchise agreement. Read your franchise agreement. Speak to other franchisees and talk to your attorney.

Signing the Lease

After you find the perfect location, the real work begins: convincing the landlord to give you a lease you can live with. Many times, landlords may be unfamiliar with your business. Worse, they may have a negative perception of your type of business. They may simply be naïve, have bad information, or possibly have had a bad experience with a past tenant who offered similar services or goods. Explain why your business is different, who your customers are, and the benefits the other tenants will receive from your business. If your concept is national in scope, give the landlord a sense of the prestige his center will receive by being part of the system.

TIP

When you're looking for sites, think of yourself as the seller, not the buyer. Your job is to *sell* the potential landlord on the merits of your business. Your franchisor should provide you with marketing materials to present to landlords. Give landlords a reason to pick you over other businesses.

By the time you're about to sign a lease, you've already decided on a location. You should be in the process of contacting the real estate or mall management company that manages the property to determine space availability and specific occupancy costs and lease terms, and to complete your site review package for your franchisor. Your franchisor may want to see a letter of intent with your landlord in the site review package.

Be financially realistic in signing a lease. A great location is no good if you can't afford it. Based on the experiences of other franchisee- and company-owned stores, a reputable franchisor is often in a good position to tell you what rent and lease conditions are reasonable.

Does the center have adequate space available for your business? Although you don't want to squeeze into a space that's too small, you also don't want to pay for space that you'll never need. Square-foot costs can vary with overall size — often, the larger the space, the lower the square-foot cost. But even with a lower per-foot cost on a larger space, the maintenance and development costs will be higher. Evaluate size based on your needs.

Confer with your franchisor regarding your proposed lease. Although most (but not all) franchisors won't negotiate your lease for you, many insist on reviewing and approving any lease before you sign it. Keep in mind that this review generally is *not* for your benefit and doesn't reflect the franchisor's judgment of whether the lease is fair or a good deal. Instead, a franchisor's review is aimed at confirming that the lease contains certain terms required by the franchisor. For example, many franchisors insist that landlords agree to assign the lease to the franchisor, at the franchisor's request, if the franchise agreement is terminated. Check your franchise agreement for any terms your franchisor requires to be included in your lease and always work with an experienced real estate lawyer in negotiating any lease.

TIP

The numerous intricacies of negotiating and signing commercial leases are well beyond the scope of this book. Check out *Negotiating Commercial Leases & Renewals For Dummies* by Dale Willerton and Jeff Grandfield (Wiley).

Meeting Your Franchise's Requirements

You'll generally be expected to develop your location to meet the site development requirements and standards of the franchisor, including layout, décor, signage, furniture, fixtures, and equipment. Although franchisors use several methods, most will provide you with a layout that they expect you to have an architect or builder recast to meet the requirements of your location.

Implementing a franchisor's designs

Every retail and restaurant franchisor has a floor plan (called a *footprint*) that may be excruciating in its exactness. Even if you think that a counter should be 2 inches longer on the left side, you have to follow the franchisor's plans — or get the franchisor's permission for a change. Even if you know for a fact that menu signs are more readable if they're placed 12 inches closer to the floor than the required 90 inches, too bad — you have to follow the plans. Review these specifications and standards with your architect and contractor.

Franchisors usually provide prototype plans for every location. Your architect must develop plans for your site that meet local ordinances and codes as well as the franchisor's standards. Don't assume that you can add improvements to the design, such as a bigger *back of house* (the kitchen and storage area).

REMEMBER

Check with your franchisor before making expensive changes that you may have to reverse.

All these specifications from the franchisor are intended to ensure consistency, which is great, but what if your particular community has some type of restriction that runs counter to your franchisor's building plans? Make sure that you notify your franchisor so that you can discuss the required changes. If the changes are important, the franchisor often personally contacts the builder or city planner to discuss the changes.

Generally the franchisor will provide you with a list of sources for the equipment, décor, and other items you'll need to purchase. Before you open your business, you will generally need the franchisor's approval that your development of your location meets its standards.

Getting approvals, permits, and licenses

Whether you're renovating an existing leased site or building a new site from scratch, you'll have to prepare preliminary plans and specifications for construction and site improvement for approval and permits from your local zoning board and building department. You'll also have to — big surprise! — submit them to your franchisor for approval. Your banker or lender will also want to see these plans.

If building a site is going to be your choice, make sure you touch base again with the local zoning board and building department before you even close on the property and certainly before you move that first shovel of dirt. You want to be in compliance with *everything* — down to local ordinances that set the hours you can hammer and saw to your heart's content. You also want to determine whether the town needs to approve any *variances* (which give you permission to do something on the land that's different from what the zoning rules allow) for the property and whether the site will support your needs for utilities, parking, and the like.

WARNING

Early discussion with the municipality is important. Even in cases where your use is permitted, the planning board may have some unusual requirements that could make the site unworkable for you. Sometimes green-space setbacks or water-retention basins, although nice for the ducks, can push your building out of sight of approaching traffic. If your business relies on impulse purchases, you would be in a tough spot.

Although your contractor or architect usually does the pre-construction legwork, seeing that it all gets done is your responsibility — not the franchisor's. Your contractor needs to obtain the following:

>> **Permits:** For construction, utilities, signs, *curb cuts* (those indentations in the sidewalk that let the cars in), and environmental matters

>> **Variances:** If you need the town to approve some specific violation of the zoning requirements for your site

>> **Certificates of occupancy:** To allow you to occupy the location

Beginning construction

After your franchisor approves your site plan, it will be your responsibility to build out the location to the franchisor's standards and to meet local building codes. Critical to the build-out process is selecting a reputable commercial contractor who has experience with meeting deadlines, securing necessary permits and approvals, and complying with the quality requirements imposed by your franchisor. Your franchisor (and other franchisees) can tell you how long the construction process typically takes.

Getting help with the opening

Many franchisors provide in-person assistance immediately before and during a location's grand opening. The amount and nature of such opening assistance varies greatly by system. Some franchisors send a single field consultant to observe and be available to answer questions during a franchisee's grand opening, whereas other franchisors send a team of field consultants who arrive up to a week before the grand opening and stay until they're comfortable that the franchisee is ready to run solo. Such pre–opening and opening assistance can include the following:

» Providing guidance on the type of marketing and advertising a franchisee should conduct for the location's market introduction and grand opening.

» Placing initial orders of opening inventory and supplies.

» Conducting additional on-site training of the franchisee and its management team. As discussed later in this chapter, many franchisors historically have provided some training to a franchisee's staff at the franchisee's location in connection with the opening; however, due to fears of being declared a joint employer of a franchisee's staff, franchisors are increasingly providing train-the-trainer programs to franchisees and then expecting franchisees to train their own staff.

» Ensuring initial compliance with brand standards.

Check your franchise agreement and Item 11 of the franchise disclosure documents (FDD) regarding the opening assistance you can expect to receive from your franchisor.

Getting the Goods: Merchandise and Supplies

Some franchisors will specify one or a just a few approved suppliers, whereas others may allow you to choose your own vendors as long as the suppliers satisfy the franchisor's required standards and specifications. Many franchisors use a combination of these approaches.

It's up to the franchisor to set brand standards and select and monitor the suppliers it chooses. Your responsibility is to follow the franchisor's contractual requirements by using only the franchisor's approved or specified suppliers when they are provided and by buying only products and ingredients that meet the franchise system's specifications.

Most franchisors look at supplier pricing as a basket of goods, and you should not expect each individual item in the basket to be at the lowest price possible. You likely might even be able to purchase some of the exact same products at lower prices by going down to the local warehouse store. When done well, the basket of goods and services is negotiated with the goal of keeping the entire basket's cost lower, but the supplier still will need to make a profit. If you were allowed to cherry-pick from the basket, the relationship between the franchise system and the supplier may be impacted — meaning the overall costs to all other franchisees could be impacted if you don't meet your obligations.

If a franchisor specifies suppliers, absent a waiver from the franchisor that allows you to purchase from someplace else, your only option is to purchase from those approved suppliers. Don't expect the franchisor to change its methods simply because you want it to. This section explores some of the more common arrangements for how franchisors enforce system standards by ensuring consistent ingredients and supplies for the franchise system.

Franchisors take supply chain violations quite seriously.

The franchisor as the sole supplier

For some goods or services, your franchisor may be your sole or exclusive source. When that occurs, the requirement usually extends only to items that are proprietary (secret recipes), contain certain key ingredients, or are branded with the franchisor's trademark. These products may be ordered directly from the company, or, in many franchise systems, the franchisor provides the products to the distributors or licenses another company to produce and oversee distribution to the system. Because these items are proprietary, don't expect any franchisor to provide you (or any supplier you recommend) with the specifications for the franchisor's proprietary ingredients or products.

Suppliers approved by the franchisor

Rather than serve as the exclusive or sole source for all required purchases, some franchisors simply give franchisees a list of approved suppliers from whom they can or must buy their items directly — and the franchisor (or one of its affiliates) may be included on that list. The franchisor and the suppliers will have agreed on what specific products can be supplied to the system as well as alternatives should any of the specified products be out of stock. The choice of alternative products is not for you as the franchisee to make. Trusting the supplier to meet system standards is an important part of why the franchisor selected the supplier in the first place. As long as the approved suppliers sell franchisees only the items approved by the franchisor — without unauthorized substitutions — a franchisor can have significant confidence that it is maintaining the control it believes is necessary over the quality of the products sold under its brand.

Compliance with quality standards is a core principle of their business, and franchisors will reject and replace any supplier that does not produce and make available products that satisfy those standards. As a check on quality and service standards, franchisees need to report to the franchisor any issues or problems they are having with an approved supplier.

TIP

Most franchisors allow franchisees to request the franchisor to approve new or alternative suppliers (or approve new products or approve new or modified product specifications). If you discover that a supplier in your market meets your franchisor's criteria and is less expensive than the franchisor's authorized suppliers, make sure to pass the information on to the franchisor. If you feel strongly that you should be able to purchase items from this supplier, make a formal request for approval of the supplier. If acceptable, the franchisor may add the supplier to the list of approved suppliers once it has vetted the supplier, often by ordering and inspecting products produced by the supplier or visiting the supplier's facilities.

WARNING

The costs for vetting requested new suppliers are often passed back to the requesting franchisee, so be discerning in your requests.

The franchisor will often reserve the right not to approve a proposed supplier for any reason, even if the supplier appears qualified to you. Keep in mind that there is more to being an acceptable supplier than the price of a single item. Smart franchisors evaluate many factors in considering whether to approve a proposed supplier. For example, does the supplier have the capacity to supply the entire franchise system with quality products on a timely basis, a proven track record, competitive prices and do they have financial stability? And if the current supplier is providing volume-based rebates or other incentives to the franchisor and the proposed supplier won't do that, the franchisor may choose not to approve the proposed alternative supplier. Also it's reasonable for any franchisor to limit how many suppliers it works with.

Rebates and upcharges

It's not unusual for franchisors to receive money based on franchisees' purchases of required goods and services. This happens either because the franchisor is selling products directly to franchisees at a markup (called an *upcharge*) or is receiving payments or benefits from the designated suppliers and distributors (a *rebate*). Franchisors frequently apply upcharges to proprietary products manufactured and supplied directly by the franchisor to cover the franchisor's product development, manufacturing, sourcing, distribution expenses, and to earn revenue.

Some franchisors may receive upfront or annual payments from suppliers and distributors in exchange for access to the system's franchisees, exclusivity to a particular product or service, or the franchisor's commitment to a long-term purchasing arrangement. Franchisors may also receive marketing fees or require equipment packages or special delivery arrangements from suppliers that benefit the system. This is common when the franchisor has agreed to feature a particular supplier's brand or products in the system's retail stores — think of Coca-Cola or Pepsi coolers or dispensers in fast food restaurants.

Many franchisors will also negotiate *volume rebates* from suppliers. These rebates are payments from vendors to the franchisor based on the number of franchisees buying from the vendor or the system's overall volume of purchases of the vendor's products.

Aggregate or total amounts of rebates and other benefits that a franchisor receives from vendors and the percentage of purchases from approved suppliers in relation to your overall investment should be disclosed in the FDD. Franchisors are not required to disclose specific rebate amounts for specific suppliers.

TIP

Review rebate information in the FDD carefully so you can get a sense of whether the franchisor is deriving significant revenue through the purchases you will make as a franchisee. Finding out in advance is important because some systems with a lower royalty rate may actually cost you more money than a system with a higher royalty rate, because the difference may be more than offset by the income the franchisor earns from your purchases. (The *royalty* is your payment to the franchisor that allows you to continue in the franchise system — it is usually based on your total sales.)

REMEMBER

The supply chain revenue received by the franchisor is generally factored in as part of the franchisor's own revenue model. Where supply chain revenue is not available, the franchisor would still require that revenue to manage the system and earn its own return on investment, which may result in higher royalties or *à la carte* fees being charged.

In addition to the information in the FDD, you should check with the franchisor about the way rebates and upcharges are handled in your system. The procedure is far from uniform among franchisors or among suppliers. Some franchisors will keep the rebates as revenue — often it offsets the costs of negotiating and monitoring the approved suppliers, but it may be used to offset franchisor expenses generally. Other franchisors will forward the rebates directly to the franchisees. Some franchisors will place some or all the rebates into a marketing fund for the benefit of the whole system. Still others will use a mix of all of the above.

It is generally acceptable for a franchisor to earn money when you purchase goods from a supplier. After all, setting up and maintaining these supplier relationships cost the franchisor, unless the system has an independent cooperative or buying group. And franchisees need to have a financially strong franchisor that can provide the services they need and want.

REMEMBER

In a perfect world, you want to find a franchise system in which the total costs of being a franchisee (royalty and other costs) are the lowest, and the services provided by the franchisor are the highest.

Many of the legal disputes over the past two decades have resulted from franchisees' perception that they are getting gouged — that is, the products they must purchase from the franchisor or its approved suppliers are excessively marked up, making the franchisee less competitive. *It is essential that prospective franchisees and the franchisor talk about supply chain policies and requirements including margins and rebates.* However, where the franchisor has properly disclosed how it conducts the supply chain before franchisees invest, franchisees have little to complain about after the fact. Understanding the supply chain relationship is important before you sign any franchise agreement.

Finding your own suppliers and requesting approval

Franchisors frequently allow and even encourage franchisees to find and choose their own vendors — as long as the franchisee complies with the product standards and specifications set by the franchisor. This practice is common in small franchise systems, but even big franchisors often allow franchisees to buy certain items locally, especially where those items are commodities, the brands for off-the-shelf items are reliable, or the franchisor is focused on local sourcing of certain items like fruits and vegetables from local farmers. If your franchisor doesn't provide you with a list of authorized suppliers, you may have to choose your own vendors. Often this can be time consuming and add some cost to your investment. Knowing which items you can choose suppliers for and the specifications that must be met is important.

TIP

Work with your field consultant and your franchisor's purchasing department to see whether they can help you identify suppliers in your market. Your local chamber of commerce may also have a list of suitable suppliers. If your franchisor offers a supplier-evaluation questionnaire, get it and use it. If not, make your own. And talk to other independent business owners in your market, including franchisees from other franchise systems. Make certain you do some basic online research on suppliers. The Internet can be a vital source of understanding how well suppliers work with their customers and what their reputation is.

When you review bids and quotations from vendors, make sure you understand the total charges. Some vendors quote a low price on a product but add on handling and delivery charges. Some reserve the right to modify or change prices unilaterally. Look for these hidden charges or reserved rights when you compare pricing.

Price is certainly one of the prime considerations, but basing your decision solely on price can be a mistake. A good price on items that are constantly out of stock or a good price from a vendor who is trying to dump outdated merchandise won't help you build your business. Consider product quality, order accuracy, and timely delivery in selecting a vendor. Having a vendor that will help you in a crisis may be more important than saving two cents a case for an item.

Receiving Merchandise

If you own any business, you have to figure out how to manage your *receipt of merchandise.* You must properly check, log in, and store all the goods, supplies, ingredients, and other merchandise entering the store. Even if you negotiate lower prices for your merchandise, you won't save any money if you don't notice unacceptable quality or shortages in shipments. To avoid these losses, you or the store manager must establish a regular receiving routine for your store. Having a routine helps to monitor vendors and reduces the chance of shortage. If your franchisor provides you with a list of recommendations and procedures for maintaining your inventory, follow it. If not, the following sections offer useful guidelines.

Considering key drop delivery

Having suppliers make their delivery through your front door during your busiest hours is going to be disruptive. Make certain you select suppliers that work with you on their hours of delivery, frequency of delivery, and how they deliver to your business.

TIP

Many reputable companies offer what's called *key drop* delivery. The vendor has a key and makes a delivery during off hours, such as at night or early in the morning. Often the business will have a refrigeration unit accessible from the outside back of the location where deliveries are made. When the delivery is made, and in situations where refrigerated or frozen products are delivered, they are placed in the middle of the cooler or freezer with the dry goods placed in middle of the stockroom floor.

In the morning, the merchandise is checked in, and if there is a disagreement a call is made and, where appropriate, a credit is issued. This type of delivery is frequently offered at a lower cost for delivery because it allows the driver to travel when there is limited traffic, allowing the driver to make his deliveries faster. In some cities there may be restrictions on the size of truck that can be making deliveries in the retail and business districts during the normal business hours.

Receiving deliveries at any kind of franchise

Suppose you have just purchased a convenience-store franchise. The new site has been built, and you're standing inside your brand-new building. The only problem is that the shelves are empty. Soon you will need to begin scheduling and receiving deliveries. Follow these general tips for receiving merchandise at any type of franchise:

>> **Make sure suppliers schedule their deliveries in advance.** Accept deliveries only during specified hours. When the location is open and operating, you want the merchandise to come during off-peak hours so that you can concentrate on accepting the delivery.

>> **Don't let vendors park in front.** Require vendors to park in an out-of-the-way spot. The front of your business is for customers.

>> **Have the delivery driver bring all products into the building before you check the items.** Some systems want their own employees to bring merchandise into the store.

>> **Confirm that the merchandise you receive is for your business.**

>> **Check all vendors in and out.** Be sure you physically see every item — don't take the driver's word. Check all cartons and boxes when the vendor is leaving to make sure they are empty and no merchandise is being carried out of the store. Unless absolutely necessary, vendor check-in should be done away from that vendor's display and away from merchandise on hand. Don't allow a vendor to both stock shelves and remove boxes unless you check both before the vendor leaves.

WARNING

>> **Watch helpers.** Some vendors have "helpers" whose main job is to distract you during the check-in process.

>> **Immediately put away all perishable products.**

>> **Check use and expiration dates.** Sometime vendors have relationships with other customers where merchandise that isn't past the expiration date is removed before that date. If you receive that merchandise, the time available to you will be shorter than you need or want.

Checking the goods after they are in your location

A truck pulls up at the back door of your franchise, and a flurry of activity follows. Suddenly, you're surrounded by boxes. The driver is completing the paperwork for your signature. This situation does not have to be scary if you know what to do.

Check the quality and condition of the merchandise before accepting it. Here are some additional tips:

» **Examine every box for signs of damage.** Look for things like tears, broken or crushed cardboard, signs of tampering, rattles, damp or wet cardboard, bad odors, dented cans, and substitutions of standard items.

» **Before signing for the boxes, open any cartons that have been opened and resealed or that you suspect have internal damage.** Note any damages on the receiving record.

» **Always check the date code on the product when it is delivered.** Make sure the product is within the code and that you can reasonably expect to sell it before the code expires.

Verifying invoices

Attending to paperwork may be the least entertaining part of business ownership, but in the case of delivery receipts, it can prove rewarding. Avoid financial losses by ensuring you get what you pay for. Check out these tips:

» **Before accepting delivery, check each item on the delivery receipt against the product that has been delivered and compare against the product ordered.** Check quantities received against quantities ordered. Count the number of cartons delivered and compare this number to the number on the driver's record or freight bill. Never sign for more cartons than you receive. Note any discrepancies on the freight bill or receiving record, or correct the errors before the vendor leaves the store.

» **Never give the delivery receipt back to the vendor.** Obtain the delivery receipt when the vendor walks in and under no circumstances return it to the vendor. Manipulating the delivery receipt is one of the most common ways that some vendors steal from franchise locations.

» **If the vendor made a substitution, call your franchisor's field consultant to verify that the substitution is valid and acceptable.** Inform the driver and note on the invoice that substitutions not approved by your franchisor are subject to return for full credit.

» **If you don't receive an item appearing on the delivery receipt, have the driver clearly mark the item "Short" along with the quantity not received.** The driver should sign the delivery receipt before you sign it.

Maintaining Inventory

Your franchisor should teach you about maintaining your inventory. Procedures vary widely, depending on the type of franchise you own. Your franchise may not even have any inventory — in that case, skip this section.

Back of the house

The *back of the house* includes the *stockroom*. It is literally in the back area of your business, and it is where you keep all the items not currently in use. Back of the house is also where you store perishables and frozen items, which means it also can be the location of a refrigerator or freezer. You will be expected to know what you have in the back, too.

Your franchisor should provide detailed back-of-the-house storage procedures that may include a *plan-o-gram* so you can readily know what you have in stock. Follow them; a plan-o-gram enables a franchisor's field consultant to quickly see how the franchisee is managing inventory because each franchisee will use the same methods for storage, and a bad stocking plan can allow for goods to be buried behind others, which can increase waste. If your franchisor doesn't provide information on back-of-the-house arrangements and procedures, the following sections provide some procedures to consider.

Dry storage

Dry storage may be wet — sorry. The term is used for items that don't require refrigeration. If you're a health-food franchisee, for example, your vitamins and sports drinks are dry-storage items. The following are some dry-storage practices:

>> Store products at least six inches off the floor on clean, nonporous surfaces to permit the cleaning of floor areas and to protect from contamination and rodents.

>> Don't store products under exposed sewer or water lines, or next to sweating walls.

>> Store all poisonous materials — including pesticides, soaps, and detergents — away from food supplies, in designated storage areas.

>> Store all open packages in closed and labeled containers.

>> Keep shelving and floors clean and dry at all times.

>> Schedule cleaning of storage areas at regular intervals.

>> Date all merchandise upon receipt and rotate inventory on a first-in-first-out basis. Place older products in front of newly received merchandise.

>> Locate the most frequently needed items on lower shelves and near the entrance.

>> Store heavy packages on low shelves.

>> Don't store any products above shoulder height.

Refrigerated storage

If you have items needing refrigeration, place them into your cold storage as soon as you can. Here are some tips for storing your refrigerated items:

>> Enclose any food or other product removed from its original container in a properly identified, clean, sanitized, and covered container.

>> Don't store foods in contact with water or undrained ice.

>> Check refrigerator and freezer thermometers regularly.

>> Store all foods so that there is free circulation of cool air on all surfaces.

>> Never store food directly on the floor.

>> Make certain the temperature setting is appropriate for the product(s) you are refrigerating.

>> Clean your equipment and refrigerated storage at regular intervals.

>> Date all merchandise upon receipt and rotate inventory on a first-in-first-out basis, placing the oldest products in front of the newly received merchandise. This step is particularly important with refrigerated products because their shelf life is usually short.

>> Establish preventive-maintenance programs for equipment.

REMEMBER

If you're using frozen products in your business, follow the appropriate steps in defrosting them. This is essential to ensure that the products you sell to your customers are safe to consume and also will have an impact on the quality of the products you serve to your customers.

Front of the house

The *front of the house* is everything that's not the back of the house. This is the area that customers see when they enter your store. Obviously, how the front of the house looks is more important for locations that are frequented by customers and less important for locations that customers never see. If you're a retail location, you'll handle your merchandise differently than you would if you were a restaurant. Still, at all times, the front of the house is your showcase — it is what customers see every time they visit your store.

Retailers need to place merchandise on shelves so that it's attractive to customers and induces them to buy. Restaurants and other businesses that sell food also need to keep their locations attractive. If you have reach-in refrigeration accessible to your customers, or if you have items on display, how you display them is just as important to you as it is to a retailer. Your franchisor should provide you with a plan-o-gram for that purpose.

To keep the front of your store in tip-top shape, make it a priority to do the following:

>> Follow your franchisor's plan-o-gram, which gives instructions on where to display products. In some systems a plan-o-gram tells the merchant how many *facings* (number of rows) they should have of each product and the amount of products on each shelf, hanger, or merchandiser. The franchisor will often specify branded merchandise at eye level with generic merchandise down by the consumer's knees.

>> Keep your shelves and *merchandisers* (displays for your merchandise) stocked, clean, and dust free.

>> Use proper product rotation by placing the oldest products in front of the newly received merchandise (first-in, first-out).

>> Price identical items the same. One benefit of point of sale (POS) technology is that you don't have to reprice each item when prices change — just change the price in the POS and on the shelf's price tag.

>> Allow adequate space between displays, as required by your local code.

>> Use only signage that is acceptable in your system. If your franchisor requires you to use professionally prepared signage, don't use hand-written signs. Equally important, make sure you keep your signage current. (Remove the Christmas posters after Santa has returned to the North Pole — before New Year's Day.)

>> Clear the floor of empty boxes, unless they're part of the design concept.

REMEMBER

The Americans with Disabilities Act requires that you keep your store arranged in a manner that makes it usable for individuals with disabilities. As a general rule, provide enough space for easy passage of a wheelchair throughout the store, make sure that the lines to your registers are accessible, and don't display merchandise in a way that makes it difficult for people with disabilities to shop. If you have no choice about how you merchandise the store, make sure that your staff is actively available to any customers who may need assistance. As the business owner, complying with all federal and local laws is your responsibility.

Getting Good Training for Yourself and Your Management

Great franchisors insist that franchisees learn the business and keep learning as the system changes and market conditions evolve. But don't expect that all you will need will come from your franchisor. Franchisors are going to deliver to you the basics, but today franchisees seek and obtain the information they need to operate their businesses from nearly unlimited sources, including the Internet, local classes, and especially from their own professional advisors.

Undergoing good initial training

A new franchisee should expect to cover a lot of ground during the initial training. Your initial training will be focused at teaching you and your managers how to produce and deliver the system's product or service consistently to brand standards, but franchisors will include other important subjects as well, including the following:

>> Site selection, design, and development (covered earlier in this chapter)

>> Supply chain, vendor relations, purchasing, receiving, stocking, and inventory management (covered earlier in this chapter)

>> Food safety and storage (if the franchise is a restaurant or a store selling food products)

>> Labor management, including recruitment, supervision, and motivation

>> Leadership and business management

>> Brand standards and operating procedures

>> An understanding of the customer experience

>> Technical operations on products and services

>> Problem-solving

>> *Brand positioning* (how the franchisor wants the public to think and feel when hearing the brand name)

- >> Merchandising

- >> Pricing strategies and methods

- >> Marketing and advertising

- >> Cleaning and maintenance

- >> Safety and security

- >> Financial management and business plan development

- >> IT, including point of sale (POS), accounting, payroll, inventory, and communications hardware and software systems

- >> "Train the trainer," to enable the franchisee to train his or her own management and staff on an ongoing basis

Good training instills in the franchisee the franchisor's brand philosophy and history, teaches franchisees things they need to know (from opening the business in the morning to closing at night), and gives them the sources for additional or emergency support.

Today, because of franchisors' concerns over claims of *joint employment*, mainly fueled by the National Labor Relations Board (NLRB) and the Department of Labor (DOL) actions in support of the Service Employees International Union (SEIU) and other unions' organizing efforts, most franchisors are moving away from directly training their franchisees' staff. Instead, franchisors are increasingly including train-the-trainer programs as part of initial training to give their franchisees the capability to train their own management and staff.

TIP

How much training a franchisee can expect to receive from its franchisor will depend on the industry, the complexity of the business, and especially on the franchisor. Your franchise agreement will provide you with information on what you should expect to receive. For details on the franchisor's initial training curriculum, look at Item 11 in the franchisor's FDD. The methods franchisors use in training their franchisees vary widely.

Although most of a franchisee's initial training will take place at a franchisor's headquarters or possibly at another training facility, more and more franchisors are including online training for franchisees. There are many benefits of online training for franchisors and franchisees. Through online training, franchisors can enhance the amount and detail of the training provided without requiring the franchisees and their management team to spend an extended period of time away from home. In addition to reducing a franchisee's travel and other costs, online training ensures that each franchisee receives consistent training and enables franchisees and their staff to go through the training at a pace best suited for themselves.

Emerging franchisors may be limited in how they deliver training to their franchisees — frequently a copy of the operations manual and a new franchisee training class are the only training assistance a new franchisee will receive. Even so, given that frequently the founders of the franchise system are still very much involved and there are few franchisees in the system that require support, franchisees can still expect to receive a significant dose of training from new franchisors.

You need to understand how much training you're going to receive from your franchisor. In some systems — even some of the largest franchise systems — a franchisee can expect to receive only a few days of training, which may be limited to working in an operating location. The amount of classroom time and the training you might expect to receive in managing your business can be very limited in those systems.

In other franchise systems, franchisees may spend months in training. That training will include both classroom and on-the-job training and will extend into additional training at the franchisees' locations before and during the opening of their business.

TIP

Don't expect every franchisor to provide the same depth and length of training. In conducting your due diligence on a franchisor, it's up to you to make certain that the training the franchisor provides is sufficient for you to operate your business. Talk to existing and experienced franchisees in the system before you sign the franchise agreement to determine whether the franchisor's training program and training staff are able to deliver what you will need. Also ask them what other training they recommend you take that may be available from sources other than the franchisor.

Receiving effective ongoing training

In established franchise systems, in addition to support that comes from the franchisor's headquarters, field support is often provided from a franchisor's regional offices. Smaller and emerging franchise systems may only have their headquarters staff available to provide franchisees with local training support and ongoing management assistance.

With the rapid changes in products, services, competition, technology, and regulations, operating a franchise today requires constant evolution and improvement. Most franchisees can't do that alone. You should not expect the franchise you invest in today to be the same exact business you will be operating next year, let alone in five years.

To help you as your business evolves, franchisees should expect their franchisor to provide more than initial training. Expect your franchisor to require you, your management team, and your training personnel to attend continuing training programs. Even when the training is only recommended and is not mandatory, smart franchisees will elect to consume every training program a franchisor has to offer. That is only being a smart businessperson — assuming your franchisor has a history of great training programs.

In some franchise systems, the franchisor's field staff is the main delivery vehicle for new training. In addition to showing up at your business armed with operational, marketing, and organizational support, they also train the franchisee and their management team on the rollout of innovations, such as the preparation of new products or the operation of new equipment.

It's the hallmark of a great franchisor to continually offer new products, updated research, state-of-the-art technology, better methods of customer service, and other improvements to continually enhance the brand in the marketplace. These changes keep a company more than one step ahead of the competition. In modern franchise systems, much of this continuing training on improvements to the brand will be provided not only by the franchisor's field staff, but also through the franchisor's intranet system online.

Chapter **4**

Starting a Home-Based Business

There are nearly 30 million businesses in the United States today. Of these businesses, 99.7 percent are *small businesses* (which the government defines as businesses with fewer than 500 employees). Of these, a little more than half — 52 percent — are home-based businesses. Now that's a lot of home-based businesses!

Owning your own home-based business may be the most rewarding experience of your entire life — and not just in a financial sense (although many home-based businesspeople find the financial rewards to be significant). Having your own home-based business is also rewarding in the sense of doing the work you love and having control over your own life.

Of course, every great journey begins with the first step. This chapter looks at the basics of home-based business — including getting started, managing your money, avoiding problems, and moving ahead. It also considers some of the good news — and the bad — about starting your own home-based business and explains how to know when it's time to make the move. It talks about starting your business from scratch and ends up with some advice on making the transition to working at your home-based business.

Looking at the Basics of Home-Based Business

Not surprisingly, a *home-based business* is a business based in a home. Whether you do all the work in your home or you do some of it on customers' or third-party premises, whether you run a franchise, a direct-sales operation, or a business opportunity, if the center of your operations is based in your home, it's a home-based business.

Determining the kind of business you want to have

After you decide you're going to start your own home-based business, you have to answer two questions:

>> What kind of home-based business do you want to start?

>> What's the best way to market your products or services?

You basically have two types of home-based businesses to choose from: businesses you start from scratch and businesses you buy. The latter category is further split into three types: franchises, direct-selling opportunities, and business opportunities. Whether you prefer to march to your own drum and start your business from the ground up or get a business-in-a-box depends on your personal preferences.

The advantage of a business you start from scratch is that you can mold it to fit your preferences and the existing and emerging markets, which provides you with a boundless variety of possibilities. Businesses started from scratch account for the majority of viable, full-time businesses — in other words, they tend to be more successful over the long run than businesses you can buy.

Each type of home business that you can buy, on the other hand, has its own spin. The following sections illustrate how the three types are different from one another.

Franchise

A *franchise* is an agreement in which one business grants another business the right to distribute its products or services. Some common home-based franchises include the following:

>> Aussie Pet Mobile (mobile pet grooming)

>> Jani-King (commercial cleaning service)

>> Jazzercise (dance/exercise classes)

>> ServiceMaster Clean (cleaning service)

>> Snap-on Tools (professional tools and equipment)

Check out Chapter 5 of Book 1 and Chapter 3 of Book 2, which cover franchising in detail.

Direct selling

Direct selling involves selling consumer products or services in a person-to-person manner, away from a fixed retail location. The two main types of direct-selling opportunities are

>> **Single-level marketing:** Making money by buying products from a parent company and then selling those products directly to customers

>> **Multi-level marketing:** Making money through single-level marketing and by sponsoring new direct sellers

Some common home-based direct-selling opportunities include the following:

>> Shaklee (household cleaning products)

>> Pampered Chef (kitchen tools)

>> Green Irene (green products and consulting)

>> Mary Kay (cosmetics)

>> Fuller Brush Company (household and personal-care products)

Business opportunity

A *business opportunity* is an idea, product, system, or service that someone develops and offers to sell to others to help them start their own, similar businesses. With a business opportunity, your customers and clients pay you directly when you deliver a product or service to them. (Another way to think of a business opportunity is that it's any business concept you can buy from someone else that isn't direct selling or franchising.) Here are several examples of business opportunities that you can easily run out of your home:

>> Astro Events of America (inflatable party rentals)

>> Debt Zero LLC (debt settlement)

>> ClosetMaid (storage and organizational products)

TIP

Interested in how to find more companies and how to get in touch with them? Entrepreneur Media (`www.entrepreneur.com`) and `www.gosmallbiz.com` have extensive information on business opportunities you can buy. You can also do a search on Google or your favorite search engine, using the keywords *business opportunity.*

After you decide on a business, you have to find the money to get it started (see Book 2, Chapter 2 for more on finding funding). Then you have to market your products or services and persuade people to buy them (the chapters in Book 5 cover the marketing gamut). You can choose conventional methods of promotion, such as advertising and public relations, or you can leverage new selling opportunities, such as the Internet, to your advantage. Or you can (and probably should) do both. It's your choice — you're the boss!

Managing your money

REMEMBER

Money makes the world go 'round, and because you're talking about your financial well-being here, it's very important that you have a handle on your business finances. To get the handle you need, do the following:

>> **Find the money you need to start your business.** The good news is that many home-based businesses require little or no money to start up. If you decide to buy a franchise or business opportunity from someone else, however, you definitely need some amount of start-up funding. To find this funding, consider all your options, including friends and family, savings, credit cards, bank loans, and more. (See Chapter 2 in Book 2.)

>> **Keep track of your money.** In most cases, keeping track of your money means using a simple accounting or bookkeeping software package (such as Quicken) to organize and monitor your business finances. Book 3 has the scoop on handling finances.

» **Set the right price for your products and services.** If you set your prices too high, you'll scare customers away; if you set them too low, you'll be swamped with customers, but you won't make enough money to stay afloat. Be sure to charge enough to cover your costs while generating a healthy profit.

» **Obtain health insurance, and plan for your retirement.** When you have your own business, you're the one who needs to arrange for health insurance and set up IRAs, 401(k)s, or other retirement plans for the day when you're ready to hang up your business and stroll off into the sunset.

» **Pay taxes.** As someone famous once said, "The only things you can count on in life are death and taxes." Well, taxes are a definite, so make sure you pay all the taxes you owe for your home-based business.

Avoiding problems

Eventually, every business — home-based or not — runs into problems. Whether the problems are being late on a delivery or hitting a snag with the Internal Revenue Service, as the owner of your own business, you need to avoid problems whenever possible and deal with them quickly and decisively when you can't avoid them. Some of the problems you may deal with include the following:

» **Legal issues:** After a good accountant, the next best friend of any business owner is a good attorney. Keep one handy to help you deal with legal issues when they inevitably arise.

» **Issues with support services:** Finding skilled and reliable outside support services — lawyers, accountants, bankers, business consultants, and insurance brokers — isn't necessarily an easy task, especially if your business is in a small town where you're pretty much stuck with what's down the road. See the section "Consult outside professionals," later in this chapter, for more information on support services.

» **Scams and rip-offs:** More and more home-based business scams seem to appear every day, so don't rush into any business opportunity. Take your time and fully explore every opportunity before you sign on the dotted line. And remember, if it looks too good to be true, it probably is.

Moving ahead

One of the best things about owning your own business is watching it develop, mature, and grow. After all, a growing business is the gift that keeps on giving — all year round, year after year. To keep your business moving ahead, consider doing the following:

>> **Make the web work for you.** Doing business and generating sales and interest in your business via the Internet is practically a given for any home-based business today. You can make the web work for you in any number of ways, from starting a blog or website (see Chapter 5 in Book 2) to networking with others through online forums or social networking sites, such as Twitter, Facebook, and LinkedIn (see Chapter 6 in Book 5).

>> **Maintain a serious business attitude.** Just because your business is located at home instead of in a big office building downtown doesn't mean you shouldn't treat it like the business it is. Although you can have fun and work all kinds of creative schedules, don't forget that the business part of your business is important, too; you have to treat your business like a business if you hope to be successful.

>> **Look for ways to grow.** For many businesses, growth can turn an operation that is doing well financially into an operation that is doing *great!* Growth allows you to take advantage of economies of scale that may be available only to larger businesses, to serve more customers, and to increase profits. For these reasons and more, growing your business should always be on your agenda.

Leaving your full-time job for your part-time business

An important, basic consideration that many fledgling, part-time home-based business owners face is whether or not to leave a full-time job in favor of a home-based business. Before you give up your full-time job, ask yourself these questions:

>> Has there been a steadily growing flow of new customers in your home-based business?

>> Has your business, even though it's only been part-time, produced a steady flow of income through seasonal or other cycles typical of the business?

>> Are you turning away business because of limits on your time? If not, do you think business would increase if you had the time to market or take on more customers?

Being able to answer at least two of these questions in the affirmative is a good sign that it would be safe to leave your full-time job. Of course, you should also be aware of any developments that could worsen the outlook for your business to grow, such as pending legislation, new technology, the movement of the kind of work you do outside the U.S. (*outsourcing* or *cloud computing*), or the decline of an industry your business depends on.

If your day job has been providing you the contacts you've needed to build your part-time business, you need to find ways to replace them before you leave your job.

TIP

Breaking the umbilical cord of a paycheck is an uncomfortable step for most people. So the closer the current income from your business is to the amount of money you need to pay your basic business and living expenses, the more confident you can be.

Examining the Good News and the Bad

Anyone can start a home-based business. You can be 10 years old or 100, male or female, rich or poor or somewhere in between, experienced in business — or not. According to a study by the Ewing Marion Kauffman Foundation, the median age of company founders is 40 years old, the majority (69.9 percent) were married when they started their first business, and more than half (51.9 percent) were the first in their families to start a business.

So how do you know whether starting a home-based business is right for you? Like most things in life, starting your own home-based business has both advantages and disadvantages, but the good news is that the advantages probably outweigh the disadvantages for most prospective home-business owners. So in the spirit of putting your best foot forward, start with the good news.

Good reasons to start a home-based business

When you start a home-based business, you may be leaving behind the relative comfort and security of a regular career or 9-to-5 job and venturing out on your own. Or you may be entering the world of work again after devoting many years of your life to raising a family. How far out you venture on your own depends on the kind of home-based business you get involved in. For example, many franchises provide extensive support and training, and *franchisees* (the people buying the franchise opportunities — you, for example) are able to seek advice from experienced franchisees or from the *franchisor* (the party selling a franchise opportunity) when they need it. This support can be invaluable if you're new to the world of home-based business.

At the other end of the spectrum, some business opportunities offer little or no support whatsoever. If you're a dealer in synthetic motor oil, for example, you may have trouble getting the huge, multinational conglomerate that manufactures the oil to return your calls, much less send you some product brochures. And you won't find any training or extensive, hands-on support if you run into the inevitable snags, either.

This wide variety of home-based opportunities brings us to the good news about starting and running your own home-based business:

>> **You're the boss.** For many owners of home-based businesses, just being their own boss is reason enough to justify making the move out of the 9-to-5 work world.

>> **You get all the benefits of your hard work.** When you make a profit, it's all yours. No one is going to try to take it away from you (except, perhaps, the tax man — see Book 3, Chapter 6).

>> **You have the flexibility to work when and where you want.** Are you a night owl? Perhaps your most productive times don't coincide with the standard 9-to-5 work schedule that most regular businesses require their employees to adhere to. And you may find that — because interruptions from co-workers are no longer an issue and the days of endless meetings are left far behind — you're much more productive working in your own workshop than in a regular office. With your own home-based business, you get to decide when and where you work.

>> **You get to choose your clients and customers.** The customers may always be right, but that doesn't mean you have to put up with the ones who mistreat you or give you more headaches than they're worth. When you own your own business, you can fire the clients you don't want to work with. Sounds like fun, doesn't it?

>> **You can put as much or as little time into your business as you want to.** Do you want to work for only a few hours a day or week? No problem. Ready for a full-time schedule or even more? Great! The more effort you put into your business, the more money you can make. As a home-based business owner, you get to decide how much money you want to make and then pick out the kind of schedule that will help you meet your goal.

These reasons to start your own home business are just the tip of the iceberg. But when you add up everything, you're left with one fundamental reason for owning your own home-based business: freedom.

The pitfalls of owning your own home-based business

Starting a home-based business isn't the solution to every problem for every person. Although many home-based businesses are successful and the people who started them are happy with the results, more than a few home-based businesses end up causing far more headaches than their owners anticipated. Some home-based business owners even go bankrupt as a direct result of the failure of their businesses. Starting your own business is hard work, and there are no guarantees for its success.

WARNING

So the next time you're lying on your sofa, dreaming of starting your own home-based business, don't forget to consider some of the potential pitfalls:

>> **The business is in your home.** Depending on your domestic situation, working in your own home — a home filled with any number of distractions, including busy children, whining spouses or significant others, televisions, loaded refrigerators, and more — can be a difficult proposition at best.

>> **You're the boss.** Yes, being the boss has its drawbacks, too. When you're the boss, you're the one who has to motivate yourself to work hard every day — no one's standing over your shoulder (except maybe your cat) watching your every move. For some people, focusing on work is very difficult when *they* are put in the position of being the boss.

>> **Health insurance may be unavailable or unaffordable.** If you've ever been without health insurance for a period of time, or if you've been underinsured and had to make large medical or dental payments, you know just how important affordable health insurance is to your health and financial well-being. According to one study, 62.1 percent of all bankruptcies are medical related, and 92 percent of these debtors had medical debts of more than $5,000. Unfortunately, when you work for yourself, finding good health insurance isn't a given. In fact, it can sometimes be downright difficult, depending on where you live and work.

>> **A home-based business is (usually) a very small business.** As a small business, you're likely more exposed to the ups and downs of fickle customers than larger businesses are. And a customer's decision not to pay could be devastating to you and your business.

>> **You may fail or not like it.** No one can guarantee that your business is going to be a success or that you're going to like the business you start. Failure may cost you dearly, including financial ruin (no small number of business owners have had to declare bankruptcy when their businesses failed), destruction of personal relationships, and worse. However, not all small businesses close because of financial problems. The Small Business Administration has found that at the time of closing, one out of three businesses is financially sound.

Regardless of these potential pitfalls, starting a home-based business remains the avenue of choice for an increasing number of people. Are you ready to join them?

Taking the Home-Based Business Quiz

Many people talk about starting home-based businesses, and many dream about becoming their own bosses. Making the transition from a full-time career to self-employment, however, is a big change in anyone's life. Are you really ready to make the move, or should you put the idea of having your own home-based business on the back burner for a while longer?

TIP

To help you decide, take the following home-based business quiz. Circle your answer to each of these questions, add up the results, and find out if you're ready to take the plunge!

1. **How strong is your drive to succeed in your own home-based business?**

   A. I can and will be a success. Period.

   B. I'm fairly confident that if I put my mind to it, I will succeed.

   C. I'm not sure. Let me think about it for a while.

   D. Did I say that I wanted to start my own business? Are you sure that was me?

2. **Are you ready to work as hard as or harder than you have ever worked before?**

   A. You bet — I'm ready to do whatever it takes to succeed!

   B. Sure, I don't mind working hard as long as I get something out of it.

   C. Okay, as long as I still get weekends and evenings off.

   D. What? You mean I'll still have to work after I start my own business? Isn't that why I hire employees?

3. **Do you like the idea of controlling your own work instead of having someone else control it for you?**

   A. I don't want anyone controlling my work but me!

   B. That's certainly my first choice.

   C. It sounds like an interesting idea — can I?

   D. Do I have to control my own work? Can't someone control it for me?

4. **Have you developed a strong network of potential customers?**

A. Yes, here are their names and numbers.

B. Yes, I have some pretty strong leads.

C. Not yet, but I've started kicking around some ideas with potential customers.

D. I'm sure that as soon as I let people know that I'm starting my own business, customers will line up.

5. **Do you have a plan for making the transition into your home-based business?**

A. Here it is — would you like to read the executive summary or the full plan?

B. Yes, I've spent a lot of time considering my options and making plans.

C. I'm just getting started.

D. I don't believe in plans — they crimp my style.

6. **Do you have enough money saved to tide you over while you get your business off the ground?**

A. Will the year's salary that I have saved be enough?

B. I have six months' expenses hidden away for a rainy day.

C. I have three months' worth.

D. I'm still trying to pay off my college student loans.

7. **How strong is your self-image?**

A. I *am* self-esteem!

B. I strongly believe in my own self-worth and in my ability to create my own opportunities.

C. I feel fairly secure with myself; just don't push too hard.

D. I don't know — what do you think?

8. **Do you have the support of your significant other and/or family?**

A. They're all on board, are an integral part of my plan, and have been assigned responsibilities.

B. They're in favor of whatever makes me happy.

C. I'm pretty sure they'll support me.

D. I'm going to tell them about it later.

9. If it's a necessary part of your plan, will you be able to start up your home-based business while you remain in your current job?

    A. Sure — in fact, my boss wants in!

    B. If I make a few adjustments in my schedule, I can't see any other reason why I can't.

    C. Would you please repeat the question?

    D. Maybe I'll be able to work on it for a couple of hours a month.

10. What will you tell friends when they ask why you quit that great job?

    A. I'm free at last!

    B. That the benefits clearly outweigh the potential costs.

    C. I don't know; maybe they won't ask.

    D. I'll pretend that I'm still working for my old organization.

Give yourself 5 points for every A answer, 3 points for every B, −3 for every C, and −5 for every D. Now tally up the numbers, and compare your results with the following ranges of numbers.

By comparing your total points with the points contained in each of the six following categories, you can find out whether you're ready to jump into your own home-based business:

25 to 50 points: Assuming you were honest with yourself as you answered the preceding questions (you were, weren't you?), you're ready! You just need to decide whether to drop your day job or work into your new business gradually.

1 to 24 points: You're definitely warming up to the idea of starting your own home-based business. Consider starting your own business in the near future, but make sure to keep your day job until you have your venture well under way.

0 points: You can go either way on this one. Why don't you try taking this test again in another month or two? Read this book in the meantime.

−1 to −24 points: Unfortunately, you don't appear to be quite ready to make the move from career to home-based business. You should read this book and then take this test again in a few months. Maybe working for someone else isn't the worst thing that can happen to you.

−25 to −50: Forget it. You were clearly born to work for someone else.

Are you ready to make the move to starting a home-based business? If the quiz indicates otherwise, don't worry — you'll have plenty of opportunities in the future. When you're ready for them, they'll be ready for you. If you're ready now, congratulations!

Starting Something from Scratch

You probably find a certain amount of pleasure in making something out of nothing with your own two hands. It's the same pleasure a sculptor gets from creating a beautiful piece of art. You may not get it right the first time — after all, it took Thomas Edison hundreds of tries before he hit on the right material for a successful light bulb filament — but when you do find the right formula for success, the feeling of satisfaction you experience is hard to beat.

Perhaps the quickest and least expensive way to start your own home-based business is to do so from scratch. No need to fill out a bunch of applications, save up money to buy into a franchise, or take weeks or months to learn some complex, proprietary way of doing business. If you really want to, there's no reason why you can't start your own business from scratch — right now. Your friends, relatives, neighbors, and co-workers are doing it, and you can, too.

When starting a business from scratch, you can use one of two main approaches: Choose to do the same kind of work you've been doing in your regular job or career, or choose to do something totally different. This section takes a closer look at each approach and the advantages each one offers you.

Doing what you've been doing in a job

As you consider the different options available to you in starting your own business, one of your first thoughts will undoubtedly be to do what you've already been doing in your full-time job.

And why not? You know the job, you're already experienced in the business, and you know exactly what to expect. You also know what your customers want and how to give it to them. You may even have a network of potential customers waiting to sign up for your products and services. Not surprisingly, doing what you've been doing has several advantages, including the following:

>> You can start your business more quickly (like right *now*) and more easily than if you choose to do something you've never done before.

>> You don't have to spend your time or money on training courses or workshops, and you don't have to worry much about a learning curve.

>> You'll be much more efficient and effective because you've already discovered the best ways to do your job, along with time-saving tricks of the trade.

>> You can capitalize on your good reputation, which may be your most important asset.

>> You can tap in to your network of business contacts, clients, and customers (when ethically appropriate) and generate business more quickly than when you start something new and different.

TIP

For many people, doing something they've been doing is the best choice. So because doing what you've been doing is often the quickest and least expensive avenue for starting your own home-based business, be sure to take a close look at this option before you consider any others.

Doing something new and different

Although doing what you've been doing in a job offers many advantages, doing something new and different has its own set of high points. If you're burned out on your current job and you dream of making radical changes in your career or lifestyle — for example, trading your high-pressure career as an attorney for a much more relaxing home-based massage business — doing something new and different may well be exactly what the doctor ordered.

The following are some key advantages of doing something new and different:

>> Getting a fresh start in your career can be an extremely energizing experience with positive repercussions for every aspect of your life, opening up exciting new possibilities and opportunities for you along the way.

>> Tapping in to new career options allows you to find work that may not have even existed when you first started your career — for example, designing smartphone apps or computer-network consulting.

REMEMBER

Many successful home-based business owners have created businesses that have nothing to do whatsoever with what they'd been doing in their full-time jobs. If you're sufficiently motivated, nothing can stand between you and success, no matter which business you choose. If you're looking to shake up the status quo or to make a break from the past, doing something completely new may well be the best option for you.

Transitioning into Your Home-Based Business

Starting your own business is exciting. For those people who have spent all their working lives employed by someone else, it's often the culmination of a dream that's lasted for years or even decades. Imagine the power and personal satisfaction you'll feel when you realize you're the boss and you call the shots — from setting your own work schedule, to deciding how to approach your work, to choosing your computer and office furniture. It's a feeling you won't soon forget.

But there's a right way and a wrong way to make the move. Your goal is to make sure you maintain a sufficient supply of cash to pay the start-up costs of your business while paying for the rest of your life — the mortgage or rent, the car loans, the health insurance, the gas and electric, your daughter's piano lessons, and the list goes on and on.

REMEMBER

The fact is, few businesses — home-based or otherwise — within the first six months of operation bring in all the money necessary to get them off the ground and keep them going for a prolonged period of time. In other words, you need *a lot of cash* — from a job, your spouse or partner's job, your savings, or loans from friends, family, or a bank — to keep both your business and your personal life going until the business generates enough revenue to take over.

Although you have to decide for yourself exactly what schedule to follow while transitioning into a home-based business, unless you're unemployed or retired, it's best to start your business on a part-time basis while you continue to hold down your regular full-time job. Why? For a number of reasons, including the following:

>> You can develop and test your new business with virtually no risk — you still have your regular job to fall back on if your new business doesn't work out (and remember, no matter how great your business idea is, there's a chance it won't work out).

>> You aren't under the intense pressure to perform and show the results that you'd have to show if your new business were your only source of income.

>> You can keep your established health insurance, retirement plan, time off, and other benefits. Given the difficulty and expense of securing a decent health care plan when you're on your own and not under the umbrella of your employer, health care alone may be reason enough to keep your day job while you start your own business.

>> You have a steady source of income you can use to pay your bills while you establish your new business.

>> You may be able to take advantage of tax benefits, like the capability to write off early losses against income.

>> You have a stronger basis for obtaining bank loans and other financing for your new business.

Of course, the decision is ultimately up to you. When starting a home-based business, follow your heart and make sure the transition fits into your schedule and your life.

This section looks at steps you need to take before you leave your regular job to devote all your time and energy to being your own boss. It also walks through the different steps involved in the process of establishing your home-based business.

Knowing what to do before leaving your day job

After you're consistently earning enough income from your part-time, home-based business to cover your bare-minimum living and business expenses, you're ready to make the jump to a full-time commitment of your time and attention. Before you turn in your resignation, however, take the following six steps:

1. **Find out when any company benefit plans you have will vest or increase in value.**

   If you have a 401(k) or other retirement plan to which your employer has been contributing, it may not be fully available to you until you've served a particular number of years of service. Finding out this information may help you determine the best time to resign. It'd be a shame, for example, if you quit two weeks before the value of your retirement benefits was set to jump from 80 to 100 percent of your current salary.

2. **Find out when you can expect to receive any bonus money or profit sharing.**

   You may, for example, be slated to receive an annual performance bonus or profit sharing a month after the end of the company fiscal year. This information can help with the financial planning for your home-based business because it lets you know when you'll have the money available to help you get your business off the ground.

3. **Get all annual health exams, have all routine procedures done, and fill all prescriptions while you and your family are still covered by your medical/dental/vision insurance.**

   Check to see whether you can convert your group coverage to an individual policy at favorable rates or what other health coverage options are open to you. (Some group plans can be converted, but be very careful about changes in coverage, co-pays, and deductibles that may actually end up costing you much more money in the long run.)

REMEMBER

Don't forget that if you work in the United States, you're likely covered by COBRA (the Consolidated Omnibus Budget Reconciliation Act of 1985), which requires your employer to allow you to continue your identical group health coverage for a period of 18 months or more. However, qualified individuals may be required to pay the entire premium for coverage up to 102 percent of the cost to the plan.

The American Recovery and Reinvestment Act of 2009 (ARRA) provides for premium reductions and additional election opportunities for health benefits under COBRA. Eligible individuals pay only 35 percent of their COBRA premiums and the remaining 65 percent is reimbursed to the coverage provider through a tax credit.

TIP

The Affordable Care Act, signed into law in 2010, may serve to help make your health insurance more portable and provides a marketplace where you can shop for new insurance on your own. Be sure to find out the latest on the law at www.healthcare.gov.

4. **If you own a house and you need some extra cash to help you through the transition, consider taking out a home equity line of credit or other loan before leaving your current job.**

Having a line of credit or loan to draw upon can be invaluable during the first two years of your new business, and your chances of getting approved for it are much greater while you're employed in a regular job. That's right — after you leave your job, you probably won't qualify for a line of credit or other loans for your business until your business has been successful for two or more years.

5. **Pay off or pay down the balance on your credit cards while you still have a steady job.**

Doing so helps your credit rating (always a good thing) and provides you with another source of potential funds to help you finance various start-up costs (and depending on the nature of your business, you may have plenty of those).

6. **Take advantage of training and educational opportunities, conferences, and meetings that can result in preparation or contacts that will prepare you for your own business.**

Doing so enables you to hit the ground running when you decide it's time to start your own business.

WARNING

Don't make your announcement or submit your resignation until you're really ready to go. Some companies are (sometimes justifiably) paranoid about soon-to-be former employees stealing ideas, proprietary data, or clients, which can make for a very hasty exit, with a personal escort, when you do resign.

After completing these steps, you're ready to take what may well be one of the most significant steps forward you'll ever take in your life: starting your own home-based business.

Understanding what you have to do to start your own home-based business

This section goes through exactly what you need to do to start up your own home-based business.

Develop a business plan

Despite what you may read on many small business websites or blogs, many home-based business owners can get by without drafting a business plan. Indeed, just the thought of having to draft a 50-page tabbed and annotated, multipart business plan is enough to scare many potential home-based business owners away from their dreams. Truth be told, most business owners today use their business plans to obtain financing from third parties, such as banks or investors, and many successful businesses — home-based or not — have been started without one.

That said, the process of drafting a business plan can be very beneficial — both to you as a business owner and to your business. Taking the time to draft a plan helps you do the right things at the right time to get your business off the ground; plus, it forces you to think through what the challenges will be and what you can do about them before they overwhelm you.

In essence, a good business plan

>> Clearly establishes your goals for the business

>> Analyzes the feasibility of a new business and its likelihood of being profitable over the long haul

>> Explores the expansion of an existing business

>> Defines your customers and competitors (very important people to know!) and points out your strengths and weaknesses

>> Details your plans for the future

REMEMBER

Even if you think your business is too small to have a business plan, it's really worth your time to see what it's all about — the process of developing the plan for your business will produce a clarity of thought that you can't find any other way. See Book 2, Chapter 1 for details on developing an effective business plan.

Consult outside professionals

As a new home-based businessperson, you need to consider establishing relationships with a number of *outside professionals* — trained and experienced people who can help you with the aspects of your business in which you may have little or no experience. By no means do you have to hire someone from each category described in this section. But if you run into questions that you can't easily answer yourself, don't hesitate to call on outside professionals for help as you go through the business start-up process.

REMEMBER

Any professional advice you get at the beginning of your business may well save you heartache and potentially expensive extra work down the road.

Here are just some of the outside professionals you may choose to consult as you start your home-based business:

» **Lawyer:** An attorney's services are an asset not only in the planning stages of your business, but also throughout its life. An attorney can help you choose your legal structure, draw up incorporation or partnership paperwork, draft and review agreements and contracts, and provide information on your legal rights and obligations. Look for an attorney who specializes in working with small businesses and start-ups. See Book 2, Chapter 6 for details on starting your business with the right legal structure.

» **Accountant:** Consult an accountant to set up a good bookkeeping system for your business. Inadequate bookkeeping is a principal contributor to the failure of small businesses. Regardless of how boring or intimidating it may seem, make sure you understand basic accounting and the bookkeeping system or software you're using, and don't forget to closely review all the regularly produced financial reports related to your business (and make sure you actually receive them!). See Book 3, Chapter 1 for the basics of setting up your books.

» **Banker:** The capital requirements of a small business make establishing a good working relationship with a local banker absolutely essential. For example, bankers can approve immediate deposit of checks that would normally be held for ten days. They're also good sources of financial information — and for obtaining cash to tide you over when times are tough or financing expansion of your business when times are good.

TIP

Establish a relationship with your banker *before* applying for a loan, not after you decide to initiate the loan process. This relationship may make the difference between getting approved for the loan you need and being turned down.

>> **Business consultant:** Every person has talents in many areas, but no one can be a master of everything. Consultants are available to assist in the areas where you need expert help. You can use business, management, and marketing consultants; promotion experts; financial planners; and a host of other specialists to help make your business more successful. Don't hesitate to draw on their expertise when you need it.

>> **Insurance agent/broker:** Many kinds of insurance options are available for business owners, and some are more necessary than others. An insurance agent or broker can advise you about the type and amount of coverage that's best for you and your business. The agent may also be able to tailor a package that meets your specific needs at reasonable rates.

REMEMBER

The relationships you establish with outside professionals during the start-up phase of your business can last for years and can be of tremendous benefit to your firm. Be sure to choose your relationships wisely. In the case of outside professionals, you often get what you pay for, so be penny-wise but don't suffer a poor-quality outside professional simply to save a dollar or two.

Choose the best legal structure for your business

Most home-based businesses begin as either sole proprietorships or partnerships because they're the easiest business structures to run and the least expensive. But as these businesses grow, many explore the transition to another kind of legal entity. Before you decide what kind of business you want yours to be, consider the pros and cons of the following legal structures:

>> **Sole proprietorship:** A *sole proprietorship* is the simplest and least regulated form of organization. It also has minimal legal start-up costs, making it the most popular choice for new home-based businesses. In a sole proprietorship, one person owns and operates the business and is responsible for seeking and obtaining financing. The sole proprietor (likely you) has total control and receives all profits, which are taxed as personal income. The major disadvantages include unlimited personal liability for the owner (if the business is sued for some reason, the owner is personally liable to pay any judgments against the company) and potential dissolution of the business upon the owner's death.

>> **Partnership:** A *partnership* is relatively easy to form and can provide additional financial resources. Each partner is an *agent* for the partnership and can borrow money, hire employees, and operate the business. Profits are taxed as personal income, and the partners are still personally liable for debts and taxes. Personal assets can be attached if the partnership can't satisfy creditors' claims. A special arrangement called a *limited partnership* allows partners to avoid unlimited personal liability. Limited partnerships must be registered and

must also pay a tax to the appropriate authorities in their jurisdiction. On the plus side, partnerships allow people to combine their unique talents and assets to create a whole greater than the sum of its parts. On the other hand, though, partnerships can become sheer living hell when partners fail to see eye to eye or when relationships turn sour.

REMEMBER

When entering into any partnership, consult a lawyer, and insist on a written agreement that clearly describes a process for dissolving the partnership as cleanly and fairly as possible.

>> **Limited liability company:** A *limited liability company* (LLC) is often the preferred choice for new operations and joint ventures because LLCs have the advantage of being treated as partnerships for U.S. income tax purposes while also providing the limited liability of corporations. However, LLCs have the disadvantage of generally being more expensive to set up than sole proprietorships or partnerships. Owners of limited liability companies, called *members,* are comparable to stockholders in a corporation or limited partners in a limited partnership. To create a limited liability company, articles of organization are filed with the secretary of state. The members must also execute an operating agreement that defines the relationship between the company and its members. Note that all 50 states and the District of Columbia have enacted LLC statutes.

>> **Corporation:** As the most complex of business organizations, the *corporation* (also known as a *C Corporation*) acts as a legal entity that exists separately from its owners. Although this separation limits the owners from personal liability, it also creates a double taxation on earnings (the corporation pays tax on net taxable income, and the shareholders pay tax on dividends distributed). A corporate structure may be advantageous because it allows the business to raise capital more easily through the sale of stocks or bonds; plus, the business can continue to function even without key individuals. The corporation also enables future employees to participate in various types of insurance and profit-sharing plans. Costs to incorporate vary from state to state — contact your secretary of state for more information.

A special type of corporation, an *S Corporation,* allows eligible domestic corporations to overcome the double taxation problem. Qualifying corporations can elect to be treated as an S Corporation under the rules of Subchapter S of the tax code. Making this election allows small corporations to be generally exempt from federal income tax. Similar to partnerships, all items of income, deduction, credit, gain, and loss are passed through on a pro rata basis to the individual S Corporation shareholders. In this way, the S Corporation passes its items of income, loss, deduction, and credits through to its shareholders to be included on their separate returns.

With C Corporations, you need to be careful you aren't erroneously classified by the government as a *professional service corporation,* which is treated much less advantageously than other C Corporations. Professional service corporations are corporations in which the owners (who are licensed professionals) substantially perform certain personal services, including accounting, actuarial science, architecture, consulting, engineering, health, veterinary services, law, and performing arts.

As you set up your new home-based business, take time to carefully think through the ramifications of your business's legal structure. Each option has many potential advantages and disadvantages for your firm, and each can make a big difference in how you run your business. If you have any questions about which kind of legal structure is right for your business, talk to an accountant or seek advice from an attorney who specializes in small businesses. Book 2, Chapter 6 discusses these legal structures in much more detail.

Decide on a name

Naming your business may well be one of the most enjoyable steps in the process of starting up your own home-based business. Everyone can get in on the action: your friends, your family, and especially your clients-to-be.

Consider your business name carefully — you have to live with it for a long time. Your business name should give people some idea of the nature of your business, it should project the image you want to have, and it should be easy to visualize. Names can be simple, sophisticated, or even silly. Try to pick one that can grow with your business and not limit you in the future.

Along with a name, many businesses develop a logo, which provides a graphic symbol for the business. As with your name, your logo needs to project the image you want, so develop it carefully. Spend a few extra dollars to have a professional graphic artist design your logo for you.

After you come up with a name, register it with your local government to make sure it isn't already in use. If you don't check first, you may have to throw out your stationery and business cards and redesign your logo and website when you eventually find out that another company has your name — and registered it 15 years before you did!

Take care of the red tape (and it will take care of you)

Taking care of all the local, state, and federal government legal requirements of starting up a business is something that too many budding home-based entrepreneurs put off or ignore. Unfortunately, ignoring the many legal requirements of going into business may put you and your business at risk.

Getting through the maze of government regulations can certainly be one of the most confusing aspects of starting up and running a business. But even though this process can be intimidating, you have to do it — and do it correctly — because noncompliance can result in costly penalties and perhaps even the loss of your business. Consider this step as one that fortifies the professionalism of your business at the same time that it helps you rest easy at night, knowing that you're following the rules. Do you want people to take you seriously? Then you need to establish your business in a professional way.

REMEMBER

Even very small or part-time businesses have certain requirements. It's your responsibility to adhere to any and all regulations that apply to your business. Fortunately, a lot of people and organizations — government small business development centers, chambers of commerce, and sometimes lawyers and certified public accountants — are willing and eager to answer questions and help you with this task. For your sake — and the sake of your business — don't hesitate to ask someone for help when you need it.

Get the insurance you need

In today's expensive, litigious world of business, insurance isn't really an option — it's essential. Without it, all your years of hard work can be lost in a minute because of a catastrophic loss.

So what kinds of insurance do you need for your business? You should talk to an insurance agent and discuss your business and its needs with him or her. Some of the most common kinds of business insurance include the following:

>> **Health insurance:** Includes medical, dental, vision, and other coverage designed to maintain and promote employee health and wellness and to protect employees against catastrophic loss in case of injury or illness

>> **Basic fire insurance:** Covers property losses due to fire and sometimes covers loss of business, as well

>> **Extended coverage:** Protects against conditions not covered by fire insurance, including storms, explosions, smoke damage, and various other disasters

>> **Liability insurance:** Covers claims against your business for bodily injury incurred on the business's premises

>> **Product liability coverage:** Covers liability for products manufactured or sold by your business

>> **Professional liability and/or errors-and-omissions insurance:** Protects the business against claims for damages incurred by customers as a result of your professional advice or recommendations

>> **Vandalism and malicious mischief coverage:** Covers against property losses resulting from vandalism and related activities

>> **Theft coverage:** Protects your business from burglary and robbery

>> **Vehicle insurance:** Covers collision, liability, and property damage for vehicles used for business

>> **Business interruption insurance:** Covers payment of business earnings if the business is closed for an insurable cause, such as fire, flood, or other natural disaster

>> **Workers' compensation:** Provides disability and death benefits to employees and others who work for you, as defined by your state law, who are injured on the job

WARNING

A homeowner's policy isn't usually enough insurance for a home-based business for a couple of reasons. First, your typical homeowner's policy provides only limited coverage for business equipment and doesn't insure you against risks of liability or lost income. Second, your homeowner's policy may not cover your business activities at all.

TIP

Insurance is the kind of thing you don't think about until you need it. And in the case of insurance, when you need it, chances are you *really* need it! Take time to set up proper coverage now — before it's too late. Call your insurance company and talk through the options it may have for your to convert or supplement your homeowner's policy to cover your business.

Decide on an accounting system

Accounting is one of those topics that makes people nervous (with visions of IRS audits dancing in their heads), but keeping books doesn't have to be complicated. In fact, simplicity is the key to a good system for home-based businesses. Keep in mind that your records need to be complete and up-to-date so that you have the information you need for business decisions and taxes.

TIP

When you establish an accounting system, pick up one of the excellent computer software programs dedicated to this purpose. Programs such as QuickBooks, FreshBooks, and Sage One do everything your home-based business will ever need — and more.

The two basic bookkeeping methods are *single entry* and *double entry.* Single entry is simpler, with only one entry required per transaction. This is probably the best method for most home-based businesses, and the vast majority can operate very well with the single-entry system. Book 3, Chapter 1 covers bookkeeping in detail.

You can also choose between two methods to keep track of the money coming in and going out of your business: *cash* or *accrual.* Most small businesses use the cash method, in which income is reported in the year it's received and expenses are deducted in the year they're paid. Under the accrual method, income is reported when it's earned, and expenses are deducted when they're incurred, whether money has changed hands yet or not.

The accounting methods you use depend on your business. You may want to talk to an accountant for help in setting up your system. Even with the support of a professional, however, you need to understand your own system thoroughly.

REMEMBER

Many home-based businesses can get by without detailed financial reporting or analysis — after all, if you can keep up with your bills and perhaps have a little bit of money to sock away in your savings account, you must be making money, right? If you really want to understand your business's financial situation, how-ever, you need some basic financial reports.

The following financial statements are the minimum necessary to understand where your business stands financially. With them in hand, you can review your business's financial strengths and weaknesses and make accurate plans for the future.

>> **Balance sheets:** *Balance sheets* show the worth of your business — the difference between its assets and its liabilities. Your balance sheet can tell you whether or not you'd have any cash left over if you shut down your business today and paid off all your bills and loans and liquidated your assets. See Chapter 3 in Book 3 for more information.

>> **Profit-and-loss statements:** *Profit-and-loss (P&L) statements,* also referred to as *income statements,* show you the difference between how much money your business is bringing in *(revenue)* and how much money it's spending *(expenses).* If you're bringing in more money than you spend, you have a profit. If you're spending more money than you bring in, you have a loss. Book 3, Chapter 2 covers P&L in detail.

>> **Cash-flow projections:** Cash-flow projections tell you where your money is going and whether or not you're likely to have sufficient money each month to pay your bills and operate the business. For many start-up companies — especially those with employees, rent, and other significant recurring expenses — a cash-flow projection is the most important financial statement of all. Check out Book 3, Chapter 4 for more on staying solvent.

Develop a marketing plan

If you want to be successful, you can't just start a business and then patiently wait for customers to walk in your door. You have to let potential customers know about your new business, get them in to have a look, and then encourage them to buy your product or service. Marketing is all of this and more. Your specific approach to marketing depends on your business, your finances, your potential client or customer base, and your goals.

Marketing sells your products and services, which brings in the cash you need to run your business. Marketing is so important to the survival (and success) of your business that it deserves a plan of its own. A *marketing plan* helps evaluate where your business currently is, where you want it to go, and how you can get there. Your marketing plan should also spell out the specific strategies and costs involved in reaching your goals. You can integrate it into your business plan as one comprehensive section. As with the business plan, you should refer to it regularly and update it as necessary.

Successful marketing for a small or home-based business doesn't happen all by itself. It requires a lot of work and careful analysis and is a terrific opportunity to use your creativity and hone your business sense. For a lot more information on marketing your home-based business, be sure to check out the chapters in Book 5.

Seek assistance when you need it

TIP

An almost unlimited number of organizations and agencies — private, public, and not-for-profit — are ready, willing, and able to help you work through the process of starting up your home-based business. Check out the websites of each of the following organizations for an incredible amount of free information and help, and know that this list is only the beginning:

>> **Small Business Development Centers:** https://www.sba.gov/tools/local-assistance/sbdc

>> **Service Corps of Retired Executives (SCORE):** www.score.org

>> **U.S. Chamber of Commerce:** www.uschamber.com

>> **Minority Business Development Agency:** www.mbda.gov

>> **Federal Business Opportunities:** www.fbo.gov

>> **International Business Innovation Association:** https://inbia.org/

>> **U.S. Patent and Trademark Office:** www.uspto.gov

Chapter **5**

Creating an Online Presence for Your Business

No matter what you sell or where you sell it — on the web, in a bricks-and-mortar store, or even on Facebook — you need to have a home base on the web, a *presence*. Not so long ago, a "home base" on the web automatically meant a website. A website is important, but you can sell online without one. That's why this chapter uses the term *presence* instead of *site*.

It's a subtle but significant difference. A presence can include a blog, ads on Craigslist, exposure for your app on iTunes, or storefronts on a variety of marketplaces.

Wherever you do business, the same basic principles work on the web just as well as they do in the bricks-and-mortar world. Attracting customers is important, but real success comes from establishing relationships with customers who come to trust you and rely on you for providing excellent products and services.

This chapter focuses on creating an organized website as part of an overall presence to attract not only first-time, but also return customers. You explore ways to achieve these goals, including making your site easy to navigate, creating compelling content, optimizing your images so they appear quickly, and building interactivity into your site so customers want to return on a regular basis.

TIP

You might think a single website is your ultimate goal. But if you want your online business to be a source of full-time income or if you hope to be in business for years to come, a website is just the start. Like many entrepreneurs, you might decide to have multiple presences in different marketplaces. The techniques described in this chapter apply to those storefronts, too.

Feng Shui-ing Your Website

Feng Shui is the art of arranging objects in an environment to achieve (among other things) success in your career, wealth, and happiness. If that's true, try practicing some Feng Shui with your online business environment — that is, your website.

Although you may be tempted to jump right into the creation of a cool website, take a moment to plan. Whether you're setting off on a road trip across the nation or building a new addition on your house, you'll progress more smoothly by first drawing a map of where you want to go. Dig down into your miscellaneous drawer until you find pencil and paper, and make a list of the elements you want to have on your site.

Look over the items on your list and break them into two or three main categories. These main categories will branch off your *home page,* which functions as the grand entrance for your online business site. You can then draw a map of your site similar to the one shown in Figure 5-1.

FIGURE 5-1:
A home page is the point from which your site branches into more specific levels of information.

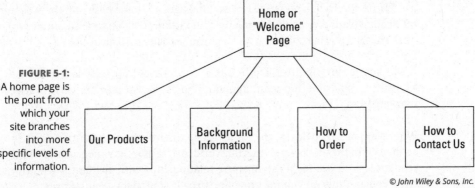

© John Wiley & Sons, Inc.

TIP

The page heading Background Information is a placeholder for detailed information about some aspect of your online business. You can write about your experience with and your love for what you buy and sell, or anything else that personalizes your site and builds trust.

The preceding example results in a very simple website. But there's nothing wrong with starting out simple. Many other businesses start with a three-layered organization for their websites. This arrangement divides the site into two sections, one about the company and one about the products or services for sale, as shown in Figure 5-2.

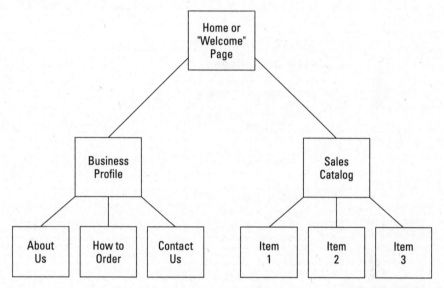

FIGURE 5-2:
This arrangement divides the site into two sections.

© *John Wiley & Sons, Inc.*

REMEMBER

Think of your home page as the lobby of a museum, where a friendly person at the information desk hands you a list of the special exhibits you can visit that day and shows you a map so you can figure out how you're going to get from here to there. Be sure to include the following items on your home page:

» The name of the store or business

» Your logo, if you have one

» Links to the main areas of your site or, if your site isn't overly extensive, to every page

» Links to your presences online — your Facebook or Twitter page, or any storefronts you have

» Contact information, such as your email address, phone/fax numbers, and (optionally) your business address so that people know where to find you in the Land Beyond Cyberspace

A mobile version of a website strips away most or all of the images and colors and simply presents the content. The presentation needs to be as straightforward as possible so that pages load quickly on a mobile device. Forget about animations or multiple columns. Isolate your most important links in a single one-column page that is easy to read on a smartphone. Figure 5-3 shows a possible arrangement.

FIGURE 5-3: A mobile site's home page needs to be simple and load quickly.

Some sites are even "smart" enough to present a limited amount of content depending on whether a touch-enabled device such as an iPad is being used.

Devising a structure for your website is only one way to organize it — the outer or top-down organizational method, you might say. Organization also comes from the inside — from the content you create. The words, images, and interactive features that help your site get organized are discussed in the following sections.

MAKING THEM FALL IN LOVE AT FIRST SITE

First impressions are critical on the web, where shoppers can jump from site to site with a click of their mouse. A few extra seconds of downtime waiting for videos or mini-computer programs — *Java applets* — to download can cause your prospective buyer to lose patience and you to lose a sale. (Keeping your site simple is especially important for mobile device users.)

How do you make visitors to your welcome page feel like they're being greeted with open arms? Here are some suggestions:

- **Remember, less is more.** Don't overload any one page with more than half a dozen images. Keep all images 50KB or less in size. You do this by saving images with a resolution of 72 dpi (dots per inch), as described in "A picture is worth a thousand words," later in this chapter.

- **Find a fast host.** Some web servers have super-fast connections to the Internet and others use slower lines. Test your site; if your pages take 10 or 20 seconds or more to appear, ask your host company why and find out whether it can move you to a faster machine. These days, cable connections of 1MB to 2MB are easy to find and affordable as well.

- **Offer a bargain.** Nothing attracts attention as much as a contest, a giveaway, or a special sales promotion. If you have something you can give away, either through a contest or a deep discount, do it.

- **Provide instant gratification.** Make sure your most important information appears at or near the top of your page. Visitors to the web don't like having to scroll through several screens' worth of material to get to the information they want.

Creating Content That Attracts Customers

What sells on the web? Look no further than the search engine you probably use on a regular basis: Google. Google proves that information sells online. Making information easy to find and organizing much of the web's content in one place has helped make this one of the most successful businesses of recent years. When it comes to a business website, you need to present the *right* content in the *right* way to make prospective clients and customers want to explore your site the first time and then come back for more.

What, you ask, is the "right" content? The "right" content

>> Helps people absorb information fast

>> Makes it easy for visitors to find out who you are and what you have to offer

>> Is friendly and informal in tone, concise in length, and clear in its organization

>> Helps develop the all-important one-to-one-relationship with customers and clients by inviting dialogue and interaction, both with you and with others who share the same interests

Begin by identifying your target audience. Envision the customers you want to attract and make your site appear to speak directly to them, person to person. Ask around and try to determine what people want from your website. Speak informally and directly to them, by using *you* rather than *we* or *us*, and make sure your site has plenty of action points — links to click, forms to fill out, or product descriptions to view. And follow the general principles outlined in the sections that follow.

Consider doing what professional marketing consultants do and write detailed descriptions of the individuals you're trying to reach. Make your customer profiles complete with fictitious names, ages, job descriptions, type of car they drive, and so on. The more detailed you get, the better you can tailor your content to those people.

Following the KISS principle: Keep it simple, sir (or sister)

Studies of how information on a web page is absorbed indicate that people don't really read the contents from top to bottom (or left to right, or frame to frame) in a linear way. In fact, most web surfers don't *read* in the traditional sense at all. Instead, they browse so quickly you'd think they have an itchy mouse finger. They "flip through pages" by clicking link after link. More and more Internet users are swiping their index fingers on tablets, smartphones, and even cars with Internet-ready computer systems. Because your prospective customers don't necessarily have tons of computing power or hours' worth of time to explore your site, the best rule is to *keep it simple.*

People who are looking for things on the web are often in a state of hurried distraction. Think about a TV watcher browsing during a commercial or a parent stealing a few moments on the computer while the baby naps. Imagine this person surfing while standing on a platform waiting for a train. He isn't in the mood to listen while you unfold your fondest hopes and dreams for success, starting with playing grocery-store cashier as a toddler. Attract him immediately by answering these questions:

>> Who are you, anyway?

>> All right, so what is your main message or mission?

>> Well, then, what do you have here for me?

>> Why should I choose your site to investigate rather than all the others that seem to be about the same?

When it comes to web pages, it pays to put the most important components first: who you are, what you do, how you stand out from any competing sites, and your contact information.

REMEMBER

People who visit a website give that site less than a minute (possibly only 20 seconds).

If you have a long list of items to sell, you probably can't fit everything you have to offer right on the first page of your site. Even if you could, you wouldn't want to: It's better to prioritize the contents of your site so that the "breaking stories" or the best contents appear at the top, and the rest of what's in your catalog is arranged in order of importance.

WARNING

Think long and hard before you use features that may scare people away instead of wow them, such as a splash page that contains only a logo or short greeting and then reloads automatically and takes the visitor to the main body of a site. Also stay away from loading your home page with Flash animations or Java applets that take your prospective customers' browsers precious seconds to load or that might not appear on an iPad, which doesn't support Flash.

Striking the right tone with your text

Business writing on the web differs from the dry, linear report writing of the corporate world. So this is your chance to express the real you: Talk about your fashion sense or your collection of salt and pepper shakers. Your business also has a personality, and the more striking you make its description on your web page, the better. Use the tone of your text to define what makes your business unique and what distinguishes it from your competition.

TIP

Satisfied customers are another source of endorsements. Ask your customers whether they're willing to provide a quote about how you helped them. If you don't yet have satisfied customers, ask one or two people to try your products or services for free, and then, if they're happy with your wares, ask permission to use their comments on your site. Your goal is to get a pithy, positive quote that you can put on your home page or on a page specifically devoted to quotes from your clients.

Making your site easy to navigate

Imagine prospective customers arriving at your website with only a fraction of their attention engaged. Making the links easy to read and in obvious locations makes your site easier to navigate. Having a row of clickable buttons at the top of your home page, each pointing to an important area of your site, is always a good idea. Such navigational pointers give visitors an idea of what your site contains in a single glance and immediately encourage them to click a primary subsection of your site and explore further. By placing an interactive table of contents up front, you direct surfers right to the material they're looking for.

The links to the most important areas of a site can go at or near the top of the page on either the left or right side.

TIP

Navigation can help with marketing: If you want to be ranked highly by search engines (and who doesn't?), you have another good reason to place your site's main topics near the top of the page in a series of links. Some search services index the first 50 or so words on a web page. Therefore, if you can get lots of important keywords included in that index, the chances are better that your site will be ranked highly in a list of links returned by the service in response to a search.

On a tablet or other mobile device, you need to arrange the most important links without flashy graphics. You don't have to design a simplified mobile version of your home page from scratch (although you can do so at www.striking.ly). Just make sure the marketplace or hosting service you choose automatically creates a mobile version of your site for you.

Open the web page you want to edit and follow these steps to create links to local files on your website by using Dreamweaver, the powerful and popular website creation software by Adobe Systems, Inc. (www.adobe.com):

1. **Select the text or image on your web page that you want to serve as the jumping-off point for the link.**

2. **Choose Insert ➪ Link or press Ctrl+L.**

3. **In the box in the Link Location section, enter the name of the file you want to link to if you know the filename.**

If the page you want to link to is in the same directory as the page that contains the jumping-off point, enter only the name of the web page. If the page is in another directory, enter a path relative to the web page that contains the link. Or click the Choose File button, locate the file in the Open HTML File dialog box, and click the Open button.

4. **Click OK.**

You return to the Composer window. If you made a textual link, the selected text is underlined and in a different color. If you made an image link, a box appears around the image.

REMEMBER

Presenting the reader with links upfront doesn't just help your search engine rankings, but also indicates that your site is content-rich and worthy of exploration.

Pointing the way with headings

Every web page needs to contain headings that direct the reader's attention to the most important contents. This book provides a good example. The chapter title (hopefully) piques your interest first. Then the section headings and subheadings direct you to more details on the topics you want to read about.

Most graphics designers label their heads with the letters of the alphabet: A, B, C, and so on. In a similar fashion, most web page–editing tools designate top-level headings with the style Heading 1. Beneath this, you place one or more Heading 2 headings. Beneath each of those, you may have Heading 3 and, beneath those, Heading 4. (Headings 5 and 6 are too small to be useful.) The arrangement may look like this (the following headings are indented for clarity; you don't have to indent them on your page):

```
Miss Cookie's Delectable Cooking School (Heading 1)
   Kitchen Equipment You Can't Live Without (Heading 2)
   The Story of a Calorie Counter Gone Wrong (Heading 2)
   Programs of Culinary Study (Heading 2)
      Registration (Heading 3)
      Course Schedule (Heading 3)
         New Course on Whipped Cream Just Added! (Heading 4)
```

TIP

You can energize virtually any heading by telling your audience something specific about your business. Instead of "Ida's Antiques Mall," for example, say something like "Ida's Antiques Mall: The Perfect Destination for the Collector and the Crafter." Instead of simply writing a heading like "Stan Thompson, Pet Grooming," say something specific, such as "Stan Thompson: We Groom Your Pet at Our Place or Yours."

YOUR WEB PAGE TITLE: THE ULTIMATE HEADING

When you're dreaming up clever headings for your web pages, don't overlook the "heading" that appears in the narrow title bar at the very top of your visitor's web browser window: the *title* of your web page.

The two HTML tags <title> and </title> contain the text that appears within the browser title bar. But you don't have to mess with these nasty HTML codes: All web page–creation programs give you an easy way to enter or edit a title for a web page. Make the title as catchy and specific as possible, but make sure it's no longer than 64 characters, including spaces. An effective title refers to your goods or services while grabbing the viewer's attention. If your business is Myrna's Cheesecakes, for example, you might make your title "Smile and Say Cheese! with Myrna's Cakes" (40 characters, including spaces).

Becoming an expert list maker

Lists are simple and effective ways to break up text and make your web content easier to digest. They're easy to create and easy for your customer to view and absorb. Suppose that you import your own decorations and want to offer certain varieties at a discount during various seasons. Rather than bury the items you're offering within an easily overlooked paragraph, why not divide your list into subgroups so that visitors find what they want without being distracted by holidays they don't even celebrate?

Lists are easy to implement. If you're using Microsoft Expression Web (a trial version is available at `www.microsoft.com/en-us/download/details.aspx?id=36179`), open your web page and follow these steps:

1. **Type a heading for your list and then select the entire heading.**

   For example, you might type and then select the words *This Month's Specials.*

2. **Choose a heading style from the Style drop-down list.**

   Your text is formatted as a heading.

3. **Click anywhere in Expression Web's Design View (the main editing window) to deselect the heading you just formatted.**

4. **Press Enter to move to a new line.**

5. **Type the first item of your list, press Enter, and then type the second item on the next line.**

6. **Repeat Step 5 until you enter all the items of your list.**

7. **Select all the items of your list (but not the heading).**

8. **Choose Format ⇨ Bullets and Numbering.**

   The List Properties dialog box appears.

9. **Choose one of the four bullet styles and click OK.**

   A bullet appears next to each list item, and the items appear closer together onscreen so that they look more like a list. That's all there is to it!

Most web editors let you vary the appearance of the bullet. For example, you can make the bullet a hollow circle rather than a solid black dot, or you can choose a rectangle rather than a circle.

Leading your readers on with links

You should interpret the preceding heading literally, not figuratively. In other words, don't make promises you can't deliver on. Rather, you should do anything you can to lead your visitors to your site and then get them to stay long enough to explore individual pages. You can accomplish this goal with a single hyperlinked word that leads to another page on your site:

More ...

This word is seen all the time on web pages that present a lot of content. At the bottom of a list of their products and services, businesses place that word in bold type: **More . . .** People are always interested in finding out what more the site could possibly have to offer them.

Magazines use the same approach. On their covers you find phrases that refer you to the kinds of stories you find inside. You can do the same kind of thing on your web pages. For example, which of the following links is more likely to get a response?

Next

Next: Paragon's Success Stories

REMEMBER

Whenever possible, tell your visitors what they can expect to encounter as a benefit when they click a link. Give them a tease — and then a big payoff for responding.

Enhancing your text with well-placed images

You can add two kinds of images to a web page: an *inline image,* which appears in the body of your page along with your text, or an *external image,* which is a separate file that visitors access by clicking a link. The link may take the form of highlighted text or a small version of the image — a *thumbnail.* You see lots of thumbnails when you do a search for images on Google Images (http://images. google.com).

The basic HTML tag that inserts an image in your document takes the following form:

```
<img src="URL">
```

This tag tells your browser to display an image (<img>) here. "URL" gives the location of the image file that serves as the source (src) for this image. Whenever possible, also include width and height attributes (as follows) because they help speed up graphics display for many browsers:

```
<img height=51 width=48 SRC="target.gif">
```

Most web page editors add the width and height attributes automatically when you insert an image. Typically, here's what happens:

1. Click the location in the web page where you want the image to appear.

2. Click an Image toolbar button or choose Insert⇨Image to display an image selection dialog box.

3. Enter the name of the image you want to add and click OK.

The image is added to your web page.

REMEMBER

A well-placed image points the way to text that you want people to read immediately. Think about where your own eyes go when you first connect to a web page. Most likely, you first look at any images on the page; then you look at the headings; finally, you settle on text to read. If you can place an image next to a heading, you virtually ensure that viewers read the heading.

Making your site searchable

A search box is one of the best kinds of content you can put on your website's opening page. A *search box* is a simple text-entry field that lets a visitor enter a word or phrase. Clicking a button labeled Go or Search sends the search term or terms to the site, where a script checks an index of the site's contents for any files that contain those terms. The script then lists documents that contain the search terms in the visitor's browser window.

Search boxes are not only found, but are expected to be found, on virtually all commercial websites. You usually see them at the top of the home page, near the links to the major sections of the site. Dummies.com, shown in Figure 5-4, includes a search box on the left side of the page.

FIGURE 5-4:
Many surfers prefer using a search box to clicking links.

© John Wiley & Sons, Inc.

Search boxes let visitors instantly scan the site's entire contents for a word or phrase. They put visitors in control right away and get them to interact with your site. They're popular for some very good reasons.

TECHNICAL STUFF

Search boxes require someone with knowledge of computer programming to create or implement a program called a CGI script to do the searching. Someone also has to compile an index of the documents on the website so that the script can search the documents. An application such as ColdFusion works well, but it's not a program for beginners.

But you can get around having to write CGI scripts to add search capabilities to your site. Choose one of these options:

>> **Let your web host do the work.** Some hosting services do the indexing and creation of the search utility as part of their services. Nearly all shopping carts and e-commerce storefront hosting services do.

>> **Use a free site search service.** The server that does the indexing of your web pages and holds the index doesn't need to be the server that hosts your site. Some services make your site searchable for free. In exchange, you display advertisements or logos in the search results you return to your visitors.

>> **Pay for a search service.** If you don't want to display ads on your search results pages, pay a monthly fee to have a company index your pages and let users conduct searches. FreeFind (www.freefind.com) has some economy packages, a free version that forces you to view ads, and a professional version that costs $19 per month for a site of 3,000 pages or less and $39 per month for a site of 6,000 pages or less. SiteMiner (http://siteminer.mycomputer.com) charges a monthly fee and lets you customize your search box and re-index your site whenever you add new content.

TIP

You say you're up to making your site searchable, but you shudder at the prospect of either writing your own computer script or finding and editing someone else's script to index your site's contents and actually do the searching? Check out FreeFind (www.freefind.com) and Webinator (www.thunderstone.com/texis/site/pages/webinator.html).

Nip and Tuck: Establishing a Visual Identity

The prospect of designing a website may be intimidating if you haven't tried it before. But it really boils down to a simple principle: *effective visual communication that conveys a particular message.* The first step in creating graphics isn't to open a painting program and start drawing, but to plan your page's message. Next, determine the audience you want to reach with that message and think about how your graphics can best communicate what you want to say. Some ways to do this are

>> **Gather ideas from websites that use graphics well.** Award-winning sites and sites created by designers who are using graphics in new or unusual ways can help you. To find some award winners, check out The Webby Awards (www.webbyawards.com) and the WebAward Competition (www.webaward.org).

>> **Use graphics consistently from page to page.** You can create an identity and convey a consistent message.

>> **Know your audience.** Create graphics that meet visitors' needs and expectations. If you're selling fashions to teenagers, go for bright colors and out-there graphics. If you're selling financial planning to senior citizens, choose a distinguished and sophisticated typeface.

TIP

How do you become acquainted with your customers when it's likely you'll never actually meet them face to face? Find newsgroups and mailing lists in which potential visitors to your site discuss subjects related to what you plan to publish on the web. Read the posted messages to get a sense of the concerns and vocabulary of your intended audience.

Choosing wallpaper that won't make you a wallflower

The technical term for the wallpaper behind the contents of a web page is its *background*. Most web browsers display the background of a page as light gray or white unless you specify something different. In this case, leaving well enough alone isn't good enough. If you choose the wrong background color (one that makes your text hard to read and your images look like they've been smeared with mud), viewers are likely to get the impression that the page is poorly designed or the author of the page hasn't put a great deal of thought into the project.

Most web page–creation programs offer a simple way to specify a color or an image file to serve as the background of a web page. For example, in the free editor Komodo Edit, you Ctrl-click the value next to the background-color command in the style sheet for the page you're working on (the section between the <style> and </style> tags). When the Color dialog box opens, click the color you want and then click OK. The hexadecimal code for your chosen color is added to the style sheet.

Color your website effective

You can use background and other colors to elicit a particular mood or emotion and convey your organization's identity on the web. The right choice of color can create impressions ranging from elegant to funky.

When selecting colors for your web pages, consider the demographics of your target audience. Do some research on what emotions or impressions are conveyed by different colors and which colors best match the mission or identity of your business. Refer to resources, such as the online essay "How to Get a Professional

Look With Color" by Webdesigner Depot (`www.webdesignerdepot.com/2009/12/how-to-get-a-professional-look-with-color`), which examines how color choices make web surfers react differently.

REMEMBER

The colors you use must have contrast so that they don't blend into one another. For example, you don't want to put purple type on a brown or blue background, or yellow type on a white background. Be sure to use light type against a dark background and dark type against a light background. That way, all your page's contents show up.

Tile images in the background

You can use an image rather than a solid color to serve as the background of a page. You specify an image in the style sheet code of your web page, and browsers automatically *tile* the image, reproducing it over and over to fill the current width and height of the browser window.

TIP

The fact is that few, if any, professional designers use background images any more. Background images worked only when they were subtle and didn't interfere with the page contents. Often, they were distracting. The emphasis these days is on easily accessible and readable content. Focus on that and make sure the background complements rather than interferes with your page's design. Choose an image with no obvious lines that create a distracting pattern when tiled. The effect you're trying to create should literally resemble wallpaper. Go to Google Images (`http://images.google.com`) and search for examples of background images that add something to a page's design.

Using web typefaces like a pro

If you create a web page and don't specify that the text be displayed in a particular font, the browser that displays the page uses its default font — which is usually Times New Roman or Helvetica (although individual users can customize their browsers by picking a different default font).

If you want to specify a typeface, the simplest option is to pick a generic font that is built into virtually every computer's operating system. This convention ensures that your web pages look more or less the same no matter what web browser or what type of computer displays them. A few choices available to you are Arial, Courier, Century Schoolbook, and Times New Roman.

However, you don't have to limit yourself to the same-old/same-old. You can exercise a degree of control over the appearance of your web page by specifying that the body type and headings be displayed in a particular nonstandard font. You have to own the font you want to use; you save it on your computer and identify the font and location in the cascading style sheets (CSS) for your website.

TIP

You can copy unusual fonts from dafont.com (`www.dafont.com`). Its creators some-times ask for donations for their work. You can generate CSS commands for such typefaces with the aid of Font Squirrel's Webfont Generator (`www.fontsquirrel.com/tools/webfont-generator`). You then copy and paste the CSS into the style sheet for your page so you can use the font for either headings or body text.

Where do you specify type fonts, colors, and sizes for the text? Again, special HTML tags or CSS commands tell web browsers what fonts to display, but you don't need to mess with these tags yourself if you're using a web page creation tool. The specific steps you take depend on what web design tool you're using. In Dreamweaver, you can specify a group of preferred typefaces rather than a single font in the Properties inspector. Check the Help files with your own program to find out how to format text and what typeface options you have.

TIP

Not all typefaces are equal in the eye of the user. Serif typefaces, such as Times New Roman, are considered more readable (at least, for printed materials) than sans-serif fonts, such as Helvetica. However, an article on the Web Marketing Today website (`http://webmarketingtoday.com/articles/html-email-fonts`) found that by a whopping 2:1 margin, the sans serif font Arial is considered more readable on a web page than Times New Roman.

TIP

If you want to make sure that a heading or block of type appears in a specific typeface (especially a nonstandard one that isn't displayed as body text by web browsers), scan it or create the heading in an image-editing program and insert it into the page as a graphic image. But make sure it doesn't clash with the generic typefaces that appear on the rest of your page.

Using clip art is free and fun

Not everyone has the time or resources to scan photos or create original graphics. But that doesn't mean you can't add graphic interest to your web page. Many web page designers use clip-art bullets, diamonds, or other small images next to list items or major web page headings that they want to call special attention to. Clip art can also provide a background pattern for a web page or highlight sales head-ings, such as Free!, New!, or Special!.

Here are some suggestions for tried-and-true sources of clip art on the web:

>> Clipart.com (`www.clipart.com/en`)

>> Clip Art Universe (`http://clipartuniverse.com`)

Be sure to read the copyright fine print *before* you copy graphics. All artists own the copyright to their work. It's up to them to determine how they want to give someone else the right to copy their work. Sometimes, the authors require you to pay a small fee if you want to copy their work, or they may restrict use of their work to nonprofit organizations.

A picture is worth a thousand words

Some customers know exactly what they want from the get-go and don't need any help from you. But most customers love to shop around or could use some encouragement to move from one item or catalog page to another. This is where images can play an important role.

Even if you use only some basic clip art, such as placing spheres or arrows next to sale items, your customer is likely to thank you by buying more. A much better approach, though, is to scan or take digital images of your sale items and provide compact, clear images of them on your site. Here's a quick step-by-step guide to get you started:

1. **Choose the right image to capture.**

   The original quality of an image is just as important as how you scan or retouch it. Images that are murky or fuzzy in print are even worse when viewed on a computer screen.

2. **Preview the image.**

   Digital cameras let you preview images so that you can decide whether to keep or delete individual pictures before downloading to your computer. If you're working with a scanner, some scanning programs let you make a quick *preview scan* of an image so that you can get an idea of what it looks like before you do the actual scan. When you click the Preview button, the optical device in the scanner captures the image. A preview image appears onscreen, surrounded by a *marquee box* (a rectangle made up of dashes).

3. **Crop the image.**

   Cropping means that you resize the box around the image to select the portion of the image that you want to keep and leave out the parts of the image that aren't essential. Cropping an image is a good idea because it highlights the most important contents and reduces the file size. Reducing the file size of an image should always be one of your most important goals — the smaller the image, the quicker it appears in someone's browser window.

Almost all scanning and graphics programs offer separate options for cropping an image and reducing the image size. By cropping the image, you eliminate parts of the image you don't want, and this *does* reduce the image size. But it doesn't reduce the size of the objects within the image. Resizing the overall image size is a separate step, which enables you to change the dimensions of the entire image without eliminating any contents.

4. **Select an input mode.**

   Tell the scanner or graphics program how you want it to save the visual data — as color, line art (used for black-and-white drawings), or grayscale (used for black-and-white photos).

5. **Set the resolution.**

   Digital images are made up of little bits (dots) of computerized information called *pixels.* The more pixels per inch, the higher the level of detail. When you scan an image, you can tell the scanner to make the dots smaller (creating a smoother image) or larger (resulting in a more jagged image). This adjustment is called *setting the resolution* of the image. (When you take a digital photo, the resolution of the image depends on your camera's settings.)

   When you're scanning for the web, your images appear primarily on computer screens. Because many computer monitors can display resolutions only up to 72 dpi, 72 dpi — a relatively rough resolution — is an adequate resolution for a web image. Using this coarse resolution has the advantage of keeping the image's file size small. Remember, the smaller the file size, the more quickly an image appears when your customers load your page in their web browsers. (Alternatively, many designers scan at a fine resolution such as 300 dpi and reduce the file size in a graphics program.)

6. **Adjust contrast and brightness.**

   Virtually all scanning programs and graphics editing programs provide brightness and contrast controls that you can adjust with your mouse to improve the image. If you're happy with the image as is, leave the brightness and contrast set where they are. (You can also leave the image as is and adjust brightness and contrast later in a separate graphics program, such as Paint Shop Pro 2019, which you can try out by downloading it from the Corel website, www.corel.com/corel.)

7. **Reduce the image size.**

   The old phrase "Good things come in small packages" is never truer than when you're improving your digital image. If you're scanning an image that is 8" x 10" and you're sure that it needs to be about 4" x 5" when it appears on your web page, scan it at 50 percent of the original size. This step reduces the file size and makes the file easier to transport, whether it's from your camera to your computer or your computer to your hosting service. Even more important, it appears more quickly in someone's web browser.

8. **Scan away!**

   Your scanner makes a beautiful whirring sound as it turns those colors into pixels. Because you're scanning only at 72 dpi, the process shouldn't take too long.

9. **Save the file.**

   Now you can save your image to disk. Most programs let you do this by choosing File ➪ Save. In the dialog box that appears, enter a name for your file and select a file format. (Because you're working with images to be published on the web, save either in GIF or JPEG format.)

TIP

Be sure to add the correct filename extension. Web browsers recognize only image files with extensions such as .gif, .jpg, or .jpeg. If you name your image product and save it in GIF format, call it product.gif. If you save it in JPEG format and you're using a PC, call it product.jpg. On a Mac, call it product.jpeg.

Creating a logo

An effective logo establishes your online business's graphic identity in no uncertain terms. A logo can be as simple as a rendering of the company name that imparts an official typeface or color. Whatever text it includes, a *logo* is a small, self-contained graphic object that conveys the group's identity and purpose.

REMEMBER

A logo doesn't have to be a fabulously complex drawing with drop shadows and gradations of color. A simple, type-only logo can be as good as gold. Pick a typeface, choose your graphic's outline version, and fill the letters with color.

Inviting Comments from Customers

Quick, inexpensive, and *personal:* These are three of the most important advantages that the web has over traditional printed catalogs. The first two are obvious pluses. You don't have to wait for your online catalog to get printed and distributed. On the web, your contents are published and available to your customers right away. Putting a catalog on the web eliminates (or, if publishing a catalog on the web allows you to reduce your print run, dramatically reduces) the cost of printing, which can result in big savings for you.

But the fact that online catalogs can be more personal than the printed variety is perhaps the biggest advantage of all. The personal touch comes from the web's potential for *interactivity.* Getting your customers to click links makes them actively involved with your catalog.

Getting positive email feedback

Playing hide-and-seek is fun when you're amusing your baby niece, but it's not a good way to build a solid base of customers. In fact, providing a way for your customers to interact with you so that they can reach you quickly may be the most important part of your website.

Add a simple mailto link like this:

Questions? Comments? Send email to: info@mycompany.com

A mailto link gets its name from the HTML command that programmers use to create it. When visitors click the email address, their email program opens a new email message window with your email address already entered. That way, they have only to enter a subject line, type the message, and click Send to send you their thoughts.

Most web page–creation programs make it easy to create a mailto link. For example, if you use Dreamweaver, follow these steps:

1. **Launch and open the web page to which you want to add your email link.**

2. **Position your mouse arrow and click the spot on the page where you want the address to appear.**

   The convention is to put your email address at or near the bottom of a web page. A vertical blinking cursor appears at the location where you want to insert the address.

3. **Choose Insert ⇨ Email Link.**

   The Insert Email Link dialog box appears.

4. **In the Text box, type the text that you want to appear on your web page.**

   You don't have to type your email address; you can also type **Webmaster, Customer Service,** or your own name.

5. **In the Email box, type your email address.**

6. **Click OK.**

   The Insert Email Link dialog box closes, and you return to the Dreamweaver Document window, where your email link appears in blue and is underlined to signify that it is a clickable link.

Other editors work similarly but don't give you a menu command called Email Link. In that case, you have to type the mailto link manually. In the WordPress editor, select the text you want to serve as the link and click the link toolbar icon.

When the Insert/Edit Link dialog box opens, in the URL box, after http:// (which is pre-entered), you type mailto:name@emailaddress.

WARNING

The drawback to publishing your email address directly on your web page is that you're certain to get unsolicited email messages (commonly called *spam*) sent to that address. Hiding your email address behind generic link text (such as Webmaster) may help reduce your chances of attracting spam.

Web page forms that aren't off-putting

You don't have to do much web surfing before you become intimately acquainted with how web page forms work, at least from the standpoint of someone who has to fill them out to sign up for web hosting or to download software.

When it comes to creating your own website, however, you become conscious of how useful forms are as a means of gathering essential marketing information about your customers. They give your visitors a place to sound off, ask questions, and generally get involved with your online business.

REMEMBER

Be clear and use common sense when creating your order form. Here are some general guidelines on how to organize your form and what you need to include:

>> **Make it easy on the customer.** Whenever possible, add pull-down menus with pre-entered options to your *form fields* (text boxes that visitors use to enter information). That way, users don't have to wonder about things such as whether you want them to spell out a state or use the two-letter abbreviation.

>> **Validate the information.** You can use a programming language — for example, JavaScript — to ensure that users enter information correctly, that all fields are completely filled out, and so on. You may have to hire someone to add the appropriate code to the order form, but the expense is worth it to save you from having to call customers to verify or correct information that they missed or submitted incorrectly.

>> **Provide a help number.** Give people a number to call if they have questions or want to check on an order.

>> **Return an acknowledgment.** Let customers know that you have received their order and will be shipping the merchandise immediately or contacting them if more information is needed.

As usual, good web page–authoring and –editing programs make it a snap to create the text boxes, check boxes, buttons, and other parts of a form that the user fills out. The other part of a form, the computer script that receives the data and processes it so that you can read and use the information, isn't as simple.

And programs like WordPress provide you with a host of add-on applications — *plugins* — that create both the text entry elements and the scripts for you.

TIP

Not so long ago, you had to write or edit a scary CGI script to set up forms processing on your website. Now you can use WordPress plugins, or if you use another application, check out a service like Response-O-Matic (`www.response-o-matic.com`) or FormMail.To (`www.formmail.to/formmail.to`). These lead you through the process of setting up a form and providing you with the CGI script that receives the data and forwards it to you.

Blogs that promote discussion

Most blogs give readers the chance to respond to individual comments the author has made. This is a standard feature to give readers the opportunity to comment on what you've written.

On blogs that attract a wide following, like Talking Points Memo (`www.talkingpointsmemo.com`), comments by multiple authors generate long discussions by a community of devoted readers.

The comments that appear at the end of an article or blog post have replaced what web designers used to call a *guestbook* — a place where visitors signed in so they could feel that they're part of a thriving community. If you use WordPress to create and manage a blog or website, you can easily give visitors the ability to comment on an article. If you have created a blog, each post is automatically "commentable." That's one of the many nice things about WordPress. You just have to make sure commenting is turned on.

Log in to WordPress and click Settings under the heading Admin Options in the narrow column on the left side of the editing window. Then click Discussion and select the Allow check box so people can post comments on new articles.

To enable comments on an individual page, follow these steps:

1. **Click Pages in the Admin settings in the narrow column on the left side of the editing window.**

   The list of pages in your WordPress site appears.

2. **Click the page you want, and if necessary, click Quick Edit.**

   The Quick Edit window for your page opens.

3. **Scroll down to the Discussion section and select the Allow check box.**

After you allow comments, be sure to log in to your site regularly to moderate them. You'll probably have to delete spam comments left by *bots* (programs that perform automated functions such as "scraping" web pages for contents) that post them automatically and respond to legitimate comments that actual human beings have left.

Chit-chat that counts

After visitors start coming to your site, the next step is to retain those visitors. A good way to do this is by building a sense of community by posting a bulletin board–type discussion area.

A discussion area takes the form of back-and-forth messages on topics of mutual interest. Each person can read previously posted messages and either respond or start a new topic of discussion. The comments areas discussed in the preceding section are the most popular ways of promoting this sort of interaction. For a more elaborate example of a discussion area that's tied to an online business, visit the EcommerceBytes (www.ecommercebytes.com) discussion areas. EcommerceBytes is a highly regarded site that provides information about the online auction indus-try. Its discussion boards give readers a place to bring up questions and issues in a forum that's independent from those provided by auction sites like eBay.

The talk doesn't have to be about your particular niche in your business field. In fact, the discussion is livelier if your visitors can discuss concerns about your area of business in general, whether it's flower arranging, boat sales, tax preparation, clock repair, computers, or whatever.

How do you start a discussion area? The basic first step is to install a special computer script on the computer that hosts your website. (Again, discussing this prospect with your web hosting service beforehand is essential.) When visitors come to your site, their web browsers access the script, enabling them to enter comments and read other messages.

Here are some specific ways to prepare a discussion area for your site:

>> Copy a bulletin board or discussion-group script from either of these sites:

   - eXtropia.com (www.extropia.com/applications.html)
   - Matt's Script Archive (www.scriptarchive.com)

>> Start your own forum on a service such as vBulletin (www.vbulletin.com)

Moving from Website to Web Presence

After you have established a visual identity through colors, images, and a logo, you can "brand" yourself by "popping up" in as many web venues as possible. Make no mistake about it: Tending to your image and building a name for yourself takes time and effort. It might take one, two, or more hours every day. And once you start blogging and building an audience, you need to keep at it every few days, if not *every* day. Otherwise, those fickle web visitors you worked so hard to cultivate will flit away to someone else's website or blog or Facebook page.

TIP

How do you "pop up" in places where people will find you? You'll find suggestions throughout this book. Here are a few ideas:

» Start up a blog and use it to comment on your area of interest. (See Chapter 6 in Book 5.)

» Twitter as much as possible; short "tweets" can advertise new products or sales you have running. (Again, see Chapter 6 in Book 5.)

» Get on Facebook and start cultivating a circle of friends. Use Facebook to point them to your website — and your blog, your tweets, and so on. (You guessed it — see Chapter 6 in Book 5.)

» Open a storefront on eBay or on a free site like eCRATER (www.ecrater.com).

The art of having a web presence is using all these sites to point to one another, so no matter where you are, shoppers are directed to your products or services, or at least prompted to find out more about you.

Chapter **6**

Starting with the Right Legal Structure

C hoosing the legal form for organizing your business is one of the important decisions you must make before launching the business. Because of changing laws, entrepreneurs today have many more choices regarding how to structure their companies. Your need for capital and protection from liability are just two reasons why understanding the options available to you is so essential.

Those changing laws are also a good reason for seeking the advice of a good attorney or certified public accountant (CPA) to make sure you're making the best choice for you and your type of business.

This chapter gives you a solid background on what you need to think about before choosing a legal form of business and what you need to understand about of the various forms available to you.

Introducing the Legal Business Classifications

All companies operate under one of four broad legal classifications:

>> Sole proprietorship

>> Partnership

>> Corporation

>> Limited Liability Company (LLC)

Many entrepreneurs assume that the best entity is always one that lets profits pass through to the owners at their personal tax rate. They further assume that incorporating in your home state is always best. These assumptions can be wrong for some entrepreneurs and for some businesses.

For example, if you know that you want to do an IPO (initial public offering) within two years, you should probably form as a C Corporation, because that form is required to go public. If you're going to use venture capital, you probably also want a C corporate form, and you may want to incorporate in California or Delaware. Why? Those states have a substantial body of law in the area of corporate governance. Choosing the wrong entity when speed is of the essence (consider the case of Internet start-ups) can mean costly delays and lost opportunities.

Understanding the various factors that come into play when you choose a particular form of legal structure is important. Seven factors affect your choice of structure. A summary comparison of these factors appears in Figure 6-1.

REMEMBER

Here the factors are presented in the form of questions you can ask yourself:

1. **Who will be the owners of the company?**

   If more than one individual owns the company, you can eliminate sole proprietorship as an option. If many people own the company, the C Corporation form is often the choice because it has an unlimited life and free transferability of interests. If you intend to have many employees, the C Corporation also lets you take advantage of pension plans and stock option plans.

2. **What level of liability protection do you require, especially for your personal assets?**

   Some forms protect you; others don't. It's a sad fact that too many businesses ignore the risks they face and don't acquire the correct forms of insurance. Just as you want to seek the advice of an attorney and accountant as you develop your business, you also want to consider the advice of an insurance broker.

Issues	Sole Proprietorship	Partnership	S Corp.	Limited Liability Company	C Corp.
Number of owners	One	No limit	100	No limit	No limit on shareholders
Liability	Owner liable for all claims against business	General partners liable for all claims. Limited partners only to amount of investment	Limited liability	Members liable as in partnerships	Shareholders liable to amount invested. Officers may be personally liable
Life of Business	Dissolution on the death of the owner	Dissolution on the death or separation of a partner unless otherwise specified in the agreement. Not so in the case of limited partners	Continuity of life	Continuity of life	No effect
Transfer of Interest	Owner free to sell	General partner requires consent of other generals to sell interest. Limiteds' ability subject to agreement	Subject to agreement	Free transferability of interests subject to agreement	Shareholders free to sell unless restricted by agreement
Distribution of Profits	Profits go to owner	Profits shared based on partnership agreement	Profits go to owners	Profits go to members	Paid to shareholders as dividends according to agreement and shareholder status
Management Control	Owner has full control	Shared by general partners according to partnership agreement	Shared by owners/ shareholders	Rests with management committee (owners or those shareholders)	Rests with the board of directors appointed by the shareholders

FIGURE 6-1:
This chart shows a summary comparison of legal categories of business organization.

© John Wiley & Sons, Inc.

3. **How do you expect to distribute the company's earnings?**

If you choose an entity allowing pass-through income and losses (partnership, S Corporation, or LLC), tax items at the entity level are allocated immediately without additional taxation, although cash may or may not be distributed. But in a C Corporation, only a salary or other forms of compensation are paid out pretax from the company to an owner.

4. **What are the operating requirements of your business and the costs of running the business under the particular form in question?**

If you own a manufacturing company that uses a lot of machinery, you have different liabilities than a service company.

5. **What are your financing plans?**

   How attractive is the form to potential investors? Are you able to offer owner-ship interests to investors and employees? In general, as already mentioned, if you're going to use venture capital, you need a corporate form. Most venture capitalists raise their money from tax-exempt entities such as pension funds, universities, and charitable organizations. These organizations can't invest in companies that have pass-through tax benefits.

6. **What will be the effect on the company's tax strategy and your personal tax strategy?**

   This includes everything from minimizing tax liability, converting ordinary income to capital gain, and avoiding multiple taxation to maximizing the benefits of startup losses.

7. **Do you expect the company to generate a profit or loss in the beginning?**

   If you think your company will lose money for the first few years (this is often true with biotech or other companies developing new products), then a pass-through option can be justified because you get to deduct your losses on your personal tax return.

Going It Alone: The Sole Proprietorship

Most businesses operating in the United States are sole proprietorships. A *sole proprietorship* is a business where the owner essentially *is* the business; that is, he or she is solely responsible for the activities of the business and is the only one to enjoy the profits and suffer the losses of the business.

Why do so many businesses start this way? Sole proprietorship is the easiest and least expensive way to form a business. If you're using your own name as the name of the business, all you need is a business license, some business cards, and you're in, uh, business.

Deciding to use another name for your business is only slightly more complex. For example, in the case of ABC Associates, you apply for a DBA, which is a certificate of Doing Business under an Assumed name. You can secure a DBA at your local government office. Securing a DBA ensures that two businesses don't operate in the same county with the same name.

Advantages of sole proprietorships

Besides being the easiest to start and least expensive form of organization, sole proprietorship also gives the owner complete control of the company. You make all the decisions and suffer all the consequences, but the income from the business is yours and you're taxed only once at your personal income tax rate.

Many professionals, such as consultants, authors, and many home-based business owners, operate as sole proprietors.

Disadvantages of sole proprietorships

WARNING

For many entrepreneurs, the sole proprietorship form of organization isn't satisfactory, for several reasons:

>> As a sole proprietor, you have unlimited liability for any claims against the business. In other words, you are putting your personal assets at risk — your home, car, bank accounts, and any other assets you may have. So, having business liability and errors and omissions insurance is extremely important. If you're producing a product, you'll need product liability insurance to protect you against lawsuits over defective products. If your company does work for other people (such as a construction company), you may be required to have bonding insurance to ensure that you complete the work specified in your contract. Because there are so many areas of liability and so many different types of insurance, you should talk to a good insurance broker.

>> Raising capital is difficult, because you're relying only on your financial statement. You are, for all intents and purposes, the business, and most investors don't like that situation.

>> You probably won't have a management team with diverse skills helping you grow your business. You may have employees, but that isn't really the same thing. Putting together an advisory board of people with skills you need may help compensate for the skills you lack.

>> Because the survival of your company depends on you being there, if something happens to you or a catastrophe strikes, the company doesn't survive. Legally, if the sole proprietor dies, so does the business, unless its assets are willed to someone.

If you intend to really grow your business, organizing as a sole proprietorship may not be a good idea, unless you're taking advantage of income and control benefits during the early stages of your business — for example, through product development.

Choosing a Partner: The Partnership

A *partnership* is two or more people deciding to share the assets, liabilities, and profits of their business. Partnering is often an improvement over the sole proprietorship because more people are sharing the responsibilities of the business and bouncing ideas off each other. Additionally, you now have multiple financial statements on which to rely and an entity that usually survives if one of the partners dies or leaves.

In terms of liability, though, you're raising the stakes, because each partner becomes liable for the obligations incurred by other partners in the course of doing business. This *doctrine of ostensible authority* works like this: Suppose one of your partners enters a contract on behalf of the partnership, purchasing certain goods from a supplier. That partner has just bound the partnership to make good on a contract even if the rest of the partners knew nothing about it. The one major exception is that personal debts of an individual partner can't attach to the rest of the partners.

On the positive side, each partner uses any property owned by the partnership and shares in the profits and losses of the partnership unless otherwise stated in the partnership agreement. Partners don't have to share equally in the profits and losses. Ownership in the partnership can be divided in any manner the partners choose. The biggest issue with partnerships is that they often are fraught with conflict in much the same way as family businesses. However, when you think about it, any business that includes a team of entrepreneurs, whether a corporation or limited liability company, has similar issues. The partnership agreement, therefore, becomes important from the beginning.

Forming a partnership

You don't have to have a written agreement when forming a partnership; a simple oral agreement works. In fact, in some cases, the conduct of the parties involved implies a partnership.

REMEMBER

Accepting a share of the profits of a business is *prima facie* (legally sufficient) evidence that you are a partner in the business, meaning that you may also be liable for its losses.

Partnerships come in several flavors. In most partnerships, entrepreneurs are general partners, meaning they share in the profits, losses, and responsibilities, and are personally liable for actions of the partnership. But other types of partners have more limited liability, including the following:

>> **Limited partners:** These partners' liability generally is limited to the amount of their investment.

>> **Secret partners:** These partners are active in the ventures but are unknown to the public.

>> **Silent partners:** These partners are usually inactive with only a financial interest in the partnership.

The partnership agreement

It's hard to overstate the importance of a partnership agreement. Many a prospective partner says things like "We've been the best of friends for years; we know what we're doing," or "How can I ask my father to sign a partnership agreement?" Well, how can you not? You must separate business from friendship and family, at least when it comes to structuring your company. This is a serious deal. No matter how well you know your partner, you probably haven't worked with him or her in this particular kind of situation. You have no way of predicting all the things that can cause a disagreement with your partner. The partnership agreement gives you an unbiased mechanism for resolving disagreements or dissolving the partnership, if it comes to that.

REMEMBER

Consulting an attorney is necessary when drawing up an agreement, so that you're not inadvertently causing yourself further problems by the way a phrase is worded in the agreement or leaving something important out. The partnership agreement addresses the following:

>> The legal name of the partnership.

>> The nature of your business.

>> How long the partnership is to last. As with any contract, it needs a stop date.

>> What each of the partners is contributing to the partnership — capital, in-kind goods, services, and so forth. This is the *initial capitalization.*

>> Any sales, loans, or leases to the partnership.

>> Who is responsible for what — the management of the partnership.

>> The sale of a partnership interest. This clause restricts a partner's right to sell his or her interest to third parties. It provides, however, a method by which a partner can divest his or her interest in the partnership.

>> How the partnership can be dissolved.

>> What happens if a partner leaves or dies.

>> How disputes will be resolved.

If you don't execute a partnership agreement, all partners are equal under the law.

Going for the Gold: The Corporation

A *corporation* is a legal entity under the law and has continuity of life. Chartered or registered by the state in which it resides, a corporation can survive the death or separation of all of its owners. It can also sue, be sued, acquire and sell real property, and lend money.

Corporation owners are called *stockholders.* They invest capital into the corporation and receive shares of stock, usually proportionate to the level of their investment. Much like limited partners, shareholders aren't responsible for the debts of the corporation (unless they have personally guaranteed them), and their investment is the limit of their liability.

This chapter covers two major types of corporations: the C Corporation (closely held, close, and public) and the S Corporation. Most corporations are C Corporations and are closely held, which means stock is held privately by a few individuals. A closely held corporation operates as any type of corporation — general, professional, or nonprofit. But in a close corporation, the number of shareholders you may have is restricted, usually to between 30 and 50 shareholders. In addition, holding directors' meetings isn't required. Such meetings are a requirement for an S Corporation. The C Corporation isn't available in every state and doesn't permit you to conduct an initial public offering. Basically, a close corporation operates much like a partnership.

Doctors, lawyers, accountants, and other professionals who previously weren't allowed to incorporate use professional corporations. This vehicle now lets professionals enjoy tax-free and tax-deferred fringe benefits. You should be aware that only members of the specific profession can be shareholders in the corporation. In a professional corporation, all the shareholders are liable for negligent or wrongful acts of any shareholder.

By contrast, in a public corporation, stock is traded on a securities exchange like the New York Stock Exchange, and the company generally has thousands (in some cases, millions) of shareholders. For space concerns, and because most people starting a business choose the C Corporation type over the S, the focus here is on C Corporations.

Three groups of individuals — shareholders, directors, and officers — make up the corporate structure. Shareholders own the corporation but they don't manage it. Shareholders exert influence through the directors they elect to serve and represent them on the board. The board of directors, in turn, manages the affairs of the corporation at a policy level and hires and fires the officers who are responsible for the day-to-day decisions of the company.

Public corporations in most states in the U.S. require only one director, but in some states, the number of shareholders you have determines the number of directors. However, you can always have more directors for many different reasons. If you are forming a corporation in a country other than the U.S., check with the local government to find out the requirements for boards of directors. The rules differ from country to country.

What is surprising for many is in the U.S., corporations comprise a small minority of all businesses, yet they generate most of the sales. Part of this surprising picture is attributable to the fact that most entrepreneurs who intend to grow their companies choose the corporate form for its many benefits.

Enjoying the benefits of a corporation

The advantages of a corporate form definitely outweigh the disadvantages. For one, the owners enjoy limited liability to the extent of their investment (the one important exception is payroll taxes that haven't been paid to the IRS). By selecting the corporate form, you also can do the following:

>> Raise capital through the sale of stock in the company.

>> Own a corporation without the public being aware of your involvement. So, if you want anonymity, it's the way to go.

>> Create different classes of stock to help you meet the various needs of investors. For example, you may want to issue nonvoting, preferred stock to conservative investors wanting to be first to recoup their investment in the event the business fails. Most stock issued is *common* stock, the owners of which enjoy voting rights and share in the profits after the preferred stock has been paid.

>> Easily transfer ownership. In a private corporation, you want assurances that your shareholders can't sell their stock to just anyone. In other words, you want to know who owns your stock. You can protect yourself by including a buy-sell clause in the stockholder's agreement. Usually, this clause specifies that the stock must first be offered to the corporation at an agreed-upon price.

>> Enter into corporate contracts and sue or be sued without the signatures of the owners.

>> Enjoy more status in the business world than other legal forms because corporations survive apart from their owners.

>> Enjoy the benefits of setting up retirement funds, Keogh and defined-contribution plans, profit sharing, and stock option plans. The corporation deducts these fringe benefits as expenses that aren't taxable to the employee.

Weighing the risks

WARNING

Every legal form has disadvantages and risks, and the corporation is no exception. Here are risks worth considering when contemplating using the corporate form:

>> Corporations are much more complex, cumbersome, and expensive to set up.

>> Corporations are subject to more government regulation.

>> A corporation pays taxes on profits regardless of whether they are distributed as dividends to stockholders.

>> Shareholders of C Corporations don't receive the tax benefits of company losses.

>> By selling shares of stock in your corporation, you're effectively giving up a measure of control to a board of directors. The reality, however, is that the entrepreneur determines who sits on that board of directors in privately held corporations.

>> You must keep your personal finances and the corporation's finances completely separate. You must conduct directors' meetings, and maintain minutes from those meetings. If you don't, you may leave your company open to what is known as piercing the corporate veil, which makes you and your officers liable personally for the company.

Where and how to incorporate

You create a corporation by filing a certificate of incorporation with the state in which you do business and issue stock, making your company a *domestic* corporation. If you incorporate in a state other than the one in which you do business, your company is a *foreign* corporation.

REMEMBER

In general, you want to incorporate in the state where you're planning to locate the business so that you don't find yourself working under the regulations of two states. When deciding where to incorporate, consider the following:

>> **The cost difference of incorporating in your home state versus doing business as a foreign corporation in another state:** In general, if you're doing business mostly in your home state, incorporating there won't subject you to taxes and annual report fees from both states.

>> **The advantages and disadvantages of the other state's corporate laws and tax structure:** For example, in some states, a corporation pays a minimum state tax regardless of whether it makes a profit, whereas other states have no minimum state tax. Likewise, if you're incorporating anywhere other than your home state and find yourself defending a lawsuit in the state of incorporation, you may incur the expense of travel back and forth during that time.

Offering Flexibility: The S Corporation, the LLC, and the Nonprofit Corporation

A number of different legal organizational forms offer flexibility for entrepreneurs in a variety of ways. This section looks at three: the S Corporation, the LLC, and the nonprofit. All the criteria used for making a decision about which form to choose apply to these as well.

Sizing up the S Corporation

An S Corporation is a corporation that elects and is eligible to choose S Corporation status, and shareholders at the time consent to the corporation's choice. In general, an S Corporation doesn't pay any income tax. Instead, the corporation's income and deductions are passed through to its shareholders. The shareholders must then report the income and deductions on their own income tax returns.

An S Corporation can provide employee benefits and deferred compensation plans. To qualify for S Corporation status, you must

1. Form your corporation with no more than 100 shareholders, none of whom may be nonresident aliens.

2. Issue only one class of stock.

3. Ensure no more than 25 percent of the corporate income is derived from passive investments like dividends, rent, and capital gains.

In addition, your S Corporation can't be a financial institution, a foreign corporation, or a subsidiary of a parent corporation. If you elect to change from an S Corporation to a C Corporate form, you can't go back to being an S Corporation form for five years.

In general, S Corporations work best

>> When you expect to experience a loss in the first year or two, and owners have other income they can shelter with that loss.

>> Where shareholders have low tax brackets (lower than the corporate rate), so the profits can be distributed as dividends without double taxation.

>> Where your business may incur an accumulated earnings penalty tax for failure to pay out its profits as dividends.

Comparing the S Corporation to the LLC

The Limited Liability Company (LLC) is the newest legal form of business organization, and although it's gaining in popularity for many entrepreneurs, it confuses the many choices they already face in structuring their companies. The LLC combines the best of partnerships (pass-through earnings) with the best of the corporate form (limited liability). LLCs have grown in popularity because they

>> Limit liability for business debts up to the amount invested.

>> Offer flexible management structure that allows the *members* (the equivalent of shareholders in a corporation) or *nonmembers* they hire to manage the organization.

>> Allow the choice of being treated as a partnership with the benefits of pass-through earnings or as a corporation, whichever provides the lowest tax liability.

>> Enable flexible distribution of profits and losses, meaning that you can divide them up any way you want among the members.

So what are the differences between an LLC and an S Corporation? Why would you choose one over the other?

>> An LLC provides for an unlimited number of owners, whereas the S Corporation limits you to 100.

>> An LLC permits you to include nonresident aliens, pension plans, partnerships, and corporations as members, whereas the S Corporation doesn't.

> » LLCs can have different classes of stock, whereas an S Corporation is generally limited to one class.

The members of an LLC are analogous to partners in a partnership or shareholders in a corporation. If the members self-manage, then the members act more like partners than shareholders, because they have a direct say in what happens within the organization. Stock in an LLC is known as *interest.*

TIP

If you're looking for more flexibility in what you're able to do in the long term, you would probably choose an LLC over an S Corporation.

Making profits in a nonprofit organization

Let's dispel the biggest myth about nonprofit organizations first. You *can* make a profit in a nonprofit company; in fact, doing so is a good idea. What you can't do is distribute those profits in the form of dividends the way other legal forms do. A nonprofit (or not-for-profit corporation) is formed for charitable, public (in other words, scientific, literary, or educational), religious, or mutual benefit (as in trade associations).

Like the C Corporation, the nonprofit is a legal entity with a life of its own and offers its members limited liability. Profits that it generates from its nonprofit activities aren't taxed as long as the company meets the state and federal requirements for exemption from taxes under IRS 501(c)(3). When you form a nonprofit, you actually give up proprietary interest in the corporation and dedicate all the assets and resources to tax-exempt activities. If you choose to dissolve the corporation, you must distribute those assets to another tax-exempt organization — you can't take them with you. Any profits you make from for-profit activities are taxed the same as any other corporation.

Nonprofit organizations derive their revenues from a variety of sources. They receive donations from corporations (which are tax deductible to the corporation) and others, conduct activities to raise money, or sell services (a for-profit activity). As entrepreneurs, founders of nonprofit, tax-exempt corporations can pay themselves a good salary, provide themselves with cars, and generally do the kinds of things you would do within a normal corporation — except distribute profits.

Most entrepreneurs who start nonprofits do so for reasons other than money — for example, a driving need to give back to the community. James Blackman founded the Civic Light Opera of South Bay Cities, Redondo Beach, California, providing a cultural arts center for the community. The opera became the third-largest musical theater in California and has won many awards. Blackman's company also provides opportunities for physically and mentally challenged children to experience music and the theater.

Benchmarking Your Best Choice

After you've gotten a good overview of what's available, Figure 6-2 offers a strategy for choosing the best legal form for your new business. Starting with the first question, work your way down, mapping an easy way to find your alternatives and organize your business.

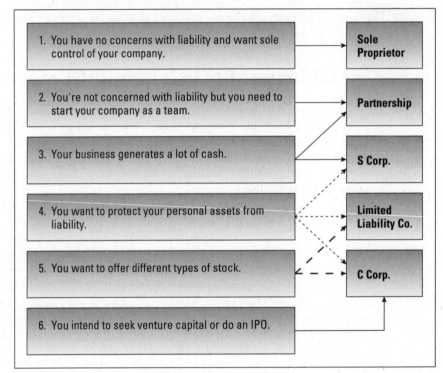

FIGURE 6-2:
Six questions point you in the right direction for choosing your legal organization.

© John Wiley & Sons, Inc.

3

Handling Your Finances

Contents at a Glance

Chapter **1**

Setting Up the Books

All businesses need to keep track of their financial transactions — that's why bookkeeping and bookkeepers are so important. Without accurate records, how can you tell whether your business is making a profit or taking a loss?

The first part of this chapter covers the key parts of bookkeeping by introducing you to the language of bookkeeping, familiarizing you with how bookkeepers manage the accounting cycle, and showing you how to understand the most difficult type of bookkeeping — double-entry bookkeeping.

Can you imagine the mess your checkbook would be if you didn't record each check you wrote? You've probably forgotten to record a check or two on occasion, but you certainly learn your lesson when you realize that an important payment bounces as a result. Yikes!

Keeping the books of a business can be a lot more difficult than maintaining a personal checkbook. Each business transaction must be carefully recorded to make sure it goes into the right account. This careful bookkeeping gives you an effective tool for figuring out how well the business is doing financially.

Bookkeepers need a road map to help determine where to record all those transactions. This road map is called the Chart of Accounts. The second half of this chapter tells you how to set up the Chart of Accounts, which includes many different accounts. It also reviews the types of transactions you enter into each type of account in order to track the key parts of any business — assets, liabilities, equity, revenue, and expenses.

Bookkeepers: The Record Keepers of the Business World

Bookkeeping, the methodical way in which businesses track their financial transactions, is rooted in accounting. *Accounting* is the total structure of records and procedures used to record, classify, and report information about a business's financial transactions. Bookkeeping involves the recording of that financial information into the accounting system while maintaining adherence to solid accounting principles.

Bookkeepers are the ones who toil day in and day out to ensure that transactions are accurately recorded. Bookkeepers need to be very detail oriented and love to work with numbers because numbers and the accounts they go into are just about all these people see all day. A bookkeeper isn't required to be a certified public accountant (CPA).

Many small business people who are just starting up their businesses initially serve as their own bookkeepers until the business is large enough to hire someone dedicated to keeping the books. Few small businesses have accountants on staff to check the books and prepare official financial reports; instead, they have bookkeepers on staff who serve as the outside accountants' eyes and ears. Most businesses do seek an accountant with a CPA certification.

In many small businesses today, a bookkeeper enters the business transactions on a daily basis while working inside the company. At the end of each month or quarter, the bookkeeper sends summary reports to the accountant, who then checks the transactions for accuracy and prepares financial statements.

In most cases, the accounting system is initially set up with the help of an accountant in order to be sure it uses solid accounting principles. That accountant periodically stops by the office and reviews the system's use to be sure transactions are being handled properly.

REMEMBER

Accurate financial reports are the only way you can know how your business is doing. These reports are developed using the information the bookkeeper enters into your accounting system. If that information isn't accurate, your financial reports are meaningless. As the old adage goes, "Garbage in, garbage out."

Wading through Basic Bookkeeping Lingo

Before you can take on bookkeeping and start keeping the books for your small business, the first things you must get a handle on are key accounting terms. The following is a list of terms that all bookkeepers use on a daily basis.

Accounts for the balance sheet

Here are a few terms you'll want to know:

REMEMBER

>> **Balance sheet:** The financial statement that presents a snapshot of the company's financial position (assets, liabilities, and equity) as of a particular date in time. It's called a balance sheet because the things owned by the company (assets) must equal the claims against those assets (liabilities and equity).

On an ideal balance sheet, the total assets should equal the total liabilities plus the total equity. If your numbers fit this formula, the company's books are in balance. (Flip to Chapter 3 in Book 3 for more about the balance sheet.)

>> **Assets:** All the things a company owns in order to successfully run its business, such as cash, buildings, land, tools, equipment, vehicles, and furniture.

>> **Liabilities:** All the debts the company owes, such as bonds, loans, and unpaid bills.

>> **Equity:** All the money invested in the company by its owners. In a small business owned by one person or a group of people, the owner's equity is shown in a Capital account. In a larger business that's incorporated, owner's equity is shown in shares of stock. Another key Equity account is *Retained Earnings,* which tracks all company profits that have been reinvested in the company rather than paid out to the company's owners. Small, unincorporated businesses track money paid out to owners in a Drawing account, whereas incorporated businesses dole out money to owners by paying *dividends* (a portion of the company's profits paid by share of common stock for the quarter or year).

Accounts for the income statement

Here are a few terms related to the income statement that you'll want to know:

» **Income statement:** The financial statement that presents a summary of the company's financial activity over a certain period of time, such as a month, quarter, or year. The statement starts with Revenue earned, subtracts out the Costs of Goods Sold and the Expenses, and ends with the bottom line — Net Profit or Loss. (See Chapter 2 in Book 3 for more about the income statement.)

» **Revenue:** All money collected in the process of selling the company's goods and services. Some companies also collect revenue through other means, such as selling assets the business no longer needs or earning interest by offering short-term loans to employees or other businesses.

» **Costs of goods sold:** All money spent to purchase or make the products or services a company plans to sell to its customers.

» **Expenses:** All money spent to operate the company that's not directly related to the sale of individual goods or services.

Other common terms

Some other common terms include the following:

» **Accounting period:** The time for which financial information is being tracked. Most businesses track their financial results on a monthly basis, so each accounting period equals one month. Some businesses choose to do financial reports on a quarterly basis, so the accounting periods are 3 months. Other businesses only look at their results on a yearly basis, so their accounting periods are 12 months. Businesses that track their financial activities monthly usually also create quarterly and *annual reports* (a year-end summary of the company's activities and financial results) based on the information they gather.

» **Accounts Receivable:** The account used to track all customer sales that are made by store credit. *Store credit* refers not to credit card sales but rather to sales in which the customer is given credit directly by the store and the store needs to collect payment from the customer at a later date.

» **Accounts Payable:** The account used to track all outstanding bills from vendors, contractors, consultants, and any other companies or individuals from whom the company buys goods or services.

- >> **Depreciation:** An accounting method used to track the aging and use of assets. For example, if you own a car, you know that each year you use the car its value is reduced (unless you own one of those classic cars that goes up in value). Every major asset a business owns ages and eventually needs replacement, including buildings, factories, equipment, and other key assets.

- >> **General Ledger:** Where all the company's accounts are summarized. The General Ledger is the granddaddy of the bookkeeping system.

- >> **Interest:** The money a company needs to pay if it borrows money from a bank or other company. For example, when you buy a car using a car loan, you must pay not only the amount you borrowed but also additional money, or interest, based on a percent of the amount you borrowed.

- >> **Inventory:** The account that tracks all products that will be sold to customers.

- >> **Journals:** Where bookkeepers keep records (in chronological order) of daily company transactions. Each of the most active accounts, including cash, Accounts Payable, and Accounts Receivable, has its own journal.

- >> **Payroll:** The way a company pays its employees. Managing payroll is a key function of the bookkeeper and involves reporting many aspects of payroll to the government, including taxes to be paid on behalf of the employee, unemployment taxes, and workers' compensation.

- >> **Trial balance:** How you test to be sure the books are in balance before pulling together information for the financial reports and closing the books for the accounting period.

Pedaling through the Accounting Cycle

Bookkeepers complete their work by completing the tasks of the accounting cycle. It's called a cycle because the workflow is circular: entering transactions, manipulating the transactions through the accounting cycle, closing the books at the end of the accounting period, and then starting the entire cycle again for the next accounting period.

The accounting cycle has eight basic steps, which you can see in Figure 1-1.

1. **Transactions:** Financial transactions start the process. Transactions can include the sale or return of a product, the purchase of supplies for business activities, or any other financial activity that involves the exchange of the

company's assets, the establishment or payoff of a debt, or the deposit from or payout of money to the company's owners. All sales and expenses are transactions that must be recorded.

2. **Journal entries:** The transaction is listed in the appropriate journal, maintaining the journal's chronological order of transactions. (The journal is also known as the "book of original entry" and is the first place a transaction is listed.)

3. **Posting:** The transactions are posted to the account that it impacts. These accounts are part of the General Ledger, where you can find a summary of all the business's accounts.

4. **Trial balance:** At the end of the accounting period (which may be a month, quarter, or year, depending on your business's practices), you calculate a trial balance.

5. **Worksheet:** Unfortunately, many times your first calculation of the trial balance shows that the books aren't in balance. If that's the case, you look for errors and make corrections called adjustments, which are tracked on a worksheet. Adjustments are also made to account for the depreciation of assets and to adjust for one-time payments (such as insurance) that should be allocated on a monthly basis to more accurately match monthly expenses with monthly revenues. After you make and record adjustments, you take another trial balance to be sure the accounts are in balance.

6. **Adjusting journal entries:** You post any corrections needed to the affected accounts once your trial balance shows that the accounts will be balanced after the adjustments needed are made to the accounts. You don't need to make adjusting entries until the trial balance process is completed and all needed corrections and adjustments have been identified.

7. **Financial statements:** You prepare the balance sheet and income statement using the corrected account balances.

8. **Closing:** You close the books for the revenue and expense accounts and begin the entire cycle again with zero balances in those accounts.

REMEMBER

As a businessperson, you want to be able to gauge your profit or loss on month by month, quarter by quarter, and year by year bases. To do that, Revenue and Expense accounts must start with a zero balance at the beginning of each accounting period. In contrast, you carry over Asset, Liability, and Equity account balances from cycle to cycle because the business doesn't start each cycle by getting rid of old assets and buying new assets, paying off and then taking on new debt, or paying out all claims to owners and then collecting the money again.

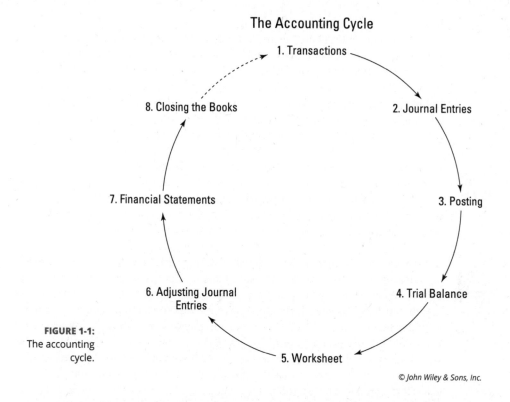

The Accounting Cycle

1. Transactions
2. Journal Entries
3. Posting
4. Trial Balance
5. Worksheet
6. Adjusting Journal Entries
7. Financial Statements
8. Closing the Books

© John Wiley & Sons, Inc.

FIGURE 1-1:
The accounting cycle.

Tackling the Big Decision: Cash-Basis or Accrual Accounting

Before starting to record transactions, you must decide whether to use cash-basis or accrual accounting. The crucial difference between these two processes is in how you record your cash transactions.

Waiting for funds with cash-basis accounting

With *cash-basis accounting*, you record all transactions in the books when cash actually changes hands, meaning when cash payment is received by the company from customers or paid out by the company for purchases or other services. Cash receipt or payment can be in the form of cash, check, credit card, electronic transfer, or other means used to pay for an item.

Cash-basis accounting can't be used if a store sells products on store credit and bills the customer at a later date. There is no provision to record and track money due from customers at some time in the future in the cash-basis accounting method. That's also true for purchases. With the cash-basis accounting method, the owner only records the purchase of supplies or goods that will later be sold when he actually pays cash. If he buys goods on credit to be paid later, he doesn't record the transaction until the cash is actually paid out.

TIP

Depending on the size of your business, you may want to start out with cash-basis accounting. Many small businesses run by a sole proprietor or a small group of partners use cash-basis accounting because it's easy. But as the business grows, the business owners find it necessary to switch to accrual accounting (see the next section) in order to more accurately track revenues and expenses.

WARNING

Cash-basis accounting does a good job of tracking cash flow, but it does a poor job of matching revenues earned with money laid out for expenses. This deficiency is a problem particularly when, as it often happens, a company buys products in one month and sells those products in the next month. For example, you buy products in June with the intent to sell them, and you pay $1,000 cash for those products. You don't sell the products until July, and that's when you receive cash for the sales. When you close the books at the end of June, you have to show the $1,000 expense with no revenue to offset it, meaning you have a loss that month. When you sell the products for $1,500 in July, you have a $1,500 profit. So, your monthly report for June shows a $1,000 loss, and your monthly report for July shows a $1,500 profit, when in actuality you had revenues of $500 over the two months.

REMEMBER

This chapter concentrates on the accrual accounting method. If you choose to use cash-basis accounting, you'll still find most of the bookkeeping information here useful, but you don't need to maintain some of the accounts listed, such as Accounts Receivable and Accounts Payable, because you aren't recording transactions until cash actually changes hands. If you're using a cash-basis accounting system and sell things on credit, though, you had better have a way to track what people owe you.

Making the switch to accrual accounting

Changing between the cash-basis and accrual basis of accounting may not be simple, and you should check with your accountant to be sure you do it right. You may even need to get permission from the IRS, which tests whether you're seeking an unfair tax advantage when making the switch. You might be required to complete and file the Application for Change in Accounting Method (Form 3115) in advance of the end of the year for which you make this change. In certain circumstances, IRS approval of change is automatic, but you should still file Form 3115 with the affected year's tax return. For example, if you started as a service business and shifted to a business that carries inventory, permission for the accounting method change should be automatically granted.

Businesses that generally shouldn't use cash-basis accounting include

>> Businesses that carry an inventory if sales exceed $1 million per year.

>> Businesses that incorporated as a C Corporation (more on incorporation in Chapter 6 of Book 2).

>> Businesses with gross annual sales that exceed $5 million.

Recording right away with accrual accounting

With *accrual accounting*, you record all transactions in the books when they occur, even if no cash changes hands. For example, if you sell on store credit, you record the transaction immediately and enter it into an Accounts Receivable account until you receive payment. If you buy goods on credit, you immediately enter the transaction into an Accounts Payable account until you pay out cash.

WARNING

Like cash-basis accounting, accrual accounting has its drawbacks. It does a good job of matching revenues and expenses, but it does a poor job of tracking cash. Because you record revenue when the transaction occurs and not when you collect the cash, your income statement can look great even if you don't have cash in the bank. For example, suppose you're running a contracting company and completing jobs on a daily basis. You can record the revenue upon completion of the job even if you haven't yet collected the cash. If your customers are slow to pay, you may end up with lots of revenue but little cash.

TIP

Many companies that use the accrual accounting method also monitor cash flow on a weekly basis to be sure they have enough cash on hand to operate the business. If your business is seasonal, such as a landscaping business with little to do during the winter months, you can establish short-term lines of credit through your bank to maintain cash flow through the lean times.

Seeing Double with Double-Entry Bookkeeping

All businesses, whether they use the cash-basis accounting method or the accrual accounting method (covered earlier in this chapter), use *double-entry bookkeeping* to keep their books. A practice that helps minimize errors and increases the chance that your books balance, double-entry bookkeeping gets its name because you enter all transactions twice.

REMEMBER

When it comes to double-entry bookkeeping, the key formula for the balance sheet (Assets = Liabilities + Equity) plays a major role.

In order to adjust the balance of accounts in the bookkeeping world, you use a combination of *debits* and *credits*. You may think of a debit as a subtraction because you've found that debits usually mean a decrease in your bank balance. On the other hand, you've probably been excited to find unexpected credits in your bank or credit card that mean more money has been added to the account in your favor. Now, forget everything you ever learned about debits or credits. In the world of bookkeeping, their meanings aren't so simple.

REMEMBER

The only definite thing when it comes to debits and credits in the bookkeeping world is that a *debit* is on the left side of a transaction, and a credit is on the *right* side of a transaction. Everything beyond that can get very muddled.

Here's an example of the practice in action. Suppose you purchase a new desk that costs $1,500 for your office. This transaction actually has two parts: You spend an asset — cash — to buy another asset — furniture. So, you must adjust two accounts in your company's books: the Cash account and the Furniture account. Here's what the transaction looks like in a bookkeeping entry:

Account	Debit	Credit
Furniture	$1,500	
Cash		$1,500

To purchase a new desk for the office

In this transaction, you record the accounts impacted by the transaction. The debit increases the value of the Furniture account, and the credit decreases the value of the Cash account. For this transaction, both accounts impacted are asset accounts, so, looking at how the balance sheet is affected, you can see that the only changes are to the asset side of the balance sheet equation:

Assets = Liabilities + Equity

Furniture increase = No change to this side of the equation

Cash decrease

In this case, the books stay in balance because the exact dollar amount that increases the value of your Furniture account decreases the value of your Cash account.

TIP

At the bottom of any journal entry, you should include a brief explanation that explains the purpose for the entry. In the first example, "To purchase a new desk for the office" indicates this entry.

To show you how you record a transaction if it impacts both sides of the balance sheet equation, here's an example that shows how to record the purchase of inventory. Suppose you purchase $5,000 worth of widgets on credit. (Haven't you always wondered what widgets are? They're just commonly used in accounting examples to represent something that's purchased.) These new widgets add value to your Inventory account (an Asset account) and also add value to your Accounts Payable account. (Remember, the Accounts Payable account is a Liability account where you track bills that need to be paid at some point in the future.) Here's how the bookkeeping transaction for your widget purchase looks:

Account	Debit	Credit
Inventory	$5,000	
Accounts Payable		$5,000

To purchase widgets for sale to customers

Here's how this transaction affects the balance sheet equation:

Assets = Liabilities + Equity

Inventory increases = Accounts Payable increases = No change

In this case, the books stay in balance because both sides of the equation increase by $5,000.

REMEMBER

You can see from the two example transactions how double-entry bookkeeping helps to keep your books in balance — as long as you make sure each entry into the books is balanced. Balancing your entries may look simple here, but sometimes bookkeeping entries can get very complex when more than two accounts are impacted by the transaction.

Differentiating Debits and Credits

Because bookkeeping's debits and credits are different from the ones you're used to encountering, you're probably wondering how you're supposed to know whether a debit or credit will increase or decrease an account. Believe it or not, identifying the difference will become second nature as you start making regular bookkeeping entries. But to make things easier, Table 1-1 is a chart that's commonly used by all bookkeepers and accountants.

TABLE 1-1

How Credits and Debits Impact Your Accounts

Account Type	Debits	Credits
Assets	Increase	Decrease
Liabilities	Decrease	Increase
Income	Decrease	Increase
Expenses	Increase	Decrease

TIP

Copy Table 1-1 and post it at your desk when you start keeping your own books. It will help you keep your debits and credits straight.

Outlining Your Financial Road Map with a Chart of Accounts

The *Chart of Accounts* is the road map that a business creates to organize its financial transactions. After all, you can't record a transaction until you know where to put it! Essentially, this chart is a list of all the accounts a business has, organized in a specific order; each account has a description that includes the type of account and the types of transactions that should be entered into that account. Every business creates its own Chart of Accounts based on how the business is operated, so you're unlikely to find two businesses with the exact same Charts of Accounts.

However, some basic organizational and structural characteristics are common to all Charts of Accounts. The organization and structure are designed around two key financial reports: the *balance sheet*, which shows what your business owns and what it owes (see Chapter 3 in Book 3), and the *income statement*, which shows how much money your business took in from sales and how much money it spent to generate those sales (see Chapter 2 in Book 3).

The Chart of Accounts starts with the balance sheet accounts, which include

» **Current Assets:** Includes all accounts that track things the company owns and expects to use in the next 12 months, such as cash, accounts receivable (money collected from customers), and inventory

» **Long-term Assets:** Includes all accounts that track things the company owns that have a lifespan of more than 12 months, such as buildings, furniture, and equipment

» **Current Liabilities:** Includes all accounts that track debts the company must pay over the next 12 months, such as accounts payable (bills from vendors, contractors, and consultants), interest payable, and credit cards payable

» **Long-term Liabilities:** Includes all accounts that track debts the company must pay over a period of time longer than the next 12 months, such as mortgages payable and bonds payable

» **Equity:** Includes all accounts that track the owners of the company and their claims against the company's assets, which include any money invested in the company, any money taken out of the company, and any earnings that have been reinvested in the company

The rest of the chart is filled with income statement accounts, which include

» **Revenue:** Includes all accounts that track sales of goods and services as well as revenue generated for the company by other means

» **Cost of Goods Sold:** Includes all accounts that track the direct costs involved in selling the company's goods or services

» **Expenses:** Includes all accounts that track expenses related to running the businesses that aren't directly tied to the sale of individual products or services

When developing the Chart of Accounts, you start by listing all the Asset accounts, the Liability accounts, the Equity accounts, the Revenue accounts, and finally, the Expense accounts. All these accounts come from two places: the balance sheet and the income statement.

TIP

This chapter reviews the key account types found in most businesses, but this list isn't cast in stone. You should develop an account list that makes the most sense for how you operate your business and the financial information you want to track. In the discussion of the Chart of Accounts here, you can see how the structure may differ for different businesses.

REMEMBER

The Chart of Accounts is a money-management tool that helps you track your business transactions, so set it up in a way that provides you with the financial information you need to make smart business decisions. You'll probably tweak the accounts in your chart annually and, if necessary, you may add accounts during the year if you find something for which you want more detailed tracking. You can add accounts during the year, but it's best not to delete accounts until the end of a 12-month reporting period.

Starting with the Balance Sheet Accounts

The first part of the Chart of Accounts is made up of balance sheet accounts, which break down into the following three categories:

>> **Asset:** These accounts are used to track what the business owns. Assets include cash on hand, furniture, buildings, vehicles, and so on.

>> **Liability:** These accounts track what the business owes, or, more specifically, claims that lenders have against the business's assets. For example, mortgages on buildings and lines of credit are two common types of liabilities.

>> **Equity:** These accounts track what the owners put into the business and the claims owners have against assets. For example, stockholders are company owners that have claims against the business's assets.

REMEMBER

The balance sheet accounts, and the financial report they make up, are so-called because they have to balance out. The value of the assets must be equal to the claims made against those assets. (Remember, these claims are liabilities made by lenders and equity made by owners.)

This section examines the basic components of the balance sheet, as reflected in the Chart of Accounts. (Check out Chapter 3 in Book 3 for details about the balance sheet.)

Tackling assets

First on the chart are always the accounts that track what the company owns — its assets: current assets and long-term assets.

Current assets

Current assets are the key assets that your business uses up during a 12-month period and will likely not be there the next year. The accounts that reflect current assets on the Chart of Accounts are:

>> **Cash in Checking:** Any company's primary account is the checking account used for operating activities. This is the account used to deposit revenues and pay expenses. Some companies have more than one operating account in this category; for example, a company with many divisions may have an operating account for each division.

>> **Cash in Savings:** This account is used for surplus cash. Any cash for which there is no immediate plan is deposited in an interest-earning savings account so that it can at least earn interest while the company decides what to do with it.

>> **Cash on Hand:** This account is used to track any cash kept at retail stores or in the office. In retail stores, cash must be kept in registers in order to provide change to customers. In the office, petty cash is often kept around for immediate cash needs that pop up from time to time. This account helps you keep track of the cash held outside a financial institution.

>> **Accounts Receivable:** If you offer your products or services to customers on store credit (meaning *your* store credit system), then you need this account to track the customers who buy on your dime.

REMEMBER

Accounts Receivable isn't used to track purchases made on other types of credit cards because your business gets paid directly by banks, not customers, when other credit cards are used.

>> **Inventory:** This account tracks the products on hand to sell to your customers. The value of the assets in this account varies depending on how you decide to track the flow of inventory in and out of the business.

>> **Prepaid Insurance:** This account tracks insurance you pay in advance that's credited as it's used up each month. For example, if you own a building and prepay one year in advance, each month you reduce the amount that you prepaid by $\frac{1}{12}$ as the prepayment is used up.

Depending upon the type of business you're setting up, you may have other current asset accounts that you decide to track. For example, if you're starting a service business in consulting, you're likely to have a Consulting account for tracking cash collected for those services. If you run a business in which you barter assets (such as trading your services for paper goods), you may add a Barter account for business-to-business barter.

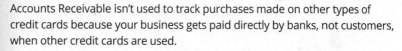

Setting Up the Books

Long-term assets

Long-term assets are assets that you anticipate your business will use for more than 12 months. This section lists some of the most common long-term assets, starting with the key accounts related to buildings and factories owned by the company:

>> **Land:** This account tracks the land owned by the company. The value of the land is based on the cost of purchasing it. Land value is tracked separately from the value of any buildings standing on that land because land isn't depreciated in value, but buildings must be depreciated. *Depreciation* is an accounting method that shows an asset is being used up.

>> **Buildings:** This account tracks the value of any buildings a business owns. As with land, the value of the building is based on the cost of purchasing it. The key difference between buildings and land is that the building's value is depreciated, as discussed in the previous bullet.

>> **Accumulated Depreciation – Buildings:** This account tracks the cumulative amount a building is depreciated over its useful lifespan.

>> **Leasehold Improvements:** This account tracks the value of improvements to buildings or other facilities that a business leases rather than purchases. Frequently when a business leases a property, it must pay for any improvements necessary in order to use that property the way it's needed. For example, if a business leases a store in a strip mall, it's likely that the space leased is an empty shell or filled with shelving and other items that may not match the particular needs of the business. As with buildings, leasehold improvements are depreciated as the value of the asset ages.

>> **Accumulated Depreciation – Leasehold Improvements:** This account tracks the cumulative amount depreciated for leasehold improvements.

The following are the types of accounts for smaller long-term assets, such as vehicles and furniture:

>> **Vehicles:** This account tracks any cars, trucks, or other vehicles owned by the business. The initial value of any vehicle is listed in this account based on the total cost paid to put the vehicle in service. Sometimes this value is more than the purchase price if additions were needed to make the vehicle usable for the particular type of business. For example, if a business provides transportation people with physical disabilities and must add additional equipment to a vehicle in order to serve the needs of its customers, that additional equipment is added to the value of the vehicle. Vehicles also depreciate through their useful lifespan.

>> **Accumulated Depreciation – Vehicles:** This account tracks the depreciation of all vehicles owned by the company.

>> **Furniture and Fixtures:** This account tracks any furniture or fixtures purchased for use in the business. The account includes the value of all chairs, desks, store fixtures, and shelving needed to operate the business. The value of the furniture and fixtures in this account is based on the cost of purchasing these items. These items are depreciated during their useful lifespan.

>> **Accumulated Depreciation – Furniture and Fixtures:** This account tracks the accumulated depreciation of all furniture and fixtures.

>> **Equipment:** This account tracks equipment that was purchased for use for more than one year, such as computers, copiers, tools, and cash registers. The value of the equipment is based on the cost to purchase these items. Equipment is also depreciated to show that over time it gets used up and

>> Accumulated Depreciation – Equipment: This account tracks the accumu-

assets that you can't touch but that company, such as organization costs, *angible assets*, and the accounts that

initial start-up expenses to get the enses can't be written off in the first egal fees must be written off over a r to depreciation, called *amortization*,

This account tracks the accumulated ring the period in which they're being

sts associated with *patents*, grants made the inventor of a product or service the ell that product or service over a set period atent costs are amortized. The value of this e company incurs to get the right to patent

ccount tracks the accumulated amortization of

>> **Copyrights:** This account tracks the costs incurred to establish copyrights, the legal rights given to an author, playwright, publisher, or any other distributor of a publication or production for a unique work of literature, music, drama, or art. This legal right expires after a set number of years, so its value is amortized as the copyright gets used up.

>> **Goodwill:** This account is only needed if a company buys another company for more than the actual value of its tangible assets. Goodwill reflects the intangible value of this purchase for things like company reputation, store locations, customer base, and other items that increase the value of the business bought.

TIP

If you hold a lot of assets that aren't of great value, you can also set up an "Other Assets" account to track them. Any asset you track in the Other Assets account that you later want to track individually can be shifted to its own account.

Laying out your liabilities

After you cover assets, the next stop on the bookkeeping highway is the accounts that track what your business owes to others. These "others" can include vendors from which you buy products or supplies, financial institutions from which you borrow money, and anyone else who lends money to your business. Like assets, liabilities are lumped into two types: current liabilities and long-term liabilities.

Current liabilities

Current liabilities are debts due in the next 12 months. Some of the most common types of current liabilities accounts that appear on the Chart of Accounts are

>> **Accounts Payable:** Tracks money the company owes to vendors, contractors, suppliers, and consultants that must be paid in less than a year. Most of these liabilities must be paid 30–90 days from billing.

>> **Sales Tax Collected:** You may not think of sales tax as a liability, but because the business collects the tax from the customer and doesn't pay it immediately to the government entity, the taxes collected become a liability tracked in this account. A business usually collects sales tax throughout the month and then pays it to the local, state, or federal government on a monthly basis.

>> **Accrued Payroll Taxes:** This account tracks payroll taxes collected from employees to pay state, local, or federal income taxes as well as Social Security and Medicare taxes. Companies don't have to pay these taxes to the government entities immediately, so depending on the size of the payroll, companies may pay payroll taxes on a monthly or quarterly basis.

- » **Credit Cards Payable:** This account tracks all credit card accounts to which the business is liable. Most companies use credit cards as short-term debt and pay them off completely at the end of each month, but some smaller companies carry credit card balances over a longer period of time. Because credit cards often have a much higher interest rate than most lines of credits, most companies transfer any credit card debt they can't pay entirely at the end of a month to a line of credit at a bank. When it comes to your Chart of Accounts, you can set up one Credit Card Payable account, but you may want to set up a separate account for each card your company holds to improve tracking credit card usage.

How you set up your current liabilities and how many individual accounts you establish depend on how detailed you want to track each type of liability. For example, you can set up separate current liability accounts for major vendors if you find that approach provides you with a better money management tool. For example, suppose that a small hardware retail store buys most of the tools it sells from Snap-On. To keep better control of its spending with Snap-On, the bookkeeper sets up a specific account called Accounts Payable – Snap-On, which is used only for tracking invoices and payments to that vendor. In this example, all other invoices and payments to other vendors and suppliers are tracked in the general Accounts Payable account.

Long-term liabilities

Long-term liabilities are debts due in more than 12 months. The number of long-term liability accounts you maintain on your Chart of Accounts depends on your debt structure. The two most common types are

- » **Loans Payable:** This account tracks any long-term loans, such as a mortgage on your business building. Most businesses have separate Loans Payable accounts for each of their long-term loans. For example, you could have Loans Payable – Mortgage Bank for your building and Loans Payable – Car Bank for your vehicle loan.

- » **Notes Payable:** Some businesses borrow money from other businesses using *notes,* a method of borrowing that doesn't require the company to put up an asset, such as a mortgage on a building or a car loan, as collateral. This account tracks any notes due.

TIP

In addition to any separate long-term debt you may want to track in its own account, you may also want to set up an account called "Other Liabilities" that you can use to track types of debt that are so insignificant to the business that you don't think they need their own accounts.

Eyeing the equity

Every business is owned by somebody. *Equity accounts* track owners' contributions to the business as well as their share of ownership. For a corporation, ownership is tracked by the sale of individual shares of stock because each stockholder owns a portion of the business. In smaller companies that are owned by one person or a group of people, equity is tracked using Capital and Drawing Accounts. Here are the basic equity accounts that appear in the Chart of Accounts:

>> **Common Stock:** This account reflects the value of outstanding shares of stock sold to investors. A company calculates this value by multiplying the number of shares issued by the value of each share of stock. Only corporations need to establish this account.

>> **Retained Earnings:** This account tracks the profits or losses accumulated since a business was opened. At the end of each year, the profit or loss calculated on the income statement is used to adjust the value of this account. For example, if a company made a $100,000 profit in the past year, the Retained Earnings account would be increased by that amount; if the company lost $100,000, then that amount would be subtracted from this account.

>> **Capital:** This account is only necessary for small, unincorporated businesses. The Capital account reflects the amount of initial money the business owner contributed to the company as well as owner contributions made after initial start-up. The value of this account is based on cash contributions and other assets contributed by the business owner, such as equipment, vehicles, or buildings. If a small company has several different partners, then each partner gets his or her own Capital account to track his or her contributions.

>> **Drawing:** This account is only necessary for businesses that aren't incorporated. It tracks any money that a business owner takes out of the business. If the business has several partners, each partner gets his or her own Drawing account to track what he or she takes out of the business.

Tracking the Income Statement Accounts

The income statement is made up of two types of accounts:

>> **Revenue:** These accounts track all money coming into the business, including sales, interest earned on savings, and any other methods used to generate income.

>> **Expenses:** These accounts track all money that a business spends in order to keep itself afloat.

The bottom line of the income statement shows whether your business made a profit or a loss for a specified period of time. This section examines the various accounts that make up the income statement portion of the Chart of Accounts. (See Chapter 2 in Book 3 for more about the income statement.)

Recording the money you make

First up in the income statement portion of the Chart of Accounts are accounts that track revenue coming into the business. If you choose to offer discounts or accept returns, that activity also falls within the revenue grouping. The most common income accounts are

>> **Sales of Goods or Services:** This account, which appears at the top of every income statement, tracks all the money that the company earns selling its products, services, or both.

>> **Sales Discounts:** Because most businesses offer discounts to encourage sales, this account tracks any reductions to the full price of merchandise.

>> **Sales Returns:** This account tracks transactions related to returns, when a customer returns a product because he or she is unhappy with it for some reason.

When you examine an income statement from a company other than the one you own or are working for, you usually see the following accounts summarized as one line item called Revenue or Net Revenue. Because not all income is generated by sales of products or services, other income accounts that may appear on a Chart of Accounts include

>> **Other Income:** If a company takes in income from a source other than its primary business activity, that income is recorded in this account. For example, a company that encourages recycling and earns income from the items recycled records that income in this account.

>> **Interest Income:** This account tracks any income earned by collecting interest on a company's savings accounts. If the company loans money to employees or to another company and earns interest on that money, that interest is recorded in this account as well.

>> **Sale of Fixed Assets:** Any time a company sells a fixed asset, such as a car or furniture, any revenue from the sale is recorded in this account. A company should only record revenue remaining after subtracting the accumulated depreciation from the original cost of the asset.

Tracking the Cost of Goods Sold

Before you can sell a product, you must spend some money to either buy or make that product. The type of account used to track the money spent is called a Cost of Goods Sold account. The most common are:

>> **Purchases:** Tracks the purchases of all items you plan to sell.

>> **Purchase Discount:** Tracks the discounts you may receive from vendors if you pay for your purchase quickly. For example, a company may give you a 2 percent discount on your purchase if you pay the bill in 10 days rather than wait until the end of the 30-day payment allotment.

>> **Purchase Returns:** If you're unhappy with a product you've bought, record the value of any returns in this account.

>> **Freight Charges:** Charges related to shipping items you purchase for later sale. You may or may not want to keep track of this detail.

>> **Other Sales Costs:** This is a catchall account for anything that doesn't fit into one of the other Cost of Goods Sold accounts.

Acknowledging the money you spend

Expense accounts take the cake for the longest list of individual accounts. Any money you spend on the business that can't be tied directly to the sale of an individual product falls under the expense account category. For example, advertising a storewide sale isn't directly tied to the sale of any one product, so the costs associated with advertising fall under this category.

REMEMBER

The Chart of Accounts mirrors your business operations, so it's up to you to decide how much detail you want to keep in your expense accounts. Most businesses have expenses that are unique to their operations, so your list will probably be longer than the one presented here. However, you also may find that you don't need some of these accounts.

On your Chart of Accounts, the expense accounts don't have to appear in any specific order. Here they're listed alphabetically. The most common are as follows:

>> **Advertising:** Tracks expenses involved in promoting a business or its products. Money spent on newspaper, television, magazine, and radio advertising is recorded here, as well as any money spent to print flyers and mailings to customers. For community events such as cancer walks or craft fairs, associated costs are tracked in this account as well.

- » **Bank Service Charges:** This account tracks any charges made by a bank to service a company's bank accounts.

- » **Dues and Subscriptions:** This account tracks expenses related to business club membership or subscriptions to magazines.

- » **Equipment Rental:** This account tracks expenses related to renting equipment for a short-term project. For example, a business that needs to rent a truck to pick up some new fixtures for its store records that truck rental in this account.

- » **Insurance:** Tracks any money paid to buy insurance. Many businesses break this down into several accounts, such as Insurance – Employees Group, which tracks any expenses paid for employee insurance, or Insurance – Officers' Life, which tracks money spent to buy insurance to protect the life of a key owner or officer of the company. Companies often insure their key owners and executives because an unexpected death, especially for a small company, may mean facing many unexpected expenses in order to keep the company's doors open. In such a case, insurance proceeds can be used to cover those expenses.

- » **Legal and Accounting:** This account tracks any money that's paid for legal or accounting advice.

- » **Miscellaneous Expenses:** This is a catchall account for expenses that don't fit into one of a company's established accounts. If certain miscellaneous expenses occur frequently, a company may choose to add an account to the Chart of Accounts and move related expenses into that new account by subtracting all related transactions from the Miscellaneous Expenses account and adding them to the new account. With this shuffle, it's important to carefully balance out the adjusting transaction to avoid any errors or double counting.

- » **Office Expense:** This account tracks any items purchased in order to run an office. For example, office supplies such as paper and pens or business cards fit in this account. As with miscellaneous expenses, a company may choose to track some office expense items in their own accounts. For example, if you find your office is using a lot of copy paper and you want to track that separately, you set up a Copy Paper expense account. Just be sure you really need the detail because the number of accounts can get unwieldy and hard to manage.

- » **Payroll Taxes:** This account tracks any taxes paid related to employee payroll, such as the employer's share of Social Security and Medicare, unemployment compensation, and workers' compensation.

- » **Postage:** Tracks money spent on stamps and shipping. If a company does a large amount of shipping through vendors such as UPS or FedEx, it may want to track that spending in separate accounts for each vendor. This option is particularly helpful for small companies that sell over the Internet or through catalog sales.

>> **Rent Expense:** Tracks rental costs for a business's office or retail space.

>> **Salaries and Wages:** This account tracks any money paid to employees as salary or wages.

>> **Supplies:** This account tracks any business supplies that don't fit into the category of office supplies. For example, supplies needed for the operation of retail stores are tracked using this account.

>> **Travel and Entertainment:** This account tracks money spent for business purposes on travel or entertainment. Some businesses separate these expenses into several accounts, such as Travel and Entertainment – Meals, Travel and Entertainment – Travel, and Travel and Entertainment – Entertainment, to keep a close watch.

>> **Telephone:** This account tracks all business expenses related to the telephone and telephone calls.

>> **Utilities:** Tracks money paid for utilities (electricity, gas, and water).

>> **Vehicles:** Tracks expenses related to the operation of company vehicles.

Setting Up Your Chart of Accounts

You can use the lists upon lists of accounts provided in this chapter to get started setting up your business's own Chart of Accounts. There's really no secret — just make a list of the accounts that apply to your business.

REMEMBER

Don't panic if you can't think of every type of account you may need for your business. It's very easy to add to the Chart of Accounts at any time. Just add the account to the list and distribute the revised list to any employees who use it. (Even employees not involved in bookkeeping need a copy of your Chart of Accounts if they code invoices or other transactions and indicate to which account those transactions should be recorded.)

The Chart of Accounts usually includes at least three columns:

>> **Account:** Lists the account names

>> **Type:** Lists the type of account — Asset, Liability, Equity, Revenue, Cost of Goods Sold, or Expense

>> **Description:** Contains a description of the type of transaction that should be recorded in the account

Many companies also assign numbers to the accounts, to be used for coding charges. If your company is using a computerized system, the computer automatically assigns the account number. Otherwise, you need to plan out your own numbering system. The most common number system is:

>> Asset accounts: 1,000 to 1,999

>> Liability accounts: 2,000 to 2,999

>> Equity accounts: 3,000 to 3,999

>> Revenue and Cost of Goods Sold accounts: 4,000 to 4,999

>> Expense accounts: 5,000 to 6,999

This numbering system matches the one used by computerized accounting systems, making it easy at some future time to automate the books using a computerized accounting system. A number of different Charts of Accounts have been developed. When you get your computerized system, whichever accounting software you use, all you need to do is review the chart options for the type of business you run included with that software, delete any accounts you don't want, and add any new accounts that fit your business plan.

TIP

If you're setting up your Chart of Accounts manually, be sure to leave a lot of room between accounts to add new accounts. For example, number your Cash in Checking account 1,000 and your Accounts Receivable account 1,100. That leaves you plenty of room to add other accounts to track cash.

Chapter **2**

Reporting Profit or Loss in the Income Statement

This chapter lifts up the hood and explains how the profit engine runs. Making a profit is the main financial goal of a business. Accountants are the profit scorekeepers in the business world and are tasked with measuring the most important financial number of a business. Be warned that measuring profit is a challenge in most situations. Determining the correct amounts for revenue and expenses (and for special gains and losses, if any) to record is no walk in the park.

Managers have the demanding tasks of making sales and controlling expenses, and accountants have the tough job of measuring revenue and expenses and preparing financial reports that summarize the profit-making activities. Also, accountants are called on to help business managers analyze profit for decision-making. And accountants prepare profit budgets for managers. This chapter explains how profit-making activities are reported in a business's external financial reports to its owners and lenders. Revenue and expenses change the financial condition of the business, a fact often overlooked when reading a profit report. Keep in mind that recording revenue and expenses (and gains and losses) and then reporting these profit-making activities in external financial reports are governed by authoritative accounting standards.

Presenting Typical Income Statements

REMEMBER

At the risk of oversimplification, businesses make profit in three basic ways:

>> **Selling products** (with allied services) and controlling the cost of the products sold and other operating costs

>> **Selling services** and controlling the cost of providing the services and other operating costs

>> **Investing** in assets that generate investment income and market value gains and controlling operating costs

Obviously, this list isn't exhaustive, but it captures a large swath of business activity. This chapter shows you typical externally reported income statements for the three types of businesses. Products range from automobiles to computers to food to clothes to jewelry. The customers of a company that sells products may be final consumers in the economic chain, or a business may sell to other businesses. Services range from transportation to entertainment to consulting. Investment businesses range from mutual funds to credit unions to banks to real estate development companies.

Looking at businesses that sell products

Figure 2-1 presents a classic profit report for a *product-oriented* business; this report, called the *income statement,* would be sent to its outside, or external, owners and lenders. (The report could just as easily be called the *net income statement* because the bottom-line profit term preferred by accountants is *net income,* but the word *net* is dropped from the title, and it's most often called the income statement.) Alternative titles for the external profit report include *earnings statement, operating statement, statement of operating results,* and *statement of earnings.* **Note:** Profit reports prepared for managers that stay inside a business are usually called *P&L* (profit and loss) statements, but this moniker isn't used much in external financial reporting.

The heading of an income statement identifies the business (which in this example is incorporated — thus the "Inc." following the name), the financial statement title ("Income Statement"), and the time period summarized by the statement ("Year Ended December 31, 2019"). Find out more about the legal organization structures of businesses in Chapter 6 of Book 2.

Typical Product Business, Inc. Income Statement For Year Ended December 31, 2019	
Sales Revenue	$26,000,000
Cost of Goods Sold Expense	14,300,000
Gross Margin	$11,700,000
Selling, General, and Administrative Expenses	8,700,000
Operating Earnings	$3,000,000
Interest Expense	400,000
Earnings Before Income Tax	$2,600,000
Income Tax Expense	910,000
Net Income	$1,690,000
Earnings Per Share	$3.38

© John Wiley & Sons, Inc.

FIGURE 2-1: Typical income statement for a business that sells products.

REMEMBER

You may be tempted to start reading an income statement at the bottom line. But this financial report is designed for you to read from the top line (sales revenue) and proceed down to the last — the bottom line (net income). Each step down the ladder in an income statement involves the deduction of an expense. In Figure 2-1, four expenses are deducted from the sales revenue amount, and four profit lines are given: gross margin, operating earnings, earnings before income tax, and net income:

>> **Gross margin (also called gross profit)** equals sales revenue minus the cost of goods (products) sold expense but before operating and other expenses are considered

>> **Operating earnings (or loss)** equals profit (or loss) before interest and income tax expenses are deducted from gross margin

>> **Earnings (or loss) before income tax** equals profit (or loss) after deducting interest expense from operating earnings but before income tax expense

>> **Net income** equals final profit for period after deducting all expenses from sales revenue, which is commonly called the "bottom line"

Although you see income statements with fewer than four profit lines, you seldom see an income statement with more.

Terminology in income statements varies somewhat from business to business, but you can usually determine the meaning of a term from its context and placement in the income statement.

TIP

Notice in Figure 2-1 that below the net income line, the *earnings per share* (EPS) amount is reported. This important number equals net income divided by the number of ownership shares the business corporation has issued and that are being held by its shareholders. All public corporations whose stock shares are traded in stock markets must report this key metric. EPS is compared to the current market price of the stock to help judge whether the stock is over- or underpriced. Private companies aren't required to report EPS, but they may decide to do so. If a private business decides to report its EPS, it should follow the accounting standard for calculating this number.

REMEMBER

The standard practice for almost all businesses is to report two-year comparative financial statements in side-by-side columns — for the period just ended and for the same period one year ago. Indeed, some companies present three-year comparative financial statements. Two-year or three-year financial statements may be legally required, such as for public companies whose debt and ownership shares are traded in a public market. Confession: The income statement in Figure 2-1 is incomplete in this regard. It should have a companion column for the year ended December 31, 2018. To ease up on the amount of numbers, however, only the most recent year is shown.

Looking at businesses that sell services

Figure 2-2 presents a typical income statement for a *service-oriented* business. The sales revenue and operating earnings are the same amount for both the product and the service businesses so you can more easily compare the two.

If a business sells services and doesn't sell products, it doesn't have a cost of goods sold expense; therefore, the company doesn't show a gross margin line. Some service businesses report a *cost of sales* expense line, but this isn't uniform at all. Even if they do, the business might not deduct this expense line from sales revenue to show a gross margin line equivalent to the one product companies report.

In Figure 2-2, the first profit line is *operating earnings*, which is profit before interest and income tax. The service business example in Figure 2-2 discloses three broad types of expenses. In passing, you may notice that the interest expense for the service business is lower than for the product business (compare with Figure 2-1). Therefore, it has higher earnings before income tax and higher net income.

Typical Service Business, Inc. Income Statement For Year Ended December 31, 2019	
Sales Revenue	$26,000,000
Marketing and Selling Expenses	4,325,000
Operating and Administrative Expenses	8,700,000
Employee Compensation Expense	9,975,000
Operating Earnings	$3,000,000
Interest Expense	200,000
Earnings Before Income Tax	$2,800,000
Income Tax Expense	980,000
Net Income	$1,820,000
Earnings Per Share	$3.64

FIGURE 2-2:
Typical income statement for a business that sells services.

© John Wiley & Sons, Inc.

TIP

The premise of financial reporting is that of *adequate disclosure,* but you find many variations in the reporting of expenses. A business — whether a product or service company or an investment company — has fairly wide latitude regarding the number of expense lines to disclose in its external income statement. A CPA auditor (assuming the company's financial report is audited) may not be satisfied that just three expenses provide enough detail about the operating activities of the business. Accounting standards do not dictate that particular expenses must be disclosed (other than cost of goods sold expense).

Public companies must disclose certain expenses in their publicly available fillings with the federal Securities and Exchange Commission (SEC). Filing reports to the SEC is one thing; in their reports to shareholders, most businesses are relatively stingy regarding how many expenses are revealed in their income statements.

Looking at investment businesses

Figure 2-3 presents an income statement for an investment business. Notice that this income statement discloses three types of revenue: interest and dividends that were earned, gains from sales of investments during the year, and unrealized gains of the market value of its investment portfolio. Instead of gains, the business could've had realized and unrealized losses during a down year, of course. Generally, investment businesses are either required or are under a good deal of pressure to report their three types of investment return. Investment companies might not borrow money and thus have no interest expense. Or they might. Interest expense is shown in Figure 2-3 for the investment business example.

Typical Investment Business, Inc. Income Statement For Year Ended December 31, 2019	
Interest and Dividends	$14,000,000
Realized Gain (Loss) from Investments	3,000,000
Unrealized Gain (Loss) on Investments	9,000,000
Total Return on Investments	$26,000,000
Marketing and Selling Expenses	4,325,000
Operating and Administrative Expenses	8,700,000
Employee Compensation Expense	9,975,000
Operating Earnings	$3,000,000
Interest Expense	200,000
Earnings Before Income Tax	$2,800,000
Income Tax Expense	980,000
Net Income	$1,820,000
Earnings Per Share	$3.38

FIGURE 2-3: Typical income statement for an investment business.

© John Wiley & Sons, Inc.

REMEMBER

Public investment companies, such as mutual funds and exchange traded securities (ETS), are heavily regulated by the SEC, as are other types of investment entities that raise capital in public offerings. The purpose in showing the income statement for an investment business (see Figure 2-3) is simply for comparison with businesses that sell products and those that sell services (see Figures 2-1 and 2-2).

Taking Care of Housekeeping Details

Accountants assume everyone knows a few things about income statements, but in fact, they are not obvious to many people. (Accountants do this a lot: They assume that the people using financial statements know a good deal about the customs and conventions of financial reporting, so they don't make things as clear as they could.) For an accountant, the following facts are second nature, but you may not be aware of them:

>> **Minus signs are missing.** Expenses are deductions from sales revenue, but hardly ever do you see minus signs in front of expense amounts to indicate that they're deductions. Forget about minus signs in income statements and

in other financial statements as well. Sometimes parentheses are put around a deduction to signal that it's a negative number, but that's the most you can expect to see.

» **Your eye is drawn to the bottom line.** Putting a double underline under the final (bottom-line) profit number for emphasis is common practice but not universal. Instead, net income may be shown in bold type. You generally don't see anything as garish as a fat arrow pointing to the profit number or a big smiley encircling the profit number — but again, tastes vary.

» **Profit isn't usually called *profit*.** As you see in Figures 2-1, 2-2, and 2-3, bottom-line profit is called *net income*. Businesses use other terms as well, such as *net earnings* or just *earnings*. (Can't accountants agree on anything?) This book uses the terms *net income* and *profit* interchangeably, but when showing a formal income statement, the book sticks to *net income*.

» **You don't get details about sales revenue.** The sales revenue amount in an income statements of a product or a service company is the combined total of all sales during the year; you can't tell how many different sales were made, how many different customers the company sold products or services to, or how the sales were distributed over the 12 months of the year. (Public companies are required to release quarterly income statements during the year, and they include a special summary of quarter-by-quarter results in their annual financial reports; private businesses may or may not release quarterly sales data.) Sales revenue does not include sales and excise taxes that the business collects from its customers and remits to the government.

Note: In addition to sales revenue from selling products and/or services, a business may have income from other sources. For instance, a business may have earnings from investments in marketable securities. In its income statement, investment income goes on a separate line and is not commingled with sales revenue. (The businesses featured in Figures 2-1 and 2-2 don't have investment income.)

» **Gross margin matters.** The *cost of goods sold* expense of a business that sells products is the cost of products sold to customers, the sales revenue of which is reported on the *sales revenue* line. The idea is to match up the sales revenue of goods sold with the cost of goods sold and show the *gross margin* (also called *gross profit*), which is the profit before other expenses are deducted. The other expenses could in total be more than gross margin, in which case the business would have a net loss for the period. (By the way, a bottom-line loss usually has parentheses around it to emphasize that it's a negative number.)

Note: Companies that sell services rather than products (such as airlines, movie theaters, and CPA firms) do *not* have a cost of goods sold expense line in their income statements, as you see in Figure 2-2. Nevertheless, some service companies report a cost of sales expense, and these businesses may also report a corresponding gross margin line of sorts. This is one more example of the variation in financial reporting from business to business that you have to live with if you read financial reports.

>> **Operating costs are lumped together.** The broad category *selling, general, and administrative expenses* (refer to Figure 2-1) consists of a wide variety of costs of operating the business and making sales. Some examples are

- Labor costs (employee wages and salaries, plus retirement benefits, health insurance, and payroll taxes paid by the business)

- Insurance premiums

- Property taxes on buildings and land

HOW BIG IS A BIG BUSINESS, AND HOW SMALL IS A SMALL BUSINESS?

One key measure of the size of a business is the number of employees it has on its payroll. Could the business shown in Figure 2-1 have 500 employees? Probably not. This would mean that the annual sales revenue per employee would be only $52,000 ($26 million annual sales revenue divided by 500 employees). But the annual wage per employee in many industries today is over $35,000 and much higher in some industries. Much more likely, the number of full-time employees in this business is closer to 100. This number of employees yields $260,000 sales revenue per employee, which means that the business could probably afford an average annual wage of $40,000 per employee or higher. Do the math to check this out.

Public companies generally disclose their numbers of employees in their annual financial reports, but private businesses generally don't. U.S. accounting standards do not require that the total number and total compensation of employees be reported in the external financial statements of a business or in the footnotes to the financial statements.

The definition of a "small business" isn't uniform. Generally, the term refers to a business with fewer than 100 full-time employees, but in some situations, it refers to businesses with fewer than 20 employees or even fewer than 10 full-time employees. Say a business has 20 full-time employees on its payroll who earn an average of $40,000 in annual wages (a relatively low amount). This costs $800,000 for its annual payroll before figuring in employee benefits (such as Social Security taxes, 401(k) matching retirement plans, health insurance, and so on). Product businesses need to earn annual gross margin equal to two or three times their basic payroll expense.

- Cost of gas and electric utilities

- Travel and entertainment costs

- Telephone and Internet charges

- Depreciation of operating assets that are used more than one year (including buildings, land improvements, cars and trucks, computers, office furniture, tools and machinery, and shelving)

- Advertising and sales promotion expenditures

- Legal and audit costs

As with sales revenue, you don't get much detail about operating expenses in a typical income statement as it's presented to the company's debtholders and shareholders. A business may disclose more information than you see in its income statement — mainly in the footnotes that are included with its financial statements. Public companies have to include more detail about the expenses in their filings with the SEC, which are available to anyone who looks up the information (probably over the Internet).

Being an Active Reader

The worst thing you can do when presented with an income statement is to be a passive reader. You should be inquisitive. An income statement is not fulfilling its purpose unless you grab it by its numbers and start asking questions.

For example, you should be curious regarding the size of the business (see the nearby sidebar "How big is a big business, and how small is a small business?"). Another question to ask is "How does profit compare with sales revenue for the year?" Profit (net income) equals what's left over from sales revenue after you deduct all expenses. The business featured in Figure 2-1 squeezed $1.69 million profit from its $26 million sales revenue for the year, which equals 6.5 percent. (The service business did a little better; see Figure 2-2.) This ratio of profit to sales revenue means expenses absorbed 93.5 percent of sales revenue. Although it may seem rather thin, a 6.5 percent profit margin on sales is quite acceptable for many businesses. (Some businesses consistently make a bottom-line profit of 10 to 20 percent of sales, and others are satisfied with a 1 or 2 percent profit on sales revenue.) Profit ratios on sales vary widely from industry to industry.

TALKING ABOUT PROFIT: THE *P* WORD

You won't be surprised to hear that the financial objective of every business is to earn an adequate profit on a sustainable basis. In the pursuit of profit, a business should behave ethically, stay within the law, care for its employees, and be friendly to the environment. But the blunt truth of the matter is that *profit* is a dirty word to many people, and the profit motive is a favorite target of many critics who blame the push for profit for unsafe working conditions, outsourcing, wages that are below the poverty line, and other ills of the economic system. The profit motive is an easy target for criticism.

You hear a lot about the profit motive of business, but you don't see the *p* word in many external financial reports. The financial press uses the term *profit* but also alternative terms — in particular, *earnings.* For example, *The Wall Street Journal* and *The New York Times* use the term *earnings reports.* If you look in financial statements, the term *net income* is used most often for the bottom-line profit that a business earns. Accountants prefer *net income,* although they also use other names, like *net earnings* and *net operating earnings.*

In short, *profit* is more of a street name; in polite company, you generally say *net income.* However, here is one exception. Caterpillar, Inc., uses the term *profit* for the bottom line of its income statement; it's one of the few companies that call a spade a spade.

REMEMBER

Accounting standards are relatively silent regarding which expenses have to be disclosed on the face of an income statement or elsewhere in a financial report. For example, the amount a business spends on advertising doesn't have to be disclosed. (In contrast, the rules for filing financial reports with the SEC require disclosure of certain expenses, such as repairs and maintenance expenses. Keep in mind that the SEC rules apply only to public businesses.)

In the product business example in Figure 2-1, expenses such as labor costs and advertising expenditures are buried in the all-inclusive *selling, general, and administrative expenses* line. (If the business manufactures the products it sells instead of buying them from another business, a good part of its annual labor cost is included in its *cost of goods sold* expense.) Some companies disclose specific expenses such as advertising and marketing costs, research and development costs, and other significant expenses. In short, income statement expense-disclosure practices vary considerably from business to business.

Another set of questions you should ask in reading an income statement concerns the *profit performance* of the business. Refer again to the product company's profit performance report (Figure 2-1). Profitwise, how did the business do? Underneath this question is the implicit question "Relative to *what?*" Generally speaking, three sorts of benchmarks are used for evaluating profit performance:

» Broad, industrywide performance averages

» Immediate competitors' performances

» The business's own performance in recent years

Deconstructing Profit

After that you've had the opportunity to read an income statement (see Figures 2-1, 2-2, and 2-3), consider this question: What *is* profit? You'll probably answer that profit is revenue less expenses. Your answer is correct, as far as it goes, but it doesn't go far enough. This answer doesn't strike at the core of profit. The answer doesn't say what profit consists of or the substance of profit.

This section explains the anatomy of profit. Having read the product company's income statement, you now know that the business earned net income for the year ending December 31, 2019 (see Figure 2-1). Where's the profit? If you had to put your finger on the profit, where would you touch?

Recording profit works like a pair of scissors: You have the positive revenue blade and the negative expenses blade. Revenue and expenses have opposite effects. This leads to two questions: What is a revenue? And what is an expense?

Figure 2-4 summarizes the financial natures of revenue and expenses in terms of impacts on assets and liabilities. Notice the symmetrical framework of revenue and expenses. It's beautiful in its own way, don't you think? In any case, this summary framework is helpful for understanding the financial effects of revenue and expenses.

FIGURE 2-4:
Fundamental
natures of
revenue and
expenses.

	Asset	Liability
Revenue	+	–
Expense	–	+

© *John Wiley & Sons, Inc.*

Revenue and expense effects on assets and liabilities

Here's the gist of the two-by-two matrix shown in Figure 2-4. In recording a sale, the bookkeeper increases a revenue account. The revenue account accumulates sale after sale during the period. So at the end of the period, the total sales revenue for the period is the balance in the account. This amount is the cumulative end-of-period total of all sales during the period. All sales revenue accounts are combined for the period, and one grand total is reported in the income statement on the top line. As each sale (or other type of revenue event) is recorded, either an asset account is increased or a liability account is decreased.

TIP

You probably follow that revenue increases an asset. For example, if all sales are made for cash, the company's cash account increases accordingly. On the other hand, you may have trouble understanding that certain revenue transactions are recorded with a decrease in a liability. Here's why: Customers may pay in advance for a product or service to be delivered later (examples are prepaying for theater or airline tickets and making a down payment for future delivery of products). In recording such advance payments from customers, the business increases cash, of course, and increases a liability account usually called *deferred revenue*. The term *deferred* simply means postponed. When the product or service is delivered to the customer — and not before then — the bookkeeper records the amount of revenue that has now been earned *and* decreases the deferred revenue liability by the same amount.

Recording expenses is rather straightforward. When an expense is recorded, a specific expense account is increased, and either an asset account is decreased or a liability account is increased the same amount. For example, to record the cost of goods sold, the expense with this name is increased, say, $35,000, and in the same entry, the inventory asset account is decreased $35,000. Alternatively, an expense entry may involve a liability account instead of an asset account. For example, suppose the business receives a $10,000 bill from its CPA auditor that it will pay later. In recording the bill from the CPA, the audit expense account is increased $10,000, and a liability account called *accounts payable* is increased $10,000.

The summary framework of Figure 2-4 has no exceptions. Recording revenue and expenses (as well as gains and losses) always follow these rules. So where does this leave you for understanding profit? Profit itself doesn't show up in Figure 2-4, does it? Profit depends on amounts recorded for revenue and expenses, of course, as shown in the next section.

Comparing three scenarios of profit

Figure 2-5 presents three scenarios of profit in terms of changes in the assets and liabilities of a business. In all three cases, the business makes the same amount of profit: $10, as you see in the abbreviated income statements on the right side. (The numbers are kept small, but you can think of $10 million instead of $10 if you prefer.)

Case A

	Asset	Liability	Income Statement	
Revenue	+ $100		Revenue	$100
Expense	- $60	+ $30	Expenses	$90
			Profit	$10

Case B

	Asset	Liability	Income Statement	
Revenue		- $100	Revenue	$100
Expense	- $60	+ $30	Expenses	$90
			Profit	$10

Case C

FIGURE 2-5:
Comparing asset
and liability
changes for three
profit scenarios.

	Asset	Liability	Income Statement	
Revenue	+ $50	- $50	Revenue	$100
Expense	- $45	+ $45	Expenses	$90
			Profit	$10

© *John Wiley & Sons, Inc.*

To find the amount of profit, first determine the amount of revenue and expenses for each case. In all three cases, total expenses are $90, but the changes in assets and liabilities differ:

>> In Case 1, revenue consists of $100 asset increases; no liability was involved in recording revenue.

>> In Case 2, revenue was from $100 decreases in a liability.

>> In Case 3, you see both asset increases and liability decreases for revenue.

REMEMBER

Revenue and expenses are originally recorded as increases or decreases in different asset and liability accounts. Cash is just one asset. The other assets and the liabilities are explained in the later section "Pinpointing the Assets and Liabilities Used to Record Revenue and Expenses."

Some businesses make sales for cash; cash is received at the time of the sale. In recording these sales, a revenue account is increased and the cash account is increased. Some expenses are recorded at the time of cutting a check to pay the expense. In recording these expenses, an appropriate expense account is increased and the cash asset account is decreased. However, for most businesses, the majority of their revenue and expense transactions don't simultaneously affect cash.

For most businesses, cash comes into play before or after revenue and expenses are recorded. For example, a business buys products from its supplier that it will sell sometime later to its customers. The purchase is paid for before the goods are sold. No expense is recorded until products are sold. Here's another example: A business makes sales on credit to its customers. In recording credit sales, a sales revenue account is increased and an asset account called *accounts receivable* is increased. Sometime later, the receivables are collected in cash. The amount of cash actually collected through the end of the period may be less than the amount of sales revenue recorded.

REMEMBER

Cash inflow from revenue is almost always different from revenue for the period. Furthermore, cash outflow for expenses is almost always different from expenses for the period. The lesson is this: Don't equate revenue with cash inflow, and do not equate expenses with cash outflows. The net cash flow from profit for the period — revenue inflow minus expense outflow — is bound to be higher or lower than the accounting-based measure of profit for the period. The income statement does not report cash flows!

This chapter lays the foundation for Chapter 4 of Book 3, which explains cash flow from profit. Cash flow is an enormously important topic in every business. Probably even Apple, with its huge treasure of marketable investments, worries about its cash flow.

Folding profit into retained earnings

REMEMBER

After profit is determined for the period, which means that all revenue and expenses have been recorded for the period, the profit amount is entered as an increase in *retained earnings*. Doing this keeps the accounting equation in balance. For Case 1 in Figure 2-5, for example, the changes in the accounting equation for the period are as follows:

+$40 Assets = +$30 Liabilities + $10 Retained Earnings

The $40 increase on the asset side is balanced by the $30 increase in liabilities and the $10 increase in retained earnings on the opposite side of the accounting equation. The books are in balance.

In most situations, not all annual profit is distributed to owners; some is retained in the business. Unfortunately, the retained earnings account sounds like an asset in the minds of many people. It isn't! It's a source-of-assets account, not an asset account. It's on the right-hand side of the accounting equation; assets are on the left side. For more information, see the sidebar "So why is it called retained earnings?"

The product business in Figure 2-1 earned $1.69 million profit for the year. Therefore, during the year, its retained earnings increased this amount because net income is recorded in this owners' equity account. You know this for sure, but what you can't tell from the income statement is how the assets and liabilities of the business were affected by its sale and expense activities during the period. The product company's $1.69 million net income resulted in some mixture of changes in its assets and liabilities, such that its owners' equity increased $1.69 million. Could be that its assets increased $1.0 million and its liabilities increased $0.69 million, but you can't tell this from the income statement.

TIP

The financial gyrations in assets and operating liabilities from profit-making activities are especially important for business managers to understand and pay attention to because they have to manage and control the changes. It would be dangerous to assume that making a profit has only beneficial effects on assets and liabilities. One of the main purposes of the statement of cash flows, which are discussed in Chapter 4 of Book 3, is to summarize the financial changes caused by the profit activities of the business during the year.

SO WHY IS IT CALLED RETAINED EARNINGS?

The ending balance reported in the retained earnings account is the amount after recording increases and decreases in the account during the period, starting with the opening balance at the start of the period, of course. The retained earnings account increases when the business makes a profit and decreases when the business distributes some of the profit to its owners. That is, the total amount of profit paid out to the owners is recorded as a decrease in the retained earnings account. (Exactly how the profit is divided among the owners depends on the ownership structure of the business; see Chapter 6 in Book 2.)

Bonus question: Why doesn't a business pay out all its annual profit to owners? One reason is that the business may not have converted all its profit into cash by the end of the year and may not have enough cash to distribute. Or the business may have had the cash but needed it for other purposes, such as growing the company by buying new buildings and equipment or spending the money on research and development of new products. Reinvesting the profit in the business in this way is often referred to as *plowing back* earnings. A business should always make good use of its cash flow instead of letting the cash pile up in the cash account. See Chapter 6 of Book 3 for more on cash flow from profit.

Pinpointing the Assets and Liabilities Used to Record Revenue and Expenses

The sales and expense activities of a business involve cash inflows and outflows, as you probably know. What you may not know, however, is that the profit-making activities of a business that sells products on credit involves four other basic assets and three basic types of liabilities. Cash is the pivotal asset. You may have heard the old saying that "all roads lead to Rome." In like manner, revenue and expenses, sooner or later, lead to cash. But in the meantime, other asset and liability accounts are used to record the flow of profit activity. This section explains the main assets and liabilities used in recording revenue and expenses.

Making sales: Accounts receivable and deferred revenue

Many businesses allow their customers to buy their products or services on credit, or "on the cuff," as they said in the old days. The customer buys now and pays later. To record credit sales, a business uses an asset account called *accounts receivable*. Recording a credit sale increases sales revenue and increases accounts receivable. The business records now and collects later. The immediate recording of credit sales is one aspect of the *accrual basis of accounting* (see Chapter 1 of Book 3). When the customer pays the business, cash is increased and accounts receivable is decreased. In most cases, a business doesn't collect all its credit sales by the end of the year, so it reports a balance for its accounts receivable in its end-of-period balance sheet (see Chapter 3 of Book 3).

In contrast to making sales on credit, some businesses collect cash before they deliver their products or services to customers. For example, suppose you pay *The New York Times* for a one-year subscription at the start of the year. During the year, the newspaper "delivers" the product one day at a time. Another example is when you buy and pay for an airline ticket days or weeks ahead of your flight. There are many examples of advance payments by customers. When a business receives advance payments from customers, it increases cash (of course) and increases a liability account called *deferred revenue*. Sales revenue isn't recorded until the product or service is delivered to the customer. When delivered sales revenue is increased, the liability account is decreased, which reflects that part of the liability has been "paid down" by delivery of the product or service.

REMEMBER

Increases or decreases in the asset *accounts receivable* and the liability account *deferred revenue* affect cash flow during the year from the profit-making activities of the business. Find out more cash flow in Chapter 4 of Book 3. Until then, keep in mind that the balance of accounts receivable is money waiting in the wings to be collected in the near future, and the balance in deferred revenue is the amount of money collected in advance from customers. These two accounts appear in the balance sheet, which is discussed in Chapter 3 of Book 3.

Selling products: Inventory

The *cost of goods sold* is one of the primary expenses of businesses that sell products. (In Figure 2-1, notice that this expense equals more than half the sales revenue for the year.) This expense is just what its name implies: the cost that a business pays for the products it sells to customers. A business makes profit by setting its sales prices high enough to cover the costs of products sold, the costs of operating the business, interest on borrowed money, and income taxes (assuming that the business pays income tax), with something left over for profit.

When the business acquires products (by purchase or manufacture), the cost of the products goes into an *inventory* asset account (and, of course, the cost is either deducted from the cash account or added to a liability account, depending on whether the business pays cash or buys on credit). When a customer buys that product, the business transfers the cost of the products sold from the inventory asset account to the *cost of goods sold* expense account because the products are no longer in the business's inventory; the products have been delivered to the customer.

In the first layer in the income statement of a product company, the cost of goods sold expense is deducted from the sales revenue for the goods sold. Almost all businesses that sell products report the cost of goods sold as a separate expense in their income statements, as you see in Figure 2-1. Most report this expense as shown in Figure 2-1 so that *gross margin* is reported. But some product companies simply report cost of goods sold as one expense among many and do not call attention to gross margin. Actually, you see many variations on the theme of reporting gross margin. Some businesses use the broader term "cost of sales," which includes cost of goods sold as well as other costs.

REMEMBER

A business that sells products needs to have a stock of those products on hand for ready sale to its customers. When you drive by an auto dealer and see all the cars, SUVs, and pickup trucks waiting to be sold, remember that these products are inventory. The cost of unsold products (goods held in inventory) is not yet an expense; only after the products are actually sold does the cost get recorded as an expense. In this way, the cost of goods sold expense is correctly matched against the sales revenue from the goods sold. Correctly matching expenses against sales revenue is the essential starting point of accounting for profit.

Prepaying operating costs: Prepaid expenses

Prepaid expenses are the opposite of unpaid expenses. For example, a business buys fire insurance and general liability insurance (in case a customer who slips on a wet floor or is insulted by a careless salesperson sues the business). Insurance premiums must be paid ahead of time, before coverage starts. The premium cost is allocated to expense in the actual periods benefited. At the end of the year, the business may be only halfway through the insurance coverage period, so it should allocate only half the premium cost as an expense. (For a six-month policy, you charge one-sixth of the premium cost to each of the six months covered.) At the time the premium is paid, the entire amount is recorded as an increase in the prepaid expenses asset account. For each period of coverage, the appropriate fraction of the cost is recorded as a decrease in the asset account and as an increase in the insurance expense account.

In another example, a business pays cash to stock up on office supplies that it may not use up for several months. The cost is recorded in the prepaid expenses asset account at the time of purchase; when the supplies are used, the appropriate amount is subtracted from the prepaid expenses asset account and recorded in the office supplies expense account.

TIP

Using the prepaid expenses asset account is not so much for the purpose of reporting all the assets of a business, because the balance in the account compared with other assets and total assets is typically small. Rather, using this account is an example of allocating costs to expenses in the period benefited by the costs, which isn't always the same period in which the business pays those costs. The prepayment of these expenses lays the groundwork for continuing operations seamlessly into the next year.

Fixed assets: Depreciation expenses

Long-term operating assets that are not held for sale in the ordinary course of business are called generically *fixed assets*; these include buildings, machinery, office equipment, vehicles, computers and data-processing equipment, shelving and cabinets, and so on. The term *fixed assets* is informal, or accounting slang. The more formal term used in financial reports is *property, plant, and equipment.* It's easier to say *fixed assets,* as in this section.

Depreciation refers to spreading out the cost of a fixed asset over the years of its useful life to a business, instead of charging the entire cost to expense in the year of purchase. That way, each year of use bears a share of the total cost. For example, autos and light trucks are typically depreciated over five years; the idea is to charge a fraction of the total cost to depreciation expense during each of the five years. (The actual fraction each year depends on the method of depreciation used.)

TIP

Depreciation applies only to fixed assets that a business owns, not those it rents or leases. If a company leases or rents fixed assets, which is quite common, the rent it pays each month is charged to *rent expense.* Depreciation is a real expense but not a cash outlay expense in the year it's recorded. The cash outlay occurred when the fixed asset was acquired.

TECHNICAL STUFF

Suppose a business records $100,000 depreciation for the period. You'd think that the depreciation expense account would be increased $100,000 and one or more fixed asset accounts would be decreased $100,000. Well, not so fast. Instead of directly decreasing the fixed asset account, the bookkeeper increases a contra asset account called *accumulated depreciation.* The balance in this negative account is deducted from the balance of the fixed asset account. In this manner, the original acquisition cost of the fixed asset is preserved, and the historical cost is reported in the balance sheet. Read about this practice in Chapter 3 of Book 3.

TIP

Take a look back at the product company income statement example in Figure 2-1. From the information supplied in this income statement, you don't know the amount of depreciation expense the business recorded in 2019. However, the footnotes to the business's financial statements and its statement of cash flows reveal this amount. In 2019, the business recorded $775,000 depreciation expense. Basically, this expense decreases the book value (the recorded value) of its depreciable assets. *Book value* equals original cost minus the accumulated depreciation recorded so far. Book value may be different — indeed, quite a bit different — compared with the current replacement value of fixed assets.

Unpaid expenses: Accounts payable, accrued expenses payable, and income tax payable

A typical business pays many expenses *after* the period in which the expenses are recorded. Following are common examples:

>> A business hires a law firm that does a lot of legal work during the year, but the company doesn't pay the bill until the following year.

>> A business matches retirement contributions made by its employees but doesn't pay its share of the latest payroll until the following year.

>> A business has unpaid bills for telephone service, gas, electricity, and water that it used during the year.

REMEMBER

Accountants use three types of liability accounts to record a business's unpaid expenses:

>> **Accounts payable:** This account is used for items that the business buys on credit and for which it receives an invoice (a bill) either in hard copy or over the Internet. For example, your business receives an invoice from its lawyers for legal work done. As soon as you receive the invoice, you record in the accounts payable liability account the amount that you owe. Later, when you pay the invoice, you subtract that amount from the accounts payable account, and your cash goes down by the same amount.

>> **Accrued expenses payable:** A business has to make estimates for several unpaid costs at the end of the year because it hasn't received invoices or other types of bills for them. Examples of accrued expenses include the following:

- Unused vacation and sick days that employees carry over to the following year, which the business has to pay for in the coming year

- Unpaid bonuses to salespeople

- The cost of future repairs and part replacements on products that customers have bought and haven't yet returned for repair

- The daily accumulation of interest on borrowed money that won't be paid until the end of the loan period

Without invoices to reference, you have to examine your business operations carefully to determine which liabilities of this sort to record.

>> **Income tax payable:** This account is used for income taxes that a business still owes to the IRS at the end of the year. The income tax expense for the year is the total amount based on the taxable income for the entire year. Your business may not pay 100 percent of its income tax expense during the year; it may owe a small fraction to the IRS at year's end. You record the unpaid amount in the income tax payable account.

Note: A business may be organized legally as a *pass-through tax entity* for income tax purposes, which means that it doesn't pay income tax itself but instead passes its taxable income on to its owners. The business referred to here is an ordinary corporation that pays income tax.

Reporting Unusual Gains and Losses

Confession time: The income statement examples in Figures 2-1, 2-2, and 2-3 are sanitized versions when compared with actual income statements in external financial reports. Suppose you took the trouble to read 100 income statements.

You'd be surprised at the wide range of things you'd find in these statements. But one thing you'd discover is certain.

Many businesses report *unusual gains and losses* in addition to their usual revenue and expenses. Remember that recording a gain increases an asset or decreases a liability. And recording a loss decreases an asset or increases a liability. The road to profit is anything but smooth and straight. Every business experiences an occasional gain or loss that's off the beaten path — a serious disruption that comes out of the blue, doesn't happen regularly, and impacts the bottom-line profit. Such unusual gains and losses are perturbations in the continuity of the business's regular flow of profit-making activities.

Here are some examples of unusual gains and losses:

» **Downsizing and restructuring the business:** Layoffs require severance pay or trigger early retirement costs. Major segments of the business may be disposed of, causing large losses.

» **Abandoning product lines:** When you decide to discontinue selling a line of products, you lose at least some of the money that you paid for obtaining or manufacturing the products, either because you sell the products for less than you paid or because you just dump the products you can't sell.

» **Settling lawsuits and other legal actions:** Damages and fines that you pay — as well as awards that you *receive* in a favorable ruling — are obviously nonrecurring losses or gains (unless you're in the habit of being taken to court every year).

» **Writing down (also called *writing off*) damaged and impaired assets:** If products become damaged and unsellable or if fixed assets need to be replaced unexpectedly, you need to remove these items from the assets accounts. Even when certain assets are in good physical condition, if they lose their ability to generate future sales or other benefits to the business, accounting rules say that the assets have to be taken off the books or at least written down to lower book values.

» **Changing accounting methods:** A business may decide to use a different method for recording revenue and expenses than it did in the past, in some cases because the accounting rules (set by the authoritative accounting governing bodies) have changed. Often, the new method requires a business to record a one-time cumulative effect caused by the switch in accounting method. These special items can be huge.

» **Correcting errors from previous financial reports:** If you or your accountant discovers that a past financial report had a serious accounting error, you make a catch-up correction entry, which means that you record a loss or gain that has nothing to do with your performance this year.

The basic tests for an unusual gain or loss are that it is unusual in nature or infrequently occurring. Deciding what qualifies as an unusual gain or loss is not a cut-and-dried process. Different accountants may have different interpretations of what fits the concept of an unusual gain or loss.

According to financial reporting standards, a business should disclose unusual gains and losses on a separate line in the income statement or, alternatively, explain them in a footnote to its financial statements. There seems to be a general preference to put an unusual gain or loss on a separate line in the income statement. Therefore, in addition to the usual lines for revenue and expenses, the income statement would disclose separate lines for these out-of-the-ordinary happenings.

WARNING

Every company that stays in business for more than a couple of years experiences an unusual gain or loss of one sort or another. But beware of a business that takes advantage of these discontinuities in the following ways:

>> **Discontinuities become continuities:** This business makes an extraordinary loss or gain a regular feature on its income statement. Every year or so, the business loses a major lawsuit, abandons product lines, or restructures itself. It reports certain "nonrecurring" gains or losses on a recurring basis.

>> **A discontinuity is used as an opportunity to record all sorts of write-downs and losses:** When recording an unusual loss (such as settling a lawsuit), the business opts to record other losses at the same time, and everything but the kitchen sink (and sometimes that, too) gets written off. This so-called *big-bath* strategy says that you may as well take a big bath now in order to avoid taking little showers in the future.

A business may just have bad (or good) luck regarding unusual events that its managers couldn't have predicted. If a business is facing a major, unavoidable expense this year, cleaning out all its expenses in the same year so it can start off fresh next year can be a clever, legitimate accounting tactic. But where do you draw the line between these accounting manipulations and fraud? Stay alert to these potential problems.

Watching for Misconceptions and Misleading Reports

One broad misconception about profit is that the numbers reported in the income statement are precise and accurate and can be relied on down to the last dollar. Call this the *exactitude* misconception. Virtually every dollar amount you see in an income statement probably would have been different if a different accountant had been in charge. It's not that some accountants are dishonest and deceitful. It's just that business transactions can get very complex and require forecasts and estimates. Different accountants would arrive at different interpretations of the "facts" and therefore record different amounts of revenue and expenses. Hopefully, the accountant is consistent over time so that year-to-year comparisons are valid.

Another serious misconception is that if profit is good, the financial condition of the business is good. At the time of writing, the profit of Apple is very good. But you can't automatically assume that its financial condition was equally good. (Actually, in Apple's balance sheet, its financial condition is very good indeed. It has more cash and marketable investments on hand than the economy of many countries.) The point is that its bottom line doesn't tell you anything about the financial condition of the business. You find this in the balance sheet, which is explained in Chapter 3 of Book 3.

The income statement occupies center stage; the bright spotlight is on this financial statement because it reports profit or loss for the period. But remember that a business reports *three* primary financial statements — the other two being the balance sheet and the statement of cash flows, which are discussed in Chapters 3 and 4 of Book 3. The three statements are like a three-ring circus. The income statement may draw the most attention, but you have to watch what's going on in all three places. As important as profit is to the financial success of a business, the income statement is not an island unto itself.

TIP

Keep in mind that financial statements are supplemented with footnotes and contain other commentary from the business's executives. If the financial statements have been audited, the CPA firm includes a short report stating whether the financial statements have been prepared in conformity with the appropriate accounting standards.

Note that an income statement you read and rely on — as a business manager, an investor, or a lender — may not be true and accurate. In most cases (perhaps even in the large majority of cases), businesses prepare their financial statements in good faith, and their profit accounting is honest. They may bend the rules a little, but basically their accounting methods are within the boundaries of generally accepted accounting principles (GAAP) even though the business puts a favorable spin on its profit number.

WARNING

But some businesses resort to accounting fraud and deliberately distort their profit numbers. In this case, an income statement reports false and misleading sales revenue and/or expenses in order to make the bottom-line profit appear to be better than the facts would support. If the fraud is discovered at a later time, the business puts out revised financial statements. Basically, the business in this situation rewrites its profit history.

The number of high-profile accounting fraud cases over the recent two decades (and longer, in fact) has been truly alarming. The CPA auditors of these companies didn't catch the accounting fraud, even though this is one purpose of an audit. Investors who relied on the fraudulent income statements ended up suffering large losses.

Anytime you read a financial report, keep in mind the risk that the financial statements may be "stage managed" to some extent — to make year-to-year reported profit look a little smoother and less erratic and to make the financial condition of the business appear a little better. Regrettably, financial statements don't always tell it as it is. Rather, the chief executive and chief accountant of the business fiddle with the financial statements to some extent.

» Categorizing business transactions

» Connecting revenue and expenses with their assets and liabilities

» Examining where businesses go for capital

» Understanding values in balance sheets

Chapter **3**

Showing Financial Condition in the Balance Sheet

This chapter explores one of the three primary financial statements reported by business and not-for-profit entities: the *balance sheet*, which is also called the *statement of financial condition* and the *statement of financial position*. This financial statement summarizes the assets of a business and its liabilities and owners' equity sources at a point in time. The balance sheet is a two-sided financial statement.

The balance sheet may seem to stand alone because it's presented on a separate page in a financial report, but keep in mind that the assets and liabilities reported in a balance sheet are the results of the activities, or transactions, of the business. *Transactions* are economic exchanges between the business and the parties it deals with: customers, employees, vendors, government agencies, and sources of capital. The other two financial statements — the income statement (Chapter 2 in Book 3) and the statement of cash flows (Chapter 4 in Book 3) — report transactions, whereas the balance sheet reports values at an instant in time. The balance sheet is prepared at the end of the income statement period.

Unlike the income statement, the balance sheet doesn't have a natural bottom line, or one key figure that's the focus of attention. The balance sheet reports various assets, liabilities, and sources of owners' equity. Cash is the most important asset, but other assets are important as well. Short-term liabilities are compared to cash and assets that can be converted into cash quickly. The balance sheet, as explained in this chapter, has to be read as a whole — you can't focus only on one or two items in this financial summary of the business. You shouldn't put on blinders in reading a balance sheet by looking only at two or three items. You might miss important information by not perusing the whole balance sheet.

Expanding the Accounting Equation

The *accounting equation* is a very condensed version of a balance sheet. In its most concise form, the accounting equation is as follows:

Assets = Liabilities + Owners' Equity

Figure 3-1 expands the accounting equation to identify the basic accounts reported in a balance sheet.

Assets	=	Liabilities	+	Owners' Equity
Cash		Accounts Payable		Invested Capital Account
Accounts Receivable		Accrued Expenses Payable		Retained Earnings
Inventory		Income Tax Payable		
Prepaid Expenses		Short-term Debt		
Fixed Assets		Long-term Debt		

FIGURE 3-1: Expanded accounting equation.

© John Wiley & Sons, Inc.

Many of the balance sheet accounts you see in Figure 3-1 are introduced in Chapter 2 of Book 3, which explains the income statement and the profit-making activities of a business. In fact, most balance sheet accounts are driven by profit-making transactions.

REMEMBER

Certain balance sheet accounts aren't involved in recording the profit-making transactions of a business. Short- and long-term debt accounts aren't used in recording revenue and expenses, and neither is the invested capital account, which records the investment of capital from the owners of the business. Transactions involving debt and owners' invested capital accounts have to do with *financing* the business — that is, securing the capital needed to run the business.

Presenting a Proper Balance Sheet

Figure 3-2 presents a two-year, comparative balance sheet for the business example that is introduced in Chapter 2 of Book 3. This business sells products and makes sales on credit to its customers. (Its income statement for the year just ended is shown in Chapter 2 of Book 3 — Figure 2-1.) The balance sheet is at the close of business, December 31, 2018 and 2019. In most cases, financial statements aren't completed and released until a few weeks after the balance sheet date. Therefore, by the time you read this financial statement, it's already somewhat out of date, because the business has continued to engage in transactions since December 31, 2019. When significant changes have occurred in the interim between the closing date of the balance sheet and the date of releasing its financial report, a business should disclose these subsequent developments in the footnotes to the financial statements.

TIP

The balance sheet in Figure 3-2 is in the vertical (portrait) layout, with assets on top and liabilities and owners' equity on the bottom. Alternatively, a balance sheet may be in the horizontal (landscape) mode, with liabilities and owners' equity on the right side and assets on the left.

The financial statement in Figure 3-2 is called a *classified* balance sheet because certain accounts are grouped into classes (groups). Although the accounts in the class are different, they have common characteristics. Two such classes are *current assets* and *current liabilities*. Notice that subtotals are provided for each class. The reasons for reporting these classes of accounts are discussed later in this chapter (see "Current assets and liabilities"). The total amount of assets and the total amount of liabilities plus owners' equity are given at the bottom of the columns for each year. You probably don't have to be reminded that these two amounts should be equal; otherwise, the company's books aren't in balance.

WARNING

If a business doesn't release its annual financial report within a few weeks after the close of its fiscal year, you should be alarmed. There are reasons for such a delay, and the reasons are all bad. One reason might be that the business's accounting system isn't functioning well and the controller (chief accounting officer) has to do a lot of work at year-end to get the accounts up to date and accurate for preparing its financial statements. Another reason is that the business is facing serious problems and can't decide on how to account for the problems. Perhaps a business is delaying the reporting of bad news. Or the business may have a serious dispute with its independent CPA auditor that hasn't been resolved.

Typical Product Business, Inc. Statement of Financial Condition at December 31, 2018 and 2019 (Dollar amounts in thousands)			
Assets	**2018**	**2019**	**Change**
Cash	$2,275	$2,165	($110)
Accounts Receivable	$2,150	$2,600	$450
Inventory	$2,725	$3,450	$725
Prepaid Expenses	$525	$600	$75
Current Assets	$7,675	$8,815	
Property, Plant, and Equipment	$11,175	$12,450	$1,275
Accumulated Depreciation	($5,640)	($6,415)	($775)
Net of Depreciation	$5,535	$6,035	
Total Assets	$13,210	$14,850	$1,640
Liabilities and Owners' Equity	**2018**	**2019**	**Change**
Accounts Payable	$640	$765	$125
Accrued Expenses Payable	$750	$900	$150
Income Tax Payable	$90	$115	$25
Short-term Notes Payable	$2,150	$2,250	$100
Current Liabilities	$3,630	$4,030	
Long-term Notes Payable	$3,850	$4,000	$150
Owners' Equity:			
Capital Stock	$3,100	$3,250	$150
Retained Earnings	$2,630	$3,570	$940
Total Owners' Equity	$5,730	$6,820	
Total Liabilities and Owners' Equity	$13,210	$14,850	$1,640

© *John Wiley & Sons, Inc.*

FIGURE 3-2:
Illustrative two-year comparative balance sheet for a product business.

REMEMBER

The balance sheet in Figure 3-2 includes a column for *changes* in the assets, liabilities, and owners' equity over the year (from year end 2018 through year end 2019). Including these changes isn't required by financial reporting standards, and in fact most businesses don't include the changes. It's certainly acceptable to report balance sheet changes, but it's not mandated, and most companies don't. The changes are included for ease of reference in this chapter. Transactions generate changes in assets, liabilities, and owners' equity, which are explained later in this chapter (see the section "Understanding That Transactions Drive the Balance Sheet").

Doing an initial reading of the balance sheet

Now suppose you own the business whose balance sheet is in Figure 3-2. (Most likely, you wouldn't own 100 percent of the ownership shares of the business; you'd own the majority of shares, giving you working control of the business.) You've already digested your most recent annual income statement (refer to Chapter 2 in Book 3 — Figure 2-1), which reports that you earned $1,690,000 net income on annual sales of $26,000,000. What more do you need to know? Well, you need to check your financial condition, which is reported in the balance sheet.

Is your financial condition viable and sustainable to continue your profit-making endeavor? The balance sheet helps answer this critical question. Perhaps you're on the edge of going bankrupt, even though you're making a profit. Your balance sheet is where to look for telltale information about possible financial troubles.

In reading through a balance sheet, you may notice that it doesn't have a punchline like the income statement does. The income statement's punchline is the net income line, which is rarely humorous to the business itself but can cause some snickers among analysts. (Earnings per share is also very important for public corporations.) You can't look at just one item on the balance sheet, murmur an appreciative "ah-ha," and rush home to watch the game. You have to read the whole thing (sigh) and make comparisons among the items.

At first glance, you might be somewhat alarmed that your cash balance decreased $110,000 during the year (refer to Figure 3-2). Didn't you make a tidy profit? Why would your cash balance go down? Well, think about it. Many other transactions affect your cash balance. For example, did you invest in new long-term operating assets (called *property, plant, and equipment* in the balance sheet)? Yes you did, as a matter of fact. These fixed assets increased $1,275,000 during the year.

Overall, your total assets increased $1,640,000. All assets except cash increased during the year. One big reason is the $940,000 increase in your retained earnings owners' equity. I explain in Chapter 2 of Book 3 that earning profit increases retained earnings. Profit was $1,690,000 for the year, but retained earnings increased only $940,000. Therefore, part of profit was distributed to the owners, decreasing retained earnings. These things and other balance sheet interpretations are discussed as you move through this chapter. For now, the preliminary read of the balance sheet doesn't indicate any earth-shattering financial problems facing your business.

TIP

The balance sheet of a service business looks pretty much the same as a product business (see Figure 3-2) — except a service business doesn't report an inventory of products held for sale. If it sells on credit, a service business has an accounts receivable asset, just like a product company that sells on credit. The size of its total assets relative to annual sales revenue for a service business varies greatly from industry to industry, depending on whether the service industry is *capital intensive* or not. Some service businesses, such as airlines, for-profit hospitals, and hotel chains, need to make heavy investments in long-term operating assets. Other service businesses don't.

REMEMBER

The balance sheet is unlike the income and cash flow statements, which report flows over a period of time (such as sales revenue that is the cumulative amount of all sales during the period). The balance sheet presents the *balances* (amounts) of a company's assets, liabilities, and owners' equity at an instant in time. Notice the two quite different meanings of the term *balance:*

>> As used in *balance sheet,* the term refers to the equality of the two opposing sides of a business — total assets on the one side and total liabilities and owners' equity on the other side, like a scale.

>> In contrast, the *balance* of an account (asset, liability, owners' equity, revenue, and expense) refers to the amount in the account after recording increases and decreases in the account — the net amount after all additions and subtractions have been entered. Usually, the meaning of the term is clear in context.

TIP

An accountant can prepare a balance sheet at any time that a manager wants to know how things stand financially. Some businesses — particularly financial institutions such as banks, mutual funds, and securities brokers — need balance sheets at the end of each day in order to track their day-to-day financial situation. For most businesses, however, balance sheets are prepared only at the end of each month, quarter, or year. A balance sheet is always prepared at the close of business on the last day of the profit period. In other words, the balance sheet should be in sync with the income statement.

Kicking balance sheets out into the real world

The statement of financial condition, or balance sheet, in Figure 3-2 is about as lean and mean as you'll ever read. In the real world, many businesses are fat and complex. Also, Figure 3-2 shows the content and format for an *external* balance sheet, which means a balance sheet that's included in a financial report released outside a business to its owners and creditors. Balance sheets that stay within a business can be quite different.

Internal balance sheets

REMEMBER

For internal reporting of financial condition to managers, balance sheets include much more detail, either in the body of the financial statement itself or, more likely, in supporting schedules. Greater detail allows for better control, analysis, and decision-making. Internal balance sheets and their supporting schedules should provide all the detail that managers need to make good business decisions.

For example, just one cash account is shown in Figure 3-2, but the chief financial officer of a business needs to know the balances on deposit in each of the business's checking accounts. As another example, the balance sheet in Figure 3-2 includes just one total amount for accounts receivable, but managers need details on which customers owe money and whether any major amounts are past due.

External balance sheets

Balance sheets presented in external financial reports (which go out to investors and lenders) don't include a whole lot more detail than the balance sheet in Figure 3-2. However, as mentioned earlier, external balance sheets must *classify* (or group together) short-term assets and liabilities. These are called *current assets* and *current liabilities,* as you see in Figure 3-2. Internal balance sheets for management use only don't have to be classified if the managers don't want the information.

REMEMBER

The term *classified,* when applied to a balance sheet, means that assets and liabilities are sorted into basic classes, or groups, for external reporting. Classifying certain assets and liabilities into *current* categories is done mainly to help readers of a balance sheet compare current assets with current liabilities for the purpose of judging the short-term solvency of a business.

Judging Liquidity and Solvency

REMEMBER

Solvency refers to the ability of a business to pay its liabilities on time. Delays in paying liabilities on time can cause serious problems for a business. In extreme cases, a business can be thrown into *involuntary bankruptcy.* Even the threat of bankruptcy can cause serious disruptions in the normal operations of a business, and profit performance is bound to suffer. The *liquidity* of a business isn't a well-defined term; it can take on different meanings. However, generally it refers to the ability of a business to keep its cash balance and its cash flows at adequate levels so that operations aren't disrupted by cash shortfalls. For more on this important topic, check out *Cash Flow For Dummies* by Tage C. Tracy and John A. Tracy (John Wiley & Sons, Inc.).

If current liabilities become too high relative to current assets — which constitute the first line of defense for paying current liabilities — managers should move quickly to resolve the problem. A perceived shortage of current assets relative to current liabilities could ring alarm bells in the minds of the company's creditors and owners.

Therefore, notice the following points in Figure 3-2 (dollar amounts refer to year-end 2019):

>> **Current assets:** The first four asset accounts (cash, accounts receivable, inventory, and prepaid expenses) are added to give the $8,815,000 subtotal for *current assets*.

>> **Current liabilities:** The first four liability accounts (accounts payable, accrued expenses payable, income tax payable, and short-term notes payable) are added to give the $4.03 million subtotal for *current liabilities*.

>> **Notes payable:** The total interest-bearing debt of the business is divided between $2.25 million in *short-term* notes payable (those due in one year or sooner) and $4 million in *long-term* notes payable (those due after one year).

Read on for details on current assets and liabilities and on the current and quick ratios.

Current assets and liabilities

Short-term, or *current*, assets include the following:

>> Cash

>> Marketable securities that can be immediately converted into cash

>> Assets converted into cash within one operating cycle, the main components being accounts receivable and inventory

The *operating cycle* refers to the repetitive process of putting cash into inventory, holding products in inventory until they're sold, selling products on credit (which generates accounts receivable), and collecting the receivables in cash. In other words, the operating cycle is the "from cash, through inventory and accounts receivable, back to cash" sequence. The operating cycles of businesses vary from a few weeks to several months, depending on how long inventory is held before being sold and how long it takes to collect cash from sales made on credit.

Short-term, or *current,* liabilities include non-interest-bearing liabilities that arise from the operating (sales and expense) activities of the business. A typical business keeps many accounts for these liabilities — a separate account for each vendor, for example. In an external balance sheet, you usually find only three or four operating liabilities, and they aren't labeled as non-interest-bearing. It's assumed that the reader knows that these operating liabilities don't bear interest (unless the liability is seriously overdue and the creditor has started charging interest because of the delay in paying the liability).

The balance sheet example in Figure 3-2 discloses three operating liabilities: accounts payable, accrued expenses payable, and income tax payable. Be warned that the terminology for these short-term operating liabilities varies from business to business.

In addition to operating liabilities, interest-bearing notes payable that have maturity dates one year or less from the balance sheet date are included in the current liabilities section. The current liabilities section may also include certain other liabilities that must be paid in the short run (which are too varied and technical to discuss here).

Current and quick ratios

The sources of cash for paying current liabilities are the company's current assets. That is, current assets are the first source of money to pay current liabilities when these liabilities come due. Remember that current assets consist of cash and assets that will be converted into cash in the short run.

The *current ratio* lets you size up current assets against total current liabilities. Using information from the balance sheet (refer to Figure 3-2), you compute the company's year-end 2019 current ratio as follows: $8,815,000 current assets divided by $4,030,000 current liabilities equals 2.2 current ratio.

TIP

Generally, businesses don't provide their current ratio on the face of their balance sheets or in the footnotes to their financial statements — they leave it to the reader to calculate this number. On the other hand, many businesses present a financial highlights section in their financial report, which often includes the current ratio.

The *quick ratio* is more restrictive. Only cash and assets that can be immediately converted into cash are included, which excludes accounts receivable, inventory, and prepaid expenses. The business in this example doesn't have any short-term marketable investments that could be sold on a moment's notice, so only cash is included for the ratio. You compute the quick ratio as follows (see Figure 3-2): $2,165,000 quick assets divided by $4,030,000 current liabilities equals 0.54 quick ratio.

REMEMBER

Folklore has it that a company's current ratio should be at least 2.0, and its quick ratio, 1.0. However, business managers know that acceptable ratios depend a great deal on general practices in the industry for short-term borrowing. Some businesses do well with current ratios less than 2.0 and quick ratios less than 1.0, so take these benchmarks with a grain of salt. Lower ratios don't necessarily mean that the business won't be able to pay its short-term (current) liabilities on time.

PREPARING MULTIYEAR STATEMENTS

The three primary financial statements of a business, including the balance sheet, are generally reported in a two- or three-year comparative format. To give you a sense of comparative financial statements, a two-year comparative format is presented in the balance sheet example in Figure 3-2. Two- or three-year comparative financial statements are *de rigueur* in filings with the Securities and Exchange Commission (SEC). Public companies have no choice, but private businesses aren't under the SEC's jurisdiction. Accounting standards favor presenting comparative financial statements for two or more years, but there are financial reports of private businesses that don't present information for prior years.

The main reason for presenting two- or three-year comparative financial statements is for *trend analysis*. The business's managers, as well as its outside investors and creditors, are extremely interested in the general trend of sales, profit margins, ratio of debt to equity, and many other vital signs of the business. Slippage in the ratio of gross margin to sales from year to year, for example, is a very serious matter.

Understanding That Transactions Drive the Balance Sheet

REMEMBER

A balance sheet is a snapshot of the financial condition of a business at an instant in time — the most important moment in time being at the end of the last day of the income statement period. The *fiscal*, or accounting, year of this chapter's business example ends on December 31. So its balance sheet is prepared at the close of business at midnight December 31. (A company should end its fiscal year at the close of its natural business year or at the close of a calendar quarter — September 30, for example.)

This freeze-frame nature of a balance sheet may make it appear that a balance sheet is static. Nothing is further from the truth. A business doesn't shut down to prepare its balance sheet. The financial condition of a business is in constant motion because the activities of the business go on nonstop.

Transactions change the makeup of a company's balance sheet — that is, its assets, liabilities, and owners' equity. The transactions of a business fall into three fundamental types:

>> **Operating activities, which also can be called profit-making activities:** This category refers to making sales and incurring expenses, and it also includes accompanying transactions that lead or follow the recording of sales and expenses. For example, a business records sales revenue when sales are made on credit and then, later, records cash collections from customers. The transaction of collecting cash is the indispensable follow-up to making the sale on credit.

For another example, a business purchases products that are placed in its inventory (its stock of products awaiting sale), at which time it records an entry for the purchase. The expense (the cost of goods sold) isn't recorded until the products are actually sold to customers.

TIP

Keep in mind that the term *operating activities* includes the associated transactions that precede or are subsequent to the recording of sales and expense transactions.

>> **Investing activities:** This term refers to making investments in assets and (eventually) disposing of the assets when the business no longer needs them. The primary examples of investing activities for businesses that sell products and services are *capital expenditures,* which are the amounts spent

Showing Financial Condition in the Balance Sheet

to modernize, expand, and replace the long-term operating assets of a business. A business may also invest in *financial assets,* such as bonds and stocks or other types of debt and equity instruments. Purchases and sales of financial assets are also included in this category of transactions.

>> **Financing activities:** These activities include securing money from debt and equity sources of capital, returning capital to these sources, and making distributions from profit to owners. Note that distributing profit to owners is treated as a financing transaction. For example, when a business corporation pays cash dividends to its stockholders, the distribution is treated as a financing transaction. The decision of whether to distribute some of its profit depends on whether the business needs more capital from its owners to grow the business or to strengthen its solvency. Retaining part or all of the profit for the year is one way of increasing the owners' equity in the business. See the later section "Financing a Business: Sources of Cash and Capital" for more information.

Figure 3-3 presents a summary of changes in assets, liabilities, and owners' equity during the year for the business example introduced in Chapter 2 of Book 3 and continue in this chapter. Notice the middle three columns, which show each of the three basic types of transactions of a business. One column is for changes caused by its revenue and expenses and their connected transactions during the year, which collectively are called *operating activities* (although you may also call them *profit-making activities*). The second column is for changes caused by its *investing activities* during the year. The third column is for the changes caused by its *financing activities.*

Note: Figure 3-3 doesn't include subtotals for current assets and liabilities; the formal balance sheet for this business is in Figure 3-2. Businesses don't report a summary of changes in their assets, liabilities, and owners' equity (though such a summary may be helpful to users of financial reports). The purpose of Figure 3-3 is to demonstrate how the three major types of transactions during the year change the assets, liabilities, and owners' equity accounts of the business during the year.

The 2019 income statement of the business is shown in Chapter 2 of Book 3. You may want to flip back to this financial statement (refer to Figure 2-1). On sales revenue of $26 million, the business earned $1.69 million bottom-line profit (net income) for the year. The sales and expense transactions of the business during the year plus the associated transactions connected with sales and expenses cause the changes shown in the operating-activities column in Figure 3-3. You can see that the $1.69 million net income has increased the business's owners' equity-retained earnings by the same amount. (The business paid $750,000 distributions from profit to its owners during the year, which decreases the balance in retained earnings.)

Typical Product Business, Inc.					
Summary of Changes in Assets, Liabilities, and Owners' Equity					
For Year Ended December 31, 2019					
(Dollar amounts in thousands)					
Assets	Beginning Balances	Operating Activities	Investing Activities	Financing Activities	Change
Cash	$2,275	$1,515	($1,275)	($350)	($110)
Accounts Receivable	$2,150	$450			$450
Inventory	$2,725	$725			$725
Prepaid Expenses	$525	$75			$75
Property, Plant, and Equipment	$11,175		$1,275		$1,275
Accumulated Depreciation	($5,640)	($775)			($775)
Totals	$13,210	$1,990	$0	($350)	$1,640
Liabilities and Owners' Equity					
Accounts Payable	$640	$125			$125
Accrued Expenses Payable	$750	$150			$150
Income Tax Payable	$90	$25			$25
Short-term Notes Payable	$2,150			$100	$100
Long-term Notes Payable	$3,850			$150	$150
Owners' Equity — Capital Stock	$3,100			$150	$150
Owners' Equity — Retained Earnings	$2,630	$1,690		($750)	$940
Totals	$13,210	$1,990		($350)	$1,640

© *John Wiley & Sons, Inc.*

FIGURE 3-3: Summary of changes in assets, liabilities, and owners' equity during the year according to basic types of transactions.

TIP

The operating-activities column in Figure 3-3 is worth lingering over for a few moments because the financial outcomes of making profit are seen in this column. Some people see a profit number, such as the $1.69 million in this example, and stop thinking any further about the financial outcomes of making the profit. This is like going to a movie because you like its title, without knowing anything about the plot and characters. You probably noticed that the $1,515,000 increase in cash in this operating-activities column differs from the $1,690,000 net income figure for the year. The cash effect of making profit (which includes the associated transactions connected with sales and expenses) is almost always different from the net income amount for the year. Chapter 4 in Book 3 explains this difference.

The summary of changes in Figure 3-3 gives you a sense of the balance sheet in motion, or how the business got from the start of the year to the end of the year. Having a good sense of how transactions propel the balance sheet is important. This kind of summary of balance sheet changes can be helpful to business managers who plan and control changes in the assets and liabilities of the business. Managers need a solid understanding of how the three basic types of transactions change assets and liabilities. Figure 3-3 also provides a useful platform for the statement of cash flow in Chapter 4 of Book 3.

Sizing Up Assets and Liabilities

When you first read the balance sheet in Figure 3-2, did you wonder about the size of the company's assets, liabilities, and owners' equities? Did you ask, "Are the balance sheet accounts about the right size?" The balances in a company's balance sheet accounts should be compared with the sales revenue size of the business. The amounts of assets that are needed to carry on the profit-making transactions of a business depend mainly on the size of its annual revenue. And the sizes of its assets, in turn, largely determine the sizes of its liabilities — which, in turn, determines the size of its owners' equity accounts (although the ratio of liabilities and owners' equity depends on other factors as well).

Although the business example that is used in this chapter is hypothetical, the numbers aren't random. The modest-sized business has $26 million in annual sales revenue. The other numbers in its income statement and balance sheet are realistic relative to each other. You can assume that the business earns 45 percent gross margin ($11.7 million gross margin ÷ $26 million sales revenue = 45 percent), which means its cost of goods sold expense is 55 percent of sales revenue. The sizes of particular assets and liabilities compared with their relevant income statement numbers vary from industry to industry and even from business to business in the same industry.

Based on the business's history and operating policies, the managers of a business can estimate what the size of each asset and liability should be; these estimates provide useful *control benchmarks* to which the actual balances of the assets and liabilities are compared. Assets (and liabilities, too) can be too high or too low relative to the sales revenue and expenses that drive them, and these deviations can cause problems that managers should try to remedy.

For example, based on the credit terms extended to its customers and the company's actual policies regarding how aggressively it acts in collecting past-due receivables, a manager determines the range for the proper, or within-the-boundaries, balance of accounts receivable. This figure is the control benchmark. If the actual balance is reasonably close to this control benchmark, accounts receivable is under control. If not, the manager should investigate why accounts receivable is smaller or larger than it should be.

This section discusses the relative sizes of the assets and liabilities in the balance sheet that result from sales and expenses (for the fiscal year 2019). The sales and expenses are the *drivers*, or causes, of the assets and liabilities. If a business earned profit simply by investing in stocks and bonds, it wouldn't need all the various assets and liabilities explained in this chapter. Such a business — a mutual fund, for example — would have just one income-producing asset: investments in securities. This chapter focuses on businesses that sell products on credit.

Sales revenue and accounts receivable

Annual sales revenue for the year 2019 is $26 million in the example introduced in Chapter 2 of Book 3 (refer to Figure 2-1). The year-end accounts receivable is one-tenth of this, or $2.6 million (see Figure 3-2). So the average customer's credit period is roughly 36 days: 365 days in the year times the 10 percent ratio of ending accounts receivable balance to annual sales revenue. Of course, some customers' balances are past 36 days, and some are quite new; you want to focus on the average. The key question is whether a customer credit period averaging 36 days is reasonable.

Suppose that the business offers all customers a 30-day credit period, which is common in business-to-business selling (although not for a retailer selling to individual consumers). The relatively small deviation of about 6 days (36 days average credit period versus 30 days normal credit terms) probably isn't a significant cause for concern. But suppose that, at the end of the period, the accounts receivable had been $3.9 million, which is 15 percent of annual sales, or about a 55-day average credit period. Such an abnormally high balance should raise a red flag; the responsible manager should look into the reasons for the abnormally high accounts receivable balance. Perhaps several customers are seriously late in paying and shouldn't be extended new credit until they pay up.

Cost of goods sold expense and inventory

In the example, the cost of goods sold expense for the year 2019 is $14.3 million. The year-end inventory is $3.45 million, or about 24 percent. In rough terms, the average product's inventory holding period is 88 days — 365 days in the year times the 24 percent ratio of ending inventory to annual cost of goods sold. Of course, some products may remain in inventory longer than the 88-day average, and some products may sell in a much shorter period than 88 days. You need to focus on the overall average. Is an 88-day average inventory holding period reasonable?

REMEMBER

The "correct" average inventory holding period varies from industry to industry. In some industries, especially heavy equipment manufacturing, the inventory holding period is long — three months or more. The opposite is true for high-volume retailers, such as retail supermarkets, that depend on getting products off the shelves as quickly as possible. The 88-day average holding period in the example is reasonable for many businesses but would be too high for others.

The managers should know what the company's average inventory holding period should be — they should know what the control benchmark is for the inventory holding period. If inventory is much above this control benchmark, managers should take prompt action to get inventory back in line (which is easier said than done, of course). If inventory is at abnormally low levels, this should be investigated as well. Perhaps some products are out of stock and should be restocked to avoid lost sales.

Fixed assets and depreciation expense

Depreciation is like other expenses in that all expenses are deducted from sales revenue to determine profit. Other than this, however, depreciation is very different from most other expenses. (Amortization expense, covered later, is a kissing cousin of depreciation.) When a business buys or builds a long-term operating asset, the cost of the asset is recorded in a specific fixed asset account. *Fixed* is an overstatement; although the assets may last a long time, eventually they're retired from service. The main point is that the cost of a long-term operating or fixed asset is spread out, or allocated, over its expected useful life to the business. Each year of use bears some portion of the cost of the fixed asset.

The depreciation expense recorded in the period doesn't require any cash outlay during the period. (The cash outlay occurred when the fixed asset was acquired, or perhaps later when a loan was secured for part of the total cost.) Rather, *depreciation expense* for the period is that quota of the total cost of a business's fixed assets that is allocated to the period to record the cost of using the assets during the period. Depreciation depends on which method is used to allocate the cost of fixed assets over their estimated useful lives.

The higher the total cost of a business's fixed assets (called *property, plant, and equipment* in a formal balance sheet), the higher its depreciation expense. However, there's no standard ratio of depreciation expense to the cost of fixed assets. The annual total depreciation expense of a business seldom is more than 10 to 15 percent of the original cost of its fixed assets. Either the depreciation expense for the year is reported as a separate expense in the income statement, or the amount is disclosed in a footnote.

REMEMBER

Because depreciation is based on the gradual charging off or writing-down of the cost of a fixed asset, the balance sheet reports not one but two numbers: the original (historical) cost of its fixed assets and the *accumulated depreciation* amount (the total amount of depreciation that has been charged to expense from the time of acquiring the fixed assets to the current balance sheet date). The purpose isn't to confuse you by giving you even more numbers to deal with. Seeing both numbers gives you an idea of how old the fixed assets are and also tells you how much these fixed assets originally cost.

In the example in this chapter, the business has, over several years, invested $12,450,000 in its fixed assets (that it still owns and uses), and it has recorded total depreciation of $6,415,000 through the end of the most recent fiscal year, December 31, 2019. The business recorded $775,000 depreciation expense in its most recent year.

You can tell that the company's collection of fixed assets includes some old assets because the company has recorded $6,415,000 total depreciation since assets were bought — a fairly sizable percent of original cost (more than half). But many businesses use accelerated depreciation methods that pile up a lot of the depreciation expense in the early years and less in the back years, so it's hard to estimate the average age of the company's assets. A business could discuss the actual ages of its fixed assets in the footnotes to its financial statements, but hardly any businesses disclose this information — although they do identify which depreciation methods they're using.

Operating expenses and their balance sheet accounts

The sales, general, and administrative (SG&A) expenses of a business connect with three balance sheet accounts: the prepaid expenses asset account, the accounts payable liability account, and the accrued expenses payable liability account (see Figure 3-2). The broad SG&A expense category includes many types of expenses in making sales and operating the business. (Separate detailed expense accounts are maintained for specific expenses; depending on the size of the business and the needs of its various managers, hundreds or thousands of specific expense accounts are established.)

Many expenses are recorded when paid. For example, wage and salary expenses are recorded on payday. However, this record-as-you-pay method doesn't work for many expenses. For example, insurance and office supplies costs are prepaid and then released to expense gradually over time. The cost is initially put in the *prepaid expenses* asset account. ("Prepaid expenses" doesn't sound like an asset account, but it is.) Other expenses aren't paid until weeks after the expenses are recorded. The amounts owed for these unpaid expenses are recorded in an *accounts payable* or in an *accrued expenses payable* liability account.

REMEMBER

For details regarding the use of these accounts in recording expenses, see Chapter 2 in Book 3. Note that the accounting objective is to match expenses with sales revenue for the year, and only in this way can the amount of profit be measured for the year. So expenses recorded for the year should be the correct amounts, regardless of when they're paid.

Intangible assets and amortization expense

Although this chapter's business example doesn't include tangible assets, many businesses invest in them. *Intangible* means without physical existence, in contrast to tangible assets like buildings, vehicles, and computers. Here are some examples of intangible assets:

>> A business may purchase the customer list of another company that's going out of business.

>> A business may buy patent rights from the inventor of a new product or process.

>> A business may buy another business lock, stock, and barrel and may pay more than the individual assets of the company being bought are worth — even after adjusting the particular assets to their current values. The extra amount is for *goodwill*, which may consist of a trained and efficient workforce, an established product with a reputation for high quality, or a very valuable location.

REMEMBER

Only intangible assets that are purchased are recorded by a business. A business must expend cash, or take on debt, or issue owners' equity shares for an intangible asset in order to record the asset on its books. Building up a good reputation with customers or establishing a well-known brand isn't recorded as an intangible asset. You can imagine the value of Coca-Cola's brand name, but this "asset" isn't recorded on the company's books. However, Coca-Cola protects its brand name with all the legal means at its disposal.

The cost of an intangible asset is recorded in an appropriate asset account, just like the cost of a tangible asset is recorded in a fixed asset account. Whether or when to allocate the cost of an intangible asset to expense has proven to be a difficult issue in practice, not easily amenable to accounting rules. At one time, the cost of most intangible assets were charged off according to some systematic method. The fraction of the total cost charged off in one period is called *amortization expense*.

Currently, however, the cost of an intangible asset isn't charged to expense unless its value has been impaired. A study of 8,700 public companies found that they collectively recorded $26 billion of write-downs for goodwill impairment in 2014. Testing for impairment is a messy process. The practical difficulties of determining whether impairment has occurred and the amount of the loss in value of an intangible asset have proven to be a real challenge to accountants. For the latest developments, search for "impairment of intangible assets" on the Internet, which will lead you to several sources. There are no technical details here; because this chapter's business example doesn't include any intangible assets, there's no amortization expense.

KEEPING A CASH BALANCE

A business's cash account consists of the money it has in its checking accounts plus the money that it keeps on hand. Cash is the essential lubricant of business activity. Sooner or later, virtually all business transactions pass through the cash account. Every business needs to maintain a working cash balance as a buffer against fluctuations in day-to-day cash receipts and payments. You can't really get by with a zero cash balance, hoping that enough customers will provide enough cash to cover all the cash payments that you need to make that day.

At year-end 2019, the cash balance of the business whose balance sheet is presented in Figure 3-2 is $2,165,000, which equals a little more than four weeks of annual sales revenue. How large of a cash balance should a business maintain? There's no simple answer. A business needs to determine how large of a cash safety reserve it's comfortable with to meet unexpected demands on cash while keeping the following points in mind:

- Excess cash balances are unproductive and don't earn any profit for the business.

- Insufficient cash balances can cause the business to miss taking advantage of opportunities that require quick action, such as snatching up a prized piece of real estate that just came on the market or buying out a competitor.

Debt and interest expense

Look back at the balance sheet shown in Figure 3-2. Notice that the sum of this business's short-term (current) and long-term notes payable at year-end 2019 is $6.25 million. From the income statement in Chapter 2 of Book 3 (refer to Figure 2-1), you see that the business's interest expense for the year is $400,000. Based on the year-end amount of debt, the annual interest rate is about 6.4 percent. (The business may have had more or less borrowed at certain times during the year, of course, and the actual interest rate depends on the debt levels from month to month.)

For most businesses, a small part of their total annual interest is unpaid at year-end; the unpaid part is recorded to bring interest expense up to the correct total amount for the year. In Figure 3-2, the accrued amount of interest is included in the *accrued expenses payable* liability account. In most balance sheets, you don't find accrued interest payable on a separate line; rather, it's included in the accrued expenses payable liability account. However, if unpaid interest at year-end happens to be a rather large amount, or if the business is seriously behind in paying interest on its debt, it should report the accrued interest payable as a separate liability.

Income tax expense and income tax payable

In its 2019 income statement, the business reports $2.6 million earnings before income tax — after deducting interest and all other expenses from sales revenue. The actual taxable income of the business for the year probably is different from this amount because of the many complexities in the income tax law. The example uses a realistic 35 percent tax rate, so the income tax expense is $910,000 of the pretax income of $2.6 million.

A large part of the federal and state income tax amounts for the year must be paid before the end of the year. But a small part is usually still owed at the end of the year. The unpaid part is recorded in the *income tax payable* liability account, as you see in Figure 3-2. In the example, the unpaid part is $115,000 of the total $910,000 income tax for the year, but it's not suggested that this ratio is typical. Generally, the unpaid income tax at the end of the year is fairly small, but just how small depends on several technical factors.

Net income and cash dividends (if any)

The business in our example earned $1.69 million net income for the year (see the income statement in Chapter 2 of Book 3 — Figure 2-1). Earning profit increases the owners' equity account *retained earnings* by the same amount. Either the $1.69 million profit stays in the business, or some of it is paid out and divided among the owners of the business.

During the year, the business paid out $750,000 total cash distributions from its annual profit. This is included in Figure 3-3's summary of transactions — look in the financing-activities column on the retained earnings line. If you own 10 percent of the shares, you'd receive one-tenth, or $75,000 cash, as your share of the total distributions. Distributions from profit to owners (shareholders) are not expenses. In other words, bottom-line net income is before any distributions to owners. Despite the importance of distributions from profit, you can't tell from the income statement or the balance sheet the amount of cash dividends. You have to look in the statement of cash flows for this information (see Chapter 4 in Book 3). You can also find distributions from profit (if any) in the *statement of changes in stockholders' equity*.

Financing a Business: Sources of Cash and Capital

REMEMBER

To run a business, you need financial backing, otherwise known as *capital*. In overview, a business raises capital needed for its assets by buying things on credit, waiting to pay some expenses, borrowing money, getting owners to invest money in the business, and making profit that is retained in the business. Borrowed money is known as *debt*; capital invested in the business by its owners and retained profits are the two sources of *owners' equity*.

How did the business whose balance sheet is shown in Figure 3-2 finance its assets? Its total assets are $14,850,000 at fiscal year-end 2019. The company's profit-making activities generated three liabilities — accounts payable, accrued expenses payable, and income tax payable — and in total these three liabilities provided $1,780,000 of the total assets of the business. Debt provided $6,250,000, and the two sources of owners' equity provided the other $6,820,000. All three sources add up to $14,850,000, which equals total assets, of course. Otherwise, its books would be out of balance, which is a definite no-no.

Accounts payable, accrued expenses payable, and income tax payable are short-term, non-interest-bearing liabilities that are sometimes called *spontaneous liabilities* because they arise directly from a business's expense activities — they aren't the result of borrowing money but rather are the result of buying things on credit or delaying payment of certain expenses.

It's hard to avoid these three liabilities in running a business; they're generated naturally in the process of carrying on operations. In contrast, the mix of debt (interest-bearing liabilities) and equity (invested owners' capital and retained earnings) requires careful thought and high-level decisions by a business. There's no natural or automatic answer to the debt-versus-equity question. The business in the example has a large amount of debt relative to its owners' equity, which would make many business owners uncomfortable.

Debt is both good and bad, and in extreme situations, it can get very ugly. The advantages of debt are as follows:

>> Most businesses can't raise all the capital they need from owners' equity sources, and debt offers another source of capital (though, of course, many lenders are willing to provide only part of the capital that a business needs).

>> Interest rates charged by lenders are lower than rates of return expected by owners. Owners expect a higher rate of return because they're taking a greater risk with their money — the business isn't required to pay them back the same way that it's required to pay back a lender. For example, a business may pay 6 percent annual interest on its debt and be expected to earn a 12 percent annual rate of return on its owners' equity.

WARNING

Here are the disadvantages of debt:

>> A business must pay the fixed rate of interest for the period even if it suffers a loss for the period or earns a lower rate of return on its assets.

>> A business must be ready to pay back the debt on the specified due date, which can cause some pressure on the business to come up with the money on time. (Of course, a business may be able to *roll over* or renew its debt, meaning that it replaces its old debt with an equivalent amount of new debt, but the lender has the right to demand that the old debt be paid and not rolled over.)

FINANCIAL LEVERAGE: TAKING A CHANCE ON DEBT

The large majority of businesses borrow money to provide part of the total capital needed for their assets. The main reason for debt is to close the gap between how much capital the owners can come up with and the amount the business needs. Lenders are willing to provide the capital because they have a senior claim on the assets of the business. Debt has to be paid back before the owners can get their money out of the business. A business's owners' equity provides a relatively permanent base of capital and gives its lenders a cushion of protection.

The owners use their capital invested in the business as the basis for borrowing. For example, for every two bucks the owners have in the business, lenders may be willing to add another dollar (or even more). Using owners' equity as the basis for borrowing is referred to as *financial leverage,* because the equity base of the business can be viewed as the fulcrum, and borrowing is the lever for lifting the total capital of the business.

A business can realize a financial leverage gain by making more EBIT (earnings before interest and income tax) on the amount borrowed than the interest on the debt. On the flip side, using debt may yield not a financial leverage gain but rather a financial leverage *loss.* Suppose EBIT equals zero for the year. Nevertheless, the business must pay the interest on its debt, so the business would have a bottom-line loss for the year.

WARNING

If a business defaults on its debt contract — it doesn't pay the interest on time or doesn't pay back the debt on the due date — it faces some major unpleasantness. In extreme cases, a lender can force it to shut down and liquidate its assets (that is, sell off everything it owns for cash) to pay off the debt and unpaid interest. Just as you can lose your home if you don't pay your home mortgage, a business can be forced into involuntary bankruptcy if it doesn't pay its debts. A lender may allow the business to try to work out its financial crisis through bankruptcy procedures, but bankruptcy is a nasty affair that invariably causes many problems and can really cripple a business.

Recognizing the Hodgepodge of Values Reported in a Balance Sheet

The values reported for assets in a balance sheet can be a source of confusion for business managers and investors, who tend to put all dollar amounts on the same value basis. In their minds, a dollar is a dollar, whether it's in accounts receivable; inventory; property, plant, and equipment; accounts payable; or retained earnings. But some dollars are much older than other dollars.

The dollar amounts reported in a balance sheet are the result of the transactions recorded in the assets, liabilities, and owners' equity accounts. (Hmm, where have you heard this before?) Some transactions from years ago may still have life in the present balances of certain assets. For example, the land owned by the business that is reported in the balance sheet goes back to the transaction for the purchase of the land, which could be 20 or 30 years ago. The balance in the land asset is standing in the same asset column, for example, as the balance in the accounts receivable asset, which likely is only 1 or 2 months old.

REMEMBER

Book values are the amounts recorded in the accounting process and reported in financial statements. Don't assume that the book values reported in a balance sheet equal the current *market values*. Generally speaking, the amounts reported for cash, accounts receivable, and liabilities are equal to or are very close to their current market or settlement values. For example, accounts receivable will be turned into cash for the amount recorded on the balance sheet, and liabilities will be paid off at the amounts reported in the balance sheet. It's the book values of fixed assets, as well as any other assets in which the business invested some time ago, that are likely lower than their current replacement values.

Also, keep in mind that a business may have "unrecorded" assets. These off-balance-sheet assets include such things as a well-known reputation for quality products and excellent service, secret formulas (think Coca-Cola here), patents that are the result of its research and development over the years, and a better trained workforce than its competitors. These are intangible assets that the business did not purchase from outside sources but, rather, accumulated over the years through its own efforts. These assets, though not reported in the balance sheet, should show up in better-than-average profit performance in the business's income statement.

WARNING

The current replacement values of a company's fixed assets may be quite a bit higher than the recorded costs of these assets, in particular for buildings, land, heavy machinery, and equipment. For example, suppose the aircraft fleet of an airline, as reported in its balance sheet, is hundreds of millions of dollars less than the current cost it would have to pay to replace the planes. Complicating matters is the fact that many of its older planes aren't being produced anymore, and the airline would replace the older planes with newer models.

Businesses aren't permitted to write up the book values of their assets to current market or replacement values. (Well, investments in marketable securities held for sale or available for sale have to be written up, or down, but this is an exception to the general rule.) Although recording current market values may have intuitive appeal, a market-to-market valuation model isn't practical or appropriate for businesses that sell products and services. These businesses do not stand ready to sell their assets (other than inventory); they need their assets for operating the business into the future. At the end of their useful lives, assets are sold for their disposable values (or traded in for new assets).

REMEMBER

Don't think that the market value of a business is simply equal to its owners' equity reported in its most recent balance sheet. Putting a value on a business depends on several factors in addition to the latest balance sheet of the business.

Chapter **4**

Reporting Cash Sources and Uses in the Statement of Cash Flows

You could argue that the income statement (Chapter 2 of Book 3) and balance sheet (Chapter 3 of Book 3) are enough. These two financial statements answer the most important questions about the financial affairs of a business. The income statement discloses revenue and how much profit the business squeezed from its revenue, and the balance sheet discloses the amounts of assets being used to make sales and profit, as well as its capital sources. What more do you need to know? Well, it's also helpful to know about the cash flows of the business.

This chapter explains the third primary financial statement reported by businesses: the *statement of cash flows.* This financial statement has two purposes: It explains why cash flow from profit differs from bottom-line profit, and it summarizes the investing and financing activities of the business during the period. This may seem an odd mix to put into one financial statement, but it actually makes sense. Earning profit (net income) generates net cash inflow (at least, it should normally). Making profit is a primary source of cash to a business. The investing and financing transactions of a business hinge on its cash flow from profit. All sources and uses of cash hang together and should be managed in an integrated manner.

Meeting the Statement of Cash Flows

The income statement (introduced in Chapter 2 of Book 3) has a natural structure:

Revenue – Expenses = Profit (Net Income)

So does the balance sheet (see Chapter 3 of Book 3):

Assets = Liabilities + Owners' Equity

The statement of cash flows doesn't have an obvious natural structure, so the accounting rule-making body had to decide on the basic format for the statement. They settled on the following structure:

± Cash Flow from Operating Activities

± Cash Flow from Investing Activities

± Cash Flow from Financing Activities

= Cash Increase or Decrease during Period

+ Beginning Cash Balance

= Ending Cash Balance

REMEMBER

The ± signs mean that the cash flow could be positive or negative. Generally, the cash flow from investing activities of product businesses is negative, which means that the business spent more on new investments in long-term assets than cash received from disposals of previous investments. And generally, the cash flow from operating activities (profit-making activities) should be positive, unless the business suffered a big loss for the period that drained cash out of the business.

REMEMBER

The threefold classification of activities (transactions) reported in the statement of cash flows — operating, investing, and financing — are the same ones introduce in Chapter 3 of Book 3, which explains the balance sheet. Figure 3-3 in that chapter summarizes these transactions for the product company example that is continued in this chapter.

In the example, the business's cash balance decreases $110,000 during the year. You see this decrease in the company's balance sheets for the years ended December 31, 2018 and 2019 (refer to Figure 3-2 in Book 3, Chapter 3). The business started the year with $2,275,000 cash and ended the year with $2,165,000. What does the balance sheet, by itself, tell you about the reasons for the cash decrease? The two-year comparative balance sheet provides some clues about the reasons for the cash decrease. However, answering such a question isn't the purpose of a balance sheet.

Presenting the direct method

REMEMBER

The statement of cash flows begins with the cash from making profit, or *cash flow from operating activities,* as accountants call it. *Operating activities* is the term accountants adopted for sales and expenses, which are the operations that a business carries out to earn profit. Furthermore, the term *operating activities* also includes the transactions that are coupled with sales and expenses. For example, making a sale on credit is an operating activity, and so is collecting the cash from the customer at a later time. Recording sales and expenses can be thought of as primary operating activities because they affect profit. Their associated transactions are secondary operating activities because they don't affect profit. However, they do affect cash flow, as explained in this chapter.

Figure 4-1 presents the statement of cash flows for the product business example introduced in Chapters 2 and 3 of Book 3. What you see in the first section of the statement of cash flows is called the *direct method* for reporting cash flow from operating activities. The dollar amounts are the cash flows connected with sales and expenses. For example, the business collected $25,550,000 from customers during the year, which is the direct result of making sales. The company paid $15,025,000 for the products it sells, some of which went toward increasing the inventory of products awaiting sale next period.

Note: Because the same business example in this chapter is used in Chapters 2 and 3 of Book 3, you may want to take a moment to review the 2019 income statement in Figure 2-1. And you may want to review Figure 3-3, which summarizes how the three types of activities changed the business's assets, liabilities, and owners' equity accounts during the year 2019. (Go ahead, take your time.)

Typical Product Business, Inc. Statement of Cash Flows for Year Ended December 31, 2019 (Dollar amounts in thousands)		
Cash Flow From Operating Activities		
Collections from sales		$25,550
Payments for products	($15,025)	
Payments for selling, general, and administrative costs	($7,750)	
Payments for interest on debt	($375)	
Payments on income tax	($885)	($24,035)
Cash Flow From Operating Activities		$1,515
Cash Flows From Investing Activities		
Expenditures on Property, Plant & Equipment		($1,275)
Cash Flows From Financing Activities		
Short-term Debt Increase	$100	
Long-term Debt Increase	$150	
Capital Stock Issue	$150	
Dividends Paid Stockholders	($750)	($350)
Decrease In Cash During Year		($110)
Beginning Cash Balance		$2,275
Ending Cash Balance		$2,165

FIGURE 4-1: The statement of cash flows, illustrating the direct method for cash flow from operating activities.

REMEMBER

The basic idea of the direct method is to present the sales revenue and expenses of the business on a cash basis, in contrast to the amounts reported in the income statement, which are on the accrual basis for recording revenue and expenses. *Accrual basis* accounting is real-time accounting that records transactions when economic events happen: Accountants record sales on credit when the sales take place, even though cash isn't collected from customers until sometime later. Cash payments for expenses occur before or after the expenses are recorded. *Cash basis* accounting is just what it says: Transactions aren't recorded until there's actual cash flow (in or out).

The revenue and expense cash flows you see in Figure 4-1 differ from the amounts you see in the accrual accounting basis income statement (refer to Figure 2-1). Herein lies a problem with the direct method. If you, a conscientious reader of the financial statements of a business, compare the revenues and expenses reported in the income statement with the cash flow amounts reported in the statement of cash flows, you may get confused. Which set of numbers is the correct one?

Well, both are. The numbers in the income statement are the "true" numbers for measuring profit for the period. The numbers in the statement of cash flows are additional information for you to ponder.

Notice in Figure 4-1 that cash flow from operating activities for the year is $1,515,000, which is less than the company's $1,690,000 net income for the year (refer to Figure 2-1). The accounting rule-making board thought that financial report readers would want some sort of explanation for the difference between these two important financial numbers. Therefore, the board decreed that a statement of cash flows that uses the direct method of reporting cash flow from operating liabilities should include a reconciliation schedule that explains the difference between cash flow from operating activities and net income.

Opting for the indirect method

Having to read both the operating activities section of the cash flow statement and a supplemental schedule gets to be rather demanding for financial statement readers. Accordingly, the accounting rule-making body decided to permit an alternative method for reporting cash flow from operating activities. The alternative method starts with net income and then makes adjustments in order to reconcile cash flow from operating activities with net income. This alternative method is called the *indirect method,* which is shown in Figure 4-2. The rest of the cash flow statement is the same, no matter which option is selected for reporting cash flow from operating activities. Compare the investing and financing activities in Figures 4-1 and 4-2; they're the same.

TIP

By the way, the adjustments to net income in the indirect method for reporting cash flow from operating activities (see Figure 4-2) constitute the supplemental schedule of changes in assets and liabilities that has to be included under the direct method. So the indirect method kills two birds with one stone: Net income is adjusted to the cash flow basis, and the changes in assets and liabilities affecting cash flow are included in the statement. It's no surprise that the vast majority of businesses use the indirect method.

The indirect method for reporting cash flow from operating activities focuses on the *changes* during the year in the assets and liabilities that are directly associated with sales and expenses. These connections between revenue and expenses and their corresponding assets and liabilities are explained in Chapter 2 of Book 3. (You can trace the amounts of these changes back to Figure 3-2.)

Both the direct method and the indirect method report the same cash flow from operating activities for the period. Almost always, this important financial metric for a business differs from the amount of its bottom-line profit, or net income, for the same period. Why? Read on.

Typical Product Business, Inc. Statement of Cash Flows for Year Ended December 31, 2019 (Dollar amounts in thousands)		
Cash Flows From Operating Activities		
Net Income		$1,690
Adjustments to Net Income For Determining Cash Flow:		
Accounts Receivable Increase	($450)	
Inventory Increase	($725)	
Prepaid Expenses Increase	($75)	
Depreciation Expense	$775	
Accounts Payable Increase	$125	
Accrued Expenses Increase	$150	
Income Tax Payable Increase	$25	($175)
Cash Flow From Operating Activities		$1,515
Cash Flows From Investing Activities		
Expenditures on Property, Plant & Equipment		($1,275)
Cash Flows From Financing Activities		
Short-term Debt Increase	$100	
Long-term Debt Increase	$150	
Capital Stock Issue	$150	
Dividends Paid Stockholders	($750)	($350)
Decrease In Cash During Year		($110)
Beginning Cash Balance		$2,275
Ending Cash Balance		$2,165

© John Wiley & Sons, Inc.

FIGURE 4-2: The statement of cash flows, illustrating the indirect method for presenting cash flow from operating activities.

Explaining the Variance between Cash Flow and Net Income

The amount of cash flow from profit, in the large majority of cases, is a different amount from profit. Both revenue and expenses are to blame. Cash collected from customers during the period is usually higher or lower than the sales revenue booked for the period. And cash actually paid out for operating costs is usually higher or lower than the amounts of expenses booked for the period. You can see this by comparing cash flows from operating activities in Figure 4-1 with sales revenue and expenses in the company's income statement (Figure 2-1 in Book 3,

Chapter 2). The accrual-based amounts (Figure 2-1) are different from the cash-based amounts (Figure 4-1).

Now, how to report the divergence of cash flow and profit? A business could present only one line for cash flow from operating activities (which in the example is $1,515,000). Next, the financial report reader would move on to the investing and financing sections of the cash flow statement. But this approach won't do, according to financial reporting standards.

REMEMBER

The premise of financial reporting is that financial statement readers want more information than just a one-line disclosure of cash flow from operating activities. The standard practice is to disclose the major factors that cause cash flow to be higher or lower than net income. Smaller factors are often collapsed on one line called "other factors" or something like that. The business example used in Chapters 2, 3, and 4 of Book 3 is traceable. You can trace all the specific reasons that cause the variance between cash flow and net income.

The business in the example experienced a strong growth year. Its accounts receivable and inventory increased by relatively large amounts. In fact, all its assets and liabilities intimately connected with sales and expenses increased; their ending balances are larger than their beginning balances (which are the amounts carried forward from the end of the preceding year). Of course, this may not always be the case in a growth situation; one or more assets and liabilities could decrease during the year. For flat, no-growth situations, it's likely that there will be a mix of modest-sized increases and decreases.

This section explains how asset and liability changes affect cash flow from operating activities. As a business owner or manager, you should keep a close watch on the changes in each of your assets and liabilities and understand the cash flow effects of these changes. Investors and lenders should focus on the business's ability to generate a healthy cash flow from operating activities, so they should be equally concerned about these changes. In some situations, these changes indicate serious problems!

TIP

You may not be too interested in the details of these changes, so at the start of each section, you are presented with the synopsis. If you want, you can just read the short explanation and move on (though the details are fascinating — well, at least to accountants).

Note: Instead of using the full phrase "cash flow from operating activities" every time, this section uses the shorter term "cash flow." All data for assets and liabilities are found in the two-year comparative balance sheet of the business (refer to Figure 3-2 in Book 3, Chapter 3).

Accounts receivable change

Synopsis: An increase in accounts receivable hurts cash flow; a decrease helps cash flow.

REMEMBER

The accounts receivable asset shows how much money customers who bought products on credit still owe the business; this asset is a promise of cash that the business will receive. Basically, accounts receivable is the amount of uncollected sales revenue at the end of the period. Cash doesn't increase until the business collects money from its customers.

The business started the year with $2.15 million and ended the year with $2.6 million in accounts receivable. The beginning balance was collected during the year, but the ending balance hadn't been collected at the end of the year. Thus, the *net* effect is a shortfall in cash inflow of $450,000. The key point is that you need to keep an eye on the increase or decrease in accounts receivable from the beginning of the period to the end of the period. Here's what to look for:

>> **Increase in accounts receivable:** If the amount of credit sales you made during the period is greater than what you collected from customers during the period, your accounts receivable increased over the period, and you need to *subtract* from net income that difference between start-of-period accounts receivable and end-of-period accounts receivable. In short, an increase in accounts receivable hurts cash flow by the amount of the increase.

>> **Decrease in accounts receivable:** If the amount you collected from customers during the period is greater than the credit sales you made during the period, your accounts receivable decreased over the period, and you need to *add* to net income that difference between start-of-period accounts receivable and end-of-period accounts receivable. In short, a decrease in accounts receivable helps cash flow by the amount of the decrease.

In the business example, accounts receivable increased $450,000. Cash collections from sales were $450,000 less than sales revenue. Ouch! The business increased its sales substantially over the last period, so its accounts receivable increased. When credit sales increase, a company's accounts receivable generally increases about the same percent, as it did in this example. (If the business takes longer to collect its credit sales, then its accounts receivable would increase even more than can be attributed to the sales increase.) In this example, the higher sales revenue was good for profit but bad for cash flow.

REMEMBER

The "lagging behind" effect of cash flow is the price of growth — business owners, managers, lenders, and investors need to understand this point. Increasing sales without increasing accounts receivable is a happy situation for cash flow, but in the real world, you usually can't have one increase without the other.

Inventory change

Synopsis: An increase in inventory hurts cash flow; a decrease helps cash flow.

Inventory is usually the largest short-term, or *current,* asset of businesses that sell products. If the inventory account is greater at the end of the period than at the start of the period — because unit costs increased or because the quantity of products increased — the amount the business actually paid out in cash for inventory purchases (or for manufacturing products) is more than what the business recorded in the cost of goods sold expense for the period. To refresh your memory here: The cost of inventory is not charged to cost of goods sold expense until products are sold and sales revenue is recorded.

In the business example, inventory increased $725,000 from start-of-year to end-of-year. In other words, to support its higher sales levels in 2019, this business replaced the products that it sold during the year *and* increased its inventory by $725,000. The business had to come up with the cash to pay for this inventory increase. Basically, the business wrote checks amounting to $725,000 more than its cost of goods sold expense for the period. This step-up in its inventory level was necessary to support the higher sales level, which increased profit even though cash flow took a hit.

Prepaid expenses change

Synopsis: An increase in prepaid expenses (an asset account) hurts cash flow; a decrease helps cash flow.

A change in the prepaid expenses asset account works the same way as a change in inventory and accounts receivable, although changes in prepaid expenses are usually much smaller than changes in the other two asset accounts.

The beginning balance of prepaid expenses is charged to expense this year, but the cash of this amount was actually paid out last year. This period (the year 2019 in the example), the business paid cash for next period's prepaid expenses, which affects this period's cash flow but doesn't affect net income until next period. In short, the $75,000 increase in prepaid expenses in this business example has a negative effect on cash flow.

REMEMBER

As a business grows, it needs to increase its prepaid expenses for such things as fire insurance (premiums have to be paid in advance of the insurance coverage) and its stocks of office and data processing supplies. Increases in accounts receivable, inventory, and prepaid expenses are the cash-flow price a business has to pay for growth. Rarely do you find a business that can increase its sales revenue without increasing these assets.

Depreciation: Real but noncash expense

Synopsis: No cash outlay is made in recording depreciation. In recording depreciation, a business simply decreases the book (recorded) value of the asset being depreciated. Cash isn't affected by the recording of depreciation (keeping in mind that depreciation is deductible for income tax).

Recording depreciation expense decreases the value of long-term, fixed operating assets that are reported in the balance sheet. The original costs of fixed assets are recorded in a *property, plant, and equipment* type account. Depreciation is recorded in an *accumulated depreciation* account, which is a so-called *contra* account because its balance is deducted from the balance in the fixed asset account (refer to Figure 3-2 in Book 3, Chapter 3). Recording depreciation increases the accumulated depreciation account, which decreases the book value of the fixed asset.

TIP

There's no cash outlay when recording depreciation expense. Sales prices should be set high enough so that the cash inflow from revenue "reimburses" the business for the use of its long-term operating assets as they gradually wear out over time. The amount of depreciation expense recorded in the period is a portion of the original cost of the business's fixed assets, most of which were bought and paid for years ago. (Chapters 2 and 3 of Book 3 explain more about depreciation.) Because the depreciation expense isn't a cash outlay this period, the amount is added to net income to determine cash flow from operating activities (refer to Figure 4-2). Depreciation is just one adjustment factor to get from net income reported in the income statement to cash flow from operating activities reported in the statement of cash flows.

For measuring profit, depreciation is definitely an expense — no doubt about it. Buildings, machinery, equipment, tools, vehicles, computers, and office furniture are all on an irreversible journey to the junk heap (although buildings usually take a long time to get there). Fixed assets (except for land) have a finite life of usefulness to a business; depreciation is the accounting method that allocates the total cost of fixed assets to each year of their use in helping the business generate sales revenue. In the example, the business recorded $775,000 depreciation expense for the year.

TIP

Instead of looking at depreciation only as an expense, consider the investment-recovery cycle of fixed assets. A business invests money in fixed assets that are then used for several or many years. Over the life of a fixed asset, a business has to recover through sales revenue the cost invested in the fixed asset (ignoring any salvage value at the end of its useful life). In a real sense, a business "sells" some of its fixed assets each period to its customers — it factors the cost of fixed assets into the sales prices that it charges its customers.

For example, when you go to a supermarket, a very small slice of the price you pay for that quart of milk goes toward the cost of the building, the shelves, the refrigeration equipment, and so on. (No wonder they charge so much!) Each period, a business recoups part of the cost invested in its fixed assets. In the example, $775,000 of sales revenue went toward reimbursing the business for the use of its fixed assets during the year.

Changes in operating liabilities

Synopsis: An increase in a short-term operating liability helps cash flow; a decrease hurts cash flow.

The business in the example, like almost all businesses, has three basic liabilities inextricably intertwined with its expenses:

» Accounts payable

» Accrued expenses payable

» Income tax payable

When the beginning balance of one of these liability accounts is the same as its ending balance (not too likely, of course), the business breaks even on cash flow for that liability. When the end-of-period balance is higher than the start-of-period balance, the business didn't pay out as much money as was recorded as an expense in the year. You want to refer back to the company's comparative balance sheet of the business in Figure 3-2 to compare the beginning and ending balances of these three liability accounts.

In the business example, the business disbursed $640,000 to pay off last year's accounts payable balance. (This $640,000 was the accounts payable balance at December 31, 2018, the end of the previous fiscal year.) Its cash this year decreased $640,000 because of these payments. But this year's ending balance sheet (at December 31, 2019) shows accounts payable of $765,000 that the business won't pay until the following year. This $765,000 amount was recorded to expense in the year 2019. So the amount of expense was $125,000 more than the cash outlay for the year, or, in reverse, the cash outlay was $125,000 less than the expense. An increase in accounts payable benefits cash flow for the year. In other words, an increase in accounts payable has a positive cash flow effect (until the liability is paid). An increase in accrued expenses payable or income tax payable works the same way.

In short, liability increases are favorable to cash flow — in a sense, the business ran up more on credit than it paid off. Such an increase means that the business delayed paying cash for certain things until next year. So you need to add the increases in the three liabilities to net income to determine cash flow, as you see in the statement of cash flows (refer to Figure 4-2). The business avoided cash outlays to the extent of the increases in these three liabilities. In some cases, of course, the ending balance of an operating liability may be lower than its beginning balance, which means that the business paid out more cash than the corresponding expenses for the period. In that case, the decrease is a negative cash flow factor.

Putting the cash flow pieces together

Taking into account all the adjustments to net income, the company's cash balance increased $1,515,000 from its operating activities during the course of the year. The operating activities section in the statement of cash flows (refer to Figure 4-2) shows the stepping stones from net income to the amount of cash flow from operating activities.

Recall that the business experienced sales growth during this period. The downside of sales growth is that assets and liabilities also grow — the business needs more inventory at the higher sales level and also has higher accounts receivable. The business's prepaid expenses and liabilities also increased, although not nearly as much as accounts receivable and inventory. Still, the business had $1,515,000 cash at its disposal. What did the business do with this $1,515,000 in available cash? You have to look to the remainder of the cash flow statement to answer this very important question.

Sailing through the Rest of the Statement of Cash Flows

After you get past the first section of the statement of cash flows, the remainder is a breeze. Well, to be fair, you *could* encounter some rough seas in the remaining two sections. But generally speaking, the information in these sections isn't too difficult to understand. The last two sections of the statement report on the other sources of cash to the business and the uses the business made of its cash during the year.

Understanding investing activities

The second section of the statement of cash flows (refer to Figure 4-1 or 4-2) reports the investment actions that a business's managers took during the year. Investments are like tea leaves indicating what the future may hold for the company. Major new investments are sure signs of expanding or modernizing the production and distribution facilities and capacity of the business. Major disposals of long-term assets and shedding off a major part of the business could be good news or bad news for the business, depending on many factors. Different investors may interpret this information differently, but all would agree that the information in this section of the cash flow statement is very important.

Certain long-lived operating assets are required for doing business. For example, FedEx and UPS wouldn't be terribly successful if they didn't have airplanes and trucks for delivering packages and computers for tracking deliveries. When these assets wear out, the business needs to replace them. Also, to remain competitive, a business may need to upgrade its equipment to take advantage of the latest technology or to provide for growth. These investments in long-lived, tangible, productive assets, which are called *fixed assets,* are critical to the future of the business. In fact, these cash outlays are called *capital expenditures* to stress that capital is being invested for the long haul.

One of the first claims on the $1,515,000 cash flow from operating activities is for capital expenditures. Notice that the business spent $1,275,000 on fixed assets, which are referred to more formally as *property, plant,* and *equipment* in the cash flow statement (to keep the terminology consistent with account titles used in the balance sheet; the term *fixed assets* is rather informal).

A typical statement of cash flows doesn't go into much detail regarding what specific types of fixed assets the business purchased (or constructed): how many additional square feet of space the business acquired, how many new drill presses it bought, and so on. Some businesses do leave a clearer trail of their investments, though. For example, in the footnotes or elsewhere in their financial reports, airlines generally describe how many new aircraft of each kind were purchased to replace old equipment or to expand their fleets.

TIP

Usually, a business disposes of some of its fixed assets every year because they reached the end of their useful lives and will no longer be used. These fixed assets are sent to the junkyard, traded in on new fixed assets, or sold for relatively small amounts of money. The value of a fixed asset at the end of its useful life is called its *salvage value.* The disposal proceeds from selling fixed assets are reported as a source of cash in the investing activities section of the statement of cash flows. Usually, these amounts are fairly small. Also, a business may sell off fixed assets because it's downsizing or abandoning a major segment of its business; these cash proceeds can be fairly large.

Looking at financing activities

Note that in the annual statement of cash flows for the business example, cash flow from operating activities is a positive $1,515,000, and the negative cash flow from investing activities is $1,275,000 (refer to Figure 4-1 or 4-2). The result to this point, therefore, is a net cash increase of $240,000, which would have increased the company's cash balance this much if the business had no financing activities during the year. However, the business increased its short-term and long-term debt during the year, its owners invested additional money in the business, and it distributed some of its profit to stockholders. The third section of the cash flow statement summarizes these *financing activities* of the business over the period.

The managers didn't have to go outside the business for the $1,515,000 cash increase generated from its operating activities for the year. Cash flow from operating activities is an *internal* source of money generated by the business itself, in contrast to *external* money that the business raises from lenders and owners. A business doesn't have to go hat in hand for external money when its internal cash flow is sufficient to provide for its growth. Making profit is the cash flow spigot that should always be turned on.

TIP

A business that earns a profit could, nevertheless, have a *negative* cash flow from operating activities — meaning that despite posting a net income for the period, the changes in the company's assets and liabilities cause its cash balance to decrease. In contrast, a business could report a bottom-line *loss* for the year yet have a *positive* cash flow from its operating activities. The cash recovery from depreciation plus the cash benefits from decreases in accounts receivable and inventory could be more than the amount of loss. However, a loss usually leads to negative cash flow or very little positive cash flow.

The term *financing* refers to a business raising capital from debt and equity sources — by borrowing money from banks and other sources willing to loan money to the business and by its owners putting additional money in the business. The term also includes the flip side — that is, making payments on debt and returning capital to owners. The term *financing* also includes cash distributions by the business from profit to its owners. (Keep in mind that interest on debt is an expense reported in the income statement.)

Most businesses borrow money for the short term (generally defined as less than one year) as well as for longer terms (generally defined as more than one year). In other words, a typical business has both short-term and long-term debt. (Chapter 3 in Book 3 explains that short-term debt is presented in the current liabilities section of the balance sheet.)

The business in the example has both short-term and long-term debt. Although this isn't a hard-and-fast rule, most cash flow statements report just the *net* increase or decrease in short-term debt, not the total amounts borrowed and total payments on short-term debt during the period. In contrast, both the total amounts of borrowing from and repayments on long-term debt during the year are generally reported in the statement of cash flows — the numbers are reported gross, instead of net.

In the example, no long-term debt was paid down during the year, but short-term debt was paid off during the year and replaced with new short-term notes payable. However, only the $100,000 net increase is reported in the cash flow statement. The business also increased its long-term debt by $150,000 (refer to Figure 4-1 or 4-2).

The financing section of the cash flow statement also reports the flow of cash between the business and its owners (stockholders of a corporation). Owners can be both a *source* of a business's cash (capital invested by owners) and a *use* of a business's cash (profit distributed to owners). The financing activities section of the cash flow statement reports additional capital raised from its owners, if any, as well as any capital returned to the owners. In the cash flow statement, note that the business issued additional stock shares for $150,000 during the year, and it paid a total of $750,000 cash dividends from profit to its owners.

Reading actively

The business lender or investor's job is to ask questions (at least in your own mind) when reading an external financial statement. You should be an active reader, not a ho-hum passive reader, when reading the statement of cash flows. You should mull over certain questions to get full value out of the financial statement.

The statement of cash flows reveals what financial decisions the business's managers made during the period. Of course, management decisions are always subject to second-guessing and criticism, and passing judgment based on reading a financial statement isn't totally fair because it doesn't capture the pressures the managers faced during the period. Maybe they made the best possible decisions in the circumstances. Then again, maybe not.

TIP

One issue comes to the forefront when reading the company's statement of cash flows. The business in the example (see Figure 4-1 or 4-2) distributed $750,000 cash from profit to its owners — a 44 percent *payout ratio* (which equals the $750,000 distribution divided by its $1,690,000 net income). In analyzing whether the payout ratio is too high, too low, or just about right, you need to look at the broader context of the business's sources of and needs for cash.

The company's $1,515,000 cash flow from operating activities is enough to cover the business's $1,275,000 capital expenditures during the year and still leave $240,000 available. The business increased its total debt $250,000. Combined, these two cash sources provided $490,000 to the business. The owners also kicked in another $150,000 during the year, for a grand total of $640,000. Its cash balance didn't increase by this amount because the business paid out $750,000 in dividends from profit to its stockholders. Therefore, its cash balance dropped $110,000.

The board of directors of this business certainly could ask the chief executive why cash dividends to shareowners weren't limited to $240,000 in order to avoid the increase in debt and to avoid having shareowners invest additional money in the business. They could probably ask the chief executive to justify the amount of capital expenditures as well.

WARNING

Some small and privately owned businesses don't report a statement of cash flows — though according to current financial reporting standards that apply to all businesses, they should. There are several small, privately owned businesses that don't go to the trouble of preparing this financial statement. Perhaps someday accounting standards for private and smaller businesses will waive the requirement for the cash flow statement. Without a cash flow statement, the reader of the financial report could add back depreciation to net income to get a starting point. From there on, it gets more challenging to determine cash flow from profit. Adding depreciation to net income is no more than a first step in determining cash flow from profit — but it's better than nothing.

Pinning Down "Free Cash Flow"

REMEMBER

The term *free cash flow* has emerged in the lexicon of finance and investing. This piece of language is *not* officially defined by the rule-making body of any authoritative accounting or financial institution. Furthermore, the term does not appear in cash flow statements reported by businesses.

Rather, *free cash flow* is street language, and the term appears in *The Wall Street Journal* and *The New York Times*. Securities brokers and investment analysts use the term freely (pun intended). Unfortunately, the term *free cash flow* hasn't settled down into one universal meaning, although most usages have something to do with cash flow from operating activities.

The term *free cash flow* can refer to the following:

>> Net income plus depreciation expense, plus any other expense recorded during the period that doesn't involve the outlay of cash — such as amortization of costs of the intangible assets of a business and other asset write-downs that don't require cash outlay

>> Cash flow from operating activities as reported in the statement of cash flows, although the very use of a different term *(free cash flow)* suggests that a different meaning is intended

>> Cash flow from operating activities minus the amount spent on capital expenditures during the year (purchases or construction of property, plant, and equipment)

>> Earnings before interest, tax, depreciation, and amortization (EBITDA) — although this definition ignores the cash flow effects of changes in the short-term assets and liabilities directly involved in sales and expenses, and it obviously ignores that interest and income tax expenses in large part are paid in cash during the period

REMEMBER

In the strongest possible terms, be very clear on which definition of *free cash flow* a speaker or writer is using. Unfortunately, you can't always determine what the term means even in context. Be careful out there.

One definition of free cash flow is quite useful: cash flow from operating activities minus capital expenditures for the year. The idea is that a business needs to make capital expenditures in order to stay in business and thrive. And to make capital expenditures, the business needs cash. Only after providing for its capital expenditures does a business have "free" cash flow that it can use as it likes. For the example in this chapter, the free cash flow is $1,515,000 cash flow from operating activities minus $1,275,000 capital expenditures: a total of $240,000 free cash flow.

In many cases, cash flow from operating activities falls short of the money needed for capital expenditures. To close the gap, a business has to borrow more money, persuade its owners to invest more money in the business, or dip into its cash reserve. Should a business in this situation distribute any of its profit to owners? After all, it has a cash *deficit* after paying for capital expenditures. But, in fact, many businesses make cash distributions from profit to their owners even when they don't have any free cash flow (as it was just defined).

Looking at Limitations of the Statement of Cash Flows

In 1987, the cash flow statement was made mandatory. Most financial report users thought that this new financial statement would be quite useful and should open the door for deeper insights into the business. However, over the years, serious problems have developed in the actual reporting of cash flows.

Focusing on cash flows is understandable. If a business runs out of money, it will likely come to an abrupt halt and may not be able to start up again. Even running low on cash (as opposed to running out of cash) makes a business vulnerable to all sorts of risks that could be avoided if it had enough sustainable cash flow. Managing cash flow is as important as making sales and controlling expenses. You'd think that the statement of cash flows would be carefully designed to make it as useful as possible and reasonably easy to read so that the financial report reader could get to the heart of the matter.

Would you like to hazard a guess on the average number of lines in the cash flow statements of publicly owned corporations? Typically, their cash flow statements have 30 to 40 or more lines of information. So it takes quite a while to read the cash flow statement — more time than the average reader probably has available. Each line in a financial statement should be a truly useful piece of information. Too many lines baffle the reader rather than clarify the overall cash flows of the business. You have to question why companies overload this financial statement with so much technical information. One could even suspect that many businesses deliberately obscure their statements of cash flows.

The main problem in understanding the statement of cash flows is the first section for cash flow from operating activities. What a terrible way to start the statement of cash flows! As it is now, the financial report reader has to work down numerous adjustments that are added or deducted from net income to determine the amount of cash flow from operating activities (refer to Figure 4-2). You could read quickly through the whole balance sheet or income statement in the time it takes to do this. In short, the first section of the cash flow statement isn't designed for an easy read. Something needs to be done to improve this opening section of the cash flow statement.

You don't hear a lot of feedback on the cash flow statement from principal external users of financial reports, such as business lenders and investors. We wonder how financial report users would react if the cash flow statement were accidently omitted from a company's annual financial report. How many would notice the missing financial statement and complain? The Securities and Exchange Commission (SEC) and other regulators would take action, of course. But in our view, few readers would even notice the omission. In contrast, if a business failed to include an income statement or balance sheet, the business would hear from its lenders and owners, that's for sure.

TIP

Instead of the statement of cash flows, consider presenting a summary of operating, investing, and financial transactions such as the one in Figure 3-3 (refer to Book 3, Chapter 3). You might compare this summary with the statement of cash flows shown in Figure 4-2. Which is better for the average financial report reader? You be the judge.

Chapter **5**

Controlling Costs and Budgeting

What's the first thing that comes to mind when you hear *cost control*? Cutting costs, right? Well, it may come as a surprise, but slashing costs is not the main theme of this chapter. Cost control is just one element in the larger playing field of profit management. The best, or optimal, cost is not always the lowest cost.

A knee-jerk reaction is that costs should be lower. Don't rush to judgment. In some situations, increasing costs may be the best path to increasing profits. It's like coaching sports: You have to play both defense and offense. You can't play on just one side of the game. Making sales is the offense side of business; defense is keeping the costs of making sales and operating the business less than sales revenue.

The planning process includes numerous elements, ranging from obtaining current market information to evaluating personnel resources to preparing budgets or forecasts. The first part of this chapter focuses on one of the most critical elements of the planning process: preparing a budget.

Budgets aren't based on the concept of "How much can I spend this year?" Rather, budgets are more comprehensive in nature and are designed to capture all relevant and critical financial data, including revenue levels, costs of sales, operating expenses, fixed asset expenditures, capital requirements, and the like. All too often, budgets are associated with expense levels and management, which represent just one element of the entire budget.

The budgeting process doesn't represent a chicken and egg riddle. From a financial perspective, the preparation of budgets, forecasts, projections, proformas, and the like represent the end result of the entire planning process. Hence, you must first accumulate the necessary data and information on which to build a forecasting model prior to producing projected financial information (for your company). There is no point in preparing a budget that does not capture your company's true economic structure.

Getting in the Right Frame of Mind

Of course, don't waste money on excessive or unnecessary costs. If possible, you should definitely save a buck here and there on expenses. There's no argument on this point. Small business owners don't particularly need tutorials on shaving costs. Rather, they need to stand back a little and rethink the nature of costs and realize that costs are pathways to profit. If you had no costs, you'd have no revenue and no profit. You need costs to make profit. You have to spend money to make money.

REMEMBER

The crucial test of a cost is whether it contributes to generating revenue. If a cost has no value whatsoever in helping a business bring in revenue, then it's truly money down the rat hole. The key management question about costs is whether the amounts of the costs are in alignment with the amount of revenue the business is generating. A business owner should ask: Are my expenses the appropriate amounts for the revenue of my business?

Getting Down to Business

Controlling costs requires that you evaluate your costs relative to your sales revenue. Suppose your business's salaries and wages expense for the year is $225,000. Is this cost too high? There's no way in the world you can answer this question, except by comparing the cost against your sales revenue for the year. The same goes for all your expenses.

In an ideal world, your customers are willing to pay whatever prices you charge them. You could simply pass along your costs in sales prices and still earn a profit. Your costs would be under control no matter how high your costs might be. Because you earn a profit, your costs are under control and need no further attention.

REMEMBER

The real world is very different, of course. But this ideal world teaches a lesson. Your costs are out of control when you can't set sales prices high enough to recover your costs and make a profit.

It's hardly news to you that small businesses face price resistance from their customers. Customers are sensitive to sales prices and changes in sales prices for the products and services sold by small businesses. In setting sales prices, you have to determine the maximum price your customers will accept before turning to lower price alternatives, or not buying at all. If the price resistance point is $125 for a product, you have to figure out how to keep your costs below $125 per unit. In other words, you have to exercise cost control.

Putting cost control in its proper context

Cost control is part of the larger management function of revenue/cost/profit analysis. So, the best place to focus is your P&L report. (Book 3, Chapter 2 explains the P&L report, also known as the income statement.) This profit performance statement summarizes your sales revenue based on the sales prices in effect during the year and your expenses for the year based on the amounts recorded for the expenses. (There are some issues regarding the accounting methods for recording certain expenses, discussed in the upcoming section "Selecting a cost of goods sold expense method.")

Suppose your business is a pass-through income tax entity, which means it doesn't pay income tax itself but passes its taxable income through to its shareholders, who then include their shares of the business's annual taxable income in their personal income tax returns for the year.

Figure 5-1 presents the income statement of a hypothetical business (you can say it's yours) for the year just ended and includes the prior year for comparison (which is standard practice). This report includes the percents of expenses to sales revenue. It also breaks out a *facilities expense* — the cost of the space used by the business — and reports it on a separate line.

	2018		2019		Change Over 2018	
Your Business Name **P&L Report** **For Years Ended December 31**						
	% of Sales Revenue		% of Sales Revenue		Amount	%
Sales revenue		$2,286,500		$2,920,562	$634,062	27.7%
Cost of goods sold expense	61.7%	$1,411,605	58.0%	$1,693,926	$282,321	20.0%
Gross margin	38.3%	$874,895	42.0%	$1,226,636	$351,741	40.2%
Operating expenses:						
Salaries, wages, commissions and benefits	27.3%	$624,590	22.7%	$662,400	$37,810	6.1%
Advertising and sales promotion	6.9%	$158,900	6.6%	$192,550	$33,650	21.2%
Depreciation	4.1%	$93,250	3.0%	$88,950	($4,300)	–4.6%
Facilities expense	3.9%	$89,545	3.2%	$94,230	$4,685	5.2%
Other expenses	1.2%	$27,255	1.5%	$42,849	$15,594	57.2%
Total operating expenses	43.5%	$993,540	37.0%	$1,080,979	$87,439	8.8%
Operating profit (loss)	–5.2%	($118,645)	5.0%	$145,657	$264,302	
Interest expense	2.1%	$47,625	1.7%	$50,006	$2,381	5.0%
Net income (loss)	–7.3%	($166,270)	3.3%	$95,651	$261,921	

© *John Wiley & Sons, Inc.*

FIGURE 5-1:
Your income
statement for
cost control
analysis.

Facilities expense includes expenditures for leases, building utilities, real estate taxes, and insurance on your premises. Depreciation isn't included in facilities expense; depreciation is an unusual expense and it's best to leave it in an expense by itself.

In this case, the business moved out of the red zone (loss) in 2018 into the black zone (profit) in 2019. Making a profit, however, doesn't necessarily mean your costs are under control. Dealing with the issue of cost control requires closer management analysis.

REMEMBER

You can attack cost control on three levels:

>> Your *business as a whole* in its entirety

>> The separate *profit centers* of your business

>> Your specific costs item by item

Figure 5-1 is the income statement for your business as a whole. At this level, you look at the forest and not the trees. It's helpful to divide your business into separate parts called profit centers. Basically, a *profit center* is an identifiable, separate stream of revenue to a business. At this level, you examine clusters or stands of trees that make up different parts of the forest.

For example, Starbucks sells coffee, sure — but also coffee beans, drinkware, food, CDs, and other products. Each is a separate profit center. For that matter, each Starbucks store is a separate profit center, so you have profit centers within profit centers. Last, you can drill down to particular, individual costs. At this level, you look at specific trees in the forest.

Beginning with sales revenue change

You increased sales $634,062 in 2019 (refer to Figure 5-1). This is good news for profit, but only if costs don't increase more than sales revenue, of course. For revenue/cost/profit analysis, it's extremely useful to know how much of your sales revenue increase is due to change in volume (total quantity sold) versus changes in sales prices. Unfortunately, measuring sales volume can be a problem.

An auto dealer can keep track of the number of vehicles sold during the year. A movie theater can count the number of tickets sold during the year, and a brewpub can keep track of the number of barrels of beer sold during the year. On the other hand, many small businesses sell a very large number of different products and services. A clothing retailer may sell several thousand different items. A hardware store in Boulder claims to sell more than 100,000 different items.

TIP

Exactly how your business should keep track of sales volume depends on how many different products you sell and how practical it is to compile sales volume information in your accounting system. In many situations, a small business can't do more than keep count of its sales transactions — number of sales rung up on cash registers, number of invoices sent to customers, customer traffic count, or something equivalent. If nothing else, you should make a rough count of the number of sales you make during the year.

In the example portrayed in Figure 5-1, you increase sales volume 20 percent in 2019 over the prior year, which is pretty good by any standard. You made much better use of the sales capacity provided by your workforce and facilities in 2019. You increased sales per employee and per square foot in 2019— see the later sections "Analyzing employee cost" and "Looking at facilities expense." The 20 percent sales volume increase is very important in analyzing your costs in 2019. A key question is whether changes in your costs are consistent with the sales volume increase.

The example portrayed in Figure 5-1 is for a situation in which product costs remain the same in both years. Therefore, cost of goods sold expense increases exactly 20 percent in 2019 because sales volume increases 20 percent over the previous year. (Of course, product costs fluctuate from year to year in most cases.)

Sales revenue, in contrast, increases more than 20 percent because you were able to increase sales prices in 2019. In Figure 5-1, note that sales revenue increases more than the 20 percent sales volume increase. Ask your accountant to calculate the average sales price increase. In the example, your sales prices in 2019 are 7.7 percent higher than the previous year.

You did not increase sales prices exactly 7.7 percent on every product you sold; that situation would be quite unusual. The 7.7 percent sales price increase is an average over all the products you sold. You should know the reasons for and causes of the average sales price increase. The higher average sales price may be due to a shift in your sales mix toward higher priced products. (*Sales mix* refers to the relative proportions that each source of sales contributes to total sales revenue.) Or perhaps your sales mix remained constant and you bumped up prices on most products.

In any case, what's the bottom line (or maybe top line, for sales revenue)? In 2019, you had $634,062 additional sales revenue to work with compared with the prior year. More than half of the incremental revenue is offset by increases in costs. But $261,921 of the additional revenue ended up in profit. How do you like that? More than 41 percent of your additional revenue goes toward profit (see Figure 5-1 for data):

$261,921 profit increase ÷ $634,062 additional sales revenue = 41.3% profit from additional revenue

This scenario may seem almost too good to be true. Well, you should analyze what happened to your costs at the higher sales level to fully understand this profit boost. Could the same thing happen next year if you increase sales revenue again? Perhaps, but maybe not.

Focusing on cost of goods sold and gross margin

For businesses that sell products, the first expense deducted from sales revenue is *cost of goods sold*. (You could argue that it should be called cost of products sold, but you don't see this term in income statements.) This expense is deducted from sales revenue to determine *gross margin*. Gross margin is also called *gross profit*; it's profit before any other expense is deducted from sales revenue. Cost of goods sold is a *direct variable* expense, which means it's directly matched against revenue and varies with sales volume.

This expense may appear straightforward, but it's more entangled than you may suspect. It's anything but simple and uncomplicated. In fact, the later section "Looking into Cost of Goods Sold Expense" explains this expense in more detail. For the moment, step around these issues and focus on the basic behavior of the expense. In the example in Figure 5-1, your business's product costs are the same as last year. Of course, in most situations, product costs don't remain constant very long. But it makes for a much cleaner analysis to keep product costs constant at this point in the discussion.

The 20 percent jump in sales volume increases your cost of goods sold expense 20 percent — see Figure 5-1. Pay special attention to the change in your gross margin ratio on sales. Your basic sales pricing strategy is to mark up product cost to earn 45 percent gross margin on sales. For example, if a product cost is $55, you aim to sell it for $100 to yield $45 gross margin. However, your gross margin is only 42.0 percent in 2019. You gave several customers discounts from list prices. But you did improve your average gross margin ratio over last year, which brings up a very important point.

How is it that your sales volume increases 20.0 percent and your sales prices increase 7.7 percent in 2019, but your gross margin increases 40.2 percent? The increase in gross margin seems too high relative to the percent increases in sales volume and sales prices, doesn't it? What's going on? Figure 5-2 analyzes how much of the $351,741 gross margin gain is attributable to higher sale prices and how much to the higher sales volume.

FIGURE 5-2:
Analyzing your gross margin increase.

2018			Change in 2019		
$2,286,500	Sales revenue	×	7.7%	Sales price increase	= $176,762
$874,895	Gross margin	×	20.0%	Sales volume increase	= $174,979
				Total increase in gross margin	= $351,741

© John Wiley & Sons, Inc.

TIP

Note that the 7.7 percent increase in sales prices causes more gross margin increase than the 20.0 percent sales volume increase. That's because of the *big base effect*; the smaller sales prices percent increase applies to a relatively large base (about $2.3 million) compared with the volume gain, which is based on a much smaller amount (about $.9 million).

Suppose you want to increase gross margin $100,000 next year. Assume that your 42.0 percent gross margin ratio on sales remains the same. If sales prices remain the same next year, then your sales volume would have to increase 8.15 percent:

$100,000 gross margin increase goal ÷ $1,226,636 gross margin in 2019 = 8.15% sales volume increase

If your sales volume remains the same next year, then your sales prices on average would have to increase just 3.42 percent:

$100,000 gross margin increase goal ÷ $2,920,562 sales revenue in 2019 = 3.42% sales price increase

In short, a 1 percent sales price increase has more profit impact than a 1 percent sales volume increase.

Controlling Costs and Budgeting

Analyzing employee cost

As the owner of a small business, your job is to judge whether the ratio of each expense to sales revenue is acceptable. Is the expense reasonable in amount? Your salaries, wages, commissions, and benefits expense equals 22.7 percent of sales revenue in 2019 (refer to Figure 5-1). In other words, your employee cost absorbs $22.70 of every $100.00 of sales revenue. This expense ratio is lower than it was last year, which is good, of course. But the fundamental question is whether it should be an even smaller percent of sales. This question strikes at the essence of cost control. It's not an easy question to answer. But, as they say, that's why you earn the big bucks — to answer such questions.

It's tempting to think first of reducing every cost of doing business. It would have been better if your employee cost had been lower — or would it? Could you have gotten by with one less employee? One less employee may have reduced your sales capacity and prevented the increase in sales revenue. In the example, you have ten full-time employees on the payroll both years. For your line of business, the benchmark is $300,000 annual sales per employee. In 2019, your sales per employee is $292,056 (see Figure 5-1 for sales revenue):

$2,920,562 annual sales revenue ÷ 10 employees = $292,056 sales revenue per employee

Summing up, your employee cost looks reasonable for 2019, assuming your sales per employee benchmark is correct. This doesn't mean that you couldn't have squeezed some dollars out of this expense during the year. Maybe you could have furloughed employees during the slow time of year. Maybe you could have fired one of your higher-paid employees and replaced him or her with a person willing to work for a lower salary. Maybe you could have cut corners and not have paid overtime rates for some of the hours worked during the busy season. Maybe you could have cut health care and vacation benefits during the year.

Business owners get paid to make tough and sometimes ruthless decisions. This is especially true in the area of cost control. If your sales prices don't support the level of your costs, what are your options? You can try to get more sales out of your costs. In fact, you did just this with employee costs in 2019 compared with 2018. Your sales revenue per employee increased significantly in 2019. But you may be at the end of the line on this course of action. You may have to hire an additional employee or two if you plan to increase sales next year.

Analyzing advertising and sales promotion costs

The total of your advertising and sales promotion costs in 2019 is just under 7 percent of sales revenue, which is about the same it was in 2018. As you probably have observed, many retail businesses depend heavily on advertising. Others don't do more than put a sign on the building and rely on word of mouth. You can advertise and promote sales a thousand different ways (see Book 5 for a lot more on marketing and promotion).

Maybe you give away free calendars. Maybe you can place ads in local newspapers. Maybe you make a donation to your local public radio or television station. Or perhaps you place ads on outdoor billboards or bus benches.

Like other costs of doing business, you need a benchmark or reference point for evaluating advertising and sales promotion costs. For the business example, the ratio is around 7 percent of annual sales. This ratio is in the typical range of the advertising and sales promotion expense of many small businesses. Of course, your business may be different. Retail furniture stores, for example, spend a lot more than 7 percent of sales revenue on advertising. Locally owned office-supply stores, in contrast, spend far less on advertising.

TIP

You should keep watch on which particular advertisements and sales promotions campaigns work best and have the most impact on sales. The trick is to find out which ads or promotions your customers respond to and which they don't. Keeping the name of your business on the customer's mind is a high marketing priority of most businesses, although measuring how your name recognition actually affects customers' purchases is difficult. Nevertheless, you should develop some measure or test of how your marketing expenses contribute to sales.

Of course, you can keep an eye on your competitors, but they aren't likely to tell you which sales promotion techniques are the most effective. You increased your advertising and sales promotion costs more than $30,000 in 2019, which is more than 20 percent over last year (see Figure 5-1). Sales revenue went up by an even larger percent, so the ratio of the expense to sales revenue actually decreased. Nevertheless, you should determine exactly what the extra money was spent on. Perhaps you bought more newspaper ads and doubled the number of flyers distributed during the year.

Appreciating depreciation expense

Depreciation expense is the cost of owning fixed assets. The term *fixed assets* includes land and buildings, machinery and equipment, furniture and fixtures, vehicles and forklift trucks, tools, and computers. These long-term operating resources aren't held for sale; they're used in the day-to-day operations of the business. Except for land, the cost of these long-term operating resources is allocated over the estimated useful lives of the assets. (Land is viewed as a property right that has perpetual life and usefulness, so its cost is not depreciated; the cost stays on the books until the land is disposed of.)

TIP

As a practical matter, the useful life estimates permitted in the federal income tax law are the touchstones used by most small businesses. Instead of predicting actual useful lives, businesses simply adopt the useful lives spelled out in the income tax law to depreciate their fixed assets. The useful life guidelines are available from the IRS at www.irs.gov/publications. Probably the most useful booklet is Publication 946, *How to Depreciate Property.* Your accountant should know everything in this booklet.

You should understand the following points about the depreciation expense:

>> The two basic methods for allocating the cost of a fixed asset over its useful life are the *straight-line method* (an equal amount every year) and an *accelerated method,* by which more depreciation expense in recorded in the earlier years than in the later years; the straight-line method is used for buildings, and either method can be used for other classes of fixed assets.

>> Businesses generally favor an accelerated depreciation method in order to reduce *taxable income* in the early years of owning fixed assets, but don't forget that taxable income will be higher in the later years when less depreciation is recorded.

>> In recording depreciation expense, a business *does not set aside money* in a fund for the eventual replacement of its fixed assets restricted only for this purpose. (A business could invest money in a separate fund for this purpose, of course, but no one does.)

>> Recording depreciation expense *does not require a decrease to cash* or an increase in a liability that will be paid in cash at a later time; rather the fixed asset accounts of the business are written down according to a systematic method of allocating the original cost of each fixed asset over its estimated useful life. (Book 3, Chapter 4 explains the cash-flow analysis of profit.)

>> Even though the *market value of real estate* may appreciate over time, the cost of a building owned by the business is depreciated (generally over 39 years).

>> The *eventual replacement costs* of most fixed assets will be higher than the original cost of the assets due to inflation; depreciation expense is based on original cost, not on the estimated future replacement cost.

>> The *estimated useful lives of fixed assets for depreciation are shorter* than realistic expectations of their actual productive lives to the business; therefore, fixed assets are depreciated too quickly, and the book values of the assets in the balance sheet (original cost less accumulated depreciation to day) are too low.

>> Depreciation expense is a real cost of doing business because fixed assets wear out or otherwise lose their usefulness to the business — although a case can be made for not recording depreciation expense on a building whose market value is steadily rising. Generally accepted accounting principles require that the cost of all fixed assets (except land) must be depreciated.

TIP

One technique used in the fields of investment analysis and business valuation focuses on EBITDA, which equals earnings before interest, tax (income tax), depreciation, and amortization. *Amortization* is similar to depreciation. Amortization refers to the allocating the cost of *intangible* assets over their estimated useful lives to the business. By and large, small businesses do not have intangible assets, so they're not discussed here.

WARNING

One last point about depreciation expense: Note in Figure 5-1 that your depreciation expense is lower in 2019 than the prior year. Yet sales revenue and all other expenses are higher than the prior year. The drop in depreciation expense is an aberrant effect of accelerated depreciation; the amount of depreciation decreases year to year. You have a year-to-year built-in gain in profit because depreciation expense drops year to year. The aggregate effect on depreciation expense for the year depends on the mix of newer and older fixed assets. The higher depreciation on newer fixed assets is balanced by the lower depreciation on older fixed assets. One advantage of the straight-line method is that the amount of depreciation expense on a fixed asset is constant year to year, so you don't get fluctuations in depreciation expense year to year that are caused by the depreciation method being used.

TIP

Ask your accountant to explain the year-to-year change in depreciation expense in your annual income statement. In particular, ask the accountant whether a decrease in the depreciation expense is due to your fixed assets getting older, with the result that less depreciation is recorded by an accelerated depreciation method.

Looking at facilities expense

The income statement shown in Figure 5-1 includes a separate line for facilities expense. You should definitely limit the number of expense lines in your income statement. But this particular expense deserves separate reporting. Basically, this expense is your cost of physical space — the square footage and shelter you need to carry on operations plus the costs directly associated with using the space. (You may prefer the term *occupancy expense* instead.)

Most of the specific costs making up facilities expense are *fixed commitments* for the year. Examples are lease payments, utilities, fire insurance on contents and the building (if owned), general liability insurance premiums, security guards, and so on. You could argue that depreciation on the building (if owned by the business) should be included in facilities expense. However, it's best to put depreciation in its own expense account.

TIP

In this example, your business uses 12,000 square feet of space, and you've determined that a good benchmark for your business is $300 annual sales per square foot. Accordingly, your space could support $3,600,000 annual sales. In 2019, your annual sales revenue is short of this reference point. Therefore, you presumably have space enough for sales growth next year. These benchmarks are no more than rough guideposts. Nevertheless, benchmarks are very useful. If your actual performance is way off base from a benchmark, you should determine the reason for the variance. Based on your own experience and in looking at your competitors, you should be able to come up with reasonably accurate benchmarks for sales per employee and sales per square foot of space.

In the business example portrayed in Figure 5-1, you use the same amount of space both years. In other words, you did not have to expand your square footage for the sales growth in 2019. The relatively modest increase in facilities expense (only 5.2 percent, as shown in Figure 5-1) is due to inflationary cost pressures. Sooner or later, however, continued sales growth will require expansion of your square footage. Indeed, you may have to relocate to get more space.

Looking over or looking into other expenses

TIP

In your income statement (refer to Figure 5-1), the last expense line is the collection of residual costs that aren't included in another expense. A small business has a surprising number of miscellaneous costs — annual permits, parking meters, office supplies, postage and shipping, service club memberships, travel, bad debts, professional fees, toilet paper, and signs, to name just a handful. A business keeps at least one account for miscellaneous expenses. You should draw the line on how large an amount can be recorded in this catchall expense account. For example, you may instruct your accountant that no outlay over $250 or $500 can be charged to this account; any expenditure over the amount has to have its own expense account.

The cost control question is whether it's worth your time to investigate these costs item by item. In 2019, these assorted costs represented only 1.5 percent of your annual sales revenue. Most of the costs, probably, are reasonable in amount — so, why spend your valuable time inspecting these costs in detail?

On the other hand, these costs increase $15,594 in 2019 (see Figure 5-1), and this amount is a relatively large percent of your profit for the year:

$15,594 increase in other expenses ÷ $95,651 net income for year = 16.3% of profit for year

TIP

Ask the accountant to list the two or three largest increases. You may see some surprises. Perhaps an increase is a one-time event that will not repeat next year. You have to follow your instincts and your experience in deciding how deep to dive into analyzing these costs. If your employees know you never look into these costs, they may be tempted to use one of these expense accounts to conceal fraud. So, it's generally best to do a quick survey of these costs, even if you don't spend a lot of time on them. It's better to give the impression that you're watching the costs like a hawk, even if you're not.

Running the numbers on interest expense

Interest expense is a financial cost — the cost of using debt for part of the total capital you use in operating the business. It's listed below the operating profit line in the income statement (see Figure 5-1). Putting interest expense beneath the operating profit line is standard practice, for good reason. *Operating profit* (also called *operating earnings*, or *earnings before interest and income tax*) is the amount of profit you squeeze out of sales revenue before you consider how your business is financed (where you get your capital) and income tax.

Obviously, interest expense depends on the amount of debt you use and the interest rates on the debt. Figure 5-3 shows the balance sheets of your business at the end of the two most recent years. At the end of 2018, which is the start of 2019, you had $400,000 of interest bearing debt ($100,000 short-term and $300,000 long-term). Early in 2019, you increased your borrowing and ended the year with $600,000 debt ($200,000 short-term and $400,000 long-term). Based on the $600,000 debt level, your interest expense for the year is 8.3 percent.

Because you negotiated the terms of the loans to the business, you should know whether this interest rate is correct. By the way, the interest expense in your income statement may include other costs of borrowing, such as loan origination fees and other special charges in addition to interest. If you have any question about what's included in interest expense, ask your accountant for clarification.

Your Business Name
Balance Sheet
At December 31

	2018	2019
Assets		
Cash	$347,779	$584,070
Accounts receivable	$136,235	$148,785
Inventory	$218,565	$250,670
Prepaid expenses	$65,230	$61,235
Total current assets	$767,809	$1,044,760
Property, plant and equipment	$774,600	$896,450
Accumulated depreciation	($167,485)	($256,435)
Cost less depreciation	$607,115	$640,015
Total assets	$1,374,924	$1,684,775
Liabilities and Owners' Equity		
Accounts payable	$286,450	$261,430
Accrued expenses payable	$67,345	$81,565
Short-term notes payable	$100,000	$200,000
Total current liabilities	$453,795	$542,995
Long-term notes payable	$300,000	$400,000
Owners' equity:		
Invested capital	$500,000	$525,000
Retained earnings	$121,129	$216,780
Total owners' equity	$621,129	$741,780
Total liabilities and owners' equity	$1,374,924	$1,684,775

FIGURE 5-3:
Your year-end
balance sheets.

Comparing your P&L numbers with your balance sheet

REMEMBER

You should compare your P&L numbers on the income statement with your balance sheet numbers. Basically, you should ask whether your sales and expenses for the year are in agreement with your assets and liabilities. Every business, based on its experience and its operating policies, falls into ruts regarding the sizes of its assets and liabilities relative to its annual sales revenue and expenses. If one of these normal ratios is out of kilter, you should find out the reasons for the deviation from normal. (See Chapter 3 in Book 3 for more about balance sheets.)

A small business owner should definitely know the proper sizes of assets and liabilities relative to the sizes of the business's annual sales revenue and expenses.

Three critical tie-ins between the income statement and balance sheet are the following:

>> **Accounts receivables/Sales revenue from sales on credit:** Your ending balance of accounts receivable (uncollected credit sales) should be consistent with your credit terms. So, if you give customers 30 days credit, then your ending balance should equal about one month of credit sales.

>> **Inventory/Cost of goods sold expense:** Your ending inventory depends on the average time that products spend in your warehouse or on your retail shelves before being sold. So, if your inventory turns six times a year (meaning products sit in inventory about two months on average before being sold), your ending inventory should equal about two months of annual cost of goods sold.

>> **Operating liabilities/Operating costs:** Your ending balances of accounts payable and accrued expenses payable should be consistent with your normal trade credit terms from vendors and suppliers and the time it takes to pay accrued expenses. So, if your average credit terms for purchases are 30 days, your ending accounts payable liability balance should equal about 30 days of purchases.

You should instruct your accountant to do these calculations and report these P&L/balance sheet ratios so that you can keep tabs on the sizes of your assets and liabilities.

WARNING

A business can develop solvency problems. One reason is that the owner keeps a close watch on the P&L but ignores what was going on in the balance sheet. Assets and liabilities were getting out of hand, but the owner thought that everything was okay because the P&L looked good.

One additional purpose for comparing your P&L numbers with your balance sheet is to evaluate your profit performance relative to the amount of capital you're using to make the profit. Your 2019 year-end balance sheet reports that your owners' equity is $741,780 (see Figure 5-3). This amount includes the capital the owners (you and any other owners) put in the business (invested capital), plus the earnings plowed back into the business (retained earnings). Theoretically, the owners could have invested this $741,780 somewhere else and earned a return on the investment. For 2019, your business earned 12.9 percent return on owners' equity:

$95,651 net income for 2019 ÷ $741,780 2019 year-end owners' equity = 12.9% return on owners' equity capital

REMEMBER

Keep in mind that the business is a pass-through tax entity. So, the 12.9 percent return on capital is before income tax. Suppose that the average income tax bracket of the owners is 25 percent (it may very well be higher). Taking out 25 percent for income tax, the return on owners' equity is 9.7 percent. You have to decide whether this percentage is an adequate return on capital for the owners (you, but also any other owners). And don't forget that the business did not pay cash dividends during the year. All the profit for the year is retained; the owners did not see any cash in their hands from the profit.

Looking into Cost of Goods Sold Expense

Small business owners have a tendency to take cost amounts reported by accountants for granted — as if the amount is the actual, true, and only cost. In contrast, small business owners are pretty shrewd about dealing with other sources of information. When listening to complaints from employees, for example, business owners are generally good at reading between the lines and filling in some aspects that the employee is not revealing. And then there's the legendary response from a customer who hasn't paid on time: The check's in the mail. Business owners know better than to take this comment at face value. Likewise, you should be equally astute in working with the cost amounts reported for expenses.

WARNING

Everyone agrees that there should be uniform accounting standards for financial reporting by businesses. Yet the accounting profession hasn't reached agreement on the best method for recording certain expenses. The earlier section "Appreciating depreciation expense" explains that a business can choose between a straight-line and an accelerated method for recording depreciation expense. And a business can choose between two or three different methods for recording cost of goods sold expense.

Selecting a cost of goods sold expense method

The cost of goods sold expense is the largest expense of businesses that sell products, typically more than 50 percent of the sales revenue from the goods sold. In the business example, cost of goods sold is 58 percent of sales revenue in the most recent year (refer to Figure 5-1). You would think that the accounting profession would have settled on one uniform method to record cost of goods sold expense. This isn't the case, however. Furthermore, the federal income tax law permits different cost of goods sold expense methods for determining annual taxable income. A business has to stay with the same method year after year (although a change is permitted in very unusual situations).

TIP

This chapter is directed to small business owners, not accountants. There's no reason for a small business owner to get into the details of the alternative cost of goods sold expense methods. Your time is too valuable. Like other issues that you deal with in running a small business, the basic question is this: What difference does it make? Generally, the method doesn't make a significant difference in your annual cost of goods sold expense — assuming that you don't change horses in the middle of the stream (in other words, that you keep with the same method year after year). Instruct your accountant to give you a heads up if your accounting method causes an unusual, or abnormal impact, on cost of goods expense for the year.

TIP

Your cost of goods sold expense accounting method affects the *book value of inventory*, which is the amount reported in the balance sheet. Under the *first-in, first out* (FIFO) accounting method, the inventory amount is based on recent costs. For example, refer to the balance sheet in Figure 5-3. Inventory at year-end 2019 is reported at $250,670. Under the FIFO method, this amount reflects costs of products during two or three months ending with the balance sheet date. Instead of using FIFO or LIFO, a business can split the difference as it were and use the *average cost* method. The average cost accounting method reaches back a little further in time compared to the FIFO method; the cost of ending inventory is based on product costs from throughout the year under the average cost method.

WARNING

If you use the last-in, first-out (LIFO) accounting method, the cost value of your year-end inventory balance could reach back many years, depending on how long you have been using this method and when you accumulated your inventory layers. For this reason, businesses that use the LIFO method disclose the current replacement cost of their ending inventories in a footnote to their financial statements to warn the reader that the balance sheet amount is substantially below the current cost of the products.

TIP

Which cost of goods sold expense method should you use, then? You might start by looking at your sales pricing policy. What do you do when a product's cost goes up? Do you wait to clear out your existing stock of the product before you raise the sales price? If so, try the first-in, first-out (FIFO) method, because this method keeps product costs in sync with sales prices. On the other hand, sales pricing is a complex process, and sales prices aren't handcuffed with product cost changes. To a large extent, your choice of accounting method for cost of goods sold expense depends on whether you prefer a conservative, higher-cost method (generally LIFO) — or a liberal, lower-cost method (generally FIFO).

Controlling Costs and Budgeting

Dealing with inventory shrinkage and inventory write-downs

Deciding which cost of goods sold expense accounting method to use isn't the main concern of many small businesses that carry a sizable inventory of products awaiting sale. The more important issues to them are losses from *inventory shrinkage* and from *write-downs of inventory* caused by products that they can't sell at normal prices. These problems are very serious for many small businesses.

WARNING

Inventory shrinkage stems from theft by customers and employees, damages caused by the handling, moving, and storing of products, physical deterioration of products over time, and errors in recording the inflow and outflow of products through the warehouse. A business needs to take a *physical inventory* to determine the amount of inventory shrinkage. A physical inventory refers to inspecting and counting all items in inventory, usually at the close of the fiscal year. This purpose is to discover shortages of inventory. The cost of the missing products is removed from the inventory asset account and charged to expense. This expense is painful to record because the business receives no sales revenue from these products. A certain amount of inventory shrinkage expense is considered to be a normal cost of doing business, which can't be avoided.

Also, at the close of the year, a business should do a *lower of cost or market test* on its ending inventory of products. Product costs are compared against the current replacement costs of the products and the current market (sales) prices of the products. This is a twofold test of product costs. If replacement costs have dropped or if the products have lost sales value, your accountant should make a year-end adjusting entry to write down your ending inventory to a lower amount, which is below the original costs you paid for the products.

Recording inventory shrinkage expense caused by missing products is cut and dried. You don't have the products. So, the cost of the products is removed from the asset account — that's all there is to it. In contrast, writing down the costs of damaged products (that are still salable at some price) and determining replacement and market values for the lower of cost or market test is not so clear-cut.

WARNING

A business may be tempted to write down its inventory too much in order to minimize its taxable income for the year. You're on thin ice if you do this, and you better pray that the IRS won't audit you.

TIP

In recording the expense of inventory shrinkage and inventory write-down under the lower of cost of market test, your accountant has to decide which expense account to charge and how to report the loss in your income statement. Generally, the loss should be included in your cost of goods sold expense in the income statement because the loss is a normal expense that sits on top of cost of goods sold.

However, when an abnormal amount of loss is recorded, your accountant should call the loss to your attention — either on a separate line in the income statement or in a footnote to the statement.

Focusing on Profit Centers

A business consists of different revenue streams, and some are more profitable than others. It would be very unusual if every different source of sales were equally profitable. A common practice is to divide the business into separate *profit centers,* so that the profitability of each part of the business can be determined. For example, a car dealership is separated into new car sales, used car sales, service work, and parts sales. Each profit center's sales revenue may be further subdivided. New vehicle sales can be separated into sedans, pickup trucks, SUVs, and other models. In the business example used in this chapter, you sell products both at retail prices to individual consumers and at wholesale prices to other businesses. Quite clearly, you should separate your two main sources of sales and create a profit center for each.

Determining how to partition a business into profit centers is a management decision. The first question is whether the segregation of sales revenue into distinct profit centers helps you better manage the business. Generally, the answer is yes. The information helps you focus attention and effort on the sources of highest profit to the business. Comparing different profit centers puts the spotlight on sources of sales that don't generate enough profit, or even may be losing money.

Generally, a business creates a profit center for each major product line and for each location (or territory). There are no hard-and-fast rules, however. At one extreme, each product can be defined as a profit center. As a matter of fact, businesses keep records for every product they sell. Many owners want a very detailed report on sales and cost of goods sold for every product they sell. This report can run many, many pages. A hardware store in Boulder sells more than 100,000 products. Would you really want to print out a report that lists the sales and cost of goods of more than 100,000 lines? The more practical approach is to divide the business into a reasonable number of profit centers and focus your time on the reports for each profit center.

A profit center is a fairly autonomous source of sales of a business, like a tub standing on its own feet. For example, the Boulder hardware store sells outdoor clothing, which is quite distinct from the other products it sells. Does the hardware store make a good profit on its outdoor clothing line of products? The first step is to determine the gross margin for the outdoor clothing department. The cost of goods sold is deducted from sales revenue for the outdoor clothing line of products. Is outdoor clothing a high gross margin source of sales? The owner of the hardware store certainly should know.

The report for a profit center doesn't stop at the gross profit line. One key purpose of setting up profit centers is, as far as possible, to match direct operating costs against the sales revenue of the profit center. *Direct operating costs* are those that can be clearly assigned to the sales activity of the profit center. Examples of direct operating costs of a profit center are the following:

>> Commissions paid to salespersons on sales of the profit center

>> Shipping and delivery costs of products sold in the profit center

>> Inventory shrinkage and write-downs of inventory in the profit center

>> Bad debts from credit sales of the profit center

>> The cost of employees who work full-time in a profit center

>> The cost of advertisements for products sold in the profit center

WARNING

Assigning direct operating costs to profit centers doesn't take care of all the costs of a business. A business has many *indirect* operating costs that benefit all, or at least two or more profit centers. The employee cost of the general manager of the business, the cost of its accounting department, general business licenses, real estate taxes, interest on the debt of the business, and liability insurance are examples of general, business-wide operating costs. Accountants have come up with ingenious methods for allocating indirect operating costs to profit centers. In the last analysis, however, the allocation methods have flaws and are fairly arbitrary. The game may not be worth the candle in allocating indirect operating costs to profit centers. Generally, there is no gain in useful information. You have all the information you need by ending the profit center report after direct operating costs.

TIP

The bottom line of a profit center report is a measure of profit before general business operating costs and interest expense (and income tax expense, if applicable) are taken into account. The bottom line of a profit center is more properly called *contribution* toward the aggregate profit of the business as a whole. The term *profit* is a commonly used label for the bottom line of a profit center report, but keep in mind that it doesn't have the same meaning as the bottom line of the income statement for the business as a whole.

Reducing Your Costs

This section covers a few cost-reduction tactics. It's not an exhaustive list, to be sure, but you may find one or two of these quite useful:

>> Have your accountant alert you to any expense that increases more than a certain threshold amount, or by a certain percent.

>> Hire a cost control specialist. Many of these firms work on a contingent fee basis that depends on how much your expense actually decreases. These outfits tend to specialize in certain areas such as utility bills and property taxes, to name just two.

>> Consider outsourcing some of your business functions, such as payroll, security, taking inventory, and maintenance.

>> Put out requests for competitive bids on supplies you regularly purchase.

>> Make prompt payments of purchases on credit to take advantage of early payment discounts. Indeed, offer to pay in advance if you can gain an additional discount.

>> Keep all your personal and family costs out of the business.

>> Keep your assets as low as possible so that the capital you need to run the business is lower, and your cost of capital will be lower.

>> Set priorities on cost control, putting the fastest rising costs at the top.

>> Ask your outside CPA for cost control ideas she or he has observed in other businesses.

Deciding Where the Budgeting Process Starts

Accounting represents more of an art than a science. This concept also holds true with the budgeting process, as it helps to be creative when preparing projections. Before creating your first budget, you should prepare by taking the following four steps:

1. Delve into your business's financial history.

To start, you should have a very good understanding of your company's prior financial and operating results. This history doesn't stretch back very far when you're starting out (obviously), but the key concept is that sound information not only should be readily available but it should be clearly understood. There is no point in attempting to prepare a budget if the party completing the work doesn't understand the financial information.

Although the history of a company may provide a basic foundation on which to develop a budget, it by no means is an accurate predictor of the future.

2. **Involve your key management.**

The budgeting process represents a critical function in most companies' accounting and financial departments — and rightfully so, because these are the people who understand the numbers best. If you have other managers looking after different departments or sections of your business, be sure to get them involved. Although the financial and accounting types produce the final budget, they rely on data that comes from numerous parties, such as marketing, manufacturing, and sales. Critical business data comes from numerous parties, all of which must be included in the budgeting process to produce the most reliable information possible.

3. **Gather reliable data.**

The availability of quality market, operational, and accounting data represents the basis of the budget. A good deal of this data often comes from internal sources. For example, when a sales region is preparing a budget for the upcoming year, the sales manager may survey the direct sales representatives on what they feel their customers will demand as far as products and services in the coming year. With this information, you can determine sales volumes, personnel levels, wages rates, commission plans, and so on.

Although internal information is of value, it represents only half the battle because external information and data is just as critical to accumulate. Having access to quality and reliable external third-party information is absolutely essential to the overall business planning process and the production of reliable forecasts. Market forces and trends may be occurring that can impact your business over the next 24 months but aren't reflected at all in the previous year's operating results.

4. **Coordinate the budget timing.**

From a timing perspective, most companies tend to start the budgeting process for the next year in the fourth quarter of their current calendar year. This way, they have access to recent financial results on which to support the budgeting process moving forward. The idea is to have a sound budget to base the next year's operations on.

On the timeline front, the following general rule should be adhered to: The nearer the term covered by the projection means more detailed information and results should be produced. That is, if you're preparing a budget for the coming fiscal year, then monthly financial statement forecasts are expected (with more detailed support available). Looking two or three years out, you could produce quarterly financial statement projections (with more summarized assumptions used).

The concept of *garbage in, garbage out* definitely applies to the budgeting process. If you don't have sound data and information, the output produced will be of little value to the owners. The data and information used to prepare your company's budgets must be as complete, accurate, reliable, and timely as possible. Though you can't be 100 percent assured that the data and information accumulated achieves these goals (because, by definition, you're attempting to predict the future with a projection), proper resources should be dedicated to the process to avoid getting bit by large information black holes.

REMEMBER

Finally, keep in mind that the projections prepared must be consistent with the overall business plans and strategies of the company. Remember, the budgeting process represents a living, breathing thing that constantly must be updated and adapted to changing market conditions. What worked two years ago may not provide management with the necessary information today on which to make appropriate business decisions.

Homing In on Budgeting Tools

After you have solid historical data in hand, you're ready to produce an actual projection model. To help start the process, you can use three simple acronyms as tools to accumulate the necessary information to build the projection model.

CART: Complete, Accurate, Reliable, and Timely

Complete, Accurate, Reliable, and Timely (CART) applies to all the data and information you need to prepare for the projection model. It doesn't matter where the information is coming from or how it's presented; it just must be complete, accurate, reliable, and timely:

» **Complete:** Financial statements produced for a company include a balance sheet (see Chapter 3 in Book 3), an income statement (see Chapter 2 in Book 3), and a cash flow statement (see Chapter 4 in Book 3). All three are needed in order to understand the entire financial picture of a company. If a projection model is incorporating an expansion of a company's manufacturing facility in a new state, for example, all information related to the new facility needs to be accumulated to prepare the budget. This data includes the cost of the land and facility, how much utilities run in the area, what potential environmental issues may be present, whether a trained workforce is available, and if not, how much will it cost to train them, and so on. Although overkill is not the objective, having access to all material information and data is.

>> **Accurate:** Incorporating accurate data represents the basis for preparing the initial budget. Every budget needs to include the price your company charges for the goods or services it sells, how much you pay your employees, what the monthly office rent is, and so on. The key to obtaining accurate information is ensuring that your accounting and financial information system is generating accurate data.

>> **Reliable:** The concepts of reliability and accuracy are closely linked but also differ as well. It may be one thing to obtain a piece of information that is accurate, but is it reliable? For example, you may conduct research and find that the average wage for a paralegal in San Diego is $24 per hour. This figure may sound accurate, but you may need a specialist paralegal who demands $37 per hour.

REMEMBER

>> **Timely:** The information and data accumulated must be done in a timely fashion. It's not going to do a management team much good if the data and information that is needed is provided six months after the fact. Companies live and die by having access to real-time information on which to make business decisions and change course (and forecasts) if needed.

SWOT: Strengths, Weaknesses, Opportunities, and Threats

Don't be afraid to utilize a Strengths, Weaknesses, Opportunities, and Threats (SWOT) analysis, which is an effective planning and budgeting tool used to keep businesses focused on key issues. The simple SWOT analysis (or matrix) in Figure 5-4 shows you how this process works.

A SWOT analysis is usually broken down into a matrix containing four segments. Two of the segments are geared toward positive attributes, such as your strengths and opportunities, and two are geared toward negative attributes, such as your weaknesses and threats. In addition, the analysis differentiates between internal company source attributes and external, or outside of the company source attributes. Generally, the SWOT analysis is meant to ensure that critical conditions are communicated to management for inclusion in the budget.

As an owner of a business, you must be able to understand the big picture and your company's key economic drivers in order to prepare proper business plans, strategies, and ultimately, forecasts. The ability to understand and positively affect the key economic drivers of your business and empower the team to execute the business plan represents the end game. Getting lost in the forest of "Why did you spend an extra $500 on the trip to Florida?" is generally not the best use of the owner's time.

Strengths	Weaknesses
(What you do well, competitive advantages)	(What you don't do well, competitive disadvantages)

Internal

Opportunities	Threats
(Potential marketplace openings, new ventures, and ideas to grow your business)	(Potential competitive, economic, or environmental factors that may hurt your business)

External

FIGURE 5-4:
A basic SWOT
analysis.

© John Wiley & Sons, Inc.

Flash reports

Flash reports are a quick snapshot of critical company operating and financial data, which is then used to support the ongoing operations of the business. All types of flash reports are used in business, and they range from evaluating a book-to-bill ratio on a weekly basis, to reporting daily sales activity during the holiday season, to looking at weekly finished goods inventory levels.

The goal with all flash reports remains the same in that critical business information is delivered to you for review much more frequently. As such, flash reports tend to have the following key attributes present:

>> **Flash reports tend to be much more frequent in timing.** Unlike the production of financial statements (which occurs on a monthly basis), flash reports are often produced weekly and, in numerous cases, daily. In today's competitive marketplace, small business owners are demanding information be provided more frequently than ever to stay on top of rapidly changing markets.

>> **Flash reports are designed to capture critical operating and financial performance data of your business or the real information that can make or break your business.** As a result, sales activities and/or volumes are almost always a part of a business's flash reporting effort. Once you have a good handle on the top line, the bottom line should be relatively easy to calculate.

>> **Flash reports aren't just limited to presenting financial data.** Flash reports can be designed to capture all kinds of data, including retail store foot volume (or customer traffic levels), labor utilization rates, and the like. Although you may want to know how sales are tracking this month, the store manager will want to keep a close eye on labor hours incurred in the process.

>> **Flash reports obtain their base information from the same accounting and financial information system that produces periodic financial statements, budgets, and other reports.** Though the presentation of the information may be different, the source of the information should come from the same transactional basis (of your company).

>> **Flash reports are almost exclusively used for internal management needs and are rarely delivered to external parties.** The information contained in flash reports is usually more detailed in nature and tends to contain far more confidential data than, say, audited financial statements, and are almost never audited.

>> **Flash reports are closely related to the budgeting process.** For example, if a company is experiencing a short-term cash flow squeeze, the owner will need to have access to a rolling 13-week cash flow projection to properly evaluate cash inflows and outflows on a weekly basis. Each week, the rolling 13-week cash flow projection is provided to the owner for review in the form of a flash report, which is always being updated to look out 13 weeks.

Flash reports should act more to "reconfirm" your company's performance rather than representing a report that offers "original" information. Granted, though a flash report that presents sales volumes for the first two weeks of February compared to the similar two–week period for the prior year is reporting new sales information, the format of the report and the presentation of the information in the report should be consistent. Thus, you should be able to quickly decipher the results and determine whether the company is performing within expectations and what to expect on the bottom line for the entire month.

Preparing an Actual Budget or Forecast

The best way to dive into preparing a budget, after all the necessary information has been accumulated, is to begin by building a draft of the budget that is more summary in nature and is focused on the financial statement, which is most easily understood and widely used. The reason more summarized budgets are developed at first is to create a general format or framework that captures the basic output desired by the parties using the budget. Offering a summarized visual version of the budget allows for reviews and edits to be incorporated into the forecasting model before too much effort is expended in including detail that may not be needed. Once the desired output reports and data points of the budget are determined, it can be expanded and adjusted to incorporate the correct level of detail.

TIP

The best way to prepare a summarized budget that is both flexible and adaptable is to build the forecasting model in software such as Excel, which is relatively easy to use and widely accepted by most businesses.

On the financial statement front, for most companies, the forecasting process tends to starts with producing a projected income statement for three primary reasons.

>> First, this financial statement tends to be the one that is most widely used and easily understood by the organization. Questions such as how much revenue can the company produce, what will the gross margin be, and how much profit will be generated are basic focal points of almost every business owner. The balance sheet and cash flow statements aren't nearly as easy to understand and produce.

>> Second, the income statement often acts as a base data point to produce balance sheet and cash flow statement information. For example, if sales volumes are increasing, it's safe to say that the company's balance in trade accounts receivable and inventory would increase as well.

>> And third, the majority of the information and data accumulated to support the budgeting process is generally centered in areas associated with the income statement, such as how many units can be sold, at what price, how many sales persons will you need, and so on.

Note also that most budgets are prepared in a consistent format with that of the current internally produced financial statements and reports utilized by your company. This achieves the dual goal of information conformity (for ease of understanding) and capturing your business's key economic drivers. To illustrate, Figure 5-5 presents a summarized budget for XYZ Wholesale, Inc., for the coming year.

XYZ WHOLESALE, INC.
UNAUDITED FINANCIAL STATEMENT — QUARTERLY PROJECTIONS

CONFIDENTIAL

Summary Balance Sheet	Actual Year End 1/1/19	Forecast Quarter End 4/1/19	Forecast Quarter End 7/1/19	Forecast Quarter End 10/1/19	Forecast Quarter End 1/1/20	Forecast Year End 1/1/20
Current Assets:						
Cash & Equivalents	$117,632	$11,364	$26,263	$38,200	$24,313	$24,313
Trade Receivables, Net	$1,271,875	$1,213,333	$1,646,667	$2,253,333	$1,610,000	$1,610,000
Inventory	$867,188	$886,667	$1,132,400	$1,248,000	$856,800	$856,800
Total Current Assets	$2,256,695	$2,111,364	$2,805,330	$3,539,533	$2,491,113	$2,491,113
Fixed & Other Assets:						
Property, Plant & Equipment, Net	$1,750,000	$1,725,000	$1,700,000	$1,675,000	$1,650,000	$1,650,000
Other Assets	$75,000	$75,000	$75,000	$75,000	$75,000	$75,000
Total Fixed & Other Assets	$1,825,000	$1,800,000	$1,775,000	$1,750,000	$1,725,000	$1,725,000
Total Assets	$4,081,695	$3,911,364	$4,580,330	$5,289,533	$4,216,113	$4,216,113
Current Liabilities:						
Trade Payables	$2,601,563	$2,340,800	$2,547,900	$2,808,000	$1,965,600	$1,965,600
Accrued Liabilities	$195,117	$234,080	$254,790	$280,800	$196,560	$196,560
Line of Credit Borrowings	$200,000	$500,000	$1,000,000	$1,100,000	$250,000	$250,000
Current Portion of Long-Term Liabilities	$300,000	$300,000	$300,000	$300,000	$300,000	$300,000
Total Current Liabilities	$3,296,680	$3,374,880	$4,102,690	$4,488,800	$2,712,160	$2,712,160
Long-Term Liabilities:						
Notes Payable, Less Current Portion	$300,000	$225,000	$150,000	$75,000	$0	$0
Other Long-Term Liabilities	$150,000	$150,000	$150,000	$150,000	$150,000	$150,000
Total Long-Term Liabilities	$450,000	$375,000	$300,000	$225,000	$150,000	$150,000
Total Liabilities	$3,746,680	$3,749,880	$4,402,690	$4,713,800	$2,862,160	$2,862,160
Equity:						
Common and Preferred Equity, $1 Per Share	$500,000	$500,000	$500,000	$500,000	$1,000,000	$1,000,000
Retained Earnings	$901,265	($164,985)	($164,985)	($164,985)	($164,985)	($164,985)
Current Earnings	($1,066,250)	($173,531)	($157,375)	$240,719	$518,938	$518,938
Total Equity	$335,015	$161,484	$177,640	$575,734	$1,353,953	$1,353,953
Total Liabilities & Equity	$4,081,695	$3,911,364	$4,580,330	$5,289,534	$4,216,113	$4,216,113

Summary Income Statement	Actual Year End 1/1/19	Forecast Quarter End 4/1/19	Forecast Quarter End 7/1/19	Forecast Quarter End 10/1/19	Forecast Quarter End 1/1/20	Forecast Year End 1/1/20
Revenue	$13,875,000	$2,800,000	$3,800,000	$5,200,000	$4,200,000	$16,000,000
Costs of Goods Sold	$10,406,250	$2,128,000	$2,831,000	$3,744,000	$3,024,000	$11,727,000
Gross Profit	$3,468,750	$672,000	$969,000	$1,456,000	$1,176,000	$4,273,000
Gross Margin	25.00%	24.00%	25.50%	28.00%	28.00%	26.71%
Selling, General & Administrative Expenses	$3,060,000	$700,000	$800,000	$900,000	$750,000	$3,150,000
Depreciation Expense	$350,000	$100,000	$100,000	$100,000	$100,000	$400,000
Interest Expense	$75,000	$20,531	$27,844	$32,906	$22,781	$104,063
Other (Income) Expenses	$1,050,000	$25,000	$25,000	$25,000	$25,000	$100,000
Net Profit Before Tax	($1,066,250)	($173,531)	$16,156	$398,094	$278,219	$518,938
Income Tax Expense (Benefit)	$0	$0	$0	$0	$0	$0
Net Profit (Loss)	($1,066,250)	($173,531)	$16,156	$398,094	$278,219	$518,938

Summary Cash Flow Statement	Actual Year End 1/1/19	Forecast Quarter End 4/1/19	Forecast Quarter End 7/1/19	Forecast Quarter End 10/1/19	Forecast Quarter End 1/1/20	Forecast Year End 1/1/20
Operating Cash Flow:						
Net Income (Loss)	($1,066,250)	($173,531)	$16,156	$398,094	$278,219	$518,938
Depreciation Expense	$350,000	$100,000	$100,000	$100,000	$100,000	$400,000
Net Operating Cash Flow	($716,250)	($73,531)	$116,156	$498,094	$378,219	$918,938
Working Capital:						
(Increase) Decrease in Trade Receivables	$471,875	$58,542	($433,333)	($606,667)	$643,333	($338,125)
(Increase) Decrease in Inventory	$1,049,194	($19,479)	($245,733)	($115,600)	$391,200	$10,388
Increase (Decrease) In Trade Payables	($81,371)	($260,763)	$207,100	$260,100	($842,400)	($635,963)
Increase (Decrease) In Accrued Liabilities	$60,971	$38,963	$20,710	$26,010	($84,240)	$1,443
Increase (Decrease) In Current Debt	$100,000	$300,000	$500,000	$100,000	($850,000)	$50,000
Net Working Capital Cash Flow	$1,600,668	$117,263	$48,743	($336,157)	($742,107)	($912,257)
Financing Capital:						
Equity Contributions	$0	$0	$0	$0	$500,000	$500,000
Additions to Long-Term Debt	$0	$0	$0	$0	$0	$0
Deletions to Long-Term Debt	($300,000)	($75,000)	($75,000)	($75,000)	($75,000)	($300,000)
Fixed Asset Additions	($600,000)	($75,000)	($75,000)	($75,000)	($75,000)	($300,000)
Change to Other Long-Term Assets	$0	$0	$0	$0	$0	$0
Change to Other Long-Term Liabilities	$10,000	$0	$0	$0	$0	$0
Net Financial Capital Cash Flow	($890,000)	($150,000)	($150,000)	($150,000)	$350,000	($100,000)
Beginning Cash	$123,214	$117,632	$11,364	$26,263	$38,200	$117,632
Ending Cash	$117,632	$11,364	$26,263	$38,200	$24,312	$24,312

FIGURE 5-5: A quarterly forecast.

© John Wiley & Sons, Inc.

A budget is shown for the year ending 12/31/20 for XYZ Wholesale, Inc. The basic budget shown in Figure 5-5 is fairly simplistic but also very informative. It captures the macro level economic structure of the company in terms of where it is today and where it expects to be at the end of next year. When reviewing the figure, notice the following key issues:

>> **The most recent year-end financial information has been included in the first column to provide a base reference point to work from.** Gaining a thorough understanding of your company's historical operating results to forecast into the future is important. Also, by having this base information, you can develop a consistent reporting format for ease of understanding.

>> **The projections are "complete" from a financial statement perspective.** That is, the income statement, balance sheet, and statement of cash flows (covered in Chapters 2, 3, and 4 of Book 3) have all been projected to assist management with understanding the entire financial picture of the company. The forecasts prepared for XYZ Wholesale, Inc., indicate that the line of credit will be used extensively through the third quarter to support working capital needs. By the end of the fourth quarter, borrowings on the line of credit are substantially lower as business slows and cash flows improve (used to pay down the line of credit).

>> **The projections have been presented with quarterly information.** You might use projections for the next fiscal year, prepared on a monthly basis to provide you with more frequent information. However, this chapter uses prepared quarterly information.

>> **The projections have been prepared and presented in a "summary" format.** That is, not too much detail has been provided, but rather groups of detail have been combined into one line item. For example, if your business has more than one location, individual budgets are prepared to support each location, but when a company-wide forecast is completed, all the sales are rolled up onto one line item. Budgets prepared in a summary format are best suited for review by external parties and managers.

>> **Certain key or critical business economic drivers have been highlighted in the projection model.** First, the company's gross margin has been called out as it increases from 24 percent in the first quarter to 28 percent in the first half of the year. The increase was the result of the company moving older and obsolete products during the first six months of the year to make way for new merchandise and products to be sold at higher prices starting in the third quarter (and then accelerating in the fourth quarter during the holidays). Second, the company's pretax net income, for the entire year, has improved significantly. This increase occurred because the company's fixed overhead and corporate infrastructure (expenses) did not need to increase nearly as much to support the higher sales (as a result of realizing the benefits of economies of scale). In addition, the company didn't have to absorb an inventory write-off of $1 million (as with 2019).

Controlling Costs and Budgeting

>> **A couple of very simple, but extremely important, references are made at the top of the projections.** The company clearly notes that the information prepared is confidential in nature. The company also notes that the information is unaudited. In today's business world, information that is both confidential and that hasn't been audited by an external party should clearly state so.

REMEMBER

The best way to prepare your first budget is to simply dive in and give it a go. There is no question that your first draft will undergo significant changes, revisions, and edits, but it's much easier to critique something that already exists than create it from scratch. The hard part is preparing the first budget. After that, the budget can then be refined, expanded, and improved to provide your organization an even more valuable tool in managing everyday challenges, stress, and growing pains.

Understanding Internal versus External Budgets

Information prepared for and delivered to external users (a financing source, taxing authorities, company creditors, and so on) isn't the same as information prepared for and utilized internally in the company. Not only does this fact apply to historically produced information, but it applies to financial information you forecast as well. The following examples show how a business can basically utilize the same information, but for different objectives:

>> **The internal sales-driven budget:** You never see a budget prepared based on sales and marketing information that is more conservative than a similar budget prepared based on operations or accounting information. By nature, sales and marketing personnel tend to be far more optimistic in relation to the opportunities present than other segments of the business (which, of course, includes the ultra-conservative nature of accountants). So, rather than attempt to have these two groups battle it out over what forecast model is the most accurate, it's a good idea to simply prepare two sets of projections. Companies often have more than one set of projections. You can use the marketing- and sales-based projection as a motivational tool to push this group but use a more conservative projection for delivery to external financing sources, which provides a "reasonable" projection so that the company isn't under enormous pressure to hit aggressive plans. Granted, this strategy has to be properly managed (and kept in balance) because one forecast shouldn't be drastically different than another.

>> **Drilling down into the detail:** When information is delivered to external parties, the level of detail is far less than what is utilized internally on a daily basis. This concept holds true for the budgeting process as well. The level and amount of detail that is at the base of the projection model will often drill down to the core elements of your business.

For example, the summary projected in Figure 5-5 displays corporate overhead expenses as one line item. This one line item could, in fact, be the summation of more than 100 lines of data and capture everything from the cost of personnel in the accounting department to the current year's advertising budget (for the company). Again, an outside party should not (and does not want to) see that level of detail because it tends to only confuse them and lead to more questions being asked than are needed. However, by being able to drill down into the detail at any given time (and provide real support for financial information presented in the budget), you can kill two birds with one stone. Internally, you have the necessary detail to hold team members responsible for expense and cost control. Externally, you can provide added confidence and creditability to your partners (for example, a financing source) that the business is being tightly managed.

Creating a Living Budget

A *living budget* is based on the idea that in today's fiercely competitive marketplace, business models change much quicker than they did a decade ago (see Book 1, Chapter 3 for more on business models). Although the budget prepared in the fourth quarter of the previous year looked good, six months later the story may change. Any number of factors, such as losing a key sales rep, having a competitor go out of business, or experiencing a significant increase in the price of raw materials to produce your products, may cause the best prepared budgets to be useless by midyear. So, you may want to keep in mind the following terminology when preparing budgets to ensure that the process doesn't become stagnant during the year:

>> **What ifs:** A what-if analysis is just as it sounds. That is, if this happens to my business or in the market, what will be the impact on my business? If I can land this new account, what additional costs will I need to incur and when to support the account? Utilizing what-if budgeting techniques is a highly effective business-management strategy that you can apply to all levels of the budgeting process.

Figure 5-6 presents a company's original budget alongside two other scenarios, one of which is a low-case scenario and the other a best-case scenario. By completing what-if budgeting, XYZ Wholesale, Inc., has provided itself with a better understanding of what business decisions need to be made in case either the low-case or high-case scenarios are realized.

CONFIDENTIAL

Summary Balance Sheet	Actual Year End 1/1/19	Forecast — Low Year End 1/1/20	Forecast — Med Year End 1/1/20	Forecast — High Year End 1/1/20
Current Assets:				
Cash & Equivalents	$117,632	$56,515	$24,313	$48,265
Trade Receivables, Net	$1,271,875	$1,550,000	$1,610,000	$2,000,000
Inventory	$867,188	$825,000	$856,800	$1,000,000
Total Current Assets	$2,256,695	$2,431,515	$2,491,113	$3,048,265
Fixed & Other Assets:				
Property, Plant & Equipment, Net	$1,750,000	$1,600,000	$1,650,000	$1,700,000
Other Assets	$75,000	$75,000	$75,000	$75,000
Total Fixed & Other Assets	$1,825,000	$1,675,000	$1,725,000	$1,775,000
Total Assets	$4,081,695	$4,106,515	$4,216,113	$4,823,265
Current Liabilities:				
Trade Payables	$2,601,563	$1,900,000	$1,965,600	$1,750,000
Accrued Liabilities	$195,117	$190,000	$196,560	$210,000
Line of Credit Borrowings	$200,000	$700,000	$250,000	$550,000
Current Portion of Long-Term Liabilities	$300,000	$300,000	$300,000	$300,000
Total Current Liabilities	$3,296,680	$3,090,000	$2,712,160	$2,810,000
Long-Term Liabilities:				
Notes Payable, Less Current Portion	$300,000	$0	$0	$0
Other Long-Term Liabilities	$150,000	$150,000	$150,000	$150,000
Total Long-Term Liabilities	$450,000	$150,000	$150,000	$150,000
Total Liabilities	$3,746,680	$3,240,000	$2,862,160	$2,960,000
Equity:				
Common and Preferred Equity, $1 Per Share	$500,000	$1,000,000	$1,000,000	$1,000,000
Retained Earnings	$901,265	($164,985)	($164,985)	($164,985)
Current Earnings	($1,066,250)	$31,500	$518,938	$1,028,250
Total Equity	$335,015	$866,515	$1,353,953	$1,863,265
Total Liabilities & Equity	$4,081,695	$4,106,515	$4,216,113	$4,823,265

Summary Income Statement	Actual Year End 1/1/19	Forecast — Low Year End 1/1/20	Forecast — Med Year End 1/1/20	Forecast — High Year End 1/1/20
Revenue	$13,875,000	$14,250,000	$16,000,000	$18,500,000
Costs of Goods Sold	$10,406,250	$10,687,500	$11,727,000	$13,597,500
Gross Profit	$3,468,750	$3,562,500	$4,273,000	$4,902,500
Gross Margin	25.00%	25.00%	26.71%	26.50%
Selling, General & Administrative Expenses	$3,060,000	$3,000,000	$3,150,000	$3,250,000
Depreciation Expense	$350,000	$350,000	$400,000	$450,000
Interest Expense	$75,000	$81,000	$104,063	$74,250
Other (Income) Expenses	$1,050,000	$100,000	$100,000	$100,000
Net Profit Before Tax	($1,066,250)	$31,500	$518,938	$1,028,250
Income Tax Expense (Benefit)	$0	$0	$0	$0
Net Profit (Loss)	($1,066,250)	$31,500	$518,938	$1,028,250

Summary Cash Flow Statement	Actual Year End 1/1/19	Forecast — Low Year End 1/1/20	Forecast — Med Year End 1/1/20	Forecast — High Year End 1/1/20
Operating Cash Flow:				
Net Income (Loss)	($1,066,250)	$31,500	$518,938	$1,028,250
Depreciation Expense	$350,000	$350,000	$400,000	$450,000
Net Operating Cash Flow	($716,250)	$381,500	$918,938	$1,478,250

Working Capital:				
(Increase) Decrease in Trade Receivables	$471,875	($278,125)	($338,125)	($728,125)
(Increase) Decrease in Inventory	$1,049,194	$42,188	$10,388	($132,813)
Increase (Decrease) in Trade Payables	($81,371)	($701,563)	($635,963)	($851,563)
Increase (Decrease) in Accrued Liabilities	$60,971	($5,117)	$1,443	$14,883
Increase (Decrease) in Current Debt	$100,000	$500,000	$50,000	$350,000
Net Working Capital Cash Flow	$1,600,668	($442,617)	($912,257)	($1,347,617)
Financing Capital:				
Equity Contributions	$0	$500,000	$500,000	$500,000
Additions to Long-Term Debt	$0	$0	$0	$0
Deletions to Long-Term Debt	($300,000)	($300,000)	($300,000)	($300,000)
Fixed Asset Additions	($600,000)	($200,000)	($300,000)	($400,000)
Change to Other Long-Term Assets	$0	$0	$0	$0
Change to Other Long-Term Liabilities	$10,000	$0	$0	$0
Net Financial Capital Cash Flow	($890,000)	$0	($100,000)	($200,000)
Beginning Cash	$123,214	$117,632	$117,632	$117,632
Ending Cash	$117,632	$56,515	$24,312	$48,265

FIGURE 5-6:
What-if forecasts.

© John Wiley & Sons, Inc.

>> **Recasts:** When you hear the term *recast,* it generally means a company is going to update its original budgets or forecasts during some point of the year to recast the information through the end of the year. Companies are constantly under pressure to provide updated information on how they think the year will turn out. Everyone wants updated information, so at the end of select periods (for example, month end or quarter end), the actual results for the company through that period are presented with recast information for the remainder of the year to present recast operating results for the entire year (a combination of actual results and updated projected results). Having access to this type of information can greatly assist business owners so that they can properly direct the company and adapt to changing conditions, not to mention provide timely updates to key external parties (on how the company is progressing).

Nobody likes surprises (more exactly, nobody likes bad ones), and nothing will get an external party, such as a bank or investor, more fired up than a business owner not being able to deliver information on the company's performance.

REMEMBER

>> **Rolling forecasts:** *Rolling forecasts* are similar to preparing recast financial results with the exception that the rolling forecast is always looking out over a period of time (for example, the next 12 months) from the most recent period end. For example, if a company has a fiscal year end of 12/31/18 and has prepared a budget for the fiscal year end 12/31/19, an updated rolling 12-month forecast may be prepared for the period of 4/1/19 through 3/31/20 once the financial results are known for the first quarter ending 3/31/19. This way, you always have 12 months of projections available to work with.

Rolling forecasts tend to be utilized in companies operating in highly fluid or uncertain times that need to always look out 12 months. However, more and more companies are utilizing rolling forecasts to better prepare for future uncertainties.

Controlling Costs
and Budgeting

Using the Budget as a Business-Management Tool

The real key to a budget lies in you, as the business owner, being able to understand the information and then act on it. This section reviews some of the most frequently relied upon outcomes from the budgeting process.

The *variance report* is nothing more than taking a look at the budget and comparing it to actual results for a period of time. Figure 5-7 presents a variance report for XYZ Wholesale, Inc., and compares the budgeted results for the quarter ending 3/31/19 against the company's actual results.

XYZ WHOLESALE, INC.
UNAUDITED FINANCIAL STATEMENT — VARIANCE ANALYSIS

Summary Income Statement	Forecast Qtr. End 4/1/19	Actual Qtr. End 4/1/19	Variance Qtr. End 4/1/19
Revenue	$2,800,000	$2,865,000	$65,000
Costs of Goods Sold	$2,128,000	$2,018,500	$109,500
Gross Profit	$672,000	$846,500	$174,500
Gross Margin	24.00%	29.55%	
Selling, General & Administrative Expenses	$700,000	$705,000	($5,000)
Depreciation Expense	$100,000	$100,000	$0
Interest Expense	$20,531	$20,000	$531
Other (Income) Expenses	$25,000	$18,500	$6,500
Net Profit Before Tax	($173,531)	$3,000	$172,469
Income Tax Expense (Benefit)	$0	$0	$0
Net Profit (Loss)	($173,531)	$3,000	$172,469

© John Wiley & Sons, Inc.

FIGURE 5-7:
Variance analysis.

Of keen importance is the increase in the company's gross margin, which helped the company break even during the quarter compared to a projected loss of $174,000. Obviously, you need to understand what caused the gross margin to increase. Was it from higher sales prices or lower product costs? Of more importance, however, is that you need to act on the information. If the market is supporting higher prices in general, then you may want to revisit pricing strategies for the second through fourth quarters to take advantage of conditions that may allow the company to further improve its annual financial performance.

Another use of the budget is to support the implementation of specific plans and action steps. For example, if your second dry cleaning store is set to open in the third quarter of the year, then you need to secure the staff to support this store in the middle of the second quarter and then train them to ensure that they're ready when the new store opens. Yes, all this data should have been accumulated and incorporated into the original budget prepared for the new store, but the idea is to turn the budget into a proactive working document (easily accessible for reference) rather than a one-time effort left on the shelf to die.

Using Budgets in Other Ways

When preparing budgets, you must remember that you can use the base data and information accumulated to support other business planning and management functions as well. For example, you can use a well-developed budget to not only prepare forecast financial statements but to prepare the estimated taxable income or loss of a company. For some companies, the difference between book and tax income is small. However for others, the difference can be significant, as the following example illustrates.

A large provider of personnel services elects to implement a strategy to self-fund its workers' compensation insurance costs. The preliminary analysis indicates that an average annual savings of 30 percent or more can be achieved if properly managed. At the end of the third year of the self-funded workers' compensation insurance program, the company had established an accrued liability for more than $1 million to account for potential future claims (to properly reflect the fact that claims made under the program through the end of the year would eventually cost the company $1 million). For book purposes, the $1 million represented an expense recorded in the financial statements, which resulted in the company producing net income of roughly zero dollars. For tax purposes, the IRS would not allow the expense until the claims were actually paid, so the taxable income of the company was $1 million (resulting in a tax liability of $400,000). If the company didn't properly budget for this business event, it may have been in for a rude surprise because, per the books, the company made nothing, yet owed $400,000 in taxes. You can be assured that this is not the type of surprise an executive business owner wants to experience on short notice.

Budgets also play a critical role in developing a business plan (see Chapter 1 in Book 2), especially when a company is attempting to secure capital to execute its strategy. Financial forecasts act as a visual or numeric display of your vision and outlook of where the company is headed. Effectively presented, financial forecasts can enhance the creditability of the management team and basis of the business plan, which, in turn, provides for fewer barriers to acceptance from potential funding sources. In effect, the financial forecasts must clearly present the "story" of the business.

You can also use the budget for other purposes as well, such as preparing information for specialized needs from external parties to training a new store manager on the basic economics of how his store should perform to ensuring that the vision of the company is properly aligned with your direct actions.

REMEMBER

The better a budget is designed and structured from the beginning, the more uses and value it will provide your business down the road.

> » **Filing taxes for corporations**
>
> » **Reporting and paying sales taxes**
>
> » **Staying on top of tax rules and strategies**
>
> » **Paying for help with your taxes**

Chapter **6**

Satisfying the Tax Man

Paying taxes and reporting income for your company are very important jobs, and the way in which you complete these tasks properly depends on your business's legal structure. From sole proprietorships to corporations and everything in between, this chapter explains how taxes are handled for each type. You also get some instruction on collecting and transmitting sales taxes on the products your company sells as well as guidance on keeping up with tax rules and paying for tax help. (See Book 2, Chapter 6 for in-depth information on what's what with all the different forms of business structure and for choosing the right legal structure for your business.)

TIP

Go to www.irs.gov to see the latest and greatest versions of the federal tax forms discussed in this chapter.

Tax Reporting for Sole Proprietors

The federal government doesn't consider sole proprietorships to be separate and distinct legal entities, so they're not taxed as such. Instead, sole proprietors report any business earnings on their individual tax returns — that's the only financial reporting they must do for income tax purposes.

Most sole proprietors file their business tax obligations as part of their individual 1040 tax return using the additional two-page form *Schedule C, Profit or Loss from Business.* On the first page of Schedule C, you report all the company's income and expenses and answer a few questions about your business. The second page is where you report information about Cost of Goods Sold and any vehicles used as part of the business.

Sole proprietors must also pay both the employee and the employer sides of Social Security and Medicare (self-employment tax) — that's double what an employee would normally pay, because the employer matches what is withheld from the employee's wages. Table 6-1 shows the drastic difference in these types of tax obligations for sole proprietors.

TABLE 6-1 ## Comparison of Tax Obligations for Sole Proprietors

Type of Tax	Amount Taken from Employees	Amount Paid by Sole Proprietors
Social Security	6.2%	12.4%
Medicare	1.45%	2.9%

Social Security and Medicare taxes are based on the net profit of the small business, not the gross profit, which means that you calculate the tax after you've subtracted all costs and expenses from your revenue. To help you figure out the tax amounts you owe on behalf of your business, use IRS form *Schedule SE, Self-Employment Tax.* On the first page of this form, you report your income sources, and on the second page, you calculate the tax due.

If you're the bookkeeper for a sole proprietor, you're probably responsible for pulling together the income, Cost of Goods Sold, and expense information needed for this form. In most cases, you then hand off this information to an accountant to fill out all the required forms.

Filing Tax Forms for Partnerships

If your business is structured as a partnership (which, by definition, has more than one owner), your business doesn't pay taxes. Instead, all money earned by the business is split up (passed through) among the partners — who then pay personal income taxes.

The bookkeeper for a partnership or an LLC choosing to be taxed as a partnership needs to provide the financial data necessary to prepare *Form 1065, U.S. Return of Partnership Income.* Typically an accurate income statement and balance sheet are all that is necessary. These financial statements should be provided to the company's accountant, who prepares Form 1065.

The partnership's income and expenses from Form 1065 are used to generate a *Schedule K-1 (Form 1065), Partner's Share of Income, Deductions, Credits, etc.* for each partner. The partnership's tax results will "pass through" to the individual partners based on the partnership agreement. The Schedule K-1 reports to each partner his or her respective share of the partnership's tax results. Using the K-1 information, each partner is then required to report the tax results on his or her tax returns.

Individuals use page 2 of *Schedule E (Form 1040), Supplemental Income and Loss* to report the K-1 information on their Form 1040. Note that Schedule E is used for other reporting purposes such as income rental real estate, income from S Corporations, and so on. Your accountant can help you with preparing Schedule E as well as making the passive and non-passive distinctions.

Paying Corporate Taxes

Corporations come in two varieties, S Corporations and C Corporations; as you may expect, each has unique tax requirements and practices. In fact, not all corporations pay taxes. Some smaller corporations have elected to be taxed as S Corporations and pass their earnings through to their stockholders. Both C and S Corporations have the same legal requirements and protections; they only vary in tax treatment.

WARNING

Check with your accountant to determine whether incorporating your business makes sense for you. Tax savings aren't the only issue you have to think about; operating a corporation also increases administrative, legal, and accounting costs. Be sure that you understand all the costs before incorporating.

Reporting for an S Corporation

An *S Corporation* must have 100 stockholders or fewer, have only one class of stock, and only have shareholders who are individuals, certain trusts, and estates. (See a professional for other, less common eligibility requirements; find out how to hire tax help later in this chapter.) An S Corporation functions like a partnership but gives owners more legal protection from lawsuits than traditional partnerships do. S Corporations still file a corporate tax return, on Form 1120S. However, the tax return is for informational purposes only, with the income on each shareholder's Form K-1 passing through to the individual's tax return on Schedule E of Form 1040, just as in the previous partnership example.

Reporting for a C Corporation

The type of corporation that's considered a separate legal entity for tax purposes is the *C Corporation*. A C Corporation is a legal entity that has been formed specifically for the purpose of running a business.

REMEMBER

The biggest disadvantage of structuring your company as a C Corporation is that your profits are taxed twice — as a corporate entity and based on dividends paid to stockholders. If you're the owner of a C Corporation, you can be taxed twice, but you can also pay yourself a salary and therefore reduce the earnings of the corporation. Corporate taxation is very complicated, with lots of forms to be filled out, so it's impossible to go into sufficient detail here about how to file corporate taxes. Be sure to consult a professional (with the help of information later in this chapter).

REMEMBER

You may think that C Corporation tax rates are a lot higher than personal tax rates, but in reality, many corporations don't pay tax at all or pay taxes at much lower rates than you do. As a corporation, you have plenty of deductions and tax loopholes to use to reduce your tax bites. So even though you, the business owner, may be taxed twice on the small part of your income that's paid in dividends, with a corporation, you're more likely to pay less in taxes overall.

Reporting for Limited Liability Companies (LLC)

LLCs, or Limited Liability Companies, are now being used extensively in business. LLCs can elect or choose their tax classification, such as being taxed as a C Corporation or as a partnership. LLCs have the same reporting requirements and file the same tax returns discussed earlier in this chapter, depending on their chosen classification.

Taking Care of Sales Taxes Obligations

Even more complicated than paying income taxes is keeping up-to-date on local and state tax rates and paying your business's share of those taxes to the government entities. Because tax rates vary from county to county, and even city to city in some states, managing sales taxes can be extremely time-consuming.

Things get messy when you sell products in multiple locations. For each location, you must collect from customers the appropriate tax for that area, keep track of all taxes collected, and pay those taxes to the appropriate government entities when due. In many states, you have to collect and pay local (for the city or county governments) and state taxes.

TIP

An excellent website for data about state and local tax requirements is the Federation of Tax Administrators (`www.taxadmin.org`). This site has links for state and local tax information for every state.

REMEMBER

States require you to file an application to collect and report taxes even before you start doing business in that state. Be sure that you contact the departments of revenue in the states you plan to operate stores before you start selling and collecting sales tax.

WARNING

All sales taxes collected from your customers are paid when you send in the Sales and Use Tax Return for your state — you must have the cash available to pay this tax when the forms are due. Any money you collected from customers during the month should be kept in an account called Accrued Sales Taxes, which is actually a Liability account on your balance sheet because it's money owed to a governmental entity. (See Chapter 3 in Book 3 for an introduction to balance sheets.)

Keeping Up with and Researching Tax Strategies and Rules

By the time you actually get around to filing your annual income tax return, it's too late to take advantage of many tax-reduction strategies for that tax year. And what can be more aggravating than — late in the evening on April 14, when you're already stressed out and unhappily working on your return — finding a golden nugget of tax advice that works great, if only you'd known about it last December!

Whether you're now faced with the daunting task of preparing your return or you're simply trying to increase your tax intelligence during the year, you're probably trying to decide how to do it with a minimum of pain and taxes owed. As you find out in the following sections, you have several options for completing your return and gaining knowledge. The best choice for you depends on the complexity of your tax situation, your knowledge about taxes, and the amount of time you're willing to invest.

REMEMBER

A minority of taxpayers may run into some nitpicky tax issues caused by unusual events in their lives or extraordinary changes in their incomes or assets. This chapter (and book) may not be enough for those folks. In such cases, you need to consider hiring a tax advisor, which is covered later in this chapter.

Using IRS publications

TIP

In addition to the instructions that come with the annual tax forms that the good old IRS prints every year, the IRS also produces hundreds of publications that explain how to complete the myriad tax forms various taxpayers must tackle. These free materials provide more detail than the basic IRS publications and are available in printed form by mail if you simply call and order them from the IRS (800-829-3676) or digitally through the IRS's website (www.irs.gov; see the later section "The Internal Revenue Service" for more on what the site has to offer). Examples of these pamphlets include

>> **Publication 17:** "Your Federal Income Tax" is designed for individual tax-return preparation.

>> **Publication 334:** "Tax Guide for Small Business" is for (you guessed it) small-business tax-return preparation for individuals who use Schedule C or C-EZ.

>> **Publication 583:** "Starting a Business and Keeping Records" is also an excellent resource.

Additionally, the IRS provides answers to common questions through its automated phone system and through live representatives.

If you have a simple, straightforward tax return, completing it on your own using only the IRS instructions may be fine. This approach is as cheap as you can get, costing only your time, patience, photocopying expenses, and postage to mail the completed tax return (unless you choose to file electronically).

WARNING

One danger in relying on the IRS staff for assistance is that it has been known to give wrong information and answers. When you call the IRS with a question, be sure to take notes about your phone conversation, thus protecting yourself in the event of an audit. Date your notes and include the IRS employee's name you spoke with, employee number, office location, what you asked, and the employee's responses. File your notes in a folder with a copy of your completed return.

The IRS also offers more in-depth booklets focusing on specific tax issues. However, if your tax situation is so complex that this book (and Publications 17 and 334) can't address it, you need to think long and hard about getting help from a tax advisor (covered later in this chapter).

REMEMBER

IRS publications present plenty of rules and facts, but they don't make finding the information and advice you really need easy. The best way to use IRS publications is to confirm facts that you already think you know or to check the little details. Don't expect IRS publications and representatives to show you how to cut your tax bill.

Buying software

If you don't want to slog through dozens of pages of tedious IRS instructions or pay a tax preparer hundreds of dollars to complete your return, you may be interested in computer software that can help you finish your IRS Form 1040 and supplemental schedules. If you have access to a computer and printer (unless you choose to file electronically), tax-preparation software can be a helpful tool.

Tax-preparation software also gives you the advantage of automatically recalculating all the appropriate numbers on your return if one number changes. Tax programs can be helpful in doing complex calculations such as determining whether you're subject to the alternative minimum tax or calculating allowable real estate passive losses. The best tax-preparation software is easy to install and use on your computer, provides help when you get stuck, and highlights deductions you may overlook.

WARNING

Before plunking down your hard-earned cash for some tax-preparation software, know that it has potential drawbacks:

>> A tax return prepared by a software program is only as good as the quality of the data you enter into it. (Of course, this drawback exists no matter who actually fills out the forms; some human tax preparers don't probe and clarify to make sure that you've provided all the right details, either.)

>> Subpar tax-preparation software programs may contain glitches that can lead to incorrect calculating or reporting of some aspect of your tax return.

TIP

TurboTax is a leading program and does a solid job of helping you through the federal tax forms. TurboTax Home & Business is designed for sole proprietors and single owner LLCs, and TurboTax Business is intended for S corporations, partnerships, C corporations, and multiple-owner LLCs.

Accessing Internet tax resources

In addition to using your computer to prepare your income tax return, you can do a number of other tax activities via the Internet. The better online tax resources are geared more to tax practitioners and tax-savvy taxpayers. But in your battle to legally minimize your taxes, you may want all the help you can get! Use the Internet for what it's best at doing — possibly saving you time tracking down factual information or forms. The following sections describe some of the better websites out there.

On the Internet, many websites provide information and discussions about tax issues. Take advice and counsel from other Net users at your peril. Don't rely on the accuracy of the answers to tax questions that you ask in online forums. The problem: In many cases, you can't be sure of the background, expertise, or identity of the person with whom you're trading messages.

The Internal Revenue Service

When you think of the Internal Revenue Service — the U.S. Treasury Department office charged with overseeing the collection of federal income taxes — you probably think of a bureaucratic, humorless, and stodgy agency. Difficult as it is to believe, the IRS website (www.irs.gov) is well organized and relatively user-friendly.

The IRS site also has links to state tax organizations, convenient access to IRS forms (including those from prior tax years), and instructions. To be able to read and print the forms, you need Adobe Acrobat Reader, which you can download for free from many Internet sites, including the IRS site or the Adobe website at www.adobe.com. To download forms from the IRS site, start browsing at www.irs.gov/forms-instructions.

You can complete your tax forms online at the IRS site using Adobe Acrobat Reader. The IRS site even features a place for you to submit comments on proposed tax regulations, with a promise that the comments are "fully considered." Is this the IRS we know and love?

Tax preparation sites

A number of websites enable you to prepare federal and state tax forms and then file them electronically. Many of these sites allow you to prepare and file your federal forms for free if you access their site through the IRS website. Just go to www.irs.gov and click the "File" and then the "Free File" links to see whether you qualify. If you access a tax-preparation site directly instead, you may have to pay a fee for a service that would be free through the Free File program.

If you don't want to use Free File, a reasonably priced alternative worth your consideration can be found at the eSmart Tax website (www.esmarttax.com), where you enter data on interview forms and calculate your tax. The premium edition, for $54.95, is designed for small business owners and self-employed folks. The service also includes tax support from professional tax advisors.

TIP

Keep in mind that if you're simply after the tax forms, plenty of the sites mentioned in this chapter offer such documents for free, as do some public libraries.

TaxTopics.net

A number of sites on the Internet claim to be directories — collections of all the best stuff on the Internet on a particular topic. However, many of these sites lack objectivity and expertise. The worst of these sites simply provide links to other sites that are willing to pay them a referral fee.

TaxTopics.net (`https://taxtopics.net/`) is a comprehensive Internet tax resource compendium organized with links by topic. It appears to be run by a California CPA and is a great online tax directory resource.

Research sites

For true tax junkies, the U.S. Tax Code On-Line (`www.fourmilab.ch/ustax/ustax.html`) is a search engine that enables you to check out the complete text of the U.S. Internal Revenue Code. Hyperlinks embedded in the text provide cross-references between sections at the click of a mouse.

And, if you really have nothing better to do with your time, check out the government sites with updated information on tax bills in Congress:

>> `www.jct.gov/`

>> `https://waysandmeans.house.gov/`

Wolters Kluwer Tax & Accounting (`https://taxna.wolterskluwer.com/`) is geared toward tax and legal professionals who need to keep up with and research the tax laws. Access to most of the site's resources comes by subscription only.

Paying for Tax Help

Simply stated, the nation's tax code is complicated and confusing. So it should come as no surprise that legions of tax preparers and advisors stand ready to be hired by you to assist you with your tax quandaries and tasks.

You can hire various types of tax pros, with varying credentials and qualifications. You want to identify possible folks to hire through trusted sources, and then you should ask them some tough questions. This section helps you make sense of your options and gives you pointers on whom to hire for what tax jobs. You also discover how to find possible candidates and get key questions that you should ask them before hiring them.

The more you know before you seek a tax advisor's services, the better able you'll be to make an informed decision and reduce your expenditures on tax preparers.

Deciding to hire tax help

Odds are quite good that you can successfully prepare your own return. Most people's returns don't vary that much from year to year, so you have a head start and can hit the ground running if you get out last year's return — which, of course, you kept a copy of, right? However, preparing your own return may not work as well whenever your situation has changed in some significant way — if you started your own business, for example.

Don't give up and hire a preparer just because you can't bear to open your tax-preparation booklet and get your background data organized. Even if you hire a tax preparer, you still need to get your stuff organized before a consultation.

TIP

As hard and as painful as it is, confront preparing your return as far in advance of April 15 as you can so that, if you feel uncomfortable with your level of knowledge, you have enough time to seek help. The more organizing you do before hiring a preparer, the less having your return prepared should cost you. If an annual compilation of tax records is too daunting, try monthly or quarterly. A more frequent effort can help if you have lots of business expenses, auto use, and charitable deductions. Avoid waiting until the last minute to hire an advisor — you won't do as thorough a job of selecting a competent person, and you'll probably pay more for the rush job. If you get stuck preparing your own return, you can get a second opinion from one of the resources discussed in this section.

If you decide to seek out the services of a tax preparer/advisor, know that tax practitioners come with various backgrounds, training, and credentials. One type of professional isn't necessarily better than another. Think of them as different types of specialists who are appropriate for different circumstances. The four main types of tax practitioners are unenrolled preparers, enrolled agents, certified public accountants, and tax attorneys.

Unenrolled preparers

Among all the tax practitioners, *unenrolled preparers* generally have the least amount of training, and more of them work part time. H&R Block is the largest and most well-known tax-preparation firm in the country. In addition, other national firms and plenty of mom and pop shops are in the tax-preparation business.

The appeal of preparers is that they're tend to be relatively less costly than the other major categories — they can do basic returns for $150 or so. The drawback is that you may hire a preparer who doesn't know much more than you do! As with financial planners, no national regulations apply to tax-return preparers, and no licensing is required, although this may change in the future. Several states (for example, California, Maryland, New York, and Oregon) require licensing of such tax preparers. In most states, almost anybody can hang a tax-preparation shingle and start preparing. Most preparers, however, complete some sort of training program before working with clients.

TIP

Preparers make the most sense for folks who don't have complicated financial lives, who are budget-minded, and who dislike doing their own taxes. If you aren't good about hanging on to receipts or don't want to keep your own files with background details about your taxes, you definitely need to shop around for a tax preparer who's going to be around for a few years. You may need all that paperwork someday for an audit, and some tax preparers keep and organize their clients' documentation rather than return everything each year. (Can you blame them for keeping your records after they go through the tedious task of sorting them all out?) Going with a firm that's open year-round may also be safer, in case tax questions or problems arise. (Some small shops are open only during tax season.)

Enrolled agents

A person must pass IRS scrutiny to be called an *enrolled agent* (EA). This license enables the agent to represent you before the IRS in the event of an audit. The training to become an EA is longer and more sophisticated than that of an unenrolled preparer. Continuing education also is required; EAs must complete at least 16 hours of continuing education each year (and 72 hours per three years) to maintain their licenses, which are renewed every three years. Some EAs offer bookkeeping and payroll tax services, and some even do financial planning.

Enrolled agents' fees tend to fall between those of an unenrolled preparer and a certified public accountant (see the next section). If you require tax return preparation and related advice and representation, and nothing more (no corporate audits or production of financial reports), an EA can provide the expertise you need for a reasonable cost.

TIP

The main difference between enrolled agents and CPAs and tax attorneys is that EAs work exclusively in the field of taxation. Not all CPAs and attorneys do. In addition to preparing your return (including simple to complex forms), good EAs can help with tax planning, represent you at tax audits, and keep the IRS off your back. You can find names and telephone numbers of EAs in your area by contacting the National Association of Enrolled Agents (toll-free 855-880-6232; www.naea.org).

Certified public accountants

Certified public accountants (CPAs) go through significant training and examination to receive the CPA credential. To maintain this designation, a CPA must complete 40 hours of continuing education classes per year.

As with any other professional service you purchase, CPA fees can vary tremendously. Expect to pay more if you live in an area with a high cost of living, if you use the services of a large accounting firm, or if your needs are involved and specialized.

TIP

Competent CPAs are of greatest value to people completing some of the more unusual and less user-friendly schedules, such as Schedule K-1 of Form 1065 for partnerships. CPAs also are helpful for people who had a major or first-time tax event during the year, such as the child-care tax-credit determination. (Good EAs and other preparers can handle these issues as well.) CPA firms are often a good choice for business owners because they're usually larger than EA firms and can offer software services beyond tax and bookkeeping, such as computer consulting.

WARNING

Whenever your return is uncomplicated and your financial situation is stable, hiring a high-priced CPA year after year to fill in the blanks on your tax returns is a waste of money. One CPA bragged that he was effectively making more than $500 per hour from some of his clients' returns that required only 20 minutes of an assistant's time to complete.

However, paying for the additional cost of a CPA on an ongoing basis makes sense if you can afford it and if your financial situation is reasonably complex or dynamic. If you're self-employed and/or you file many other schedules, hiring a CPA may be worth it. But you needn't do so year after year. If your situation grows more complex one year and then stabilizes, consider getting help for the perplexing year and then using other preparation resources discussed in this chapter or a lower-cost preparer or enrolled agent in the future.

TIP

If you desire more information about CPAs in your area, use the "For the Public" link on the American Institute of Certified Public Accountants' website at `www.aicpa.org/forthepublic/findacpa.html`. If you're considering hiring a CPA, be sure to ask how much of his or her time is spent preparing individual income tax returns and returns like yours.

Tax attorneys

Unless you're a super-high-income earner with a complex financial life, hiring a tax attorney to prepare your annual return is prohibitively expensive. In fact, many tax attorneys don't prepare returns as a normal practice. Because of their level of specialization and training, tax attorneys tend to have high hourly billing rates — $200 to $400-plus per hour isn't unusual, and rumor has it that some attorneys in a major metropolitan area have just crossed the $1,000-per-hour threshold.

Tax attorneys sometimes become involved in court cases dealing with tax problems, disagreements, or other complicated matters, such as the purchase or sale of a business. However, other good tax advisors also can help with these issues.

Who's best qualified?

Who is best qualified to prepare your return? That really depends on the individual you want to hire. The CPA credential is just that, a credential. Some people who have the credential try to persuade you not to hire someone without it.

What about all the non-CPAs, such as EAs, who do a terrific job helping prepare their clients' returns and tax plans throughout the year?

If you can afford to and want to pay hundreds of dollars per hour, hiring a large CPA firm can make sense. But for the vast majority of taxpayers, spending that kind of money is unnecessary and wasteful. Many EAs and other tax preparers are out there doing outstanding work for less.

REMEMBER

The more training and specialization a tax practitioner has (and the more affluent the clients), generally the higher the hourly fee. Select the tax pro who best meets your needs. Fees and competence at all levels of the profession vary significantly. If you aren't sure of the quality of work performed and the soundness of the advice, get a second opinion.

Finding tax advisors

Your challenge is to locate a tax advisor who does terrific work, charges reasonable fees, and thus is too busy to bother calling to solicit you! Here are some resources to find those publicity-shy, competent, and affordable tax advisors:

>> **Friends and family:** Some of your friends and family members probably use tax advisors and can steer you to a decent one or two for an interview.

>> **Coworkers:** Ask people in your field what tax advisors they use. This strategy can be especially useful if you're self-employed.

>> **Other advisors:** Financial and legal advisors also can be helpful referral sources, but don't assume that they know more about the competence of a tax person than you do.

WARNING

Beware of a common problem: Financial or legal advisors may simply refer you to tax preparers who send them clients.

>> **Associations:** EAs and CPAs maintain professional associations that can refer you to members in your area. See the relevant earlier sections for EAs and CPAs.

REMEMBER

Never decide to hire a tax preparer or advisor solely on the basis of someone else's recommendation. To ensure that you hire a competent advisor with whom you'll work well, take the time to interview at least two or three candidates (with the help of the following section).

Interviewing prospective tax advisors

When you believe that your tax situation warrants outside help, be sure to educate yourself as much as possible before searching for assistance. The more you know, the better able you'll be to evaluate the competence of someone you may hire.

Ask the right questions to find a competent tax practitioner whose skills match your tax needs. The following questions/issues are a great place to start.

REMEMBER

When all is said and done, make sure that you feel comfortable with a tax advisor. If you're feeling uneasy and can't understand what your tax advisor says to you in the early stages of your relationship, trust your instincts and continue your search.

What tax services do you offer?

Most tax advisors prepare tax returns. This chapter uses the term *tax advisors* because most tax folks do more than simply prepare returns. Many advisors can help you plan and file other important tax documents throughout the year. Some firms can also assist your small business with bookkeeping and other financial reporting, such as income statements (covered in Chapter 2 of Book 3) and balance sheets (covered in Chapter 3 of Book 3). These services can be useful when your business is in the market for a loan or if you need to give clients or investors detailed information about your company.

As a small business owner, seek out tax advisors who work with a large number of small businesses. Doing so should comprise a significant portion of their practice.

TIP

Ask tax advisors to explain how they work with clients. You're hiring the tax advisor because you lack knowledge of the tax system. If your tax advisor doesn't explore your situation, you may experience "the blind leading the blind." A good tax advisor can help you make sure that you don't overlook deductions or make other costly mistakes that may lead to an audit, penalties, and interest. Beware of tax preparers who view their jobs as simply plugging your information into tax forms.

What are your particular areas of expertise?

This question is important because you want to find an advisor who's a good match for your situation. For example, if a tax preparer works mainly with people who receive regular paychecks from an employer, the preparer probably has little expertise in helping small business owners best complete the blizzard of paperwork that the IRS requires.

TIP

Find out what expertise the tax advisor has in handling whatever unusual financial events you're dealing with this year — or whatever events you expect in future years.

What other services do you offer?

Ideally, you want to work with a professional who is 100 percent focused on taxes. It may be difficult to imagine that some people choose to work at this full time, but they do — and lucky for you!

WARNING

A multitude of problems and conflicts of interest crop up when a person tries to prepare tax returns, sell investments, and appraise real estate all at the same time. That advisor may not be fully competent or current in any of those areas.

By virtue of their backgrounds and training, some tax preparers also offer consulting and financial planning services for business owners and other individuals. Because such preparers already know a great deal about your personal and tax situation, they may be able to help in these areas. Just make sure that this help is charged on an hourly consulting basis. Avoid tax advisors who sell financial products that pay them a commission — this situation inevitably creates conflicts of interest.

Who will prepare my return?

If you talk to a solo practitioner, the answer to this question should be simple — the person you're talking to should prepare your return. But if your tax advisor has assistants and other employees, make sure that you know what level of involvement these different people will have in the preparation of your return.

It isn't necessarily problematic if a junior-level person does the preliminary tax return preparation that your tax advisor reviews and finalizes. In fact, this procedure can save you money in tax-preparation fees if the firm bills you at a lower hourly rate for a junior-level person.

Be wary of firms that charge you a high hourly rate for a senior tax advisor who then delegates most of the work to a junior-level person.

How aggressive or conservative are you regarding interpreting tax laws?

Some tax preparers, unfortunately, view their role as enforcement agents for the IRS. This attitude often is a consequence of one too many seminars put on by local IRS folks, who admonish and sometimes intimidate preparers with threats of audits.

On the other hand, some preparers are too aggressive and try tax maneuvers that put their clients on thin ice — subjecting them to additional taxes, penalties, interest, and audits.

Assessing how aggressive a tax preparer is can be difficult. Start by asking what percentage of the preparer's clients gets audited (see the next question). You can also ask the tax advisor for references from clients for whom the advisor helped unearth overlooked opportunities to reduce tax bills.

What's your experience with audits?

As a benchmark, you need to know that the IRS audits about 1 percent of all taxpayer returns. Small business owners and more affluent clients can expect a higher audit rate — somewhere in the neighborhood of 2 percent to 4 percent.

If a tax preparer proudly claims no audited clients, be wary. Among the possible explanations, any of which should cause you to be uncomfortable in hiring such a preparer: She isn't telling you the truth, she has prepared few returns, or she's afraid of taking some legal deductions, so you'll probably overpay your taxes.

A tax preparer who has been in business for at least a couple of years will have gone through audits. Ask the preparer to explain her recent audits, what happened, and why. This explanation sheds light not only on her work with clients but also on her ability to communicate with you in plain English.

How does your fee structure work?

Tax advisor fees, like attorney and financial planner fees, are all over the map — from about $50 to $300 or more per hour. Many preparers simply quote you a total fee for the preparation of your tax return.

Ultimately, the tax advisor charges you for time, so ask what the hourly billing rate is. Alternatively, you can ask for a time estimate to complete your tax return.

If the advisor balks at answering such questions, try asking what his fee is for a one-hour consultation. You may want a tax advisor to work on this basis if you've prepared your return yourself and want it reviewed as a quality-control check. You also may seek an hourly fee if you're on top of your tax preparation in general but have some specific questions about an unusual or one-time event, such as making some major purchases for your business or possibly selling your business.

Clarify whether the preparer's set fee includes follow-up questions that you may have during the year or covers IRS audits on the return. Some accountants include these functions in their set fee, but others charge for everything on an as-needed basis. The advantage of the all-inclusive fee is that it removes the psychological obstacle of your feeling that the meter's running every time you call with a question. The drawback can be that you pay for additional services (time) that you may not need or use.

What qualifies you to be a tax advisor?

REMEMBER

Tax advisors come with a variety of backgrounds. The more tax and business experience they have, usually the better. But don't be overly impressed with credentials. As discussed earlier in this chapter, tax advisors can earn certifications such as CPAs and EAs. Although gaining credentials takes time and work, these certifications are no guarantee that you get quality, cost-effective tax assistance or that you won't be overcharged.

Generally speaking, more years of experience are better than fewer, but don't rule out a newer advisor who lacks gray hair or who hasn't yet slogged through thousands of returns. Intelligence and training can easily make up for less experience.

Newer advisors also may charge less to build up their practices. Be sure, though, that you don't just focus on each preparer's hourly rate (which of course can change over time). Ask each practitioner you interview how much total time she expects your tax return to take. Someone with a lower hourly fee can end up costing you more if she's slower than a more experienced and efficient preparer with a higher hourly rate.

Do you carry liability insurance?

A tax advisor making a major mistake or giving poor advice could cost you thousands of dollars. The greater your income, assets, and the importance of your financial decisions, the more financial harm that can be done.

Your tax advisor needs to carry what's known as *errors and omissions* or *liability* insurance. You can, of course, simply sue an uninsured advisor and hope the advisor has enough personal assets to cover a loss, but don't count on it. Besides, you'll have a much more difficult time getting due compensation that way!

You may also ask the advisor whether he has ever been sued and how the lawsuit turned out. Asking this type of question doesn't occur to most people, so make sure that you tell your tax advisor that you're not out to strike it rich on a lawsuit!

TIP

Another way to discover whether a tax advisor has gotten into hot water is by checking with appropriate professional organizations to which that preparer may belong. You can also check whether any complaints have been filed with your local Better Business Bureau (BBB), although this is far from a foolproof screening method. Most dissatisfied clients don't bother to register complaints with the BBB, and you should also know that the BBB is loath to retain complaints on file against companies that are members.

Can you provide references of clients similar to me?

You need to know that the tax advisor has handled cases and problems like yours. For example, if you're a small business owner (and it's assumed that by picking up this book, you either are or want to be), ask to speak with other small business owners. But don't be overly impressed by tax advisors who claim that they work mainly with one occupational group, such as retailers or physicians. Although there's value in understanding the nuances of a profession, tax advisors are ultimately generalists — as are the tax laws.

When speaking with a tax advisor's references, be sure to ask what work the advisor performed and what the client's satisfaction was with it.

4

Managing Your Business

Contents at a Glance

Chapter **1**

Tackling the Hiring Process

Finding and hiring the best candidate for a job has never been easy. Your challenge as a business owner is to figure out how to not just find the best candidates for your job openings, but also to convince them that your company is the best place to work. This chapter guides you through both sides of that challenge.

Starting with a Clear Job Description

Is the position new, or are you filling an existing one? In either case, before you start the recruiting process, you need to ask yourself some questions. Do you know exactly what standards you're going to use to measure your candidates? Do you have a designated pay range for this position? The clearer you are about what you need and the boundaries you need to work within, the easier and less arbitrary your selection process becomes.

If you're filling an existing position, you probably already have a detailed job description available. Review it closely and make changes where necessary. Again, ensure that the job description reflects exactly the tasks and requirements of the position. When you hire someone new to fill an existing position, you start with a clean slate. For example, you may have had a difficult time getting a former employee to accept certain new tasks — say, taking minutes at staff meetings or filing travel vouchers. By adding these new duties to the job description before you open recruitment, you make the expectations clear and you don't have to struggle with your new hire to do the job.

If the job is new, now is your opportunity to design your ideal candidate. Draft a job description that fully describes all the tasks and responsibilities of the position and the minimum necessary qualifications and experience. If the job requires expertise in addition and subtraction, for example, say so. You're not going to fill the position with the right hire if you don't make certain qualifications a key part of the job description. The more work you put into the job description now, the less work you have to do after you bring in your new hire.

Finally, before you start recruiting, use the latest-and-greatest job description to outline the most important qualities you're seeking in your new hire. Consult and compare notes with other owners of similar businesses to get input on your descriptions, and ask employees for their feedback as well. Use this outline to guide you in the interview process. Keep in mind, however, that job descriptions may give you the skills you want, but they don't automatically give you the kind of employee you want — finding the right person is much more difficult (and is the reason you spend so much time recruiting in the first place).

TIP

Making an *interview outline* carries an additional benefit: You can easily document why you didn't hire the candidates who didn't qualify for your positions. An interview outline is your personal summary of your impressions of the candidate — a memory trigger, based on your notes taken before, during, and after the interview. Pay close attention here. If a disgruntled job candidate ever sues you for not hiring him — and such lawsuits are more common than you may suspect — you'll be eternally thankful that you did your homework in this area of the hiring process. One more thing: Don't make notes on the résumé — your comments could be used in a lawsuit.

Defining the Characteristics of Desirable Candidates

Employers look for many qualities in candidates. The following list gives you an idea of the qualities employers consider most important when hiring new employees. Other characteristics may be particularly important to you, your company, and the job you're looking to fill. This list gives you a good start in identifying them:

>> **Hard working:** Hard work can often overcome a lack of experience or training. You want to hire people who are willing to do whatever it takes to get the job done. Conversely, no amount of skill can make up for a lack of initiative or work ethic. Although you won't know for sure until you make your hire, carefully questioning candidates can give you some idea of their work ethic (or, at least, what they want you to believe about their work ethic). Of course, hard work alone isn't always the end-all, be-all of hiring. People can generate a lot of work, but if the work doesn't align with your business's strategies or isn't within the true scope of their role, then it's wasted effort. Be careful to note the difference as you assess your candidates.

>> **Good attitude:** Although what constitutes a "good" attitude differs for each person, a positive, friendly, willing-to-help perspective makes life at the office much more enjoyable and makes everyone's job easier. When you interview candidates, consider what they'll be like to work with for the next five or ten years. Skills are important, but attitude is even more important. This is the mantra for the success of Southwest Airlines: "Hire for attitude, train for skill."

>> **Experienced:** Some candidates may naively think they should be hired immediately based on the weight of their institution's diploma. However, they may lack a critical element that's so important in the hiring process: experience. An interview gives you the opportunity to ask pointed questions that require your candidates to demonstrate that they can do the job.

>> **Self-starter:** Candidates need to demonstrate an ability to take initiative to get work done. Initiative ranks as a top reason employees are able to get ahead where they work.

>> **Team player:** Teamwork is critical to the success of today's organizations that must do far more with far fewer resources than their predecessors. The ability to work with others and to collaborate effectively is a definite must for employees today.

>> **Smart:** Smart people can often find better and quicker solutions to the problems that confront them. In the world of business, work smarts are more important than book smarts (present book excepted, of course).

>> **Responsible:** You want to hire people who are willing to take on the responsibilities of their positions. Questions about the kinds of projects your candidates have been responsible for and the exact roles those projects played in their success can help you determine this important quality. Finer points, like showing up for the interview and remembering the name of the company they're interviewing for, can also be key indicators of your candidates' sense of responsibility.

>> **Flexible/resilient:** Employees who are able to multitask and switch direction if necessary in a seamless manner are real assets to any organization in today's fast-changing world.

>> **Cultural fit:** Every business has its own unique culture and set of values. The ability to fit into this culture and values is key to whether candidates can succeed within a particular business (assuming that they already have the technical skills).

>> **Stable:** You don't want to hire someone today and then find out he's already looking for the next position tomorrow. No business can afford the expense of hiring and training a new employee, only to have that person leave six months later. You can get some indication of a person's potential stability (or lack thereof) by asking pointed questions about how long candidates worked with a previous employer and why they left. Be especially thorough and methodical as you probe this particular area.

REMEMBER

Hiring the right people is one of the most important tasks business owners face. You can't have a great organization without great people. Unfortunately, business owners traditionally give short shrift to hiring, devoting as little time as possible to preparation and the actual interview process. As in much of the rest of your life, the results you get from the hiring process are usually in direct proportion to the amount of time you devote to it.

Finding Good People

People are the heart of every business. The better people you hire, the better business you'll have. Some people are just meant to be in their jobs. You may know such individuals — someone who thrives as a receptionist or someone who lives to sell. Think about how great your organization would be if you staffed every position with people who lived for their jobs.

WARNING

Likewise, bad hires can make working for an organization an incredibly miserable experience. The negative impacts of hiring the wrong candidate can reverberate both inside and outside an organization for years. If you, as a business owner, ignore the problem, you put yourself in danger of losing your good employees — and one word, per conventions sheet clients, business partners, and vendors. Would you rather spend a few extra hours upfront to find the best candidates, or later devote countless hours trying to straighten out a problem employee?

Of course, as important as the interview process is to selecting the best candidates for your jobs, you won't have anyone to interview if you don't have a good system for finding good candidates. So, where can you find the best candidates for your jobs? The simple answer is *everywhere*.

REMEMBER

Take a long-term view of the hire: a broad search and long hiring cycle that involves other employees in the process. The short-term, "We've gotta have somebody right away" approach often results in selecting an applicant who is the lesser of a number of evils — and whose weaknesses soon become problems for the organization.

Going through traditional recruiting channels

Your job is to develop a recruitment system that helps you find the kinds of people you want to hire. Here are some of the best ways to find candidates for your positions:

>> **Internal candidates:** In most organizations, the first place to look for candidates is within the organization. If you do your job training and developing employees (see Chapter 1 in Book 6), you probably have plenty of candidates to consider for your job openings. Only after you exhaust your internal candidates should you look outside your organization. Not only is hiring people this way less expensive and easier, but you also get happier employees, improved morale, and new hires who are already familiar with your organization.

>> **Personal referrals:** Whether from co-workers, professional colleagues, friends, relatives, or neighbors, you can often find great candidates through referrals. Who better to present a candidate than someone whose opinion you already value and trust? You get far more insight about the candidates' strengths and weaknesses from the people who refer them than you ever get from résumés alone. Not only that, but research shows that people hired through current employees tend to work out better, stay with the company longer, and act happier.

TIP

When you're getting ready to fill a position, make sure you let people know about it. Your employees and co-workers may well mount their own Twitter and Facebook campaigns for you, getting the word out to a wide audience.

>> **Temporary agencies:** Hiring *temps,* or temporary employees, has become routine for many companies. When you simply have to fill a critical position for a short period of time, temporary agencies are the way to go — no muss, no fuss. And the best part is that when you hire temps, you get the opportunity to try out employees before you buy them. If you don't like the temps you get, no problem. Call the agency, and it sends replacements before you know it. But if you like your temps, most agencies allow you to hire them at a nominal fee or after a minimum time commitment. Either way, you win.

One more point: If you're using temps, you can complete your organization's necessary work while you continue looking for the right full-time employee. Doing so buys you more time to find the best person for the job without feeling pressure to hire someone who doesn't really meet all your needs.

>> **Professional associations:** Most professions have their accompanying associations that look out for their interests. Whether you're a doctor (and belong to the American Medical Association) or a truck driver (and belong to the Teamsters), you can likely find an affiliated association for whatever you do for a living. Association newsletters, magazines, websites, blogs, and social networking sites are great places to advertise your openings when you're looking for specific expertise, because your audience is already prescreened for you.

>> **Employment agencies:** If you're filling a particularly specialized position, are recruiting in a small market, or simply prefer to have someone else take care of recruiting and screening your applicants, employment agencies are a good, albeit pricey alternative (with a cost of up to a third of the employee's first-year salary, or more). Although employment agencies can usually locate qualified candidates in lower-level or administrative positions, you may need help from an executive search firm or *headhunter* (someone who specializes in recruiting key employees away from one firm to place in a client's firm) for your higher-level positions.

>> **Want ads:** Want ads can be relatively expensive, but they're an easy way to get your message out to a large cross-section of potential candidates. You can choose to advertise in your local paper, in nationally distributed publications such as *The Wall Street Journal,* or on popular job-search websites (see the next section for suggestions). On the downside, you may find yourself sorting through hundreds or even (gulp) thousands of unqualified candidates to find a few great ones.

Leveraging the power of the Internet

The proliferation of job search tools, corporate web pages, and online employment agencies has brought about an entirely new dimension in recruiting. Your own website lets you present almost unlimited amounts and kinds of information about your business and your job openings — in text, audio, graphic, and video formats. Your site works for you 24 hours a day, 7 days a week.

Consider a few of the best ways to leverage the power of the Internet in your own hiring efforts:

TIP

» **Websites and blogs:** If you don't already have a great recruiting page on your company website, you should. In addition to this baseline item, also consider setting up company blogs where employees can describe what they do and how they do it. This gives prospective job candidates insight into your organization, helping them decide for themselves whether yours is the kind of organization they want to actively pursue. Be sure to include a function where people can supply their email address or sign up for an RSS feed to be updated as new positions open. Prices to set up a website or blog vary from free to a few thousand dollars a year, depending on how many bells and whistles you require.

» **Email campaigns:** If you set up the email function on your website just mentioned, you'll soon collect a large number of addresses from potential job candidates. Don't just sit there — use them! Be sure to email an announcement to everyone on your list every time you have a job opening. Even if the people who receive your email message aren't interested, they may know someone who is and may forward your announcement.

» **Social networking sites:** Two, in particular, deserve your attention if you hope to broaden your search for good candidates: Facebook (`www.facebook.com`) and LinkedIn (`www.linkedin.com`). Many millions of people have established accounts at both of these sites; however, LinkedIn was specifically designed to help job seekers network with one another to find new job opportunities. This makes it a particularly effective way for you to get the word out about your open positions. Although Facebook isn't specifically set up for job networking, you can set up a fan page there and use it as an effective recruiting platform. There's no charge to set up and use a Facebook or LinkedIn account.

» **Twitter:** Many organizations today are using Twitter (`www.twitter.com`) as a real-time platform for getting out information to anyone interested in getting it. This includes prospective job applicants. The variety of information you can send out to the world is limited only by your imagination — and by the character limit for individual tweets. There's no charge to set up and use your Twitter account.

» **Traditional job-hunting sites:** A number of job-hunting sites have become popular with people looking for new positions. This makes them good platforms from which to pitch your own job openings. Popular ones include Career Builder (`www.careerbuilder.com`), Indeed (`www.indeed.com`), Simply Hired (`www.simplyhired.com`), and Monster (`www.monster.com`). You'll likely have to pay to post your jobs on these sites — prices vary. For a free option, don't forget your local Craigslist (`www.craigslist.com`).

Becoming a Great Interviewer

After you narrow the field to the top three or five applicants, the next step is to start interviewing. What kind of interviewer are you? Do you spend several hours preparing for interviews — reviewing résumés, looking over job descriptions, writing and rewriting questions until each one is as finely honed as a razor blade? Or are you the kind of interviewer who, busy as you already are, starts preparing for the interview when you get the call from your receptionist that your candidate has arrived?

REMEMBER

The secret to becoming a great interviewer is to be thoroughly prepared for your interviews. Remember how much time you spent preparing to be interviewed for a job you really wanted? You didn't just walk in the door, sit down, and get offered the job, did you? You probably spent hours researching the company, its products and services, its financials, its market, and other business information. You probably brushed up on your interviewing skills and may have even done some role-playing with a friend or in front of a mirror. Don't you think you should spend at least as much time getting ready for the interview as the people you're going to interview?

Asking the right questions

More than anything else, the heart of the interview process is the questions you ask and the answers you get in response. You get the best answers when you ask the best questions. Lousy questions often result in lousy answers that don't really tell you whether the candidate is right for the job.

A great interviewer asks great questions. According to Richard Nelson Bolles, author of the perennially popular job-hunting guide *What Color Is Your Parachute?*, you can categorize all interview questions under one of the following headings:

>> **Why are you here?** Why is the person sitting across from you going to the trouble of interviewing with you today? You have just one way to find out — ask. You may assume that the answer is because he or she wants a job with your firm, but what you find may surprise you.

Consider the story of the interviewee who forgot that he was interviewing for a job with Hewlett-Packard. During the entire interview, the applicant referred to Hewlett-Packard by the name of one of its competitors. He didn't get the job.

>> **What can you do for us?** Always an important consideration! Of course, your candidates are all going to dazzle you with their incredible personalities, experience, work ethic, and love of teamwork — that almost goes without

saying. However, despite what many job seekers seem to believe, the question is not, "What can your firm do for me?" — at least, not from your perspective. The question that you want an answer to is, "What can you do for us?"

» **What kind of person are you?** Few of your candidates will be absolute angels or demons, but don't forget that you'll spend a lot of time with the person you hire. You want to hire someone you'll enjoy being with during the many work hours, weeks, and years that stretch before you — and the holiday parties, company picnics, and countless other events you're expected to attend. You also want to confirm a few other issues: Are your candidates honest and ethical? Do they share your views regarding work hours, responsibility, and so forth? Are they responsible and dependable employees? Would they work well in your company culture? Of course, all your candidates will answer in the affirmative to mom-and-apple-pie questions like these. So how do you find the real answers?

TIP

You might try to "project" applicants into a typical, real-life scenario and then see how they'd think it through. For example, ask the prospect what she would do if a client called at 5 p.m. with an emergency order that needed to be delivered by 9 a.m. the next morning. This way, there's no "right" answer and candidates are forced to expose their thinking process: what questions they'd ask, what strategies they'd consider, which people they'd involve, and so forth. Ask open-ended questions and let your candidates do most of the talking.

» **Can we afford you?** It does you no good to find the perfect candidate but, at the end of the interview, discover that you're so far apart in pay range that you're nearly in a different state. Keep in mind that the actual wage you pay to workers is only part of an overall compensation package. You may not be able to pull together more money for wages for particularly good candidates, but you may be able to offer them better benefits, a nicer office, the option of working from home, extra time off, a more impressive title, or a key to the executive sauna.

Following interviewing do's

So what can you do to prepare for your interviews? The following handy-dandy checklist gives you ideas on where to start:

» **Review the résumés of each interviewee the morning before interviews start.** Not only is it extremely poor form to wait to read your interviewees' résumés during the interview, but you miss out on the opportunity to tailor your questions to those little surprises you invariably discover in the résumés.

>> **Become intimately familiar with the job description.** Are you familiar with all the duties and requirements of the job? Surprising new hires with duties that you didn't tell them about — especially when they're major duties — isn't a pathway to new-hire success.

>> **Draft your questions before the interview.** Make a checklist of the key experience, skills, and qualities that you seek in your candidates, and use it to guide your questions. Of course, one of your questions may trigger other questions that you didn't anticipate. Go ahead with such questions, as long as they give you additional insights into your candidate and help illuminate the information you're seeking with your checklist.

>> **Select a comfortable environment for both of you.** Your interviewee will likely be uncomfortable regardless of what you do. You don't need to be uncomfortable, too. Make sure that the interview environment is well ventilated, private, and protected from interruptions. You definitely don't want your phone ringing off the hook or employees barging in during your interviews. You get the best performance from your interviewees when they aren't thrown off track by distractions.

REMEMBER

As you have no doubt gathered by now, interview questions are one of your best tools for determining whether a candidate is right for your company. Although some amount of small talk is appropriate to help relax your candidates, the heart of your interviews should focus on answering the questions just listed. Above all, don't give up. Keep asking questions until you're satisfied that you have all the information you need to make your decision.

REMEMBER

Take lots of notes as you interview your candidates. Don't rely on your memory when it comes to interviewing candidates for your job. If you interview more than a couple of people, you can easily forget who said exactly what, as well as what your impressions were of their performances. Not only are your written notes a great way to remember who's who, but they're an important tool to have when you're evaluating your candidates.

And try to avoid the temptation to draw pictures of little smiley faces or that new car you've been lusting after. Write the key points of your candidates' responses and their reactions to your questions. For example, if you ask why your candidate left her previous job, and she starts getting really nervous, make a note about this reaction. Finally, note your own impressions of the candidates:

>> *Top-notch performer — the star of her class.*

>> *Fantastic experience with developing applications in a client/server environment. The best candidate yet.*

>> *Geez, was this one interviewing for the right job?*

Avoiding interviewing don'ts

If you've gone through the hiring process a few times already, you know that you can run into tricky situations during an interview and that certain questions can land you in major hot water if you make the mistake of asking them.

Some interviewing don'ts are merely good business practice. For example, accepting an applicant's invitation for a date is probably not a good idea. Believe it or not, it happens. After a particularly drawn-out interview at a well-known high-tech manufacturer, a male candidate asked out a female interviewer. The interviewer considered her options and declined the date; she also declined to make Prince Charming a job offer.

Avoid playing power trips during the course of the interview. Forget the old games of asking trick questions, turning up the heat, or cutting the legs off their chairs (yes, some people still do this game playing) to gain an artificial advantage over your candidates. Get real — it's the 21st century.

WARNING

Some blunders are the major legal type — the kind that can land you and your company in court. Interviewing is one area of particular concern in the hiring process as it pertains to possible discrimination. For example, although you can ask applicants whether they are able to fulfill job functions, in the United States, you can't ask them whether they have disabilities. Because of the critical nature of the interview process, you must know the questions that you absolutely should never ask a job candidate. Here is a brief summary of the kinds of topics that may get you and your business into trouble, depending on the exact circumstances:

>> Age

>> Arrest and conviction record

>> Debts

>> Disability

>> Gender or gender identity

>> Height and weight

>> Marital status

>> National origin

>> Race or skin color

>> Religion (or lack thereof)

>> Sexual orientation

REMEMBER

Legal or illegal, the point is that none of the preceding topics is necessary to determine applicants' ability to perform their jobs. Therefore, ask questions that directly relate to the candidates' ability to perform the tasks required. To do otherwise can put you at definite legal risk. In other words, what *does* count is job-related criteria — that is, information that's directly pertinent to the candidate's ability to do the job (you clearly need to decide this *prior* to interviewing!).

Evaluating Your Candidates

Now comes the really fun part of the hiring process — evaluating your candidates. If you've done your homework, then you already have an amazing selection of candidates to choose from, you've narrowed your search to the ones showing the best potential to excel in your position, and you've interviewed them to see whether they can live up to the promises they made in their résumés. Before you make your final decision, you need a bit more information.

Checking references

Wow! What a résumé! What an interview! What a candidate! Would you be surprised to find out that this shining employee-to-be didn't really go to Yale? Or that he really wasn't the account manager on that nationwide marketing campaign? Or that his last supervisor wasn't particularly impressed with his analytical skills?

A résumé and interview are great tools, but a reference check is probably the only chance you have to find out before you make a hiring decision whether your candidates are actually who they say they are. Depending on your organization, you may be expected to do reference checks. Or maybe your human resources department takes care of that task.

WARNING

Depending on your industry and level of security consciousness, you may want to run a background check on your prospects before hiring them. The legal and privacy implications of doing so vary from state to state. You can check out www.privacyrights.org/small-business-owner-background-check-guide for an overview of the process of doing a background check. But you should definitely consult a lawyer licensed to practice in your state before doing your first background check.

REMEMBER

The twin goals of checking references are to verify the information that your candidates have provided and to gain some candid insight into who your candidates really are and how they behave in the workplace. When you contact a candidate's references, limit your questions to topics related to the work to be done. As in the interview process, asking questions that can be considered discriminatory to your candidates isn't appropriate.

Here are some of the best ways to do your reference checking:

>> **Check academic references.** A surprising number of people exaggerate or tell outright lies when reporting their educational experience. Start your reference check here.

>> **Call current and former supervisors.** Getting information from employers is getting more difficult. Many businesspeople are rightfully concerned that they may be sued for libel or defamation of character if they say anything negative about current or former subordinates. Still, it doesn't hurt to try. You get a much better picture of your candidates if you speak directly to their current and former supervisors instead of to their company's human resources department — especially if the supervisors you speak to have left their firms. The most you're likely to get from the HR folks is a confirmation that the candidate worked at the company during a specific period of time.

>> **Check your network of associates.** If you belong to a professional association, union, or similar group of like-minded careerists, you have the opportunity to tap into the rest of the membership to get the word on your candidates. For example, if you're a certified public accountant (CPA) and want to find out about a few candidates for your open accounting position, you can check with the members of your professional accounting association to see whether anyone knows anything about them.

>> **Do some surfing.** On the web, that is. Google your candidate's name, perhaps along with the name of the company where the person last worked or the city where she lives. Or do a search for your candidate on Facebook (www.facebook.com) or LinkedIn (www.linkedin.com). You might be surprised by how much information you can uncover about a job candidate — good and bad — doing just a few simple web searches.

WARNING

But be careful. Many people have the same name. Make sure you have the right person!

Reviewing your notes

You did take interview notes, didn't you? Now's the time to drag them back out and look them over. Review the information package for each candidate — one by one — and compare your findings against your predetermined criteria. Take a look at the candidates' résumés, your notes, and the results of your reference checks. How do they stack up against the standards you set for the position? Do you see any clear winners at this point? Any clear losers? Organize your candidate packages into the following stacks:

>> **Winners:** These candidates are clearly the best choices for the position. You have no hesitation in hiring any one of them.

>> **Potential winners:** These candidates are questionable for some reason. Maybe their experience isn't as strong as that of other candidates, or perhaps you weren't impressed with their presentation skills. Neither clear winners nor clear losers, you hire these candidates only after further investigation or if you can't hire anyone from your pool of winners.

>> **Losers:** These candidates are clearly unacceptable for the position. You simply don't consider hiring any of them.

Conducting a second (or third) round

When you're a busy business owner, you have pressure to get things done as quickly as possible, and you're tempted to take shortcuts to achieve your goals. It seems that everything has to be done yesterday — or maybe the day before. When do you have the opportunity to really spend as much time as you want to complete a task or project? Time is precious when you have ten other projects crying for your attention. Time is even more valuable when you're hiring for a vacant position that's critical to your organization and needs to be filled right now.

REMEMBER

Hiring is one area of business where you must avoid taking shortcuts. Remember, hire slowly and fire quickly (but within the rules). Finding the best candidates for your vacancies requires an investment of time and resources. Your company's future depends on it. Great candidates don't stay on the market long, though, so don't allow the process to drag on too long. Make sure the candidates know your required time frame, and stick to it.

Depending on your organization's policies or culture, or if you're undecided on the best candidate, you may decide to bring candidates in for several rounds of interviews. But keep in mind that the timeline for an offer differs depending on the job you're interviewing for. Lower-level job hunters cannot afford to be unemployed (if they are) for long, and they often get and accept job offers quickly. A higher-level position — say, a general manager — gives you more time.

The ultimate decision on how many rounds and levels of interviews to conduct depends on the nature of the job itself, the size of your company, and your policies and procedures. If the job is simple or at a relatively low level in the company, a single phone interview may be sufficient to determine the best candidate.

However, if the job is complex or at a relatively high level in the organization, you may need several rounds of testing and personal interviews to determine the best candidate.

Checking employment eligibility

With today's increased emphasis on national security and immigration status, employers are required to take some steps to verify the eligibility of employees to work in the U.S. You should obtain USCIS Form I-9 (Employment Eligibility Verification) from prospective employees. This form is used to collect information on the employee and document the verification steps. Be aware: An employer can be fined for failing to follow the process. In addition, there is a program called E-Verify, which allows employers to verify an applicant's work status online. You can obtain Form I-9 and related information from the U.S. Citizenship and Immigration Services (USCIS) website at www.uscis.gov. The E-Verify program is free, and you can find out more about it at www.e-verify.gov.

Immigrants can be a good source of workers, and you may be able to sponsor employees through various programs. For example, there are H-1B visas for specialty occupations, such technical or scientific workers. The USCIS website mentioned in the preceding paragraph has additional information about these and other employer-sponsored worker visas.

TIP

You should be aware of possible federal tax credits available for hiring certain targeted workers. For example, the American Taxpayer Relief Act of 2012 extended the Work Opportunity Tax Credit, which provided tax credits for hiring qualified veterans. You can find current information at www.irs.gov/businesses/small-businesses-self-employed/work-opportunity-tax-credit.

Hiring the Best (and Leaving the Rest)

Rank your candidates within the groups of winners and potential winners that you established during the evaluation phase of the hiring process (see the earlier section "Reviewing your notes"). You don't need to bother ranking the losers because you wouldn't hire them anyway — no matter what. The best candidate in your group of winners is first, the next best is second, and so on. If you've done your job thoroughly and well, the best candidates for the job are readily apparent at this point.

The next step is to get on the phone and offer your first choice the job. Don't waste any time — you never know whether your candidate has interviewed with other employers. It would be a shame to invest all this time in the hiring process only to find out that your top choice accepted a job this morning with one of your competitors. If you can't come to terms with your first choice in a reasonable amount of time, go on to your second choice. Keep going through your pool of winners until you either make a hire or exhaust the list of candidates.

The following sections give you a few tips to keep in mind as you rank your candidates and make your final decision.

Being objective

In some cases, you may prefer certain candidates because of their personalities or personal charisma, regardless of their abilities or work experience. Sometimes the desire to like these candidates can obscure their shortcomings, while a better qualified, albeit less socially adept, candidate may fade in your estimation.

Be objective. Consider the job to be done, as well as the skills and qualifications that being successful requires. Do your candidates have these skills and qualifications? What would it take for your candidates to be considered fully qualified for the position?

Don't allow yourself to be unduly influenced by your candidates' looks, bubbly personalities, high-priced hairstyles, or fashion-forward clothing ensembles. None of these characteristics can tell you how well your candidates will actually perform the job. The facts are present for you to see in your candidates' résumés, interview notes, and reference checks. If you stick to the facts, you can still go wrong, but the chances are diminished.

REMEMBER

One more thing: Diversity in hiring is positive for any organization. Check your bias at the door.

Trusting your gut

Sometimes you're faced with a decision between two equally qualified candidates, or with a decision about a candidate who is marginal but shows promise. In such cases, you have weighed all the objective data and given the analytical side of your being free rein, but you still have no clear winner. What do you do in this kind of situation?

Listen to yourself. Although two candidates may seem equal in skills and abilities, do you have a feeling that one is better suited to the job? If so, go with it. As much as you may want your hiring decision to be as objective as possible, whenever you introduce the human element into the decision-making process, a certain amount of subjectivity is naturally present.

In reality, rarely are two candidates equally qualified, although often one or more people seem to have more to bring to the job than anticipated (for example, industry focus, fresh ideas, previous contacts, and so forth). This is again where your pre-work can be so valuable in keeping you focused. Can they both do the job? If so, the bonus traits can tip the scale.

Other options:

>> Give them each a nonpaid assignment and see how they do.

>> Try them each on a paid project.

Keep in touch with other top candidates as additional needs arise or in case your first choice doesn't work out.

Revisiting the candidate pool

What do you do if, heaven forbid, you can't hire anyone from your group of winners? This unfortunate occurrence is a tough call, but no one said hiring is an easy task. Take a look at your stack of potential winners. What would it take to make your top potential winners into winners? If the answer is as simple as a training course or two, then give these candidates serious consideration — with the understanding that you can schedule the necessary training soon after hiring. Perhaps a candidate just needs a little more experience before moving into the ranks of the winners. You can make a judgment call on whether you feel that someone's current experience is sufficient until that person gains the experience you're looking for. If not, you may want to keep looking for the right candidate. After all, this person may be working with you for a long time — waiting for the best candidate only makes sense.

If you're forced to go to your group of almost-winners and no candidate really seems up to the task, don't hire someone simply to fill the position. If you do, you're probably making a big mistake. Hiring employees is far easier than unhiring them. The damage that an inappropriate hire can wreak — on co-workers, your customers, and your organization (not to mention the person you hired) — can take years and a considerable amount of money to undo. Not only that, but it can be a big pain in your neck! Other options are to redefine the job, reevaluate other current employees, or hire on a temporary basis to see whether a risky hire works out.

Chapter **2**

Setting Goals

I f you created a list of the most important duties of management, "setting goals" would likely be near the top of the list. In most small and start-up companies, the owner sets the overall purpose — the vision — of the organization. The owner then has the job of developing goals and plans for achieving that vision. Owners and employees work together to set goals and develop schedules for attaining them.

As a business owner, you're probably immersed in goals — not only for yourself, but also for your employees and your organization. This flood of goals can cause stress and frustration as you try to balance the relative importance of each one:

> *Should I tackle my goal of improving turnaround time first, or should I get to work on finishing the budget? Or maybe the goal of improving customer service is more important. Well, I think I'll just try to achieve my own personal goal of setting aside some time to eat lunch today.*

Sometimes having too many goals is as bad as not having any goals. This chapter helps you understand why setting strong, focused goals is essential to your success and that of your employees. It also guides you in communicating visions and goals and keeping both you and your employees on track to meet established goals.

REMEMBER

Goals provide direction and purpose. Don't forget, if you can see it, you can achieve it. Goals help you see where you're going and how you can get there. And the *way* you set goals can impact how motivating they are to others.

Knowing Where You're Going

Believe it or not, Lewis Carroll's classic book *Alice's Adventures in Wonderland* offers lessons that can enhance your business relationships. Consider the following passage, in which Alice asks the Cheshire Cat for advice on which direction to go.

> "Would you tell me, please, which way I ought to go from here?"
>
> "That depends a good deal on where you want to go," said the Cat.
>
> "I don't much care where —," said Alice.
>
> "Then it doesn't matter which way you go," said the Cat.
>
> " — so long as I get *somewhere*," Alice added as an explanation.
>
> "Oh, you're sure to do that," said the Cat, "if you only walk long enough."

REMEMBER

It takes no effort at all to get *somewhere*. Just do nothing, and you're there. (In fact, everywhere you go, there you are.) However, if you want to get somewhere meaningful and succeed as a business owner, you first have to know where you want to go. And after you decide where you want to go, you need to make plans for how to get there. This practice is as true in business as in your everyday life.

For example, suppose that you have a vision of starting up a second dry cleaning store in a nearby suburb so that you can grow your business. How do you go about achieving this vision? You have three choices:

>> An unplanned, non-goal-oriented approach

>> A planned, goal-oriented approach

>> A hope and a prayer

Which choice do you think is most likely to get you to your goal? Go ahead, take a wild guess. If you guessed the unplanned, non-goal-oriented approach to reaching your vision, shame on you. Please report to study hall. Your assignment is to write 500 times: *A goal is a dream with a deadline.*

If you guessed the planned, goal-oriented approach, you've earned a big gold star.

Why should you set goals?

Following are the main reasons to set goals whenever you want to accomplish something significant:

» **Goals provide direction.** To get something done, you have to set a definite vision — a target to aim for and to guide the efforts of you and your organization. You can then translate this vision into goals that take you where you want to go. Without goals, you're doomed to waste countless hours going nowhere. With goals, you can focus your efforts and your team's efforts on only the activities that move you toward where you're going — in this case, opening another dry cleaning location.

» **Goals tell you how far you've traveled.** Goals provide milestones to measure how effectively you're working toward accomplishing your vision. If you determine that you must accomplish several specific milestones to reach your final destination and you complete a few of them, you know exactly how many remain. You know right where you stand and how far you have yet to go.

» **Goals help make your overall vision attainable.** You can't reach your vision in one big step — you need many small steps to get there. If, again, your vision is to open a second dry cleaning location, you can't expect to proclaim your vision on Friday and walk into a fully staffed and functioning store on Monday. You must accomplish many goals — from shopping for business space, to hiring staff, to getting the word out via advertising — before you can attain your vision. Goals enable you to achieve your overall vision by dividing your efforts into smaller pieces that, when accomplished individually, add up to big results.

» **Goals clarify everyone's role.** When you discuss your vision with your employees, they may have some idea of where you want to go but no idea of how to go about getting there. As your well-intentioned employees head off to help you achieve your vision, some employees may duplicate the efforts of others, some employees may focus on the wrong strategies and ignore more important tasks, and some employees may simply do something else altogether (and hope that you don't notice the difference). Setting goals with your team clarifies what the tasks are, who handles which tasks, and what is expected from each employee and, ultimately, from the entire team.

» **Goals give people something to strive for.** People are typically more motivated when challenged to attain a goal that's beyond their normal level of performance — this is known as a *stretch goal*. Not only do goals give people a sense of purpose, but they also relieve the boredom that can come from performing a routine job day after day. Be sure to discuss the goal with them and seek feedback where appropriate to gain their commitment and buy-in.

What makes goals effective?

For goals to be effective, they have to link directly to the owner's final vision. To stay ahead of the competition — or simply to maintain their current position in business — business owners create compelling visions, and then they and their employees work together to set and achieve the goals to reach those visions.

REMEMBER

When it comes to goals, the best ones

>> Are few in number but very specific and clear in purpose.

>> Are stretch goals. They're attainable, but they aren't too easy or too hard.

>> Involve people. When you involve others in a collaborative, team-based process, you get buy-in so it becomes their goal, not just yours.

Identifying SMART Goals

You can find all kinds of goals in all types of organizations. Some goals are short term and specific ("Starting next month, we will increase production by two units per employee per hour"); others are long term and vague ("Within the next five years, we will become a learning organization"). Employees easily understand some goals ("Line employees will have no more than 20 rejects per month"), but other goals can be difficult to measure and subject to much interpretation ("All employees are expected to show more respect to each other in the next fiscal year"). Still other goals can be accomplished relatively easily ("Reception staff will always answer the phone by the third ring"), whereas others are virtually impossible to attain ("All employees will master the five languages that our customers speak before the end of the fiscal year").

How do you know what kind of goals to set? The whole point of setting goals, after all, is to achieve them. It does you no good to go to the trouble of calling meetings, hacking through the needs of your organization, and burning up precious time only to end up with goals that aren't acted on or completed. Unfortunately, this scenario describes what far too many business owners do with their time.

Breaking down the meaning of SMART

The best goals are *smart* goals — actually, SMART goals is the acronym to help you remember them. SMART refers to a handy checklist for the five characteristics of well-designed goals:

>> **Specific:** Goals must be clear and unambiguous; broad and fuzzy thinking has no place in goal setting. When goals are specific, they tell employees exactly what's expected, when, and how much. Because the goals are specific, you can easily measure your employees' progress toward their completion.

>> **Measurable:** What good is a goal that you can't measure? If your goals aren't measurable, you never know whether your employees are making progress toward their successful completion. Not only that, but your employees may have a tough time staying motivated to complete their goals when they have no milestones to indicate their progress.

>> **Attainable:** Goals must be realistic and attainable by average employees. The best goals require employees to stretch a bit to achieve them, but they aren't extreme. That is, the goals are neither out of reach nor set too low. Goals that are set too high or too low become meaningless, and employees naturally come to ignore them.

>> **Relevant:** Goals must be an important tool in the grand scheme of reaching your company's vision and mission. You may have heard that 80 percent of workers' productivity comes from only 20 percent of their activities. You can guess where the other 80 percent of work activity ends up. This relationship comes from Italian economist Vilfredo Pareto's 80/20 rule. This rule, which states that roughly 80 percent of effects come from 20 percent of causes, has been applied to many other fields. Relevant goals address the 20 percent of workers' activities that has such a great impact on performance and brings your organization closer to its vision, thereby making it, and you, a success.

>> **Time-bound:** Goals must have starting points, ending points, and fixed durations. Commitment to deadlines helps employees focus their efforts on completing the goal on or before the due date. Goals without deadlines or schedules for completion tend to be overtaken by the day-to-day crises that invariably arise in the workplace.

REMEMBER

SMART goals make for smart businesses. Many owners and managers neglect to work with their employees to set goals together. And for the ones that do, goals are often unclear, ambiguous, unrealistic, immeasurable, uninspiring, and unrelated to the organization's vision. By developing SMART goals with your employees, you can avoid these traps while ensuring the progress of your business and your team.

Developing SMART goals

Although the SMART system of goal setting provides guidelines to help you frame effective goals, you have additional considerations to keep in mind. The following considerations help you ensure that anyone in your organization can easily understand and act on the goals you and your employees agree on:

>> **Ensure that goals are related to your employees' role in the business.** Pursuing an organization's goals is far easier for employees when those goals are a regular part of their jobs and they can see how their contributions support the company. For example, suppose that you set a goal for employees who solder circuit boards to raise production by 2 percent per quarter. These employees spend almost every working moment pursuing this goal, because the goal is an integral part of their job. However, if you give the same employees a goal of "improving the diversity of the organization," what exactly does that have to do with your line employees' role? Nothing. The goal may sound lofty and may be important to your business, but because your line employees don't make the hiring decisions, you're wasting both your time and theirs with that particular goal.

>> **Whenever possible, use values to guide behavior.** What's the most important value in your organization? Honesty? Fairness? Respect? Whatever it is, ensure that you and any other leaders in the business model this behavior and reward employees who live it.

>> **Simple goals are better goals.** The easier your goals are to understand, the more likely the employees are to work to achieve them. Goals should be no longer than one sentence; make them concise, compelling, and easy to read and understand.

TIP

Goals that take more than a sentence to describe are actually multiple goals. When you find multiple-goal statements, break them into several individual, one-sentence goals. Goals that take a page or more to describe aren't really goals; they're books. File them away and try again.

Setting Goals: Less Is More

Big businesses love to plan. When the last planning meetings are over, the managers often congratulate each other over their collective accomplishment and go back to their regular office routines. Before long, the goals they hammered out together are forgotten, and the pages they were recorded on are neatly folded and stored away in someone's file cabinet. Meanwhile, business goes on as usual, and the long-range planning effort goes into long-term hibernation. You probably don't have this problem, but the lesson is there for you to learn all the same, because even in a small business, it can be tempting to create goals and then let them slide as you resume your normal day-to-day work.

REMEMBER

Don't let all your hard work be in vain. When you go through the exercise of setting goals, keep them to a manageable number that can realistically be followed up on. And when you finish one goal, move on to the next.

The following guidelines can help you select the right goals — and the right number of goals — for your business:

>> **Pick two to three goals to focus on.** You can't do everything at once — at least not well — and you can't expect your employees to, either. Attempt to complete only a few goals at any one time. Setting too many goals dilutes the efforts of you and your staff and can result in a complete breakdown in the process.

>> **Pick the goals with the greatest relevance.** Certain goals bring you a lot closer to attaining your vision than do other goals. Because you have only so many hours in your workday, it clearly makes sense to concentrate your efforts on a few goals that have the biggest payoff rather than on a boatload of goals with relatively less impact to the business.

>> **Focus on the goals that tie most closely to your organization's mission.** You may be tempted to take on goals that are challenging, interesting, and fun to accomplish but that are far removed from your organization's mission. Don't do it.

>> **Regularly revisit the goals and update them as necessary.** Business is anything but static, and regularly assessing your goals is important in making sure that they're still relevant to the vision you want to achieve. Put in quarterly or midyear review schedules. If the goals remain important, great — carry on. If not, meet with your employees to revise the goals and the schedules for attaining them.

REMEMBER

Avoid creating too many goals in your zeal to get as many things done as quickly as you can. Too many goals can overwhelm you — and they can overwhelm your employees, too. You're far better off setting a few significant goals and then concentrating your efforts on attaining them. Don't forget that your management skill isn't measured by one huge success after another. Instead, it involves successfully meeting daily challenges and opportunities — gradually but inevitably improving the business in the process.

Communicating Your Vision and Goals to Your Team

Having goals is great, but how do you get the word out to your employees? As you know, goals should align with your vision for your business. Establishing goals helps you ensure that employees focus on achieving the vision in the desired time frame and with the desired results. You have many possible ways to communicate goals to your employees, but some ways are better than others. In every case, you must communicate goals clearly, the receiver must understand the goals, and the relevant parties must follow through on achieving the goals.

Communicating your organization's vision is as important as communicating specific goals. You can communicate the vision in every way possible, as often as possible, throughout your organization and to significant others such as clients, customers, suppliers, and so forth.

REMEMBER

When you communicate vision and goals, do it with energy and a sense of urgency and importance. You're talking about the future of your business and your employees, not the score of last night's game. If your team doesn't think that you care about the vision, why should they? Simply put, they won't.

Announcing your vision

Companies usually announce their visions to employees — and the public — in ways that are designed to maximize the impact. Companies commonly communicate their vision in these ways:

- » By conducting employee rallies where the vision is unveiled in an inspirational presentation

- » By branding their vision on anything possible — business cards, letterhead stationery, posters hung in the break room, employee name tags, and more

- » By proudly emblazoning their vision statements within company websites; on Facebook fan pages; and via electronic media campaigns, Twitter tweets, and other Internet-enabled methods of communication

- » By mentioning the corporate vision in newspaper, radio, television, and other media advertising

- » By encouraging managers to "talk up" the vision in staff meetings or other verbal interactions with employees and during recruiting

TIP

To avoid a cynical "fad" reaction from employees who may be suspicious of management's motives when unveiling a new initiative, making consistent, casual, and genuine reference to it is much more effective than hosting a huge, impersonal event. Again, in this case, less is often better.

Communicating goals

Unlike visions, goals are much more personalized to the department or individual employees, and you must use more formal and direct methods to communicate them. The following guidelines can help:

>> **Write down your goals.** Putting them down on paper or in a Word document makes them alive and real. They are no longer abstract, in-your-head ideas.

>> **Conduct one-on-one, face-to-face meetings with your employees to introduce, discuss, and assign goals.** If you can't conduct a face-to-face meeting, conduct your meeting over the phone. The point is to make sure that your employees hear the goals, understand them and your expectations, and have the opportunity to ask for clarifications.

>> **Call your team together to introduce team-related goals.** You can assign goals to teams instead of solely to individuals. Get the team together and explain the role of the team and each individual in the successful completion of the goal. Make sure that all team members understand exactly what they are to do and whether a leader or co-leaders are ultimately responsible for the goals' completion. Get employee buy-in and try to make the goals resonate with each person. (Book 4, Chapter 5 discusses teams in more detail.)

>> **Gain the commitment of your employees, whether individually or on teams, to work toward the successful accomplishment of their goals.** Ask your employees to prepare and present plans and milestone schedules explaining how they can accomplish the assigned goals in the agreed-upon timeline. After your employees begin working on their goals, regularly monitor their progress to ensure that they're on track, and collaborate with them to resolve any problems.

Juggling Priorities: Keeping Your Eye on the Ball

After you've decided what goals are important to you and your organization, you come to the difficult part. How do you, the owner, maintain the focus of your employees — and yourself, for that matter — on achieving the goals you've set?

The process of goal setting can generate excitement and engage employees in the inner workings of the business, whether the goals are set individually or by function. This excitement can quickly evaporate, though, when employees return to their desks. You, the owner, must take steps to ensure that the organization's focus remains centered on the agreed-upon goals, not on other matters (which are less important but momentarily more pressing). Of course, this task is much easier said than done.

Falling into the activity trap

Staying focused on goals can be extremely difficult — particularly when you're a busy person and the goals compound your regular responsibilities. How often do you sit down at your desk in the morning to prioritize your day, only to have your priorities completely changed five minutes later when you get a call from an angry customer? How many times has an employee unexpectedly come to you with a problem? Have you ever gotten caught in a so-called quick meeting that lasts for hours?

In unlimited ways, you or your employees can get derailed and lose the focus you need to get your organization's goals accomplished. One of the biggest problems employees face is confusing activity with tangible results. Do you know anyone who works incredibly long hours — late into the night and on weekends — but never seems to get anything done? These employees always seem busy, but they're working on the wrong things. This is called the *activity trap,* and it's easy for you and your employees to fall into.

Remember the 80/20 rule? The flip side is when you consider that only 20 percent of workers' productivity comes from 80 percent of their activity. This statistic illustrates the activity trap at work. What do you do in an average day? More important, what do you do with the 80 percent of your time that produces so few clear results? You can get out of the activity trap and take control of your schedules and priorities. However, you have to be tough, and you have to single-mindedly pursue your goals.

REMEMBER

Achieving your goals is all up to you. No one can make it any easier for you to concentrate on achieving your goals. You have to take charge and find an approach that works for you. If you aren't controlling your own schedule, you're simply letting everyone else control your schedule for you.

Getting out of the activity trap

TIP

Following are some tips to help you and your employees get out of the activity trap:

>> **Complete your top-priority task first.** With all the distractions that compete for your attention, with the constant temptation to work on the easy stuff first and save the tough stuff for last, and with people dropping into your office just to chat or to unload their problems on you, concentrating on your top-priority task is always a challenge. However, if you don't do your top priority first, you're almost guaranteed to find yourself caught in the activity trap. That is, you'll find the same priorities on your list of tasks to do day after day, week after week, and month after month. If your top-priority task is too large, divide it into smaller chunks and focus on the most important piece first.

>> **Get organized.** Getting organized and managing your time effectively are both incredibly important pursuits for anyone in business. If you're organized, you can spend less time trying to figure out what you should be doing and more time just doing it.

>> **Just say no.** If someone tries to make his or her problems your problems, just say no. If you're a small business owner, you probably like nothing more than taking on new challenges and solving problems. However, the conflict arises when solving somebody else's problems interferes with your own work. You have to fight the temptation to lose control of your day. Always ask yourself, "How does this help me achieve my goals?"

Using Your Power for Good: Making Your Goals Reality

After you create a set of goals with your employees, how do you make sure they get done? How do you turn your priorities into your employees' priorities? The best goals in the world mean nothing if they aren't achieved. You can choose to leave this critical step to chance or you can choose to get involved.

REMEMBER

You have the power to make your goals happen.

Power has gotten a bad rap lately. In reaction to the highly publicized leadership styles that signified greed and unethical behavior in American corporations, employees have increasingly demanded — and organizations are recognizing the need for — management that is principle centered and has a more compassionate, human face.

Nothing is inherently wrong with power — everyone has many sources of power within. Not only do you have power, but you also exercise power to control or influence people and events around you on a daily basis (hopefully in a positive way). Generally, well-placed power is a positive thing. However, power can be a negative thing when abused or when someone acts in only self-interest. Manipulation, exploitation, and coercion have no place in the modern workplace.

You can use your positive power and influence to your advantage — and to the advantage of the people you lead — by tapping into it to help achieve your organization's goals. People and systems often fall into ruts or nonproductive patterns of behavior that are hard to break. Power properly applied can redirect people and systems and move them in the right direction — the direction that leads to the accomplishment of goals.

Everyone has five primary sources of power, as well as specific strengths and weaknesses related to these sources. Recognize your strengths and weaknesses and use them to your advantage. As you review the five sources of power that follow, consider your own personal strengths and weaknesses:

>> **Personal power:** This is the power that comes from within your character. Your passion for greatness, the strength of your convictions, your ability to communicate and inspire, your personal charisma, and your leadership skills all add up to personal power.

>> **Relationship power:** Everyone has relationships with people at work. These interactions contribute to the relationship power that you possess in your organization. Sources of relationship power include close friendships with top executives, partners, owners, people who owe you favors, and co-workers who provide you with information and insights that you wouldn't normally receive.

>> **Knowledge power:** To see knowledge power in action, just watch what happens the next time your organization's computer network goes down. You'll see who really has the power in your organization — in this case, your computer network administrator. Knowledge power comes from the special expertise and knowledge gained during the course of your career. Knowledge power also comes from obtaining academic degrees (think MBA) or special training.

>> **Task power:** Task power is the power that comes from the job or process you perform at work. As you've probably witnessed, people can facilitate or impede the efforts of their co-workers and others by using their task power. For example, when you submit a claim for payment to your insurance company and months pass with no action ("Gee, we don't seem to have your claim in our computer — are you sure you submitted one? Maybe you should send us another one just to be safe!"), you're on the receiving end of task power.

>> **Position power:** This kind of power derives strictly from your rank or title in the organization and is a function of the authority that you wield to command human and financial resources. Whereas the position power of the receptionist in your organization may be low, the position power of you, the owner, is at the top of the position power chart. But the best leaders seldom rely on position power to get things done today.

If you identify weakness in certain sources of power, you can strengthen them. For example, work on your weakness in relationship power by making a concerted effort to know your employees better. Instead of passing on the invitations to get together after work, join them once in a while — have fun and strengthen your relationship power at the same time. (Just never forget you're the boss. Try to keep such social gatherings as low-key as you can. If things start getting a little loose and rowdy, it's likely time for your departure.)

REMEMBER

Be aware of the sources of your power and use your power in a positive way to help you and your employees accomplish the goals of your organization. For getting things done, a little power can go a long way.

Chapter **3**

Embracing Corporate Social Responsibility

Corporate social responsibility — CSR, for short — is a way of doing business that's rapidly gaining in popularity both in the United States and around the world. *Corporate social responsibility* is conducting your business in a way that has a positive impact on the communities you serve. CSR affects many different aspects of operating a business — from recycling, to ethics, to environmental laws, and much more.

Ethics and office politics are powerful forces in any organization. *Ethics* is the framework of values that employees use to guide their behavior. You've seen the devastation that poor ethical standards can lead to — witness the string of business failures attributed to less than sterling ethics in more than a few large, seemingly upstanding businesses. Today more than ever, business owners are expected to model ethical behavior, to ensure that their employees follow in their footsteps, and to purge employees who refuse to align their own standards with the business owners' standards.

This chapter looks at adopting a corporate social responsibility strategy, building an ethical organization, and determining the nature and boundaries of your political environment.

Understanding Socially Responsible Practices

CSR has been gaining traction within businesses of all kinds in recent years. At one time, CSR was the sole province of socially progressive companies like ice-cream maker Ben & Jerry's and organic yogurt manufacturer Stonyfield Farm, but this is no longer the case. Today even small, local, start-up companies have adopted CSR practices and strategies.

REMEMBER

Depending on the exact approach you take and how you implement it, you may have to spend a significant amount of money to conduct your business in a socially responsible way, but the benefits nearly always outweigh the costs. The consumer is changing. People want to buy products and services from companies that are socially responsible and that are making a positive impact on their communities. What's more, they want to *work for* companies that are socially responsible and that are making a positive impact on their communities. Finally, becoming a socially responsible company can actually reduce costs. For these reasons and others like them, CSR has taken the business world by storm.

Figuring out how you can employ CSR

As mentioned earlier, CSR involves conducting your business in a way that has a positive impact on the communities you serve. But what exactly does that look like in the real world? Consider some of the traits of a socially responsible business:

>> Takes responsibility for the conditions in which its products are manufactured, whether domestically or internationally, and whether by the company itself or by subcontractors.

>> Promotes recycling, environmental responsibility, and natural resources used in more efficient, productive, and profitable ways.

>> Views employees as assets instead of costs and engages them in their jobs by involving them in decision making. In the event of layoffs or job eliminations, it is viewed as a company that treats people fairly.

>> Is committed to diversity in hiring and selection of vendors and employees.

>> Adopts strong internal management and financial controls.

>> Meets or exceeds all applicable social and environmental laws and regulations.

>> Supports its communities through volunteerism, philanthropy, and local hiring.

>> Promotes sustainability — that is, meeting the needs of the present without compromising the ability of future generations to meet their needs.

REMEMBER

As a business owner, you will develop or lead the development of your company's CSR goals. The exact goals you select must be aligned with both your company's core business objectives and its core competencies. Some of the traits in the preceding list may or may not fit with your company's culture, objectives, or competencies. To be effective, your approach to CSR must make sense for your company and its employees, customers, and other stakeholders.

Consider for a moment the six Guiding Principles that coffee purveyor Starbucks embraces. The company's CSR strategy strongly influences these Guiding Principles:

>> Provide a great work environment and treat each other with respect and dignity.

>> Embrace diversity as an essential component in the way we do business.

>> Apply the highest standards of excellence to the purchasing, roasting, and fresh delivery of our coffee.

>> Develop enthusiastically satisfied customers all the time.

>> Contribute positively to our communities and our environment.

>> Recognize that profitability is essential to our future success.

Enjoying the net benefits of socially responsible practices

The best corporate social responsibility is tightly integrated into a company's business operations; this strong connection can have a positive impact on the bottom line. Many CSR activities can reduce the cost of doing business while drawing new customers into the company's orbit, increasing the top line. The younger generation of employees now entering the workplace wants to make a difference in the world, too. Companies that practice CSR are more attractive to these talented men and women, who will remain loyal to their employers as long as they continue to have an opportunity to make a difference.

Starbucks presents a strong business case for adopting a corporate social responsibility strategy in its Corporate Social Responsibility Annual Report:

>> **Attracting and retaining partners (employees):** Starbucks believes that its commitment to CSR contributes to overall retention and higher-than-usual levels of partner satisfaction and engagement. The company's comprehensive benefits package also motivates partners to stay at Starbucks.

>> **Customer loyalty:** Studies have revealed that customers prefer to do business with a company they believe to be socially responsible, when their other key buying criteria are met. One customer survey found that 38 percent associate Starbucks with good corporate citizenship. The vast majority (86 percent) of customers surveyed indicated being extremely or very likely to recommend Starbucks to a friend or family. Customers' loyalty has been instrumental to the company's ability to grow.

>> **Reducing operating costs:** Many environmental measures, such as energy-efficient equipment or lighting, involve initial investments but deliver long-term environmental and cost-saving benefits.

>> **Creating a sustainable supply chain:** Starbucks has made significant investments in supply chains, with the long term in mind. The focus has been to ensure that suppliers of today will have the capacity to supply Starbucks tomorrow. Their sustainability is critically linked to the company's growth and success. This is especially true of those who supply core products or ingredients, such as coffee, tea, and cocoa.

>> **License to operate:** Having a strong reputation as a socially responsible company makes it more likely that Starbucks will be welcomed into a local community. In one customer survey, nearly half of the respondents indicated extremely or very positive attitudes about having a Starbucks in their neighborhood, while only 7 percent expressed negative attitudes.

REMEMBER

Long story short, adopting socially responsible business practices is a net benefit to the companies that adopt them. Why not try them in your organization and see what happens?

Developing a CSR Strategy for Implementation

Adopting CSR in an effective manner requires developing a strategy for its implementation. The spectrum of possible CSR initiatives available to a company is mind-boggling. You can start with a barebones approach — say, replacing disposable (and environmentally unfriendly) Styrofoam coffee cups with washable and infi-nitely reusable porcelain coffee mugs — or you can go all the way to a multiphase international CSR strategy that touches every part of your organization and has a direct and significant impact on the world.

Kellie McElhaney is the founding faculty director of the Center for Responsible Business at the Haas School of Business, University of California, Berkeley. In her book *Just Good Business: The Strategic Guide to Aligning Corporate Social Responsibility and Brand* (Berrett-Koehler), Kellie describes seven rules to consider when devel-oping an effective CSR strategy:

>> **Know thyself.** Your CSR strategy must be authentic and must ring true for your organization. The best way to ensure that this is the case is to closely match it to your company's mission, vision, and values. Employees, customers, and others will know when it's not authentic, and your CSR strategy won't have the desired effect.

>> **Get a good fit.** The goals you select for your CSR strategy must fit your company and its products and services. For example, if your business is a boutique selling women's clothing, then actively supporting breast cancer research is a good fit.

>> **Be consistent.** Be sure that everyone in your organization knows what your CSR strategy and goals are and that everyone can express them consistently to one another — and to the general public. Your CSR efforts are multiplied when everyone in your company has a clear understanding of his or her role and is completely aligned with the program.

>> **Simplify.** In developing and implementing a CSR strategy, simpler is usually better. Organic yogurt maker Stonyfield Farm's mantra is simple: "Healthy food, healthy people, healthy planet." Anyone can understand what the company is committed to accomplishing, and customers feel tremendous brand loyalty because they want to be a part of what Stonyfield is doing.

>> **Work from the inside out.** Your CSR strategy isn't worth the paper it's written on if you haven't engaged your employees in the process of developing and implementing it. Instead of forcing a CSR strategy on your employees, invite their active participation in creating it and then rolling it out. You'll get better results and your employees will be pleased that you thought highly enough about them to involve them in the process.

>> **Know your customer.** When developing a CSR strategy, it's better to address the immediate needs of your customers before you try to solve all the prob-lems of the world. These customer needs often boil down to the most basic of human needs: safety, love and belonging, self-esteem, and self-actualization. If you can address these customer needs, you'll have a customer for life.

>> **Tell your story.** When you have your CSR strategy in place, don't be afraid to publicize your efforts to be socially responsible along with your successes. Again, many people (including prospective customers, clients, and employees) are attracted to companies that operate in a socially responsible way. If you don't get out the word about your programs, you'll lose this powerful advantage. So tell your story — as often as you can — to your employees and to the general public. Use company newsletters and brochures, your website, and online social media such as Twitter, Facebook, LinkedIn, and YouTube.

REMEMBER

Above all, don't spend hours, days, or weeks laboring over a CSR strategy, only to file it away and forget all about it. Integrate your strategy into your everyday business operations. In this way, you'll gain the full benefit of corporate social responsibility — a benefit that can give you a distinct competitive advantage in the marketplace.

Doing the Right Thing: Ethics and You

Each year or two, the leaders of some company somewhere trigger a huge scandal due to some ethical lapse. These lapses are often so egregious that you wonder whether people in charge know the difference between right and wrong — or, if they do know the difference, whether they care.

Despite appearances to the contrary, many business leaders do know the difference between right and wrong. Now more than ever, businesses and the leaders who run them are trying to do the right thing, not just because the right thing is politically correct, but because it's good for the bottom line.

Defining ethics on the job

Do you know what ethics are? In case you're a bit rusty on the correct response, the long answer is that *ethics* are standards of beliefs and values that guide conduct, behavior, and activities — in other words, a way of thinking that provides boundaries for your actions. The short answer is that ethics are simply doing the right thing.

Although all people come to a job with their own sense of ethical values — based on their own upbringing and life experiences — organizations and leaders are responsible for setting clear ethical standards.

When you have high ethical standards on the job, you generally exhibit some or all of the following personal qualities and behaviors:

>> Accountability

>> Dedication

>> Fairness

>> Honesty

>> Impartiality

>> Integrity

>> Loyalty

>> Responsibility

REMEMBER

Ethical behavior starts with you. As the owner, you're the leader of your organization, and you set an example — both for any managers you have reporting to you and for the many workers who are watching your every move. When others see you behaving unethically, you're sending the message loud and clear that ethics don't matter. The result? Ethics won't matter to them, either.

However, when you behave ethically, others follow your example and behave ethically, too. And if you practice ethical conduct, it also reinforces and perhaps improves your own ethical standards. Small business owners have a responsibility to try to define, live up to, and improve their own set of personal ethics.

Creating a code of ethics

Although most people have a pretty good idea about which kinds of behavior are ethical and which aren't, ethics are somewhat subjective and open to interpretation by the individual employee. For example, one worker may think that making unlimited personal phone calls from the office is okay, whereas another worker may consider that to be inappropriate.

So what's the solution to ethics that vary from person to person in an organization? A code of ethics. By creating and implementing a code of ethics, you clearly and unambiguously spell out for all employees — from the very top to the very bottom — your organization's ethical expectations. A code of ethics isn't a substitute for company policies and procedures; the code complements them. Instead of leaving your employees' definition of ethics on the job to chance — or someone's upbringing — you clearly spell out that stealing, sharing trade secrets, sexually harassing a co-worker, and engaging in other unethical behavior is unacceptable and may be grounds for dismissal. And when you require your employees to read and sign a copy acknowledging their acceptance of the code, your employees can't very well claim that they didn't know what you expected of them. The ethics policy should be reviewed and agreed to annually so that it remains top-of-mind for all employees.

Four key areas form the foundation of a good code of ethics:

» Compliance with internal policies and procedures

» Compliance with external laws and regulations

» Direction from organizational values

» Direction from individual values

Of course, a code of ethics isn't worth the paper it's printed on if it doesn't address some very specific issues, as well as generic ones. The following are some of the most common issues addressed by typical codes of ethics:

» Conflicts of interest

» Diversity

» Employee health and safety

» Equal opportunity

» Gifts and gratuities

» Privacy and confidentiality

» Sexual harassment

In addition to working within an organization, a well-crafted code of ethics can be a powerful tool for publicizing your company's standards and values to people outside your organization, including vendors, clients, customers, investors, potential job applicants, the media, and the general public. Your code of ethics tells others that you value ethical behavior and that it guides the way you and your employees do business.

Of course, simply having a code of ethics isn't enough. You and your employees must also live it. Even the world's best code of ethics does you no good if you file it away and never use it.

Making ethical choices every day

You may have a code of ethics, but if you never behave ethically in your day-to-day business transactions and relationships, what's the purpose of having a code in the first place? Ethical challenges abound in business — some are spelled out in your company's code of ethics, or in its policies and procedures, and some aren't. For example, what would you do in these situations?

>> One of your favorite employees gives you tickets to a baseball game.

>> An employee asks you not to write her up for a moderate infraction of company policies.

>> You sold a product to a client that you later found out to be faulty, but the client seems unaware of the problem.

>> You find out that your star employee actually didn't graduate from college, as he claimed in his job application.

>> You know that a product you sell doesn't actually do everything your company claims it does.

REMEMBER

People make ethical choices on the job every day; how do you make yours? Consider this framework comprising six keys to making better ethical choices:

>> **Evaluate** circumstances through the appropriate filters. (Filters include culture, laws, policies, circumstances, relationships, politics, perception, emotions, values, bias, and religion.)

>> **Treat** people and issues fairly within the established boundaries. *Fair* doesn't always mean *equal*.

>> **Hesitate** before making critical decisions.

>> **Inform** those affected of the standard or decision that has been set.

>> **Create** an environment of consistency for yourself and your working group.

>> **Seek** counsel when you have any doubt (but from those who are honest and whom you respect).

Chapter **4**

Managing with Technology

You've gotta love technology. Unfortunately, like everything else in life, technology has its good and bad points. On the upside, computers make our work lives much easier and more efficient, right? As long as your computer doesn't crash, it remembers everything you've done and makes completing repetitive tasks (like merging a letter with a 1,000-person mailing list) a snap. On the downside, computers can be an enormous waste of time. Instead of working, some people spend a significant portion of their workdays checking their Facebook accounts, watching cat videos on YouTube, and keeping track of the latest celebrity gossip.

You may automatically assume that your employees are more productive because they have computers at their fingertips, but are you (and your fledgling business) really getting the most out of this innovative and expensive technology? Given how much money most start-ups invest in their information technology (IT) systems, hardware, and software, that can be an expensive question.

This chapter explains how to harness IT — technology used to create, store, exchange, and use information in its various forms. It examines the technology edge and considers how technology can help or hinder a new organization. It looks at how technology can improve efficiency and productivity, and how to get the most out of it. Finally, it describes how to create a technology plan.

Weighing the Benefits and Drawbacks of Technology in the Workplace

Think for a moment about the incredible progress of information technology just in your lifetime. With so many tools at your fingertips, can you believe that, only several decades ago, the personal computer hadn't yet been introduced commercially? Word processing used to mean a typewriter and a lot of correction fluid or sheets of messy carbon paper. Computers have revolutionized the way businesspeople can manipulate text, graphics, and other elements in their reports and other documents. Mobile phones, the Internet, broadband wireless connections, and other business technology essentials are all fairly recent innovations.

You can't turn back the clock on technology. To keep up with the competition — and beat it — you must keep pace with technology and adopt tools that can make your employees more productive, while improving products and services, customer service, and the bottom line. You really have no other choice.

Making advances, thanks to automation

IT can have a positive impact on your business in two important ways, both related to the practice of automation:

>> **Automating processes:** Not too many years ago, business processes were manual. For example, your bookkeeper may have calculated payroll entirely by hand with the assistance of only a ten-key adding machine. What used to take hours, days, or weeks can now be accomplished in minutes or even seconds. Other processes that are commonly automated are inventory tracking, customer service, call analysis, and purchasing.

>> **Automating personal management functions:** More people than ever are moving their calendars and personal planners onto computers. Although paper-based planners aren't going to die completely, many folks are finding that computers are much more powerful management tools than their manual counterparts. Small business owners use computers to schedule meetings, track projects, analyze numbers, manage business contact information, conduct employee performance evaluations, and more.

REMEMBER

Before you run off and automate everything, keep this piece of information in mind: If your manual system is inefficient or ineffective, simply automating the system isn't necessarily going to make your system perform any better. In fact, automating it can make your system perform worse than the manual version.

When you automate, review the process in detail. Cut out any unnecessary steps and make sure your system is optimized for the new, automated environment. The time you take now to improve your processes and functions is going to pay off when you automate.

Improving efficiency and productivity

The explosion of IT accompanies the shift in business from old-school standards, such as cigar stores, video rental shops, and shoe repair outfits, to those producing web design, app development, and online retail products and services. The personal computer industry, still in its infancy a few decades ago, has grown into a market worth many billions of dollars in annual sales.

REMEMBER

The idea that businesspeople who best manage information have a competitive advantage in the marketplace seems obvious enough. The sooner you receive information, the sooner you can act on it. The more effectively you handle information, the easier you can access that information when and where you need it. The more efficiently you deal with information, the fewer expenses you incur for managing and maintaining your information.

New business owners often cite the preceding reasons, and others like them, as justification for running up huge start-up costs to buy computers, install email and voice-mail systems worthy of much larger organizations, and train employees to use these new tools of the Information Age. But have all these expenditures made your own workers more productive? If not, perhaps you aren't taking the right approach to implementing IT within your business.

Before spending the money, a business owner should take time to identify the questions that need an answer:

>> Who needs the answer? (customer, supplier, employee, owner)

>> How fast do they need the answer? (real time, one minute, one hour, one day)

>> How frequently do they need the answer? (daily, weekly, monthly)

When the answers to these questions become clear, you have a rational basis for evaluating alternate technologies based on how well they meet the criteria needed for your "answers." A lot of technology seems to be designed to provide a real-time answer to a question that may need to be asked only once a month.

When planned and implemented wisely, IT can improve an organization's efficiency and productivity. Recent studies are beginning to show a relationship between the implementation of IT and increased productivity. Examples like the following bear out this relationship:

>> Implementing a computerized inventory-management system at Warren, Michigan–based Duramet Corporation — a manufacturer of powdered metal and now a part of the Cerametal Group — helped the company double sales over a three-year period without hiring a single new salesperson.

>> By using IT to provide employees with real-time information about orders and scheduling that cuts through the traditional walls within the organization, M.A. Hanna, a manufacturer of polymers that merged with Geon Company to form PolyOne Corporation, reduced its working capital needs by a third to achieve the same measure of sales.

WARNING

Although evidence is beginning to swing toward productivity gains, studies indicate that merely installing computers and other IT doesn't automatically lead to gains in employee efficiency. As a business owner, you must take the time to improve your work processes before you automate them. If you don't, office automation can actually lead to decreases in employee efficiency and productivity. Instead of the usual lousy results that you get from your manual system, you end up with something new: garbage at the speed of light. Don't let your organization make the same mistake.

Taking steps to neutralize the negatives

Just as information technology can help a business, it can also hinder it. Consider a few examples of the negative side of IT:

>> Widespread worker abuse of Internet access has reduced worker productivity.

>> Hackers have sent periodic waves of computer viruses and malicious attacks through the business world, leaving billions of dollars of damage and lost productivity in their wake.

>> Email messages can be unclear and confusing, forcing workers to waste time clarifying their intentions or covering themselves in case of problems.

>> Employees are forced to wade through spam and junk email messages.

>> The slick, animated, sound-laden, computer-based, full-color presentations so common today can take longer to prepare than the simple text and graphs that were prevalent a few years ago — especially if you're not technologically savvy.

REMEMBER

You have to take the bad with the good. But don't take the bad lying down. You can maximize the positives of IT while minimizing the negatives:

>> **Stay current on the latest information innovations and news.** You don't need to become an expert on how to install a network server or configure your voice-mail system, but you do need to become conversant in the technology behind your business systems.

>> **Hire experts.** Although you must have a general knowledge of IT, plan to hire experts to advise you in the design and implementation of critical IT-based systems.

>> **Manage by walking around.** Make a habit of dropping in on employees — wherever they're located — and observe how they use your organization's IT. Solicit their feedback and suggestions for improvement. Research and implement changes as soon as you discover the need.

Using Technology to Your Advantage

Information technology is all around us today, and it touches every aspect of our lives — at home and at work. Computers and telecommunications technology are essential tools for any business. Even the most defiant, old-school entrepreneurs can now be seen glued to their smartphones. IT can give you and your business tremendous advantages. As an owner, you must capitalize on them — before your competition does.

Before you act, you must become technology savvy. The following sections recommend the four basic ways for doing just that.

Know your business

Before you can design and implement IT in the most effective way, you have to completely understand how your business works. What work is being done? Who's doing it? What do employees need to get their work done?

TIP

One way to know your business is to approach it as an outsider. Pretend you're a customer and see how your company's people and systems handle you. Do the same with your competitors to see how their people and systems handle you. What are the differences? What are the similarities? How can you improve your own organization using IT as a result of what you've discovered?

Create a technology-competitive advantage

Few business owners understand how technology can become a competitive advantage for their businesses. They may have vague notions of potential efficiency gains or increased productivity, but they're clueless when dealing with specifics.

Information technology can create real and dramatic competitive advantages over other businesses in your markets, specifically by doing the following:

>> Competing with large companies by marketing on a level playing field (the Internet)

>> Helping to build ongoing, loyal relationships with customers

>> Connecting with strategic partners to speed up vital processes, such as product development and manufacturing

>> Linking with everyone in the company, as well as with necessary sources of information both inside and outside the organization

>> Providing real-time information on pricing, products, and so forth to vendors, customers, and original equipment manufacturers (OEMs)

REMEMBER

Now is the time to create advantages over your competition. Keep in mind that the winner isn't the company that *has* the most data, but the company that *manages* that data best.

Develop a plan

If you're serious about using IT as an edge, you must have a plan for its implementation. When it comes to the fast-changing area of technology, having a *technology plan* — a plan for acquiring and deploying IT — is a definite must. Many businesses buy bits and pieces of computer hardware, software, and other technology without considering the technology that they already have in place and without looking very far into the future. Then when they try to hook everything together, they're surprised that their thrown-together system doesn't work.

Business owners who take the time to develop and implement technology plans aren't faced with this problem, and they aren't forced to spend far more money and time fixing the problems with their systems.

TIP

Technology is no longer an optional expense; it's a strategic investment that can help push your company ahead of the competition. And every strategic investment requires a plan. In their book *eBusiness Technology Kit For Dummies* (John Wiley & Sons, Inc.), Kathleen Allen and Jon Weisner recommend that you take the following steps in developing your technology plan:

1. **Write down your organization's core values.**

    For example, core values might be to provide customers with the very best customer service possible, or to always act ethically and honestly.

2. **Picture where you see your business ten years from now. Don't limit yourself.**

    Will you be in the same location or perhaps some new ones? What products and services will you offer, and to whom will you offer them? How many employees will you have? 1? 10? 50?

3. **Set a major one-year goal for the company that is guided by your vision.**

    This goal might be to create a system that tracks customer service complaints and gets them in front of you in real time.

4. **List some strategies for achieving the goal.**

    A strategy to achieve the preceding one-year goal might be to hire a consultant to develop a set of recommended solutions within three months.

5. **Brainstorm some tactics that can help you achieve your strategies.**

    Specific tactics to achieve the preceding strategy might include assigning responsibility for the project to a specific employee or vendor, and setting milestones and deadlines for completion and reporting of results.

6. **Identify technologies that support your strategies and tactics.**

    Provide some guidance by bounding the technologies to use in achieving the one-year goal, strategies, and tactics. For example, you may require that any new system work with existing systems or that the new system be web based.

Gather your thoughts — and your employees' thoughts — and write them down. Create a concise document, perhaps no more than five to ten pages, that describes your IT strategies as simply and exactly as possible. After you create your plan, screen and select vendors that can help you implement your plan. Close out the process by monitoring performance and adjusting the plan as needed to meet the needs of your organization and employees, and to produce optimal performance.

TIP

Keep the following points in mind as you navigate the planning process:

>> **Don't buy technology just because it's the latest and greatest thing.** Shopping for the latest whiz-bang gizmo is fun. Unfortunately, just because an item is new, has lots of flashing lights, and makes cool noises doesn't mean it's right for your business. It could be too big or too small, too fast or too slow, too expensive or too cheap. Or it might not even be compatible with the systems you've already got. Be sure that whatever technology you include in your plan makes sense for your business.

>> **Check in with your IT guru.** Make sure your planned purchase is compatible with existing systems. You also want to find out whether the program you're thinking of buying will be obsolete within a couple months.

>> **Plan for the right period of time.** Different kinds of businesses require different planning *horizons,* the time periods covered by their plans. If you're in a highly volatile market such as smartphone app development, your planning horizon may be only six months or so out. If you're in a stable market such as plumbing or garage door repair, your planning horizon may extend three to five years into the future.

>> **Consider the benefits of outsourcing.** You may be able to save significant amounts of money by outsourcing appropriate functions to further streamline systems and create efficiencies.

>> **Make the planning process a team effort.** You're not the only one who's going to be impacted by all this new technology that you bring into your company. Make employees, customers, and vendors a part of your planning team. If you take time to involve them in the process and get their buy-in ahead of time, your technology rollout will go much more smoothly.

Get some help

If you're a fan of technology and pretty knowledgeable in it, that's great — you have a head start on the process. But if you're not, get help from people who are experts in IT. Are any of your employees knowledgeable about IT? Can you hire a technician or technology consultant to fill in the gaps? Whatever you do, don't try it alone. Even if you're a full-fledged techno-geek, recruit others for your cause. Technology is changing incredibly fast and on every front. No one person can be an expert in every aspect of the IT necessary to run and grow your business.

Getting the Most Out of Company Networks

The personal computer began revolutionizing business decades ago, shifting the power of computing away from huge mainframes and onto the desks of individual users. Then computer networks brought about a new revolution in business. Although the personal computer is a self-sufficient island of information, when you link these islands in a network, individual computers have the added benefit of sharing with every computer on the network.

So does networking have any benefits? You bet it does. See what you think about these reasons:

>> **Networks improve communication.** Computer networks allow anyone in an organization to communicate with anyone else quickly and easily. With the click of a button, you can send messages to individuals or groups of employees. You can send replies just as easily. Furthermore, employees on computer networks can access financial, marketing, and product information to do their jobs from throughout the organization.

>> **Networks save time and money.** In business, time is money. The faster you can get something done, the more tasks you can complete during the course of your business day. Email allows you to create messages, memos, and other internal communications and files and send them instantaneously to as many co-workers as you want. Even better, these co-workers can be located across the hall or out in the marketplace making account calls.

>> **Networks improve market vision.** Information communicated via computer networks is, by nature, timely and direct. In the old world of business communication, many layers of employees filtered, modified, and slowed the information as it traveled from one part of the organization to another. With direct communication over networks, no one filters, modifies, or slows the original message. What you see is what you get. The sooner you get the information that you need and the higher its quality is, the better your market vision can be.

Chapter **5**

Delegating to Get Things Done

After you grow beyond a one-person shop, the power of your business comes not from your efforts alone, but from the sum of all the efforts of your employees. If you're responsible for only a few employees, with extraordinary effort, you perhaps can do the work of your entire group if you so desire — and if you want to be a complete stranger to your friends and family. When you're talking about more than a few employees, you simply can't do all the work if you tried. Besides, you don't want to be known as a *micromanager* who gets too involved in the petty details of running things. And your employees may take less responsibility for their work because you're always there to do it (or check it) for them. They will be less engaged in their work, and morale will plummet. Why should they bother trying to do their best job if you don't trust them enough to do it?

Managers — even ones who are also business owners — assign responsibility for completing tasks through *delegation*. But simply assigning tasks and then walking away isn't enough. To delegate effectively, you must also give employees authority and ensure that they have the resources necessary to complete tasks effectively. You must also monitor the progress of their employees, if they have direct reports of their own, toward meeting their assigned goals.

Delegating: The Manager's Best Tool

As a business owner, you're required to develop skills in many different areas. You need good technical, analytical, and organizational skills, but most important, you also must have good people skills. Of all the people skills, the one skill that can make the greatest difference in your effectiveness is the *ability to delegate well*. Delegating is the number one management tool, and the inability to delegate well is the leading cause of management failure.

Why do you have a hard time delegating? A variety of possible reasons exist:

>> You're too busy and just don't have enough time.

>> You don't trust your employees to complete their assignments correctly or on time.

>> You're afraid to let go.

>> You're concerned that you'll no longer be the center of attention.

>> You have no one to delegate to (lack of resources).

>> You don't know how to delegate effectively.

Consider these reasons why you must let go of your preconceptions and inhibitions and start delegating today:

REMEMBER

>> **Your success depends on it.** Business owners who can successfully manage team members — each of whom has specific responsibilities for a different aspect of the team's performance — are the ones who enjoy the most success.

>> **You can't do it all.** No matter how great a manager you are, shouldering the entire burden of achieving your goals isn't in your best interest unless you want to work yourself into an early grave. Besides, wouldn't it be nice to see what life is like outside the four walls of your office?

>> **You have to concentrate on the jobs that you can do and your staff can't.** You're the manager — not a software programmer, truck driver, accounting clerk, or customer service representative. Do your job, and let your employees do theirs.

>> **Delegation gets workers more involved.** When you give employees the responsibility and authority to carry out tasks — whether individually or in teams — they respond by becoming more involved in the day-to-day operations of the organization. Instead of acting like drones with no responsibility or authority, they become vital to the success of the business. And if your employees succeed, you succeed.

WARNING

>> **Delegation gives you the chance to develop your employees.** If you make all the decisions and come up with all the ideas, your employees never learn how to take initiative and see tasks through to successful completion. And if they don't learn, guess who's going to get stuck doing everything forever? (Hint: Take a look in the mirror.) In addition, doing everything yourself robs your employees of a golden opportunity to develop their work skills. Today's employees increasingly report learning and development opportunities as one of the top motivators. (See Chapter 1 in Book 6 for more about employee development.)

Suppose, for example, that you're running a health care consulting firm. When the firm had only a few employees and sales of $100,000 a year, it was no problem for you to personally bill all your customers, cut checks to vendors, run payroll, and take care of the company's taxes every April. However, now you've grown to 20 employees and sales are at $3 million a year. Face it, you can't even pretend to do it all — you don't have enough hours in the day. You now have specialized employees who take care of accounts payable, accounts receivable, and payroll, and you have farmed out the completion of income tax work to a CPA.

Each employee to whom you've assigned a specific work function has specialized knowledge and skills in a certain area of expertise. If you've made the right hiring decisions (see Book 4, Chapter 1), each employee is a talented and specialized pro in a specific field. Sure, you could personally generate payroll if you had to, but you've hired someone to do that job for you. (By the way, your payroll clerk is probably a lot better and quicker at it than you are.)

On the other hand, you're uniquely qualified to perform numerous responsibilities in your organization. These responsibilities may include developing and monitoring your operations budget, conducting performance appraisals, and helping to plan the overall direction of your company's acquisitions. The section "Sorting Out What to Delegate and What to Do Yourself," later in this chapter, suggests which tasks to delegate to your employees and which ones to retain.

Debunking Myths about Delegation

Admit it, you may have many different rationalizations for why you can't delegate work to your employees. Unfortunately, these reasons have become part of the general folklore of being a manager. And they're guaranteed to get in the way of your ability to be effective.

You can't trust your employees to be responsible

If you can't trust your employees, whom can you trust? Assume that you're responsible for hiring at least a portion of your staff. Now, forgetting for a moment the ones you didn't personally hire, you likely went through quite an involved process to recruit your employees (as described in Book 4, Chapter 1). Remember the mountain of résumés you had to sift through and then divide into winners, potential winners, and losers? After hours of sorting and then hours of interviews, you selected the best candidates — the ones with the best skills, qualifications, and experience for the job.

You selected your employees because you thought they were the most talented people available and deserved your trust. Now your job is to give them that trust without strings attached.

REMEMBER

You usually reap what you sow. Your staff members are ready, willing, and able to be responsible employees — you just have to give them a chance. Sure, not every employee is going to be able to handle every task you assign. If that's the case, find out why. Does someone need more training? More time? More practice? Maybe you need to find a task that's better suited to an employee's experience or disposition. Or perhaps you simply hired the wrong person for the job. If that's the case, face up to the fact and fire or reassign the employee before you lose even more time and money. To get responsible employees, you have to give responsibility.

You'll lose control of a task and its outcome

If you delegate correctly, you don't lose control of the task or its outcome. You simply lose control of the way the outcome is achieved. Picture a map of the world. How many different ways can a person get from San Francisco to Paris? One? One million? Some ways are quicker than others. Some are more scenic, and others require a substantial resource commitment. Do the differences in these ways make any of them inherently wrong? No.

REMEMBER

In business, getting a task done doesn't mean following only one path. Even for tasks that are spelled out in highly defined steps, you can always leave room for new ways to make a process better. Your job is to describe to your employees the outcomes that you want and then let them decide how to accomplish the tasks. Of course, you need to be available to coach and counsel them so that they can learn from your past experience, if you want, but you need to let go of controlling the *how* and instead focus on the *what* and the *when*.

You're the only one with all the answers

You're joking, right? As talented as you may be, unless you're the only employee, you can't possibly have the only answer to every question in your organization.

On the other hand, a certain group of people deals with an amazing array of situations every day. The group talks to your customers, your suppliers, and each other — day in and day out. Who are these people? They are your employees.

REMEMBER

Your employees have a wealth of experience and knowledge about your business contacts and the intimate, day-to-day workings of the organization. They are often closer to the customers and problems of the company than you are. They've seen things you haven't. To ignore their suggestions and advice is not only disrespectful, but also shortsighted and foolish. Don't ignore this resource. You're already paying for it, so use it.

You can do the work faster by yourself

You may think that you're completing tasks faster when you do them than when you assign them to others, but this belief is merely an illusion. Yes, discussing a task and assigning it to one of your employees may require more of your time when you first delegate that task, but if you delegate well, you'll spend significantly less time the next time you delegate that same task.

What else happens when you do it yourself instead of delegating it? When you do the task yourself, you're forever doomed to doing the task — again and again and again. When you teach someone else to do the task and then assign that person the responsibility for completing it, you may never have to do it again. Your employee may even come to do it faster than you can. Who knows? That employee may actually improve the way that you've always done it, perhaps reducing costs or increasing customer satisfaction.

Delegation dilutes your authority

Delegation does the exact opposite of what this myth says — it actually *extends* your authority. You're only one person, and you can do only so much by yourself. Now imagine all 5, 10, 20, or 100 members of your team working toward your common goals. You still set the goals and the timetables for reaching them, but each employee chooses her own way of getting there.

Do you have less authority because you delegate a task and transfer authority to an employee to carry out the task? Clearly, the answer is no. What do you lose in this transaction? Nothing! Your authority is extended, not diminished. The more authority you give to employees, the better able your employees are to do the jobs you hired them to do.

REMEMBER

As you grant others authority, you gain an efficient and effective workforce — employees who are truly empowered, feel excited by their jobs, and work as team players. You also gain the ability to concentrate on the issues that deserve your undivided attention.

You relinquish the credit for doing a good job

Letting go of this belief is one of the biggest difficulties in the transition from being a doer to being a manager of doers. When you're a doer, you're rewarded for writing a great report, developing an incredible market analysis, or programming an amazing piece of computer code. When you're a manager, the focus of your job shifts to your performance in reaching an overall company or project goal through the efforts of others. The skills required are quite different, and your success is a result of the indirect efforts of others and your behind-the-scenes support.

REMEMBER

Wise managers know that when their employees shine, they shine, too. The more you delegate, the more opportunities you give your employees to shine. Give your workers the opportunity to do important work — and do it well. And when they do well, make sure you tell everyone about it. If you give your employees credit for their successes publicly and often, they'll more likely want to do a good job for you on future assignments. Don't forget, when you own a business that employs others, your business's success is primarily measured on your employees' performance, not what you're personally able to accomplish.

Delegation decreases your flexibility

When you do everything yourself, you have complete control over the progress and completion of tasks, right? Wrong! How can you, when you're balancing multiple priorities at the same time and dealing with the inevitable crisis (or two or three) of the day? Being flexible is pretty tough when you're doing everything yourself. Concentrating on more than one task at a time is impossible. While you're concentrating on that one task, you put all your other tasks on hold. Flexibility? Not!

REMEMBER

The more people you delegate to, the more flexible you can be. As your employees take care of the day-to-day tasks necessary to keep your business running, you're free to deal with those surprise problems and opportunities that always seem to pop up at the last minute.

Taking the Six Steps to Delegate

Delegation can be scary, at least at first. But as with anything else, the more you do it, the less scary it gets. When you delegate, you're putting your trust in another individual. If that individual fails, you're ultimately responsible — regardless of whom you give the task to. When you delegate tasks, you don't automatically abdicate your responsibility for their successful completion.

As a part of this process, you need to understand your employees' strengths and weaknesses. For example, you probably aren't going to delegate a huge task to someone who has been on the job for only a few days. As with any other task that you perform as a manager, you have to work at delegating — and keep working at it. Ultimately, delegation benefits both workers and managers when you do it correctly.

REMEMBER

Follow these six steps for effectively delegating:

1. **Communicate the task.**

   Describe exactly what you want done, when you want it done, and what end results you expect. Ask for any questions your employee might have.

2. **Furnish context for the task.**

   Explain why the task needs to be done, its importance in the overall scheme of things, and possible complications that may arise during its performance.

3. **Determine standards.**

   Agree on the standards you plan to use to measure the success of a task's completion. Make these standards realistic and attainable.

4. **Grant authority.**

   You must grant employees the authority to complete the task without constant roadblocks or standoffs with other employees.

5. **Provide support.**

   Determine the resources necessary for your employee to complete the task, and then provide them. Successfully completing a task may require money, training, or the ability to check with you about progress or obstacles as they arise.

6. **Get commitment.**

   Make sure your employee has accepted the assignment. Confirm your expectations and your employee's understanding of and commitment to completing the task.

Sorting Out What to Delegate and What to Do Yourself

In theory, you can delegate anything you're responsible for to your employees. Of course, if you delegate all your duties, what are you going to do? The point is, there are some things you are better able to do, and some things your employees are better able to do. As a result, some tasks you make an effort to delegate to your employees and other tasks you retain for yourself.

REMEMBER

When you delegate, begin with simple tasks that don't substantially impact the business if they aren't completed on time or within budget. As your employees gain confidence and experience, delegate higher-level tasks. Carefully assess the level of your employees' expertise and assign tasks that meet or slightly exceed that level. Set schedules for completion and then monitor your employees' performance against them. This is a good opportunity to see if an employee isn't being challenged or is bored. When you get the hang of it, you'll find that you have nothing to be afraid of when you delegate.

Pointing out appropriate tasks for delegation

Certain tasks naturally lend themselves to being delegated. Take every opportunity to delegate the following kinds of work to your employees.

Detail work

As a business owner, you have no greater time-waster than getting caught up in details — you know, tasks such as double-checking pages, spending days troubleshooting a block of computer code, or personally auditing your employees' timesheets. The Pareto Principle holds that 20 percent of the results come from 80 percent of the work. You can no doubt run circles around almost anyone on those detailed technical tasks that you used to do all the time.

But when you're the owner, your duty is to orchestrate the workings of a team toward a common goal — not just to perform an individual task. So leave the details to your employees, but hold them accountable for the results. Concentrate your efforts on tasks that have the greatest payoff and that allow you to most effectively leverage the work of all your employees.

Information gathering

Browsing the web for information about your competitors, spending hours poring over issues of *Fortune* magazine, and moving into your local library's reference stacks for weeks on end isn't an effective use of your time. Still, many business owners can get sucked into the trap. Not only is reading newspapers, reports, books, magazines, and the like fun, but it also gives you an easy way to postpone the more difficult tasks of managing your company. Your responsibility is to look at the big picture — to gather a variety of inputs and make sense of them. You can work so much more efficiently when someone else gathers needed information, freeing you to take the time you need to analyze the inputs and devise solutions to your problems.

Repetitive assignments

What a great way to get routine tasks done: Assign them to your employees. Many of the jobs in your company arise again and again; checking inventory levels and placing orders for more product, reviewing your biweekly report of expenditures versus budget, and approving your monthly phone bill are just a few examples. Your time is much too important to waste on routine tasks that you mastered years ago.

If you find yourself involved in repetitive assignments, first take a close look at their particulars. How often do the assignments recur? Can you anticipate the assignments in sufficient time to allow an employee to successfully complete them? What do you have to do to train your employees in completing the tasks? When you figure all of this out, develop a schedule and make assignments to your employees.

Surrogate roles

Do you feel that you have to be everywhere all the time? Well, you certainly can't be everywhere all the time — and you shouldn't even *try*. Every day, your employees have numerous opportunities to fill in for you. Presentations, conference calls, client visits, and meetings are just a few examples. In some cases, you may be required to attend. However, in many other cases, whether you attend personally or send someone to take your place really doesn't matter.

The next time someone calls a meeting and requests your attendance, send one of your employees to attend in your place. This simple act benefits you in several different ways. Not only do you have an extra hour or two in your schedule, but also your employee can present you with only the important outcomes of the meeting. In any case, your employee has the opportunity to take on some new responsibilities, and you have the opportunity to spend the time you need on your most important tasks. Your employee may even discover something new in the process.

Future duties

As a business owner, you must always be on the lookout for opportunities to train your staff in their future job responsibilities. For example, one of your key duties may be to develop your annual budget. By allowing one or more of your employees to assist you — perhaps in gathering basic market or research data, or analyzing trends in previous-year budgets — you can give your employees a taste of what goes into putting together a budget.

REMEMBER

Don't fall into the trap of believing that the only way to train your employees is to sign them up for an expensive class taught by someone with a slick color brochure who knows nothing about *your* business. Opportunities to train your employees abound within your own business. An estimated 90 percent of all development occurs on the job. Not only is this training free, but also by assigning your employees to progressively more important tasks, you build their self-confidence and help pave their way to progress in the organization. (See Chapter 1 in Book 6 for more about employee development.)

Knowing what tasks should stay with you

Some tasks are part and parcel of the job of being the owner. By delegating the following work, you fail to perform your basic management duties.

Long-term vision and goals

Your position at the top provides you with a unique perspective on the organization's needs. One of the key functions of management is vision. Although employees at any level can give you input and make suggestions that help shape your perspectives, developing the business's long-term vision and goals is up to you. Employees can't collectively decide the direction in which you should move. An organization is much more effective when everyone moves together in the same direction.

Positive performance feedback

Rewarding and recognizing employees when they do good work is an important job for every manager. If this task is delegated to lower-level employees, however, the workers who receive it won't value the recognition as much as if it came from the owner. The impact of the recognition is therefore significantly lessened.

Performance appraisals, discipline, and counseling

In a busy small business, a strong relationship between owner and employee is often hard to come by. Most owners are probably lucky to get off a quick "Good morning" or "Good night" between the hustle and bustle of a typical workday. Given everyone's hectic schedules, you may have times when you don't talk to one or more of your employees for days at a time.

However, sometimes you absolutely have to set time aside for your employees. When you discipline and counsel your employees, you're giving them the kind of input that only you can provide. You set the goals for your employees, and you set the standards by which you measure their progress. Inevitably, you decide whether your employees have reached the marks you've set or whether they've fallen short. You can't delegate away this task effectively — everyone loses as a result.

Politically sensitive situations

Some situations are just too politically sensitive to assign to your employees. For example, say you're auditing the expenses for your business. The results of your review show that someone has gone to way too many lunches on company funds. Do you assign a worker the responsibility of reporting this explosive situation? No! You're in the best position to deal with this information.

REMEMBER

Not only do such situations demand your utmost attention and expertise, but placing your employee in the middle of the line of fire in a potentially explosive situation is also unfair. Being the owner may be tough sometimes, but you're paid to make the difficult decisions and to take the political heat that your work generates.

Confidential or sensitive circumstances

WARNING

You're privy to information that your staff isn't, such as wage and salary figures, proprietary data, and personnel assessments. Releasing this information to the wrong individuals can be damaging to a business. For example, salary information should remain confidential. Similarly, if your competitors get their hands on some secret process that your company has spent countless hours and money to develop, the impact on your organization and employees can be devastating. Unless your staff has a compelling need to know, retain assignments involving these types of information.

5
Marketing and Promotion

Contents at a Glance

Chapter **1**

Optimizing Your Marketing Program

Marketing is all the activities that contribute to building ongoing, profitable relationships with customers to grow your business. The traditional goal of marketing is to bring about healthy sales through advertising, brand development, and other activities. A more long-term goal is to become increasingly useful or valuable to a growing number of customers so as to ensure your future success. Watch both short-term sales and long-term development of value to make your organization a growing success.

Your *marketing program* is the right mix of products or services, pricing, promotions, branding, sales, and distribution that will produce immediate sales and also help you grow over time. You'll know when you've found the right mix for you and your organization because it will produce profitable sales and enough demand to allow you to grow at a comfortable rate.

This chapter serves as a jumping-off point into the world of marketing. By reading it, you can begin to design a marketing program that works for you. The rest of the chapters in Book 5 can help you refine the program that meets your needs.

Know Yourself, Know Your Customer

To make your marketing program more profitable and growth-oriented, think about how to reach and persuade more of the right customers. When you understand how your customers think and what they like, you may find better ways to make more sales. The following sections help you get better acquainted with what you have to offer and start communicating those offerings to your customers.

Asking the right question

Traditional marketers ask just one key question:

> What do we need to tell customers to make the sale?

Then they flood the environments (both virtual and actual) with competing claims, trying to outdo each other in their efforts to prove that they have what customers want. This barrage of noisy advertising and one-up salesmanship is inefficient, wasteful, and, to many, an unfortunate source of social pollution.

A better initial question to ask is this:

> What do I/we have uniquely to offer?

REMEMBER

When you start right off by examining yourself in the mirror and identifying your genuine, honest-to-yourself strength(s), you're many laps ahead of most marketers, whether you're selling something as simple as your résumé, as complex as a new high-tech product, or anything in between. Your unique strengths form the core of your offering, and you should keep building your strengths in ways that are true to your identity.

Whether you're marketing yourself (perhaps you're a consultant or someone else who offers individualized services) or a business, you can't make consistent and efficient headway by deceiving yourself and trying to deceive others. The more true to your core the marketing message is, the more effective it is. If you can't find any unique qualities to advertise, postpone those media purchases and work on self-improvement or product development. (Perhaps you simply need to listen harder to what your customers say and make sure they're so happy that they recruit new customers!) Then come back to your program with a stronger set of claims that any customer can clearly see are of benefit — that is, unique benefit, not just a run-of-the-mill, everybody-does-it-that-way benefit.

TIP

If you draw a large enough circle around your market, you'll probably encompass competitors who are better than you. There are so many people out there, working hard and innovating, just like you. So as you work to improve your offerings and become ever more unique and special, draw that circle appropriately. It's the equivalent of your bar, so don't set it too high. Perhaps you should try to be the best distributor of alternative, organic, and local foods in just one city. After you have that city sewed up, expand to the next closest market. Don't, however, try to advertise and distribute across a ten-state area right out of the starting block. Knowing yourself means knowing your limitations as well as your strengths.

Marketing programs communicate *benefits*. Benefits are the qualities that your customers value. For example, your product may offer benefits such as convenience, ease of use, brand appeal, attractive design, local sourcing, healthiness, or a lower price than the competition. A service business, or an individual who provides services like consulting, may list benefits such as expertise, friendliness, and availability. The right mix of benefits can make your product or service particularly appealing to the group of customers who value those benefits. Make your list now: What are your core benefits, things that you can honestly say you're good at and that customers may value?

REMEMBER

Even if you're better from a logical or rational perspective, customers may still choose the competition. Say your new soda scores better in blind taste tests or is made of organic ingredients. So what? Who wants to buy an unknown soda rather than the brand they know and love? No, this trust issue isn't rational, but it still affects the purchase — which is why you absolutely must take a look at the emotional reasons people may or may not buy from you. Is your brand appealing? Do you use an attractive design for your packaging? Is your presentation professional and trustworthy? Do people know you or your business and look upon you favorably? Positive image isn't hard to build for free when you market locally or regionally; you just need to show up consistently in ways that demonstrate your concern for the community.

Image isn't everything in marketing, but it *is* just about everything when it comes to the emotional impact you make. So pay close attention to your image when you're looking for ways to boost sales (see Chapter 3 of Book 5 for more about taking stock of your business image). To truly know your customers, you also need to explore the answers to these two questions:

>> **What do customers think about my product?** Do they understand it? Do they think its features and benefits are superior to the competition and can meet their needs? Do they feel that my product is a good value given its benefits and costs? Is it easy for them to buy the product when and where they need it?

>> **How do customers feel about my product?** Does it make them feel good? Do they like its personality? Do they like how it makes them feel about themselves? Do they trust me?

To answer these questions, find something to write on and draw a big *T* to create two columns. Label the left column "What Customers Know About," and put the name of your brand, company, or product in the blank. Label the right column "How Customers Feel About," and fill in as much as you can from your own knowledge before asking others to give you more ideas. Keep working on this table until you're sure you have an exhaustive list of both the logical thoughts and facts and the emotional feelings and impressions that customers have.

Then, if you have access to a friendly group of customers or prospective customers, tell them you're holding an informal focus group with complimentary drinks and snacks (doing so helps with your recruiting) and ask them to help you understand your marketing needs by reviewing and commenting on your table. The goal is to see whether your lists of what customers know and feel about your product agree with theirs. Do they concur with how you described their emotional viewpoint and/or their factual knowledge base?

Filling the awareness gap

Are prospective customers even aware that you exist? If not, then you need to bump up your marketing communications and get in front of them somehow to reduce or eliminate the *awareness gap,* which is the percentage of people in your target market who are unaware of your offerings and their benefits. If only one in ten prospective customers knows about your brand, then you have a 90 percent awareness gap and need to get the word out to a lot more people.

REMEMBER

If you need to communicate with customers more effectively and often, you have some options for bumping up the impact of your marketing communications and reducing the awareness gap:

>> **You can put in more time.** For example, if customers lack knowledge about your product, more sales calls can help fill this awareness gap.

>> **You can spend more money.** More advertisements help fill your awareness gap, but of course, they cost money.

>> **You can communicate better.** A strong, focused marketing program with clear, consistent, and frequent communications helps fill the awareness gap with information and a positive brand image, which then allows interest and purchase levels to rise significantly. Communicating better is usually the best approach, because it substitutes to some degree for time and money. See Chapter 5 of Book 5 for more about marketing communications.

>> **You can become more popular.** Sometimes you can create a buzz of talk about your product. If people think it's really cool or exciting, they may do some of the communicating for you, spreading the news by word of mouth and via social media (this is sometimes referred to as *viral marketing*). If your customers are active on any social media, then you need to be, too; see Chapter 6 of Book 5 for more information.

Focusing on your target customer

Your *target customer* is the person for whom you design your product and marketing program. If you don't already have a clear profile of your target customer, make one now; otherwise, your marketing program will be adrift in a sea of less-than-effective options.

TIP

To craft your target customer profile, assemble any and all facts about your target customer on a large piece of poster paper: age, employer, education level, income, family status, hobbies, politics (if relevant), favorite brand of automobile, or anything else that helps you focus on this person. Also list your target customer's motivations: what he or she cares about in life and how you can help him or her achieve those goals. Finally, cut and paste one to three pictures out of magazine ads to represent the face or faces of your target customer. This is the audience you have to focus your marketing program on. Everything from product design or selection to the content, timing, and placement of ads must specifically target these people.

You can further increase your focus on your target customer by deciding whether he or she prefers marketing that takes a rational, information-based approach; an emotional, personality-based approach; or a balanced mix of the two. By simply being clear about whom to target and whether to market to them in an informational or emotional manner, you ensure that your marketing program has a clear focus.

TIP

You can further target your audience by knowing their specific generation. Times, technologies, channels, and needs have changed and so, too, has the way you connect, engage, and sell to your customers. With all this change, the gap or differences in the various generations is getting wider as people's attitudes, perspectives, and the way they live, shop, and engage with brands is redefined by technology, media channels, and social trends. The primary "shopping" generations are roughly broken down as follows:

>> **Millennials:** born 1981-1996

>> **Generation X:** born 1965-1980

>> **Baby boomers:** born 1946-1964

Although a ton of information about each generation is available — from books to white papers to videos and more — the main thing marketers need to understand is what each generation thinks of brands, what they expect about brands, and what they respond to in terms of values and stimuli.

REMEMBER

Each generation has a unique way of looking at the same brands and assigns different expectations for how it wants to be served.

Millennials (see Table 1-1) don't trust brands or authority in the same way their parents did and do, and they have high standards for how brands should behave toward consumers, employees, and the greater good, which is a strong trend in consumerism.

TABLE 1-1　　**Marketing to Millennials**

Value	Suggested Response
Want self-expression.	Involve in user-generated content.
Respect is earned, not given.	Use statistics, industry knowledge, and experiences to position your marketing leadership and authority.
Trust equity is low because many don't trust brands to be truthful or operate in others' best interests.	Be transparent. If you don't have the best product, don't say you do. If your customer service is poor, fix it before making promises. Listen and admit to wrongdoing when you've made mistakes.

Value	Suggested Response
Crave change.	Keep your brand energetic and change things up to add interest and novelty.
Respond to bold colors, ideas, humor, and interaction.	Use digital channels that provide interaction, such as games and bright colors that fit their energy level, and engage them in disruptive events, like guerilla marketing tactics.
Seek relevance.	Your products, not just your marketing, need to fit their lifestyle and add value. Marketing should demonstrate how.
Open-minded, intelligent, responsible.	Always communicate with transparency, and never talk down or misrepresent the value of an offer or product. When trust is broken, you won't get a second chance.
Expectations for brands.	Involve them in user-generated content and product design and respond to them promptly.

Table 1-2 focuses the values of Generation X and how you can respond to them.

TABLE 1-2   **Marketing to Generation Xers**

Value	Suggested Response
Want to feel they are contributing to something worthwhile.	Involve in volunteerism and corporate social responsibility (CSR) initiatives.
Like recognition for what they do.	Send thank-you emails, invite to VIP clubs, and reward with experiences, content, discounts, or products.
Thrive on autonomy, freedom.	Give them options for pricing, packages, service agreements, and product inventory. Enable communications options as well.
Seek a balanced life.	Align your brand's values with their values and personal life.
Accept authority but are skeptical.	Position your leadership and authority in an objective manner.
Skeptical about economy, fearful of job loss and financial setbacks, and skeptical of big business.	Communicate the security, comfort, and peace of mind that your product and brand deliver. Be transparent about pricing and product claims. Design brand offerings around their need to feel in control and have peace of mind.
Entrepreneurial.	Appeal to their desire to initiate new programs, ideas, and movements.

Baby Boomers, their values, and suggested responses to those values are the focus of Table 1-3.

TABLE 1-3 **Marketing to Baby Boomers**

Value	Suggested Response
Want to feel they are in control of their choices and lives.	Provide information that informs, provides guidance, and assists in decision processes.
Like recognition for what they do.	Thank them for their business, invite to VIP loyalty programs, and reward frequently.
Thrive on prosperity.	Because they have worked hard for years and want to enjoy the perks of successful careers and financial planning, promote perks, pampering, and themes around "you deserve this."
Seek self-actualization.	Align your messaging and experiences with what matters most, such as leaving legacies, making an impact, achieving personal goals, and recognition.
Collaborative.	Invite to your causes centered on your common goals associated with charity, environment, and so on.
Optimistic.	They see good in communities and people and like to believe people can be trusted to be who they say they are.
Goal oriented.	They like to set goals and have a plan and a purpose.

Identifying and playing up your strengths

One of the best steps you can take as a marketer is to find your chief strengths and build on them so you can add an additional degree of focus and momentum to your marketing program. The key is to always think about what you do well for the customer (don't get hung up on shortcomings) and make sure you build on your strengths in everything you do.

For example, imagine that customers say your pricing isn't as good as larger competitors, and you also feel that your brand name isn't very well known. That's the bad news, but the good news is that existing customers are loyal because they like your product and service. The thing to do here is build on this strength by creating a loyalty program for customers, asking for and rewarding referrals, and including testimonials in your marketing materials and on your website. Also, remind customers and prospects that you are the local alternative. "Shop Locally to Support Your Community" may be a good phrase to sneak into every marketing communication, whether on paper, signs, your vehicles, or the web. Building on your strength in this manner can help you overcome the weaknesses of your higher pricing and lesser name recognition.

TIP

Focus on your strengths by clearly and succinctly defining what your special strength or advantage is. Grab a piece of paper and a pen and start your sentence like this: "My product (or service) is special because . . .." Take a minute to think about what makes your firm or product special and why customers have been attracted to you in the past. Then make sure you talk about your strengths or show them visually whenever you communicate with customers.

Discovering the best way to find customers

Another aspect of your customer focus is deciding whether you want to emphasize attracting new customers or retaining and growing existing customers. One or the other may need to dominate your marketing program, or perhaps you need to balance the two. Marketing to new prospects is usually a different sort of challenge from working with existing customers, so knowing which goal is most important helps you improve the focus of your marketing.

"What's your best way to attract customers?" Here are some of the most common answers — things that marketers often say are most effective at bringing them customers:

>> **Referrals:** Your customers may be willing to help you sell your product.

>> **Social media:** Your presence as a provider of helpful or interesting content can't be underestimated in its potential impact on brand development and as a source of customer leads, so try to get ever more comfortable with blogging, Twitter, Facebook, and similar options (see Book 5, Chapter 6 for more on marketing and social media).

>> **Trade shows and professional association meetings:** Making contacts and being visible in the right professional venue may be a powerful way to build your business.

>> **Sales calls:** Salespeople sell products, so make more calls yourself, or find a way to put commissioned salespeople or sales representatives to work for you.

>> **Advertising:** Advertising sells the product, but only if you do it consistently and frequently, whether in print, on radio and TV, outdoors, or on the web.

>> **Product demonstrations, trial coupons, or distribution of free samples:** If your product is impressive, let it sell itself.

>> **Placement and appearance of buildings/stores:** Location is still one of the simplest and best formulas for marketing success.

As the preceding list indicates, every business has a different optimal formula for attracting customers. However, in every case, successful businesses report that one or two methods work best. Their programs are therefore dominated by one or two effective ways of attracting customers. They put between one-third and two-thirds of their marketing resources into their primary way of attracting customers and then use other marketing methods to support their most effective method.

TIP

To find your business's most effective way of reaching out to customers, you need to ask yourself this important question: What's my best way to attract customers, and how can I focus my marketing program to take fuller advantage of it? You can't look up the answer in a book, but you can take heart from the fact that, with persistence, you'll eventually work out what your winning formula is, and then you may have to make only minor changes from year to year to keep your program working well.

When you answer this question, you're taking yet another important step toward a highly focused marketing program that leverages your resources as much as possible. Your marketing program can probably be divided into four tiers of activities:

>> Major impact

>> Helpful; secondary impact

>> Minor impact

>> Money loser; very low impact

If you reorganize last year's budget into these categories, you may find that your spending isn't concentrated near the top of your list. If that's the case, then you can try to move up your focus and spending. Cut the bottom tier, where your marketing effort and spending isn't paying off. Reduce the next level of spending and shift your spending to one or two activities with the biggest impact.

This is the *marketing pyramid.* Marketers should try to move their spending up the pyramid so their marketing resources are concentrated near the top (which reflects the most effective activities). Ideally, the pyramid gets turned upside down, with most of the spending on the top floor rather than the bottom. What does your marketing pyramid look like? Can you move up it by shifting resources and investments to higher-impact marketing activities? Ideally, your marketing pyramid should have clear distinctions between the primary, secondary, and tertiary activities so you know where to concentrate your resources for best effect.

If you haven't done much marketing yet, go forth and ask nosey questions. Find marketers who sell something at least remotely similar to what you plan to sell, and ask them what activities bring them customers. First, draw out a list of at least six different things they do to find or close customers. Then ask them which are the most and least effective. Combine all this data into a speculative marketing pyramid, and begin to get quotes on and experiment with the methods yourself. Hopefully, the benchmark information you gathered will get you closer to an effective program the first time around, but plan on testing and refining your methods. Each marketer's winning formula is unique. There is no one surefire marketing plan that everybody can use.

Finding Your Marketing Formula

A marketing program should be based on a *marketing strategy,* which is the big-picture idea driving your success (if you don't have one yet, check out Book 5, Chapter 2). The marketing program is all the coordinated activities that together make up the tactics to implement that strategy. To make both strategy and program clear, write them up in a *marketing plan.*

For example, a general contractor (builder) may choose the strategy of renovating and building residential homes close to downtown areas in appealing smaller cities and larger suburbs in their region to take advantage of a trend where professional couples are moving out of the suburbs and back to revitalized downtowns. Stating this strategy clearly is a great way to bring focus to the marketing program. You now know what kinds of projects to talk about in blogs and to local media and acquaintances and to show in your website portfolio. And you know who your customers are and will soon be brainstorming ways to find more of them (for example, by networking to local realtors who help relocate them).

You don't have to get fully into the technicalities of strategies and plans right now. This chapter goes over a lot of simpler, quicker actions you can take to leverage your marketing activities into a winning program. The following sections require you to think about and write down some ideas, so get out your pencil and paper or tablet to jot down notes while you're reading.

Analyzing your four Ps

Every marketing plan needs to address the four Ps — *price, product, promotion,* and *place* — because, essentially, they represent the foundation of your business and the assets you have to sell and market your goods. You need to flesh out your product and pricing strategies, place of distribution strategies, and promotions so you can compare your strengths to your competitors', monitor your progress in each of these areas, and see how your efforts get you closer to or further from your goals.

REMEMBER

The purpose of your marketing plan is really to outline the actionable items most likely to push your *product* forward in the market, building out your *places* of distribution as efficiently as possible, *pricing* your products for trial and loyalty, and *promoting* your product and brand using the channels and tactics that best reach and influence your customers and their influencers. These may include print and digital ads, content marketing, engagement, and events, online and offline, to create awareness and sales and to build customer acquisition and retention.

Price

List the aspects of *price* that influence customer perception. What does it cost the customer to get and use your product? The list price is often an important element of the customer's perception of price, but it isn't the only one. Discounts and special offers belong on your list of price-based influence points, too. And don't forget any extra costs the customer may have to incur, like the cost of switching from another product to yours; extra costs can really affect a customer's perception of how attractive your product is. (If you can find ways to make switching from the competitor's product to yours easier or cheaper, you may be able to charge more for your product and still make more sales.)

Product

Determine which aspects of the *product* itself are important and have an influence on customer perception and purchase intentions. List all tangible features plus intangibles, such as personality, look and feel, and packaging — these are the aspects (both rational features and emotional impressions) of your product that influence customer perception.

REMEMBER

First impressions are important for initial purchase, but performance of the product over time is more important for repurchase and referrals.

Promotion

List all the ways you have to *promote* your offering by communicating with customers and prospects. Do you have a website? Do you routinely update your blog, Facebook page, and Instagram feed? Do you advertise? Send mailings?

Hand out brochures? What about the visibility of signs on buildings or vehicles? Do distributors or other marketing partners also communicate with your customer? If so, include their promotional materials and methods in your marketing program because they help shape the customer's perception, too. And what about other routine elements of customer communication, like bills? They're yet another part of the impression your marketing communications make.

TIP

The web hasn't finished revolutionizing promotion, and you can innovate to get messages out creatively and inexpensively in a lot of ways (see Book 5, Chapter 6 for details).

Place

List the aspects of *place* or distribution (in both time and space) that influence the accessibility of your product. When and where is your product available to customers? Place is a big influence, because most of the time, customers aren't actively shopping for your product. Nobody runs around all day every day looking for what you want to sell her. When someone wants something, she's most strongly influenced by what's available to her. Getting the place and timing right is a big part of success in marketing and often very difficult.

The web allows you to define your market narrowly and locally, or globally, or (and this is the really exciting idea that many businesses haven't yet picked up on) in local markets other than your physical one. For example, if you have a bookstore specializing in children's and young adult titles, then you would do best to be present in the local areas where there are the most children and young adult readers. The web can narrowly target the top five cities for your product.

Refining your list of possibilities

You need to find efficient, effective ways to positively influence customer perception. You want to use elements of your marketing program to motivate customers to buy and use your product (service, firm, whatever). The list of your current influence points for each of your four Ps (see the previous sections) is just a starting point on your journey to an optimal marketing program.

Now ask yourself the following questions: What can be subtracted because it isn't working effectively? What can be emphasized or added? Think about each of the four Ps and try to add more possible influence points. Look to competitors or successful marketers from outside your product category and industry for some fresh ideas. The longer your list of possibilities, the more likely you are to find really good things to include in your marketing program. But in the end, don't forget to focus on the handful of influence points that give you the biggest effect.

To craft your own winning formula, think of one or more new ways to reach and influence your customers and prospects in each of the four Ps and add them to your list as possibilities for your next marketing program.

Avoiding the pricing trap

WARNING

Don't be tempted to make price the main focus of your marketing program. Many marketers emphasize discounts and low prices to attract customers. But price is a dangerous emphasis for any marketing program because you're buying customers rather than winning them. That's a very, very hard way to make a profit. So unless you actually have a sustainable cost advantage (a rare thing in business), don't allow low prices or coupons and discounts to dominate your marketing program. Price reasonably, use discounts and price-off coupons sparingly, and look for other tactics to focus on in your marketing program.

Controlling Your Marketing Program

Little details can and do make all the difference in closing a sale. Does your marketing program display inconsistencies and miss opportunities to get the message across fully and well? If so, you can increase your program's effectiveness by eliminating these pockets of inconsistency to prevent out-of-control marketing.

Consider the numerous eBay sellers who fail to take and post high-quality photographs of the products they're trying to sell and then wonder why they get few bidders and have to sell for low prices. These sellers can easily upgrade their photography, but they fail to recognize the problem, so they allow this critical part of their marketing mix to remain poorly managed.

Given the reality that some of your influence points may be partially or fully uncontrolled right now, draw up a list of inconsistent and/or uncontrolled elements of your marketing program. You'll likely find some inconsistencies in each of the four Ps of your program (don't worry, though, that's common!). If you can make even one of your marketing elements work better and more consistently with your overall program and its focus, you're improving the effectiveness of your marketing. Answer the questions in Table 1-4 to pinpoint elements of your marketing mix that you need to pay more attention to.

TABLE 1-4   **Getting a Grip on Your Marketing Program**

Customer Focus
Define your customers clearly: Who are they? Where and when do they want to buy?
Are they new customers, existing customers, or a balanced mix of both?
Understand what emotional elements make customers buy: What personality should your brand have? How should customers feel about your product?
Understand what functional elements make customers buy: What features do they want and need? What information do they need to see to make their decision?

Product Attraction

What attracts customers to your product?
What's your special brilliance that sets you apart in the marketplace?
Do you reflect your brilliance throughout all your marketing efforts?

Most Effective Methods

What's the most effective thing you can do to attract customers?
What's the most effective thing you can do to retain customers?
Which of the four Ps (price, product, promotion, place) is most important in attracting and retaining customers?

Controlling Points of Contact

What are all the ways you can reach and influence customers?
Are you using the best of these right now?
Do you need to increase the focus and consistency of some of these points of contact with customers?
What can you do to improve your control over all the elements that influence customer opinion of your product?

Action Items

Draw up a list of things you can do based on this analysis to maximize the effectiveness of your marketing program.

Refining Your Marketing Expectations

When you make improvements to your marketing program, what kind of results can you expect? As a general rule, the percentage change in your program will at best correspond with the percentage change you see in sales. For example, if you change only 5 percent of your program from one year to the next, you can't expect to see more than a 5 percent increase in sales. Check out the following sections for help refining what to expect from your marketing plan.

Projecting improvements above base sales

Base sales are what you can reasonably count on if you maintain the status quo in your marketing. If, for example, you've seen steady growth in sales of 3 to 6 percent per year (varying a bit with the economic cycle), then you may reasonably project sales growth of 4 percent next year, presuming everything else stays the same. But things rarely do stay the same, so you may want to look for threats from new competitors, changing technology, shifting customer needs, and so on. Also, be careful to adjust your natural base downward if you anticipate any such threats materializing next year. If you don't change your program, your base may even be a negative growth rate, because competitors and customers tend to change even if you don't.

WARNING

After you have a good handle on what your base may be for a status quo sales projection, you can begin to adjust it upward to reflect any improvements you introduce. Be careful in doing this, however, because some of the improvements are fairly clearly linked to future sales, whereas others aren't. If you've tested or tried something already, then you have some real experience upon which to project its impact. If you're trying something that's quite new to you, be cautious and conservative about your projections until you have your own hard numbers and real-world experience to go on.

Preparing for (ultimately successful) failures

Start small with new ideas and methods in marketing so you can afford to fail and gain knowledge from the experience; then adjust and try again. Effective marketing formulas are developed through a combination of planning and experimentation, not just from planning alone. In marketing, you don't have to feel bad about making mistakes, as long as you recognize the mistakes and take away useful lessons.

What can go wrong, will go wrong . . . and you'll be fine. Try to avoid being too heavily committed to any single plan or investment. Keep as much flexibility in your marketing programs as you can. For example, don't buy ads too far in advance even though that would be cheaper, because if sales drop, you don't want to be stuck with the financial commitment to a big ad campaign. Monthly commissions for salespeople and distributors is preferable because then their pay is variable with your sales and goes down if sales fall — so you don't have to be right about your sales projections.

REMEMBER

Flexibility, cautious optimism, and contingency planning give you the knowledge that you can survive the worst. That knowledge, in turn, gives you the confidence to be a creative, innovative marketer and the courage to grow your business and optimize your marketing program. And you can afford to profit from your mistakes.

Revealing More Ways to Maximize Your Marketing Impact

You can improve a marketing program and increase your business's sales and profits in an infinite number of ways. Following are just some of the ideas you may be able to put to use; keep searching for more ideas and implement as many good ones as you can.

>> **Talk to some of your best customers.** Do they have any good ideas for you? (Ignore the ideas that are overly expensive, however. You can't count on even a good customer to worry about your bottom line.)

>> **Thank customers for their business.** A friendly "thank you" and a smile, a card or note, or a polite cover letter stuffed into the invoice envelope — all are ways to tell customers that you appreciate their business. People tend to go where they're appreciated.

>> **Change your marketing territory.** Are you spread too thin to be visible and effective? If so, narrow your focus to your core region or customer type. But if you have expansion potential, try broadening your reach bit by bit to grow your territory.

>> **Get more referrals.** Spend time talking to and helping out folks who can send customers your way. And make sure you thank anyone who sends you a lead. Positive reinforcement increases the behavior.

>> **Make your marketing more attractive (professional, creative, polished, clear, well written, and well produced).** You can often increase the effectiveness of your marketing programs by upgrading the look and feel of all your marketing communications and other components. (Did you know that the

best-dressed consultants get paid two to five times as much as the average in their fields?) See Chapter 5 of Book 5 for more about marketing communications.

» **Smile to attract and retain business.** Make sure your people have a positive, caring attitude about customers. If they don't, their negativity is certainly losing you business. Don't let people work against your marketing program. Spend time making sure they understand that they can control the success of the program, and help them through training and good management so they can take a positive, helpful, and productive approach to all customer interactions.

» **Offer a memorable experience for your customer or client.** Make sure doing business with you is a pleasant experience. Also, plan to do something that makes it memorable (in a good way, please!).

» **Know what you want to be best at and invest in being the best.** Who needs you if you're ordinary or average? Success comes from being clearly, enticingly better at something than any other company or product. Even if it's only a small thing that makes you special, know what it is and make sure you keep polishing that brilliance. It's why you deserve the sale.

» **Try to cross-sell additional products (or related services) to your customer base.** Increasing the average size of a purchase or order is a great way to improve the effectiveness of your marketing program. But keep the cross-sell soft and natural. Don't sell junk that isn't clearly within your focus or to your customer's benefit.

» **Take advantage of the increasingly local options for advertising on the web.** Don't think of the web as worldwide. Google ads can be tailored to customers in your region who are looking for services or products like yours. Now, that's incredibly local, and often an inexpensive way to get leads. There are lots of ways to localize your reach on the web.

» **Debrief customers who complain or who desert you.** Why are they unhappy? Can you do something simple to retain them? (But ignore the customers who don't match your target customer profile, because you can't be all things to all people. Target customers are discussed earlier in this chapter.)

REMEMBER

Every time you put your marketing hat on, seek to make at least a small improvement in how marketing is done in your organization and for your customers.

IN THIS CHAPTER

» **Determining your market's growth rate**

» **Operating for growth**

» **Looking at market segmentation**

» **Implementing market share and positioning strategies**

» **Giving growth hacking a try**

» **Staying innovative**

Chapter **2**

Laying a Foundation for Growth

A mantra from the Native American belief says that elements of nature provide important guiding lessons for life. For one, we're taught that we should live our life like a river, always flowing and moving forward; otherwise, we stop progressing and become stagnant, like a pond that can be compromised by moss, fungus, and other elements that hinder growth.

As a business owner, you need to look at your business from this same perspective. Where are the white water rapids, or the growth waves, and can you ride them to capitalize your business?

The simplest and most reliable marketing strategy you can prepare for your business or product is to go where the growth is. One of your top priorities should be finding opportunities that exist today and riding those *growth waves* as long as you can. Doing so will better enable you to operate at a profit so you can capitalize your next round of product development, marketing campaigns, and expansion into new markets or new distributor relationships.

This chapter helps you determine what the growth rate of your market is and evaluate opportunities to find the best options for both short- and long-term growth.

Measuring the Growth Rate of Your Market

Typically, only a few markets are growing rapidly at any given time in a given economy. Some are actually shrinking. Knowing how quickly or slowly your market is growing is vital because it's a key driver of your sales growth and profits.

Continuously monitor and evaluate the current growth rate and future growth potential of your primary market and the opportunities or threats it presents to you. These factors should be part of your brand and competitive SWOT analyses, which will help you better determine your brand's *strengths, weaknesses, opportunities,* and *threats.*

REMEMBER

Your core market should be experiencing a 5 to 10 percent overall annual growth. Anything slower than 5 percent makes it difficult for any business to thrive. If your primary market isn't growing fast enough to support your business goals, or is at risk of slowing down soon due to growth in other business sectors, you may need to find new markets you can serve, reinvent your business, or adapt your product line.

To assess your market's growth potential, you can use simple indicators of your market's current overall growth rate to guide you. These include

>> Year-over-year trends in industry-wide sales

>> An increase or decrease in the number of customers in the market

>> Changes in the type and size of purchases per customer

Mapping out these growth indicators for the past one to three years can help you see what's happening and what to expect. Although these indicators will give you rudimentary guidelines that aren't based on statistical formulas or predictive analytics, they'll give you indications of growth nonetheless.

Here are a couple of examples of the kind of information you get on various markets from Statista (www.statista.com), a statistics portal that provides data about numerous industries and markets from more than 22,500 sources. Its reports share findings on industry growth year over year, projections for future years, and more.

>> If you're in the home furnishings space, you can review statistics on furniture sales for a given year. Statista's reports break down revenue per type of store and show the market share, revenue, and sales of top leading companies in the space. And much more.

>> If you're selling mineral water, you can see growth charts for the United States and other world markets, revenue per capita, and consumption per capita, in addition to growth projections and other insightful data.

TIP

Explore its reports and those of other market information providers to see whether you can get breakdowns for specific regions you're targeting. Analyst firms like Forrester (https://go.forrester.com/) and Gartner (www.gartner.com/en), chambers of commerce, and trade associations are also good sources of marketing growth trends.

Also pay attention to the business news in specific cities in which you sell your products. Follow the trends on home sales, new construction, real estate development, job growth or decline, and other economic indicators.

REMEMBER

If you find that your primary market is shrinking or static, then it's time to look for growth opportunities and prepare for change.

Responding to a Flat or Shrinking Market

When faced with a flat or declining market, consider the following adjustments:

>> Reduce retail stores and other major investments to avoid losses.

>> Look for ways to move your sales online to expand your market reach beyond your current borders. This one step works quickly and powerfully if you're willing to invest in an e-commerce infrastructure. Be sure you find ways to efficiently fulfill and ship online orders before going this route to preserve your profit margins.

Laying a Foundation for Growth

>> Eliminate low-margin products from your physical store sales and put those online only. This will help you cut waste from inventory not moving off your shelves while not disappointing customers with fewer options. You see Walmart and Target doing this quite effectively because it helps maximize revenue per foot and lowers overhead costs.

>> Look for other places to sell your product by exploring new distributors, intermediaries, online channels, and collaborators. You can also look to renegotiate your terms with existing partners to help increase your margins. The win for them is that they don't lose a client, end up with less to sell, or have to replace you with another account.

REMEMBER

By keeping an eye on market growth rates and your focus on growth markets, you set yourself up to grow your sales and profit potential at the same time. Slow-growth and no-growth markets are brutally competitive. To win sales in either case, you often have to slash prices, ruining your profit margins. That's why smart marketers make a strategic point of focusing on growth markets and pay close attention to growth rates in all their markets so they stay alert to slowdowns that may indicate a need to move on.

Figuring out how to reinvent yourself before you have to is critical to staying profitable and alive. Never assume that you can glide on your successes. There is no rest for the successful business executive or enterprise that seeks sustainable growth.

TIP

Grow revenue by adding services to support your products. Look for services that appeal to all or specific segments. The goal is to add valuable new revenue streams in case your customer acquisition stagnates. Consider these examples:

>> Utility companies now offer ancillary services such as home delivery of air filters for furnaces and air conditioners, surge protection for appliances and electronics in case of lightning strikes, and more. These subscription-based services increase customer lifetime value and current revenue.

>> Software companies engage in licensing, or SaaS (software as a service) models, which ensures revenue flow every month instead of one-time big chunks of income by selling their systems for a high price one transaction at a time. In the long term, this typically adds up to much more than they could have charged outright.

In addition, look at the geographic areas you target most to assess their economic health and strength. If your current market isn't growing, look for nearby markets with stronger population growth and economic projections. Look also at a market's workforce to ensure that it has the skills you need at affordable salaries. In recent years, Utah has become a hotbed for high-tech and software companies because the workforce is highly educated and the cost of living still relatively low. As a result, companies can operate at lower costs than Silicon Valley and make more profits without compromising quality of operations or human capital.

Finding Your Best Growth Strategies

Market growth and expansion are clearly the most common strategies in marketing and the foundations of sustainable brands. The ideas, respectively, are to get your product to customers as efficiently as possible and to start selling to new groups of prospective customers, in terms of demographics and geography, to grow and sustain profitability.

Clearly, your marketing strategies will differ if you're new to an established market, are an existing brand looking for growth, or are launching new products within an established brand to grow new revenue streams. The following sections cover some tactics for achieving success in these and other scenarios.

Go to market

A go-to-market (GTM) strategy is your blueprint for getting your product to the end customer and achieving a high level of sales and awareness at the same time. Pricing, distribution, and publicity are key to GTM strategies. Following are some innovative ways to take a product to market that get you noticed and help you build your base.

Build a presence

Large companies with much to invest in new product launches may start out with their own retail stores to ensure that they reach their target customers and have total control over the product demo and buying experience. Apple carefully created the shopping experience and built a brand persona at its own retail stores before allowing its products to be sold elsewhere, like Amazon and Best Buy. If you have the money, this is a great way to build a strong platform on which a new brand can grow.

Crowdfunding

Even though campaigns on Kickstarter and other crowdfunding sites are designed to raise funds over selling products, they can help create a strong base of champions to help spread the word. If you create a strong campaign with product demos and great videos and gets lots of media talking about your campaign, awareness will skyrocket without having to pay for most of it. Additionally, if your campaign can create enough emotional enthusiasm to succeed, you'll likely have a lot of excited backers who want you to succeed and thus are willing to tell your story and promote your products and brand to their networks. And if each of those people has a network of 500 people on just Facebook, Twitter, and LinkedIn, that's a lot of valuable publicity via the most credible channel ever — consumer-to-consumer communications.

Beta testing

Beta testing can work really well. For example, one particular new business got off the ground recently, and one of the ways it did so was through a beta program. Instead of offering introductory or discounted pricing to get off the ground, because it's hard to raise it even after a launch price, people were invited to apply to be part of the beta test whereby they received reduced pricing if they allowed their success stories in the business's marketing materials. It worked brilliantly.

People often want to be part of a test to find a new way to do something better, but they shy away from "introductions" because they don't want to be the first to buy an unproven product. And deeply discounted products can send a signal that it's not worth much anyway, and you're just full of hype.

TIP

If you invite consumers to participate in a test, offer to share some information about your category or a how-to guide that is related to the product being tested so that the value of participation is more than price-oriented.

TIP

After your pilot stage is completed, send participants a report and insights about next steps. Consider offering them a small discount on their next purchase or to renew a subscription to your services as a way to get them to remain an active customer.

Different experiences

Marketing today isn't about the price, special offer, or even the promise and function of a product as much as it is the experience. An experience is what creates the feelings that make people want to come back for more. The experience can come from using the product, trying the service, or from appreciating the service and kinship that follows after the sale. To spark a new feeling of excitement for a new product, guerilla marketing can play a big role.

Grow what you have for higher profitability

Two powerful ways to expand your market position and sales involve introducing more products into the market and using a bestseller to draw more customers to your brand and expanded product line. The sections that follow highlight how you can go about accomplishing both.

Offering more products

Introducing new products is a strong way to expand your share of a particular market — eventually. If you sold only 10 products last year and you offer 20 this year, you just may find that your sales double. Of course, there's a good chance your new products won't sell as well as your old ones at first, but if you persist, you should be able to ramp up their sales over the course of a few years.

When looking to offer more products, you have two options:

>> Add new products simply by reselling or distributing products that complement your current line and meet some need of your current customer base.

>> Innovate to create one or more new products that nobody else sells.

Either way, you have the twofold challenge of informing customers that you have something new to offer and convincing them to take a look — and then getting them to buy it before a bigger competitor gets wind of your idea and decides to offer its own version of a similar product, too. If this happens, the competitor is likely to undercut you on price and overwhelm you on distribution due to greater resources.

These reasons alone illustrate why being especially visible and persistent in the first few months of a new product launch or market expansion is so critical. A concentrated blast of marketing communications (see Chapter 5 of Book 5) is the key to opening a new market successfully. With all the content management systems available today, doing this is getting more and more efficient.

TIP

Create visibility by showing people your brand or product often and in a consistent, professional manner. You can do this through publicity efforts to get visibility on blogs, news channels, and so on, advertising, direct mail, email blasts, search engine marketing, signage (such as billboards and transit ads), sales calls, or presence at conferences and trade shows.

Another great way to introduce a new product for both an existing brand or a new one is to sell it at kiosks, which are less expensive and often more visible than retail stores in shopping malls. Anson Calder, a luxury travel accessories brand, launched by opening a kiosk in a busy New York City building, which let people see its products firsthand. By doing this, it was able to introduce its style and quality and drive sales to the website, which is its primary commerce channel.

TIP

If your product is different, set up a demo station and offer coffee or snacks to keep people lingering longer and staying for the whole demo. Free food and drink have stopping power at malls or even stores like Costco. Collect email and other usable information before giving away that free coffee so you can build your database at the same time.

WARNING

Risks and costs increase when you experiment with *new products* — anything you're not accustomed to making and marketing. Consequently, you should discount your first year's sales projections for a new market by some factor to reflect the degree of risk. A good general rule is to cut back the sales projections by 20 to 50 percent, depending on your judgment of how new and risky the product is to you and your team. It may also cost you double the time and money to make each sale when entering a new market, because your new prospects won't be familiar with your brand, and you likely won't have a well-defined marketing formula at the start. Budget accordingly.

Riding a bestseller to the top

If you have a *bestseller* — a product that substantially outsells your other products — it may make sense to put a lot of your resources toward maximizing sales for this product and using the profits to grow other areas of your business. Some marketing experts look for bestsellers to achieve sales that are at least ten times the norm; outstanding bestsellers can achieve a hundred or more times the normal level of sales for a product in their category. If you have just one bestseller in your line, growing your revenues and profits is fairly easy as long as it remains popular.

You can expand demand for a top-selling product by creating new experiences around it or partnering with others to help package or bundle your products with their products. Partnering or bundling works well with software and in retail. If you sell comfy throw blankets, for example, partner with a company that makes fuzzy slippers or single-serve coffee machines to help round out the cozy-at-home experience.

TIP

How do you create a bestselling product? First, look for one. Don't be content with products that sell moderately well. Keep looking for something that has more excitement and potential. Test many alternatives. When you find one that seems to have momentum (you'll know it has momentum when early sales figures surprise you by their rapid growth), quickly refocus your marketing efforts on that product. Make it the heart of sales calls and ads, feature it at the top of your website's home page, talk to the media about it, and offer specials for new customers who try it. Bestsellers are found and made by marketers who believe in them. Be a believer!

When you have a product with bestseller potential, your marketing strategy should be to ride it as hard and as far as you can. Write a marketing plan that puts the majority of your budget and efforts behind the bestseller and gives the rest of your product line as minimal a budget as you think you can get away with. The bestseller will tend to lift all sales by attracting customers to your brand, which will likely have a strong reputation for quality and service due to your bestseller, so you won't have to worry as much about the rest of your products.

After you have a bestseller, you should see your profits grow. Use some of these profits to look for the next bestseller because, like all good things, your current bestseller will eventually lose its momentum. Always be looking for your next top product so you can have it ready and waiting in the wings. Test ideas and options, and be patient. If you can't find another bestseller, switch to another marketing strategy. You don't have to have a bestseller to succeed, but it sure is nice if you can find a product that fits this strategy.

TIP

While your products are selling and your customer satisfaction is high, referral marketing and reward programs are critical to maximize your sales and profit potential. Reward your customers who continue to buy your products by giving them discounts for repeat purchases. Also consider giving referring customers a financial reward and see what that alone can do for profits. System Pavers pays $500 for each customer referred who completes a qualifying project. It puts no limit on how much one customer can make in referrals. This act of reciprocity not only makes current customers happy, but also keeps the brand and new products on their minds. And it has helped grow profits very successfully as well.

So if, for example, a company paid out just $1 million in referral rewards, that is 2,000 projects. If a company's average sale is $10,000, that adds up to $20 million! With no advertising costs involved, that's a pretty amazing return.

Making a hot product even hotter

Another strategy is to influence the supply and demand for a product that's showing signs of being another one of your top sellers. You can influence sales and pricing by how you choose to distribute your product after it has established a stronghold in your market. One way to do this is to release a limited amount of product to specialty stores so that people have to seek out your product. If you distribute through the mass retailers, you lose the chance to build a competitive edge with exclusivity or scarcity. You also have the freedom to change your price as demand increases, which you often give away when you contract with Walmart or another mass retailer that demands fixed prices.

Beanie Babies are a great example of this strategy. Creator Ty Warner released his Beanie Babies for short periods of time and then retired them, making them collector items that made people want them even more. And for some of his creations, he produced only a couple of hundred bears, making them instant and rare collector items. The value of some of his bears at the peak of the Beanie Baby frenzy reached upwards of $3,000.

Take a look at your distribution strategies for your top products. Can you produce less and make them more valuable? Can you change your access points to make them seem more exclusive? Or do you just want to keep selling a product until it doesn't sell anymore and pocket the profits while you can?

WARNING

There are many considerations for how to maximize the profitability of your top-selling products. Just remember, what's hot now may not be hot in a matter of weeks. In the case of Beanie Babies, they were one of the biggest frenzies and crashes of the 1990s, as described by Zac Bissonnette, who wrote *The Great Beanie Baby Bubble: Mass Delusion and the Dark Side of Cute*. When the company announced that it would stop producing the toys that had become collectors' obsessions — leading to a murder and a custody battle in court over a divorcing couple splitting their "babies" — the frenzy almost dried up as quickly as it had heated up. Those big-priced little Beanie Babies on eBay lost value quickly, and the fad faded to where today many consumers don't really know what a Beanie Baby is or was.

REMEMBER

Whatever your plan for maximizing the growth of your current top-selling products, have an exit strategy in mind, too. Be prepared to answer the following questions:

>> At what point will you cease production before you end up producing more than you can sell if trends and fads change?

>> At what point are you willing to let your product become a commodity, selling at a fixed price?

>> At what point will you replace this product with a new one that is likely to have the same appeal to the same consumers so that you have an opportunity to create another highly profitable product and cycle?

Growing a Market Segmentation Strategy

To succeed, a *market segmentation strategy* needs to be more than just sorting customers into like groups so you can build marketing around specific personas that appeal to each group with relevance. It involves messaging on psychological influences and producing relevant content for each segment, often simultaneously, to keep sales moving in large quantities rather than periodic spurts.

You can create segments along numerous lines. The key is to sort them in ways that make sense for how people process decisions to buy, past transactions, attitudes, and so on, and how you're set up to reach each segment efficiently. Digital asset management platforms that enable you to create new versions and release content for all channels simultaneously are key to enabling you to communicate to all segments at the same time with high efficiencies.

REMEMBER

Step one in a segmentation strategy is to have a strong content marketing system that can automatically adapt your digital and print marketing material for each segment and enable you to put all versions in market at the same time instead of staggering sales promotions that can delay your sales and overall success.

The advantage of a segmentation strategy is that it allows you to tailor your product and your entire marketing effort to a clearly defined group with uniform, specific characteristics. If you find that one segment strongly outperforms all others consistently over time, you may want to consider a niche strategy whereby you drop your focus on all other segments and channel all your resources on the one segment. In a world that's looking for more customization and personalized service, niche marketing might just make the most sense. It helps you better compete with larger businesses because you can specialize and personalize in ways they can't.

Customer segments

One of the most proven and common segmentation strategies is based on RFM — recency, frequency, and monetary value of customers. When you sort customers accordingly, you identify those customers with the highest propensity for repeat sales and profitability for your business and establish groups with like values to which you can communicate with "mass personalization." RFM is one of the basic fundamentals of a strong data-driven marketing strategy.

You may build customer segments on the following:

>> RFM

>> Products purchased

>> Transaction value

>> Frequency of purchase

>> Generational attitudes

>> Trust equity in brand and/or category

>> Emotional selling proposition (ESP) profiles

>> Conversion channel (did they come in via social, web, retail, referral, or other?)

>> Purchasing and browsing patterns

>> Demographics (education, gender, income)

>> Geography

>> Relationship with brand (warm lead, cold call, or established customer)

With a strong database program and analytics tools, you can find out about your current customers and how you can build segments to capture growth trends or better nurture future leads. For example, if a subset of your customers is growing faster than the rest, consider specializing in those types of customers to gain more of their business or purchasing more lists that replicate that customer set. You can also adjust your product, pricing, promotion, or distribution plans for each segment. If you do this, you need to adapt your marketing content for each group.

TIP

If your customer base is shrinking or your current segments aren't responding as desired, consider adding a new segment. For example, a consulting firm specializing in coaching healthcare executives can decide to start offering a similar service to nonprofits, expanding its market base without having to change its core competencies or budget for expensive new product development.

Niche marketing

Specializing in a specific market segment can give you the momentum you need to power past your competition, but it may not always be the right approach for your operation. The niche strategy may work well for you if

>> You think your business can be more profitable by specializing in a more narrowly defined segment than you do now.

>> You face too many competitors in your broader market and can't seem to carve out a stable, profitable customer base of your own.

>> It takes better advantage of things you're good at.

>> You're too small to be one of the leaders in your overall market or industry. Maybe you can be the leader in a specific segment of your market.

Developing a Market Share Strategy

Scaling your business is obviously the best way to improve your ability to compete with larger, more established brands and increase your market share. *Market share* is, very simply, your sales as a percentage of total sales for your product category in your market (or in your market segment if you use a segmentation strategy). If you sell $2 million worth of widgets and the world market totals $20 million per year, then your share of market is 10 percent. It's that simple. Or is it?

Following are some insights on market share and how you can implement one effectively.

Define your metrics

Before you can completely determine your market share, determine the metrics that matter most to you. Is it better to determine market share by dollars earned, containers shipped, or units sold? Pick whatever seems to make sense for your product and the information you have access to.

Establish a benchmark

To effectively increase your market share, you must have an accurate picture of where you stand currently. Here's a simple method for estimating market size and share.

1. **Estimate the number of customers in your market.**

   For instance, guess how many people in your country are likely to buy toothpaste or how many businesses in your city buy consulting services. With companies like Statista (www.statista.com), a consumer statistics portal, and D&B Hoovers (www.hoovers.com), a commercial database of businesses and executives, you can get fairly precise insights on the size, sales, and market leaders for any industry.

2. **Estimate how much each customer buys a year, on average.**

   Does each customer buy six tubes of toothpaste? Fifteen hours of consulting services? You can check your sales records for specific data for your brand or turn to industry research for specific information and year-over-year growth data.

3. **Multiply the two figures together to get the total size of the annual market and then divide your unit sales into it to get your share.**

You can also look at information compiled by the U.S. Census Data (www.census.gov) to get information about population and economic trends to help you with forecasting and growth plans.

Alternatively, you may estimate, for example, that three-quarters of the wholesalers handle low-cost, inexpensive teas and therefore don't compete directly with your specialty tea business. In that case, you can calculate your market share of the quarter of total sales that are similar specialty teas as $0.525 \div (0.25 \times 3.886)$, which gives you 54 percent. That's a much larger share based on a narrower definition of the market. Estimating your market share helps you determine which market share numbers are correct.

REMEMBER

To create a market share strategy, you need to clearly identify and define your product and where it fits into your market. In other words, you need to know your *product category* — the general grouping of competitive products to which your product belongs (be it merchandise or a service). Knowing your product category is extremely important. If you don't know where your product fits into the market, you can't begin to develop a strategy to build on and increase your existing market share. For example, if you're a boutique business selling specialty teas from physical retail locations, you need to determine the following:

>> Are you competing with mass-market brands?

>> How do you compete with other specialty tea shops with physical locations that offer a gathering place rather than just a product?

>> Are you losing market share to online sellers?

>> Are there better opportunities for growth by selling as a wholesaler instead of a retailer?

You can learn about consumptions patterns and project consumer behavior by studying reports from trade associations, Statista data, and other sources that can guide you on what's happening and what to expect in your industry.

Do the math

If your goals are to increase market share by a certain percentage or dollar value, you need to do some calculations to determine what those figures really are. For example: If you own a tea store in Shanghai, you could have a goal of increasing share of tea sales by 1.5 percentage points. If each point of share is worth roughly $40,000 in annual sales (1 percent of the total sales in the market), then you'll likely need a plan that involves spending, say, an extra $25,000 to win that 1.5 percent share gain. If it works, you can gain an extra $60,000. But will it work?

To be cautious, you, as the marketer, may want to discount this projection of $60,000 in additional sales by a risk factor of, say, 25 percent, which cuts your projected gain back to $45,000. If you exceed it, you can enjoy the reward. If not, you avoid setting your business up for missed sales projections, which can affect profitability and your own credibility.

Be realistic about the time it takes to reach market share goals. A sales projection starting at the current level of sales in the first month and ramping up to the projected increase by, say, the sixth month, may be reasonable. Dividing $45,000 by 12 to find the monthly value of the risk-discounted 1.5 share point increase gives you $3,750 in extra monthly sales for the sixth month and beyond. Lower increases apply to earlier months when the program is just starting to kick in. But the marketing expenses tend to be concentrated in the early months, reflecting the need to invest in advance to grow your market share.

REMEMBER

Market share gives you a simple way of comparing your progress to your competitors' from period to period. If your share drops, you're losing; if your share grows, you're winning. It's that simple. Base your goals on realistic, actionable items that you can measure. For example, if your goal is to increase share from 5 to 7 percent with a product upgrade and trial-stimulating special offers, be sure you can attribute market share growth to those actions so you know what's working and what isn't.

Designing a Positioning Strategy

A *positioning strategy* reflects the emotional fulfillment and psychological relevance of building ESPs (emotional selling propositions) over USPs (unique value propositions) because "unique" isn't a sustainable strategy. It's too easy for a competitor with more resources or a quicker time-to-market process to duplicate and take away a "unique" advantage. A successful positioning strategy focuses on getting customers or prospects to see your product by the emotional and functional values it offers, to trust your claims about quality and service, and to try your products before considering competitors' offerings.

REMEMBER

Your positioning strategy needs to reflect your ESP strategy. As you plan for growth, identify new markets where your ESP and positioning will stand out and be appealing to consumers. Do you need to adapt your ESP or how you position it and your other promises for various cultures or demographics that you're trying to penetrate or dominate? The more you know about each market you operate in, the more effective you'll be.

Envisioning your position: An exercise in observation and creativity

Good positioning means your product has mind share among consumers, which will in turn help you gain market share. Your positioning statement should be believable and actionable. It should reflect the core values of what you offer and make a statement about how you differ from competitors' or even functional alternatives.

TIP

As you do your competitive analysis, compare your positioning strategy against competitors to see whether you're saying the same thing in different words or whether your promise and emotional value really stand out. Just as important, do your product, sales, and service processes fulfill the promise you make in your positioning statements, sales promises, and other marketing materials?

Aligning your positioning strategy with growth initiatives

After you've defined the emotional value you offer in addition to the product value or competitive difference that sets you apart, you can start building growth plans accordingly. For example, if you produce and sell organic healthy snack foods for children that replace the abundance of junk food marketed to kids daily, your positioning could reflect the health benefits and emotional relief parents gain by knowing that they're not jeopardizing their child's growth by giving into demands for food that isn't healthy. As a result of having a healthier but tasty snack food for children, you can expand to niche and specialty markets that are showing big growth opportunity. Sometimes these may be geographical markets. Health food and fitness services are big in Boulder, Colorado, but may not be so big in some parts of the south where less healthy types of food are consumed regularly.

For a product such as this, you can target influencers who are directly related to parents who are highly concerned about the physical and mental impact of poor nutrition. Influencers whom you can target for resellers may include, for example, allergists, pediatricians, youth sports clubs, and associations and government bodies focused on nutritional research and education.

For any given industry, you can find a long list of organizations with whom you can build alliances for reselling your products, referring others, or introducing you to consumers who are right for what you offer, which leads to another critical strategy in today's world of many options and confusing alternatives: *growth hacking* (see the next section).

Growth Hacking to Build Leads and Market Share

Although the term *growth hacking* may be relatively new to this generation of marketing, the concept isn't. It's just a highly concentrated process for reaching out to your networks to build direct leads and increase your visibility and position in a marketplace by linking to others' social and digital assets and creating collaborative opportunities.

It's also about gaining mind share by taking advantage of the social and digital tools that enable people to find your brand ahead of others. The following sections offer some tips about growth-hacking strategies that cost little to execute but can pay off in a big way.

Search

Know what and who is getting the most attention in your market. Through tools as simple as Google's Search console, you can discover what websites are getting the most impressions and highest click-through rates and what keywords in your industry are getting the same. Pay attention to how the brands getting the most impressions are marketing themselves and what keywords are most popular for consumer searches in your industry. Make sure you include these in your positioning and marketing messages. And make sure you build your own search engine optimization (SEO) and search engine marketing (SEM) strategies around the keywords and products most searched by your core consumers. These will change and change frequently, so keeping current on these trends is critical.

Build links

There's a reason LinkedIn is growing in size and value to marketers in all industries and of businesses of all sizes. Take stock of your own network (if you're not on LinkedIn, get on it now; see Chapter 6 of Book 5 for details). How big is your network? Do you have 1,000 or more connections? How many of those can you name? And for how many of those do you have personal or work email addresses? Probably "not a lot" is your answer to both of those final questions.

TIP

In today's world of digital networks, if you're not mining your network connections, you're likely walking away from a gold mine. You need to create templates for communicating with members in ways that get them to respond. Try emailing connections on LinkedIn and asking whether they'd be interested in a free white paper or participating in a brief survey. For either of these, they need to share their email address with you, which you can then add to your database for content marketing. You've just gained a critical email address and sparked a direct relationship that you or your sales team can nurture.

Fish for emails

Although *phishing* most often refers to unethical scams designed to get personal contact information to exploit consumers, *fishing* — the kind that uses bait to hook people on your brand — is still good and pays off. Fishing for emails is as simple as offering something of value to consumers in exchange for their email address. You don't need click bait to get people to participate if you offer something real and of real value.

For example, if you're a marketing consultant and you design a banner ad or email that says, "Need help calculating your customer lifetime value?" you can require people to click on a form in your marketing template that sends their email address directly to you. Bam! You've got another email for your growth marketing campaigns and a lead with whom you've just started a new relationship.

Try tripwires

Tripwire is yet another new term, relatively speaking, for marketing tactics but not a new concept or strategy. Tripwire marketing is simply the act of offering something people can't refuse. It's one of those "big blowout sales" used car lots have been using for years. You see these all the time in infomercials on TV and now through digital channels all over the web. You sell someone on the benefit it offers and then offer it for a limited time as a free trial ("get now, pay later if you keep it" approach) or for such a low price that no one can say no. The trick according to Neil Patel, a growth marketing guru, is to keep your price pretty low (less than $50) and to offer a more expensive, better value product at checkout. According to Patel, at least 30 percent of your shoppers should end up buying the higher-end product or better value, which you can position as your "best value."

Hire a growth hacker

So how do you go about integrating these tactics into your growth strategy given that many are time-consuming? Simple. Hire a growth hacker who can dedicate her days to sending out templates for invitations to connects, offers for white papers, and other messages for you. If you have a well-connected sales or executive team, open their networks for your growth hacker. Your goal should be to establish a connection with about 20 percent of those to whom you reach out. Again, if you have a network of 3,000 people on your social sites, 20 percent is 600. Now multiply that number by five executives on your team and you'll have a new database of 3,000 highly qualified leads to nurture and grow.

TIP

To read more about growth hacking, follow Neil Patel's blog at www.neil patel.com.

Selling Innovative Products

Every product category has a limited life. At least in theory — and usually in all-too-real reality — some new type of product comes along to displace the old one. The result is called *the product life cycle*, a never-ending cycle of birth, growth, and decline, fueled by the endless inventiveness of competing businesses. Product categories arise, spread through the marketplace, and ultimately decline as replacements arise and begin their own life cycles. If you're marketing an innovative product that's just beginning to catch on (in what marketers call the growth phase of the life cycle), you can expect rapid growth in sales and profits.

REMEMBER

Your growth strategy and actions will be only as good as your product. If you don't keep up with changing technology, consumer needs, and demands, no plan for growth will pay off. Imagine trying to sell a typewriter when personal computers were taking off and coming down in price. No amount of imagination, linking, connecting, and lead generation can overcome an out-of-date product that has no value in the current world. Your strategic imagination is the only limitation to your growth.

Chapter **3**

Taking Stock of Your Business Image

Right now, even if you're not doing much marketing, your business is making an impression. Somewhere, someone is encountering your ad, seeing your logo, calling your company, visiting your website, reading a review or article about your business, or walking through your door. Maybe someone is driving by the sign on your locked-up shop at night or running across your business name in a web search.

As a result, right now people are drawing conclusions about your business. Based on what they're seeing or hearing, they're deciding whether your business looks like a top-tier player, an economical alternative, or a struggling start-up — all based on impressions that you may not even be aware that you're making.

This chapter is about where and when your business makes impressions and how you can align your communications so that people form the opinion you want them to have.

Making First Impressions

You've heard the saying a thousand times: "You never get a second chance to make a first impression." The advice is self-evident and sounds easy enough to follow until you realize that your business most often makes its first impressions when you're nowhere to be found. In your stead is your website, your Facebook page, your voicemail message, your ad or direct mailing, your business sign, your employees, some customer's review or rating, or maybe your logo on the back of a Little League player's uniform.

Ask yourself the following questions as you assess whether the impressions you're making on customers represent you well:

>> When people receive multiple impressions of your business, do they see and hear evidence of a consistent, reliable, well-managed, successful enterprise?

>> Do your communications look and sound like they all represent the same company?

>> Does your logo always look the same? What about your use of typestyles and color scheme? How about the sound and smell of your business? And the tone or voice of your communications?

REMEMBER

People form impressions through all senses. Be sure you're consistent through all encounters.

>> If you use a tagline or slogan, is it always the same or does it change from one presentation to the next?

>> Do search engines deliver results that are consistent with the image you want customers to see and believe about your business?

TIP

To evaluate what kinds of impressions you're making, begin by tracking the ways in which customers approach your business. Then work backward to determine what marketing efforts led to their arrivals. After that, work forward to determine what kinds of impressions customers form when they actually "meet" your business, whether that first contact is made in person, over the phone, or online.

Encountering your business through online searches

What customers see online is fundamental to their impressions of what you and your business are and offer. Book 5, Chapter 6 is all about connecting with customers online. This section is about assessing what customers see when they search online and whether their search results align with what you want them to believe about your business.

Study search results for your name and the name of your company and products. First, Google your name, and then search with Bing, DuckDuckGo, and other search engines. Here's what to look for:

>> Does the name you're searching for appear prominently in the first few pages of results — which is as far as most people look?

>> Are you happy with what you see? Do links to your name lead to sites with information that's relevant to the brand image you want to project? (See Book 5, Chapter 4 for more on your brand.)

>> Do top results lead straight to your business website or to a map or phone number for your company?

>> When you search your name in online images and video, are you happy with what you see or are results inconsistent with the image you want your business to project?

Arriving at your website

To people shopping online, your website *is* your business. To everyone else, it's a gateway to your business. Here are some quick points to keep in mind as you develop an online presence that supports your business image:

REMEMBER

>> **You have to work to be found online.** With the web already hosting at least a trillion pages, and the number of URLs or site addresses increasing by hundreds of thousands each day, any business now needs the following:

- A website with its own name in the site address

- Social media pages

- A network of online links that point web users to the business site

- A commitment to optimizing the site's visibility in search engine results

- A communication effort that features links to all major online locations in all ads and marketing materials

TIP

>> **People arriving at your site may not know where they are.** They may be coming from search engine results or online links that send them to an internal page of your site, so be sure that every page features your name or logo, along with a link to your home page.

>> **Realize that most customers are channel agnostics.** They migrate between online and offline encounters and expect continuity as they travel. Whether they see your Facebook page, your website or blog, your traditional media ads, your display windows, or you and your staff members in person, they expect a single business image. Be sure your online identity meshes with your offline identity, right down to the style of typeface you use, the kinds of messages you present, and the way you display your business name and logo.

REMEMBER

Don't ignore the fact that more than eight out of ten smartphone owners search from their phones while they're shopping, traveling, or otherwise away from their computers, even when they're in their own homes. Be sure to create a simplified mobile version of your website (see Book 2, Chapter 5 for more details).

Managing email impressions

Sometime in the late 1990s (in other words, ancient history), the number of email messages eclipsed the volume of traditional letters sent by businesses. Yet while businesses routinely format, proofread, print, and file traditional correspondence, they send email messages spontaneously, often with no standard policy and rarely with a company record for future referral. Such an informal approach to email is fine for thank-you notes or quick updates to customers, but what if the message includes a fee estimate or a notice that client-requested changes will result in an additional thousand dollars of expense? And what if the staff member who sent the email is no longer with your company when the customer questions the bill?

TIP

For the sake of your business, set a few email guidelines:

>> **Unify all company emails by use of a common signature.** A *signature* or *sig* is a few lines of text that appear at the end of every email message. The signature usually includes

- The name of the person sending the message

- Your business logo

- A tagline that tells what your business does

- Your business address, phone number, and website URL

- Often a promotional message or offer

Note: You can create a signature in almost any email program. Go to the help function for instructions.

>> **Set a tone and style for email messages.** In well-managed businesses, traditional letters go out on company letterhead, use a consistent typeface and style, and employ clear, professional language. Consider email a dressed-down version of your formal correspondence. It can be more relaxed and more spontaneous, and it can (and should) be more to the point — but it can't be impolite or unprofessional.

>> **Respond to email within four hours, even if your response is simply a one-line note that offers a complete answer within days.** An email that isn't answered promptly falls into the same category as phone calls that are placed on endless hold or long, slow-moving lines at the cash register. The customer service impact is devastating.

>> **Back up email messages so they're easily accessible.** This is especially important should an employee quit or not be available when a customer questions a pricing, delivery, or other promise made through email communications.

>> **Consider establishing business-wide email standards.** Keep email messages short, encourage the use of greetings and standard punctuation, and limit the use of emoticons. Also avoid colored backgrounds or graphics that make messages slow to download on customer computers or mobile devices.

Arriving by telephone

Often, with no prompting at all, callers will tell you how they found your number: "John Jones suggested I call," or "I'm curious about the new whatchamacallits I see in your ad," or "I was on your website, but I couldn't tell whether your business is open Sundays." If the conversation doesn't naturally disclose how the person obtained your phone number, take a few seconds (but only a few seconds) to ask something like, "I'm glad you called us. We're always working to improve our communications, and I'd love to note how you got our phone number."

The responses help you see what is and isn't working to generate phone calls. They also help you determine which first impression points bring qualified prospects into your business and which ones reel in people who are "just looking." In the latter case, realize that the problem is rarely with the caller and most often with the impression point.

For example, a real estate brokerage that specializes in high-end residential properties continuously fields calls from shoppers trying to buy homes in a much lower price tier than those listed by the realty company. Upon questioning, the real estate agents discover that most of the mismatched callers found the phone number in a regional real estate guide in which the company's ad read, "We have your dream home." The agents realize that their ad message is appealing to the wrong target market. As a result, they amend their ad to read, "Specialists in fine properties and estate homes."

REMEMBER To get the right prospects to call your business, be sure to target your communications carefully, help customers understand what you offer, make your phone number appropriately large and bold, give people a reason to dial it, and then be ready to treat every call as a valuable business opportunity.

REMEMBER All marketing communications — whether through advertising, direct mail, email, networking, presentations, social media, or website visits — aim to achieve a single goal: a personal contact and the opportunity to make a sale. Chapter 5 in Book 5 has more information on marketing communications that work.

When the hard-won call comes, don't fumble the opportunity:

» **Answer calls promptly.** Pick up after the first or second ring whenever possible. Even if you have a receptionist, train others to serve as backups, answering any call that reaches a third ring.

» **Transfer calls as quickly as you answer them.** Be prompt about getting the caller to the appropriate person in your business. If that person isn't available, say so immediately. Offer to take a message, put the caller through to voicemail, or find someone else to help.

On hold is a dangerous and costly place to leave valuable prospects.

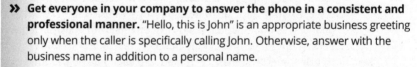

WARNING » **Get everyone in your company to answer the phone in a consistent and professional manner.** "Hello, this is John" is an appropriate business greeting only when the caller is specifically calling John. Otherwise, answer with the business name in addition to a personal name.

» **Keep voicemail messages brief and friendly.** Use wording that conveys your business purpose and personality and offer no more than three options so callers can quickly jump to the option they seek. For example:

"Thank you for calling 20/20 Vision. We're focusing on eye exams and frame selections right now, but please press 1 for our hours and location, or press 2 to leave a message. We promise to call you back within the hour."

TIP » **Ask your phone company to monitor and report on your hang-up rate.** Multiple rings, lengthy hold times, and voicemail responses are reasons for callers to abandon their efforts to reach your business.

TIP

Consider placing mirrors near the phones if your business relies heavily on telephone contact. People instinctively smile at themselves in mirrors because it makes them look more attractive, and a smile also makes a voice more attractive — more natural, friendly, and enthusiastic. You'll be able to hear the difference, and so will the person on the other end of the line.

Approaching your business in person

If a person walks into your business, looks around, and asks, "What kind of a business is this?" you can make an educated guess that the drop-in was unplanned and triggered only by a look at your signage or window displays. (You may want to improve these impression points to better address this obvious question.)

TIP

Many businesses boast that their signage is their most effective means of attracting first-time visitors. But before banking on your sign to draw people in, realize that when people respond only to your signage, they're making spur-of-the-moment, drop-in visits — perhaps at a time when they're short on both time and money. Instead, work to achieve *destination visits* by making impressions and cultivating interest well in advance of prospects noticing your sign and walking through your door.

Leading people to your business

If your business relies on consumer visits, convey directions on your website and in ads, mailings, and other advance communications. Build a mobile version of your website to quickly help on-the-go customers reach your location (see Chapter 5 in Book 2 for details). Invest in directional road signs or billboards if appropriate. Also, be sure that when visitors arrive at your business, whether you're located in a high-rise building or a home office, they see a sign with your business name and instructions on how to reach your front door.

Parking

Is your business's parking area clean, well marked, well lit, and capable of making a good impression? If a parking fee is involved, do you have a validation program that customers know about in advance? Have you saved the nearest spots for customers rather than for your car or your employees' cars? (How many times have you driven into a parking lot only to see the spot nearest to the door marked "Reserved for Manager"? And what do those three simple words tell you about your standing as a customer?)

Nearing your front door

As a prospect approaches your entrance, does your business look open and inviting? Here's a list of questions to consider:

TIP

>> Is your signage visible, clean, and professional?

>> Do signs and window displays clearly indicate what your business does?

>> Is your business well lit?

>> Is the entrance easy to find?

>> Is your entryway signage welcoming or is it papered with negatives such as "No UPS," "No Smoking," "Deliveries Use Back Door," or "No Outside Food or Beverages"? With just a little editing, you can state your rules in a positive way. "Let us hold your umbrella and packages while you shop" sure beats "No backpacks."

>> If your business success relies on foot traffic, do your windows have show-stopping capacity? Stand back and look hard. If necessary, adjust lighting to improve visibility or to cut glare. Replace small objects with big, bold items that are magnets for attention. Use mirrors to slow people down and also to help them adjust their dispositions (as noted earlier in this chapter, people automatically put on a friendly face when they look in the mirror), both of which are likely to benefit your business.

The moment of arrival

Walk through the process of approaching and entering your business. Forget for a minute that this is *your* business. Imagine how it feels to a stranger. Does it convey the right set of impressions? Consider the following:

TIP

>> Is your entry area impeccably clean?

>> Is the entry area decorated to make a strong statement about the nature of your business, its customers, and its products?

Do your surroundings present and promote *your* company, or do they inadvertently promote other companies whose logos happen to appear on calendars, posters, coffee cups, and other items that sneak their way into your environment? Rather than making your lobby a display for others, turn it into a showcase of your own products, your clients, or your staff. If you want customers to be proud to associate with your business, proudly spotlight your offerings.

>> Does your business have a clear "landing area" — a place where a visitor can pause upon entry and receive a good first impression?

>> Does your business offer an obvious greeting, either by a person or a welcoming display?

>> If you have a customer waiting area, do people head straight for it, or do they pause and look for an invitation before entering? In some businesses, a coffeemaker, a stack of logo ID cups, and a welcoming sign are all it takes to break the ice. Other times, you may need to remodel or at least redecorate to break down obstacles and enhance the sense of welcome.

TIP

If customers consistently stop in a certain area or study a particular display, consider that area as prime marketing real estate and think of ways that you can enhance it to deliver the strongest possible statement on behalf of your business.

What it's like to be a customer in your business

In designing your business environment, balance your operations and internal needs against the wants and needs of your most important asset: your customers. Follow the path that customers take through your business to figure out where you need to make adjustments to improve their experience. Take the following steps, and then repeat the process in fact-finding visits to a few of your competitors, if such visits are possible:

>> **Stop where customers stop.** Stand in an inconspicuous spot and watch what people do when they enter your business.

- How long do they wait until someone greets them?

- Do they look around for a clue regarding what to do next?

- If you're a retailer, do they see a bottleneck at the cash register as their first impression?

- How many people make a U-turn and leave before they make a purchase, and where do they seem to most frequently lose interest?

>> **Shop like they shop.** Study what it's like to purchase your product. How many different people or departments do customers deal with, and does each contribute value rather than require an annoying duplication of customer input? Where do points of concern or resistance arise? How can you eliminate obstacles that hinder your customers' decisions to buy or their ability to enjoy dealing with your business?

- If you have a service business and customers want to know how your charges add up, be ready with answers. Create a brochure or handout describing your services and fee structure.

- If they want to touch the merchandise, build appropriate displays.

- If they need to try before they buy, offer samples, fitting rooms, before-and-after photos, or other ways to experience your product.

- If they want to browse, display products at eye level and give them room to stop and shop, realizing that narrow aisles and tight spaces drive people — especially women — right out the door.

>> **Wait where they wait and for as long.** Test your customer service from a customer's viewpoint. Look at how customers react to the way your company serves and treats them.

- Have you provided chairs in areas where they end up waiting?

- In areas where customers pause, have you placed displays that move them toward buying decisions?

- If spouses, children, or friends accompany customers, have you created entertainment areas and appropriate diversions?

- If their visits consistently last longer than an hour, do you provide some form of refreshment?

WARNING

- Watch for nonverbal complaints about a lack of attentiveness. Do customers glance at their watches or fidget while waiting for employees to handle phone calls, deal with other customers, or complete paperwork? Be aware that customers use waiting time as the single most important factor in gauging your customer service, so plan accordingly.

Auditing the Impressions Your Business Makes

The only way you can be sure you're making consistently good impressions in your marketplace is to take inventory and assess every contact with prospects, customers, and others who deal with your business.

Surveying your marketing materials and communications

Start by pulling samples of stationery, ads, signs, brochures, coffee cups, T-shirts, online communications, and any other items that represent your business. Line them all up and evaluate them using these questions:

>> Does your business name and logo look the same every time you make an impression?

>> Do you consistently use the same colors?

>> Do you consistently use the same typeface?

>> Do your marketing materials present a consistent image in terms of look, quality, and message?

Study your samples and isolate those that don't fit with the others, perhaps because they use outdated or inaccurate versions of your name or logo. Or maybe the colors are wrong or the tone is inconsistent. Possibly the message is witty or silly when the rest of your communications are fact-filled and serious. Or the caliber may be unprofessional compared to the rest of your materials.

Cull the inappropriate items and then look at what's left.

>> **Does the consistent portion of your marketing materials accurately reflect your business?**

>> **Do your marketing materials adequately appeal to your target market?**

- For example, if you know that your customers value top quality, do your marketing materials convey a top-quality company? Do your ads convey quality? Do you apply your logo only to prestigious advertising items? If you're a retailer, are your shopping bags the finest you can afford? If you're a service company, do you present your proposals in a manner that reinforces the caliber of your firm while affirming your customer's taste level?

- If your customers value economy, do your materials look too upscale? If so, they may telegraph the wrong message.

- If your customers choose you primarily for convenience, do your materials put forth that assurance? Or, if customers value your reliability, do you convey that attribute through a flawless commitment to a reliably consistent projection of your identity?

REMEMBER

In forming opinions about your company, your market relies on the impressions it gets from your communications. See Chapter 5 in Book 5 for details on creating marketing communications that work.

Creating an impression inventory

TIP

Your business makes impressions in person, online, in ads and marketing materials, in correspondence . . . the list goes on and on. Every contact is capable of contributing to or detracting from the image you want people to hold in their minds about your business. Try the following tips:

>> **Define your company's impression points.** Using the provided entries, check all impression points that apply to your business, and add any additional ways your business comes into contact with customers and prospective customers. No item is too small to include. If your ad is a work of art but your proposal cover is flimsy, the negative impact of one cancels out the positive impact of the other. Every impression counts.

>> **Define the target market for each impression point.** Is it to develop a new prospect or to communicate with an existing customer — or maybe a little bit of both? If your business has a number of customer types or product lines, you may want to get even more specific. For instance, one ad for an insurance brokerage may target property insurance prospects and another may target life insurance prospects. By defining the different purposes, the brokerage is able to gauge how much it invests in the development of each product line.

>> **Rate the quality of each impression your business makes.** Give each of your communication vehicles a grade of Good, Average, or Poor, based on your assessment of how well it conveys your business image, message, look, and style.

>> **Who's in charge of each impression point?** Many impressions that affect a company's image are made by those who don't think of themselves as marketers. Nine times out of ten, no one is thinking about marketing when a cost estimate is presented, a bill is sent, or a purchase order is issued. The key is to think about the marketing impact far in advance so that you create materials, processes, and systems that advance a positive image for your company.

>> **Evaluate the costs involved.** What does each communication cost in terms of development, media, printing, or other expenses? After you know the answer, you can add up what you're spending on business development, customer retention, and marketing of each product line. You may be surprised to find that you're over-supporting some functions and under-supporting others, and you can adjust accordingly.

Improving the impressions you're making

Ask yourself the following questions to assess the quality and effectiveness of the impressions your business makes:

>> **Are you allocating your efforts well?** Are you spending enough on efforts to keep current customers happy, or are your efforts too heavily weighted toward getting new people through the door — or vice versa?

>> **Do your communications fit your image and objectives?** Answer this question for every item, whether it's an ad or a logo-emblazoned coffee cup. Be sure that each contributes to the image you're trying to etch in your marketplace rather than to some decision made long ago based on the powerful presentation by a sales representative.

>> **Is your image consistent, professional, and well suited to the audiences that matter most to your business?**

TIP

Use your inventory as you fine-tune your communications. Keep it on hand. If you ever decide to change your name, logo, or overall look, this list will remind you of all the items that you need to update.

REMEMBER

Use your impression inventory to guide changes as you strengthen the image you project to your market. Work to phase out and replace any impression points you rate as poor and to adjust and improve the quality of any impression points you rate as average.

Chapter **4**

Forging Your Brand

"We're just a small business," you may be thinking. "We're not Coca-Cola or Nike, with a bazillion-dollar ad budget and a global market. We're just 12 people trying to build a half million dollars in sales. We hardly need a brand."

Guess what? A brand isn't some mysterious, expensive treasure available only to the rich and famous. And it isn't just for mega-marketers, though they all have one.

Branding simply (well, maybe not all *that* simply) involves developing and consistently communicating a set of positive characteristics that consumers can relate to your name. If those characteristics happen to fill a meaningful and available position in their minds — a need they've been sensing and trying to fill — then you just scored a marketing touchdown, and that half-million-dollar sales goal will be way easier to reach.

Recognizing What Brands Are and What They Do

REMEMBER

Keep in mind the following two facts about what brands are and aren't:

>> A brand is a set of beliefs. It's a promise that customers believe.

>> A brand isn't a logo. A logo is a symbol that identifies a brand. When people see your logo or hear your name, a set of images arises. Those images define your brand in their minds.

Your brand isn't what *you* think it is. Your brand is whatever mental image those in your target audience automatically unlock when they encounter your name or logo. Your brand is what they believe about you based on everything they've ever seen or heard — whether good or bad, true or false.

REMEMBER

If you make impressions in your marketplace, whether proactively or unconsciously, you're building your brand. In fact, you're likely building two brands at once — a business brand for your company and a personal brand for yourself, a brand balancing act featured later in this chapter.

Something as basic as your street or online address contributes to how people perceive your brand. For that matter, customers, prospective customers, job applicants, reporters, bankers, suppliers, and those who refer people to you and your business form impressions every time they walk through your front door, visit your website, meet an employee, see your ad, or scan an online review or search results.

All those impressions accumulate to become your brand image in your customer's mind, which is where brands live.

Unlocking the power and value of a brand

If you need a motivating fact to boot you into branding action, here it is: Branding makes selling easier because people want to buy from those they know and like, and those they trust will deliver on commitments. A good brand puts forth that promise.

With a well-managed brand, your company hardly needs to introduce itself. Within your target market, people will already know your business, its personality, and the promise it makes to customers — all based on the positive set of impressions you've made and they've stored in their minds.

WARNING

Without a well-managed brand, you'll spend a good part of every sales opportunity trying to introduce your business, while some well-known brand down the street can spend that time actually making the sale.

Brands fuel success in three ways:

>> Brands lead to name awareness, which sets your business apart from all the contenders your audience has never heard of.

>> Brands prompt consumer selection because people prefer to work with those they've heard of and heard good things about.

>> Brands unlock profitability because people pay premium prices for products (or, in the case of personal brands, for people) that they trust will deliver higher value than lesser-known alternatives.

As a result of the advantages they deliver, brands increase the odds of business success, which makes them especially valuable in a world where half of all businesses fail in the first five years, nine out of ten products don't make it to their second anniversary, and too many people are vying for the same jobs, sales, and opportunities.

Tipping the balance online

Without a brand, you have to build the case for your business before every sale. Doing that is tough work in person and even tougher online, because you can't be there to make introductions, inspire confidence, counter resistance, or break down barriers.

Brands are essential to online and offline success for very different reasons:

>> **For those who sell online, brands are necessary for credibility.** People buy everything online — from contact lenses to cars — all without the benefit of personal persuasion, hands-on evaluation, or test drives. Why? Because customers arrive at websites with confidence in the brands they buy. When they see a brand they know and like, they check the price and terms, click to buy, and move on to checkout. If your business takes place primarily online, your brand is your key to sales.

>> **For those who sell offline, brands are necessary for findability.** Anymore, nearly every brand needs to be findable, prominent, and credible online. The rare exceptions are those that serve a target market that never goes online and that's never influenced by those that do. For every other brand, Chris Anderson, author of *The Long Tail* (Hachette Books), says, "Your brand is what Google says it is." If customers can't find your business in an online search, they conclude that you either don't exist or aren't a top player in your arena.

REMEMBER

Branding facilitates sales and spurs success, whether your cash register is online or on Main Street.

Building a Powerful Brand

Your small business will probably never have a globally recognized "power brand" simply because you don't have (and for that matter don't need) the marketing muscle that would fuel that level of awareness.

But you *can* be the most powerful brand in your target market. All it takes is the following:

» Knowing the brand image that you want to project

» Developing a distinct point of difference that's relevant and beneficial to your target audience

» Having commitment and discipline to project your brand well

» Spending what's necessary to get your message to your target market

» Managing your marketing so that it makes consistent impressions that etch your desired brand image into the mind of your target prospect

Being consistent to power your brand

To build a strong brand, project a consistent look, tone, and level of quality through each point of customer contact, whether in person or through marketing and whether online or offline.

Then stick with the brand you build. People in your target audience are exposed to thousands of images every day. To manage the marketing clutter, they filter out all but the messages and images that are relevant and familiar. The quickest route to making your brand image one they recognize and trust is to present it consistently — without fail.

Don't try to change your brand image unless you're certain that it's no longer appropriate for the market. (And if that's the case, you'd better be prepared to change your business, because your brand is the public representation of your business.) Imagine how tired the people at Campbell's Soup must be of their label, but imagine what would happen to their sales if they abandoned it simply because a fickle marketing manager said, "Let's try something new." Remember "New Coke"?

REMEMBER

Consistency builds brands, and brands build business.

Taking six brand-management steps

Building a well-managed brand follows certain steps:

1. Define why you're in business.

What does your business do? Or, if you're building a personal brand, what do you do? How do you do it better than anyone else? Put into writing the reason that your business exists and the positive change you aim to achieve.

2. Consider what you want people to think when they hear your name.

What do you want current and prospective employees to think about your business? What do you want prospects, customers, suppliers, associates, competitors, and friends to think?

REMEMBER

You can't be different things to each of these groups and still have a well-managed brand. For example, you can't have an internal company mindset that says "economy at any price" and expect consumers to believe that no one cares more about product quality and customer service than you do.

Figure out what you want people to think when they hear your name. Then ask yourself whether that brand image is believable to each of the various groups with whom you communicate. If it isn't, decide how you need to alter your business to make achieving your brand image possible.

3. Think about the words you want people to use when defining your business.

TIP

Ask your employees, associates, and customers this question: When people hear our name, what images do you think come into their minds? If everyone says the same thing, and if those words are the words you *want* associated with your name, you have a well-managed brand. If gaps occur, you have your brand-management work cut out for you.

List words that you want people to link to your business and be certain that you live up to that desired image. Then lead people to the right conclusions by presenting those characteristics — that brand image — consistently and repeatedly in your marketing communications. Choose messages and graphic symbols that support the image you want to project. For example, Rolex maintains its luxury brand image by featuring a crown as its logo and by giving its signature watch collection the name *Oyster*.

4. Pinpoint the advantages you want people to associate with your business.

Figuring out these distinctions leads to your definition of the position you want to own in consumer minds.

5. **Define your brand.**

   Look at your business through a customer's or prospect's eyes as you define your brand. What do people say and think about your company and the unique benefits they count on it to deliver? Why do they choose your business and prefer to buy from you again and again? How would they define your brand and the promise it makes?

   Boil your findings down to one concept — one brand definition — that you honestly believe you can own in the minds of those who deal with your business. The following are examples of how three widely known brands are generally perceived by the public:

   - Volvo: The safest car

   - CNN: The middle-of-the-road, all-news channel

   - Google: The top Internet search engine

6. **Build your brand through every impression that you make.**

   Flip to Book 5, Chapter 3 for advice on auditing your brand's impression points. Rate whether each impression enhances or detracts from the brand you're building, depending on how well it projects your brand with clarity and consistency.

Your Market Position: The Birthplace of Your Brand

Brands live in consumer minds. But just like you need to find an empty lot if you want to build a home to live in, you need to find an empty mind space if you want to embed your brand in your customer's brain.

Positioning involves figuring out what meaningful and available niche in the market — and in your customer's head — your business is designed to fill, and then filling it and performing so well that people have no reason to allow anyone else into the space in their minds they hold for your brand.

Seeing how positioning happens

When people learn about your business, they subconsciously slot you into a business hierarchy composed of the following:

>> **Me-too businesses:** If the mind slot — or position — that you want for your business is already taken, you have to persuade consumers to switch allegiances on your behalf, and that's a tough job. The best advice for a "me-too" business is to find a way to become a "similar-but-different" business by targeting an unserved market niche or providing a differentiating benefit.

>> **Similar-but-different businesses:** These businesses market a meaningful difference in a crowded field. Depending on the nature of your business, your positioning distinction may be based on pricing, inventory, target market, service structure, or company personality. For example, instead of simply opening your town's umpteenth pizza shop, open the only one in a trendy new neighborhood, the only one that offers New York–style pizza by the slice, or the only one that uses recipes from Southern Italy in a trattoria setting. Your distinction had better be compelling, though, because you have to convince people the difference is worth hearing about, sampling, and changing for.

>> **Brand-new offerings:** If you can be the first to fill a market's needs, you have the easiest positioning task of all. Just don't expect that marketing to seize that brand-new position will be a cakewalk. First-in-market businesses need to educate consumers about what the new offering is and why they should care. Then they have to promote skillfully and forcefully before competitors enter the fray.

WARNING

First-in-a-market businesses and first-of-a-kind products have to market fast and fastidiously because, in the end, being first isn't as important as being first to seize a positive position in the consumer's mind.

Determining your positioning strategy

The simplest way to figure out what position you hold is to determine what your business offers that your customers would have a hard or impossible time finding elsewhere. Some questions that will lead to your positioning statement include the following:

>> How is our offering unique or at least difficult to copy?

>> Is our unique offering something that consumers really want?

>> Is our offering compatible with economic and market trends?

>> How is our offering different — and better — than available options?

>> Is our claim believable?

Don't aim for a position that requires the market to make a leap of faith on your behalf. If a restaurant is known for the best burgers in town, it can't suddenly decide to try to jump into the position of "the finest steakhouse in the state." Leapfrogging doesn't work well when the game is positioning.

Develop your position around the distinct attributes that have made your business successful to date. Here are a few positioning examples:

>> Skyliner is a community offering families the finest view in town.

>> Treetops is an inn hosting the most pampered ski vacationers in the East.

>> *Starting a Business All-in-One For Dummies* is a friendly guide packed with advice and tools to help small business leaders achieve success by planning, launching, and managing their businesses.

See how it works? A positioning statement is easy to construct — just apply the formula you see in Figure 4-1.

FIGURE 4-1:
This formula helps you build a positioning statement.

Your Name + Your Business Description + Your Point of Distinction + Your Market Description = Your Positioning Statement

© *John Wiley & Sons, Inc.*

As you write your statement, avoid these traps:

>> **Don't try to duplicate a position in an already crowded category.** Opening the third shoe repair shop in a small town requires more than a location and announcement. You need to convince customers who are already committed to the other shops that your store is better — because of its location, service, or other distinguishing attributes.

>> **Don't base your distinction on a pricing or quality difference that a competitor can take from you.** For instance, you're only egging on your competitors if you position yourself as "the lowest priced" or "the most creative." With effort, a competitor can beat you on either front.

>> **Don't hang your hat on a factor you can't control.** Too many resorts have ended up red-faced after positioning themselves as "the region's only five-star resort," only to lose a star or have a competitor gain one. Instead, communicate distinctions that matter to your customers and then back them up with

definitions and promises. For example, instead of making a vague promise about "best service," Alaska Air says it's the first major U.S. airline with a 20-minute baggage service guarantee.

>> **Don't settle for a generic positioning statement.** Be sure you can answer no to this question: Could another business say the same thing?

Conveying Your Position and Brand through Taglines

Your *tagline* or *slogan* is a quick, memorable phrase that helps consumers link your name to your business brand and position. Your positioning statement tells the unique market niche and mind space you aim to occupy. Your tagline converts that statement to a line that matters to consumers.

You need a tagline if your brand name benefits from some explanation. For instance, Jiffy Lube doesn't need a tagline but BMW does, because if you'd never heard of BMW, its name alone wouldn't tell you what it is and does.

As you develop a tagline for your brand, follow some advice from Eric Swartz, who calls himself a *verbal branding professional* and *master wordslinger,* and who lives up to his self-description on both counts. He's created thousands of brand expressions, including corporate taglines, city mottoes, campaign slogans, company and product names, headlines, and other short-form messages.

REMEMBER

His business, TagLine Guru (www.taglineguru.com), is summed up by the tagline, "It's your brand on the line." Here's what he says you need to know as you write a tagline for your brand:

>> **A tagline should say something essential about who you are, what makes you special, and why the world should care.** It should confer marquee value on your brand and illustrate the value and appeal of your organization. Think of your tagline as a final exclamation point that wraps up your 30-second elevator pitch.

>> **Because taglines aren't written in stone, you can easily update or replace them if your organization or message undergoes a shift.** Use your tagline to reflect a change in positioning, launch a marketing or brand-awareness campaign, forge a relationship with a new audience, define a new direction, or highlight a key benefit or attribute.

Swartz lists the following 12 characteristics of great taglines:

>> **Original:** Make it your own

>> **Believable:** Keep it real

>> **Simple:** Make it understandable

>> **Succinct:** Get to the point

>> **Positive:** Elevate their mood

>> **Specific:** Make it relevant

>> **Unconventional:** Break the mold

>> **Provocative:** Make them think

>> **Conversational:** Make it personable

>> **Persuasive:** Sell the big idea

>> **Humorous:** Tickle their funny bone

>> **Memorable:** Make a lasting impression

TIP

Not all taglines incorporate all 12 characteristics — obviously, a legal or accounting firm wouldn't aim to convey humor — but this list can help during the tagline brainstorming process.

After you adopt a tagline, include it in all marketing communications so that when people see your brand name, they also see the tagline that translates your brand promise into a descriptive and memorable phrase. (See Chapter 5 in Book 5 for more about marketing communications.)

Balancing Personal and Business Brands

Most people build two brands at once: one for their business and one for themselves, personally. Between the two, you need to maintain balance.

To rate your personal/business brand balance, answer these questions:

>> Online and within your personal and business community, is one of your brands — your personal brand or your business brand — significantly more visible and credible than the other?

>> If you sold your business or left your current position tomorrow, is your personal brand strong enough to transport you into new business opportunities?

>> If you own your business, is your business brand strong enough to survive without the weight of your personal brand behind it?

TIP

Based on your answers, you can take one of two steps:

>> **Strengthen your personal brand if it's weak in comparison to your business brand.** Especially if you own your company, your personal brand helps you humanize your business and take it places where only people go, such as into networking events and community or industry leadership positions.

- Follow the six brand management steps earlier in this chapter to develop your personal brand in addition to your business brand.

- Develop heightened personal-brand awareness within your business, industry, and community, and especially online, which is where most brand research starts.

- Create and maintain a personal online home base — your own website, a blog, or pages on social networks. (See Book 5, Chapter 6 for help with this step.)

>> **Strengthen your business brand if it's eclipsed by your personal brand.** This is especially important if you hope to one day sell your business or develop it into an enterprise that can survive without you.

- If your business doesn't have a website, get one (see Book 2, Chapter 5 for advice). And if it doesn't rank well in search results, broaden its online presence to improve its visibility.

- If your personal brand is monopolizing your business image, make way for others on your team to get more visible with clients, on projects, in media, and within your community and industry. Online, instead of personally representing your business, create separate social media accounts for yourself and your company. Then invite members of your team to add their voices (with guidance) to your business blog and social media pages so people view your company as an enterprise larger than one visible person.

- Make a conscious effort to direct interest in you, personally, to your business. Feature your business prominently in your personal communications and introductions. Even consider using your business logo instead of a personal photo on your personal online pages, where business contacts may be searching.

REMEMBER

Especially if you're planning to grow or sell your business, strengthen your business brand. If you want to pursue personal career opportunities or to humanize your business, strengthen your personal brand. In between, the best approach is to keep your two brands nicely in balance.

Maintaining and Protecting Your Brand

For something so powerful, brands are surprisingly vulnerable. They thrive with consistency and they wither under the attack of zigs and zags in message, experience, and management. The best way to grow a healthy brand is to follow two steps:

>> Establish your brand message and creative strategy.

>> Put controls in place to protect your brand and ensure its consistent presentation.

Staying consistent with your brand message and creative strategy

Your *creative strategy* is the plan that directs the development of all your marketing communications. It defines

>> Your target market

>> The believable and meaningful benefit you offer to your market

>> The way you present your personality in your communications

Writing your creative strategy

You can write your creative strategy in three sentences that define the purpose, approach, and personality that will guide the creation of your marketing communications, following this formula:

1. **"The purpose of our marketing communications is to convince** [insert a brief description of your target market] **that our product is the most** [describe the primary benefit you provide to customers].**"**

2. **"We will prove our claim by** [insert a description of why your distinct benefit is believable and how you'll prove it in your marketing].**"**

3. **"The mood and tone of our communications will be** [insert a description of the personality that your communications will convey].**"**

Following is a sample strategy for a fictitious business:

> **Glass Houses, a window-washing service:** The purpose of our marketing communications is to convince affluent homeowners in our hometown that our service is the easiest and most immediately gratifying way to beautify their homes. We will prove our claim by guaranteeing same-week and streak-free service, by promising four-month callback reminders, and by offering special, three-times-a-year rates so that homeowners never have to think about window cleaning after their first call to us. The mood and tone of our communications will be straightforward and clean — like our service.

Using your creative strategy

Every time you create an ad, a mailer, a voicemail recording, or even a business letter or an employee uniform or dress code, be 100 percent certain that your communication is consistent with the creative strategy that you've established to guide your business personality. Here are some ways to do so:

>> **Use your creative strategy to guide every representation of your business — and your brand.** Start by looking around your business to see that your physical space projects the tone and develops the image you want for your business. If your creative strategy stipulates a discreet image for your business, you don't want prospects to encounter a rowdy atmosphere with music blaring when they walk into or call your business. Carry that same discipline into every marketing communication.

>> **Create each new marketing communication with your creative strategy in mind.** Whether you're developing a building sign, a website, or a major ad campaign, insist that the final product adheres to your creative strategy.

>> **Fine-tune your creative strategy annually.** Review your creative strategy. You may decide to reach out to a different target market or to present a different marketing message based on your assessment of market opportunities. But hold tight to your definition of the mood and tone of your communications. (Flip to the earlier section "Being consistent to power your brand" for a reminder of why your look and tone need to be reliable indicators of your brand image.)

Controlling your brand presentation

Well-branded organizations have rules — called style guidelines — that determine how their logos may be presented, what typestyles and colors may be used in marketing materials, how certain words are used, and when and how taglines, copyrights, and trademark indicators apply.

Create style guidelines to protect the consistency of your brand image, too. Then, before a print shop, specialty-advertising producer, staff designer, outside marketing firm, or any other supplier creates marketing materials on your behalf, share your style guidelines to steer the outcome of their efforts.

Managing your logo presentation

Your logo is the face of your business on marketing materials. Ensure that it's presented cleanly and without unnecessary alteration by asking and answering the following questions in your style guidelines:

» When your logo appears in black ink, what color backgrounds may be used?

» When your logo appears in white ink (called a *reverse*), what color backgrounds may be used?

» When your logo appears in color, what ink color or colors may be used?

» What's the smallest size that can be used for your logo?

REMEMBER

Indicate in your guidelines that your logo must be reproduced from original artwork or a professionally produced reproduction and never from a photocopy or previously printed piece, because the quality will be inferior. If a professional designed your logo, be sure to request the EPS or vector art files. JPG and PNG files may look fine online, but they appear fuzzy when stretched for large-scale use. Also, get professional guidance on which colors to use, whether your logo translates well in reverse treatments, and other presentation advice.

Deciding on your typestyle

A quick way to build consistency is to limit the typestyles you use in your ads, web pages, brochures, signs, and all other communications. Choose one typeface (also called a *font*) for headlines and one for ad copy. If your company prints technical materials (instruction guides, warranties, operating or assembly instructions, or other copy-intensive pieces), you might designate a third, easy-to-read font for small print and long-text applications or for online use where your selected brand fonts may not display well.

TIP

When choosing fonts for your marketing materials, aim to reflect your brand's personality. If you want to convey an old-fashioned or traditional tone, you probably need a *serif* type, which is also the best choice for use in large bodies of type. But if you want your materials to appear informal or very clean and straightforward, *sans serif* type is an appropriate choice.

In addition to specifying fonts, you may want to define usage preferences, taking the following points into consideration:

>> Type featuring both uppercase and lowercase letters is easier to read than copy printed in all capital letters. For legibility, avoid using all capital letters unless the headline or copy block is extremely short and easy for the eyes to track.

>> If your target market has aging vision, keep text or body copy no smaller than 10 points in size.

>> Avoid reversed type — white type on black or dark backgrounds — if you expect people to read your words easily. If, for design purposes, you decide to reverse type, keep the type size large.

>> Use only two fonts in any single marketing piece, unless you're trying through your design to create a cluttered look.

Establishing copy guidelines

Copy refers to the words, text, or content of your marketing materials. As you establish style guidelines, also define how you want your copy prepared, taking these points into consideration:

>> If certain words in your marketing materials require copyright (©), trademark (™), or registered trademark (®) symbols, list these words in your style guidelines.

>> Indicate in your guidelines whether you want your marketing materials to carry a copyright notice in small (usually 6-point) type. For example: © 2019 John Doe. (Go to www.copyright.gov for more information.)

>> If you plan to send printed materials over national borders, ask your attorney whether you need to include a line reading "Printed in U.S.A." If so, include the instructions in your guidelines.

>> Decide which words you prefer to have capitalized. For example, perhaps your style preference is to say your business is located in "Southern California" and not "southern California." Or maybe you want your business to be "The Candy Factory" and not "the Candy Factory."

>> Determine whether you want to ban certain words. For example, a real estate developer may prohibit the word *lots* in favor of the word *homesites*. A public relations firm may insist that the term *PR* be spelled out to read *public relations*. A business with a down-to-earth image might rule out any word that ends in "-ize," saying "see" instead of "visualize" or "make the most of" instead of "maximize."

Chapter **5**

Creating Marketing Communications That Work

Creative. The very word turns confident people queasy and rational people giddy. It prompts marketers to say such outrageous things as "Let's dress up like chickens" or such well-intended but pointless things as "Let's cut through the noise" or "Let's think outside the box." Far less often will you hear the conversation turn strategic, with statements like "Let's talk in terms that matter to our customers" or "Let's define what we're trying to accomplish."

This chapter helps you set communication objectives and steer past the mistakes that shoot too many ad efforts into the great abyss, where wasted dollars languish.

Note: The first three sections of this chapter apply to small business owners doing your own marketing, whether you present your marketing communications in person, online, with print or broadcast ads, or through direct mail. If you place ads in traditional mass media outlets such as newspapers, magazines, and broadcast stations, stick with this chapter to the end for information on scheduling and evaluating your ads. For info on using social media, turn to Book 5, Chapter 6.

Starting with Good Objectives

Copywriters and designers are talented and creative, but they're rarely telepathic. They can't create marketing materials that meet specific objectives if their instructions don't include what they're expected to accomplish.

So who is supposed to define the objective, set the strategy, and steer the creative process? Well, get ready, because that task falls to the person responsible for marketing, which is probably, well, *you*.

Defining what you want to accomplish

You can hit your marketing target almost every time if you take careful aim. Consider the following examples of creative instructions and note the differences:

> **Example 1:** "We need to build sales. Let's run some ads."

> **Example 2:** "We need a campaign to convince teenagers that by shopping after school on weekdays they'll enjoy our best prices in a club atmosphere because we feature live music, two-for-one cafe specials, and weekday-only student discounts."

Example 1 forces those creating the ad to guess what message to project — and toward whom. It'll likely lead to round after round of revisions as the creative team makes best guesses about the target market, promotional offer, and creative approach.

Example 2 tells the ad creators precisely which consumers to target, what message and offer to project, and what action to prompt. It guides the project toward an appropriate concept and media plan — probably on the first try.

REMEMBER

As the business owner, it's your job to give those who produce your marketing communications the information they need to do the job right the first time.

WARNING

An old saying among marketers concludes that half of all ad dollars are wasted, but no one knows which half. You can move the dividing line between what works and what doesn't by avoiding three wasteful errors:

>> **Mistake #1:** Producing marketing materials without first defining your marketing objectives, leading to materials that address neither the target prospect nor the marketing objective.

>> **Mistake #2:** Creating messages that are too "hard-sell" — asking for the order without first reeling in the prospect's attention and interest.

>> **Mistake #3:** Creating self-centered communications that focus more on what your business wants to say about itself than on the benefits that matter to a prospective customer.

A good ad can inform, persuade, sell, or connect with consumers, but it can't do all those things at once. Nor is it likely to move the right target audience to the desired consumer action if the audience and objective aren't clearly established before ad creation begins.

REMEMBER

Before you undertake any marketing effort, define the audience you aim to influence, the action you're working to inspire, the message you want to promote, and the way that you'll measure effectiveness, whether by leads, web or store traffic, inquiries, social media likes or follows, or other actions you can prompt and monitor.

TIP

When setting the objective for your marketing communication, use the following template by inserting the appropriate text in the brackets.

> **This** [ad/brochure/sales call/speech/trade booth display] **will convince** [describe the target market for this communication] **that by** [describe the action that you intend to prompt] **they will** [describe the benefit the target audience will realize] **because** [state the facts that prove your claim, which form the basis of the message you want the communication to convey].

Putting creative directions in writing

Your communication objective defines *what* you're trying to accomplish. A *creative brief* provides the instructions for *how* you'll get the job done. Answer the following seven questions, and your briefing instructions will be complete.

Who is your target audience for this communication?

Start with everything you know about your prospective customers and then boil down your knowledge into a one-sentence definition that encapsulates the geographic location, the lifestyle facts, and the purchasing motivators of those you want to reach.

Here's an example:

> The target audience is comprised of Montana residents, age 40+, married with children living at home, with professional careers, upper-level income, and an affinity for travel, outdoor recreation, status brands, and high levels of service.

What does your target audience currently know or think about your business and offering?

Use research findings (if available), your own instincts, and input from your staff and colleagues to answer the following questions:

» Have prospects heard of your business?

» Do they know what products or services you offer?

» Do they know where you're located or how to reach you?

» Do they see you as a major player? If they were asked to name three suppliers of your product or service, would you be among the responses?

» How do they rate your service, quality, pricing, accessibility, range of products, and reputation?

» Do you have a clear brand and market position or a mistaken identity in their minds?

REMEMBER

Be candid with your answers. Only by acknowledging your real or perceived shortcomings can you begin to address them through your marketing efforts. If your prospects haven't heard of your business, you need to develop awareness. If they're clueless about your offerings, you need to present meaningful facts. If they hold inaccurate impressions, you need to persuade them to think differently.

Here's an example:

> The majority of those in our target audience aren't aware of our existence, but among those familiar with our name, we're known to provide an experience competitive with the best contenders in our field. We need to reinforce the opinions of our acquaintances while also developing awareness and credibility with prospective customers and especially with opinion leaders whose recommendations are most valued by our affluent and socially connected target market.

What do you want your target audience to think and do?

Don't get greedy. In each communication, present one clear idea and chances are good that you'll *convey* one clear idea. If you try to present two or three messages, you'll likely communicate nothing at all.

REMEMBER

Four out of five consumers read only your headline, absorb no more than seven words off of a billboard, and take only one idea away from a broadcast ad — provided they don't tune out or skip over the ad altogether.

What single idea do you want prospects to take away from this particular marketing effort? As you answer, follow this process:

1. **Step out of your own shoes and stand in those of your prospect.**

2. **Think about what your prospect wants or needs to know.**

3. **Develop a single sentence describing what you want people to think and what motivating idea you want them to take away from this communication.**

Here's the desired outcome for a computer retailer targeting senior citizens:

> We want senior citizens to know that they're invited to our Computer 101 open houses every Wednesday afternoon this month, where they can watch computer and Internet demonstrations, receive hands-on training, and learn about our special, first-time computer owner packages.

WARNING

Be careful what you ask for. Be sure that you're prepared for the outcome you say you desire. If you aren't geared up to handle the online traffic, answer the phone, manage the foot traffic, or fulfill the buying demand that your ad generates, you'll fail strategically even though you succeeded — wildly — on the advertising front.

Consider this example: A one-man painting company decides to rev up business by placing a series of clever, small-space newspaper ads touting impeccable service, outstanding quality, affordable estimates, and prompt response. The ads win attention, action, and advertising awards. The problem is, the painter can't keep up with the phone calls, the estimates, or the orders. Prospects — who had been inspired by the great ads — end up signing contracts with the painter's competitors instead.

The moral of the story is to expect a miracle from good advertising and to be prepared to get what you ask for.

Why should people believe you and take the proposed action?

To be believable, your marketing materials need to make and support a claim. They can do so in either an easy way or an effective way:

>> **The easy way** is to list features: the oldest moving company in the East, under new management, the only manufacturer featuring the X2000 widget, the winner of the industry's top award, yada yada yada.

>> **The effective way** is to turn those features into benefits that you promise to your customers. The difference between features and benefits is that features are facts and benefits are personal outcomes.

Table 5-1 shows you exactly what this crucial difference means.

TABLE 5-1   **Features versus Benefits**

Product	Feature	Benefit	Emotional Outcome
Diet soda	One calorie	Lose weight	Look and feel great
Flower arrangements	Daily exotic imports	Send unique floral presentations	Satisfaction that your gift stands out and draws attention
Automobile	Best crash rating	Reduce risk of harm in accidents	Security that your family is safe
Miniature microwave	1.5 cubic feet in size	Save dorm room space	Make room for the floor's only big-screen TV

REMEMBER

Every time you describe a *feature* of your product or service, you're talking to yourself. Every time you describe the *benefit* that your product or service delivers, you're talking to your prospect. Consumers don't buy the feature — they buy what the feature does for them. Here are some examples:

>> Consumers don't buy V-8 engines. They buy speed.

>> They don't buy shock-absorbing shoes. They buy walking comfort.

>> They don't buy the lightest tablet computer. They buy the freedom to get online wherever they want.

TIP

Follow these steps to translate features into benefits:

1. **State your product or business feature.**

2. **Add the phrase "which means."**

3. **Complete the sentence by stating the benefit.**

For example, a car has the highest safety rating (that's the feature), *which means* you breathe a little easier as you hand the keys over to your teenager (that's the benefit).

What information must your communication convey?

Be clear about your must-haves. Those who create ads, websites, mailers, and other communications call it "death by a thousand cuts" when marketers respond to every creative presentation with, "Yes, but we also have to include. . .."

If you know that you need to feature a certain look, specific information, or artwork, say so upfront — not after you see the first creative presentation. And keep the list of requirements as short as possible. Here are some guidelines:

>> **Must-have #1:** Every communication has to advance your brand image (refer to Book 5, Chapter 4 for help with defining your brand). Provide your image style guide whenever you assign a staff person or outside professional to help with the development of marketing materials.

>> **Must-have #2:** Be sparing with all other "musts." Every time you start to say, "We have to include . . ." check yourself with this self-test:

● Is this element necessary to protect our brand?

● Is it necessary to protect our legal standing?

● Is it necessary to prompt the marketing action we want to achieve?

● Is it necessary to motivate the prospect?

REMEMBER

Let necessity — not history — guide your answers. Any ad designer will tell you that less is more. The more stuff you try to jam into an ad, the less consumer attention it draws. Include no more information than is necessary to arouse interest and lead people to the next step in the buying process.

How will you measure success?

Small business leaders are critical of their marketing efforts — after the fact. Instead, before creating any marketing communication, set your expectations and define your measurement standard in your creative brief.

After an ad has run its course, you'll hear such criticism as, "That ad didn't work, it didn't make the phone ring, and it sure didn't create foot traffic." Yet if you examine the ad, you'll often find that it includes no reason to call, no special offer, a phone number that requires a magnifying glass, and no address whatsoever.

What's your time frame and budget?

Know the specifications of your job before you start producing it, especially if you assign the production task to others. Here are some guidelines:

>> **Set and be frank about your budget.** Small business owners often worry that if they divulge their budgets, the creative team will spend it all — whether it needs to or not. But the never-reveal-the-budget strategy usually backfires. If suppliers *don't* know the budget, they *will* spend it all — and then some — simply because no one gave them a not-to-exceed figure to work within. The solution is to hire suppliers you trust, share your budget with them (along with instructions that they can't exceed the budget without your prior approval), and count on them to be partners in providing a cost-effective solution.

>> **Know and share deadlines and material requirements.** If you've already committed to a media buy, attach a media rate card to your creative brief so your designer can obtain the specifications directly rather than through your translation.

>> **Define the parameters of nonmedia communication projects.** For example, if you ask for speechwriting assistance, know the length of time allocated for your speech. If you request materials for a sales presentation, know the audio-visual equipment availability and the number of handouts you want to distribute.

REMEMBER

What the creative team doesn't know can cost you dearly in enthusiasm and cost overruns if you have to retrofit creative solutions to fit production realities. Communicate in advance for the best outcome.

TIP

Whether you're creating an ad, writing a speech, making a sales presentation, planning a brochure, posting on an online network, or composing an important business letter, start by running through the questions on the creative brief to focus your thinking. For all major projects — or for any project that you plan to assign to a staff member, freelance professional, vendor, or advertising agency — take the time to put your answers in writing. Pass them along so they can serve as a valuable navigational aid. Then monitor success by counting inquiries, click-throughs to landing pages, coupon redemptions, or other measurable actions prompted by your communications — and share your findings so your creative team can benefit from the knowledge of what worked well.

Developing Effective Marketing Communications

Whether delivered in person, through promotions, or via traditional media, direct mail, or email, all marketing communications need to accomplish the same tasks:

>> Grab attention.

>> Impart information the prospect wants to know.

>> Present offers that are sensitive to how and when the prospect wants to take action.

>> Affirm why the prospect would want to take action.

>> Offer a reason to take action.

>> Launch a relationship, which increasingly means fostering interaction and two-way communication between you and your customer.

Good communications convince prospects and nudge them into action without any apparent effort. They meld the verbiage with the visual and the message with the messenger so the consumer receives a single, inspiring idea.

Creative types will tell you that making marketing communications look easy takes a lot of time and talent, and they're right. If you're spending more than $10,000 on an advertising effort or developing a major marketing vehicle such as a website, ad campaign, or product package, bring in pros to help you out.

Steering the creative process toward a "big idea"

After you establish your objectives and prepare your creative brief (see the earlier section "Putting creative directions in writing"), it's time to develop your creative message.

No matter which target audience you're reaching out to, the people in that audience are busy and distracted by an onslaught of competing messages. That's why great communicators know that they need to project big ideas to be heard over the marketplace din.

The *big idea* is to advertising what the brake, gas pedal, and steering wheel are to driving. (See why they call it *big?*) Here's what the big idea does:

>> It stops the prospect.

>> It fuels interest.

>> It inspires prospects to take the desired action.

Advertising textbooks point to Volkswagen's "Think Small" ad campaign as a historic example of a big idea. Volkswagen used it to stun a market into attention at a time when big-finned, lane-hogging gas guzzlers ruled the highways. "Think Small" — two words accompanied by a picture of a squat, round Volkswagen Beetle miniaturized on a full page — stopped consumers, changed attitudes, and made the Bug chic.

In addition, "Got Milk?" was a big idea that juiced up milk sales, and "Smell like a Man, Man" worked like magic for Old Spice.

But big ideas aren't just for big advertisers. In Portland, Oregon, quirky Voodoo Doughnut's big idea that "The magic is in the hole" has gained international appeal for an eight-outlet (though expanding) enterprise.

Big ideas are

>> Appealing to your target market

>> Attention-getting

>> Capable of conveying the benefit you promise

>> Compelling

>> Memorable

>> Persuasive

WARNING

An idea qualifies as a big idea only if it meets *all* the preceding qualifications. Many advertisers quit when they hit on an attention-getting and memorable idea. Think of it this way: A slammed door is attention-getting and memorable, but it's far from appealing, beneficial, compelling, or persuasive.

Brainstorming ideas

Brainstorming is an anything–goes group process for generating ideas through free association and imaginative thinking with no grandstanding, no idea ownership, no evaluation, and definitely no criticism.

TIP

The point of brainstorming is to put the mind on automatic pilot and see where it leads. You can improve your brainstorming sessions by doing some research in advance:

>> Study websites and magazines for inspiration. Pick up copies of *Advertising Age, Adweek,* or *Communication Arts* (available at newsstands and in most libraries) for a look at the latest in ad trends. Also include fashion magazines, which are a showcase for big ideas and image advertising.

>> Check out competitors' ads and ads for businesses that target similar audiences to yours. If you sell luxury goods, look at ads for high-end cars, jewelry, or designer clothes. If you compete on price, study ads by Target and Walmart.

>> Look at your own past ads.

>> Think of how you can turn the most unusual attributes of your product or service into unique benefits.

>> Doodle. Ultimately, great marketing messages combine words and visuals. See where your pencil leads your mind.

>> Widen your perspective by inviting a customer or a front-line staff person to participate in the brainstorming session.

REMEMBER

If you're turning your marketing project over to a staff member or to outside professionals, you may or may not decide to participate in the brainstorming session. If you do attend, note that a brainstorming session has no boss, and every idea is a good idea. Bite your tongue each time you want to say, "Yes, but . . ." or, "We tried that once and . . ." or, "Get real, that idea is just plain dumb."

At the end of the brainstorm, gather up and evaluate the ideas:

>> Which ideas address the target audience and support the objectives outlined in your creative brief?

>> Which ones best present the consumer benefit?

>> Which ones can you implement with strength and within the budget?

Any idea that wins on all counts is a candidate for implementation.

Following simple advertising rules

The following rules apply to *all* ads, regardless of the medium, the message, the mood, or the creative direction:

>> Know your objective and stay on strategy.

>> Be honest.

>> Be specific.

>> Be original.

>> Be clear and concise.

>> Don't overpromise or exaggerate.

>> Don't be self-centered or, worse, arrogant.

>> Don't hard-sell.

>> Don't insult, discriminate, or offend.

>> Don't turn the task of ad creation over to a committee.

WARNING

Committees are great for brainstorming, but when it comes to developing head-lines, they round the edges off of strong ideas. They eliminate any nuance that any committee member finds questionable, and they crowd messages with details that matter more to the marketers than to the market. An old cartoon popular in ad agencies is captioned, "A camel is a horse designed by committee."

Making Media Selections

Even back in the day when advertisers chose from among three TV networks, a couple of local-market AM radio stations, and a single hometown newspaper, deciding where to place ads was a nail-biting proposition.

Now add in cable TV channels, dozens of radio stations in even the smallest market areas, thousands of consumer and online magazines, countless alternative newspapers, and constantly emerging online advertising options, and you can see why placing ads sometimes feels like a roll of the dice.

The upcoming two sections help tip the odds in your favor with an overview of today's advertising channels and advice about how to select the best vehicles for your advertising messages.

Selecting from the media menu

Marketing communications are delivered in one of two ways:

>> *Mass media* channels, which reach many people simultaneously

>> *One-to-one marketing* tools, which reach people individually, usually through direct mail or email

When people talk about *media*, it's usually mass media they're talking about, which traditionally has been divided into three categories, with a fourth category later added:

>> **Print media:** Includes newspapers, magazines, and print directories.

>> **Broadcast media:** Includes TV and radio.

>> **Outdoor media:** Includes billboards, transit signs, murals, and signage.

>> **Digital media:** Back in the day, the digital-media category was usually called "new media," but it's not new anymore, and its usage, popularity, and effectiveness increase almost by the moment. Exactly as its name implies, digital media includes any media that's reduced to digital data that can be communicated electronically. That means Internet advertising, webcasts, web pages, mobile and text ads, and interactive media, including social media networks.

Each mass-media channel comes with its own set of attributes and considerations, which are summarized in Table 5-2.

Deciding which media vehicles to use and when

Face it: Sorting through pitches from local newspapers, local radio stations, daily-deal coupon sites, and industry-specific publications can consume entire days if you let it. Plus there's the elephant in the room — social media (see Book 5, Chapter 6).

TABLE 5-2   **Mass Media Comparisons**

Media Channel	Advantages	Considerations
Newspapers, which reach a broad, geographically targeted market	Involve short timelines and low-cost ad production	You pay to reach the total circulation, even if only a portion fits your prospect profile
Magazines, which reach target markets that share characteristics and interests	Good for developing awareness and credibility through strong visual presentations	Require long advance planning and costly production; ads are viewed over long periods of time
Directories, which reach people at the time of purchase decisions	Increasingly available for free in digital versions; good for prompting selection over unlisted competitors	Print versions are impossible to update between editions and increasingly eclipsed by digital directories
Radio, which reaches targeted local audiences (if they're tuned in)	Cost is often negotiable; good for building immediate interest and response	You must air ads repeatedly to reach listeners; airtime is most expensive when most people are tuned in
TV, which reaches broad audiences of targeted viewers (if they're tuned in)	Well-produced ads engage viewer emotions while building awareness and credibility	Ad production is costly; reaching large audiences is expensive; ads must be aired repeatedly; options such as DVRs and streaming services erode effectiveness
Digital media, which reaches people on-demand via any digital device	Allows two-way communication with customers; allows convergence of content by linking among digital sources; low cash investment	Requires targeting of customers and keywords and a significant time investment to create, monitor, and evaluate online visibility and interaction

Your media options are seemingly infinite, but your time and budget aren't. So before considering media proposals for any given communication or campaign, answer the following questions:

>> **What do you want this marketing effort to accomplish?**

REMEMBER

If you want to develop general, far-reaching awareness and interest, use mass-media channels that reach a broad and general market. If you want to talk one-to-one with targeted prospective customers, bypass mass media in favor of targeted online communications and direct mail or other one-to-one communication tools.

>> **Where do the people you want to reach turn for information?**

When it comes to purchasing ad space and time, trying to be all-inclusive is a bankrupting proposition. The more precisely you can define your prospect, the more precisely you can determine which media that person uses and, therefore, which media channels you should consider for your marketing program.

TIP

When in doubt, ask customers how they like to be reached with marketing messages. Ask whether they read the local newspaper, tune in to local broadcast stations, or notice transit or outdoor ads. Ask whether they use social media networks and which ones. Ask whether they like or dislike marketing messages sent by text message or email. Talking directly with customers is your great advantage as a small business. Ask directly if you can or use the free survey tools available through sites like SurveyMonkey (www.surveymonkey.com) to poll customers.

By finding out the media habits of your established customers, you get a good idea of the media habits of your prospective customers because they likely fit a very similar customer profile. After you're clear about who your customers are and how they use media, you'll know which media channels to target.

>> **What information do you want to convey and when do you want to convey it?**

TIP

Be clear about your message urgency and content, and then refer to Table 5-2 to match your objectives with media channels. For example:

- If you're promoting an offer with a close deadline, such as a one-week special event, you obviously want to steer away from monthly magazines that are in circulation long after your offer is history.

- If you want to show your product in action, you want to feature video in TV ads or on your website or YouTube channel, to which you can lead customers by including the link in your promotional materials, ads, and social media posts.

>> **How much money is in your media budget?**

REMEMBER

Set your budget before planning your media buy. Doing so forces you to be realistic with your media choices and saves you an enormous amount of time because you don't have to listen to media sales pitches for approaches that are outside your budget range.

The Making of a Mass Media Schedule

When advertising on all mass media except digital media, the amount of money you spend and how you spend it depends on how you balance three scheduling considerations: *reach, frequency,* and *timing.*

Balancing reach and frequency

Your ad schedule needs to achieve enough reach (that is, your message needs to get into the heads of enough readers or viewers) to generate a sufficient number of prospects to meet your sales objective. It also needs to achieve enough frequency to adequately impress your message into those minds — and that rarely happens with a single ad exposure.

>> *Reach* is the number of individuals or homes exposed to your ad. In print media, reach is measured by circulation counts. In broadcast media, reach is measured by *gross rating points*.

>> *Frequency* is the number of times that an average person is exposed to your message.

TIP

If you have to choose between frequency and reach — and nearly every small business works with a budget that forces that choice — limit your reach to carefully selected target markets and then spend as much as you can on achieving frequency within that area.

The case for frequency

Ad recall studies prove that people remember ad messages in direct proportion to the number of times they encounter them. Here are some facts about frequency:

REMEMBER

>> **One-shot ads don't work, unless you opt to spend more than five million dollars to air a 30-second ad during the Super Bowl.** Even then, part of the audience will be away from the tube, replenishing the guacamole dish or grabbing a beer from the refrigerator.

>> **On most broadcast channels, you need to place an ad as many as nine times to reach a prospect even once.** That means you need to place it as many as 27 times in order to make contact three times — the number of exposures it takes before most ad messages sink in. If your ad airs during a program that people tune into with regular conviction, the placement requirement decreases, but especially in the case of radio ads, the 27-time schedule generally holds true.

Why? Because each time your ad airs, a predictably large percentage of prospects aren't present. They're either tuned out or distracted, or maybe your creative approach or offer failed to grab their attention.

>> **Multiple exposures to your ad results in higher advertising effectiveness.**
By achieving frequency, you increase the number of people who see your ad, resulting in increased recognition for your brand, increased consumer reaction to your message, and increased responsiveness to your call to action.

Reach creates awareness, but frequency changes minds.

The case for limiting reach by using only a few media channels

Frequency and limited-reach, concentrated ad campaigns go hand in hand. A *concentrated campaign* gains exposure using only a few media outlets.

Instead of running an ad one time in each of six magazines that reach your target market, a concentrated campaign schedules your ad three times each in two of the publications. Or instead of running a light radio schedule and a light newspaper schedule, a concentrated campaign bets the full budget on a strong schedule that builds frequency through one medium or the other.

A concentrated ad campaign offers several benefits:

>> It allows you to take advantage of media volume discounts.

>> It can give you dominance in a single medium, which achieves a perception of strength and clout in the prospect's mind.

>> It allows you to limit ad production costs.

>> It ensures a higher level of frequency.

Timing your ads

No small business has enough money to sustain media exposure 52 weeks a year, 24/7. Instead, consider the following mass media scheduling concepts:

>> **Flighting:** Create and sustain awareness by running ads for a short period, then go dormant before reappearing with another *flight* of ads.

>> **Front-loading:** Announce openings, promote new products, and jump-start sales by running a heavy schedule of ads before pulling back to a more economical schedule that aims to maintain awareness.

>> **Heavy-up scheduling:** Synchronize ad schedules with seasonal business or market activity using schedules that include heavy buys several times a year during what's called *ad blitzes.*

>> **Pulsing:** Maintain visibility with an on-and-off schedule that keeps your ad in media channels on an intermittent basis with no variations.

After setting your schedule, leverage your buy by using email and social media to alert customers to watch for your ads, or post the ad on your website and pages to make your investment go further.

Evaluating Your Efforts

Armchair quarterbacking is a popular and pointless after-the-ad-runs activity. Instead, set objectives and plan your evaluation methods early on — not after the play has taken place.

The quickest way to monitor ad effectiveness is to test a couple of great headlines online and measure the clicks they generate. The next-easiest way to monitor ad effectiveness is to produce ads that generate responses and then track how well they do, following this advice:

>> Give your target audience a time-sensitive invitation to take action, a reason to respond, and clear, easy instructions to follow. For example, if you're measuring phone calls, make your phone number large in your ad and be ready for call volume; if you're measuring website visits, present an easy-to-enter site address that leads to a landing page tied to your ad message.

>> Measure media effectiveness by assessing the volume of responses that each media channel generates compared to the investment you made in that channel. Also measure ad effectiveness by tracking the volume of responses to various ad headlines.

TIP

>> Produce your ads to make tracking possible by including a *key,* which is a code used to differentiate which ads produce an inquiry or order. Here are ways to key your ads:

• Direct calls to a unique phone extension keyed to indicate each medium or ad concept. Train those who answer the phone to record the responses to each extension so you can monitor media and ad effectiveness.

- Add a key to coupons that you include in print ads and direct mailers. For direct mailers, the key might indicate the mailing list from which the inquiry was generated. For print ads, the code could match up with the publication name and issue date. For example, BG0214 might be the key for an ad that runs on Valentine's Day in *The Boston Globe.*

- Feature different post office box numbers or email addresses on ads running in various media channels. When receiving responses, attach the source as you enter names in your database so you can monitor not only the number of responses per medium but also the effectiveness of each medium in delivering prospects who convert to customers.

» Test headline or ad concepts by placing several ads that present an identical offer. Track responses to measure which ads perform best.

» Compare the cost effectiveness of various media buys by measuring the number of responses against the cost of the placement.

Chapter **6**

Social Marketing: Facebook, Twitter, Instagram, LinkedIn, and Pinterest

Marketing with digital channels today is somewhat like trying to hit a moving target as the tools, tactics, and trends change more quickly than most can imagine. And because nearly all marketing today is connected to a digital channel, platform, analytics tool, or device, the term *digital marketing* is somewhat of an oxymoron.

No matter what business you're in, the role you play, or the size and scope of your market, you need to understand and stay on top of digital marketing tools to succeed on any level.

Although digital technology introduces exciting opportunities to open new markets and engage with customers like never before, it also comes with the following challenges:

>> Digital tools are constantly changing. As soon as marketers master one, another comes up.

>> Because of the ability that digital technology offers for highly personalized communications, customers have grown to expect it, making traditional marketing methods less effective and putting more pressure on marketers to keep up with rapidly changing technological developments that enhance customers' overall experience.

>> Being able to manage the breadth and depth that digital channels offer marketers for communicating to customers any time and any place is another challenge. In the old days of marketing, brand managers just had to worry about developing a clever campaign with a good offer and getting a good media buyer to negotiate ad buys with magazines, newspapers, radio and television stations, and outdoor companies. Now, you have to identify the best opportunities within numerous channel categories for several customer segments and then customize versions of all elements of each campaign to be personalized for every customer segment or persona, adapt the format for every channel you plan to use, and then deploy quickly and frequently. Oh, and then you have to monitor social media dialogue and online review sites and respond quickly to avoid losing consumer interest, your reputation, or sales.

Mind-boggling! But thankfully, manageable. The trick is to map out a detailed plan based on how your customers use and respond to digital channels to guide how you spend your time and resources communicating, placing ads, and creating meaningful experiences online. Otherwise, you can keep yourself busy and not really go anywhere.

After you have a plan in place as to which channels you need to use and how you need to use them, you then need to have a plan for which technology investments make the most sense for your desired reach, outcomes, and budget.

This chapter provides some insights on several digital channels that drive customer engagement and sales and some tips for how you can integrate these into your marketing plan.

TIP

If you want more in-depth information on the channels discussed here, check out *Social Media Marketing All-in-One For Dummies*, 4th Edition, by Jan Zimmerman and Deborah Ng (John Wiley & Sons, Inc.).

Using Facebook for Engagement That Builds Sales

Facebook is an incredibly important marketing tool. To effectively use Facebook for customer conversations, promotions, and relationship building, you need to build a content marketing plan specific to this channel and an advertising plan. Don't post anything just because you can. Posting without a messaging plan may actually do more harm than good because if it's not meaningful, you'll lose likes, follows, and readership, and each of these is hard to build back.

Following are some guidelines for putting together a content and advertising plan for Facebook; however, this planning guide applies to all other social media channels mentioned in this chapter. Instead of repeating these tips for each channel, use the following as your guide for building a presence and dialogues with your customers on Twitter, Instagram, LinkedIn, and other sites.

Developing a successful Facebook plan

Facebook is where many people document their life story and share their greatest moments. It's also a great place for brands to tell their stories and do so in ways that support the values of their core customers. As you build a plan to tell your story and engage in dialogue with core customers, keep in mind that Facebook is for stories, not sales pitches. Using this channel the way consumers use it will help you achieve greater success and return on the time you spend posting, sharing, liking, and more.

Here are some key elements you need to establish as you work on your Facebook marketing plan:

>> **Define your purpose.** Do you want your Facebook page to be a place where you have meaningful dialogues with your customers? Or a site that promotes your products, provides promotional codes and discount coupons, announces your sales, and the like? Or is your page a place to share stories about your people and business to better humanize your brand? When you answer and prioritize these questions and others like them, you're better poised to make your Facebook efforts pay off.

>> **Set your goals.** Facebook offers many different opportunities and outcomes for businesses in all areas. The trick is to set specific goals and have a plan to help you measure your progress toward achieving them while using your time wisely.

Some goals you can achieve through Facebook include

- Discovering what trends, attitudes, and needs are important to your customers at a given time

- Interacting with customers to discover what they like about your products and brand and what else you can be doing

- Attracting more prospects by posting about relevant topics

- Driving customers and prospects to your website, where you can better direct them toward a transaction

- Growing your email permission database through Facebook promotions

- Communicating with customers and prospects for whom you don't have an email address

- Building your social presence and prospect base through likes, comments, and shares of your current followers

- Creating a stronger brand image

- Putting together a community, or a hive, around your brand

REMEMBER

These same steps apply to other social media pages and channels, so just repeat the steps that apply when building out your brand's digital presence.

The following sections present some tips and examples that will enable you to succeed at reaching many of these goals. But first, keep in mind that you can't achieve any of these goals unless you have followers and friends connected to your page. Use all your social channels to invite people to connect with you on Facebook (and others like LinkedIn), and post content that's worth sharing with their friends to build your base. Always include links for your page on your website, emails, content elements, and in marketing materials.

TIP

Consider doing an email campaign for the sole purpose of getting people to follow you on Facebook and other channels. Let consumers know what they'll gain in terms of insights and interaction if they choose to follow or connect with you.

Determine your metrics

Like any program, make sure you have a mechanism to measure the impact of your efforts toward your goals so you can see whether you need more resources to keep up with the opportunities created or need to make some changes to have a better impact.

TIP

Facebook Insights — a dashboard with metrics and analytics for your page — is available on business pages and provides valuable insights to help you see what your followers liked and didn't like, engagement level per post, which posts got the most likes, and whether you got likes from searches, shares from others, or Facebook advertisements, and more. It's important to pay attention to trends and comments on your page so you can discover what matters most and identify problems before they escalate.

Learn

Opportunities to learn valuable and actionable insights on Facebook are many. For example, you can find out what matters most to your followers and what drives behavior from the dialogue you create, the questions you post, the comments you get back, the posts your customers like or don't like, games your customers play, and by watching what your competitors are doing.

TIP

Ask questions. Most people like to comment on Facebook and have their voice heard. Just look at all the "talk" during a political season, surrounding a common cause, or about a sports matchup. Posting questions for your followers can provide some great insights from their answers and comments.

For example, if you're a carpet cleaning company, here are some questions you may want to ask:

>> When it comes to cleaning your carpets, what motivates you most?

- Having your house look clean and fresh?
- Getting rid of germs that can affect your health?
- Getting that brand new look back again?

People often respond if they like you, want to voice their opinion, or if you offer an incentive. Facebook has a poll application (find it at www.facebook.com/simple.polls) you can use to create and post and monitor results, making it easy to analyze. Or you can just post a question and see what kind of dialogue it inspires. With Facebook's poll application, you can share your poll by email, which helps increase traffic to your page.

TIP

If you have a small following, be careful about using the polls app versus just posting questions to spark dialogue. If few people respond to your poll, it can send a signal that you aren't worth following on Facebook.

Make your question or poll open-ended and thought provoking rather than a yes-or-no question. Instead of, "Do you like watching soccer?" ask, "What do you like most about watching women's soccer matches?" Doing so will help you discover your customers' values and motivators.

REMEMBER

You need to monitor your page and control the content instead of letting others control it for you. You don't want customers to go to your Facebook page and see customer complaints to which no one responded. When this happens, newcomers to your site see a good reason not to do business with you and no explanation or resolution that could inspire them to still give you a chance.

Interact

Clearly, you can interact with customers in many ways on Facebook; you're really just limited by your time and imagination. Because Coca-Cola has one of the most liked and followed Facebook pages, with more than 117 million likes and followers, its page is a good one from which to gain ideas and inspiration.

Coke interacts with Facebook fans by frequently posting about things that matter to them. On November 15, 2018, for example, a post about supporting wildfire relief efforts in California got nearly 500 likes and 124 shares. And when someone posts about Coke, the brand responds. One fan commented on how he liked the little Coke cans but couldn't find them. Coke responded by asking for his zip code (in a personal message, of course) so it could help him find them. On another occasion, a fan asked whether Santa would give him a job. Regardless of whether this was sarcastic or serious, Coke responded with a link to its employment page.

REMEMBER

The key to building relationships on Facebook is twofold:

>> Post content worth reading and commenting on.

>> Respond to the good, the bad, the funny, and the serious.

If consumers feel ignored or invisible on your page, you'll lose them.

If you want shares to help build your reach, the most effective way is to post things that are fun, engaging, humorous, or just really cool. Cool photos, funny videos, and inspirational stories seem to get the most shares.

Build

Keep in mind that the best content isn't always about driving a sale but more about engaging and creating rapport, trust, and communications with your followers. When you achieve these attributes, sales will follow. The best content strategy is to post fun, positive, inspiring, and relatable content that tells a story in which your customers can see themselves.

Creating content that gets a response, dialogue, and leads

Creating a story in which readers can easily see themselves is the best way to spark interaction, dialogue, and new leads. But simply posting a well-written status update isn't likely going to fill up your inbox with new prospects waiting to be sold something. However, if you post content that invites response and interaction that includes others' thoughts, feedback, and expertise, you will be more likely to start a conversation that could get you the right kinds of leads for your business.

Here are some tips for lead-generating content on Facebook:

- **Be brief.** Note that people typically have short attention spans, which seem to be getting shorter all the time with all the distractions and demands on their attention. To up engagement, keep your content short. If you want to provide more information about a topic in a post, provide a link to a full article.

- **Direct to your website.** Directing people to your website for more information on a post you shared is always a good idea, and then be sure to follow up by asking people for their email to get the full story. Offer white papers, links to columns, links to news coverage for your brand, and so on. You can also post about special sales and discounts available on your website.

- **Invite a response.** Don't just post a point, an opinion, or a fact. Spark dialogue by asking fans what they think. Do they agree? Share your stories and encourage followers to do the same. One comment often inspires another, which makes your page more interesting and gives fans more attention for their own voice, too.

- **Provide tips.** People like how-to tips and will often follow a site just to get more. If you have something of value that's actionable and helps others, post it. If you can, break up your list of how-to tips into a series to give you content that inspires people to come back for more.

- **Use hashtags.** Hashtags simply give your post more chances of getting seen, on Facebook and on other channels. Include at least one but not too many, and some research says that two work best.

REMEMBER

Prepare a content plan and stick with it. It's easy to spend all day posting and reading comments on your page and others' pages and accomplish little, if anything, else. To avoid wasting your time and that of your followers and friends, make your content meaningful and actionable.

WARNING

Facebook is best used for interacting and building relationships. If you use it too much to promote sales and offers, you risk losing credibility and fans.

Advertising on Facebook

If you're not able to build your base through the tactics in the previous sections, or you want to get to mass quickly, consider advertising on Facebook. You can do this through boosting your post for a nominal fee or by purchasing Page Like or Offer ads. Here's the difference:

» **Boosting post:** You pay a nominal free to get your post pushed out to people in a demographic you choose. The more you pay, the more people see your post.

» **Page like ads:** These are ads with a Like button for your page that are sent to audiences of your choice. If they "like" the button, they become followers of your page.

» **Offer ads:** You can use an Offer function provided by Facebook to post offers on your page. You can pay to have that offer boosted to people not following you to get more exposure for it. If you have a Facebook page, you likely see these in your News Feed quite a bit.

Building Your Twitter Presence

Although Twitter can be frustrating for the long-winded because you have to keep your posts to 280 characters or less, it does add value for building your brand's presence. For one, Twitter helps start conversations with followers and can be used to post links to your more in-depth content on LinkedIn, Facebook, and, of course, your website. (Flip to Chapter 5 in Book 2 for more about building your own website.)

A key advantage of Twitter is that it helps you find people with similar interests by suggesting people you can follow. And if you post enough interesting content on a given topic, Twitter encourages others to follow you, too.

You can build your Twitter base by doing the following:

>> Searching a keyword related to your brand and then clicking on People associated with that term. For example, searching "consumer behavior" on Twitter results in dozens upon dozens of people to follow.

>> Including hashtags for your tweets so that people can find your posts.

>> Posting your Twitter handle in your email signature, on your web page, and on handouts for trade shows and live events. Encourage followers on your other social channels to follow you on Twitter as well.

>> Creating an interesting profile page and tweeting regularly about things that are of interest to consumers interested in your product and brand.

>> Tweeting about something more than just your latest offer or white paper. Start conversations on objective themes to attract like-minded people.

>> Linking your Twitter account to your Facebook account so that your tweets show up on Facebook, too.

REMEMBER

Twitter has more than 300 million monthly global users and is still growing. It keeps you connected in real time to your customers and maintains your presence in channels that consumers use daily in all industries.

Igniting Your Social Presence on Instagram

Instagram is a photo-centric social network that lets you tell your story through imagery — photos and videos. It's popular among younger audiences and omits a lot of the chatter, good and bad, from other social sites. As of June 2018, Instagram had around 1 billion monthly active users, making it another must-use site for reaching today's consumers.

Because a picture can be "worth a thousand words," Instagram is a great way to communicate quickly about brand events or happenings and to tell your story through the power of images. Most people access it via their smartphone, which limits your reach, but it helps boost your mobile strategy and share your brand stories.

REMEMBER

The best way to be successful on Instagram is to use high-quality photos that are interesting, inspiring, and engaging. You can also upload your Instagram photos to other social sites, including Facebook, Twitter, Flickr, and Foursquare.

Expanding Your Network through LinkedIn

Although many people use LinkedIn to advance their careers and build far-reaching professional networks, LinkedIn also serves a valuable role for businesses. It's different from other social media channels and needs to be treated as such, or it can backfire on you. For one, LinkedIn is *not* for promoting products and attracting leads; it's for promoting your industry expertise, knowledge, insights, and business happenings and for posting your job openings. LinkedIn is widely used by B2B brands to identify decision makers at companies with whom they'd like a relationship and to strike up a meaningful conversation. Many companies in the B2C space use it to promote their workplace culture and attract new employees because it has a popular job center, which attracts job seekers and employers.

As of this writing, LinkedIn has more than 600 million members, making it another must channel for businesses, especially B2B. IBM's page is a great example of how businesses can use LinkedIn. It has more than 5.2 million followers and keeps the content on target and worth reading.

Here's a brief overview of the fundamental elements of a LinkedIn page for businesses:

» **About Us:** Like personal profiles on LinkedIn, your page starts with a summary of your business. You can state whatever you want to about your company and change it as often as you want to.

» **Connections:** LinkedIn shows visitors to your page any common connections you both have so they can see who else values your page and whom they can reach out to for an introduction or conversation. Having a big network makes you and your brand more valuable to others and sends a signal that you're successful at what you do because people want to follow your insights.

» **Showcase pages:** You can add showcase pages to your main page that provide details about your product lines. For example, IBM has 14 showcase pages, which include IBM Watson Health, IBM Watson Internet of Things, and IBM Mobile.

» **Updates:** Your updates are your posts, articles, links to articles, insights you want to share, and other information that helps define your brand. For a business, these may include inspirational quotes from your CEO, financial results, announcements about live events on other channels, such as Facebook, and insights about your product and development and of your corporate social responsibility.

The following sections explore some of the best features on LinkedIn for businesses and marketers alike.

Groups

A good use of LinkedIn is to create your own group. Find a topic of interest in which you're a thought leader and start a group to share insights and exchange ideas. If you start a group, your role is to set the rules, monitor posts, manage posts, initiate conversations, and keep it going. Every time a new post is made on your group page, all members get an email notification, which helps to keep your topic and expertise on members' minds. A group is tough to keep up with if you're stretched for time, so make sure you have a plan for keeping your group active and inspired.

Here are some tips for getting a group going:

» **Define the purpose.** Is this group for exchanging ideas about innovations, solutions, trends, breakthroughs, and case studies on a given topic?

» **Set the rules.** Put your purpose and rules on your site for all to see. If your rules are no job posts or promotions of any kind, follow through. As the manager, you can delete posts and eliminate violators.

» **Invite members of your network to join, and promote your group on your individual page as well as other social channels.** Keep inviting people to join regularly, because the bigger the group, the greater your network and reach.

» **Monitor all activity.** If you set your group up to be an open group, you'll likely get a lot of fake accounts and spam posts. If you don't delete these, you may lose the members you value.

» **Post often.** Post articles, insights, links to white papers, videos, research findings, event coverage, and personnel news. Keep your content business-oriented and leave the promotional, fun posts for other channels like Facebook and Twitter.

Engagement

The best way to get noticed on LinkedIn is to post meaningful articles or updates several times a week if possible. Topics that get engagement include articles you've written, news coverage of your brand, events, trade shows, personnel news, how-to guides, checklists, and links to your blog or new information on your website.

Here are some tips for driving engagement:

>> Include a link to a landing page in your posts; by doing so, you can double your engagement.

>> Post thoughtful questions and encourage others to share their insights.

>> Add an image. LinkedIn claims that images can result in a 98 percent higher comment rate.

>> Link to your videos on YouTube, which will play directly in your LinkedIn feed and could increase your share rate by 75 percent.

>> Respond to comments in a way that encourages more comments and gets more people commenting.

TIP

For every post, LinkedIn provides analytics, such as the number of impressions, clicks, interactions, and percentage of engagement to help you see which topics do best. Like other sites, you can pay to sponsor an update for more money and more exposure.

Promoting Your Brand with Pinterest

With an average monthly active user number of around 250 million, Pinterest can't be ignored, especially by B2C businesses that want their products and creative uses of their products to go viral. Pinterest is widely used as a bookmark of ideas for recipes, home decorating, crafts, holiday décor and goodies, fashion, and do-it-yourself projects.

Per a recent report posted on www.expandedramblings.com, a site that posts stats about various social channels, 60 percent of Pinterest users are female and roughly 40 percent are male. Around 55 percent of online shoppers in the United States claim that Pinterest is their favorite social media platform.

So if you cater to women who like to make, bake, follow fashion trends, and the like, Pinterest just might be for you. If users like your post, they can really increase your exposure by sending it to their email and Facebook contacts or sharing it on other social channels.

REMEMBER

Pinterest is an idea board. You pin what you like, and your pins get communicated via other social channels, giving the creators of those ideas added exposure. The better the picture and the most clever the ideas, the greater the number of pins you'll receive.

You can create boards of images and ideas of interest to you and include images from others on these boards. If people click on these images, they can be directed away from your page so be careful about sending viewers to other pages or sites.

TIP

Pinterest can also be a good place to sell your products. You can promote your pin like on other sites and even set up a shopping cart so people can purchase from you without leaving Pinterest. The shopping cart works much like those on Amazon.com and eBay. You're buying from a seller using its platform. If you use Pinterest for business, make sure you set up a business account so you can get analytics about your most popular pins, shares, repins, likes, and demographic information about those visiting your Pinterest account.

6

Staying in Business

Contents at a Glance

» Breaking down the employee development process

» Building basic coaching skills

» Understanding the power of mentoring

Chapter **1**

Developing Employees Through Coaching and Mentoring

As a business owner, if you have employees, you're by definition a manager. That may not be your goal when you first imagine starting your own business, but unless you can do everything yourself, you need people to help get the work done. Managing people can be tricky, and the ways in which it's been successfully accomplished through the years have changed dramatically.

One recurring theme of today's new management reality is the role of managers as people who support and encourage their employees instead of telling them what to do (or, worse, simply expecting them to perform). The best managers take time to develop their employees by staying actively involved in employee progress and development, helping to guide them along the way. The best managers also are *coaches* — that is, individuals who guide, discuss, and encourage others on their journey. With the help of coaches, employees can achieve outstanding results and organizations can perform better than ever.

Employee development doesn't just happen. Managers and employees must make a conscious, concerted effort. The best employee development is ongoing and requires that you support and encourage your employees' initiative. Recognize, however, that all development is self-development. You can really develop only yourself. You can't force your employees to develop; they have to want to develop themselves. You can, however, help set an environment that makes it more likely that they will want to learn, grow, and succeed. This chapter guides you through employee development, coaching, and mentoring, pointing to the large and small things you can do to help improve your employees' performance and position them for future success.

REMEMBER

As the maxim goes . . .

Tell me . . . I forget.

Show me . . . I remember.

Involve me . . . I learn.

Understanding Why Employee Development Is Important

Many good reasons exist for helping your employees develop and improve themselves. Perhaps the number one reason is that they'll perform more effectively in their current jobs. However, despite all the good reasons, development boils down to one important point: As a manager, you're the one person in the best position to provide your employees with the support they need to develop in your organization. You can provide them with not only the time and money required for training, but also unique on-the-job learning opportunities and assignments, mentoring, team participation, and more. Besides, you'll need *someone* capable of running things when you go on a vacation, right? Employee development involves a lot more than just going to a training class or two. In fact, approximately 90 percent of development occurs on the job.

REMEMBER

The terms *training* and *development* can have two distinctly different meanings. *Training* usually refers to teaching workers the short-term skills they need to know right now to do their jobs. *Development* usually refers to teaching employees the kinds of long-term skills they'll need in the future as they progress in their careers. For this reason, employee development is often known as *career development.*

Now, in case you're still not sure why developing your employees is a good idea, the following list provides just a few reasons:

>> **You may be taking your employees' knowledge for granted.** Have you ever wondered why your employees continue to mess up assignments that you know they can perform? Believe it or not, your employees may not know how to do those assignments. Have you ever actually seen your employee perform the assignments in question?

Suppose you give a pile of numbers to your assistant and tell him you want them organized and totaled within an hour. But instead of presenting you with a nice, neat computer spreadsheet, your employee gives you a confusing mess. No, your assistant isn't necessarily incompetent; he may not know how to put together a spreadsheet on his computer. Find out! The solution may be as simple as walking through your approach to completing the assignment with your employee and then having him give it a try.

>> **Employees who work smarter are better employees.** Simply put, smarter employees are better employees. If you could help your employees develop and begin to work smarter and more effectively — and doubtless you can — why wouldn't you?

REMEMBER

No one in your organization knows everything there is to know. Find out what your employees don't know about their jobs and then make plans for getting them help with what they need to know. When your employees have achieved their development goals, they'll work smarter, your business will reap the benefits in greater employee efficiency and effectiveness, and you'll sleep better at night — all good things when you're a business owner.

>> **Someone has to be prepared to step into your shoes.** Do you ever plan to take a vacation? Or do you need to travel for your business, to seek new suppliers or attend conferences? How are you going to go anywhere or do anything outside the office if you don't prepare your employees to take on the higher-level duties that are part of your job? Some owners are so worried about what's going on at the office when they're on vacation that they call in for a status update several times a day. No matter where they are, they spend more time worrying about the office than they do enjoying themselves.

The reason many business owners *don't* have to call their offices when they're on vacation is that they make it a point to develop their employees to take over when they're gone. You can do the same, too. The future of your company depends on it — really.

>> **Your employees win, and so does your business.** When you allocate funds to employee development, your employees win by learning higher-level skills and new ways of viewing the world — and your company wins because of

increased employee motivation and improved work skills. When you spend money for employee development, you actually double the effect of your investment because of this dual effect. Most important, you prepare your employees to fill the roles your business will need them to move into in the future.

>> **Your employees are worth your time and money.** New employees cost a lot of money to recruit and train. You have to consider the investment not only in dollars, but also in time.

When you have a trained employee, you must do everything to keep that person. Constantly training replacements can be disruptive and expensive.

REMEMBER

When employees see that you have their best interests at heart, they're likely to want to work for you and learn from you. As a result, your business will attract talented people. Invest in your employees now, or waste your time and money finding replacements later. The choice is yours.

>> **The challenge stimulates your employees.** Face it, not every employee is fortunate enough to have the kind of exciting, jet-setting, make-it-happen job you have. Right? For this reason, some employees occasionally become bored, lackadaisical, and otherwise indisposed. Employees constantly need new challenges and new goals to maintain interest in their jobs. And if you don't challenge your employees, you're guaranteed to end up with either an unmotivated, low-achievement workforce or employees who jump at offers from employers who will challenge them. Which option do you prefer?

Getting Down to Employee Development

Employee development doesn't just happen all by itself. It takes the deliberate and ongoing efforts of employees with the support of their supervisor — you. If either employees or you drop the ball, employees don't develop and your business suffers the consequences of employees who aren't up to the challenges of the future. This outcome definitely isn't good. As a business owner, you want your company to be ready for the future the moment it arrives, not always trying to catch up to it.

The employees' role is to identify areas where development can help make them better and more productive workers and then to relay this information to their managers. After identifying further development opportunities, managers and employees can work together to schedule and implement them.

REMEMBER

As a business owner who directly supervises employees, your role is to be alert to the development needs of your employees and to keep an eye out for potential development opportunities. You're also the one who determines where the organization will be in the next few years. Armed with that information, you're responsible for finding ways to ensure that employees are available to meet the needs of the future organization. Your job is then to provide the resources and support required to develop employees so that they're able to fill your company's needs.

Taking a step-by-step approach

To develop your employees to meet the coming challenges within your business, follow these steps:

1. **Meet with an employee about her career.**

   After you assess your employee, meet with her to discuss where you see her in the organization and also to find out where in the organization she wants to go. This effort has to be a joint one. Having elaborate plans for an employee to rise up the company ladder in sales management doesn't do you any good if she hates the idea of leaving sales to become a manager of other salespeople.

2. **Discuss your employee's strengths and weaknesses.**

   Assuming that, in the preceding step, you discover that you're on the same wavelength as your employee, the next step is to have a frank discussion regarding her strengths and weaknesses. Your main goal here is to identify areas the employee can leverage — that is, strengths she can develop to continue her upward progress in the organization and to meet the future challenges your business faces. Focus most of your development efforts and dollars on these opportunities.

   REMEMBER

   Most important, you need to spend more time developing her strengths than improving her weaknesses. She can excel in an area that comes easy to her, resulting in more value for you and your organization than if you forced her to be merely adequate at tasks others excel in.

3. **Assess where your employee is now.**

   The next step in the employee-development process is to determine the current state of your employee's skills and talents. Does Jane show potential for supervising other warehouse employees? Which employees have experience in doing customer demos? Is the pool of line cooks and expediters adequate enough to accommodate a significant upturn in business? If not, can you develop internal candidates, or will you have to hire new employees from outside the organization? Assessing your employees provides you with an overall road map to guide your development efforts.

4. **Create a career development plan.**

   A career development plan is an agreement between you and your employee that spells out exactly what formal support (tuition, time off, travel expenses, and so on) she'll receive to develop her skills and when she'll receive it. Career development plans include milestones. (See the next section for more on these plans.)

5. **Follow through on your agreement, and make sure your employee follows through on hers.**

   Don't break the development plan agreement! Provide the support that you agreed to provide. Make sure that your employee upholds her end of the bargain, too. Check on her progress regularly. If she misses a schedule because of other priorities, reassign her work as necessary to ensure that she has time to focus on her career development plans.

So when is the best time to sit down with your employees to discuss career planning and development? The sooner the better. Unfortunately, many organizations closely tie career discussions to annual employee performance appraisals. On the plus side, doing so ensures that a discussion about career development happens at least once a year; on the minus side, development discussions become more of an afterthought than the central focus of the meeting. Because of that limitation, along with the current rapid changes in competitive markets and technology, once a year just isn't enough to keep up.

TIP

Conducting a career development discussion twice a year with each of your employees definitely isn't too frequent, and quarterly is even better. Include a brief assessment in each discussion of the employee's development needs. Ask your employee what she can do to fulfill them. If those needs require additional support, determine what form of support the employee needs and when to schedule the support. Career development plans are best adjusted and resources best redirected as necessary.

Creating career development plans

The career development plan is the heart and soul of your efforts to develop your employees. Unfortunately, many business owners don't take the time to create development plans with their employees. Instead, they trust that, when the need arises, they can find training to accommodate that need. This kind of reactive thinking ensures that you're always playing catch-up to the challenges your organization will face in the years to come.

Why wait for the future to arrive before you prepare to deal with it? Are you really so busy that you can't spend a little of your precious time planting the seeds that your business will harvest years from now? No! Although you do have to take care of the seemingly endless crises that arise in the here and now, you also have to prepare yourself and your employees to meet the challenges of the future. To do otherwise is an incredibly shortsighted and ineffective way to run your company.

All career development plans must contain at least the following key elements:

>> **Specific learning goals:** When you meet with an employee to discuss development plans, you identify specific *learning goals.* And don't forget, every employee in your organization can benefit from having learning goals. Don't leave anyone out.

>> **Resources required to achieve the designated learning goals:** After you identify your employee's learning objectives, you have to decide how he will reach them. Development resources include a wide variety of opportunities that support the development of your employees. Continuing education classes, job shadowing, *stretch assignments* (assignments that aren't too easy or too hard and that involve some learning and discomfort), formal training, and more may be required. Formal training may be conducted by outsiders, by internal trainers, or perhaps in a self-guided series of learning modules. If the training requires funding or other resources, identify those resources and make efforts to obtain them.

>> **Employee responsibilities and resources:** Career development is the joint responsibility of an employee and his manager. A business can and does pay for training and development opportunities, but so can employees (as any employee who has paid out of her own pocket to get a college degree can attest). A good career development plan should include what the employee is doing on her own time.

TIP

>> **Required date of completion for each learning goal:** Plans are no good without a way to schedule the milestones of goal accomplishment and progress. Each learning goal must have a corresponding date of completion. Don't select dates that are so close that they're difficult or unduly burdensome to achieve, or so far into the future that they lose their immediacy and effect. The best schedules for learning goals allow employees the flexibility to get their daily tasks done while keeping ahead of the changes in the business environment that necessitate the employees' development in the first place.

>> **Standards for measuring the accomplishment of learning goals:** For every goal, you must have a way to measure its completion. Normally, the manager assesses whether the employees actually use the new skills they've been taught. Whatever the individual case, make sure that the standards you use to measure the completion of a learning goal are clear and attainable and that both you and your employees are in full agreement with them.

EASY WAYS TO DEVELOP EMPLOYEES

Although you can develop employees in many different ways, some are definitely better than others. Here are some of the best — and easiest:

1. Give employees opportunities to learn and grow.

2. Be a mentor to an employee.

3. Let an employee fill in for you sometimes, starting with some non-critical task.

4. Allow employees to pursue and develop any idea they have.

5. Give employees more say in how they do their jobs.

6. Send an employee to a seminar on a new topic.

7. Bring an employee with you when you call on customers.

8. Give employees special assignments.

9. Allow an employee to shadow you during your workday.

Coaching Employees to Career Growth and Success

Coaching plays a critical part in the learning process for employees who are developing their skills, knowledge, and self-confidence. Your employees don't learn effectively when you simply tell them what to do. In fact, they usually don't learn at all.

With the right guidance, anyone can be a good coach. This section considers what effective coaches do and how they do it so that you can coach your employees toward successful results.

Serving as both manager and coach

Even if you have a pretty good sense of what it means to be a manager, do you really know what it means to be a coach? A coach is a colleague, counselor, and cheerleader, all rolled into one. Based on that definition, are you a coach? Why or why not?

Surely you're familiar with the role of coaches in other realms. A drama coach, for example, is almost always an accomplished actor or actress. The drama coach's job is to conduct auditions for parts, assign roles, schedule rehearsals, train and direct cast members throughout rehearsals, and support and encourage the actors and actresses during the final stage production. These roles aren't all that different from the roles managers perform in a business, are they?

Coaching a team of individuals isn't easy, and certain characteristics make some coaches better than others. Fortunately, as with most other business skills, you can discover, practice, and improve the traits of good coaches. You can always find room for improvement, and good coaches are the first to admit it. Following are key characteristics and tasks for coaches:

REMEMBER

>> **Coaches set goals.** Whether a small business's vision is to become the leading pizza franchise in the city, to increase revenues by 20 percent a year, or simply to get the break room walls painted this year, coaches work with their employees to set goals and deadlines for completion. They then go away and allow their employees to determine how to accomplish the goals.

>> **Coaches support and encourage.** Employees — even the best and most experienced — can easily become discouraged from time to time. When employees are learning new tasks, when a long-term account is lost, or when business is down, coaches are there, ready to step in and help the team members through the worst of it. "That's okay, Kim. You've learned from your mistake, and I know that you'll get it right next time!"

>> **Coaches emphasize team success over individual success.** The team's overall performance is the most important concern, not the stellar abilities of a particular team member. Coaches know that no one person can carry an entire team to success; winning takes the combined efforts of all team members. The development of teamwork skills is a vital step in an employee's progress in a company.

>> **Coaches can quickly assess the talents and shortfalls of team members.** The most successful coaches can quickly determine their team members' strengths and weaknesses and, as a result, tailor their approach to each. For example, if one team member has strong analytical skills but poor presentation skills, a coach can concentrate on providing support for the employee's development of better presentation skills. "You know, Mark, I want to spend some time with you to work on making your viewgraph presentations more effective."

>> **Coaches inspire their team members.** Through their support and guidance, coaches are skilled at inspiring their team members to the highest levels of human performance. Teams of inspired individuals are willing to do whatever it takes to achieve their organization's goals.

>> **Coaches create environments that allow individuals to succeed.** Great coaches ensure that their workplaces are structured to let team members take risks and stretch their limits without fear of retribution if they fail.

REMEMBER

Coaches are available to advise their employees or just to listen to their problems, as needed. "Carol, do you have a minute to discuss a personal problem?"

>> **Coaches provide feedback.** Communication and feedback between coach and employee is a critical element of the coaching process. Employees must know where they stand in the company — what they're doing right and what they're doing wrong. Equally important, employees must let their coaches know when they need help or assistance. And both parties need this dialogue in a timely manner, on an ongoing basis — not just once a year in a performance review.

WARNING

Firing someone doesn't constitute effective feedback. Unless an employee has engaged in some sort of intolerable offense (such as physical violence, theft, or intoxication on the job), a manager needs to give the employee plenty of verbal and written feedback before even considering termination. Giving employees several warnings offers them opportunities to correct deficiencies that they may not be able to see.

Identifying a coach's tools

Coaching isn't a one-dimensional activity. Because every person is different, the best coaches tailor their approach to their team members' specific, individualized needs. If one team member is independent and needs only occasional guidance, recognize where she stands and provide that level of support. This support may consist of an occasional, informal progress check while making the rounds of the office. On the other hand, if another team member is insecure and needs more guidance, the coach must recognize this employee's position and assist as needed. In this case, support may consist of frequent, formal meetings with the employee to assess progress and provide advice and direction as needed.

REMEMBER

Although you have your own coaching style, the best coaches employ certain techniques to elicit the greatest performance from their team members:

>> **Make time for team members.** Managing is primarily a people job. Part of being a good manager and coach is being available to your employees when they need your help. If you're not available, your employees may seek out other avenues to meet their needs — or simply stop trying to work with you. Always keep your door open to your employees and remember that they are your first priority. Manage by walking around. Regularly get out of your office and visit your employees at their workstations. "Do I have a minute, Elaine? Of course, I always have time for you and the other members of my staff."

» **Provide context and vision.** Instead of simply telling employees what to do, effective coaches explain the why. Coaches provide their employees with context and a big-picture perspective. Instead of spouting long lists of do's and don'ts, they explain how a system or procedure works and then define their employees' parts in the scheme of things. "Chris, you have a very important part in the financial health and vitality of our company. By ensuring that our customers pay their invoices within 30 days after we ship their products, we're able to keep our cash flow on the plus side, and we can pay our obligations such as rent, electricity, and your paycheck on time."

» **Transfer knowledge and perspective.** A great benefit of having a good coach is the opportunity to learn from someone who has more experience than you do. In response to the unique needs of each team member, coaches transfer their personal knowledge and perspective. "We faced this exact situation about five years ago, Dwight. I'm going to tell you what we did then, and I want you to tell me whether you think it still makes sense today."

» **Be a sounding board.** Coaches talk through new ideas and approaches to solving problems with their employees. Coaches and employees can consider the implications of different approaches to solving a problem and role-play customer or client reactions before trying them out for real. By using active listening skills, coaches can often help their employees work through issues and come up with the best solutions themselves. "Okay, Priscilla, you've told me that you don't think your customer will buy off on a 20 percent price increase. What options do you have to present the price increase, and are some more palatable than others?"

» **Obtain needed resources.** Sometimes coaches can help their employees make the jump from marginal to outstanding performance simply by providing the resources those employees need. These resources can take many forms: money, time, staff, equipment, or other tangible assets. "So, Gene, you're confident that we can improve our cash flow if we throw a couple more clerks into collections? Okay, we'll give it a try."

» **Offer a helping hand.** For an employee who is learning a new job and is still responsible for performing her current job, the total workload can be overwhelming. Coaches can help workers through this transitional phase by reassigning current duties to other employees, authorizing overtime, or taking other measures to relieve the pressure. "Phoebe, while you're learning how to troubleshoot that new network server, I'm going to assign your maintenance workload to Rachel. We can get back together at the end of the week to see how you're doing."

Teaching through show-and-tell coaching

Besides the obvious coaching roles of supporting and encouraging employees in their quest to achieve an organization's goals, managers as coaches also teach their employees how to achieve an organization's goals. Drawing from your experience, you lead your workers step by step through work processes or procedures. After they discover how to perform a task, you delegate full authority and responsibility for its performance to them.

For the transfer of specific skills, you can find no better way of teaching, and no better way of learning, than the *show-and-tell* method. Developed by a post–World War II American industrial society desperate to quickly train new workers in manufacturing processes, show-and-tell is beautiful in its simplicity and effectiveness.

REMEMBER

Show-and-tell coaching has three steps:

1. **You do, you say.** Sit down with your employees and explain the procedure in general terms while you perform the task.

2. **They do, you say.** Now have the employees do the same procedure as you explain each step in the procedure.

3. **They do, they say.** Finally, as you observe, have your employees perform the task again as they explain to you what they're doing.

TIP

As you go through these steps, have employees create a "cheat sheet" of the new steps to refer to until they become habit.

Making turning points big successes

Despite popular impressions to the contrary, 90 percent of management isn't the big event — the blinding flash of brilliance that creates markets where none previously existed, the magnificent negotiation that results in unheard-of levels of union-management cooperation, or the masterful stroke that catapults the firm into the big leagues. No, 90 percent of a manager's job consists of the daily chipping away at problems and the shaping of talents.

REMEMBER

The best coaches are constantly on the lookout for *turning points* — the daily opportunities to succeed that are available to all employees.

The big successes — the victories against competitors, the dramatic surges in revenues or profits, the astounding new products — are typically the result of building a foundation of countless small successes along the way. Making a phone-prompt system more responsive to your customers' needs, sending an employee to a seminar on time management, writing a great sales agreement, conducting a meaningful performance appraisal with an employee, meeting a prospective client for lunch — all are turning points in the average business day. Although each event may not be particularly spectacular on its own, when aggregated over time, they can add up to big things.

This is the job of a coach. Instead of using dynamite to transform the business in one fell swoop (and taking the chance of destroying their business, their employees, or themselves in the process), coaches are like the ancient stonemasons who built the great pyramids of Egypt. The movement and placement of each individual stone may not have seemed like a big deal when considered as a separate activity. However, each was an important step in achieving the ultimate result — the construction of awe-inspiring structures that have withstood thousands of years of war, weather, and tourists.

Incorporating coaching into your day-to-day interactions

REMEMBER

Coaches focus daily on spending time with employees to help them succeed — to assess their progress and to find out what they can do to help the employees capitalize on the turning points that present themselves every day. Coaches complement and supplement the abilities and experience of their employees by bringing their own abilities and experience to the table. They reward positive performance and help their employees learn important lessons from making mistakes — lessons that, in turn, help the employees improve their future performance.

For example, suppose you have a young and inexperienced, but bright and energetic, sales trainee on your staff. Your employee has done a great job of contacting customers and making sales calls, but she hasn't yet closed her first deal. When you talk to her about this, she confesses that she's nervous about her own personal turning point: She's worried that she may become confused in front of the customer and blow the deal at the last minute. She needs your coaching.

TIP

The following guidelines can help you, the coach, handle any employee's concerns:

>> **Meet with your employee.** Make an appointment with your employee as soon as possible for a relaxed discussion of the concerns. Find a quiet place free of distractions, and put your phone on hold or forward it to voice-mail.

>> **Listen!** One of the most motivating things one person can do for another is to listen. Avoid instant solutions or lectures. Before you say a word, ask your employee to bring you up-to-date with the situation, her concerns, and any possible approaches or solutions she's considered. Let her do the talking while you do the listening.

TOP COACHING WEBSITES

Here are a few places on the web where you can learn a lot more about coaching:

- The Coaching and Mentoring Network: www.coachingnetwork.org.uk
- International Coach Federation: www.coachfederation.org
- Global Coach Connect: http://coachingconnection.wordpress.com
- Find a Mentor: http://findamentor.com

>> **Reinforce the positive.** Begin by pointing out what your employee did right in the particular situation. Let your employee know when she's on the right track. Give her positive feedback on her performance.

>> **Highlight areas for improvement.** Point out what your employee needs to do to improve and tell her what you can do to help. Agree on the assistance you can provide, whether your employee needs further training, an increased budget, more time, or something else. Be enthusiastic about your confidence in the employee's ability to do a great job.

>> **Follow through.** After you determine what you can do to support your employee, do it! Notice when she improves. Periodically check up on the progress your employee is making and offer your support as necessary.

REMEMBER

Above all, be patient. You can't accomplish coaching on your terms alone. At the outset, understand that everyone is different. Some employees catch on sooner than others and some employees need more time to develop. Differences in ability don't make certain employees any better or worse than their co-workers — they just make them different. Just as you need time to build relationships and trust in business, your employees need time to develop skills and experience.

Finding a Mentor, Being a Mentor

Someone who's already been there and seen what it takes to succeed and who takes a special interest in helping someone else learn what you should and shouldn't do as you work your way up is called a *mentor*. As a new business owner, you may want to find an established business owner to advise you. And as you become established, you may want to help out someone else who is just starting out.

Isn't a manager supposed to be a mentor? No. A mentor is most typically not someone's boss. A manager's job is clearly to coach and help guide employees. Although managers certainly *can* act as mentors for their own employees, mentors most often act as confidential advisers and sounding boards to their chosen employees and, therefore, aren't typically in the employee's direct chain of command.

The day that a mentor takes you under his wing is a day for you to celebrate. Why? Not everyone is lucky enough to find a mentor. And someday you'll be in the position to be a mentor to someone else. When that day comes, don't be so caught up in your busy business life to neglect to reach out and help someone else find his way up in the business.

Here are some of the things mentors do:

>> **Mentors explain how the business really works.** Mentors are a great way to find out what's really going on. There is often a difference between what's formally announced to employees and what really goes on in the business. A mentor can convey that knowledge (at least, the knowledge that isn't confidential).

>> **Mentors teach by example.** A mentor has likely already seen it all and can help an employee discover the most effective and efficient ways to get things done. Why reinvent the wheel or get beaten up by the powers-that-be when you don't have to? This aspect of mentoring is particularly relevant if you choose to seek out an established business owner to be your mentor.

>> **Mentors provide growth experiences.** A mentor can help guide someone to activities above and beyond formal career development plans that are helpful to growth as an employee. For example, a mentor may strongly suggest joining a group such as Toastmasters to improve public-speaking skills. A mentor makes this suggestion because he knows that public-speaking skills are important to future career growth.

>> **Mentors provide career guidance and discussion.** A mentor knows which career paths are dead ends and which offer the most rapid advancement. This knowledge can be incredibly important to an employee's future when making career choices. The advice a mentor gives can be invaluable.

TIP

Within a business, the mentoring process often happens when a more experienced employee takes a professional interest in a new or inexperienced employee. Employees can also initiate the mentoring process by engaging the interest of potential mentors while seeking advice or working on projects together. Recognizing the potential benefits for the development of their employees, many organizations have formalized the mentoring process and made it available to a wider range of employees than the old informal process ever could. You may want consider doing the same in your business.

Chapter **2**

Keeping Your Customers Loyal

A huge factor in your business's long-term success is not only attracting but also satisfying and retaining customers. As a small-business owner, you may be on the front lines of dealing with your business's customers. However, if you have employees, they'll likely be dealing with customers, too. Therefore, the importance of providing excellent customer service must be clear to *everyone* in your organization who has any impact (direct or indirect) on customer satisfaction. This includes the receptionist, the accounts receivable clerk, the delivery truck driver, and many others.

This chapter offers some helpful advice for providing excellent customer service. Here, you discover many strategies for keeping your current customers, whether they're satisfied or dissatisfied.

WARNING

Although the level of customer service in many American businesses falls short, only a foolish business owner would assume that unhappy customers will continue to tolerate poor service or buy products that don't perform. Consumers generally have many choices, so if you and your employees don't satisfy your customers' needs, you'll likely face these unpleasant results:

>> **Competitive threats:** Now more than ever, customers have many options for buying what your company has to offer. For the vast majority of businesses, competition is intense at the global, national, state, regional, and local levels.

It's only a matter of time before your unhappy customers become your competitors' newest customers.

>> **Negative word-of-mouth:** Even worse than losing dissatisfied customers to the competition is *negative word-of-mouth,* whereby unhappy customers post negative reviews online and talk, telling other consumers why they wouldn't buy your products and services. Furthermore, your competitors are more than happy to recount the negative stories they've heard from your disgruntled customers. All this talk will certainly tarnish your business's reputation.

>> **Potential lawsuits:** As if losing customers and tarnishing your business's reputation aren't enough, disgruntled customers can initiate (gasp!) lawsuits. Even if those litigious customers don't prevail in court, they can cause you to face large legal bills, and your business can suffer further damage to both its profitability and its reputation.

Retaining Your Customer Base

As the owner of a small business, you should strive to keep your customers happy. How? Well, you have an enormous impact on your customers' satisfaction through your company's products and services and the way in which you present them. This section provides you with the keys to keeping your customers satisfied. Of course, not all customers will stay satisfied and loyal to your business, so you also discover how you can learn from customer defections to minimize their happening in the future.

Getting it right the first time

As a small-business owner, if you don't get your product or service right the first time, you may not have a second chance with customers. Customers aren't stupid, and if you sell them inferior merchandise or services — especially when better merchandise or services are available from other sources — they won't come back the next time they're in the market for the products and services you offer.

What's more, some of your customers who suffered bad experiences with your company will tell others of their lousy experiences. Large companies usually have enough cash reserves built up to weather a storm, but the typical small-business owner doesn't.

Continuing to offer more value

Getting your product or service right the first time isn't enough to keep customers coming back in the long run. Like life, the business world keeps changing. Because of the ever-present threat of competition, resting on your laurels is foolish — and perhaps fatal. In addition to initially developing a top-notch, quality product or service, you must regularly examine how you can offer even more value — improved products or services at the same or lower cost. If you don't, competitors who faithfully keep up with market forces will gradually eat your lunch.

Suppose that you're a dry cleaner. A new dry-cleaning technology that allows dry-cleaning establishments to get their work done 20 percent faster and 30 percent cheaper has been introduced in the marketplace. If you fail to take advantage of this improvement in your industry, you may discover the hard way, when your customers leave you for your competitors, that they want the value this new technique offers. As your competitors cut prices and reap greater numbers of customers and profits, you lose business and experience shrinking profit margins.

Knowing that company policy is meant to be bent

Flexibility is paramount in any organization, but it's especially important in a small business, where responsive and personally tailored service can set you apart from the larger companies. One place where you should be flexible is in your company policy. If a customer has a problem but you have a rule or regulation preventing you from resolving that problem, forget the rule or regulation. Bend it. Skirt it. Find a loophole in it.

For example, put yourself in the following situations:

>> You're an electrical contractor who needs material to complete a job. Your electrical wholesaler tells you that he has a problem with the order-entry system and can't process your order right now, so you'll have to come back tomorrow to place your order.

>> You're a regular customer at a dry cleaner. It's Wednesday, and you need your tuxedo dry-cleaned by Friday night. The dry cleaner informs you that it won't be ready until Saturday because of the firm's three-day turnaround policy.

What are the common threads here?

>> The electrical wholesaler and the dry cleaner apparently have cast-in-stone rules and regulations that dictate the way they do business, and they won't bend those rules to solve a customer's problem.

>> The two businesses are in danger of alienating a customer.

How can these business owners become more flexible to satisfy the customer? The electrical wholesaler can give the contractor the material today and run the transaction through his order-entry system tomorrow. The dry cleaner can put the customer's tuxedo in front of someone else's order, no matter what the company's operations manual dictates.

These are the moments of truth in any business — the times when what the business says it will do conflicts with what the business actually does. These times differentiate the business that *says* the customer is king from the business that *acts* as if the customer is king.

REMEMBER

This policy doesn't mean that you should always provide extra service casually or for free. In some situations, you may want to charge more for a special service. Consider the special favor and the one-time transaction when you set your pricing strategy. Also, you don't want to tell your employees to feel free to break any rule at any time; that's the road to chaos and lack of standards, quality control, and profitability. But flexibility helps keep customers feeling happy and coming back — and recommending you to others. Let your managers and other employees know that you stand behind this philosophy, and you'll empower them to always provide good customers with top-notch service.

Taking away lessons from customer defections

The costs of acquiring a new customer are often significant. After spending the marketing effort and dollars needed to secure a new customer for your business (see Book 5 for the skinny on marketing), you will want to keep that customer coming back to your business for many years. If you experience much customer turnover, your cost of doing business will rise significantly as you try to attract replacement customers, so you need to take action quickly. After all, customer turnover can indicate major problems with your company's products or services and customer service.

A popular action within a business is to celebrate successes rather than examine failures. However, as a small-business owner, you'll stick around much longer if you scrutinize your failures and make positive changes to correct them. Take the time to examine customer defections and their underlying causes. The following sections dig deeper into this topic.

Examining the value of customer loyalty

Frederick Reichheld is a management consultant who specializes in understanding, and working with corporations on, customer loyalty. He's the author of several books on customer loyalty, and his research has produced the following powerful insights and facts:

>> The average company today loses half of its customers in five years.

>> The typical *Fortune* 500 company has an average annual *real growth* (that is, growth in excess of the rate of inflation) of 2.5 percent. If such a company retained just 5 percent more of its customers each year, its real growth would jump to 7.5 percent.

>> A 5 percent increase in customer retention in a typical company generally translates into an increase in profits of more than 25 percent. In some industries, good, long-standing customers are worth so much that reducing customer defections by 5 percent can double profits.

Clearly, retaining customers — particularly your best customers — has an enormous bottom-line impact. Given how important and valuable retaining customers is, you may think that if a business were losing many of its customers, it would seek to understand why and to correct the underlying problems. Well, if that were the case, customer loss wouldn't be as high as it is in many businesses.

Tracking customer defections

In his consulting work and research, Reichheld has also found that, not surprisingly, many businesses don't learn from their customer losses. He says,

> "Psychologically and culturally, it's difficult and sometimes threatening to look at failure too closely. Ambitious managers want to link their careers to successes; failures are usually examined for purposes of assigning blame rather than detecting and eradicating the systemic causes of poor performance."

The good news for you, the small-business owner, is that you don't have to be concerned with bosses and organizational politics when addressing the problem of customer defections. After all, you're the boss. However, it's a natural human tendency to spend more time chasing and celebrating successes than investigating and learning from failures and losses.

TIP

Make a commitment to track the customers that you lose and ask why. (This is the customer equivalent to the exit interview that you should always perform with departing employees.) Knowing that you've lost customers isn't enough; you must find out *why* you lost them. Doing so can help keep you in business and help keep your business growing (see Chapter 3 of Book 6 for more on growing your business).

Consider, for example, one particular automotive oil-change business. The business boasted that you can get your oil changed within ten minutes and be on your merry way. On one visit to the establishment, a customer pulled into the entrance and got out of his car. He was then ignored for the next ten minutes — and not because the business was too busy. The people who were checking in new customers moved at a snail's pace, and one employee even spent several minutes on a personal phone call.

When it was the customer's turn, the employee who checked him in was rude. He left during the oil change to do some shopping nearby rather than sit in the poorly ventilated, exhaust-infested garage. Upon his return, he had to wait another ten minutes because, although his car had finally been serviced, the paperwork wasn't done. The same employee who checked him in took another 15 minutes to finish the paperwork and kept his unfriendly and surly attitude all the while.

Throughout this poor-service experience, the customer didn't utter a word of complaint, but guess which shop he bypassed the next time his car needed an oil change? A gas station closer to the customer's home started offering oil changes, which were about 20 percent less costly than the other place. The attendant who checked him in at the service station was friendly and polite, and his car and paperwork were ready when promised.

REMEMBER

Make it part of your company's culture that you don't expect employees to be perfect and that making mistakes won't necessarily lead to an employee's immediate firing. However, make it clear that you won't tolerate employees who provide sub-par service, display poor attitudes, and drive good customers away from your business.

Recognizing and practicing customer service

All businesses have products or services to sell. Sometimes businesses get too focused on those products and services, giving short shrift to the accompanying customer service that customers expect.

Maybe you can't readily define the term *customer service*, but you probably know what it is when you get it or don't get it. For example, you surely recognize customer service in a company you do business with when

>> Its receptionist (or at least its telephone system) connects you with your party quickly and efficiently.

>> Its bookkeeper politely answers a question you have about an invoice.

>> Its shipping clerk quickly traces your order and tells you exactly when to expect it.

>> Its salesperson gets back to you quickly with the quotes and delivery schedules you requested.

REMEMBER

In each of these situations, the company is solving your problem or addressing your need in a manner that meets or exceeds your expectations, which is, after all, the definition of *customer service*. Customer service is solving your customers' problems or meeting their needs.

When you ask an employee for help in a business that you frequent, have you ever felt that her behavior was essentially saying to you, "That's not my department or responsibility"? In a business — large or small — that recognizes the value of customer service, the correct response to a customer question is, "Let me find the solution for you." The solution may ultimately rest in the hands of another employee, another department, or even another business, but the employee has accepted responsibility for solving your problem.

Some larger companies have distinctly identified *customer service departments* — a person or group of people whose sole purpose is to solve customer problems. In such a company, all customer telephone calls are routed through to the customer service department. In smaller companies, however, many — perhaps even all — employees are involved in customer service. In the examples from the previous bulleted list, the telephone operator, the bookkeeper, the shipping clerk, and the salesperson are providing customer service. If you, the boss and Grand Poobah, get involved in solving a customer's problem, you, too, are focused on customer service. The same is true for the janitor or the night watchman.

The challenge is for your employees to understand that they're on the job to solve your customers' problems. After all, they may believe (because this is the way their job descriptions read) that their role is simply to answer the telephone, keep the books, ship products, or sell services. Although these functions accurately describe the employees' assigned *activities*, they don't define the employees' assumed *responsibilities*.

REMEMBER

You and your employees are on the job — just as your entire company exists — for one reason and one reason only: to solve your customers' problems.

Smart business owners know that customer service (and the accompanying problem solving) begins before a sale is made, continues during the sale, and continues long after the sale is complete. Keep in mind that customers aren't just coming to your business for your products and services. The attentiveness you show toward your customers' needs — before, during, and after the sale — that comes with what you sell is an integral part of the package. Treat your customers as you would a good friend.

The following sections break down the stages of customer service so that you can see what you and your employees need to do to keep your customers coming back.

Customer service before the sale

When a customer goes to buy a product or service, part of what can close the sale or blow the deal is the quality (or lack thereof) of the customer service before the moment the customer decides to buy. When a customer schedules an appointment, she's buying not only the service provider's expertise but also the "proper care and handling" before the service is provided. And when a potential customer enters your store for a product, she wants the store to be clean, well maintained, and conveniently arranged. That's all part of the customer service experience.

Consider the last time you bought something, whether it was a car, a bag of groceries, a medical exam, or a haircut. With each of these purchases, you interacted with the business provider before you committed to buy the product or service.

If you're like most people, you probably have some bad memories about slick salespeople who accosted you the moment you walked onto an auto dealer's lot. Many car salespeople spend more time selling than they do listening and educating. The salesperson isn't trying to solve *your* problem — figuring out which car to purchase. He's trying to solve *his* problem — how to make a hefty commission to meet his next mortgage payment. Because of poor customer service at the point of sale in the car business, many people turn around and take their business elsewhere.

Customer service during the sale

After a customer commits to buying a product or service, the customer service must continue. Never halt your efforts to satisfy customers. When a customer forks over the dough for your wares and you don't meet the customer's service expectations, even if the sale is finalized, you may lose repeat business and the opportunity for referrals to other customers.

For example, after your doctor arrives in the examination room, you'll pay close attention to how well she listens to you and how she treats you. If the doctor is abrupt, bad at listening, and arrogant in asserting her opinion — instead of showing a willingness to discuss options and consider your needs — you may choose to find another physician.

Likewise, after you decide to buy a car, you won't be overjoyed if completing the transaction takes several hours. Even though you may be happy with the selection of the car, the hassle in getting on your way may make you less glowing in your recommendation to others.

Customer service after the sale

After a customer has purchased your company's products or services, your relationship with that customer, at least as it relates to that transaction, isn't over. The customer may have follow-up questions that you need to answer or problems down the road with your products or services.

WARNING

If you or your employees treat your customers as if they're bothering you and you aren't attentive to after-sales service, you may discourage customers from making more purchases and referring others to your business. Poor after-sales service communicates to your customers that after you have their money, you don't really care what happens to them.

In addition to being attentive to all your customers' questions and concerns, be sure to solicit feedback (possibly through a formal survey) from your customers as to the quality of the customer service that your business offered them.

REMEMBER

In some businesses, you must be careful not to give away valuable support that you can and should charge for. For example, if follow-up exams or appointments are expected, you should build the cost of those expected services into your upfront pricing or set a pricing schedule for the cost of the follow-up. Be sure that at the time customers buy from you, they know the cost of such follow-up work. Customers don't like negative surprises, especially when they affect their pocketbooks.

Showing that you care — the old-fashioned way

In the age of technology, you may be tempted to discard some of the personal touches that today's customers still appreciate. Although technology certainly answers many of your business's needs, it can never replace the following personal touches in the eyes of customers:

>> **Handwriting notes:** A handwritten note is always the best way to say "thank you."

>> **Thanking customers personally:** Having the owner of a company call and say "thank you" (as opposed to having an assistant or salesperson send out an email) makes a positive impression.

>> **Handling mistakes honestly and quickly:** Don't waste one second trying to cover your tracks after mistakes are made. Come clean, fess up, and solve the problem. Provide personal customer service representatives — not voicemail boxes that allow you to avoid dealing with problems. Approached correctly, mistakes can provide an opportunity to improve your business, impress your customers, and reward their loyalty.

Dealing with Dissatisfied Customers

You can have the best products and services, offer competitive prices, and provide terrific customer service, and you'll still end up with the occasional unhappy customer. How you handle complaints — both justified and unjustified — is vital to the long-term reputation and health of your business. The following sections contain our time-tested advice for dealing with your unhappy and sometimes troublesome customers.

Here's a tip to help you maintain your sanity: Keep in mind that you have your own way of doing things, that yours isn't a perfect product or service, and that you can't meet *all* your customers' needs and expectations *all* the time.

Listen, listen, listen

Most people like to believe that they're terrific listeners. The reality is that most of them aren't. And even if you *are* a good listener, you have moments when, for any number of reasons, you don't listen well. You get busy and stressed out with the competing demands on your time from work, family, friends, daily chores, and obligations. You also have days when you're tired, not feeling well, or have been on the receiving end of bad news or bad experiences.

Another impediment to good listening is that you may be convinced that an upset customer is simply being a troublemaker. As with all personal relationships, however, your preconceived notions about others can keep you from hearing legitimate and real concerns and reasons for being dissatisfied.

Before you (or one of your employees) lose your temper with a complaining customer, take a deep breath. Try to set aside all your personal issues, your opinions about the situation, and your preconceived notions about the customer and her right to be unhappy. Stop and listen. Try to find out what the customer is unhappy about and why. Different people, not surprisingly, get upset about different things. You have no way to know and understand what's upsetting a particular customer until you take the time to ask and truly listen.

To ensure that you've really heard what your upset customer has said, paraphrase the concerns you've heard and tell the customer that you're sorry that she's unhappy. (Keep in mind that this isn't an admission of wrongdoing or guilt on your part, especially if you're worried about landing in court and being sued for product liability.) Then work on developing a solution with the customer (see the following section for how to do so).

WARNING

The absolute worst thing that you (or your employees) can do to a customer with a complaint is to interrupt and argue when she's trying to convey dissatisfaction with your products or services. And don't be defensive. This is easier said than done, but you'll do far more long-term damage to your business's reputation by further upsetting an already-unhappy customer. Even if you're 100 percent certain that the customer is the biggest yahoo you've ever dealt with and that you don't want her as a future customer, treat her with respect and try to solve her problem. Otherwise, you may end up with negative online reviews and word-of-mouth advertising, and possibly a lawsuit.

Develop a solution

When a customer complains, keep in mind that he's complaining because of dissatisfaction with the deal that he received. The next step, after listening to the customer's complaints, is to develop a solution that addresses the complaints.

REMEMBER

You have two ways to arrive at a solution:

>> **Ask the customer what solution he would propose and then see how it compares with what you can do.** The advantage of asking the customer for a solution is the same as with any other form of negotiation (which, after all, is what's going on in this situation). If you let the dissatisfied customer make the opening offer, you know exactly where you stand and what you have to do to satisfy him.

Imagine the benefit you can derive when the customer's solution is less costly than what you were about to offer. In such a circumstance, the opportunity suddenly exists for you to take an unpleasant situation and turn it into an opportunity to strengthen the complaining customer's loyalty to your business.

>> **Propose a solution yourself and then wait for the customer to counter with a solution that he thinks is better.** If you go this route, you don't propose a solution until the customer doesn't have, or refuses to come up with, one.

For example, suppose that you run a professional service business and you're responsible for missing a customer's appointment — either because of a scheduling mistake or because you're behind schedule and the customer simply couldn't wait any longer. You quickly determine that the customer is really angry about having been stood up after he has taken valuable time out of his workday.

Your solution to ease the customer's unhappiness can go something like this:

1. **Apologize for the time he wasted.**

2. **Ask for his recommended solution.**

3. **If he doesn't have a solution, offer a discount (perhaps 15 or 20 percent off the appointment price when he reschedules).**

4. **When the customer returns for the rescheduled appointment, be absolutely certain that he's seen on time and provided with the best possible service.**

The key to understanding your customers' complaints (and your employees' complaints, really) is your ability to put yourself in their shoes. After you've figured out how to view your business through the eyes of a customer, you'll find that you can solve problems the vast majority of the time.

Now suppose that your company sells products, and a customer comes in to say that a product you sold her broke and isn't worth the packaging it came in. In this case, you can offer a replacement product, fix the broken one, or offer the customer a refund. But if you're certain that the customer misused the product and that her mistake subsequently led to the breakage, you have a dilemma on your hands. You have to decide whether this person adheres to your definition of what a "good" customer should be.

Even in those situations in which you determine that this person isn't what you consider to be a good customer, try to make the parting of your ways as harmonious and conflict-free as possible. It's okay if an unmanageable customer doesn't do business with you anymore. Just do everything you can to ensure that he doesn't go away angry and tell others that your business offers a lousy service or product.

Chapter **3**

Cultivating a Growing Business

Given the choice, most small-business owners would prefer that their companies grow rather than not grow, stagnate, or even fail. After all, growth *is* the American way — not to mention it's also one of the typical entrepreneur's primary motivators.

This chapter is for you if your business is presently on a growth track or (you hope) soon will be. It provides you with insights into what awaits you on your journey, along with tips on how to survive the trip and prosper as you go. However, be aware that growth — especially that of the consistent and relentless variety — can feel like a climb up an uncharted mountain. And the climb becomes even steeper if you set out on the journey unprepared to make the change that has eluded so many small-business owners before you: the transition from entrepreneur to manager.

The changes to your growth-fueled business will be apparent everywhere. Five years from now, your customers will be different, their demands and needs will be different, and many of the products and services you offer them will be different. You'll also have a number of brand-spanking-new superstar employees, and employee-related matters will take up more and more of your time. (Sadly, some of your earlier hires will have departed or won't have the skills to keep up with your growth.)

Finally, you — the founder — will be constantly in the midst of change, engrossed in the not-always-enjoyable-but-always-necessary process of making the transition from entrepreneur to manager. Along the way, you'll adopt skills such as delegation, focus, and holding people accountable — skills that every successful manager must eventually acquire to effectively lead a growing team of employees. And your financial, communication, and leadership skills will be tested and, we hope, improved. In other words, you won't be the same Grand Poobah you are today!

The only characteristics of your business that won't change as your company grows are its ethics and principles. However, if your top management (which is probably just you at this point) changes during the business's growth years, as happens in so many growing entrepreneurial companies, even your company's ethics and principles may be subject to change. Growth holds nothing sacred!

Recognizing Growth Stages

Small-business success doesn't just happen. Some fairly predictable but not very orderly stages characterize its evolution. Most entrepreneurs caught up in the day-to-day goings on in a business don't recognize these stages until they've passed. Well, it's time to open your eyes. The following sections describe the three stages of business evolution.

The start-up years

The *start-up years* are the period when survival motivates your thoughts and actions. Everything that happens within the business is dominated by you; words such as *delegation, team,* and *consensus* generally aren't yet part of the business's vocabulary. These are the hands-on years. For some owners, they're the most enjoyable years of the business; for all owners, they're an integral part of the learning process.

The work during this time is hard — often the physically and emotionally draining kind of hard. The hours are long and sometimes tedious, but by the end of the day, you can hopefully see, touch, and feel at least some of the progress you've made. The gratification is instantaneous.

The duration of this first stage varies greatly from business to business. Some fly through the start-up stage in less than a year, but most spend anywhere from one to three years growing out of this stage. Others — often those in the more competitive niches — can spend as many as five or more years in the start-up stage.

REMEMBER

You know you've graduated from the start-up stage when profitability and orderliness become a dependable part of your business. The hectic days of worrying about survival are replaced by the logical and orderly days of planning for success.

The growth years

The *growth years* are the years when your business achieves some sense of order, stability, and profitability. Your evolving business has survived the mistakes, confusion, and chaos of the start-up years, and now optimism, camaraderie, and cooperation should play an important role in the organization. Key employees surface, efficient administrative systems and controls become part of the business's daily operating procedures, and the need to depend on you for everything that happens diminishes.

The business of doing business remains fun for most small-business owners in this stage, because increasing sales translate into increasing profits — every small-business owner's dream. The balance sheet puts some flesh on its scraggly bones as you generate cash as a result of profitability. You figure out how to delegate many of those unpleasant tasks that you performed in the past. And survival is no longer your primary motivator. At last, the daily choices you make can be dictated by strategic goals rather than day-to-day survival.

REMEMBER

Here is some more good news: This stage can last a long time if the growth remains under control and if you manage the business and its expanding population of employees properly. (For information on out-of-control growth, see the nearby sidebar "Is your business growth healthy?") More than likely, however, this stage will last anywhere from a few years to six or seven years or so before the next stage raises its ugly head.

The transition stage

The third stage, the *transition period*, can also be called the *restructuring stage* or the *diversification stage*. By the time this stage begins, something basic to the success of the growth years has changed or gone wrong. As a result, in order for the business to survive, a strategic change in direction is required. (See the later section "Redefining Your Role in an Evolving Business" for more on this topic.)

IS YOUR BUSINESS GROWTH HEALTHY?

Growth is good, as long as it's healthy growth. Here are two ways to figure out whether your business's growth is trending toward healthy or unhealthy:

- Using your income (profit and loss) statement (see Chapter 2 in Book 3), compute the percentage growth of your sales. Then compute the percentage growth of your earnings. If your sales are growing faster than your earnings, your business is showing an early sign of unhealthy growth. The bigger the spread, the more unhealthy the trend.

- Using your balance sheet (see Chapter 3 in Book 3), compute the combined percentage growth of your key noncash asset categories: accounts receivable, inventory, and equipment. If the combined percentage growth of these three categories exceeds the percentage growth of your sales (see the preceding bullet point), your business is showing another early sign of unhealthy growth. Again, the bigger the spread, the more unhealthy the trend.

For your business's long-term growth to be trending in a healthy direction, two things should be taking place:

- Your percentage growth in earnings should keep up with, or exceed, your percentage growth in sales.

- The combined percentage increase in the key asset categories (accounts receivable, inventory, and equipment) should be less than your percentage increase in sales.

The financially astute small-business owner is no different from the financially astute homeowner. The homeowner must figure out how to keep his expenditures in line with his income. The small-business owner must figure out how to keep her income in line with her sales (which amounts, in large part, to controlling her expenses), all while controlling the purchase of those key assets (inventory, receivables, and equipment) — the increase in which must be paid for by cash generated through future earnings.

WARNING

Many factors can bring about this transition stage, including the following:

- **Relentless growth:** Relentless sales growth requires relentless improvement in the business's employees, systems, procedures, and infrastructure, and many businesses simply can't keep up with such pressures.

- **Shrinkage of sales and the disappearance of profits, or even prolonged periods of stagnation:** This is the opposite of growth. The causes for this shrinkage or stagnation can come from anywhere and everywhere, and they often include such uncontrollable factors as new competitors, a changing economy, new technology, and changes in consumer demand.

The solution to transition-stage problems lies in making a strategic change — a transition — in the fundamentals of the company. This transition often involves a change in top management. It isn't unusual for a rapidly growing company to outgrow its founding entrepreneur (that's you!). Additionally, the transition may involve the introduction of new products or services, the establishment of new distribution systems, the adoption of new technology, or the paring of the under-performing assets of the business.

TIP

The good news to a displaced founding entrepreneur: If yours was a profitable company and you can sell it on the way out, you can then afford to go back to what you do well and what you enjoy. You can go back to the life of an entrepreneur and start all over again. Or, if you're financially able, you can move on to other pursuits.

Resolving Human Resources Issues

The day that you hire your first employee is the same day that the bottomless pit of human resources (or HR) issues appears on your path (flip to Chapter 1 in Book 4 for an introduction to hiring). After all, that newly hired employee has needs, privileges, and rights — the last of which, lest you forget, are protected by a host of watchdog government agencies and lawyers. The following sections raise some important HR concerns you'll face and provide suggestions on how to handle them.

Identifying important HR concerns

Consider, if you will, a partial list of HR issues, the mere mention of which can make a government inspector's (and attorney's) mouth water:

>> Sexual harassment

>> Discrimination

>> Wrongful discharge

>> Hiring violations

>> Workplace safety violations

>> Working conditions violations

>> Wage and hour violations

Unfortunately, much of the concern for the employee's welfare that you hear about today is well founded and necessary, because of a minority of greedy and uncaring business owners over the years who have created the need for such scrutiny. This means that law-abiding and people-caring small-business owners like you must pay the price in the form of red tape and regulations. And the more your company grows, the larger that total price generally becomes.

Dealing with HR issues in three stages

How do you deal with such a wide spectrum of HR issues? The answer depends on which of the three stages of HR development your company happens to be in.

Stage 1: Handling HR issues yourself

Stage 1 is the start-up stage when your business has, for example, fewer than ten employees and you have no one on the payroll to whom you can delegate the wide variety of HR issues. In this stage, you must defer the activities that you probably prefer performing (sales, product development, and customer service) and deal with those that you don't (working conditions, drug and alcohol policies, and employee conduct).

Stage 1 is the hands-on stage when you're up to your eyeballs in the day-to-day details of running a business (see the earlier section "The start-up years"). The good news is that the HR lessons you learn at this stage of your business will benefit you forever. The bad news is that dealing with some HR issues may consume an extraordinarily large part of your time.

REMEMBER

When dealing with those sticky issues that have the potential to become even stickier — harassment, wrongful termination, employee theft, and the like — consult a professional (a human resources consultant or lawyer) before you act.

Stage 2: Delegating HR responsibilities to others

As the number of employees in your company grows, you should look for the opportunity to offload some of HR's details onto someone else in the business — most likely a full-time bookkeeper or the person who manages your office — or consider outsourcing your HR to a professional employer organization. Whatever option you choose, the basic HR functions will remain as a part of your day-to-day business procedures until your business enters Stage 3.

Stage 3: Hiring an HR professional

You may think you're in heaven when your business grows to the point when you can finally afford the small-business owner's greatest luxury: your very own

Director of HR. (This typically happens when you have somewhere between 50 and 100 employees.) You may find it hard to believe that people make a 9-to-5 living dealing with, and actually enjoying, the seemingly endless details involved in HR. Imagine, someday you can have that person on your payroll!

TIP

Strangely, people capable of becoming HR directors are similar to consultants: There seems to be one on every street corner. Run an ad for an HR director in one of the many online resources (for example, LinkedIn, Glassdoor, Indeed, Monster, ZipRecruiter) and you can expect to measure your responses in the dozens. Among those dozens, you can reasonably expect to find a number of quality applicants. (See Chapter 1 in Book 4 for tips on how to hire the best one.)

Addressing Time-Management Issues

The faster a company grows and the bigger it becomes, the more important time-management issues become. The increased size of an organization requires increased communication between its members — which in turn increases the demands on your time and that of your employees.

REMEMBER

Time, and the efficient use of it, is one of those cultural issues that starts at the small-business owner's desk. You, by way of your actions, determine how your business utilizes its time. If you ensure that meetings start on time, that the workday begins at 8:30 a.m. sharp, and that prolonged gatherings around the copy machine are unacceptable behavior, your company is bound to develop a culture of efficient time management. On the other hand, if you don't pay attention to such issues, human nature will take its course, which doesn't bode well for your business's efficient use of time.

Here are just a few of the ways that a small-business team can waste time:

>> Missed deadlines and appointments

>> Meetings that last an hour when they should last only ten minutes

>> People who arrive late to meetings

>> Meetings that shouldn't be held in the first place

>> Long voice-mail messages, unreturned phone calls, unanswered phone calls, and unnecessary calls

>> Unnecessary or long-winded emails

>> Employees who conduct personal matters on the job (texting and making calls to friends, shopping online, surfing their Facebook page, and so on)

>> People who take 15 minutes to say what can be said in 5

>> Time spent waiting — in waiting rooms, outside offices, or for someone to get off the phone or away from the copier

>> Equipment that malfunctions, systems that don't work, and supplies that run out of whatever is needed at that instant

Imagine what your company would be like if everyone practiced effective time management. How much additional work would each employee get done? How much time would he or she save? Five hours a week? Ten? What can every employee do with another 5 hours a week — 250 hours a year? And what can your company do with those 250 hours a year, multiplied by the number of employees you have?

REMEMBER

To increase efficiency in your small business, you should insist on employee attitudes and behavior that value rather than abuse time. For example, you should insist on a culture within your business that

>> Requires people to be on time for the start of the day, for meetings, for conferences, for whatever.

>> Doesn't hold unnecessary meetings and disbands meetings that are unnecessary.

>> Requires every employee to use a time-management system, whether it's a simple to-do list, an intricate store-bought system, or contained on the latest handheld device.

>> Has definitive rules governing such issues as surfing the web for personal purposes and/or playing computer games on company time.

>> Deals with its in-house nonstop talkers and time abusers (every office has them).

>> Requires that telephones be picked up after the first or second ring, voice-mail messages be shortened, and telephone calls be returned promptly.

>> Respects visitors' time. (How do you like it when you visit another business and you wait in the lobby for half an hour?)

>> Encourages thoughtful delegation. (Don't waste your time doing a task that someone else can do faster — and often better.)

>> Understands that shorter and quicker is better when it comes to meetings, memos, emails, letters, manuals, and rules.

>> Insists on employee accountability. You should be able to count on employees to perform such detail-ridden tasks as keeping the supply inventory at adequate levels, maintaining equipment to minimize downtime, and designing and implementing workable internal systems and controls.

>> Uses time-proven technology efficiently.

Time management itself is impossible to measure. What you *can* measure are results — results when compared to plans, budgets, and goals. You can usually figure that whenever you see improving results in areas you *can* measure, your management of time is improving, too.

REMEMBER

You alone can make effective time management a part of your company's culture. After hiring the best people that you can (see Chapter 1 in Book 4), you need to set the right example. Your employees will take it from there. (If they don't, you've hired the wrong employees.)

Choosing Your Management Tools

So, what are you, the small-business owner who's looking for ways to continue growing your company, supposed to do when you think your business is ready for a dose of something new? What management tools should you use to ensure continued growth? Whose advice should you take? And how can you possibly know which of the latest fads to glom onto?

The truth of the matter is that no one management tool will turn your company around. Just as no one strategy will produce profitable customers, no one tool will change your culture, correct your infrastructure, or unite your employees.

When you're considering adopting the latest management tool (or system), let someone else be the pioneer. Other organizations have needed restructuring, other employees have needed motivating, and other cultures have needed change. (As someone once said, "You can always tell the pioneers — they're the ones with the arrows in their backs.") In other words, be aware of the fads making the rounds, and don't bet the farm on the latest one. Feel free to cherry-pick the key components of a tool that make the most sense to you and your business.

Use the following tips to help you determine whether a newly adopted management system will work for you:

>> **Don't be the first kid on the block.** Determine which similarly sized businesses have already pioneered the system and/or utilized any of its most appropriate tools and then solicit their suggestions and advice. This step is particularly important when you're considering new, costly, software-driven applications. Make sure the program you're considering has been time-tested and has many satisfied users. Also do your due diligence to ensure that the software company will be around to service and upgrade the system you buy.

>> **Make sure your key employees agree with the need for and the basic elements of the new tools before you introduce them.** Include your key employees in the purchasing, planning, and especially the implementation processes.

>> **Consider the downsides as well as the upsides of utilizing the new tools.** Be sure you know what it will cost to pull the plug midstream if the tools don't work as you planned.

>> **Understand the time frame needed to implement the tools and measure their success.** Ensure that you can live within the time frame. Whatever figure you come up with, you generally can multiply that number by two.

>> **Be certain that you, the owner and chief culture-setter of your business, have the time and energy to devote to the proper implementation of the new management tool you select.** The implementation of new tools always requires the total commitment of the owner; if you aren't willing — or able — to make that commitment, don't even think about introducing a new management system.

If your business is working well (as measured primarily by profitability), don't break it. (You can, however, bend it.) If your business isn't working well, consider a change. One of your many responsibilities is to be the systems and tools matchmaker. Be sure to stay current with the latest and greatest management systems and the tools within them, and then match your business's need for change with the applicable system.

Consider, for instance, the management tools in the following sections. Each of the tools has at least one key management component that makes sense — ranging from setting goals to redefining processes, from paring expenses to sharing financial information. Every tool offers a degree of management wisdom and an accompanying management component, but that doesn't mean you need to adopt the entire system. Cherry-pick as you see fit.

Management by objective

An old-timer for sure, the basic components of *management by objective* (MBO) — setting and reaching goals — have endured and are still used by many successful businesses. The process of goal-setting is discussed at length in Chapter 2 of Book 4. Most successful businesses — small and large — use goal-setting in one form or another; so should yours.

Participatory management

The primary characteristic of *participatory management* is that all employees take part in determining the direction and policies of the company. Great in theory, this approach can work wonders when organized carefully and phased in over long periods of time. The participatory tools inherent in such a system work for two reasons:

>> Given a voice in the decision-making process, employees are much more likely to make a personal commitment to the decisions reached.

>> Given the fact that employees see the business through different eyes and often more frequent experiences with customers than the owners, their input enhances the quality of the decisions made.

WARNING

But don't give away the keys to your business too soon. Figuring out how to grow a small business takes years of training and preparation. Besides, not all employees *want* the responsibility that goes with management positions. Employee participation takes time and patience, neither of which is a common trait of most entrepreneurs.

Employee ownership

There is motivation inherent in offering employees the opportunity to own a piece of the company (in other words, *employee ownership*), but sharing the pie isn't always as easy as it sounds. Sometimes you don't have enough pie to go around; sometimes the pie isn't divided the way everyone would like it to be; and sometimes some of your employees would rather bet their futures on T-bills rather than on small-business pie. Besides, minority shareholders can be a pain in the rear.

But for many people, ownership is one of the best motivators available. That's why, despite the problems that come with sharing the pie, more and more pie-sharing is going on today than ever before. Even the federal government recognizes this fact, which is why it offers a number of incentives to companies who want to establish such employee-empowering tools as Employee Stock Ownership Plans (ESOPs).

Quality circles

Quality circles are ad hoc groups or temporary teams (also known as *ad hoc committees*) of employees assembled to solve specific problems. Most successful businesses use forms of this team approach to problem solve. In many cases, businesses assemble specially formed teams to solve a problem and then quickly disband the team after the issue has been resolved.

The appeal of the problem solving tool inherent in quality circles is the age-old theory that two heads are better than one. This is especially true when those two (or more) heads are focused on solving a specific problem and when those heads bring differing perspectives to the problem solving table.

Open-book management

Open-book management dictates that informed employees can make key decisions usually reserved for management — within, that is, their areas of expertise. An *informed employee* is one who's privy to nearly everything that goes on within the company, including a variety of tools usually reserved for management, such as using and understanding financial statements.

Similar to any other management system, the open-book management system has an upside and a downside:

WARNING

» The downside is that your employees may discover things you'd prefer they didn't know, like how much you spend on travel and entertainment in a year and how much your new sports car costs the company.

» The upside is that informed employees tend to make better day-to-day decisions than uninformed ones. Informed employees are also more likely to be committed to the cause — in this case, to increasing the profitability of the company.

Troubleshooting Your Business Challenges

From time to time, businesses call in small-business consultants to troubleshoot. Although troubleshooting can be an effective tool any time, many small-business owners use it only when their growing business suddenly slows down. Consultants can help a struggling business by evaluating important areas of the business — such as finances, employee morale, and business appearance — and then making suggestions for improvement. Find out how in the following sections.

Filling out a troubleshooting checklist

Most consultants use checklists to help them determine the seriousness of a business's problems. Here's a checklist used by one particular troubleshooting consultant.

Rank each of the following categories from 1 to 10:

_____ **Quality of cash-management procedures (cash flow reporting and forecasting) (1 = poor, 10 = excellent)**

_____ **Quality of financial reporting (profit and loss statement and balance sheet) (1 = poor, 10 = excellent)**

_____ **Quality of financial forecasting (budgets) (1 = poor, 10 = excellent)**

_____ **Dependence on borrowed funds (1 = heavy, 10 = none)**

_____ **Late with payroll tax deposits (1 = often, 10 = never)**

_____ **Lag between sales growth and profit growth (1 = substantial, 10 = none)**

_____ **Employee turnover (1 = heavy, 10 = nonexistent)**

_____ **Quality and frequency of strategic planning (1 = never, 10 = regular and dependable)**

_____ **Owner has more work to do than time to do it (1 = too much work, 10 = balances time efficiently)**

_____ **Owner's feelings about the business (1 = hates it, 10 = loves it)**

If you were your own troubleshooting consultant, how would you rate your business overall? What areas would you target for improvement? Use this checklist to determine how your business checks out. How many items would receive close to a 10? How many areas would receive something less than a 5?

TIP

Although there's no overall key to grading your answers, consider giving immediate attention to working on any answer that received a 5 or below. For the 6s and 7s, put the issue on your long-range to-do list. For the 8s and above, pat yourself on the back and make sure that the employees responsible for the rating are publicly recognized and, where possible, rewarded.

Taking the five-minute appearance test

Your business's appearance is important, especially to your customers. With this in mind, check out the following appearance test. Five minutes are all you need to take it.

Start with a business other than your own. For instance, you can offer to give a friend's business the following five-minute appearance test. Or use the test on a business you frequent, such as your dry cleaner. Simply drive into the parking lot, walk into the customer service or office area, peek into a few doors here and there, step into the restroom for a quick look around, and then check out the areas around the coffeemaker and copy machines before you go.

Note the following as you go, ranking your observations from 1 (poor) to 5 (excellent):

THE EXTERIOR

_____ **Parking lot:** Well cared for and clean

_____ **Grounds and exterior:** Well maintained, trimmed, and inviting

_____ **Windows:** Clean, unsmeared, and uncluttered when viewed from the outside

_____ **Signage:** Well maintained, readable, and understandable

THE INTERIOR

_____ **General neatness:** Desks and working areas neat and uncluttered

_____ **Restrooms:** Neat and clean

_____ **Expense awareness:** Unnecessary lights and unused equipment turned off, no original van Goghs in the lobby

_____ **Time-management:** Employees appear focused and busy, no gossipy gatherings around the coffeemaker or copy machines

_____ **Employee attitudes:** Polite, alert, attentive, and focused

_____ **Employee appearance:** Neat, clean, and dressed appropriately

_____ **Sense of urgency:** Employees going about their business at a pace that indicates they don't have time to waste

THE BEST AND THE WORST

The one thing I saw that impressed me the most:

_____

The one thing I saw that bothered me the most:

_____

Then give the questionnaire to the owner and ask her to repay you the favor. Your business could use the five-minute appearance test, too.

Redefining Your Role in an Evolving Business

Owning a business is like raising a teenager: As it grows, the business is sure to get into trouble, yet you can never be sure what the trouble will be, how severe it will be, and how the company will weather the experience. Whether the business (and the teenager) will survive and subsequently thrive or fail depends on the quality of leadership provided.

That leadership, in the case of your business, anyway, must come from you.

REMEMBER

So why is growth, especially that of the rapid variety, so hard on the typical small-business owner? The reasons are twofold:

>> **Most small-business owners aren't prepared for the managerial demands of a growing business.** In most cases, the owner's expertise is in a specialized area, such as sales or accounting, or is related to his craft or to the product or service that the company offers. As a result, he's untrained and unskilled in the management aspects of running a business. To make matters worse, many of the management skills required to run a growing business are usually counter to the way the owner is accustomed to doing things.

>> **The bigger your company becomes, the farther you fade from the center of the action.** Visions get blurred as a result of that distance, missions fade, and communications falter. Also, the more the business grows, the more layers you have between you and your customers, vendors, and employees. With this distance comes misdirection — unless your management skills, as delegated to your key employees, can keep pace with the growth.

A proficient manager requires a number of traits, but most of these traits aren't required for a successful start-up; they come into play only as a company grows. The ability, or inability, of the entrepreneur to adopt these skills determines the ultimate success of the business.

Making the transition to manager

Here's a popular entrepreneurial axiom: "The day you hire your first employee is the same day you begin making the transition to manager." This transition isn't an easy one to make because many of the personal traits of the typical small-business owner run counter to those of a successful manager.

REMEMBER

Consider the following required traits and job descriptions of the successful manager — traits that aren't always near the top of the typical entrepreneur's list of skills:

>> **Focus:** The successful manager focuses on the project at hand, no matter what else is going on around him. The typical entrepreneur stops in the middle of the task to respond to the latest opportunity or crisis.

>> **Attention to detail:** The successful manager devoutly dots her *i*'s and crosses her *t*'s. The typical entrepreneur is often too busy or simply isn't the type that enjoys dealing with details.

>> **Follow-up:** The successful manager understands that employees need to know that their work will be evaluated. The typical entrepreneur doesn't think that employees' work should have to be followed up; he believes that the employees should do it right the first time.

>> **Conflict resolution:** The successful manager views resolving conflict as an important part of her job description. The typical entrepreneur sees it as an intrusion on her time.

>> **Training:** The successful manager views training as an investment. The typical entrepreneur sees it as an expense.

Of course, not all small-business owners fit this entrepreneur's profile. You can make changes in some, if not all, of the managerial traits that you lack. However, the transition to manager isn't an easy one, and it involves some basic — and often wrenching — changes in the entrepreneur who originally founded the business.

Implementing strategic changes

WARNING

The *Peter Principle*, which says that managers rise to their level of incompetence, constantly creeps up on all small-business owners as their companies grow. For one entrepreneur, it may arrive when his company has only one employee; for others, it may creep up when their companies reach 1,000 employees. But everyone has limitations — managerial and otherwise. Having limitations doesn't make you a bad person; it only means that, where the management of your business is concerned, there may come a time when you should either move over or move on.

Once you notice that the Peter Principle is hanging over your management skills and you're having a difficult time making the transition from entrepreneur to manager (you'll know it's happening when your business isn't fun anymore), take some time to consider the four alternatives in the following sections.

Downsizing your business

Downsizing involves shrinking your business back to the point where you're able to spend your time doing those things you enjoy and are best at. For example, you may decide to limit your customer base to only those within your market area, thereby cutting your sales and allowing you to shrink the number of employees you must manage.

Before making the decision to downsize, ask yourself the following questions:

» What are the downsides of shrinking the business (losing income, reducing the market value of the business, letting go of customers, and possibly laying off employees)?

» Will you be able to emotionally and financially cope with these losses?

If the answer to the second question is no, consider the alternative in the following section.

Taking a personal inventory

Taking a personal inventory includes assembling your own *managerial defect list* — a list of the traits that make managing your business difficult, such as inattention to detail or fear of conflict. Consider which entries on the list you can, and would, change in order to make the managerial transition.

TIP

Ask your spouse, friends, and key employees to help you make your managerial defect list.

After you make your list, ask yourself the following questions:

» How many of the traits on your managerial defect list can you hire around?

» How many of the traits can you train around?

» How many of the traits can you delegate around?

» Of those traits that you can't hire, train, or delegate around, which ones can you reasonably expect to change?

This exercise will tell you what you need to do to improve your managerial skills and how you can go about doing so. Assuming that, as a result of the answers given, you decide you can make the transition, get busy! Start hiring, training, delegating, and, where applicable, making changes in your organizational structure (see the earlier section "Choosing Your Management Tools").

If you decide that you can't — or won't — make the managerial transition, consider the following alternative.

Hiring a replacement

Hiring a replacement includes hiring a president or Chief Operating Officer (COO) to run your company while you become Chief Executive Officer (CEO). The president or COO takes control of the day-to-day management of the business, while you concentrate on the things you're good at, such as sales or product development or strategy. (See Chapter 1 in Book 4 for details on how to hire the right person for the job.)

Before hiring a replacement, ask yourself the following:

>> Is your company big enough and profitable enough to afford a president or COO?

>> Are you capable of letting go and keeping your nose out of the day-to-day operating functions of your business? In other words, can you keep yourself from micromanaging your company?

If the answer to either of these questions is no, you have two options:

>> Go back to the preceding alternatives (downsizing your business or making personal changes) and decide how to adapt one (or both) of them to your situation.

>> Consider the fourth alternative.

Selling the business

Before you decide to take such a big step as selling your business, ask yourself the following questions:

>> Will you emotionally be able to sell and walk away from the company you've built?

>> Is your company salable at a price that works for you?

Ultimately, you may decide to sell your business and move on to something you're better suited for or more ready to do. Or, most importantly, something you'll enjoy doing.

Index

A

academic references, 399

accelerated method, 340

Account column, in Chart of Accounts, 260

accountants, 187, 263

accounting cycle, 241–243

accounting equation, 288

accounting methods, 192–193, 283

accounting period, 240

accounts payable, 240, 254, 281–282, 303

accounts receivable, 240, 251, 278–279, 301, 318

accrual-basis accounting, 193, 244–245, 314

accrued expenses payable, on statement of cash flows, 281–282

accrued expenses payable liability account, 303, 305

Accrued Payroll Taxes account, 254

accumulated depreciation

  about, 302–303

  buildings account, 252

  equipment account, 253

  furniture and fixtures account, 253

  leasehold improvements account, 252

  on statement of cash flows, 320–321

  vehicles account, 253

action plan, 106

activity trap, 414–415

actual budgeting, 357–360

adequate disclosure, 267

adjusting journal entries, as step in accounting cycle, 242, 243

adjustments, 242

Adobe Dreamweaver, 202–203, 215

advanced entrepreneurship, 46

advertising

  analyzing costs of, 338–339

  on Facebook, 548

  finding customers with, 461

  simple rules of, 532

  timing, 537–538

Advertising account, 258

Advertising Age (magazine), 531

Adweek (magazine), 531

Affordable Care Act (2010), 185

Allen, Kathleen (author)

  eBusiness Technology Kit For Dummies, 435

Amazon, 55, 61

American Institute of Certified Public Accountants (website), 378

American Recovery and Reinvestment Act (ARRA, 2009), 185

American Taxpayer Relief Act (2012), 401

Americans with Disabilities Act, 163

Amgen, 60

amortization

  on balance sheet, 304

  defined, 341

  organization costs account, 253

  patents account, 253

analyzing

  advertising costs, 338–339

  employee cost, 338

  influence points, 463–466

  sales promotion cost, 338–339

  shortfalls, 565

  talents, 565

anatomy, of business plans, 105–107

angels, finding, 122–123

Angie's List, 73

annual reports, 240

answering phones, 496

anticipated upsell business model, 51

appearance of buildings/stores, finding customers with, 461

W

About the Authors

Kathleen R. Allen, PhD, is an authority on entrepreneurship and small business technology and is the author of *Entrepreneurship For Dummies, The Complete MBA For Dummies* (with Peter Economy), *eBusiness Technology Kit For Dummies* (with Jon Weisner), *Launching New Ventures* (Cengage Learning), and *Growing and Managing a Small Business* (South-Western College Pub), as well as several other books. She has also written for popular business magazines and newspapers (*Inc., Los Angeles Times, Los Angeles Business Journal,* and *The New York Times*) and is called upon by *The Wall Street Journal,* CNN, CNBC, and a variety of other media for expert opinion in the field of entrepreneurship.

Peter Economy is a home-based business author, ghostwriter, publishing consultant, and the author or coauthor of more than 50 books, including *Home-Based Business For Dummies* with Paul and Sarah Edwards, *Managing For Dummies* and *Consulting For Dummies* with Bob Nelson, and *Writing Children's Books For Dummies* with Lisa Rojany Buccieri (John Wiley & Sons, Inc.). Peter is also associate editor for the Apex Award-winning magazine *Leader to Leader.* Peter invites you to visit his website at www.petereconomy.com.

Paul and Sarah Edwards are award-winning authors of 17 books with more than two million books in print. Sarah, a licensed clinical social worker with a PhD in ecopsychology, and Paul, a licensed attorney, are recognized as pioneers in the working-from-home field. With the emergence of a global economy that challenges the environment and everyone's personal, family, and community well-being, they are focusing their efforts on finding pathways to transition to a sustainable Elm Street economy in which home business plays a vital role. Paul and Sarah hosted the *Working From Home* show on HGTV and have been regular commentators on CNBC. They're the coauthors of *Home-Based Business For Dummies* (John Wiley & Sons, Inc.).

Lita Epstein, who earned her MBA from Emory University's Goizueta Business School, enjoys helping people develop good financial, investing, and tax planning skills. While getting her MBA, Lita worked as a teaching assistant for the financial accounting department and ran the accounting lab. After completing her MBA, she managed finances for a small nonprofit organization and for the facilities management section of a large medical clinic. She designs and teaches online courses on topics such as accounting and bookkeeping and starting your own business. She's written more than 35 books, including *Bookkeeping For Dummies, Reading Financial Reports For Dummies, Trading For Dummies, The Business Owner's Guide to Reading and Understanding Financial Statements,* and *Financial Decision Making* (Bridgepoint Education).

Alexander Hiam helps organizations (including nonprofits and government agencies) think through their branding and marketing strategies and their leadership development programs. He has served on the boards of directors of a variety of organizations and also as an instructor in the Isenberg School of Management at UMass Amherst. Alex earned his BA from Harvard and his MBA in marketing and strategic planning from the Haas School at UC Berkeley. He has led creative retreats for top consumer and industrial firms to facilitate innovative thinking about strategic plans, branding, naming, and product ideas. He also writes novels and believes that all good writing (including advertising) is, at heart, good storytelling. He is the author of *Business Innovation For Dummies* and early editions of *Marketing For Dummies* (John Wiley & Sons, Inc.).

Greg Holden started the small business Stylus Media, which is a group of editorial, design, and computer professionals who produce both print and electronic publications. The company's name comes from the recording stylus, which reads the traces left on a disk by voices or instruments and translates those signals into electronic data that can be amplified and enjoyed by listeners. Greg has been a freelance writer since 1996, and is also a novelist. Over the years, he has been a regular contributor to CNET and to EcommerceBytes. He received a Master of Arts degree in English from the University of Illinois at Chicago, and he writes general-interest books, short stories, and poetry. He is the author of *Starting an Online Business For Dummies* (John Wiley & Sons, Inc.).

Peter Jaret has written for *The New York Times, Newsweek, National Geographic, Health, Reader's Digest,* and dozens of other magazines. He is the coauthor, along with Steven D. Peterson and Barbara Findlay Schenck, of *Business Plans Kits For Dummies* (John Wiley & Sons, Inc.). He is also the author of other books, including *In Self-Defense* (Harcourt), *Impact: From the Frontlines of Global Health* (National Geographic), *Nurse: A World of Care* (Emory University), *Active Living Every Day* (Human Kinetics). He has developed written materials for the Electric Power Research Institute, Lucas Arts, The California Endowment, WebMD, BabyCenter, Stanford University, Collabria, Home Planet Technologies, and others. In 1992, he received the American Medical Association's first-place award for medical reporting. In 1997 and again in 2007, he won James Beard Awards for food and nutrition writing. He holds degrees from Northwestern University and the University of Virginia.

Jeanette Maw McMurtry, MBA, first became obsessed with marketing when she stumbled upon a marketing textbook just before graduating with her college degree in journalism. Having realized her passions lie in creativity and analytics, she pursued jobs in marketing upon graduation and eventually landed at DDB Worldwide and Ketchum, where she learned the science and art of advertising and public relations. After career positions at American Express, Intermountain Health Care, and a few high-tech start-ups, she became a CMO for a direct marketing agency in Denver, Colorado, where she became entrenched in database marketing and personalization. She then started her own consulting firm and emerged as a leading authority on psychology-based marketing, helping brands trigger the unconscious mind in order to achieve "unthinkable" ROI. She is the author of *Marketing For Dummies*, 5th Edition (John Wiley & Sons, Inc.).

Joyce Mazero is partner and co-chair of the Global Supply Network at Gardere Wynne Sewell LLP. With a legal career spanning more than 35 years, Joyce has established an international reputation as a strong and strategic lawyer and a trusted business advisor in the franchising, supply chain, food service, restaurant, and retail industries. At Gardere she leads the team and its interdisciplinary group of professionals, all of whom advise national and multinational franchised and independent businesses on building and expanding chains across the globe. She is the coauthor of *Franchise Management For Dummies* (John Wiley & Sons, Inc.).

Jim Muehlhausen, JD, like most entrepreneurs, has an eclectic background, ranging from CPA to franchisee, attorney, business owner, consultant, franchisor, public speaker, university professor, and book author. While still attending the Indiana University School of Law, he became the youngest franchisee in Meineke Discount Muffler history (1987–1991). After successfully selling that business, Jim founded an automotive aftermarket manufacturing concern. During his nine-year tenure with that business, the company achieved recognition from Michael Porter of the Harvard Business School and *Inc.* magazine in the IC 100 Fastest Growing Businesses. In 2009, he founded the Business Model Institute, which is devoted to the innovation and study of business models. Jim writes several articles for the Institute each year as well as contributing to publications such as *Inc., The Small Business Report, Entrepreneur, BusinessWeek,* and various business journals. He is the author of *Business Models For Dummies* (John Wiley & Sons, Inc.).

Bob Nelson, PhD, is president of Nelson Motivation Inc., a management training and consulting company that specializes in helping organizations improve their management practices, programs, and systems. He has sold more than 3.5 million books on management and motivation, which have been translated in more than 35 languages, including 1001 Ways to Reward Employees (Workman Publishing Co.), The 1001 Rewards & Recognition Fieldbook (Workman Publishing Co.), 1001 Ways to Take Initiative at Work (Workman Publishing Co.), Keeping Up in a Down Economy (Nelson Motivation), Ubuntu: An Inspiring Story of an African Prinicple of Teamwork and Collaboration (Crown Business), and (with Peter Economy) *The Management Bible, Managing For Dummies,* and *Consulting For Dummies* (John Wiley & Sons, Inc.). He holds an MBA in organizational behavior from UC Berkeley and received his PhD in management with Dr. Peter F. Drucker at the Drucker Graduate Management School of Claremont Graduate University. For more information about available products or services offered by Nelson Motivation Inc., including registration for Dr. Nelson's free Tip of the Week, visit www.nelson-motivation.com.

Steven D. Peterson is founder and CEO of Strategic Play, a management training company specializing in software tools designed to enhance business strategy, business planning, and general management skills. He's the creator of the Protean Strategist, a business simulation that reproduces a dynamic business environment where participant teams run companies and compete against each other in a fast-changing marketplace. He is the coauthor, along with Peter Jaret and

Barbara Findlay Schenck, of *Business Plans Kits For Dummies.* He is also the coauthor, along with Paul Tiffany, of *Business Plans For Dummies,* which was nominated as one of the best business books of the year by the *Financial Times.* He holds advanced degrees in mathematics and physics and received his doctorate from Cornell University.

Jim Schell hasn't always been a grizzled veteran of the small-business wars, contrary to what some people may think. Growing up in Des Moines, Iowa, and earning a BA in Economics at the University of Colorado, Jim served in the U.S. Air Force in Klamath Falls, Oregon. Jim's entrepreneurial genes eventually surfaced when he and three Minneapolis friends started The Kings Court, at the time the nation's first racquetball club. Two years later, Jim bought General Sports, Inc., a struggling sporting-goods retailer and wholesaler. After another two years, he started National Screenprint, and, finally, he partnered with an ex-employee in Fitness and Weight Training Corp. Each of the start-ups was bootstrapped, and each was privately held. For a period of exhausting years, Jim involved himself in the management of all four businesses at the same time. His third business, National Screenprint, ultimately grew to $25 million in sales and 200 employees. Relocating to San Diego, Jim began a long-simmering writing career, authoring four books (The Brass Tacks Entrepreneur [Owlet], Small Business Management Guide [Henry Holt & Co.], The Small Business Answer Book [John Wiley & Sons], and Understanding Your Financial Statements [Visuality]) and numerous columns for business and trade magazines. Citing culture shock, Jim and his wife, Mary — a sales trainer and longtime business partner — relocated to Bend, Oregon, where he continued his writing career. He is the coauthor of *Small Business For Dummies.*

Barbara Findlay Schenck has spent her career helping business owners start, grow, market, and brand their companies. She's worked internationally in community development, served as a college administrator and instructor in Hawaii, and cofounded an advertising agency in Oregon. She writes marketing advice columns for MSN and participates in programs that help businesses adapt to their ever-changing media and consumer markets. She is the author of *Small Business Marketing Kit For Dummies* and *Selling Your Business For Dummies* and is the coauthor of *Branding For Dummies* and *Business Plans Kit For Dummies* (John Wiley & Sons, Inc.). For more information on her background, books, and business advice, visit her website at www.bizstrong.com.

Michael H. Seid is founder and managing director of Michael H. Seid & Associates (MSA), the nation's leading consulting firm specializing in franchising and other methods of distribution. During his 25+ years in franchising, Michael has been a senior operations and financial executive or consultant for companies within the franchise, retail, hospitality, restaurant, and service industries. He has also been a franchisee. Michael is the past chairman of the International Franchise Association (IFA) Supplier Forum, a former member of the IFA's executive committee, and the first supplier ever directly elected to the IFA's board of directors. Michael is a CFE (Certified Franchise Executive) and a nonpracticing CPA. Michael is a noted author of numerous articles on franchising, an oft-quoted expert in the field, and a frequent lecturer on the subject of franchising. For more information on the services offered by MSA, including speaking or consulting services, visit MSA's website at www.msaworldwide.com. He is the coauthor of *Franchise Management For Dummies*.

John A. Tracy, CPA, is Professor of Accounting, Emeritus, at the University of Colorado in Boulder. Before his 35-year tenure at Boulder, he was on the business faculty for four years at the University of California at Berkeley. He served as staff accountant at Ernst & Young and is the author of several books on accounting and finance, including *Accounting For Dummies, Accounting Workbook For Dummies, The Fast Forward MBA in Finance,* and *How to Read a Financial Report,* and is coauthor with his son, Tage, of *How to Manage Profit and Cash Flow* as well as *Small Business Financial Management Kit For Dummies.* He received his B.S.C. degree from Creighton University and earned his MBA and PhD degrees from the University of Wisconsin. He is a CPA (inactive) in Colorado.

Tage C. Tracy, CPA, is the principal owner of TMK & Associates, an accounting, financial, and strategic business planning consulting firm focused on supporting small- to medium-sized businesses since 1993. Tage received his baccalaureate in accounting in 1985 from the University of Colorado at Boulder with honors. Tage began his career with Coopers & Lybrand (now merged into Pricewaterhouse Coopers). More recently, Tage coauthored *Small Business Financial Management Kit For Dummies* and *How to Manage Profit and Cash Flow* with his father, John Tracy.

Eric Tyson, MBA, has been a personal financial writer, lecturer, and counselor for the past 25+ years. As his own boss, Eric has worked with and taught people from a myriad of income levels and backgrounds, so he knows the small-business ownership concerns and questions of real folks just like you. After toiling away for too many years as a management consultant to behemoth financial-service firms, Eric decided to take his knowledge of the industry and commit himself to making personal financial management accessible to everyone. Despite being handicapped by a joint BS in Economics and Biology from Yale and an MBA from Stanford, Eric remains a master at "keeping it simple." An accomplished freelance personal-finance writer, Eric is the author or coauthor of numerous *For Dummies* national bestsellers on personal finance, investing, for seniors, and home buying, including *Small Business For Dummies* and *Small Business Taxes For Dummies,* and is a syndicated columnist. His book *Personal Finance For Dummies* won the Benjamin Franklin Award for Best Business Book. His website is www.erictyson.com.

Publisher's Acknowledgments

Senior Acquisitions Editor: Tracy Boggier

Compilation Editor: Georgette Beatty

Project Manager: Linda Brandon

Copy Editor: Chad R. Sievers

Technical Editor: James Floyd Kelly

Production Editor: Magesh Elangovan

Cover Image: © PeopleImages/Getty Images